A Classical Mind

C. A. R. Hoare, Series Editor

BACKHOUSE, R. C., *Program Construction and Verification*
BACKHOUSE, R. C., *Syntax of Programming Languages*
DEBAKKER, J. W., *Mathematical Theory of Program Correctness*
BARR, M. and WELLS, C., *Category Theory for Computing Science*
BEN-ARI, M., *Principles of Concurrent and Distributed Programming*
BEN-ARI, M., *Mathematical Logic for Computer Science*
BIRD, R. and WADLER, P., *Introduction to Functional Programming*
BORNAT, R., *Programming from First Principles*
BOVET, D. and CRESCENZI, P., *Introduction to the Theory of Complexity*
BUSTARD, D., ELDER, J. and WELSH, J., *Concurrent Program Structures*
CLARK, K. and McCABE, F. G., *Micro-Prolog: Programming in Logic*
CROOKES, D., *Introduction to Programming in Prolog*
DAHL, O.-J., *Verifiable Programming*
DROMEY, R. G., *How to Solve It by Computer*
DUNCAN, E., *Microprocessor Programming and Software Development*
ELDER, J., *Construction of Data Processing Software*
ELLIOTT, R. J. and HOARE, C. A. R. (eds), *Scientific Applications of Multiprocessors*
FREEMAN, T. L. and PHILLIPS, R. C., *Parallel Numerical Algorithms*
GOLDSCHLAGER, L. and LISTER, A., *Computer Science: A modern introduction (2nd edn)*
GORDON, M. J. C., *Programming Language Theory and its Implementation*
GRAY, P. M. D., KULKARNI, K. G. and PATON, N. W., *Object-oriented Databases*
HAYES, I. (ed), *Specification Case Studies (2nd edn)*
HEHNER, E. C. R., *The Logic of Programming*
HENDERSON, P., *Functional Programming: Application and implementation*
HOARE, C. A. R., *Communicating Sequential Processes*
HOARE, C. A. R., and GORDON, M. J. C. (eds), *Mechanized Reasoning and Hardware Design*
HOARE, C. A. R., and JONES, C. B. (eds), *Essays in Computing Science*
HOARE, C. A. R., and SHEPHERDSON, J. C. (eds), *Mechanical Logic and Programming Languages*
HUGHES, J. G., *Database Technology: A software engineering approach*
HUGHES, J. G., *Object-oriented Databases*
INMOS LTD, *Occam 2 Reference Manual*
JACKSON, M. A., *System Development*
JOHNSTON, H., *Learning to Program*
JONES, C. B., *Systematic Software Development Using VDM (2nd edn)*
JONES, C. B. and SHAW, R. C. F. (eds), *Case Studies in Systematic Software Development*
JONES, G., *Programming in Occam*
JONES, G. and GOLDSMITH, M., *Programming in Occam 2*
JONES, N. D., GOMARD, C. K. and SESTOFT, P., *Partial Evaluation and Automatic Program Generation*
JOSEPH, M., PRASAD, V. R. and NATARAJAN, N., *A Multiprocessor Operating System*
KALDEWAIJ, A., *Programming: The derivation of algorithms*
KING, P. J. B., *Computer and Communications Systems Performance Modelling*
LALEMENT, R., *Computation as Logic*
LEW, A., *Computer Science: A mathematical introduction*
McCABE, F. G., *Logic and Objects*
McCABE, F. G., *High-Level Programmer's Guide to the 68000*
MEYER, B., *Introduction to the Theory of Programming Languages*
MEYER, B., *Object-oriented Software Construction*
MILNER, R., *Communication and Concurrency*
MITCHELL, R., *Abstract Data Types and Modula 2*
MORGAN, C., *Programming from Specifications*
PEYTON JONES, S. L., *The Implementation of Functional Programming Languages*
PEYTON JONES, S. and LESTER, D., *Implementing Functional Languages*
POMBERGER, G., *Software Engineering and Modula-2*
POTTER, B., SINCLAIR, J. and TILL, D., *An Introduction to Formal Specification and Z*
REYNOLDS, J. C., *The Craft of Programming*
RYDEHEARD, D. E. and BURSTALL, R. M., *Computational Category Theory*
SLOMAN, M. and KRAMER, J., *Distributed Systems and Computer Networks*
SPIVEY, J. M., *The Z Notation: A reference manual (2nd edn)*
TENNENT, R. D., *Principles of Programming Languages*
TENNENT, R. D., *Semantics of Programming Languages*
WATT, D. A., *Programming Language Concepts and Paradigms*
WATT, D. A., *Programming Language Processors*
WATT, D. A., WICHMANN, B. A. and FINDLAY, W., *ADA: Language and methodology*
WELSH, J. and ELDER, J., *Introduction to Modula 2*
WELSH, J. and ELDER, J., *Introduction to Pascal (3rd edn)*
WELSH, J., ELDER, J. and BUSTARD, D., *Sequential Program Structures*
WELSH, J. and HAY, A., *A Model Implementation of Standard Pascal*
WELSH, J. and McKEAG, M., *Structured System Programming*
WIKSTRÖM, Å., *Functional Programming Using Standard ML*

A Classical Mind
Essays in Honour of C. A. R. Hoare

Edited by

A. W. Roscoe
Oxford University Computing Laboratory

Prentice Hall
New York   London   Toronto   Sydney   Tokyo   Singapore

First published 1994 by
Prentice Hall International (UK) Limited
Campus 400, Maylands Avenue
Hemel Hempstead
Hertfordshire, HP2 7EZ
A division of
Simon & Schuster International Group

Printed and bound in Great Britain at
The University Press, Cambridge

Library of Congress Cataloging-in-Publication Data

Available from the publisher

British Library Cataloguing in Publication Data

A catalogue record for this book is available from
the British Library

ISBN 0-13-294844-3

1 2 3 4 5   98 97 96 95 94

Contents

Foreword

For a group of people who share in some enterprise, to celebrate the birthday of a person who has given much of his life to it with resounding effect is a matter for pure rejoicing. Everyone – the person, the group, the enterprise itself – has gained; it should be like a harvest festival.

Such a festival means nothing without what went before; the discipline, struggle and vision which led to the harvest. In the quarter-century since I first met Tony Hoare I came to know his particular vision well, and to be drawn on by it. He approached the foundations of computing not with a preconceived mathematical tool-kit, but with two more important things; an unexcelled power of analysis, arising no doubt from his training in the classics, and a first-hand experience of a human activity which urgently needed to be organised – namely, computer systems engineering. Progress in this field owes much to his insistence that it be organised as a science. If you read the excellent collection of his writings edited by Cliff Jones, *Essays in Computing Science* (Prentice Hall), you see the development of his own great efforts toward this goal. In particular, everyone should read the plea in his Turing Award lecture to fight against prejudice and baroque practices; a fine piece of writing, yes, but a ruthless exposure of the dangers of avoiding fundamental thinking in computer science.

In that collection you will also find a foreword by David Gries, of Cornell University, who analyses the importance of Tony Hoare's own contributions to this fundamental thinking. If I tried to do the same I would repeat a lot of Gries' analysis; instead let me commend it to you, and mention one or two achievements which best represent Hoare's ability to join theory to practice, and which may for that reason give him the greatest satisfaction. First, the occam language and its industrial implementation. The design and implementation of occam was a team effort led by David May at Inmos Limited, and the project was a direct reification of Hoare's theory of Communicating Sequential Processes. Moreover the language is not only a vehicle for real application work on transputer networks, but is *itself* a theory; for it has an equational axiomatisation worked out by Hoare and Roscoe. This is a new standard for computer languages; it is only when one of them reaches this standard, as occam did, that the others are seen to fall short.

The second achievement I want to mention gives me a chance to recall some of my direct experience of Tony Hoare at work. I remember the beginning of his ideas on the *failures* model for CSP, at the end of the 1970s. I was thinking hard about exactly when two interactive processes should be considered behaviourally equal. I had rejected the traditional equivalence of automata theory since it is insensitive to deadlock, which makes it inadequate as a guide for system design. I adopted the much more refined model which I called observation equivalence; some thought it *too* refined, but I doubted the existence of a good model strictly intermediate in refinement. I was therefore deeply impressed when Tony, with Bill Roscoe and Steve Brookes, produced the failures model, and my respect for it has steadily increased. We know now that it has a special place in concurrency theory; it is, precisely, the weakest congruence that respects deadlock. Moreover it has led to a stream of practical applications, progressively more substantial.

I saw him at work on this model at first hand, because he shared some of his thoughts on it with me (though I didn't see where they led). I was struck by the sheer intensity of his pursuit of the notion. In a sense he *knew* it was there, and couldn't rest until it was laid bare. I had met this complete dedication years earlier, in 1972, on a flight to the International Symposium on Theoretical Programming at Novosibirsk, Siberia. I had come from California, through London; on changing planes in London after losing a night's sleep I fell in with Tony, starting his journey nice and fresh. I forget what idea he pursued when we had taken our seats, but it was a hot pursuit as usual. Alas, I nodded off in mid-(Hoare)-sentence. What seemed like hours later, he saw my eyes open again. 'Furthermore', he continued.

One might excuse Tony Hoare, as a leading innovator, from devoting a large part of his effort time to leadership in a teaching department. But he did not excuse himself. Quite the opposite; he clearly relished continuing after Christopher Strachey at Oxford, developing both the science and the teaching of it, and at the same time shouldering the burdens of a department Head in a growing discipline. He followed Strachey in making sure that theories are relevant to practice, so he must be proud to lead a department which not only builds theories but can also win the Queen's Award for Industry. It is clear to everyone who visits Oxford how highly his colleagues value this leadership, not just for its intellectual but also for its humane quality.

Among his research colleagues worldwide, too, the rich assembly of contributors to this volume provides clear evidence of loyalty and admiration. In his 'envoi' at the end of *Essays in Computing Science* Tony Hoare tells us how much he enjoys writing, as is fully evident from what he writes. In giving him this book we hope that he will enjoy reading it, too; and since his work is by no means finished, we hope to return the favour by reading more of his insights over the next decade or so. In fact, Tony: Many happy returns!

Robin Milner
University of Edinburgh

Preface

The most difficult part of editing this volume was selecting the list of people who were invited to contribute. In assembling this list, with the assistance of Cliff Jones and Helen Martin, I was acutely aware of the disappointment we would cause to the many distinguished names we were unable to include for lack of space. This is just one measure of Tony's distinction, and the regard in which he is held in our community. This was also apparent in the high acceptance rate of invitations to submit, and in how simple it has been for me to assemble such an impressive range of papers in a very tight schedule: the project was only conceived in October 1992.

Authors were invited to submit some piece of work of up to 25 pages. We believed – as has been borne out – that this would give space for some substantial and interesting contributions. I accepted jointly-written papers with one other author; in these cases, at my request, the original invitee is always the first-named.

I would like to thank Robin Milner for writing the foreword, and all the authors for making my task so easy. I am most grateful to Cliff and Helen for their advice and help throughout this project. Jill Jones made the suggestion which led to me thinking of the title – a problem that had taxed me for months. Most authors used the LaTeX style we sent round to prepare their chapters, but they also used an astonishing variety of macros and fonts I had never seen before. Jim Davies has brought it all together into a coherent whole – I would have been in trouble without him.

October 1994 will see another great achievement for Tony: the arrival of the first undergraduates on the new Honour School of Computation at Oxford. We hope to use the proceeds of this book to establish a prize in his honour for the best student each year on this course.

A. W. R.
October 1993

List of Contributors

S. Abramsky. Department of Computing, Imperial College, 180 Queen's Gate, London SW7 2BZ, UK.

R. S. Bird. Programming Research Group, Oxford University Computing Laboratory, The Wolfson Building, Parks Road, Oxford OX1 3QD, UK.

D. Bjørner. UNU/IIST, P.O. Box 3058, Macau.

S. D. Brookes. Department of Computer Science, Carnegie-Mellon University, Schenley Park, Pittsburgh PA 15213, USA.

R. Burstall. Department of Computer Science, University of Edinburgh, The King's Buildings, Mayfield Road, Edinburgh, UK.

O.-J. Dahl. Department of Informatics, University of Oslo, Postboks 1080 Blindern, 0316 Oslo 3, Norway.

R. Diaconescu. Programming Research Group, Oxford University Computing Laboratory, The Wolfson Building, Parks Road, Oxford OX1 3QD, UK.

E. W. Dijkstra. Department of Computer Sciences, The University of Texas at Austin, Austin TX 78712-1188, USA.

J. A. Goguen. Programming Research Group, Oxford University Computing Laboratory, The Wolfson Building, Parks Road, Oxford OX1 3QD, UK.

M. J. C. Gordon. Department of Computer Science, Cambridge University, Corn Exchange Street, Cambridge, UK.

D. Gries. Department of Computer Science, Cornell University, Ithaca NY 14850, USA.

He Jifeng. Programming Research Group, Oxford University Computing Laboratory, The Wolfson Building, Parks Road, Oxford OX1 3QD, UK.

E. C. R. Hehner. Computer Systems Research Institute, University of Toronto, Sandford Fleming Building, 10 Kings College Road, Toronto M5S 1A4, Canada.

M. A. Jackson. 101 Hamilton Terrace, London NW8 9QX, UK.

C. B. Jones. University of Manchester, Department of Computer Science, Oxford Road, Manchester, UK.

D. E. Knuth. Department of Computer Science, Stanford University, Stanford, CA 94305-2140, USA.

B. W. Lampson. Digital Equipment Corporation, One Kendall Square, Bldg. 700, Cambridge MA 02139, USA.

D. Lehmann. Institute of Computer Science, The Hebrew University of Jerusalem, Jerusalem, Israel.

Li Xiaoshan. Software Institute, the Chinese Academy of Sciences, P. O. Box 8718, Beijing, China.

G. Malcolm. Programming Research Group, Oxford University Computing Laboratory, The Wolfson Building, Parks Road, Oxford OX1 3QD, UK.

M. D. May. Inmos Ltd, 1000 Aztec West, Almondsbury, Bristol, UK.

J. Misra. Department of Computer Sciences, The University of Texas at Austin, Austin TX 78712-1188, USA.

R. Milner. Department of Computer Science, University of Edinburgh, The King's Buildings, Mayfield Road, Edinburgh, UK.

O. de Moor. Programming Research Group, Oxford University Computing Laboratory, The Wolfson Building, Parks Road, Oxford OX1 3QD, UK.

C. C. Morgan. Programming Research Group, Oxford University Computing Laboratory, The Wolfson Building, Parks Road, Oxford OX1 3QD, UK.

M. O. Rabin. Aiken Computation Lab, Harvard University, Cambridge MA 02138, USA, *and* Institute of Computer Science, The Hebrew University of Jerusalem, Jerusalem, Israel.

A. W. Roscoe. Programming Research Group, Oxford University Computing Laboratory, The Wolfson Building, Parks Road, Oxford OX1 3QD, UK.

J. E. Stoy. Programming Research Group, Oxford University Computing Laboratory, The Wolfson Building, Parks Road, Oxford OX1 3QD, UK.

R. D. Tennent. Department of Computer Science, Queen's University, Kingston, Ontario, Canada.

J. Welsh. Department of Computer Science, University of Queensland, St. Lucia, Brisbane 4067, Australia.

Zhou Chaochen. UNU/IIST, P.O. Box 3058, Macau. On leave of absence from the Software Institute, the Chinese Academy of Sciences.

Chapter 1

Interaction Categories and Communicating Sequential Processes

Samson Abramsky

1.1   Introduction

The first lectures I heard on concurrency were given by Tony Hoare as part of a summer school held at the University of California at Santa Cruz in August 1979. The contents of those lectures are well represented by the paper [11]. Their spirit is suggested by the following quotation from that paper:

> The primary objective of this paper is to give a simple mathematical model of communicating sequential processes ... As the exposition unfolds, the examples begin to look like programs, and the notations begin to look like a programming language. Thus the design of a language seems to emerge naturally from its formal definition, in an intellectually pleasing fashion.

I still remember the excitement I felt at seeing how computational modelling, conceptual clarity and mathematical elegance could be brought together in a fundamental study of concurrency. Although the limitations of the model presented in [11], particularly as regards non-determinism, are made clear in that paper, and a more refined semantics was subsequently developed by Hoare, Brookes and Roscoe, the attitudes underlying the work in [11] made a permanent impression on me.

Semantic paradigms 1: denotational semantics   The most influential and longest established of current paradigms for the semantics of computation is Denotational Semantics. It is this paradigm which best approximates by far to the ideal of a mathematical theory of computation in the sense of McCarthy [14] or Scott [17].

The criticism I wish to lodge is one of scope. Despite its pretensions to universality, Denotational Semantics has an inherent bias towards a particular computational paradigm, that of *functional computation*. By this I mean, not only functional programming languages, but that whole sphere of computation in which the behaviour of the program is adequately abstracted as the computation of a function. This view of programs as functions is built into the basic mathematical framework on which Denotational Semantics is founded: a category of "sets" (domains) to interpret types, and certain functions between these sets to interpret programs.

Within the sphere of functional computation, Denotational Semantics has worked extremely well, serving not merely to describe, but to lead the way in language design and programming methods: think e.g. of types and type-checking, higher-order functions, recursive types, polymorphism, continuations, monads. These semantic insights have gone hand-in-hand with the canonical formal calculus for functional computation provided by the λ-calculus.

However, it is by now widely recognized that functional computation is just one, rather limited, part of the computational universe, into which e.g. distributed systems, real-time systems and reactive systems don't really fit. The success of denotational semantics outside the sphere of functional computation has been much more limited.

Semantic paradigms 2: process calculi   A different family of semantic paradigms has been developed for reactive systems. The most notable of these is the process calculus paradigm, pioneered by Hoare and Milner, and exemplified by CSP [12] and CCS [16]. The great achievement of this paradigm over the past 15 years has been to develop an algebraic theory of concurrency, as a basis for structural methods of description of concurrent systems. The major limitation is that no canonical theory or calculus for concurrency has emerged; there is a veritable Babel of formalisms, combinators, equivalences. This may suggest that the current methodologies for concurrency are insufficiently constrained, or perhaps that some key ideas are still missing. Some secondary, but also significant, limitations of the paradigm follow:

- It is type-free; a good notion of type for concurrent processes would be very desirable, but has proved elusive.
- There has been an over-emphasis on what processes *are* – as in the extensive literature on process equivalences – rather than on what structure they must possess collectively. One may compare this to the emphasis in the early days of set-theoretical foundations on which sets numbers *were*, as opposed to the modern emphasis on universal properties e.g. for Natural Numbers objects.
- Partly because of the lack of a good notion of a type, there has been a fairly systematic confusion between specifications and processes. One obvious place where this has caused problems has been in the discussion of *fairness*.
- The early design decisions of the pioneers have been copied so often that they have become almost invisible; yet there are quite basic points which may be questioned. For example, there is the rôle of *names* in process calculi; these are typically used as proper names (constants), which tends to give these calculi a highly syntactic, intensional slant from the outset.

The great bifurcation   These two leading semantic paradigms have developed separately. After 15 years this separate development must be regarded as a major open problem: how can we combine our understanding of the functional and concurrent process paradigms, with their associated mathematical underpinnings, in a single unified theory? Such a unification is required to obtain sound foundations for languages combining concurrent processes and communication on the one hand, with types, higher-order constructs and polymorphism on the other. It is also needed as a basis for useful type systems for concurrency, which would allow interface constraints for concurrent modules (or objects) to be expressed. Such type systems are of prime importance. After all, it is only worth while to make some subsystem into a "black box" (a module or object) if we can describe its interface to its environment in some fashion significantly simpler than a detailed description of the internals of the black box.

Calculi vs. semantic universes   At this point it will be useful to contrast the methodology implicit in presenting theories of concurrency as formal "process calculi", with that in which one presents a "semantic universe" in the form of a categorical model. The formal calculus approach starts from a set of combinators generating a syntax; then one may define a structured operational semantics or a model, various notions of equivalence, etc.

The weakness of this methodology is in the very first step; why this set of combinators rather than any other? If in fact a consensus had been reached that some calculus was canonical for concurrency in the same way and for the same kind of reasons that λ-calculus enjoys this status for functional computation, then this would not have been a problem. History has turned out otherwise, and should caution us to beware of availing ourselves too readily of the seductive freedoms of BNF.

In the categorical semantic approach, we define

- "objects" (types) A, B, C
- "morphisms" (programs) $f : A \to B$
- composition

$$\frac{f : A \to B \quad g : B \to C}{f\,;g : A \to C}$$

Composition is the fundamental primitive of category theory, in the same sense that membership is the fundamental primitive of set theory. Once we have said what this bare framework of typed arrows closed under composition is, an enormous amount of further structure is then determined uniquely up to isomorphism. Thus the various type constructions of interest will typically be characterized by universal properties, which means: axiomatized in terms of their behaviour under composition in such a way that, if they exist at all, it can only be in (essentially) one way. For example, once we have specified a category $\mathbb{C}$ there is *only one way* it can be a Cartesian closed category, and hence canonically model λ-calculus; the bare structure of composition determines all the possibilities for manipulation of higher-order functions by abstraction and application. To paraphrase Picasso: *we do not seek, we find.* Thus, in contrast to the formal calculus approach, there is a major shift from stipulation to observation of structure. Part and parcel of this is that the categorical framework imposes much more severe constraints on what counts as an acceptable definition: functoriality, naturality, universality, etc.

The interaction category paradigm   We propose *Interaction Categories* as a new paradigm for the semantics of computation. In place of sets, functions, and function composition, an Interaction Category is a semantic universe where

- Types are *process specifications* A, B, C
- Morphisms are *processes* $p : A \to B$
- Composition is *interaction*

$$\frac{p : A \to B \qquad q : B \to C}{p \mathbin{;} q : A \to C}$$

(Roughly speaking, interaction should be understood as "parallel composition + hiding/restriction" in process calculus terms.)

At first sight, the reader will probably find it rather hard to accept a view of processes as arrows. Part of this is no doubt just the psychological association of the arrow notation with functions. A more substantial objection is that process interaction is symmetric and bidirectional in character. However, the reader surely had no difficulty in adjusting to the idea of a category of sets and relations; but relations have as much symmetry and no more intrinsic directionality than do communicating processes. Relations acquire a direction as arrows by convention; this meshes conveniently with the use of positional notation (ordered n-tuples) to access the components of the instances of a relation.

We take a similar view of a process *qua* morphism

$$p : A \to B$$

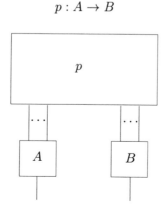

We think of p as a concurrent module, with its interface to the environment represented as a bunch of wires. The types A, B *partition* the interface of p; moreover, each one may be highly structured, grouping various wires together. By accessing this interface positionally, we can get combinators that let us do process algebra *name-free*. Returning to our analogy with relations, we can contrast the name-free positional approach to the traditional use of names in process algebra as analogous to positional access via n-tuples $\langle a_1, \ldots, a_n \rangle$ vs. the labelled records representation

$$[l_1 \Rightarrow a_1 \; ; \cdots ; l_n \Rightarrow a_n]$$

Again, we can draw an analogy with categorical combinators for Cartesian-closed categories, which yield variable-free translations of the λ-calculus.

Because the partitioning of the interface is merely conventional, we can get a duality

$$\frac{A \xrightarrow{p} B}{A^\perp \xleftarrow{p^\perp} B^\perp}$$

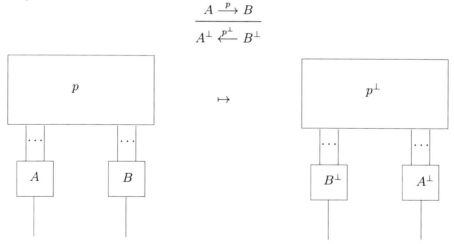

such that $p^{\perp\perp} = p$. Often, it will be the case that $A^\perp = A$, i.e. the duality is trivial on objects; compare relational converse.

Furthermore, we can use categorical type structure to control and repartition the interface. For grouping wires together, we can introduce a tensor product $A \otimes B$

$$\frac{p : A \to B \quad q : A' \to B'}{p \otimes q : A \otimes A' \to B \otimes B'}$$

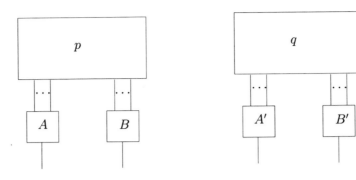

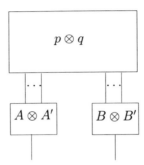

where $p \otimes q$ is a disjoint parallel composition of p and q – there is no interaction between them. This tensor product should be *functorial*; while housekeeping on the grouping of wires is done positionally by canonical isomorphisms

$$
\begin{aligned}
\mathsf{assoc}_{A,B,C} : \quad & (A \otimes B) \otimes C && \cong && A \otimes (B \otimes C) \\
\mathsf{symm}_{A,B} : \quad & A \otimes B && \cong && B \otimes A \\
\mathsf{unit}_A : \quad & A \otimes I && \cong && A
\end{aligned}
$$

satisfying some standard coherence equations. All of this says that we should have the structure of a *symmetric monoidal category* [13].

Repartitioning of the interface is catered for by *currying*:

$$
\frac{p : A \otimes B \to C}{\Lambda(p) : A \to (B \multimap C)}
$$

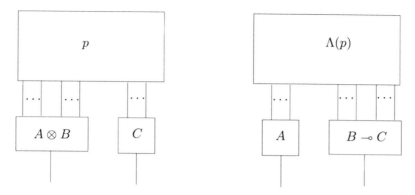

together with application

$$\mathsf{Ap}_{A,B} : (A \multimap B) \otimes A \to B$$

This tensor structure gives us

Interpretation of the multiplicatives of Linear Logic [10]; "Linear λ-calculus" [1].	Static operations of process calculus [15] (in name-free form).

If $A = A^\perp$ holds (or more generally if $A \otimes B = (A^\perp \otimes B^\perp)^\perp$, i.e. the category is *compact closed*) then we can use this type structure to build arbitrary process interconnection networks, including cycles.

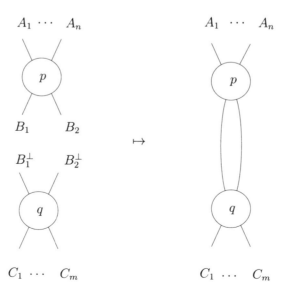

As a typing rule, this is

$$\frac{\vdash \Gamma, B_1, B_2 \qquad \vdash \Delta, B_1^{\perp}, B_2^{\perp}}{\vdash \Gamma, \Delta}$$

It is justified by the calculation

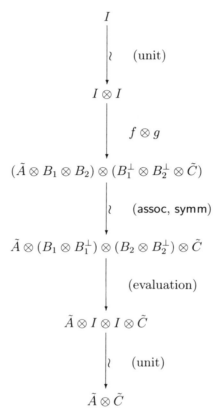

where

$$\Gamma = \tilde{A} = A_1 \otimes \cdots \otimes A_m, \quad \Delta = \tilde{C} = C_1 \otimes \cdots \otimes C_n$$

and f, g are the interpretations of the proofs of the premises of the above rule.

Continuing with our programme, we can define products and coproducts by universal properties, yielding

Additives of Linear Logic: conditionals, pairing and projections, injections and case expressions.	(disjointly) guarded sums of process algebra.

If $A = A^{\perp}$ holds (or more generally if products and coproducts coincide, so we have *biproducts*) this gives rise to an interpretation of non-determinism: if

$p, q : A \to B$ then we can define their non-deterministic combination by

$$
\begin{aligned}
p + q &= A \xrightarrow{\Delta} A \oplus A \xrightarrow{[p,q]} B \\
&= A \xrightarrow{\langle p,q \rangle} B \oplus B \xrightarrow{\nabla} B
\end{aligned}
$$

(This is the standard derivation of a semi-additive structure from biproducts; see [13, 8].) The pairing of f and g will be a "disjointly guarded", and hence deterministic, combination of p and q; the type confusion between products and coproducts allows us to compose this with the codiagonal, which removes the tags rendering p and q disjoint, so that $p + q$ does indeed represent the non-deterministic mingling of p and q.

So we get a common core structure, supporting key elements of *both* functional programming *and* communication and concurrency.

We can go further, to introduce the exponentials of Linear Logic, yielding the ability to define the full typed λ-calculus on the functional side, and replication on the process calculus side; polymorphism and recursive types; and constructs to articulate the temporal structure of processes, in the form of certain monads. In this fashion, we can obtain all the ingredients for combining the functional and communicating processes paradigms at a fundamental level, with substantial *sharing of structure* – the same formal structure being used to account for elements of both paradigms.

Concrete examples of interaction categories   The ideas sketched in the previous sub-section should be understood as an informal outline of an axiomatic development of Interaction Categories. Two concrete examples of Interaction Categories have been developed in some detail:

- **SProc**: an Interaction Category for synchronous processes. Some basic details of **SProc** are described in [2]; a much fuller account is given in [3]. My students Simon Gay and Rajagopal Nagarajan have applied **SProc** to modelling a number of real-time synchronous languages including ESTEREL, LUSTRE and SIGNAL [9, 5].
- **ASProc**: an Interaction Category for asynchronous processes. This will be described in detail in a forthcoming paper [4]. A brief account is given in the following section.

1.2   A Simplified Introduction to ASProc

In this section, we briefly give the basic definitions of **ASProc**, an Interaction Category for asynchronous processes. To simplify the discussion we shall model processes by sets of traces as in [11] rather than by labelled transition systems modulo weak bisimulation, as in the "official" definition.

As in [11], a basic notion is that of a *trace* of a process. However, we differ from [11] in allowing traces to record simultaneous occurrences of events. Thus a trace on a given alphabet Σ is a finite sequence of non-empty subsets of Σ. We write $\mathtt{Tr}(\Sigma)$ for the set of traces on Σ. If $s \in \mathtt{Tr}(\Sigma)$ and $X \subseteq \Sigma$, we define $s{\upharpoonright}X$ inductively:

$$\varepsilon{\upharpoonright}X \;=\; \varepsilon$$
$$(ms){\upharpoonright}X \;=\; \left\{ \begin{array}{ll} (m \cap X)(s{\upharpoonright}X), & (m \cap X \neq \varnothing) \\ s{\upharpoonright}X & (m \cap X = \varnothing) \end{array} \right.$$

An *object* of **ASProc** is a pair $A = (\Sigma_A, S_A)$ where Σ_A is a *sort* or *alphabet*, and $S_A \subseteq \mathtt{Tr}(\Sigma_A)$ is a non-empty prefix-closed subset of $\mathtt{Tr}(\Sigma_A)$, a *safety property* [7].

We define $A^\perp = A$, and $A \otimes B$ by

$$\Sigma_{A \otimes B} \;=\; \Sigma_A + \Sigma_B$$
$$S_{A \otimes B} \;=\; \{s \in \mathtt{Tr}(\Sigma_{A \otimes B}) \mid s{\upharpoonright}\Sigma_A \in S_A, s{\upharpoonright}\Sigma_B \in S_B\}$$

Note that $A^\perp = A$ implies that $A \otimes B = A \multimap B = A\,\wp\,B$.

A process of sort Σ is a non-empty prefix-closed subset of $\mathtt{Tr}(\Sigma)$. We write $p \models A$ if p is a process of sort Σ_A such that $p \subseteq S_A$.

We write $p : A \to B$ iff $p \models A \multimap B$. A morphism of **ASProc** is a tuple (A, p, B) such that $p : A \to B$ (compare a careful definition of the category of sets and relations, which also requires the domain and codomain of a morphism to be explicitly recorded).

Given $p : A \to B$, $q : B \to C$, we define $p\,;q : A \to C$ by:

$$p\,;q = \{s{\upharpoonright}\Sigma_A, \Sigma_C \mid s \in \mathtt{Tr}(\Sigma_A + \Sigma_B + \Sigma_C), s{\upharpoonright}\Sigma_A, \Sigma_B \in p, s{\upharpoonright}\Sigma_B, \Sigma_C \in q\}$$

Compare this to the definition of $[p\|q]$ (parallel composition + hiding) in [11].

Identities are defined by:

$$1_A = \{s \in \mathtt{Tr}(\Sigma_A + \Sigma_A) \mid \exists t \in S_A.\, \forall i.\, s_i = \mathtt{inl}(t_i) \cup \mathtt{inr}(t_i)\}.$$

That is, at each stage, the identity simultaneously offers any possible actions of A at both ends of its interface – it behaves like a wire:

$$a \;\overline{\qquad 1_A \qquad}\; a$$

Allowing simultaneous actions plays a crucial rôle at this point.

We can specify the composition in terms of labelled transitions by:

$$\frac{p \xrightarrow{m} p'}{p\,;q \xrightarrow{m} p'\,;q}\, m \cap \Sigma_B = \varnothing \qquad\qquad \frac{q \xrightarrow{n} q'}{p\,;q \xrightarrow{n} p\,;q'}\, n \cap \Sigma_B = \varnothing$$

$$\frac{p \xrightarrow{m} p' \quad q \xrightarrow{n} q'}{p\,;q \xrightarrow{(m \cup n)\backslash \Sigma_B} p'\,;q'}\, m \cap \Sigma_B = n \cap \Sigma_B$$

Proposition 1.2.1 **ASProc** is a category.

Note that parallel composition plus hiding in CSP, and parallel composition plus restriction in CCS, are *not associative*. That is why composition and hiding are separated out in these calculi. The use of types in **ASProc** allows associativity to be retrieved, so that a different choice of primitives is possible.

We can extend tensor to a functor by:

$$\frac{p : A \to B \qquad q : A' \to B'}{p \otimes q : A \otimes A' \to B \otimes B'}$$

$$p \otimes q = \{s \in \mathtt{Tr}(\Sigma_{A \otimes A' \multimap B \otimes B'}) \mid s{\restriction}\Sigma_A, \Sigma_B \in p, \, s{\restriction}\Sigma_{A'}, \Sigma_{B'} \in q\}$$

In terms of transitions:

$$\frac{p \xrightarrow{m} p'}{p \otimes q \xrightarrow{m} p' \otimes q'} \qquad\qquad \frac{q \xrightarrow{n} q'}{p \otimes q \xrightarrow{n} p' \otimes q'}$$

$$\frac{p \xrightarrow{m} p' \qquad q \xrightarrow{n} q'}{p \otimes q \xrightarrow{m \cup n} p' \otimes q'}$$

The tensor unit I is the trivial type:

$$I = (\varnothing, \{\varepsilon\}).$$

All the further structure of a $*$-autonomous category can be defined on **ASProc**.

Proposition 1.2.2 **ASProc** is a compact-closed category.

To illustrate these constructions, we show how to represent the standard CSP operations of composition and hiding. Given a type $A = (\Sigma_A, \Sigma_A^*)$, processes $p, q : I \longrightarrow A$, and a synchronization alphabet $L \subseteq \Sigma_A$, we define $p \parallel_L q$ by

$$p \parallel_L q = I \cong I \otimes I \xrightarrow{p \otimes q} A \otimes A \xrightarrow{m} A$$

where m is defined recursively by

$$
\begin{aligned}
m \;=\; & \textstyle\bigsqcup_{a \in L}\{\mathtt{inl}(\mathtt{inl}(a)), \mathtt{inl}(\mathtt{inr}(a)), \mathtt{inr}(a)\} \to m \\
\sqcap \;& \textstyle\bigsqcup_{a \notin L}\{\mathtt{inl}(\mathtt{inl}(a)), \mathtt{inr}(a)\} \to m \\
\sqcap \;& \textstyle\bigsqcup_{a \notin L}\{\mathtt{inl}(\mathtt{inr}(a)), \mathtt{inr}(a)\} \to m
\end{aligned}
$$

The idea is that m is the CSP "synchronization algebra", which is composed with the independent parallel composition of p and q to force synchronization exactly on actions in L.

Similarly, hiding can be defined by

$$p/L = I \xrightarrow{p} A \xrightarrow{\rho_L} A$$

where

$$\rho_L = \bigsqcup_{a \in L} \{\mathtt{inl}(a), \mathtt{inr}(a)\} \to \rho_L \;\sqcap\; \bigsqcup_{a \notin L} \{\mathtt{inl}(a)\} \to \rho_L$$

We now turn to the interpretation of the additives in **ASProc**. In fact, **ASProc** only has *weak* products (which are necessarily weak biproducts by the self-duality). These are described as follows. We define

$$\Sigma_{A \oplus B} = \Sigma_A + \Sigma_B + \{l, r\}$$
$$S_{A \oplus B} = \{\varepsilon\} \cup \{\{l\}s \mid s \in S_A\} \cup \{\{r\}t \mid t \in S_B\}$$

so we have

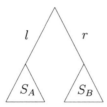

For the weak coproduct diagram

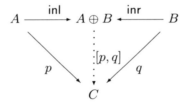

we proceed as follows. Firstly, if $p \subseteq \mathtt{Tr}(\Sigma)$ and $f : \Sigma \to \Sigma'$ we define *relabelling* of p by f:

$$p[f] = \{\bar{f}(s) \mid s \in p\}$$

where $\bar{f} : \mathtt{Tr}(\Sigma) \to \mathtt{Tr}(\Sigma')$ is the canonical extension of f.

Now we define

$$\mathsf{inl} = l.1_A[i] \quad \mathsf{inr} = r.1_B[j]$$

where

$$i : \Sigma_A + \Sigma_A \to \Sigma_A + \Sigma_{A \oplus B}, \quad j : \Sigma_B + \Sigma_B \to \Sigma_B + \Sigma_{A \oplus B}$$

are the canonical injections, and

$$[p, q] = l.p[m] \cup r.q[n]$$

where

$$m : \Sigma_C + \Sigma_A \to \Sigma_C + \Sigma_{A \oplus B}, \quad n : \Sigma_C + \Sigma_B \to \Sigma_C + \Sigma_{A \oplus B}$$

are the canonical injections, and e.g.

$$l.p = \{\varepsilon\} \cup \{\{l\}s \mid s \in p\}$$

Proposition 1.2.3 These definitions yield a weak biproduct, i.e. we have

$$\mathsf{inl} \,;\, [p, q] = p, \quad \mathsf{inr} \,;\, [p, q] = q.$$

These definitions easily extend to weak biproducts of arbitrary set-indexed families of types $\bigoplus_{i \in I} A_i$.

Note that in process algebra terms, these constructions yield *disjointly guarded sums*: if $p_i : I \to A_i$ then (using the weak product structure now)

$$\langle p_i \rangle_{i \in I} : I \to \bigoplus_{i \in I} A_i$$

is given by

$$\langle p_i \rangle_{i \in I} = \prod_{i \in I} a_i \to p_i \quad (i \neq j \Rightarrow a_i \neq a_j)$$

in CSP terms. Note that our combinators are name-free; the names are controlled indirectly via the types.

Furthermore, if we apply the general definition of non-determinism as semi-additivity, we obtain

$$p + q = p \cup q$$

which is the interpretation of non-determinism in the trace model as given e.g. in [11]. (In the more refined version of **ASProc** in which processes are synchronisation trees modulo weak bisimulation, then $p + q$ is the CSP "internal choice" $p \sqcap q$ [12].)

1.3 Types and Specifications

We have only considered very rudimentary safety specifications in this paper; indeed, the very simple model of programs we have adopted leaves almost no scope for more refined properties. However, the full version of the theory provides a framework in which more refined properties can be introduced. Examples for **ASProc** include:

- liveness properties relativized to fairness constraints (this makes full use of the distinction between specifications and processes incorporated in our framework),
- deadlock freedom, based on a novel combination of ideas from concurrency theory (ready sets) and Linear realizability [6],
- causal independence, giving access to "true concurrency" ideas.

As we introduce these more refined specifications, the type degeneracies disappear, so that all the Linear types receive distinct interpretations. The net effect is that we obtain a working version of Propositions as Types for concurrency. Moreover, the familiar typing rule for composition

$$\frac{p : A \to B \quad q : B \to C}{p \,;\, q : A \to C}$$

becomes a true compositional proof rule for parallel composition.

Further details of these ideas will appear in [3, 4].

References

[1] S. Abramsky. Computational Interpretations of Linear Logic. *Theoretical Computer Science*, 111:3–57, 1993. Earlier version appeared as Imperial College Technical Report DOC 90/20, October 1990.

[2] S. Abramsky. Interaction Categories (Extended Abstract). In G. L. Burn, S. J. Gay, and M. D. Ryan, editors, *Theory and Formal Methods 1993: Proceedings of the First Imperial College Department of Computing Workshop on Theory and Formal Methods*. Springer-Verlag Workshops in Computer Science, 1993. To appear.

[3] S. Abramsky. Interaction Categories I: Synchronous processes. Paper in preparation, 1993.

[4] S. Abramsky. Interaction Categories II: Asynchronous processes. Paper in preparation, 1993.

[5] S. Abramsky, S. J. Gay, and R. Nagarajan. Interaction Categories: Illustrative examples, 1993. Abstract of talk given at the CONFER Workshop, University of Edinburgh, UK.

[6] S. Abramsky and R. Jagadeesan. New foundations for the geometry of interaction. *Information and Computation*. To appear.

[7] B. Alpern and F. B. Schneider. Defining liveness. *Information Processing Letters*, 21(4):181–185, 1985.

[8] P. J. Freyd and A. Scedrov. *Categories, Allegories*, volume 39 of *North-Holland Mathematical Library*. North-Holland, 1990.

[9] S. J. Gay and R. Nagarajan. Synchronous dataflow in Interaction Categories, 1993. Submitted to the Thirteenth Conference on the Foundations of Software Technology and Theoretical Computer Science, Bombay, India.

[10] J.-Y. Girard. Linear Logic. *Theoretical Computer Science*, 50(1):1–102, 1987.

[11] C.A.R. Hoare. A model for communicating sequential processes. In R.M. McKeag and A.M. Macnaghten, editors, *On the Construction of Programs*. Cambridge University Press, 1980.

[12] C.A.R. Hoare. *Communicating Sequential Processes*. Prentice Hall, 1985.

[13] S. Mac Lane. *Categories for the Working Mathematician*. Springer-Verlag, Berlin, 1971.

[14] J. McCarthy. A basis for a mathematical theory of computation. In P. Braffort and D. Hirschberg, editors, *Computer Programming and Formal Systems*, pages 33–69. North Holland, 1963.

[15] R. Milner. *A Calculus for Communicating Systems*, volume 92 of *Lecture Notes in Computer Science*. Springer-Verlag, Berlin, 1980.

[16] R. Milner. *Communication and Concurrency*. Prentice Hall, 1989.

[17] D.S. Scott. Outline of a mathematical theory of computation. In *4th Annual Princeton Conference on Information Sciences and Systems*, pages 169–176, 1970.

Chapter 2

Relational Program Derivation and Context-free Language Recognition

Richard Bird and Oege de Moor

2.1 Introduction

By way of paying tribute to the instincts and intuitions of Tony Hoare, we would like to begin our contribution to his Festschrift with a little of its history. About the middle of 1990 we had written a paper on the calculation of Earley's algorithm [8, 12] for general context-free language recognition. The idea was to improve on existing treatments (see e.g. [14, 21]) by exploiting the algebraic calculus of functions developed in [3, 4, 5, 17] to give a short and mathematical calculation of the basic recursive form of the algorithm. However, as necessary preparation we had to set up a fair amount of machinery for stating various properties of set-valued functions, Cartesian product, Kleisli composition, closure and inversion. This machinery was not specific to language recognition, so its cost could be charged to general theory development, but in the end we set the work aside because the effort demanded of the reader was arguably too great for what was achieved.

A couple of years earlier, Tony Hoare had suggested to us that a move from functions to relations might result in a mathematical calculus better suited to program derivation. The primary reason at that stage was the unsatisfactory treatment of nondeterminism in a purely functional calculus. At the time, one of us (Bird) resisted Hoare's suggestion because of reluctance to break the direct link to functional programming, and the feeling that equational reasoning was too important to be abandoned lightly. Nevertheless, by 1989 the spirit of relational calculi for software – or hardware – development was in the air, and enthusiastically embraced by De Moor (who was then Bird's research student), Roland Backhouse [1], Geraint Jones and Mary Sheeran [15], and others.

At about the same time, Hoare's lectures [13] on category theory at the 1988 Marktoberdorf Summer School brought the subject to a wider audience than before. A number of computing scientists, in particular Malcolm [16], Spivey [22], and Wadler [23], argued convincingly that the rules of program derivation could be structured in terms of categorical concepts, and also that the categorical treatment of datatypes enabled a smoother and more general presentation of many derivations. In particular, De Moor exploited a categorical treatment of relations in his thesis on dynamic programming [20], using a number of results from Freyd and Scedrov [11] which had just appeared. The notational and conceptual advantages of relations were sufficiently apparent to render further objections pointless, and for the past two years we have been using them in a mathematical investigation of various principles and techniques of algorithm design [6, 7].

Recently, we returned to language recognition to see how it would look in the new relational setting. The result, elaborated below, was a simpler calculation than before. The basic reason was that the isomorphism between relations and set-valued functions could be invoked at the end of the calculation, rather than having to be imposed from the beginning. Furthermore, the categorical approach to data types served to simplify and unify notation.

So, Tony Hoare's instincts and intuitions were right on both counts. But then they usually are, which is why we are honoured to contribute to this book celebrating his 60th birthday.

2.2   A Calculus of Relations

We begin with a brief and incomplete review of the relational calculus, leaving out various important pieces not actually needed in the problem of language recognition. The calculus is based on Freyd's theory of *allegories* [11]; basically, an allegory is a category with additional axioms designed to capture the essential facts about relations. We will not take a fully axiomatic approach here, relying instead on appeal to naive set theory, but we do assume a nodding acquaintance with categories and functors.

2.2.1   Relations

The basis of the calculus is a category *Rel* whose objects are sets and whose arrows are relations. Arrows go backwards: we write $R : A \leftarrow B$ to denote that R is a relation of type 'A from B'; we can think of R as a subset of $A \times B$. Relational composition, like its functional counterpart, also goes backwards: $R \cdot S$ is pronounced 'R after S'. Composition is associative with the identity relation $id : A \leftarrow A$ as unit, all of which says *Rel* is a category. For any A and B there exists a smallest relation $0 : A \leftarrow B$, which is the zero of composition, and a largest relation $\Pi : A \leftarrow B$.

Each relation $R : A \leftarrow B$ has a *converse* relation $R^\circ : B \leftarrow A$, which preserves identities but reverses composition (so $(R \cdot S)^\circ = S^\circ \cdot R^\circ$), all of which says that converse is a contravariant functor from *Rel* to itself. By assumption, the converse functor is its own inverse, $R^{\circ\circ} = R$, and so is an isomorphism.

For each A and B the arrows $A \leftarrow B$ form a complete lattice with union $\cup$ and intersection $\cap$. These arrows can be compared with a partial order $\subseteq$, where $R \subseteq S$ denotes $R = R \cap S$. Converse preserves $\subseteq$ and composition distributes over (arbitrary) unions, but only weakly distributes over intersection in that

$$R \cdot (S \cap T) \ \subseteq \ (R \cdot S) \cap (R \cdot T).$$

We will suppose that composition binds more tightly than $\cup$ or $\cap$, so the right-hand side could have been written without brackets. Using the given properties of converse, we get from the above inequation a second one:

$$(R \cap S) \cdot T \ \subseteq \ (R \cdot T) \cap (S \cdot T).$$

These two inequations say that composition is monotonic in both arguments under $\subseteq$.

One further inequation, called the *modular law*, is adjoined to the other axioms to give a weak converse of distributivity over intersection:

$$(R \cdot S) \cap T \ \subseteq \ R \cdot (S \cap R^\circ \cdot T).$$

Again, taking converses, we get the symmetric version

$$(R \cdot S) \cap T \ \subseteq \ (R \cap T \cdot S^\circ) \cdot S.$$

2.2.2 Entire and simple relations

There are three subcategories of *Rel* of particular interest: the entire (or total) relations, the simple (or single-valued) relations, and functions (which are both entire and simple). A relation $R : A \leftarrow B$ is *entire* if $id \subseteq R^\circ \cdot R$, and *simple* if $R \cdot R^\circ \subseteq id$. Identity arrows are both entire and simple, and composition preserves both properties, so both kinds of relations form subcategories of *Rel*. It follows that the category *Fun* of functions is also a subcategory of *Rel*. Functions will be denoted by lower case identifiers, $f, g, \ldots$ and so on.

To illustrate these definitions, let us prove that

$$(R \cap S) \cdot f \ = \ (R \cdot f) \cap (S \cdot f)$$

for all functions f. We argue

$\quad (R \cap S) \cdot f$
$\subseteq \quad \{\text{distributing composition over } \cap\}$
$\quad (R \cdot f) \cap (S \cdot f)$
$\subseteq \quad \{\text{modular law}\}$
$\quad ((R \cdot f \cdot f^\circ) \cap S) \cdot f$
$\subseteq \quad \{\text{monotonicity of composition, since } f \cdot f^\circ \subseteq id\}$
$\quad (R \cap S) \cdot f.$

Note that we used only the fact that f was simple.

2.2.3   Relators

A functor $\mathsf{F} : Rel \leftarrow Rel$ is said to be *monotonic* if $R \subseteq S$ implies $\mathsf{F}R \subseteq \mathsf{F}S$. Monotonic functors have many nice algebraic properties, most of which can be derived from the fact that they preserve converse, that is, $\mathsf{F}(R^\circ) = (\mathsf{F}R)^\circ$. Monotonic functors take entire relations to entire relations, simple relations to simple ones, and so functions to functions. Furthermore, any functor $\mathsf{F} : Fun \leftarrow Fun$ has at most one monotonic extension $\mathsf{F} : Rel \leftarrow Rel$ that coincides with F on functions. Following Backhouse [1], we will call such a functor a *relator*, also using this term just as an abbreviation for monotonic functor.

2.2.4   Products and coproducts

Recall that in a category an object $A \times B$ with two arrows $outl : A \leftarrow A \times B$ and $outr : B \leftarrow A \times B$ is called a *product* if for all C and arrows $f : A \leftarrow C$, $g : B \leftarrow C$ there is a unique arrow $\langle f, g \rangle : A \times B \leftarrow C$ such that $outl \cdot \langle f, g \rangle = f$ and $outr \cdot \langle f, g \rangle = g$. The category *Fun* has products and the product bifunctor $\times$ is defined by

$$f \times g \;=\; \langle f \cdot outl, g \cdot outr \rangle.$$

This functor is a binary relator whose unique extension to relations is given by $R \times S = \langle R \cdot outl, S \cdot outr \rangle$, where

$$\langle R, S \rangle \;=\; (outl^\circ \cdot R) \cap (outr^\circ \cdot S).$$

However, *outl*, *outr* and $\langle -, - \rangle$ do not satisfy the conditions of a categorical product in *Rel* since, for example, $outl \cdot \langle R, 0 \rangle = 0$ for all R. This is not a problem, for we said only that functional product has a unique extension in *Rel*, not that this extension should also be a product in *Rel*. However, we do have $outl \cdot \langle R, S \rangle = R$ and $outr \cdot \langle S, R \rangle = R$ whenever S is entire, so $outl \cdot (R \times S) = R \cdot outl$ and $outr \cdot (S \times R) = R \cdot outr$ whenever S is entire.

Dually, in a category an object $A + B$ with two arrows $inl : A + B \leftarrow A$ and $inr : A + B \leftarrow B$ is called a *coproduct* if for all C and arrows $f : C \leftarrow A$, $g : C \leftarrow B$ there is a unique arrow $[f, g] : C \leftarrow A + B$ such that $[f, g] \cdot inl = f$ and $[f, g] \cdot inr = g$. The category *Fun* also has coproducts and the coproduct bifunctor $+$ is defined by

$$f + g \;=\; [inl \cdot f, inr \cdot g].$$

The coproduct is also a binary relator with extension $R + S = [inl \cdot R, inr \cdot S]$, where

$$[R, S] \;=\; (R \cdot inl^\circ) \cup (S \cdot inr^\circ).$$

Unlike the case of products, *inl*, *inr* and $[-, -]$ do form a proper coproduct in *Rel*. For example, $[R, S] \cdot inl = R$ for all S. Also, from the definition of coproduct we get

$$[R, S] \cdot [U, V]^{\circ} \;=\; R \cdot U^{\circ} \,\cup\, S \cdot V^{\circ},$$

which will be needed below. Relators built up from constants, finite products and coproducts are called *polynomial*, and all polynomial functors are relators.

2.2.5 Algebras and catamorphisms

Let F be a relator. By definition, an F–*algebra* is a relation of type $A \leftarrow FA$. The set A is called the *carrier* of the algebra. A F–*homomorphism* from an algebra $S : B \leftarrow FB$ to an algebra $R : A \leftarrow FA$ is a relation $\phi : A \leftarrow B$ such that

$$\phi \cdot S \;=\; R \cdot F\phi.$$

Identity arrows are homomorphisms, and the composition of two homomorphisms is again a homomorphism, so F–algebras form the objects of a category whose arrows are homomorphisms. For many relators (in particular, the polynomial ones), this category has an initial object, which we shall denote by $\alpha : T \leftarrow FT$. For any other F–algebra $R : A \leftarrow FA$ the unique homomorphism from α to R will be denoted by $(\![R]\!)$, so $(\![R]\!) : A \leftarrow T$ is characterised by

$$\phi \cdot \alpha = R \cdot F\phi \;\equiv\; \phi = (\![R]\!).$$

Homomorphisms of the form $(\![R]\!)$ are called *catamorphisms* [18], and the initial algebra $\alpha : T \leftarrow FT$ is called a *datatype*.

2.2.6 Promotion

The initial algebra α is an isomorphism [10], meaning $\alpha \cdot \alpha^{\circ} = id$ and $\alpha^{\circ} \cdot \alpha = id$, so we can rewrite the above equivalence as an assertion about unique fixed points:

$$\phi = R \cdot F\phi \cdot \alpha^{\circ} \;\equiv\; \phi = (\![R]\!).$$

It follows from the Knaster–Tarski fixpoint theorem that the unique solution (if it exists) of $X = F(X)$ is also the least solution of $X \supseteq F(X)$ and the greatest solution of $X \subseteq F(X)$. Using these facts we get the following consequences of the existence of α, known collectively as the *promotion* rules:

$$\phi = R \cdot F\phi \cdot \alpha^{\circ} \;\equiv\; \phi = (\![R]\!)$$
$$\phi \subseteq R \cdot F\phi \cdot \alpha^{\circ} \;\Rightarrow\; \phi \subseteq (\![R]\!)$$
$$\phi \supseteq R \cdot F\phi \cdot \alpha^{\circ} \;\Rightarrow\; \phi \supseteq (\![R]\!).$$

The typical use of promotion is when $\phi = S \cdot (\![T]\!)$. In particular, the following calculation gives a useful condition for expressing $S \cdot (\![T]\!)$ as a catamorphism:

$$S \cdot (\![T]\!) = (\![R]\!)$$
$$\equiv \quad \{\text{promotion}\}$$
$$S \cdot (\![T]\!) \cdot \alpha = R \cdot \mathsf{F}(S \cdot (\![T]\!))$$
$$\equiv \quad \{\text{definition of } (\![T]\!)\}$$
$$S \cdot T \cdot \mathsf{F}(\![T]\!) = R \cdot \mathsf{F}(S \cdot (\![T]\!))$$
$$\Leftarrow \quad \{\mathsf{F} \text{ is a functor}\}$$
$$S \cdot T = R \cdot \mathsf{F}S.$$

That is, if S is a homomorphism from T to R, then $S \cdot (\![T]\!) = (\![R]\!)$. Use of this, or similar, conditions in calculations will be signalled with the hint 'promotion'.

2.2.7   Datatypes

Datatypes and initial algebras are named by type declarations. For example,

$$Nat \quad ::= \quad zero \mid succ\, Nat$$

declares $[zero, succ] : Nat \leftarrow \mathsf{F}\, Nat$ to be the initial F-algebra, where F is the functor $\mathsf{F}A = \bot + A$ and $\mathsf{F}h = id_\bot + h$. Here, $\bot$ is the terminal object of Rel and $zero : Nat \leftarrow \bot$ is a constant.

Datatypes are often parameterised. For example,

$$\mathsf{list}\, A \quad ::= \quad nil \mid snoc\, (\mathsf{list}\, A, A)$$

declares $[nil, snoc] : \mathsf{list}\, A \leftarrow \mathsf{F}_A(\mathsf{list}\, A)$ to be the initial F_A-algebra, where the functor F is given by $\mathsf{F}_A(B) = \bot + (B \times A)$ and $\mathsf{F}_A(f) = id_\bot + (f \times id_A)$. One could write $\mathsf{F}(A, B)$ instead of $\mathsf{F}_A(B)$, in which case we think of F as a *bifunctor*.

Above we wrote list in sans serif font, which is our convention for denoting functors. This was intended: with every type constructor T is associated a certain functor, called a *type* functor. For example, the type functor list is just the familiar *map* operation of functional programming. The function $\mathsf{list}\, f$ is defined over snoc lists by

$$\mathsf{list}\, f \quad = \quad (\![nil, snoc \cdot (id \times f)]\!).$$

Using the characterisation of catamorphisms, this definition expands to the recursion equations

$$\mathsf{list}\, f\, [\,] \quad = \quad [\,]$$
$$\mathsf{list}\, f\, (snoc\, (x, a)) \quad = \quad snoc\, (\mathsf{list}\, f\, x, f\, a)$$

more familiar in functional programming. In fact, $([e, f])$ translates to the standard higher-order function *foldl f e*. Note that we write $([e, f])$ rather than the more clumsy $([[e, f]])$.

Type functors are relators and the case of lists illustrates how they are defined in general: given an initial algebra $\alpha : \mathsf{T}A \leftarrow \mathsf{F}(A, \mathsf{T}A)$, the type functor T is defined by

$$\mathsf{T}\,R \;=\; ([\alpha \cdot \mathsf{F}(R, id)]).$$

Further examples of datatypes and catamorphisms appear below in our treatment of language recognition.

2.2.8 Lists

We have already started to record some basic facts about lists and, since we will need them below, we give a few more.

First of all, the function *cat* : list $A \leftarrow$ list $A \times$ list A concatenates two lists and is defined on snoc-lists by the recursive equations

$$
\begin{aligned}
cat \cdot (id \times nil) &= outl \\
cat \cdot (id \times snoc) &= snoc \cdot (cat \times id) \cdot assoc.
\end{aligned}
$$

Here, *assoc* is the natural isomorphism from $A \times (B \times C)$ to $(A \times B) \times C$. These equations are 'pointless' translations of the equations

$$
\begin{aligned}
x + [\,] &= x \\
x + snoc(y, b) &= snoc(x + y, b)
\end{aligned}
$$

where $+$ is infix notation for *cat*.

The function *snoc* is related to *cat* in that $snoc = cat \cdot (id \times wrap)$, where the function *wrap* 'wraps' a symbol into a singleton list and is defined by $wrap\ a = snoc(nil, a)$ or, more shortly, $wrap\ a = [a]$. Thus we have $snoc(x, a) = x + [a]$.

Finally, the function *concat* : list $A \leftarrow$ list(list A) concatenates a list of lists and is defined by

$$concat \;=\; ([nil, cat]).$$

All the above is, of course, familiar territory in functional programming; what is mainly of interest here are the names and the pointless versions of definitions and equations.

2.2.9 Powersets

It is an important feature of the calculus that we can move between a relation $R : A \leftarrow B$ and the corresponding set-valued function $\Lambda R : \mathsf{P}A \leftarrow B$. Formally, the isomorphism between these two representations of relations can be described in the following suitably abstract form. For every set A there exists a set $\mathsf{P}A$, called the *powerset* of A, and a relation $\in : A \leftarrow \mathsf{P}A$, called the *membership* relation on A. The powerset $\mathsf{P}A$ and the relation $\in$ are characterised by the following property. For every relation $R : A \leftarrow B$, there exists a function $\Lambda R : \mathsf{P}A \leftarrow B$ such that

$$(f = \Lambda R) \;\equiv\; (\in \cdot f = R) \quad \text{for all } f : \mathsf{P}A \leftarrow B.$$

The function ΛR is called the *power transpose* of R and can be defined in set theory by

$$(\Lambda R)\, b \;=\; \{\, a \mid aRb \,\}.$$

Λ sets up an isomorphism between relations and set-valued functions since $\Lambda R = \Lambda S$ if and only if $R = S$. A large part of set theory can be recovered using just the above equivalence together with the axioms of the relational calculus, but we will need only the following properties of Λ, explained afterwards:

$$
\begin{aligned}
\Lambda(R \cdot S) &= \mathit{Union} \cdot \mathsf{P}(\Lambda R) \cdot \Lambda S \\
\Lambda(R \,\cup\, S) &= \mathit{union} \cdot \langle \Lambda R, \Lambda S \rangle \\
\Lambda(R \times S) &= \mathit{cross} \cdot (\Lambda R \times \Lambda S).
\end{aligned}
$$

First of all, $\mathit{Union} = \Lambda(\in \cdot \in)$ is the big union operation of set theory with type $\mathit{Union} : \mathsf{P}A \leftarrow \mathsf{PP}A$. The powerset functor $\mathsf{P} : \mathit{Fun} \leftarrow \mathit{Fun}$ is defined by $\mathsf{P}f = \Lambda(f \cdot \in)$ and applies f to every element of a set; in other words, P is the *map* operator for sets. The powerset functor is a relator, though we will not need its extension to relations in this paper. (A detailed discussion of P and its algebraic properties can be found in [20].) The particular combination $\mathit{Union} \cdot \mathsf{P}f \cdot g$ of two set-valued functions f and g is known as *Kleisli* composition and is sometimes written $f \circ g$. Kleisli composition is associative and has unit τ, the function that turns an object into a singleton set.

The function $\mathit{union} : \mathsf{P}A \leftarrow \mathsf{P}A \times \mathsf{P}A$ is defined by $\mathit{union} = \Lambda(\in \cdot \mathit{outl} \,\cup\, \in \cdot \mathit{outr})$ and returns the union of two set-valued functions. Finally, the function $\mathit{cross} : \mathsf{P}(A \times B) \leftarrow \mathsf{P}A \times \mathsf{P}B$ is defined by $\mathit{cross} = \Lambda(\in \times \in)$ and takes the cross-product of two sets.

2.2.10   Least fixed points

Finally, we record here certain notation and results about least fixed points that will be needed in the sequel. Most of the material is well-known; an early reference is [2], and a more modern account can be found in [9]. The reader is referred to these papers for a more detailed discussion of the calculus of least fixed points.

In what follows $F(X)$, $F(X, Y)$, and so on, denote arbitrary relational expressions monotonic in X and Y.

The least solution of the equation $X = F(X)$ will be denoted by $(\mu X : F(X))$. This is also the least solution of $X \supseteq F(X)$, as we mentioned earlier. The two conditions characterising least fixed points are that it is a fixed point:

$$F\left(\mu X : F(X)\right) \;=\; (\mu X : F(X)),$$

and that it is a least one:

$$F(Y) \subseteq Y \;\;\Rightarrow\;\; (\mu X : F(X)) \subseteq Y.$$

The facts we need are as follows:

$$
\begin{aligned}
(\mu X : F(X, X)) &= (\mu X : (\mu Y : F(X, Y))) & (2.1) \\
(\mu X : F(X, X)) &= (\mu X : F(X, \mu Y : F(Y, Y))) & (2.2) \\
F\left(\mu X : G\left(F(X)\right)\right) &= (\mu X : F\left(G(X)\right)) & (2.3) \\
(\mu X : F\left(\mu Y : G(X, Y)\right)) &= F\left(\mu X : G\left(F\,X,\,X\right)\right) & (2.4)
\end{aligned}
$$

Proofs are straightforward applications of the characterisation of least fixed points and we omit details.

2.3 Context-free Grammars and Languages

Now let us return to the problem of context-free language recognition in which many of the above concepts are illustrated. Context-free grammars can be defined in terms of three quantities: a finite alphabet A of symbols, a designated 'start' symbol a_0 in A, and a relation $P : \mathsf{list}\,A \leftarrow A$ which specifies the production rules. The non-terminal symbols are just those symbols in the domain of P. There are two ways this information can be used to describe context-free languages. One approach involves building syntax trees, while the other takes the reflexive transitive closure of a 'derives' relation. We will consider both methods below.

2.3.1 Syntax trees

Syntax trees can be introduced with the type definition

$$\mathsf{tree}\,A \;\;::=\;\; tip\,A \mid fork(A, \mathsf{list}(\mathsf{tree}\,A)).$$

This declares $[tip, fork] : \mathsf{tree}\,A \leftarrow \mathsf{G}_A(\mathsf{tree}\,A)$ to be the initial G_A–algebra, where G is the functor $\mathsf{G}_A(B) = A + (A \times \mathsf{list}\,B)$ and $\mathsf{G}_A(f) = id_A + (id_A \times \mathsf{list}\,f)$. As we saw earlier, list is the type functor associated with snoc-lists.

The function $tips : \mathsf{list}\,A \leftarrow \mathsf{tree}\,A$ returns the list of tips of a given tree in left to right order:

$$tips \;=\; (\!\![wrap, concat \cdot outr]\!\!). \tag{2.5}$$

As practice, we will expand this definition. The characterisation of catamorphisms gives

$$tips \cdot [tip, fork] \;=\; [wrap, concat \cdot outr] \cdot (id + (id \times \mathsf{list}\ tips)),$$

and simplifying this equation we get the recursion equations

$$
\begin{aligned}
tips(tip\ a) &= wrap\ a\\
tips(fork(a, ts)) &= concat\ (\mathsf{list}\ tips\ ts).
\end{aligned}
$$

Next, the relation *generate* : $\mathsf{tree}\ A \leftarrow A$ generates a syntax tree from a given symbol. This tree is labelled with the given symbol, and conforms to the syntax of the grammar in that each subtree with label a and list x of labels of its immediate subtrees satisfies xPa. The relation *generate* is defined formally as the converse of a relational catamorphism:

$$generate \;=\; (\!(id, step^\circ)\!)^\circ, \tag{2.6}$$

where $step = \langle id, P\rangle$, so $(a, x)step(a)$ just in the case xPa. The reader should study (2.6) carefully, as it illustrates the descriptive power of relational catamorphisms and their converses very forcefully.

Finally, the language relation $L : \mathsf{list}\ A \leftarrow A$ is defined by

$$L \;=\; tips \cdot generate \tag{2.7}$$

and derives a string from a given symbol by first generating some syntax tree and then extracting its tips.

2.3.2   Closure

The second way of defining the language relation L is by taking the reflexive transitive closure of a relation $D : \mathsf{list}\ A \leftarrow \mathsf{list}\ A$ that extends P to sequences. This relation describes a single 'parallel' derivation step in which every symbol is rewritten simultaneously – possibly to itself. For the rest of this section we will suppose that $wrap \subseteq P$, so that each symbol can produce itself. Then we have $D = concat \cdot \mathsf{list}\ P$. Equivalently, using promotion, D is the catamorphism

$$D \;=\; (\!(nil, cat \cdot (id \times P))\!).$$

We now define

$$L \;=\; D^\star \cdot wrap, \tag{2.8}$$

so L is the reflexive transitive closure (explained below) of D applied to a singleton list.

To complete this definition we need to say what $D^\star$ is. For any relation $R : A \leftarrow A$ there exists a smallest reflexive and transitive relation $R^\star$ containing R.

Formally, we define $R^\star = (\mu X : id \cup X \cdot R)$, though an alternative definition is that $R^\star = (\mu X : id \cup R \cdot X)$. A fact we will use below generalises this second characterisation:

$$R^\star \cdot S \;=\; (\mu X : S \cup R \cdot X). \tag{2.9}$$

Taking $S = id$ gives the earlier result.

Equations (2.7) and (2.8) look quite different, though they do define the same relation. The latter is more familiar in formal language theory – where $y D^\star x$ is usually written $x \Rightarrow^\star y$ – but the former is more useful in dealing with questions of parsing.

2.4 Hylomorphisms

Equation (2.7) defines L as a catamorphism after the converse of a catamorphism. Such a combination is known in the trade as a *hylomorphism* (Meijer [19]). Hylomorphisms can be characterised as least fixed points of certain equations. More precisely,

Proposition 1 *Suppose* $R : A \leftarrow \mathsf{F}\,A$ *and* $S : B \leftarrow \mathsf{F}B$ *for some functor* F. *Then* $(\!(R)\!) \cdot (\!(S)\!)^\circ : A \leftarrow B$ *is given by*

$$(\!(R)\!) \cdot (\!(S)\!)^\circ \;=\; (\mu X : R \cdot \mathsf{F}X \cdot S^\circ).$$

Using this result, we obtain from (2.5), (2.6) and (2.7) that

$$L \;=\; (\mu X : [wrap, concat \cdot outr] \cdot \mathsf{G}X \cdot [id, step^\circ]^\circ). \tag{2.10}$$

We simplify the right-hand side in two stages. First

$$
\begin{aligned}
&\quad [wrap, concat \cdot outr] \cdot \mathsf{G}X \\
&= \quad \{\text{definition } \mathsf{G}X = id + (id \times \mathsf{list}\,X) \text{ and coproduct}\} \\
&\quad [wrap, concat \cdot outr \cdot (id \times \mathsf{list}\,X)] \\
&= \quad \{\text{since } outr \cdot (id \times R) = R \cdot outr\} \\
&\quad [wrap, concat \cdot \mathsf{list}\,X \cdot outr].
\end{aligned}
$$

Second

$$
\begin{aligned}
&\quad [wrap, concat \cdot \mathsf{list}\,X \cdot outr] \cdot [id, step^\circ]^\circ \\
&= \quad \{\text{since } [R, S] \cdot [U, V]^\circ = R \cdot U^\circ \cup S \cdot V^\circ\} \\
&\quad wrap \cup concat \cdot \mathsf{list}\,X \cdot outr \cdot step \\
&= \quad \{\text{since } step = \langle id, P\rangle \text{ and } outr \cdot \langle id, P\rangle = P\} \\
&\quad wrap \cup concat \cdot \mathsf{list}\,X \cdot P.
\end{aligned}
$$

Hence we have shown

$$L = (\mu X : wrap \ \cup \ concat \cdot \text{list } X \cdot P). \tag{2.11}$$

This is a characterisation of L solely in terms of lists: the syntax trees, having served their purpose as an intermediate data structure, have been eliminated from further consideration.

2.4.1   Closure as a hylomorphism

Practically every relation of interest can be specified as a hylomorphism. Let us digress for a moment and define closure as a hylomorphism. To start with, let $\text{list}^+ A$ denote the non-empty snoc lists over A, defined by

$$\text{list}^+ A \quad ::= \quad wrap \ A \mid snoc(\text{list}^+ A, A).$$

The identifiers *wrap* and *snoc* have been used before in the context of possibly empty lists, but the ambiguity is harmless.

Next, for $S : A \leftarrow A$ consider the function *chain* $S : \text{list}^+ A \leftarrow A$ which, given an element $a \in A$, returns some sequence $[a_0, a_1, \ldots, a_n]$ with $a_n = a$ and $a_j S a_{j+1}$ for $0 \leq j < n$. Like *generate* we can define *chain* as the converse of a catamorphism:

$$chain \ S \ = \ (\!(id, step^\circ)\!)^\circ,$$

where $step = \langle S, id \rangle$.

Next, let *first* : $A \leftarrow \text{list}^+ A$ return the first element of a list:

$$first \ = \ (\!(id, outl)\!).$$

Finally, define $S^\star$ as the hylomorphism

$$S^\star \ = \ first \cdot chain \ S.$$

Following the earlier calculation for expressing hylomorphisms as least fixed points, we find $S^\star = (\mu X : id \ \cup \ X \cdot S)$, which is the standard definition.

So, it is not surprising that the two definitions of a context-free language are connected, although we will not pause to prove they are indeed equivalent.

2.5   The Recognition Problem

The recognition problem is to determine whether or not xLa_0 for a given x. To solve it, we will turn (2.11) into a well-founded recursion for computing ΛL° and then see whether $a_0 \in \Lambda L^\circ(x)$. Such a strategy is indicated because ΛL might return infinite sets, whereas ΛL° returns finite sets since the alphabet of symbols is assumed to be finite.

Because converse preserves order and relators preserve converse, we can take the converse of (2.11), obtaining

$$L^\circ \;=\; (\mu X : wrap^\circ \;\cup\; P^\circ \cdot \mathsf{list}\, X \cdot concat^\circ). \tag{2.12}$$

It follows that L° satisfies

$$L^\circ \;=\; wrap^\circ \;\cup\; P^\circ \cdot \mathsf{list}\, L^\circ \cdot concat^\circ.$$

However, this equation cannot serve directly as an implementation of L° since the recursion is not well-founded: for example, $[x]\, concat^\circ\, x$, $[[\,], [x]]\, concat^\circ\, x$, and so on. To deal with this problem, we need to simplify the term $P^\circ \cdot \mathsf{list}\, X \cdot concat^\circ$ of (2.12). If we could express $P^\circ \cdot \mathsf{list}\, X$ as a catamorphism, then $P^\circ \cdot \mathsf{list}\, X \cdot concat^\circ$ would be a hylomorphism, so we could appeal to Proposition 1 to rewrite it as a recursion equation.

Since $\mathsf{list}\, X = (\![nil, snoc \cdot (id \times X)]\!)$, promotion gives $P^\circ \cdot \mathsf{list}\, X = (\![R, S]\!)$ provided

$$P^\circ \cdot [nil, snoc \cdot (id \times X)] \;=\; [R, S \cdot (P^\circ \times id)].$$

We can take $R = P^\circ \cdot nil$ and $S = op \cdot (id \times X)$, provided op is such that

$$P^\circ \cdot snoc \;=\; op \cdot (P^\circ \times id).$$

Unfortunately, no such identity holds. The key step in developing Earley's algorithm is to generalise P° to a relation Q that does satisfy such an identity.

Suppose we define Q by $(a, y)\, Q x = a P^\circ (x \,+\!\!+\, y)$. In words, Q returns possible start symbols together with what is expected next. We have $a P^\circ x = (a, [\,])\, Q x$ or, equivalently,

$$P^\circ \;=\; q \cdot Q \quad \text{where} \quad q = outl \cdot (id \times nil^\circ), \tag{2.13}$$

so Q generalises P. Note in particular that $Q \cdot nil = \{(a, x) \mid x P a\}$. Furthermore,

$$(a, y)\, Q(x \,+\!\!+\, [b]) \;=\; a P^\circ (x \,+\!\!+\, [b] \,+\!\!+\, y) \;=\; (a, [b] \,+\!\!+\, y)\, Q x,$$

so we get what we want:

$$Q \cdot snoc \;=\; op \cdot (Q \times id), \tag{2.14}$$

where op is the partial function $op((a, [b] \,+\!\!+\, y), b) = (a, y)$. Now we replay the reasoning above:

$$\begin{aligned}
&\quad P^\circ \cdot \mathsf{list}\, X \\
&= \quad \{\text{equation (2.13)}\} \\
&\quad q \cdot Q \cdot \mathsf{list}\, X \\
&= \quad \{\text{equation (2.14) and promotion}\} \\
&\quad q \cdot (\![Q \cdot nil, op \cdot (id \times X)]\!).
\end{aligned}$$

Hence

$$L^\circ = (\mu X : wrap^\circ \cup q \cdot R), \tag{2.15}$$

where R is the hylomorphism $R = (\!\![Q \cdot nil, op \cdot (id \times X)]\!\!) \cdot concat^\circ$. Proposition 1 plus a little simplification of the kind we saw earlier now gives

$$R = (\mu Y : Q \cdot nil \cdot nil^\circ \cup op \cdot (Y \times X) \cdot cat^\circ).$$

Using the substitution lemma (2.4) of the μ–calculus, we obtain that $L^\circ = wrap^\circ \cup q \cdot R$, where

$$R = (\mu X : Q \cdot nil \cdot nil^\circ \cup op \cdot (X \times (wrap^\circ \cup q \cdot X)) \cdot cat^\circ).$$

Expanding the second term using $snoc = cat \cdot (id \times wrap)$, we find

$$R = (\mu X : Q \cdot nil \cdot nil^\circ \cup op \cdot (X \times id) \cdot snoc^\circ \cup op \cdot (X \times q \cdot X) \cdot cat^\circ).$$

We have made progress but there still remains the problem that this recursion is not well-founded: we have $([\,], x)\, cat^\circ\, x$ and $(x, [\,])\, cat^\circ\, x$ for all x.

The final step is to break the *cat* into pieces, using the identity

$$cat = outl \cdot (id \times nil^\circ) \cup outr \cdot (nil^\circ \times id) \cup catp,$$

where $x\, catp(y, z)$ if and only y and z are nonempty lists and $x = y +\!\!+ z$. We then get

$$
\begin{aligned}
(X \times q \cdot X) \cdot cat^\circ = {}& (X \times (q \cdot X \cdot nil)) \cdot outl^\circ \cup \\
& ((X \cdot nil) \times (q \cdot X)) \cdot outr^\circ \cup \\
& (X \times (q \cdot X)) \cdot catp^\circ.
\end{aligned}
$$

The first two terms involve the constant $X \cdot nil$, that is, a relation with domain $\bot$, and can be rewritten using the identities

$$
\begin{aligned}
(A \cdot B \times C) \cdot outl^\circ &= \langle A, C!\rangle \cdot B \\
(C \times A \cdot B) \cdot outr^\circ &= \langle C!, A\rangle \cdot B,
\end{aligned}
$$

where C is a constant and $C! = C \cdot !$. Here $! :\bot\leftarrow A$ is the unique arrow from A to the terminal object, so $C!$ is a relation with constant range. The result is

$$
\begin{aligned}
(X \times q \cdot X) \cdot cat^\circ = {}& (\langle id, q \cdot X \cdot nil!\rangle \cup \langle X \cdot nil!, q\rangle) \cdot X \cup \\
& (X \times (q \cdot X)) \cdot catp^\circ.
\end{aligned}
$$

Now, introducing

$$S = op \cdot (\langle id, q \cdot R \cdot nil!\rangle \cup \langle R \cdot nil!, q\rangle), \tag{2.16}$$

and using equation (2.2) of the μ–calculus, we obtain

$$
\begin{aligned}
R = {}& (\mu X : S \cdot X \cup Q \cdot nil \cdot nil^\circ \cup op \cdot (X \times id) \cdot snoc^\circ \\
& \cup op \cdot (X \times q \cdot X) \cdot catp^\circ).
\end{aligned}
$$

The end is in sight: using equation (2.1) of the μ–calculus, together with (2.9), we get the final result

$$
\begin{aligned}
R \;=\; & (\mu X : S^{\star} \cdot (Q \cdot nil \cdot nil^{\circ} \;\cup\; op \cdot (X \times id) \cdot snoc^{\circ} & \text{(2.17)} \\
& \cup\; op \cdot (X \times q \cdot X) \cdot catp^{\circ}).
\end{aligned}
$$

This is a well-founded recursion for R. In effect, we have isolated the source of non-well-foundedness in a single equation, namely the equation

$$
R \cdot nil \;=\; \mu X : Q \cdot nil \;\cup\; op \cdot \langle X, q \cdot X \rangle \tag{2.18}
$$

for computing the constant $R \cdot nil : \mathsf{list}\, A \leftarrow \perp$. We need $R \cdot nil$ to define S but, once we have S, the values of R for nonempty arguments can be computed using (2.17). And, having computed R, we can compute $L^{\circ} = wrap^{\circ} \cup q \cdot R$.

Equation (2.17) is the essence of the basic form of Earley's algorithm for general context-free language recognition, omitting the so-called 'predictor' stage. The predictor stage improves on the basic algorithm by further restricting the range of R to those values which contribute to the computation of $(a_0, []) \in \Lambda R(x)$. Although prediction is important in practice, the details depend on a specific implementation strategy for R and will not be considered further here.

In the remaining section we will outline how to convert (2.17) into a recursion for computing ΛR and also show how to implement the recursion efficiently by a bottom-up tabulation scheme.

2.6   Tabulation

To turn (2.17) into an effective program for computing ΛR we use the identities given in Section 2.2.9, and then represent the (finite) set-valued functions by list-valued ones. (To avoid lengthy explanations, familiarity with functional programming and its repertoire of list-processing operations will be assumed in what follows.) In particular, the function $\Lambda catp^{\circ}$ is represented by a function *splits*, where $splits\, x = zip\, (inits^{+}\, x, tails^{+}\, x)$, and

$$
\begin{aligned}
inits^{+}\, [a_1, a_2, \ldots, a_n] \;&=\; [[a_1], [a_1, a_2], \ldots, [a_1, \ldots, a_{n-1}]] \\
tails^{+}\, [a_1, a_2, \ldots, a_n] \;&=\; [[a_2, \ldots, a_n], \ldots, [a_{n-1}, a_n], [a_n]]
\end{aligned}
$$

return the lists of proper initial and tail segments of a list, respectively. The result is a recursive definition of a function f (that is, ΛR) of the following general form:

$$
\begin{aligned}
f\, [a] \;&=\; g\, a \\
f\, (x \mathbin{+\!\!+} [a]) \;&=\; h\, (f\, x, a) \mathbin{+\!\!+} j\, [(f\, u, f\, v) | (u, v) \leftarrow splits\, (x \mathbin{+\!\!+} [a])].
\end{aligned}
$$

To explain briefly where the various functions g, h and j come from, let *star* denote the list valued function corresponding to $Union \cdot \mathsf{P}(\Lambda S^{\star})$, let *qnil* be the constant list corresponding to $(\Lambda Q)\,[\,]$, and *rnil* the constant list corresponding to $(\Lambda R)\,[\,]$.

The list *qnil* is given as input, $qnil = [(a, x) \mid xPa]$, and we have $rnil = star\ qnil$. Now we get

$$
\begin{aligned}
g\ a &= star\ [(b, tail\ y) \mid (b, y) \leftarrow rnil, head\ y = a] \\
h\ (xs, a) &= star\ [(b, tail\ y) \mid (b, y) \leftarrow xs, head\ y = a] \\
j\ (xs, ys) &= star\ [(b, tail\ y) \mid (b, y) \leftarrow xs, y \neq [\,], (head\ y, [\,]) \leftarrow ys]
\end{aligned}
$$

Direct execution of the program for f requires exponential time, but a suitably chosen tabulation scheme can bring this down to cubic time. The tabulation scheme is not specific to language recognition but arises in many examples of dynamic programming. For this reason we will give details of its synthesis.

In order to compute $f\ x$ we need also to compute $f\ w$ for every nonempty segment w of x. Define

$$
\begin{aligned}
fis\ x &= [f\ u \mid u \leftarrow inits\ x] \\
fts\ x &= [f\ v \mid v \leftarrow tails\ x] \\
fss\ x &= [fis\ v \mid v \leftarrow tails\ x],
\end{aligned}
$$

where *inits* x and *tails* x return the nonempty initial and tail segments of a list, respectively. For nonempty x we have $inits\ x = inits^+\ x \mathbin{+\!\!+} [x]$ and $tails\ x = [x] \mathbin{+\!\!+} tails^+\ x$. Furthermore, $f = last \cdot head \cdot fss$ on nonempty lists, so it is sufficient to show how to compute *fss*.

Since $tails\ [\,] = [\,]$ we have $fss\ [\,] = [\,]$. For the general case we calculate

$$
\begin{aligned}
&fss\ (x \mathbin{+\!\!+} [a]) \\
={}& \quad \{\text{definition}\} \\
&[fis\ v \mid v \leftarrow tails\ (x \mathbin{+\!\!+} [a])] \\
={}& \quad \{\text{since } tails\ (x \mathbin{+\!\!+} [a]) = [v \mathbin{+\!\!+} [a] \mid v \leftarrow tails\ x \mathbin{+\!\!+} [[\,]]]\} \\
&[fis\ (v \mathbin{+\!\!+} [a]) \mid v \leftarrow tails\ x \mathbin{+\!\!+} [[\,]]] \\
={}& \quad \{\text{definition of } fis\} \\
&[fis\ v \mathbin{+\!\!+} [f\,(v \mathbin{+\!\!+} [a])] \mid v \leftarrow tails\ x \mathbin{+\!\!+} [[\,]]] \\
={}& \quad \{\text{unzipping, writing } zipc = zipwith\ snoc\} \\
&zipc\ ([fis\ v \mid v \leftarrow tails\ x \mathbin{+\!\!+} [[\,]]], [f\,(v \mathbin{+\!\!+} [a]) \mid v \leftarrow tails\ x \mathbin{+\!\!+} [[\,]]]) \\
={}& \quad \{\text{definition of } fss \text{ and } fts\} \\
&zipc\ (fss\ x \mathbin{+\!\!+} [[\,]], fts(x \mathbin{+\!\!+} [a])).
\end{aligned}
$$

This gives a recursive definition for *fss* in terms of *fts*. Aiming now to express *fts* in terms of *fss*, we see that $fts\ [a] = [g\ a]$ and

$$
fts\ (x \mathbin{+\!\!+} [a]) = [f\ (x \mathbin{+\!\!+} [a])] \mathbin{+\!\!+} [f\ v \mid v \leftarrow tails^+\ (x \mathbin{+\!\!+} [a])].
$$

Now we can argue

$$
f(x \mathbin{+\!\!+} [a])
$$

$$
\begin{aligned}
&= \quad \{\text{definition}\} \\
&\quad h(f\,x,a) \mathbin{+\!\!+} j\,[(f\,u,f\,v) \mid (u,v) \leftarrow \mathit{splits}\,(x \mathbin{+\!\!+} [a])] \\
&= \quad \{\text{definition of } \mathit{splits} \text{ and unzipping, writing } k = j \cdot \mathit{zip}\} \\
&\quad h(f\,x,a) \mathbin{+\!\!+} k([f\,u \mid u \leftarrow \mathit{inits}^+(x \mathbin{+\!\!+} [a])],[f\,v \mid v \leftarrow \mathit{tails}^+(x \mathbin{+\!\!+} [a])]) \\
&= \quad \{\text{definitions of } \mathit{fis}, \mathit{fts} \text{ and } f = \mathit{last} \cdot \mathit{fis}\} \\
&\quad h(\mathit{last}(\mathit{fis}\,x),a) \mathbin{+\!\!+} k(\mathit{fis}\,x, \mathit{fts}(\mathit{tail}(x \mathbin{+\!\!+} [a]))) \\
&= \quad \{\text{since } \mathit{fis} = \mathit{head} \cdot \mathit{fss}\} \\
&\quad h(\mathit{last}\,\mathit{xs},a) \mathbin{+\!\!+} k(\mathit{xs},\mathit{ys}),
\end{aligned}
$$

where $\mathit{xs} = \mathit{head}(\mathit{fss}\,x)$ and $\mathit{ys} = \mathit{fts}(\mathit{tail}(x \mathbin{+\!\!+} [a]))$. Hence, with these values of xs and ys, we obtain

$$
\mathit{fts}\,(x \mathbin{+\!\!+} [a]) \;=\; [h(\mathit{last}\,\mathit{xs},a) \mathbin{+\!\!+} k(\mathit{xs},\mathit{ys})] \mathbin{+\!\!+} \mathit{ys},
$$

and so we get

$$
\begin{aligned}
\mathit{fts}\,(x \mathbin{+\!\!+} [a]) \;=\;\; & \mathit{foldr}\,(\oplus)\,[g\,a]\,(\mathit{fss}\,x) \\
& \text{where } \mathit{xs} \oplus \mathit{ys} = [h(\mathit{last}\,\mathit{xs},a) \mathbin{+\!\!+} k(\mathit{xs},\mathit{ys})] \mathbin{+\!\!+} \mathit{ys}.
\end{aligned}
$$

Using this in the derived expression for $\mathit{fss}\,(x \mathbin{+\!\!+} [a]$, we get

$$
\mathit{fss}\,(x \mathbin{+\!\!+} [a]) \;=\; \mathit{zipc}\,(\mathit{fss}\,x \mathbin{+\!\!+} [[\,]], \mathit{foldr}\,(\oplus)\,[g\,a]\,(\mathit{fss}\,x)).
$$

Thus, fss can be expressed as a catamorphism on snoc-lists. Such catamorphisms are expressed using foldl, so we get the final program for f on nonempty lists:

$$
\begin{aligned}
f \;&=\; \mathit{last} \cdot \mathit{head} \cdot \mathit{fss} \\
\mathit{fss} \;&=\; \mathit{foldl}\,(\otimes)\,[\,] \\
\mathit{xss} \otimes a \;&=\; \mathit{zipc}(\mathit{xss} \mathbin{+\!\!+} [[\,]], \mathit{foldr}\,(\oplus)\,[g\,a]\,\mathit{xss}) \\
& \quad\;\; \text{where } \mathit{xs} \oplus \mathit{ys} = [h(\mathit{last}\,\mathit{xs},a) \mathbin{+\!\!+} k(\mathit{xs},\mathit{ys})] \mathbin{+\!\!+} \mathit{ys}.
\end{aligned}
$$

Computation of fss on a list of length n requires n evaluations of $\otimes$, and evaluation of $\mathit{xss} \otimes a$ when xss has length m requires $O(m)$ evaluations of $\oplus$. Assuming g, h and j take constant time, evaluation of $\mathit{xs} \oplus \mathit{ys}$ when the length of xs and ys is p requires $O(p)$ steps, so the total is

$$
\sum_{m=1}^{n} \sum_{p=1}^{m} O(p) \;=\; O(n^3)
$$

steps.

2.7 Summary and Conclusions

There are three points worth noting about the above derivation. First there is the descriptive power of relational catamorphisms and their converses. This is perhaps the most pleasing part of the approach. With very little machinery one can define and manipulate syntax trees as easily as lists, so it would be possible to treat the parsing problem in the same way. Second, there is the maneuvering to achieve a well-founded recursion. This is perhaps the least pleasing aspect. It all would have been much simpler if we had banned productions with empty right-hand sides, and therefore excluded the empty list from consideration. This is sometimes done in formal treatments of Earley's algorithm, but it sidesteps one of its main features. Finally, there is the change of calculus from relations to functions when reasoning about a suitable tabulation scheme. When it comes down to questions of implementation and optimisation some change into an executable notation is necessary. And at least the transition to a functional programming framework is fairly smooth.

Acknowledgment The authors are very grateful to Carroll Morgan for a careful reading of a draft of this paper and for suggesting a number of changes to improve the presentation. Any mistakes or obscurities that remain are, of course, our sole responsibility.

References

[1] R. C. Backhouse, P. J. de Bruin, G. Malcolm, E. Voermans, and J. C. S. P. van der Woude. Relational Catamorphisms. In B. Moller, editor *Proceedings of the IFIP TC2/WG2.1 Working Conference on Constructing Programs from Specifications*, 287–318, 1991.

[2] J. W. de Bakker and W. P. de Roever. A calculus for recursive program schemes. In M. Nivat, editor *Automata, Languages and Programming*, North-Holland, 167–196, 1973.

[3] R. S. Bird. An introduction to the theory of lists. In M. Broy, editor, *Logic of Programming and Calculi of Discrete Design*, volume 36 of *NATO ASI Series F*, pages 3–42. Springer-Verlag, 1987.

[4] R. S. Bird. A calculus of functions for program derivation. In D. A. Turner, editor, *Research Topics in Functional Programming*, 1987 University of Texas Year of Programming Series, Addison-Wesley, 287–308, 1990.

[5] R. S. Bird. Lectures on constructive functional programming. In M. Broy, editor, *Constructive Methods in Computing Science*, Springer-Verlag NATO ASI Series F:Computer and System Sciences, vol 5, 151–216, 1989.

[6] R. S. Bird and O. de Moor. From dynamic programming to greedy algorithms. To appear in *Proceedings of the State-of-the-Art Seminar on Formal Program Development*, Rio de Janeiro, 1992.

[7] R. S. Bird and O. de Moor. Solving optimisation problems with catamorphisms. *Proceedings of the Oxford Mathematics of Program Construction Conference 1992*, Springer-Verlag LNCS 669, 1993.

[8] J. Earley. An efficient context-free parsing algorithm. *Communications of the ACM*, 13(2):94–102, February 1970.

[9] W. H. J. Feijen. ETAC's exploration of JAN177 Department of Mathematics and Computing Science, Eindhoven University of Technology, Technical Note WF152, 1992.

[10] M. M. Fokkinga. Law and order in Algorithmics. Ph. D. Thesis, University of Twente, The Netherlands, 1992. ISBN 90-9004816-2.

[11] P. J. Freyd and A. Ščedrov. *Categories, Allegories*, volume 39 of *Mathematical Library*. North-Holland, 1990.

[12] S. L. Graham, M. A. Harrison, and W. L. Ruzzo. An improved context-free recognizer. *ACM Transactions on Programming Languages and Systems*, 2(3):415–462, July 1980.

[13] C. A. R. Hoare. Lectures on Category Theory. In M. Broy, editor, *Constructive Methods in Computing Science*, Springer-Verlag NATO ASI Series F:Computer and System Sciences, vol 5, 1989.

[14] C. B. Jones. *Software Development – A Rigorous Approach*. Prentice-Hall, 1980.

[15] Geraint Jones and Mary Sheeran. *Circuit design in Ruby*, in Jørgen Staunstrup (ed.), *Formal methods for VLSI design*, North-Holland, 1990. pp. 13–70.

[16] Grant Malcolm. Homomorphisms and promotability. In J. Snepscheut, editor *1989 Groningen Mathematics of Program Construction Conference*. Springer-Verlag LNCS 375, 335-347, 1989.

[17] L. G. L. T. Meertens. Algorithmics – towards programming as a mathematical activity. In J. W. de Bakker, M. Hazewinkel, and J. K. Lenstra, editors, *Mathematics and Computer Science. CWI Symposium, November 25, 1983*, volume 1 of *CWI Monographs*, pages 289–334. North-Holland, 1986.

[18] L. G. L. T. Meertens. Paramorphisms. *Formal Aspects of Computing*, vol 4, no 5, 413–424, 1992.

[19] Erik Meijer, Maarten Fokkinga Ross Paterson. Programming with bananas, lenses, envelopes and barbed wire. in *Proceedings of the 1991 ACM Conference on Functional Programming and Computer Architecture*Springer-Verlag LNCS 523 , 1991

[20] O. de Moor. Categories, relations and dynamic programming. D.Phil. thesis. Technical Monograph PRG-98, Computing Laboratory, Oxford, 1992. Also *Theoretical Computer Science*, to appear 1993.

[21] H. Partsch. Structuring transformational developments: A case study based on Earley's recognizer. *Science of Computer Programming*, 4:17–44, 1984.

[22] M. Spivey. A categorical approach to the theory of lists. In J. Snepscheut, editor *1989 Groningen Mathematics of Program Construction Conference* Springer-Verlag LNCS 375, 399-420, 1989.

[23] P. L. Wadler. Theorems for free. *Proceedings 1989 ACM Conference on Lisp and Functional Programming*, 347-359, 1989.

Chapter 3

Formal Model of Robots: Geometry and kinematics

Dines Bjørner

3.1 Introduction

3.1.1 Background

A *robot* is a *re-programmable multi-functional mechanical manipulator,* with external sensors, *designed to move material, parts, tools, or specialized devices, through variable programmed motions for the performance of a variety of tasks*[1]. An essential part of this definition implies that there is one or more computers involved in the robot – and that this (or these) computer(s), in their monitoring and controlling software, somehow contain a model of the robot, its environment and its task description. The aim of this paper is to lay a foundation for the concise, terse abstraction of exactly these models.

A *robot system*, according to [13], generally consists of three subsystems: a *motion* subsystem, a *recognition* subsystem (with sensors), and a *control* subsystem. An aim of this paper is to start laying a foundation for understanding, in the form of "complete", abstract models, the interplay between these three parts.

Robotics is the study of basic organisation and operation of robots (robot systems). Five areas characterize robotics research: (i) *manipulators* (their design (including geometry), kinematics, dynamics, locomotion, and control), (ii) *sensors* (contact and non-contact), (iii) *programming systems*, (iv) *planning systems* and, summarizing these, (v) *systems architecture*. The aim of this paper is to contribute to the area of programming systems by proposing computable, systems architecture models of manipulators.

Robotics is in need, we find, of having the treatment of one of its core subjects be structured according to the disciplines of computing science. Computer and computing science deals with <u>what</u> objects can exist inside the computer, their behaviour (complexity, computability, etc.), respectively <u>how</u> such efficient, computable objects are efficiently constructed. (In the program and software field of

---

[1]This *italicized* definition is due to the *Robot Institute of America* [7].

the computation sciences there is no distinction between design and construction. They coincide.)

3.1.2   Short term objective

The short term objective, only partly reached by this paper, is to develop a "closed model" of "any" robot, a model that may serve as the basis for analysis (modelling and simulation) and synthesis (design).

We wish to demonstrate the validity of our approach. We wish to *improve* the otherwise competent treatment of robotics ([10, 2, 13, 8, 9, 11, 12]) found in standard text-books. These text-books usually treat their overall subject: the mechanics and control of robots in fragments. All the parts are there: material on robot *geometry*, *forward* (or *direct*) and *inverse kinematics*, *dynamics*, *motion planning* – including *trajectories* and their *generation* – robot *mechanism design*, robot (*feedback loop*) *control* design, *force control design*, and, usually, a little bit on the side on off- and on-line *robot programming*.

But there is nothing *formal* that "ties" the whole thing together. For each of the above mentioned *italicized* concepts there is a fine treatment, in the classical style of mathematics. That is: for each of the robot concepts there is, what has classically been expected from any engineering science, namely one or more *mathematical models*.

But: there is no model that connects all the fragments – all the various disciplines – together. It is a short term objective of this paper to offer such a model.

3.1.3   Structure of paper

The treatment of this paper is primarily based on [10, 2, 13, 9, 11, 12, 8]   – notably [2].

The structure of the remaining parts of the paper is as follows.

In three stages of *specification development* we propose a model-oriented definition of the *geometric* (Section 3.2) and the *kinematic components* (Section 3.4).

Section 3.3 defines abstract algorithms for computing *static positions*. Likewise Section 3.5 defines abstract algorithms for computing *inverse kinematics*.

The model of later sections enriches those of former sections.

3.2   Geometry

Geometry is the science of properties and relations of magnitudes in space – such as lines, surfaces and solids.

In this paper we will only treat what we call *abstract geometry. Concrete geom-*

etry deals the physical three-dimensional dimensions of the solid link bodies, and will be needed for *dynamics of robots* and for visual animation.

The geometry of a robot is that of its directed links, the fact that certain links are joined (but not the [kinematic] nature of the joint), and the position and orientation of links.

First we model graph-like properties of robots. Then we augment by incorporating frame (position and orientation) information, etc. Thus we believe that only two stages of specification development are necessary to capture all of the relevant geometry of a large class of robots. Further stages of specification development then enriches the obtained models with kinematic data.

3.2.1 A graph model of robot geometries

Initial class description
Let links be uniquely identified, with identifiers $l{:}L$. We model L as a class of further unspecified tokens:

  1.0 $l{:}L$ = TOKEN

The fact that links are connected, and that they form an acyclic graph, usually a partial order, can be modelled by:

  2.0 $g{:}GEO$ $= L\xrightarrow{m}L\text{-}\mathbf{set}$

that is: the geometry of a robot, $g{:}GEO$, can be modelled as an acyclic graph, and this graph is here modelled as a function $(\xrightarrow{m})$ from links to sets of successor links. We refer to GEO as the class of most abstract robot geometries.

Figure 3.1 shows two figures, on the sides, and a formula, in the middle. They abstractly model a robot with 7 links – where links $l_1-l_3-l_5$ and links $l_1-l_2-l_4-l_5$ form a loop. We do not show it, but the direction of the links is, in this example, upwards! The abstract model, of which the formula expression in the middle of Figure 3.1 is an example, can be thought of as either modelling links or modelling joints. The two pictures at the sides of Figure 3.1 illustrate this.

Initial geometry constraints
We must ensure that our graph model of robots is *well-formed:* that it satisfies a number of constraints. So far these are: (3.2) all links that are connected to a link (that is: used in the range of the graph function), must be defined (that is: in the domain of the graph function); and, defining *reachable links* as any set of links forming a succession (i.e. the links of an *arm* or a *link path* (4)), then, in an acyclic graph, no such arm (also called a *kinematic chain*) must contain the same link twice (3.3):

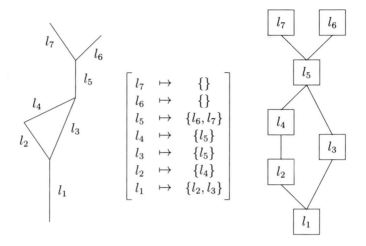

Figure 3.1 Graph Lines are Links, respectively Joints.

3.0   **type** : **inv-** *GEO: GEO* →BOOL
3.1   **inv-** *GEO(g)* ≜
 .2   **union rng** *g* ⊂ **dom** *g*
3.3   ∧ *(∀l∈* **dom** *g)(l∉ ReachableLinks(g,l))*

where:

4.0   **type** : *ReachableLinks: GEO×L→L-***set**
4.1   *ReachableLinks(g,l)* ≜
 .2   **let** *ls = g(l)∪{l'|l'∈* **dom** *g: (∃l″ ∈ ls)(l' ∈ g(l″))}* **in**
4.3   *ls*

If no link has more than at most one predecessor, that is, if, in (3.) no two different
links has successors in common:

5.0   *(∀l₁,l₂ ∈* **dom** *g)*
5.1   *(l₁≠l₂ ⊃(g(l₁)∩g(l₂))={ })*

then (5.) defines a total order on the links of a robot.

   If the robot geometry is such that it has a unique *base link* and that all links
can be reached from that base, then we have to further augment (3.):

6.0   *(∃!l∈**dom** g)*
  .1   *((∀l' ∈**dom** g)(l∉ g(l')*
6.2   *∧(ReachableLinks(g,l)=**dom** g\\{l}))*

The above (3.–5.–6.) define the constraints that must be satisfied by most single robots.

Criterion (5.) is independent of criterion (6.), and the former is less often satisfied. Thus there are robots where two different arms may lead to the same (third) link. Typically one may have *parallelogram robots*

An auxiliary function
A function which given an invariant robot geometry *g:GEO* and a link *l* computes all *arms* starting with *l* is defined next:

7.0   **type** : *Arms: GEO×L ⇸L⁺* **-set**
7.1   *Arms(g,l)* ≜
  .2   *{<l>ˆll‖ll∈L*:ll=<>∨*
7.3   *((g(l)≠{ })⊃(ll∈**union**{Arms(g,l')|l' ∈g(l)}))*
7.4   **pre-**: *l∈**dom** g*

The *ll* can be an either empty or a non-empty arm (chain) in each invocation of *Arms*. This ensures that the resulting link sequences are prefix closed.

3.2.2   Some definitions

Abstract and concrete links: An *abstract link* supports two axes. A *concrete link* – the rigid body mentioned above – usually consists of one or more abstract links.

Link length: An abstract link thus supports two joint axes. These are defined by lines in space. The *length* of an abstract link is measured as the length a of the line mutually perpendicular to the two axis lines of the abstract link.

Henceforth we shall refer only to abstract links.

Link twist: One joint axis of a link may be *twisted* wrt the other joint axis. This *link twist* is defined as follows. Let the line perpendicular to both link joint axes be the normal of a plane. Project onto this plane the two joint axes. The link twist α is now the angle between these two axis projections – measured right-hand wise wrt some ordering of the links.

Link offset: Two adjacent links define a joint with a common axis. The *link offset* is the distance d along this common axis from one link to the other. The offset is measured as the distance between the perpendiculars of the two links, one wrt a *predecessor link*, the other wrt a successor link. (For the case of closed loop linkages various, reasonably logical, conventions are applied to identify appropriate links.)

Joint angle: Finally the *joint angle* θ describes the rotation about the common axis of a first link wrt a second link.

Joint variable: For a *revolute joint* θ is the *joint variable*, whereas for a *prismatic joint* d is the *joint variable*.

Link parameters: The three remaining characteristics (link length, link twist and link offset, respectively joint angle) are called the *link parameters*.

Position and orientation: For each link we are – alternatively – interested in its position and orientation. To each link we can attach its position and orientation usually wrt a predecessor link. How we do this is described next.

Frame: The link attribute pair of position and orientation defines a *frame*. Frames can be thought of as orthogonal coordinate systems affixed to links. The relationships between neighbouring link frames thus define the relative position and orientation of the links.

Usually the Z axis of a link frame is coincident with its first (of two) joint axes, whether revolute or prismatic. The X axis points along the perpendicular (a) for the joint axis of this link and 'the next', and 'towards the next'. If $a = 0$ then X is the normal to the plane of the two joint Z axes lines. The origin of the XYZ coordinate system (for a link) is placed where the line perpendicular to the two link axes ('this' and the 'next') intersects the first of these.

Standard frames: There is a *base* frame: the origin ('begin') of the robot – and we assume in our model that there is a unique such base.

There is a *station* frame: the general location of the object being manipulated by the robot.

There is a *wrist* frame: an 'end' link of the robot to which is attached the *tool*.

So there is a *tool frame*, that is: *end-effector frame*.

The object being manipulated 'around' the station is the *goal* – and with it is likewise associated a frame.

Frame versus link parameters and joint variables: One way of characterizing a robot, geometrically, is by means of the four quantities: link length a, link twist α, link offset d and joint angle θ – two link descriptors and two joint descriptors, respectively. All these can be represented with respect to the frames.

Let $i-1$, i and $i+1$ be three, ordered adjacent links. The link parameters and joint variables are now measured as follows wrt the $X_{i-1}Y_{i-1}X_{i-1}$, $X_iY_iX_i$, and $X_{i+1}Y_{i+1}X_{i+1}$ frames:

- length a_i is the distance from Z_i to Z_{i+1} measured along X_i,
- twist α_i is the angle between Z_i and Z_{i+1} measured about X_i,
- offset d_i is the distance from X_{i-1} to X_i measured along Z_i, and
- angle θ_i is the angle between X_{i-1} and X_i measured about Z_i.

From the above we conclude that we need, in general, to refer to three frames when defining a link. We shall see this reflected in our second robot geometry model. If i refers to the base frame, then we model $i - 1$ as **nil**. If i is the wrist frame, then we model $i+1$ as **nil**. The frames for these **nil**s are coincident with their successor, respectively predecessor!

3.2.3   A position and orientation model

We model position and orientation by means of link and joint attributes.

Figure 3.2, page 44 illustrate, more concretely, the robot abstracted in Figure 3.1 (page 40).

We observe that the common link l_5 has two "incoming" joints E, F – and that joints G, H can be characterized either wrt E or wrt F. The thin lines shown in Figure 3.2 shall indicate the link parameters and joint variable of one, the "upper", joint wrt to another, the "lower" joint.

The rule for affixing the base frame, here A, mandates that – for example – π_A^C be the 4-by-4 identity matrix $\mathcal{I}_{(4,4)}$, and hence that frames A and C coincide.

This leads us to the geometry abstraction given next.

Enriched geometry class description

8.0	$g{:}GEO\,'$	$= L_i \overrightarrow{m}(L_{i+1} \overrightarrow{m}(L_{i-1} \overrightarrow{m}PaO))$
9.0	L_i	$= L$
10.0	L_{i-1}, L_{i+1}	$= [L]$
11.0	$\pi{:}PaO$	$= \underline{\textbf{s-}}lnk{:}(\underline{\textbf{s-}}len{:}\textbf{REAL}\times\underline{\textbf{s-}}twi{:}\textbf{ANG})$
12.0		$\times \underline{\textbf{s-}}jnt{:}(\underline{\textbf{s-}}off{:}\textbf{REAL}\times\underline{\textbf{s-}}ang{:}\textbf{ANG})$

We regret to be unable to draw you a proper picture that more clearly illustrates the three-dimensional nature of robots. The one shown may seem "flat", but need not be! We refer to Figures 3.18 (page 88 of the 1989 edition) of [2] for a good, "three dimensional" picture of a robot, and to its Figure 3.5 (page 75) for a fine picture showing all relevant link and joint parameters.

Definitions (11.0) and (12.0) introduces the **s-**$link$, **s-**len and **s-**twi, respectively the **s-**jnt, **s-**off and **s-**ang selector functions.

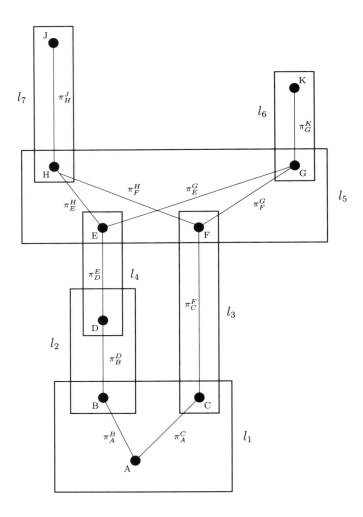

Figure 3.2 A Closed Loop Robot

Before commenting on the model we show how the picture of Figure 3.2 can be formally represented as an expression in Domain $GEO\,'$:

$$
\begin{bmatrix}
l_1 \mapsto \begin{bmatrix} l_2 \mapsto \begin{bmatrix} \mathbf{nil} \mapsto \pi_A^B \end{bmatrix} \\ l_3 \mapsto \begin{bmatrix} \mathbf{nil} \mapsto \pi_A^C \end{bmatrix} \end{bmatrix} \\
l_2 \mapsto \begin{bmatrix} l_4 \mapsto \begin{bmatrix} l_1 \mapsto \pi_B^D \end{bmatrix} \end{bmatrix} \\
l_3 \mapsto \begin{bmatrix} l_5 \mapsto \begin{bmatrix} l_1 \mapsto \pi_C^F \end{bmatrix} \end{bmatrix} \\
l_4 \mapsto \begin{bmatrix} l_5 \mapsto \begin{bmatrix} l_2 \mapsto \pi_D^E \end{bmatrix} \end{bmatrix} \\
l_5 \mapsto \begin{bmatrix} l_6 \mapsto \begin{bmatrix} l_4 \mapsto \pi_E^G \\ l_3 \mapsto \pi_F^G \end{bmatrix} \\ l_7 \mapsto \begin{bmatrix} l_4 \mapsto \pi_E^H \\ l_3 \mapsto \pi_F^H \end{bmatrix} \end{bmatrix} \\
l_6 \mapsto \begin{bmatrix} \mathbf{nil} \mapsto \begin{bmatrix} l_4 \mapsto \pi_H^J \end{bmatrix} \end{bmatrix} \\
l_7 \mapsto \begin{bmatrix} \mathbf{nil} \mapsto \begin{bmatrix} l_4 \mapsto \pi_G^K \end{bmatrix} \end{bmatrix}
\end{bmatrix}
$$

The above model takes base and end-effector links into account – and models them through **nil** values in the L_{i-1}, respectively the L_{i+1} map domain 'positions'.

The model also permits closed loops to converge at distinct joints – as illustrated in Figure 3.2.

Abstraction function
The enrichment that $GEO\,'$ represents over GEO is considerable – nevertheless it is possible, in this case without first considering invariance of the $GEO\,'$ objects (g'), to define the *retrieval* or *abstraction function* which to enriched objects in $GEO\,'$ relates their abstracted object in GEO.

13.0   **type** : **retr-**GEO: $GEO\,'{\rightarrow}GEO$

13.1   **retr-**$GEO(g') \triangleq [\,l{\mapsto}g'(l)\backslash\{\mathbf{nil}\}\,|\,l\in\mathbf{dom}\,g'\,]$

The retrieval of $GEO\,'$ objects is not guaranteed to yield invariant GEO objects, and the abstraction function **retr-**GEO is, in this case, defined on objects that do not satisfy the invariance of $GEO\,'$ objects.

Geometry constraints
A number of Domain constraints must be satisfied for $GEO\,'$ to define well-formed robots:

1. The "underlying" robot abstraction must remain invariant.
2. There must be exactly one, hence a unique, base link (frame) – that is: the set of *In-Degree-0* nodes of the robot graph(s) has cardinality 1.

3. In the model the base link has no predecessors, and is – hence – the only link in the domain of any g' whose predecessor (L_{i-1}) 'positions' are all **nil**.
4. Only the set of *Out-Degree-0* nodes have **nil** in their L_{i+1} successor 'positions'.
5. For any successor l_s of a link l_p, that link l_s shall have l_p as a predecessor and vice versa. That is: in objects of the Domain *GEO'*, if l_s occurs in the L_{i+1} 'position' of a domain (i.e. L_i) element l_p, then l_p will occur in the L_{i-1} 'position' of domain (i.e. L_i) element l_s.
6. If two or more distinct arms lead to the same joint it shall have the same position and orientation wrt any joint in the two arms.

Except for the sixth condition – which we are not quite ready to tackle yet – we shall formalize the above.

Invariance

14.0	**type** : **inv-**GEO': GEO'→BOOL	
14.1	**inv-**$GEO'(g') \triangleq$	
.2	**inv-**$GEO(\text{\textbf{retr-}}GEO(g'))$	1
.3	$\wedge UniqueBase(g')$	2
.4	$\wedge ProperBase(g')$	3
.5	$\wedge ProperTools(g')$	4
.6	$\wedge ProperPredecessors(g')$	5-a
.7	$\wedge ProperSuccessors(g')$	5-b
.8	$\wedge ProperArms(g')$	6
14.9	$\wedge Stiff(g')$	

Because of the way we are modelling links and joints we need to add a further invariant condition on the model: stiffness of links. With reference to Figure 3.2 stiffness amounts to securing that the non-link "links" *BC*, *EF*, and *GH* have constant lengths. We leave it as an exercise to the reader to define the *Stiff*ness predicate.

Auxiliary predicates

15.0	**type** : *UniqueBase*: GEO'→BOOL
15.1	*UniqueBase(g')* $\triangleq$
.2	**card** *In-Degree-0*(**retr-**$GEO(g')$) = 1

16.0   **type** : *ProperBase: GEO '→*BOOL

16.1   *ProperBase(g') ≜*
.2   **let** *{b} = In-Degree-0(***retr-***GEO(g'))* **in**
.3   *(∀l∈* **dom** *(g'(b)))*
16.4   *(***dom***((g'(b))(l)) = {***nil***})*

17.0   **type** : *ProperTools: GEO '→*BOOL

17.1   *ProperTools(g') ≜*
.2   **let** *tls = Out-Degree-0(***retr-***GEO(g'))* **in**
.3   *(∀m∈* **rng***(g'\tls))(***nil** *∈***dom** *m)*   must – and
17.4   *∧(∀tl∈tls)(***dom** *(g'(tl)) = {***nil***})*   must only

18.0   **type** : *ProperPredecessors: GEO '→*BOOL

18.1   *ProperPredecessors(g') ≜*
.2   *(∀l_i ∈***dom** *g')*
.3   *(∀l_{i+1} ∈* **dom***(g'(l_i)))*
.4   **let** *m = g'(l_{i+1})* **in**
.5   *(∀l_{i+2} ∈* **dom** *m)*
18.6   *(l_i ∈* **dom***(m(l_{i+2})))*

19.0   **type** : *ProperSuccessors: GEO '→*BOOL

19.1   *ProperSuccessors(g') ≜*
.2   *(∀l_i ∈* **dom** *g'\In-Degree-0(***retr-***GEO(g')))*
.3   *(∀l_{i+1} ∈* **dom** *(g'(l_i)))*
.4   *(***dom***((g'(l_i))(l_{i+1}))*
19.5   *= Predecessors(l_i,***retr-***GEO(g')))*

Auxiliary functions

We can define the set of closed link circuits of a robot as a set of distinct pairs of arms that have first link and last link in common:

20.0   **type** : *Loops: GEO →(L^+ × L^+)***-set**

20.1   *Loops(g) ≜*
.2   **union***{{ (ar,ar')|*
.3   *ar,ar' ∈ Arms(g,l):*
.4   *ar[1]=ar'[1]∧ar[***len** *ar]=ar'[***len** *ar'] ∧ar≠ar'}|*
.5   *l∈* **dom** *g}*

3.3   Static Positions

Given geometric models of robots – such as those of the previous section – we can now model how to compute static positions of robots.

This section will contain two kinds of formulas: informal formulas of mathematics proper and formal formulas of the VDM meta-language Meta-IV. We use the former in order to explain aspects of robots informally. We use the latter in order to define, formally, data models and functions over data models – that is: formal models of robots.

The informal mathematics formulas are unnumbered, or numbered in the right margin. The Meta-IV formulas are numbered in the left margin.

3.3.1   Mathematical modelling

In this subsection we only deal with the modelling of the computations required to express robot positions.

Position and orientation reviewed
Every point p in three-dimensional space can be characterized by its position (x, y, z) wrt some origin XYZ co-ordinate system, and by its orientation, that is: a rotation – at the point of interest – of the origin XYZ co-ordinate system. From linear algebra we know that rotations can be formulated in terms of 3-by-3 matrices – and these express the projection on the translated origin co-ordinate system of the unit axes of the re-oriented co-ordinate system of the point of interest.

We wish to compute, given a robot, with all its links, each with their link parameters and joint variables – together (a, α, d, θ) and with the origin base frame, the position and orientation of any link and joint.

The link parameters and joint variables are ideal quantities – not directly suitable for efficient computations. Hence we turn via the frame model to the idea of the *homogenous transform*.

The frame model reviewed – and more
The frame concept models the position and orientation in terms of vectors and matrices that express translations and rotations of link co-ordinate systems – one wrt to a previous.

The frame concept can be modelled in various ways. First we model the frame as a pair: (P, R) – where P is the (x, y, z) vector of the position and R the 3-by-3 rotation matrix.

P and R are expressed relative to some co-ordinate system. Since we shall operate with several co-ordinate systems, and since the points of interest usually become the origin of other new co-ordinate systems it is convenient to introduce a notation for such systems.

Some vector and matrix notation

Let point P in frame A have (column vector) coordinates $(^A x, ^A y, ^A z)$ – abbreviated $^A P$.

Let $^A_B R$ denote the rotation matrix that expresses the rotation R of frame B wrt frame A.

Let there be given two frames: A and B and a point P. Let the origin of B wrt A be the column vector $(^A x_B, ^A y_B, ^A z_B)$ – abbreviated $^A P_{B_{org}}$.

Translation

Let the orientation of P be the same as that of frame A. The vector addition:

$$^A P \ = \ ^B P \oplus {}^A P_{B_{org}} \tag{3.1}$$

now expresses the *translation mapping* of a vector from one frame (B) to another (A) having the same orientation.

Rotation

Let the two frames A and B have their origin coincide, but with B rotated $^A_B R$ wrt A. The matrix-vector multiplication:

$$^A P \ = \ {}^A_B R \otimes {}^B P \tag{3.2}$$

now expresses the *rotation mapping* of vector P in frame B wrt frame A.

Transformation

In general:

$$^A P \ = \ {}^A_B R \otimes {}^B P \oplus {}^A P_{B_{org}} \tag{3.3}$$

expresses the *general transformation mapping* of a vector from its description in one frame (B) to its description in another frame (A).

Homogenous transform

The general situation is that of transformation ($=$ rotation $+$ translation!). Instead of expressing transformation as matrix-vector multiplication followed by vector-vector addition we can represent the frame pair $(^A_B R, ^A P_{B_{org}})$ as a 4-by-4 matrix such that:

$$^A P \ = \ {}^A_B R \otimes {}^B P \oplus {}^A P_{B_{org}} \tag{3.4}$$

now becomes expressed as:

$$^{A}P' \;=\; {}^{A}_{B}T \otimes {}^{B}P'$$
(3.5)

where the first and last 4 element column vectors and the middle 4-by-4 matrix above are defined below:

$$
\begin{bmatrix} {}^{A}P \\ \cdots \cdots \\ 1 \end{bmatrix}
=
\begin{bmatrix}
& & \vdots & \\
& {}^{A}_{B}R & \vdots & {}^{A}P_{B_{org}} \\
& & \vdots & \\
\cdots & \cdots\cdots & \cdots & \cdots\cdots \\
0 & 0 \quad 0 & \vdots & 1
\end{bmatrix}
\otimes
\begin{bmatrix} {}^{B}P \\ \cdots\cdots \\ 1 \end{bmatrix}
$$
(3.6)

The dotted horizontal and vertical "lines" ($\ldots\ldots$, respectively $\vdots$) shall informally indicate "boundaries" between 3 element column vectors, and the 3-by-3 matrix, and the "added" 0's and 1's.

Let link $i-1$ precede link i and be connected to this link by a joint.

We now wish to express the above homogenous transform, ${}^{A}_{B}T$, that is: ${}^{i-1}_{i}T$, in terms of the link parameters and joint variable (a_{i-1}, α_{i-1}, d_i, θ_i) that define link i relative to link $i-1$.

One can show that:

$$
{}^{i-1}_{i}T \;=\;
\begin{bmatrix}
\cos\theta_i & -\sin\theta_i & 0 & a_{i-1} \\
\sin\theta_i \times \cos\alpha_{i-1} & \cos\theta_i \times \cos\alpha_{i-1} & -\sin\alpha_{i-1} & -\sin\alpha_{i-1} \times d_i \\
\sin\theta_i \times \sin\alpha_{i-1} & \cos\theta_i \times \sin\alpha_{i-1} & \cos\alpha_{i-1} & \cos\alpha_{i-1} \times d_i \\
0 & 0 & 0 & 1
\end{bmatrix}
$$
(3.7)

Given a robot geometry g (as so far defined), and given a link pair, (l_{i-1}, l_i) (that is: an abstract link), we can extract link parameters and joint variable and define a function $\mathcal{T}$ which when applied to these will compute the above homogenous transform ${}^{i}_{i+1}T$:

21.0   **let** $((a_{i-1},\alpha_{i-1}),(d_i,\theta_i)) = ((g'(l_i))(l_{i+1}))(l_{i-1})$ **in**
21.1   **let** ${}^{i}_{i+1}T = \mathcal{T}((a_{i-1},\alpha_{i-1}),(d_i,\theta_i))$ **in**
21.2 $\ldots$

3.3.2   Formal modelling

The homogeneous transform matrices above can be put into a Domain, (22.0), and the function which applies to link parameters and joint variables can be defined.

We can then define the static position wrt any frame of any other thereby linked frame.

Finally we can complete the invariant (14.) given on page 46.

Auxiliary domain and function

22.0 $\quad {}_n^m T \qquad = (\text{REAL}^4)^4$

23.0 $\quad$ **type** $: \mathcal{T}: ((\text{REAL}\times\text{REAL})\times(\text{REAL}\times\text{REAL})) \to {}_n^m T$

23.1 $\quad \mathcal{T}((a,\alpha),(d,\theta)) \triangleq$

.2 $\qquad <<\cos\theta, -\sin\theta, 0, a>,$

.3 $\qquad\quad <\sin\theta\cdot\cos\alpha, \cos\theta\cdot\cos\alpha, -\sin\alpha, -\sin\alpha\cdots d>,$

.4 $\qquad\quad <\sin\theta\cdot\sin\alpha, \cos\theta\cdot\sin\alpha, \cos\alpha, \cos\alpha\cdots d>,$

23.5 $\qquad <0,0,0,1>>$

The iterated static position computation

Let g' be a robot of the kind $(GEO\,')$ so far formalized. Let m be an arm consisting of links $<l_{i_1}, l_{i_2}, \ldots, l_{i_n}>$. We wish to formally define the computation of the position and orientation of frame i_n wrt frame i_1, that is:

$$ {}_{i_2}^{i_1}T \otimes {}_{i_3}^{i_2}T \otimes \cdots {}_{i_n}^{i_{n-1}}T \tag{3.8}$$

Recalling that we need insert an appropriate predecessor link, which may be **nil**, the above arm becomes: $<l_{i_0}, l_{i_1}, l_{i_2}, \ldots, l_{i_n}>$, referred to as *arm* below.

The following recursively defined (*static positioning*) function will perform this composite transformation:

24.0 $\quad$ **type** $: Sta\text{-}Pos:\ GEO\,'\times L^+ \overset{\sim}{\to} {}_n^m T$

24.1 $\quad Sta\text{-}Pos(g',arm) \triangleq$

.2 $\qquad$ **if** **len** $arm=2$

.3 $\qquad$ **then** $\mathcal{I}_{(4,4)}$

.4 $\qquad$ **else** **let** $lpjv = ((g'(\mathbf{hd\ tl}\ arm))(\mathbf{hd\ tl\ tl}\ arm))(\mathbf{hd}\ arm)$ **in**

.5 $\qquad\qquad$ **let** $tra = \mathcal{T}(lpjv)$ **in**

24.6 $\qquad\qquad tra \otimes Sta\text{-}Pos(g',\mathbf{tl}\ arm)$

24.7 $\quad$ **pre-**$:\ arm\in Arms(g')(\mathbf{hd}\ arm)$

where $\mathcal{I}_{(4,4)}$ is the 4-by-4 identity matrix which is also a member of the result Domain.

Proper arms

If there is a loop then computing the static position one way around the loop shall equal the static position computed any other way around:

25.0 $\quad$ **type** $: ProperArms:\ GEO\,' \to \text{BOOL}$

25.1 $\quad ProperArms(g') \triangleq$

.2 $\qquad (\forall (ar,ar')\in Loops(g'))$

25.3 $\qquad\quad (Sta\text{-}Pos(g',ar) = Sta\text{-}Pos(g',ar'))$

3.4   Kinematics

The kinematics model must now *enrich* the geometry model. The basis for performing kinematics calculations is what we have to model – not these calculations themselves. Our model is, however, going to be such that, given an instantiation, that is: an abstract robot representation, in the form here defined, we can also specify the kinematics calculations themselves – but that is not the purpose of this paper. We hope that future papers will document such specifications – such that crucial implementations of kinematics calculations can be proven correct. That is: we also want to have robotics engineers develop their software properly.

The geometry model included the frame model of robots, but not whether a joint was *revolute* or *prismatic*. The second geometry model thus expressed the current position and orientation of all links.

We now have to model revolute (or rotating) and prismatic (or linear) joints. In our kinematics model we also include the representation of an *initial state* (that is: value of all joint variables). For rotating joints we have to model the angles between which rotations can occur and the initial and present angles. For linear joints we have to model 'extremes' between which a sliding movement can occur and the initial and present offsets.

The *(position,orientation)* model of the previous section already covers much of the ground. So we need only a few adjustments.

3.4.1   Kinematics class description

26.0	$k{:}KIN$	$= L_i \overrightarrow{m} (L_{i+1} \overrightarrow{m} (L_{i-1} \overrightarrow{m} PaO'))$	
27.0	L_i	$= L$	
28.0	L_{i-1}, L_{i+1}	$= [L]$	
29.0	$\pi'{:}PaO'$	$= \underline{\textbf{s}}\text{-}\pi{:}PaO \times \underline{\textbf{s}}\text{-}typ{:}RoP$	
30.0	$\pi{:}PaO$	$= \underline{\textbf{s}}\text{-}lnk{:}(\underline{\textbf{s}}\text{-}len{:}\text{REAL} \times \underline{\textbf{s}}\text{-}twi{:}\text{ANG})$	
31.0		$\times\ \underline{\textbf{s}}\text{-}jnt{:}(\underline{\textbf{s}}\text{-}off{:}\text{REAL} \times \underline{\textbf{s}}\text{-}ang{:}\text{ANG})$	current
32.0	$rop{:}RoP$	$= REV|PRI$	range+initial
33.0	REV	$::\ \underline{\textbf{s}}\text{-}lo{:}\text{ANG} \times \underline{\textbf{s}}\text{-}hi{:}\text{ANG} \times \underline{\textbf{s}}\text{-}init{:}\text{ANG}$	
34.0	PRI	$::\ \underline{\textbf{s}}\text{-}lo{:}\text{REAL} \times \underline{\textbf{s}}\text{-}hi{:}\text{REAL} \times \underline{\textbf{s}}\text{-}init{:}\text{REAL}$	

Definitions (33.0 and 34.0) introduce the **mk-**REV, respectively the **mk-**PRI, *constructor functions* – as well as a number of new *selector functions* (**s-**).

3.4.2   Retrieval

35.0   **type** : **retr-**GEO': $KIN \to GEO'$

35.1   **retr-**$GEO'(k) \triangleq$

35.2 $[l_i \mapsto [l_{i+1} \mapsto [l_{i-1} \mapsto \textbf{s-}\pi(((k)(l_i))(l_{i+1}))(l_{i-1})|$

.3 $l_{i-1} \in \textbf{dom}\,((k)(l_i))(l_{i+1})]|$

.4 $l_{i+1} \in \textbf{dom}\,k(l_i)]|$

.5 $l_i \in \textbf{dom}\,k\,]$

3.4.3   Invariant

First we tackle the "smaller" Domains:

36.0   **inv-**$PaO'(,(,ang),\textbf{mk-}REV(lo,hi,)) \triangleq lo \leq ang \leq hi$

36.1   **inv-**$PaO'(,(off,),\textbf{mk-}PRI(lo,hi,)) \triangleq lo \leq off \leq hi$

36.2   **inv-**$REV(\textbf{mk-}REV(lo,hi,init)) \triangleq lo < hi \land lo \leq init \leq hi$

36.3   **inv-**$PRI(\textbf{mk-}PRI(lo,hi,init)) \triangleq lo < hi \land lo \leq init \leq hi$

Given that the above holds we can concentrate on the entire Domain:

37.0   **inv-**$KIN(k) \triangleq$ **inv-**$GEO'(\textbf{retr-}GEO'(k))$

3.5   Kinematic Positions

In this section we will illustrate the idea of inverse kinematics. Rather than, as in the previous sections, defining predicates and functions explicitly, we shall here additionally illustrate the definition of functions by **pre-/post-** conditions.

3.5.1   Inverse kinematics

There is given a robot, according to the kinematics model (KIN).

The robot may have more than one wrist frame – so we treat the general case, but build it up from the case of just one wrist.

Now let there, in general, be given a set of target frames S_{tf} – ostensibly for the wrists of a robot, but it could as well be for any set of identified link frames.

S_{tf} expresses a desired position and orientation of points wrt to one other frame, typically the base frame F_b. Each of the target frames is identified wrt to the desired wrist:

$$S_{tf} : \{(w_1, t_1), (w_2, t_2), \ldots, (w_n, t_n)\}$$

where the set $\{w_1, w_2, \ldots, w_n\}$ is the set of *Out-Degree-0* nodes, that are defined by the set of all wrists of a given robot.

The problem of *inverse kinematics* is now that of finding the set of all *joint variable vectors* that makes the identified wrist frames coincident with the corresponding target frames.

To compute this is not straightforward. Different kinds of computations are possible. Amongst these are: numeric approximations, and algebraic and geometric calculations. We are not going to express abstract algorithms for either of these kinds of computations. Instead we shall *characterize* what it means for such a computation to have solved the problem!

A projection function

In order to compute whether a robot can have its joint variables attain such values that the static position of, for example, a wrist, wrt the base, coincides with a desired position and orientation, we have to ignore the current values of joint variables (offset for prismatic joints, angle for revolute joints).

Ignoring, to us, means to *project* a kinematic model of a robot onto one where there is no specification, say *holes,* **nil**, for the current value of the joint variables.

We therefore define the Domain $KIN_{\mathbf{nil}}$ of such "robots" and the projection function:

$$
\begin{array}{llll}
38.0 & k{:}KIN_{\mathbf{nil}} & = L_i \underset{\overrightarrow{m}}{} (L_{i+1} \underset{\overrightarrow{m}}{} (L_{i-1} \underset{\overrightarrow{m}}{} PaO'')) & \\
39.0 & L_i & = L & \\
40.0 & L_{i-1}, L_{i+1} & = [L] & \\
41.0 & \pi'{:}PaO'' & = \underline{\mathbf{s}\text{-}}\pi{:}PaO \times \underline{\mathbf{s}\text{-}}typ{:}RoP & \\
42.0 & \pi{:}PaO & = \underline{\mathbf{s}\text{-}}lnk{:}(\underline{\mathbf{s}\text{-}}len{:}\text{REAL} \times \underline{\mathbf{s}\text{-}}twi{:}\text{ANG}) & \\
43.0 & & \times \underline{\mathbf{s}\text{-}}jnt{:}(\underline{\mathbf{s}\text{-}}off{:}[\text{REAL}] \times \underline{\mathbf{s}\text{-}}ang{:}[\text{ANG}]) & \text{current} \\
44.0 & rop{:}RoP & = REV | PRI & \text{range+initial} \\
45.0 & REV & :: \underline{\mathbf{s}\text{-}}lo{:}\text{ANG} \times \underline{\mathbf{s}\text{-}}hi{:}\text{ANG} \times \underline{\mathbf{s}\text{-}}init{:}\text{ANG} & \\
46.0 & PRI & :: \underline{\mathbf{s}\text{-}}lo{:}\text{REAL} \times \underline{\mathbf{s}\text{-}}hi{:}\text{REAL} \times \underline{\mathbf{s}\text{-}}init{:}\text{REAL} & \\
\end{array}
$$

We define no invariant on the Domain of $KIN_{\mathbf{nil}}$ objects since they are always projected from well-formed *KIN* objects.

$$
\begin{array}{ll}
47.0 & \mathbf{type} : Project{:}\ KIN \overset{\sim}{\to} KIN_{\mathbf{nil}} \\
47.1 & Project(k) \triangleq \\
.2 & \quad [\, l_i \mapsto [l_{i+1} \mapsto [l_{i-1} \mapsto Proj((k(l_i))(l_{i+1}))(l_{i-1}) \\
.3 & \quad\quad\quad l_{i-1}\ \mathbf{dom}\ ((k(l_i))(l_{i+1}))] \\
.4 & \quad\quad l_{i+1}\ \mathbf{dom}\ (k(l_i))] \\
47.5 & \quad l_i \in \mathbf{dom}\ k\,]
\end{array}
$$

48.0   **type** : *Proj: PaO′→PaO″*

48.1   *Proj(((a, α), (d, θ)),rop)* ≙

  .2   **is-***REV(rop)* → *(((a, α), (d, **nil**)),rop)*

48.3   **is-***PRI(rop)* → *(((a, α), (**nil**, θ)),rop)*

In lines (48.2–.3) we use the **is-** *Domain test predicate* introduced by definitions (33.0), (45.0), (34.0), and (46.0). In fact, any Domain definition, whether of the "*A = . . .*" form (or the "*B ∷ . . .*", constructor form, see below), defines a predicate **is-***A*, which when applied to a non-functional object will determine whether it is of that Domain (*A*) or not.

Robot equivalence

Two robots having the same link structure, and having the same link parameters and the same ranges and initial values for joint variables – for pairwise the same links – will therefore be *equivalent* no matter what the current values of joint variables may be.

49.0   **type** : *EquivRobot: KIN× KIN⇸*BOOL

49.1   *EquivRobot(k,k′)* ≙ *Projection(k)=Projection(k′)*

49.2   **pre-***:* **inv-***KIN(k)*∧**inv-***KIN(k′)*

The inverse kinematic functions

We are now ready to formulate the special *inverse kinematics* problem.

> Given a robot *k* (with a unique base) and given a wrist identifier *w* and a target frame *t* does there exist an equivalent robot *k′* such that the static position of wrist *w* wrt the base is *t*?

A function which generates all such equivalent robots is now defined:

50.0   **type** : *ComputeInverse: L× PaO× KIN ⇸KIN-**set***

50.1   **pre-***ComputeInverse(w,,k)* ≙

  .2   *w*∈ **dom** *k*

50.3   **post-***ComputeInverse((w,π,k),ks)* ≙

  .4   *(∀k′ ∈ ks)*

  .5   *(EquivRobot(k,k′) ∧OK-Position(w,π,k′))*

  .6   ∧¬*(∃k″ ∈ KIN\ks)*

50.7   *(EquivRobot(k,k″) ∧OK-Position(w,π,k″)))*

The above **pre-post** specification characterizes solutions. The set *ks* is the set of all robots equivalent to the given but with its wrist *w* positioned at *π*. Clause (50.6–50.7) guarantees "all".

51.0   **type** : *OK-Position: L×PaO× KIN*→BOOL
51.1   *OK-Position(w,π,k)* ≜
.2   **let** *g′*= **retr-** *GEO ′(k)* **in**
.3   **let** *g* = **retr-** *GEO(g′)* **in**
.4   **let** *{b}* = *In-Degree-0(g)* **in**
.5   **let** *arm* ∈ *Arms(g,b)* **be** **s.t.** *arm[len arm]=w* **in**
51.6   *Sta-Pos(g′,arm)* = $\mathcal{T}(π)$

The general problem is now:

52.0   **type** : *ComputeInverse$_g$: (L$_{\overrightarrow{m}}$PaO) × KIN* $\Rightarrow$ *KIN*-**set**
52.1   **pre-** *ComputeInverse$_g$(wπs,k)* ≜
.2   **dom** *wπs* ⊆ **dom** *k*
52.3   **post-** *ComputeInverse$_g$((wπs,k),ks)* ≜
.4   *(∀k′ ∈ ks)*
.5   *(EquivRobot(k,k′) ∧OK-Position$_g$(wπs,k′))*
.6   *∧¬(∃k″ ∈ KIN\ks)*
52.7   *(EquivRobot(k,k″) ∧OK-Position$_g$(wπs,k″)))*

53.0   **type** : *OK-Position$_g$: (L$_{\overrightarrow{m}}$PaO) × KIN*→BOOL
53.1   *OK-Position$_g$(wπs,k)* ≜
.2   **let** *g′*= **retr-** *GEO ′(k)* **in**
.3   **let** *g* = **retr-** *GEO(g′)* **in**
.4   **let** *{b}* = *In-Degree-0(g)* **in**
.5   *(∀w∈ **dom** wπs)*
.6   *(**let** arm ∈ Arms(g,b) **be** **s.t.** arm[len arm]=w **in***
53.7   *Sta-Pos(g′,arm)* = $\mathcal{T}(wπs(w)))$

3.5.2   Discussion

One thing, as we have done, is to *characterize properties* of what *inverse kinematics* is, another thing is to *compute constructive solutions* to the inverse kinematics problem. Various approaches are used, and some of these are already covered in the text-book literature. We envisage a need for formalizing even these approaches – using techniques similar to the ones of this paper – in order to secure their orderly, correct, full and efficient implementation.

3.6   Conclusion

The papers by John E. Hopcroft ([3, 4]) take the position that robotics and its strong dependence on computer science *necessitates changes in computer science curricula.* We concur. We also believe that the "reverse" can be claimed: that the advent of robotics necessitates changes in mechanical engineering curricula – at least in the direction of computer science!

3.6.1   Summary

We have established a geometry and kinematics model of a large class of robots, and we have defined a number of invariant properties and computations over such robots – notably those associated with the static positioning (direct or forward kinematics) and inverse kinematics of robots.

3.6.2   Discussion

The robot model given readily allows for a robot to consist of several disjoint robots. A Russian Moon robot thus consisted initially of three "robots", which assembled on the Moon into one robot, and, after the mission, disassembled itself into a smaller that returned to Earth (while leaving the rest as "rubbish")! The *assembly/disassembly* functions can also readily be modelled as simple extensions to our model. Likewise we can readily model *multi-legged* robots.

3.6.3   Future work

Immediate work should incorporate *trajectory generation and motion planning:* desired paths for robot wrists and required (sets of sequences of alternative) positions and orientations for all joints.

Next one should incorporate dynamics into the models: thus exhibiting such attributes as mass, center-of-gravity, actuator force: momentum and torque, etc., so as to be able to select, from sets of sequences of alternative positions and orientations, motions which result in smooth operation, and to generate the commands that actuate revolute and prismatic joint motors.

The model given can thus be viewed as an interpreter for a very wide class of robots. Given the data that characterize a specific robot one can *partially evaluate* ([1]) the model into one that, in some sense, "compiles" into software "optimal" for the given robot. Changes, in the design, during the life-time of such a robot, can then more readily be reflected into the controlling software. To properly develop such a "compiler-compiler" is yet another future task.

3.7   Acknowledgements

The author thanks Dr Lars Fleckenstein Nielsen for patiently helping him make the first steps into the realm of robotics. It was Dr Tom Østerby who first brought the two together. We also acknowledge early comments from Prof. Erik Trostmann. All of the above are colleagues at the Technical University of Denmark.

But my deepest thanks goes to Tony Hoare. I cannot overemphasize the extent to which his work, and inspiration from having worked with him, has helped me formulate and pursue what I think is important in our exciting field: computing science.

References

[1] D. Bjørner, A.P. Ershov, and N.D. Jones, editors. *Partial Evaluation and Mixed Computation*, Gl. Avernæs, Denmark, October 1987 1988. IFIP TC2 Working Conference, North-Holland Publ. Co., Amsterdam, The Netherlands.

[2] J.J. Craig. *Introduction to ROBOTICS – Mechanics and Control*. Electrical and Computer Engineering: Control Engineering. Addison-Wesley Publishing Company, 2nd. edition, (1986) 1989.

[3] J.E. Hopcroft and D. Krafft. *The Challenge of Robotics for Computer Science*. Lawrence Erlbaum Associates, Hillsdale, N.J., USA, 1987.

[4] J.E. Hopcroft. The Impact of Robotics on Computer Science. *Communications of the ACM*, 29(6):486–498, June 1986.

[5] C.S. George Lee. Robot Arm Dynamics. In C.S.G. Lee, R.C. Gonzalez, and K.S. Fu, editors, *see [7]*, pages 93–102. IEEE Computer Society Press, 1983.

[6] C.S. George Lee. Robot Arm Kinematics. In C.S.G. Lee, R.C. Gonzalez, and K.S. Fu, editors, *see [7]*, pages 47–65. IEEE Computer Society Press, 1983.

[7] C.S.G. Lee, R.C. Gonzalez, and K.S. Fu, editors. *Tutorial on Robotics (see [6, 5])*, IEEE Computer Society, P.O.Box 80452, Worldway Postal Center, Los Angeles, California 90080, USA, 1983. IEEE Computer Society Press.

[8] P. McKerrow. *Introduction to ROBOTICS*. Addison-Wesley Publishing Company, 1990.

[9] Y. Nakamura. *Theory of ROBOTICS*. Addison-Wesley Publishing Company, 1990.

[10] R.C. Paul. *Robot Manipulators: Mathematics, Programming, and Control*. The MIT Press Series in Artificial Intelligence. The MIT Press, Cambridge, Mass. and London, England, 1981.

[11] R.C. Schilling. *Fundamentals of Robotics, Analysis and Control*. Prentice-Hall International, Inc., 1990.

[12] S. Tsuji. *AI-Based ROBOTICS*. Addison-Wesley Publishing Company, 1990.

[13] T. Yoshikawa. *Foundations of Robotics*. The MIT Press, 1990.

Chapter 4

Fair Communicating Processes

Stephen Brookes

4.1 Introduction

In an article published in August 1978 Tony Hoare introduced the programming language CSP (Communicating Sequential Processes) [6]. Although Hoare himself stated that the concepts and notations used in this paper "should not be regarded as suitable for use as a programming language, either for abstract or for concrete programming", these concepts and notations have had significant impact on the design of languages such as Ada [9] and occam [10]. In addition Hoare's ideas have stimulated much research on the development of semantic models and proof methodologies for parallel languages.

The original CSP language is a simple yet powerful and elegant generalization of Dijkstra's guarded commands [4], permitting parallel execution of sequential commands ("processes"). Processes have disjoint "local" states and may communicate by synchronized message-passing: communication occurs when one process names another as destination for output and the second process names the first as source for input, whereupon they perform a synchronized handshake. The syntax of CSP was closely based on Dijkstra's notation for guarded commands, generalized to permit communication guards, and using an n-ary parallel composition of named sequential processes. Nested parallel compositions were not allowed, and only input commands were allowed as guards. These restrictions were imposed mainly for pragmatic reasons, and have often been relaxed or removed in later developments. For instance, it is common to permit output guards; *occam* uses channel names rather than process names, has a binary associative form of parallel composition, and allows nested parallelism; Plotkin [14] discusses a variant of CSP with a more general scoping facility for process names.

Hoare's work on semantic models for communicating processes has focussed mainly on a more abstract process language, which has come to be known as Theoretical CSP (or TCSP) [2, 8]. Like Milner's Calculus of Communicating Systems (CCS) [12], TCSP provides a collection of primitive processes and operations (like parallel composition) for building complex processes from simpler ones. Atomic actions (like input and output) are treated as events drawn from some given alphabet. Processes may be characterized in terms of the sequences of events (or traces) that they may perform. Thus, in the *trace model* of [7] the denotation of a process is taken to be a non-empty, prefix-closed set of finite sequences of events.

In many applications it is reasonable to assume that programs executing in parallel are not delayed forever. This is known as a *fairness* assumption [5]. Hoare remarked in [6] that "an efficient implementation (of CSP) should try to be reasonably fair and should ensure that an output command is not delayed unreasonably often after it first becomes executable". Hoare also stated that he was "fairly sure"[1] that a programming language definition should not specify that an implementation *must* be fair, and that the programmer should be responsible for proving that his program terminates correctly without relying on fairness in the implementation.

Hoare's trace model [7] was not designed to incorporate fairness; indeed, this model ignores the possibility of infinite computation and it is difficult to reconcile fair infinite traces with the prefix-closure assumption. The problem remained of finding a satisfactory semantic account of communicating processes that accurately supports reasoning about programs under fairness assumptions. This is the problem addressed by our paper.

We propose a mathematically straightforward trace semantics for a language of fair communicating processes, and we explore some of its properties. We build on the foundational work of David Park, who gave a semantics for a fair shared variable parallel programming language, based on an elegant characterization of a "fairmerge" operation on finite and infinite sequences [13]. Park's model is tailored specifically to the purpose of modelling the interactions of parallel programs that share a global state. Since we focus on a CSP-like language, with no sharing of state, a rather different model is appropriate. We adapt and generalize Park's definitions in a natural way.

The language discussed in this paper is essentially a hybrid derived from the original CSP and CCS. As in CSP we require that processes have disjoint local states. As in occam we permit nested parallelism and communication uses named channels rather than process names. We also prefer an abstract syntax less closely tied to the guarded command notation, using a binary form of parallel composition. Thus we obtain a language in which processes themselves may be parallel combinations of processes, so that it might be preferable to refer to "communicating parallel processes".

We give an operational semantics, then a denotational semantics, and we show that the two semantic definitions essentially coincide. We then prove that the denotational semantics is *fully abstract* [11] with respect to a natural notion of program behavior. This means that the semantics distinguishes between two commands if and only if they induce different behavior in some program context. We discuss a few well known examples, and we suggest directions for further research.

---

[1]The pun was (presumably) intended.

4.2 Syntax

The abstract syntax of our programming language is defined as follows. There are five syntactic sets: **Ide**, the set of identifiers, ranged over by I; **Exp**, the set of expressions, ranged over by E; **BExp**, the set of boolean expressions (or conditions), ranged over by B; **Chan**, the set of channel names, ranged over by h; and **Com**, the set of commands, ranged over by C. The abstract syntax for identifiers, channel names, expressions and conditions will be taken for granted; all we assume is that identifiers and expressions denote integer values, boolean expressions denote truth values, and the language contains the usual arithmetic and boolean operators and constants. For commands we specify the following grammar:

$$C \; ::= \; \textbf{skip} \mid I\!:=\!E \mid C_1; C_2 \mid \textbf{if } B \textbf{ then } C_1 \textbf{ else } C_2 \mid \textbf{while } B \textbf{ do } C \mid$$
$$h?I \mid h!E \mid C_1 \| C_2 \mid \sum_{i=1}^{k}(\rho_i \to C_i) \mid C \backslash h,$$

where the ρ_i each have one of the forms $h?I$ or $h!E$.

We refer to $h?I$ as an *input command* and $h!E$ as an *output command*. The form $\sum_{i=1}^{k}(\rho_i \to C_i)$ corresponds to a guarded command whose guards involve input or output[2]. The command $C \backslash h$ is C restricted on channel h: it will behave like C except that its ability to communicate on channel h is removed. Note that processes may have *internal* actions (like assignments to local variables) in addition to communication capabilities.

Parallel composition is denoted $C_1 \| C_2$, and we impose the syntactic constraint that in all such commands the components C_1 and C_2 must have disjoint sets of variables. Formally, we make use of the set free$[\![C]\!]$ of identifiers occurring free in C, given as usual by structural induction on C:

> free$[\![\textbf{skip}]\!] = \{\}$
> free$[\![I\!:=\!E]\!] = \{I\} \cup$ free$[\![E]\!]$
> free$[\![C_1; C_2]\!] =$ free$[\![C_1]\!] \cup$ free$[\![C_2]\!]$
> free$[\![\textbf{if } B \textbf{ then } C_1 \textbf{ else } C_2]\!] =$ free$[\![B]\!] \cup$ free$[\![C_1]\!] \cup$ free$[\![C_2]\!]$
> free$[\![\textbf{while } B \textbf{ do } C]\!] =$ free$[\![B]\!] \cup$ free$[\![C]\!]$
> free$[\![h?I]\!] = \{I\}$
> free$[\![h!E]\!] =$ free$[\![E]\!]$
> free$[\![C_1 \| C_2]\!] =$ free$[\![C_1]\!] \cup$ free$[\![C_2]\!]$
> free$[\![\sum_{i=1}^{k}(\rho_i \to C_i)]\!] = \bigcup_{i=1}^{k}($free$[\![\rho_i]\!] \cup$ free$[\![C_i]\!])$
> free$[\![C \backslash h]\!] =$ free$[\![C]\!]$

We say that C is well-formed iff for every sub-command of C with form $C_1 \| C_2$ we have free$[\![C_1]\!] \cap$ free$[\![C_2]\!] = \{\}$. For example, $(a?x; x\!:=\!x + 1; a!x) \| (y\!:=\!0; a!y; a?z)$

---

[2]We omit "mixed" guards with an additional boolean component, since this permits a simpler presentation.

is well formed, but $x:=0; [a?x \| x:=x+1]$ is not. Throughout the paper we assume that we deal with well-formed commands.

We also define chans$[\![C]\!]$, the finite set of channel names occurring in C, by structural induction on C:

$$\text{chans}[\![\textbf{skip}]\!] = \{\}$$
$$\text{chans}[\![I{:=}E]\!] = \{\}$$
$$\text{chans}[\![C_1; C_2]\!] = \text{chans}[\![C_1]\!] \cup \text{chans}[\![C_2]\!]$$
$$\text{chans}[\![\textbf{if } B \textbf{ then } C_1 \textbf{ else } C_2]\!] = \text{chans}[\![C_1]\!] \cup \text{chans}[\![C_2]\!]$$
$$\text{chans}[\![\textbf{while } B \textbf{ do } C]\!] = \text{chans}[\![C]\!]$$
$$\text{chans}[\![h?I]\!] = \{h\}$$
$$\text{chans}[\![h!E]\!] = \{h\}$$
$$\text{chans}[\![C_1 \| C_2]\!] = \text{chans}[\![C_1]\!] \cup \text{chans}[\![C_2]\!]$$
$$\text{chans}[\![\textstyle\sum_{i=1}^{k} (\rho_i \to C_i)]\!] = \textstyle\bigcup_{i=1}^{k} (\text{chans}[\![\rho_i]\!] \cup \text{chans}[\![C_i]\!])$$
$$\text{chans}[\![C \backslash h]\!] = \text{chans}[\![C]\!] - \{h\}$$

4.3   Operational Semantics

A state is a finite partial function from identifiers to integer values. We use N for the set of integers, and we let $S = [\textbf{Ide} \to_p N]$ denote the set of states. A typical state will be written in form $[I_1 = n_1, \ldots, I_k = n_k]$. We use s as a meta-variable ranging over S, and we write $[s \mid I = n]$ for the state which agrees with s except that it gives identifier I the value n. The *domain* of a state, denoted dom(s), is the set of identifiers for which the state has a value. Two states s_1 and s_2 are *disjoint*, if and only if their domains do not overlap:

$$\text{disjoint}(s_1, s_2) \iff \text{dom}(s_1) \cap \text{dom}(s_2) = \{\}.$$

We assume for simplicity that expression evaluation always terminates and causes no side-effects, and we assume given the evaluation semantics for boolean and integer expressions: we write $\langle E, s \rangle \to^* n$ to indicate that E evaluates to value n in state s, with a similar notation for boolean expressions.

For commands, in order to model communication properly we use a *labelled transition system*, much as in [14]. Configurations have the form $\langle C, s \rangle$, where s is a state defined at least on the free identifiers of C[3]:

$$\textbf{Conf} = \{\langle C, s \rangle \mid \text{free}[\![C]\!] \subseteq \text{dom}(s)\}.$$

We decorate transitions with a label indicating the type of atomic action involved: ϵ represents an internal action, $h?n$ represents receiving value n on channel h, and $h!n$ represents sending value n along channel h. We let Λ be the set of all labels:

---

[3]This means that we need not be concerned with the possibility of uninitialized identifiers in our semantics.

$$\langle \mathbf{skip}, s \rangle \mathrm{term}$$

$$\frac{\langle E, s \rangle \rightarrow^* n}{\langle I{:=}E, s \rangle \xrightarrow{\epsilon} \langle \mathbf{skip}, [s \mid I = n] \rangle}$$

$$\frac{\langle C_1, s \rangle \xrightarrow{\lambda} \langle C_1', s' \rangle}{\langle C_1; C_2, s \rangle \xrightarrow{\lambda} \langle C_1'; C_2, s' \rangle}$$

$$\frac{\langle C_1, s \rangle \mathrm{term}}{\langle C_1; C_2, s \rangle \xrightarrow{\epsilon} \langle C_2, s \rangle}$$

$$\frac{\langle B, s \rangle \rightarrow^* \mathtt{tt}}{\langle \mathbf{if}\ B\ \mathbf{then}\ C_1\ \mathbf{else}\ C_2, s \rangle \xrightarrow{\epsilon} \langle C_1, s \rangle}$$

$$\frac{\langle B, s \rangle \rightarrow^* \mathtt{ff}}{\langle \mathbf{if}\ B\ \mathbf{then}\ C_1\ \mathbf{else}\ C_2, s \rangle \xrightarrow{\epsilon} \langle C_2, s \rangle}$$

$$\langle \mathbf{while}\ B\ \mathbf{do}\ C, s \rangle \xrightarrow{\epsilon} \langle \mathbf{if}\ B\ \mathbf{then}\ C; \mathbf{while}\ B\ \mathbf{do}\ C\ \mathbf{else}\ \mathbf{skip}, s \rangle$$

Figure 4.1 Transition rules for sequential constructs.

$\Lambda = \{\epsilon\} \cup \{h?n, h!n \mid n \in N, h \in \mathbf{Chan}\}$. We use λ as a meta-variable ranging over action labels, and we write

$$\langle C, s \rangle \xrightarrow{\lambda} \langle C', s' \rangle$$

to indicate that command C in state s can perform an action labelled λ, leading to C' in state s'. Two labels λ_1 and λ_2 *match* iff one has form $h?n$ and the other $h!n$ for some channel name h and value n; when this holds we write match(λ_1, λ_2).

We identify the *successfully terminated* (or *terminal*) configurations by means of a predicate *term*. The termination predicate and the transition relations $\xrightarrow{\lambda}$ ($\lambda \in \Lambda$) are defined to be the least relations on configurations satisfying the axioms and rules of Figures 4.1 and 4.2. The rules specify that a parallel composition terminates when all of its components have terminated[4].

Parallel execution is modelled by interleaving, but with the extra possibility of communication. The transition rule for communication between parallel processes is carefully constructed so as to make precise the intuitive description given earlier

---

[4]We do not model the "distributed termination convention" used in the original paper on CSP.

$$\frac{}{\langle h?I, s\rangle \xrightarrow{h?n} \langle \mathbf{skip}, [s \mid I = n]\rangle} \quad \text{for each } n \in N$$

$$\frac{\langle E, s\rangle \rightarrow^* n}{\langle h!E, s\rangle \xrightarrow{h!n} \langle \mathbf{skip}, s\rangle}$$

$$\frac{\langle \rho_i, s\rangle \xrightarrow{\lambda} \langle \mathbf{skip}, s'\rangle}{\langle \sum_{j=1}^{k}(\rho_j \rightarrow C_j), s\rangle \xrightarrow{\lambda} \langle C_i, s'\rangle} \quad \text{for each } i \in 1 \ldots k$$

$$\frac{\langle C, s\rangle \xrightarrow{\lambda} \langle C', s'\rangle}{\langle C\backslash h, s\rangle \xrightarrow{\lambda} \langle C'\backslash h, s'\rangle} \quad \text{if } \lambda \notin \{h?n, h!n \mid n \in N\}$$

$$\frac{\langle C, s\rangle \text{term}}{\langle C\backslash h, s\rangle \text{term}}$$

$$\frac{\langle C_1, s\rangle \xrightarrow{\lambda} \langle C_1', s'\rangle}{\langle C_1 \| C_2, s\rangle \xrightarrow{\lambda} \langle C_1' \| C_2, s'\rangle}$$

$$\frac{\langle C_2, s\rangle \xrightarrow{\lambda} \langle C_2', s'\rangle}{\langle C_1 \| C_2, s\rangle \xrightarrow{\lambda} \langle C_1 \| C_2', s'\rangle}$$

$$\frac{\langle C_1, s_1\rangle \xrightarrow{\lambda_1} \langle C_1', s_1'\rangle \quad \langle C_2, s_2\rangle \xrightarrow{\lambda_2} \langle C_2', s_2'\rangle}{\langle C_1 \| C_2, s_1 \cup s_2\rangle \xrightarrow{\epsilon} \langle C_1' \| C_2', s_1' \cup s_2'\rangle}$$
$$\text{provided match}(\lambda_1, \lambda_2) \text{ and disjoint}(s_1, s_2)$$

$$\frac{\langle C_1, s\rangle \text{term} \quad \langle C_2, s\rangle \text{term}}{\langle C_1 \| C_2, s\rangle \text{term}}$$

Figure 4.2 Transition rules for parallel constructs.

of the synchronized handshake mechanism. The disjointness assumption on states s_1 and s_2, together with the implicit requirement that free$[\![C_1]\!] \subseteq \text{dom}(s_1)$ and free$[\![C_2]\!] \subseteq \text{dom}(s_2)$, are enough to make the communication rule unambiguous. (To make this precise, we should first note that commands can only affect and be affected by the values of their free identifiers.)

We will write Λ^* for the set of finite sequences of communications:

$$\Lambda^* = \{\epsilon\} \cup \{h?n, h!n \mid n \in N, h \in \textbf{Chan}\}^+,$$

where A^+ is the set of non-empty sequences over A. This definition of Λ^* is a slight abuse of notation, since the usual form of Kleene star operation would include "mixed" sequences containing communications and occurrences of ϵ; our definition absorbs such occurrences of ϵ, and this corresponds to the fact that ϵ represents the empty sequence, which is a unit for concatenation. We also define (with a similar abuse of notation)

$$\Lambda^\omega = \{\alpha\epsilon^\omega \mid \alpha \in \Lambda^*\} \cup \{h?n, h!n \mid n \in N, h \in \textbf{Chan}\}^\omega.$$

Again this definition builds in the property that ϵ is a unit for concatenation (even for infinite sequences). However, it is important to note that ϵ^ω is not the same as ϵ; the former represents divergence, the latter represents termination. Finally, we let $\Lambda^\infty = \Lambda^* \cup \Lambda^\omega$. For $\alpha \in \Lambda^\infty$ we denote by $\text{chans}(\alpha)$ the set of channel names occurring in α.

We now define generalized transition relations $\stackrel{\alpha}{\Longrightarrow}$, where $\alpha \in \Lambda^\infty$:

- For finite α, $\langle C, s\rangle \stackrel{\alpha}{\Longrightarrow} \langle C', s'\rangle$ means that C from state s may perform the sequence of communications α, leading to the configuration C' in state s'; finitely many ϵ-transitions are permitted between communications. Note the special case when α is ϵ, representing a finite (possibly empty) sequence of ϵ-transitions.
- For infinite α, $\langle C, s\rangle \stackrel{\alpha}{\Longrightarrow}$ means that there is a *fair* infinite computation of C from initial state s in which the action labels form the sequence α. The special case $\alpha = \epsilon^\omega$ indicates that C has a fair infinite internal computation starting from s.

To be precise about fairness we should tag each transition with an indication of which sub-commands are responsible for the atomic action that causes it, and ensure that the interleaving operation takes proper account of tags. For instance, see [5, 1].

4.4 Examples

1. Let a be a channel name. Then the possible transition sequences of $a?x\|a!0$ from an initial state in which the value of x is 1 are:

$$\langle a?x\|a!0, [x=1]\rangle \stackrel{a?n}{\longrightarrow} \langle \textbf{skip}\|a!0, [x=n]\rangle \stackrel{a!0}{\longrightarrow} \langle \textbf{skip}\|\textbf{skip}, [x=n]\rangle$$
$$\langle a?x\|a!0, [x=1]\rangle \stackrel{a!0}{\longrightarrow} \langle a?x\|\textbf{skip}, [x=1]\rangle \stackrel{a?n}{\longrightarrow} \langle \textbf{skip}\|\textbf{skip}, [x=n]\rangle$$
$$\langle a?x\|a!0, [x=1]\rangle \stackrel{\epsilon}{\longrightarrow} \langle \textbf{skip}\|\textbf{skip}, [x=0]\rangle$$

In each case the final configuration is terminal.

2. In contrast, restricting on a in the previous example forces the communication to take place:

$$\langle (a?x\|a!0)\backslash a, [x = 1] \rangle \xrightarrow{\ \epsilon\ } \langle (\mathbf{skip}\|\mathbf{skip})\backslash a, [x = 0] \rangle.$$

Again the final configuration is terminal.

3. Let B_1, B_2, B_{12} be the processes defined by:

$$\begin{aligned}
B_1 &= \mathbf{while\ true\ do}\ (in?x; link!x) \\
B_2 &= \mathbf{while\ true\ do}\ (link?y; out!y) \\
B_{12} &= [B_1\|B_2]\backslash link
\end{aligned}$$

Intuitively, B_1 behaves like a buffer of capacity 1, repeatedly inputting a value on channel in and outputting it on channel $link$. Similarly, B_2 is a buffer with input $link$ and output out. B_{12} behaves like a buffer from input in to output out, with capacity 2. A discussion of similar processes (in a non-imperative setting) occurs in [8].

4. The program $[C_1\|C_2\|C_3]\backslash left\backslash right$, where

$$\begin{aligned}
C_1 &= \mathbf{while\ true\ do}\ (left?x \rightarrow out!x) + (right?x \rightarrow out!x) \\
C_2 &= \mathbf{while\ true\ do}\ left!0 \\
C_3 &= \mathbf{while\ true\ do}\ right!1,
\end{aligned}$$

performs a "merge" of a sequence of 0's with a sequence of 1's. According to the transition rules, this program has an infinite transition sequence corresponding to the sequence of communications $out!0$. This is an *unfair* computation sequence for this program, because it cannot be obtained by fairly interleaving communication traces for each of the constituent processes: the only way for this sequence to arise is by ignoring the communication capability for C_3. The fair communication traces of this program have form $out!v_0.out!v_1.out!v_2....out!v_n...$, where $v_0v_1...v_n...$ is a fair merge of 0^ω and 1^ω, so that it contains infinitely many 0's and infinitely many 1's.

5. Consider the processes C_1 and C_2 given by

$$C_1 = (a?x \rightarrow ((b!x \rightarrow \mathbf{skip}) + (c!x \rightarrow \mathbf{skip})))$$

$$C_2 = (a?x \rightarrow b!x) + (a?x \rightarrow c!x)$$

Each can perform the sequence of communications $a?nb!n$ and can perform $a?nc!n$, for each $n \in N$. But the second process has two essentially different $a?n$ transitions, leading to configurations where either the only possible next step involves channel b or the only possible next step involves c. In the first process, after doing input on channel a it will be possible to do output on b or on c.

4.5   Program Behavior

The only important attribute of an expression in the transition system for commands (Figures 4.1 and 4.2) is its value. We therefore define evaluation functions $\mathcal{E} : \mathbf{Exp} \to \mathcal{P}(S \times N)$ and $\mathcal{B} : \mathbf{BExp} \to \mathcal{P}(S \times V)$, where $V = \{\mathtt{tt}, \mathtt{ff}\}$ is the set of truth values:

$$\mathcal{E}[\![E]\!] = \{(s, n) \mid \langle E, s \rangle \to^* n\}$$
$$\mathcal{B}[\![B]\!] = \{(s, v) \mid \langle B, s \rangle \to^* v\}.$$

We want to be able to reason about the effect of command execution, including whether or not it terminates successfully, assuming fair execution. We therefore define the "state transformation" behavior of a command C, denoted $\mathcal{M}[\![C]\!]$, as follows:

Definition 4.5.1 The behavior function $\mathcal{M} : \mathbf{Com} \to \mathcal{P}(S \times S_\perp)$ is defined by:

$$\mathcal{M}[\![C]\!] = \{(s, s') \mid \langle C, s \rangle \overset{\epsilon}{\Longrightarrow} \langle C', s' \rangle \text{term}\} \cup \{(s, \perp) \mid \langle C, s \rangle \overset{\epsilon^\omega}{\Longrightarrow}\}.$$

$\bullet$

We use $\perp$ to represent non-termination, and $S_\perp = S \cup \{\perp\}$. A command C has a fair infinite computation (involving only internal actions) from state s if and only if $(s, \perp) \in \mathcal{M}[\![C]\!]$.

We have defined this behavioral notion by reference to the transition system given above: this is an operational characterization. It is obvious that $\mathcal{M}$ cannot be defined compositionally, since (for instance) $\mathcal{M}[\![C_1 \| C_2]\!]$ cannot be determined from $\mathcal{M}[\![C_1]\!]$ and $\mathcal{M}[\![C_2]\!]$. We now give a compositional notion of behavior generalizing $\mathcal{M}$ in a natural way.

Definition 4.5.2 The trace semantic function $\mathcal{T} : \mathbf{Com} \to \mathcal{P}(S \times \Lambda^\infty \times S_\perp)$ is characterized operationally by:

$$\mathcal{T}[\![C]\!] = \{(s, \alpha, s') \mid \langle C, s \rangle \overset{\alpha}{\Longrightarrow} \langle C', s' \rangle \text{term}\} \cup \{(s, \alpha, \perp) \mid \alpha \in \Lambda^\omega \,\&\, \langle C, s \rangle \overset{\alpha}{\Longrightarrow}\}.$$

$\bullet$

In contrast to [7], our traces are adapted to the imperative setting: we model state changes explicitly. Moreover, since we focus only on the *terminal* finite traces we do not impose the prefix-closure condition on trace sets. Nor do we require that an infinite trace be included in a trace set if each of its prefixes is present in the set: this would be incompatible with our desire to model fairness properly. From now on, we use the term *trace* for a triple of form (s, α, s') (where $s' \in S_\perp$) and we will refer to the α component as a *communication trace*.

The state transformation behavior of a command is derivable from its traces:

$$\mathcal{M}[\![C]\!] = \{(s, s') \mid (s, \epsilon, s') \in \mathcal{T}[\![C]\!]\} \cup \{(s, \perp) \mid (s, \epsilon^\omega, \perp) \in \mathcal{T}[\![C]\!]\}.$$

This obvious property will be useful later.

4.6　Denotational Semantics

We now show that $\mathcal{T}$ can be defined compositionally. This gives a denotational characterization to complement the operational characterization just given.

To start, notice that we can regard the semantic domain $\mathcal{P}(S \times \Lambda^\infty \times S_\perp)$ as a complete partial order (in fact, a complete lattice), with set inclusion as the underlying order.

We begin by defining a semantic analogue to the syntactic operation of sequential composition. For trace sets T_1 and T_2 we define

$$T_1; T_2 = \{(s, \alpha\beta, s'') \mid \exists s'.(s, \alpha, s') \in T_1 \ \& \ (s', \beta, s'') \in T_2\}$$
$$\cup\{(s, \alpha, \perp) \mid (s, \alpha, \perp) \in T_1\},$$

where concatenation of communication sequences is defined as usual, so that $\alpha\beta = \alpha$ when α is infinite.

Next we generalize from concatenation to iteration. For a trace set T we define T^n, the n-fold iteration of T, by induction on n:

$$T^0 \ = \ \{(s, \epsilon, s) \mid s \in S\}$$
$$T^{k+1} \ = \ T; T^k \qquad (k \geq 0).$$

We then define T^* and T^ω by:

$$T^* \ = \ \bigcup_{n=0}^\infty T^n$$
$$T^\omega \ = \ \{(s_0, \alpha_0\alpha_1 \ldots \alpha_n \ldots, \perp) \mid \forall n.(s_n, \alpha_n, s_{n+1}) \in T\}.$$

Note that $\{(s, \epsilon, s) \mid s \in S\}$ is a unit for sequential composition of trace sets, and $T^1 = T$ for all trace sets T.

Parallel composition is modelled by a form of interleaving of traces, allowing for synchronized communication. We need to define a fairmerge operator on traces, so that we only include interleavings corresponding to fair behaviors. The following definitions are based on [13], adapted to deal with communicating processes and synchronization. Let T_1 and T_2 represent the trace sets of disjoint processes. Then we define $T_1 \| T_2$, the set of all *fair synchronizing merges* of a trace from T_1 and a trace in T_2, as follows:

$$T_1 \| T_2 \ = \ \{(s_1 \cup s_2, \gamma, s'_1 \cup s'_2) \mid \exists (s_1, \alpha, s'_1) \in T_1, (s_2, \beta, s'_2) \in T_2.$$
$$disjoint(s_1, s_2) \ \& \ (\alpha, \beta, \gamma) \in fairmerge\},$$

where

$$fairmerge \ = \ (L^*RR^*L)^\omega \ \cup \ (L \cup R)^*A,$$
$$L \ = \ \{(\lambda, \epsilon, \lambda) \mid \lambda \in \Lambda\} \cup M,$$
$$R \ = \ \{(\epsilon, \lambda, \lambda) \mid \lambda \in \Lambda\} \cup M,$$
$$M \ = \ \{(\lambda_1, \lambda_2, \epsilon) \mid \text{match}(\lambda_1, \lambda_2)\},$$
$$A \ = \ \{(\alpha, \epsilon, \alpha), (\epsilon, \alpha, \alpha) \mid \alpha \in \Lambda^\infty\}.$$

In this definition we extend the set-theoretic union operator to $S_\perp \times S_\perp$ in the obvious way, defining $\perp \cup s = s \cup \perp = \perp$. We also extend the concatenation operation to triples of traces in the obvious componentwise way and we use the pointwise extension to sets of triples.

When $(\alpha, \beta, \gamma) \in fairmerge$ we say that γ is a fair synchronizing merge of α and β. Intuitively, the definition is intended to specify that γ is constructed from α and β by a combination of interleaving and synchronization of matching input and output, and in the construction all actions from α and β are used up. If α is finite then as soon as all of α has been used up there is no further fairness requirement to fulfil, and similarly if β is finite; all such cases give rise to triples (α, β, γ) expressible in the form $(L \cup R)^*A$. The term $(L^*RR^*L)^\omega$ deals with the cases where α and β are both infinite. Apart from the difference in the underlying notion of atomic action, this fairmerge definition is obtained from Park's by adding states, taking advantage of the disjointness assumption (so that states may be combined using union), and by including a component M dealing with synchronization. Note that a synchronized pair of communications produces an ϵ-step and counts as an atomic action by both of the participating processes; this is important in ensuring a proper account of fair execution.

For example, the possible fair merges of $a?n$ and $a!0$ are $a?n.a!0$, $a!0.a?n$ and ϵ. The fair merges of $a?0.b?0.a?0$ and $a!0$ include $b?0.a?0$, $a?0.b?0$, $a?0.b?0.a?0.a!0$, but not $a!0.b?0.a?0$ and not $a!0.a?0.b?0$. The only fair merge of ϵ^ω with β is β itself if β is infinite, and $\beta\epsilon^\omega$ if β is finite. The fair merges of $(a?0)^\omega$ and $(a!0)^\omega$ include $(a?0)^n\epsilon^\omega$ and $(a!0)^n\epsilon^\omega$ (for all $n \geq 0$), but not $(a?0)^\omega$ or $(a!0)^\omega$.

With these definitions in hand, it is now easy to give a denotational description of $\mathcal{T}$.

Proposition 4.6.1 The trace semantics $\mathcal{T} : \mathbf{Com} \to \mathcal{P}(S \times \Lambda^\infty \times S_\bot)$ is characterized by the following clauses:

$$
\begin{aligned}
\mathcal{T}[\![\mathbf{skip}]\!] &= \{(s, \epsilon, s) \mid s \in S\} \\
\mathcal{T}[\![I{:=}E]\!] &= \{(s, \epsilon, [s \mid I = n]) \mid (s, n) \in \mathcal{E}[\![E]\!]\} \\
\mathcal{T}[\![C_1; C_2]\!] &= \mathcal{T}[\![C_1]\!]; \mathcal{T}[\![C_2]\!] \\
\mathcal{T}[\![\mathbf{if}\ B\ \mathbf{then}\ C_1\ \mathbf{else}\ C_2]\!] &= \mathcal{T}[\![B]\!]; \mathcal{T}[\![C_1]\!] \cup \mathcal{T}[\![\neg B]\!]; \mathcal{T}[\![C_2]\!] \\
&\quad \text{where } \mathcal{T}[\![B]\!] = \{(s, \epsilon, s) \mid (s, \mathbf{tt}) \in \mathcal{B}[\![B]\!]\} \\
\mathcal{T}[\![\mathbf{while}\ B\ \mathbf{do}\ C]\!] &= (\mathcal{T}[\![B]\!]; \mathcal{T}[\![C]\!])^*; \mathcal{T}[\![\neg B]\!] \cup (\mathcal{T}[\![B]\!]; \mathcal{T}[\![C]\!])^\omega \\
\mathcal{T}[\![h?I]\!] &= \{(s, h?n, [s \mid I = n]) \mid s \in S, n \in N\} \\
\mathcal{T}[\![h!E]\!] &= \{(s, h!n, s) \mid (s, n) \in \mathcal{E}[\![E]\!]\} \\
\mathcal{T}[\![\textstyle\sum_{i=1}^{k}(\rho_i \to C_i)]\!] &= \bigcup_{i=1}^{k}(\mathcal{T}[\![\rho_i]\!]; \mathcal{T}[\![C_i]\!]) \\
\mathcal{T}[\![C\backslash h]\!] &= \{(s, \alpha, s') \in \mathcal{T}[\![C]\!] \mid h \notin \mathrm{chans}(\alpha)\} \\
\mathcal{T}[\![C_1\|C_2]\!] &= \mathcal{T}[\![C_1]\!] \| \mathcal{T}[\![C_2]\!]
\end{aligned}
$$

Proof: It is straightforward to show, for each command C, that the operational description of $\mathcal{T}[\![C]\!]$ coincides with the set $\mathcal{T}[\![C]\!]$ prescribed by this denotational definition. The details for parallel composition rely on the operational characterization of fair infinite computation. ∎

This semantic description makes certain equivalences obvious. For instance, writing $C_1 \equiv C_2$ to mean that C_1 and C_2 have the same trace semantics, it is easy to verify the following laws:

$$C; \mathbf{skip} \ \equiv \ C$$
$$\mathbf{skip}; C \ \equiv \ C$$
$$\mathbf{while} \ B \ \mathbf{do} \ C \ \equiv \ \mathbf{if} \ B \ \mathbf{then} \ (C; \mathbf{while} \ B \ \mathbf{do} \ C) \ \mathbf{else} \ \mathbf{skip}$$
$$(h?I \| h!E) \backslash h \ \equiv \ I{:=}E$$
$$C \| \mathbf{skip} \ \equiv \ C$$
$$C_1 \| C_2 \ \equiv \ C_2 \| C_1$$
$$(C_1 \| C_2) \| C_3 \ \equiv \ C_1 \| (C_2 \| C_3)$$
$$(C \backslash h_1) \backslash h_2 \ \equiv \ (C \backslash h_2) \backslash h_1$$
$$(C \backslash h) \backslash h \ \equiv \ C \backslash h$$

The last two laws allow us to write $C \backslash \{h_1, \ldots, h_k\}$ for $(C \backslash h_1) \ldots \backslash h_k$, the result of restricting C on a finite set of channels.

The following result is an easy consequence of the fact that all operations on trace sets used in these semantic clauses are monotone with respect to set inclusion. A program context $P[-]$ is a program containing a hole (denoted $[-]$) into which a command may be inserted; $P[C]$ denotes the program obtained by inserting C into the hole. We restrict attention to contexts $P[-]$ and commands C such that $P[C]$ is well-formed.

Proposition 4.6.2 For every program context $P[-]$ and all commands C and C', we have the following "contextual monotonicity" property:

$$\mathcal{T}[\![C]\!] \subseteq \mathcal{T}[\![C']\!] \ \Rightarrow \ \mathcal{T}[\![P[C]]\!] \subseteq \mathcal{T}[\![P[C']]\!].$$

4.7   Examples

1. It is easy to check the following details, illustrating the correspondence between the denotational and operational definitions of $\mathcal{T}$:

$$\mathcal{T}[\![a?x]\!] = \{(s, a?n, [s \mid x = n]) \mid s \in S \ \& \ n \in N\}$$
$$\mathcal{T}[\![a!0]\!] = \{(s, a!0, s) \mid s \in S\}$$
$$\mathcal{T}[\![a?x \| a!0]\!] = \{(s, \epsilon, [s \mid x = 0]) \mid s \in S\}$$
$$\cup \{(s, a?n.a!0, [s \mid x = n]) \mid s \in S \ \& \ n \in N\}$$
$$\cup \{(s, a!0.a?n, [s \mid x = n]) \mid s \in S \ \& \ n \in N\}$$
$$\mathcal{T}[\![(a?x \| a!0) \backslash a]\!] \ = \ \{(s, \epsilon, [s \mid x = 0]) \mid s \in S\}.$$

2. Recall the processes B_1, B_2, B_{12} discussed earlier:

$$B_1 \ = \ \mathbf{while} \ \mathbf{true} \ \mathbf{do} \ (in?x; link!x)$$
$$B_2 \ = \ \mathbf{while} \ \mathbf{true} \ \mathbf{do} \ (link?y; out!y)$$
$$B_{12} \ = \ [B_1 \| B_2] \backslash link$$

One can use the denotational semantics to show that B_1 and B_2 behave like 1-place buffers and B_{12} behaves like a 2-place buffer.

3. Consider again the program $[C_1 \| C_2 \| C_3] \backslash left \backslash right$, where

$$
\begin{aligned}
C_1 &= \textbf{while true do } (left?x \to out!x) + (right?x \to out!x) \\
C_2 &= \textbf{while true do } left!0 \\
C_3 &= \textbf{while true do } right!1.
\end{aligned}
$$

The traces of $C_2 \| C_3$ have form

$$ (left!0)^\omega \| (right!1)^\omega = ((left!0)^* right!1 (right!1)^* left!0)^\omega, $$

each containing infinitely many *left* and infinitely many *right* steps. The traces of C_1 have form $(h_n?v_n.out!v_n)_{n=0}^\infty$, where each $h_n \in \{left, right\}$ ($n \geq 0$). The only fair merges of a trace of C_1 with a trace of $C_2 \| C_3$, restricted so as to contain no *left* and *right* steps, must therefore involve all synchronization steps. The possible sequences of values output on channel *out* will therefore correspond to the extended regular expression $(0^*11^*0)^\omega$. As required, this is the set of sequences of 0's and 1's that contain infinitely many of each.

4. The loop **while true do skip** diverges:

$$ \mathcal{T}[\![\textbf{while true do skip}]\!] = \{(s, \epsilon^\omega, \bot) \mid s \in S\}. $$

4.8 Full Abstraction

Having presented a denotational description of $\mathcal{T}$ it is clear that we can use traces to reason compositionally about the communication sequences of fair parallel programs: $\mathcal{T}$ distinguishes between a pair of commands C_1 and C_2 if and only if there is a context $P[-]$ such that $\mathcal{T}[\![P[C_1]]\!]$ and $\mathcal{T}[\![P[C_2]]\!]$ differ. The proof of this is almost trivial, using the contextual monotonicity property mentioned above.

Since the behavior $\mathcal{M}[\![C]\!]$ can be extracted from $\mathcal{T}[\![C]\!]$ the trace semantics also supports compositional reasoning about behavior. In fact, we obtain full abstraction: $\mathcal{T}$ distinguishes between C_1 and C_2 if and only if there is a context $P[-]$ such that $\mathcal{M}[\![P[C_1]]\!]$ and $\mathcal{M}[\![P[C_2]]\!]$ differ.

Proposition 4.8.1 The trace semantics $\mathcal{T}$ is (inequationally) fully abstract with respect to $\mathcal{M}$:

$$ \mathcal{T}[\![C]\!] \subseteq \mathcal{T}[\![C']\!] \iff \forall P[-].(\mathcal{M}[\![P[C]]\!] \subseteq \mathcal{M}[\![P[C']]\!]). $$

Proof: The proof of the forward implication follows easily by contextual monotonicity and the fact that the behavior of a program is extractable from its trace set.

For the reverse implication we rely on the following key facts:

1. For a finite communication sequence α containing k output actions, and k distinct identifiers $z_1, \ldots, z_k$, there is a command $D0_\alpha(z_1, \ldots, z_k)$ that performs a sequence of communications matching α and uses the z_i to store the values output in α.

2. For an infinite sequence α, $\langle C', s \rangle$ cannot perform α if and only if there is some finite prefix β of α such that either $\alpha = \beta \epsilon^\omega$ and no β-derivative of $\langle C', s \rangle$ can do ϵ^ω; or α has the form $\beta \lambda \gamma$ where λ is a communication (not ϵ), and no β-derivative of $\langle C', s \rangle$ can do λ.

3. For any configuration $\langle C, s \rangle$, and any finite communication trace α the set $\{ C'' \mid \exists s''.\langle C, s \rangle \overset{\alpha}{\Longrightarrow} \langle C'', s'' \rangle \}$ is finite.

If (s, α, s') is a trace of C but not of C' there is a finite prefix β of α after which a behavioral difference is detectable, and we may use a parallel context containing a command of form $DO_\beta(z_1, \ldots, z_k)$ to distinguish between C and C'.

∎

As an immediate corollary, we obtain (equational) full abstraction: two commands have the same trace sets if and only if they may be interchanged in all program contexts without altering the behavior of the overall program. Thus all of the semantic equivalences validated by this model can be used in any program context with the guarantee that replacing any command by an equivalent one has no effect on program behavior.

4.9 Conclusions

We have presented a semantic model, based on fair traces, for a CSP-like language of communicating processes. We have shown that this semantics is fully abstract with respect to a natural notion of program behavior, so that the semantics exactly supports compositional reasoning about behavior.

A configuration is *deadlocked* iff it is not terminal but has no transitions. For a trivial example, the command $h!0\backslash h$ is deadlocked in any state.

Trace models like this are well suited to reasoning about safety properties but inadequate for reasoning about the possibility of *deadlock*. A non-terminal configuration is deadlocked if it has no transitions. Traces do not provide enough information to distinguish between a process that may either deadlock or perform a communication and the corresponding deadlock-free process. It is not even enough to augment the trace model with extra traces representing communication sequences that lead to deadlock. This is easily seen in one of the examples discussed earlier: the two commands

$$C_1 = (a?x \rightarrow ((b!x \rightarrow \mathbf{skip}) + (c!x \rightarrow \mathbf{skip})))$$
$$C_2 = (a?x \rightarrow b!x) + (a?x \rightarrow c!x).$$

have the same successful traces and no deadlock traces, but they induce different deadlock traces in the context $[-\|b?y]\backslash b\backslash c$: only the second command may deadlock after doing $a?0$.

One way to add appropriate extra structure to the semantic model is to work with *failure sets* [2]: a failure of a process is a (finite) trace together with a set of events that the process may be able to refuse after having performed the trace. The possibility of deadlock is represented by the ability to refuse all events. To extend this idea to the imperative setting we need to incorporate a suitable treatment of program states, perhaps along the lines discussed by Roscoe in [15]. The two commands C_1 and C_2 have different failure sets: only C_2 has the failure $(s, a?0, [s \mid x = 0], \{b!0\})$, corresponding precisely to the behavioral difference noted above.

We plan to investigate further the full abstraction problem for communicating processes and various natural notions of program behavior, including partial and total correctness and deadlock-freedom. The analogous problems for a shared variable parallel language were discussed in [3].

References

[1] K. R. Apt and E.-R. Olderog. *Verification of Sequential and Concurrent Programs.* Springer-Verlag, 1991.

[2] S. Brookes, C.A.R. Hoare, and A.W Roscoe. A theory of communicating sequential processes. *JACM*, volume 31, number 3, pages 560–599, July 1984.

[3] S. Brookes. Full abstraction for a shared variable parallel language. In *Proc. 8th Annual IEEE Symposium on Logic in Computer Science.* IEEE Computer Society Press, June 1993.

[4] E. W. Dijkstra. Cooperating sequential processes. In F. Genuys, editor, *Programming Languages: NATO Advanced Study Institute*, pages 43–112. Academic Press, 1968.

[5] N. Francez. *Fairness.* Springer-Verlag, 1986.

[6] C. A. R. Hoare. Communicating Sequential Processes. *CACM*, 21(8):666–677, August 1978.

[7] C. A. R. Hoare. A model for communicating sequential processes. Technical Report PRG-22, Oxford University, Programming Research Group, 1981.

[8] C. A. R. Hoare. *Communicating Sequential Processes.* Prentice-Hall International, 1985.

[9] J. D. Ichbiah. Reference manual for the Ada programming language. ANSI MIL-STD-1815A-1983, 1983.

[10] INMOS Ltd. *The occam programming manual.* Prentice-Hall, 1984.

[11] R. Milner. Fully abstract models of typed lambda-calculi. *Theoretical Computer Science*, 4:1–22, 1977.

[12] R. Milner. *A Calculus of Communicating Systems*, volume 92 of *LNCS*. Springer-Verlag, 1980.

[13] D. Park. On the semantics of fair parallelism. In D. Bjørner, editor, *Abstract Software Specifications*, volume 86 of *Lecture Notes in Computer Science*, pages 504–526. Springer-Verlag, 1979.

[14] G. D. Plotkin. An operational semantics for CSP. In D. Björner, editor, *Formal Description of Programming Concepts II*, pages 199–225. North-Holland, 1982.

[15] A. W. Roscoe. Denotational semantics for occam. In *Seminar on Concurrency*, volume 197 of *Lecture Notes in Computer Science*. Springer-Verlag, 1984.

Chapter 5

Hiding and Behaviour: An institutional approach

Rod Burstall and Răzvan Diaconescu

Theories with hidden sorts provide a setting to study the idea of behaviour and behavioural equivalence of elements. But there are variants on the notion of theory: many sorted algebras, order sorted algebras and so on; we would like to use the theory of institutions to develop ideas of some generality. In this paper we formulate the notion of behavioural equivalence in a more abstract and categorical way, and we give a general explication of "hiding" in an institution. We use this to show that both hidden many sorted algebras and hidden order sorted algebras yield institutions.

This work was carried out at the Programming Research Group. We would like to thank Tony Hoare, in whose honour this volume appears, for his creation of an environment there which we both greatly appreciate, one of us as a frequent visitor and the other as a PhD student.

5.1 Introduction

An institution [5] is an abstract definition of a logic system, which has proved useful in studying specification languages. It consists of a category of signatures with functors defining sentences and models for each signature, together with a satisfaction relation between sentences and models. Our aim is to explicate the notion of object[1] in the context of institutions, or since the notion of object is very rich, we should more modestly seek to contribute to such an explication. The aspects which we study are:

- The unary nature of objects – they have unary operations on a "state" which produce a new state;
- This state is "hidden" – different states can only be distinguished by their "visible" behaviour

---

[1] It turns out that the world is full of objects; here we mean 'object-oriented' objects.

Our work takes as its starting point Goguen's representation of objects by "hidden many sorted algebras" [3, 6], with which he seeks to capture the two aspects described above. A hidden many sorted signature has "hidden" and "visible" sorts. The visible sorts and the operations on them have a fixed interpretation for all algebras, but the interpretation of hidden sorts may vary from algebra to algebra. The operations on hidden sorts are unary in the sense that they take at most one argument of hidden sort – they cannot act on two states.

We may remark that Goguen's terminology might be made more explicit, albeit more cumbersome, by referring to "hidden *monadic* many sorted algebras", since the unary aspect is important as well as the hidden aspect. Indeed one might better refer to them as many sorted *object* algebras. However we will stick to Goguen's terminology here.

In [3], Goguen defines the hidden many sorted equational institution to have as signatures the usual many sorted signatures with the sorts divided into "hidden" and "visible" ones and a restriction to unary operations on hidden sorts. The sentences and models are the same as for many sorted institutions, but the satisfaction relation is different. A model now satisfies an equation if the left hand side gives the same result as the right hand side in all visible contexts. Here a *visible context* means a term with one free variable and a visible result sort. We shall call this *behavioural satisfaction*. The definition of morphism for hidden many sorted signatures has some restrictions. We shall make all this precise later.

Given a hidden many sorted algebra, A, it behaviourally satisfies a set of sentences just if a certain quotient algebra satisfies the sentences in the usual sense. This quotient algebra identifies elements which are behaviourally indistinguishable, that is there is no visible context which discriminate between them.

Consider the following example of a many sorted signature. The comments in parentheses are just for motivation.

```
Sorts
   Nat            (Naturals)
   NzNat          (Nonzero Naturals)
   R
```

```
Operations
   _+_,_*_ : Nat Nat -> Nat           (addition and multiplication)
   _+_,_*_ : NzNat NzNat -> NzNat     (addition and multiplication)
   _div_ : Nat NzNat -> Nat           (division ignoring remainder)
   natof : NzNat -> Nat               (injection)
   in : NzNat -> R                    (injection)
   _*_ : R Nat -> R
   _/_ : R NzNat -> R
   wh : R -> Nat                      (whole part)
```

Based on this example, we can define a hidden many sorted signature, by defining the sort R to be hidden, Nat and NzNat to be visible. The interpretation of the visible sorts is fixed thus $|\text{Nat}| = \omega$, the set of natural numbers, $|\text{NzNat}| = \omega_+$, the set of nonzero natural numbers and the interpretation of the operations on these is the standard one.

There are many hidden sorted algebras for this signature. A particular familiar one is obtained by interpreting the hidden sort R as $|\text{R}| = \omega \times \omega_+$. Using $n, n', \ldots$ for elements of ω, $d, d', \ldots$ for elements of ω_+ and $r, r', \ldots$ for elements of $|\text{R}|$, we define the operations

```
in(n) = (n,1)
(n,d) * n´ = (n*n´,d)
(n,d) / d´ = (n, d*d´)
wh(n,d) = n div d
```

We think of n as the numerator and d as the denominator. Now r and r' are *behaviourally equivalent* iff any term of sort Nat involving r and the corresponding term involving r' have the same value. (As it happens, our signature has no terms of sort NzNat, the other visible sort.)

For example, (3,2) is behaviourally equivalent to (6,4) since $\text{wh}(3,2) = 1 = \text{wh}(6,4)$, and $\text{wh}[(3,2) \times 10] = 15 = \text{wh}[(6,4) \times 10]$, and so on for all terms. But (3,2) is not behaviourally equivalent to (7,4) since $\text{wh}[(3,2) \times 10] = 15 \neq 17 = \text{wh}[(7,4) \times 10]$. It is not hard to see that (n, d) is behaviourally equivalent to (n', d') iff the rationals n/d and n'/d' are equal, that is, $n \times d' = n' \times d$. This algebra is not quite the nonnegative rationals, since it has many (n, d) pairs corresponding to each rational.

Another hidden sorted algebra could be defined by taking $|\text{R}|$ to be $\mathbb{Q}^{nn}$, the nonnegative rationals with the operations in, *, /, and wh interpreted in the usual way. Now, r and r' are behaviourally equivalent if and only if they are equal. This algebra with $|\text{R}| = \mathbb{Q}^{nn}$ is actually a quotient of the algebra above with $|\text{R}| = \omega \times \omega_+$. This quotienting will play a central role in our investigation, since a hidden many sorted algebra gives rise by quotienting to a many sorted algebra which in a sense represents its behaviour.

A more object oriented example may give more computational motivation:

```
Sorts
    int
    counter   [hidden]

Operations
    _+_,_-_ : int int -> int
    0,1 : -> int
    incr,decr : counter -> counter
    init : -> counter
    read : counter -> int
```

Now we can have an algebra where |counter| is pairs of natural numbers (the number of increments and the number of decrements) or an algebra where |counter| is integers (the difference between these numbers). The latter is a quotient of the former.

5.1.1   Behaviour algebras

In order to describe the notion of behaviourally indistinguishable concisely we may convert a hidden many sorted algebra into another kind of algebra which is simpler and has a concise formulation of "behaviour". This is what we shall call a *behaviour algebra*; it somewhat reminiscent of the Lawvere notion of algebra for an algebraic theory. Like a Lawvere algebra, it is a functor from a category to **Set**, but here the category has a distinguished object and this object has a fixed interpretation. The distinguished object will represent the totality of visible sorts. We are able to show that hidden many sorted algebras convert to behaviour algebras and back again and that there are terminal behaviour algebras. The morphism to the terminal object yields the required behavioural quotient. We may say that the category algebras explicate our notion of *object*.

From a hidden sorted signature we can derive a category playing the role of a signature for behaviour algebras. The derivation should be intuitively natural; it will be spelled out formally later. We first convert the signature to a graph, whose nodes are the hidden sorts plus a distinguished node representing all the visible sorts. Each operation on a hidden sort gives a family of edges in the graph. Now the paths on this graph, or possibly a quotient of them, yield a category. So here is the graph corresponding to the hidden sorted signature in the "rationals" example presented above.

- Nodes: R and u
- Edges: $*_n$, $/_d$: R → R for each $n \in \omega$, $d \in \omega_+$, and wh : R → u.

Thus the *binary* operator * :   R Nat -> R becomes a family of *unary* operators $*_n$: R -> R, taking one argument of hidden sort.

For the signature of the behaviour algebras we will take the path category of this graph. A typical arrow is $*_3; *_4; /_2;$ wh : R → u. We can think of each path ending in the visible sort u as a possible experiment. An interpretation of the graph nodes as sets and the edges as functions extends to an interpretation the path category, assigning to each path the composition of the functions for the edges making up the path; we call this an algebra of the path category. It is what we called a behaviour algebra above.

In the case of the rational numbers example, as an interpretation for u we take $|u| = \omega$ (strictly, in our construction given below, $|u| = \omega + \omega_+$, but, since there are no terms of sort NzNat, we can simplify this to ω and avoid a boring injection of ω into $\omega + \omega_+$). We can think of $|u|$ as the set of answers. Corresponding to the first hidden sorted algebra given above we have the behaviour algebra given as follows:

- $|R| = \omega \times \omega_+$
- $*_{n'}(n, d) = (n*n', d)$
- $/_{d'}(n, d) = (n, d*d')$
- $\text{wh}(n, d) = n \text{ div } d$

The interpretation of a path to $|u|$ (an experiment) is a function; when this function is applied to a value in the interpretation of R it gives an answer to the experiment. It turns out that the collection of all functions from experiments to answers is itself a behaviour algebra, indeed the terminal behaviour algebra.

Two elements of the hidden sort $|R|$ are indistinguishable by observation if all experiments give the same answer. We can now quotient the algebra by this observation equivalence, obtaining in fact the behaviour algebra corresponding to the second hidden sorted algebra given above, that interprets R as the nonnegative rationals. We obtain this quotient by factorising the unique morphism to the terminal algebra.

5.1.2 Making a hidden version of an institution

We use this to develop a way of taking an institution equipped with some extra data and producing an object version of the institution (or as Goguen calls it a "hidden" version). The extra data shows how the models of the institution can be viewed as representing behaviour algebras. So you might take the institution of many sorted algebras and produce the institution of hidden many sorted algebras. Or you might start with order sorted algebras and produce hidden order sorted algebras.

Here is the idea in outline. We take an institution $\mathcal{I}$ plus the extra data and produce an institution $\mathcal{H}$, thus:

- We have a notion of $\mathcal{H}$ signature, and each $\mathcal{H}$ signature should have a corresponding $\mathcal{I}$ signature.
- The models of the $\mathcal{H}$ signature are a subcategory of the models of the $\mathcal{I}$ signature.
- For each model M of an $\mathcal{H}$ signature Σ we can derive a behaviour algebra.
- We compute a quotient of this behaviour algebra by equating elements which have the same observable behaviour
- We convert this quotient algebra back into an $\mathcal{H}$ model $\beta_\Sigma(M)$.

- The satisfaction relation in $\mathcal{H}$ between the model M and any sentence e is defined as the satisfaction in $\mathcal{I}$ between $\beta_\Sigma(M)$ and e.

All this should work smoothly when you change signatures so that we get appropriate functors and natural transformations, so that we get an institution $\mathcal{H}$ equipped with an institution morphism to $\mathcal{I}$.

5.1.3   The order sorted institution

Goguen also wishes to define a hidden version of the order sorted institution. We use the machinery outlined above to accomplish this. The translation from an order sorted signature to a category again uses the path category, but because of the inclusions induced by the ordering on sorts certain paths have to be identified. It is for this reason that we preferred to define a behaviour algebra as a functor rather than taking an algebra to be a morphism from a graph to **Set**; this simpler notion would have sufficed to translate many sorted algebras, but not order sorted ones.

Acknowledgments

We would like to express our gratitude to Joseph Goguen for posing the main question of the paper and for introducing the authors to the connection between object orientation and hidden sorted logics. The exciting discussions which we have had with him greatly helped our understanding of these topics, and his strong influence on this paper will be evident. We also have to thank several people for help with Latex, including Claire Jones, James McKinna and Healf Goguen.

The research reported in this paper has been supported in part by grants from the SERC, the EC 'Types, proofs and programs' basic research project, and the Information Technology Promotion Agency, Japan, as part of the R & D of Basic Technology for Future Industries "New Models for Software Architecture" project sponsored by NEDO.)

Rod Burstall wishes to dedicate his work presented here to the memory of his wife Sissi and her unfailing love.

5.2   Preliminaries

5.2.1   Institutions

An adequate formalisation of logic as used in Computing Science must achieve a delicate balance between syntax and semantics. Tarski's semantic definition of truth for first order logic [12] is a traditional reconciliation of these two aspects of logics, based on the notion of *satisfaction* as a binary relation between models and sentences. Some such notion is needed for the very basic notions of *soundness* and *completeness* of logical systems, because these notions depend in an essential way upon the relationship between provability (which is syntactic) and satisfaction (which is semantic, i.e., concerns "truth" in Tarski's sense). These notions, in turn, are basic to classical treatments of the adequacy of rules of deduction for logical systems; soundness and completeness with respect to an intuitively plausible class of models give us far greater confidence in a set of rules of deduction, and make their range of applicability more precise.

In a series of papers beginning in 1979, Goguen and Burstall developed institutions to formalise the intuitive notion of a logical system; the most recent and complete exposition is [5]. This approach allows us to discuss the crucial relationship between theories and models without commitment to either side at the expense of the other. Institutions are much more abstract than Tarski's model theory, and they also add another basic ingredient, namely signatures and the possibility of translating sentences and models from one signature to another. A special case of this translation may be familiar from first order model theory: if $\Sigma \rightarrow \Sigma'$ is an inclusion of first order signatures, and if M is a Σ'-model, then we can form $M|_\Sigma$, called the *reduct* of M to Σ. Similarly, if e is a Σ-sentence, then we can always view it as a Σ'-sentence (but there is no standard notation for this). The key axiom, called the Satisfaction Condition, says that *truth is invariant under change of notation*, which is surely a very basic intuition for traditional logic.

Definition 1 An **institution** consists of

1. a category $Sign$, whose objects are called **signatures**,
2. a functor $Sen : Sign \rightarrow \textbf{Set}$, giving for each signature a set whose elements are called **sentences** over that signature,
3. a functor $\textsc{Mod} : Sign^{op} \rightarrow \textbf{Cat}$ giving for each signature Σ a category whose objects are called Σ-**models**, and whose arrows are called Σ-(**model**) **morphisms**, and
4. a relation $\models_\Sigma \subseteq |\textsc{Mod}(\Sigma)| \times Sen(\Sigma)$ for each $\Sigma \in |Sign|$, called Σ-**satisfaction**,

such that for each morphism $\phi : \Sigma \rightarrow \Sigma'$ in $Sign$, the **Satisfaction Condition**

$$M' \models_{\Sigma'} Sen(\phi)(e) \quad \text{iff} \quad \textsc{Mod}(\phi)(M') \models_\Sigma e$$

holds for each $M' \in |\textsc{Mod}(\Sigma')|$ and $e \in Sen(\Sigma)$. □

The notion of institution morphism is especially relevant for comparing different logical sytems and eventually for transfering results from one logical system to another [5], or from one theorem prover built on the top of one particular logical system to another theorem prover built on the top of another logical system. Here is its original definition as given by [5]:

Definition 2   Let $\mathcal{I}$ and $\mathcal{I}'$ be institutions. Then an **institution morphism** $\Phi: \mathcal{I} \to \mathcal{I}'$ consists of

1. a functor $\Phi: \text{SIGN} \to \text{SIGN}'$,
2. a natural transformation $\alpha: \Phi; Sen' \Rightarrow Sen$, and
3. a natural transformation $\beta: \text{MOD} \Rightarrow \Phi; \text{MOD}'$

such that the following **Satisfaction Condition** holds

$$M \models_\Sigma \alpha_\Sigma(e') \quad \text{iff} \quad \beta_\Sigma(M) \models'_{\Phi(\Sigma)} e'$$

for any Σ-model M from $\mathcal{I}$ and any $\Phi(\Sigma)$-sentence e' from $\mathcal{I}'$. $\square$

5.2.2   Many sorted algebra

An important institution in Computing Science is that of many sorted equational logic, which played a major role in the theory of algebraic specifications [2], semantics of imperative programming languages [10], and theorem proving [4]:

Definition 3 [4] A **many sorted (algebraic) signature** is a pair (S, Σ), where S is a set of sorts and Σ is a family of sets of operator names, indexed by $S^* \times S$. A **morphism of many sorted signatures** $\phi: (S, \Sigma) \to (S', \Sigma')$ consists of a map $S \to S'$ of sorts and an $S^* \times S$-indexed family of maps $\phi_{w,s}: \Sigma_{w,s} \to \Sigma'_{\phi w, \phi s}$.
   A **many sorted algebra** A over the signature (S, Σ) is an S-sorted set $\langle A_s \mid s \in S \rangle$ together with an interpretation of operator names as functions $\langle A_\sigma: A_w \to A_s \mid \sigma \in \Sigma_{w,s} \rangle$ (by A_w we mean the cartesian products of all A_v for all elements v of w). A **homomorphism** $h: A \to A'$ of many sorted algebras over the signature (S, Σ) is an S-sorted map $A \to A'$ such that for all σ in $\Sigma_{w,s}$ and all $a = a1 \ldots an$ in A_w, $h_s(A_\sigma a) = A'_\sigma(h_{s1} a1 \ldots h_{sn} an)$. $\square$

Definition 4 [4] An **equation** e for the many sorted signature (S, Σ) is a triple $\langle X, l, r \rangle$, where X is an S-sorted set, where l and r are terms over X having the same sort $s \in S$. A many sorted algebra A over (S, Σ) **satisfies** the equation $\langle X, l, r \rangle$ iff for all valuations $v: X \to A$, $v^\#(l) = v^\#(r)$ (where $v^\#$ is the unique extension of v to a homomorphism from the term algebra over X to the algebra A). In this case we write $A \models_\Sigma \langle X, l, r \rangle$. $\square$

[5] describes the way equations are translated and models are "reduced" along many sorted signature morphisms and proves the Satisfaction Condition for many sorted equational logic.

5.3 Behaviour Algebras and Observations

Definition 5 A **behaviour signature** is a category with distinguished object u such that there are no arrows whose source is the distinguished object except the identity; we let a morphism of behaviour signatures be a functor preserving the distinguished object and such that distinguished objects are the only objects mapped to distinguished objects. Let $\mathbf{Cat}_u$ denote the category of behaviour signatures.

We write a behaviour signature as a pair (C, u) where C is a category and u is its distinguished object. We use h and h' for objects different from u, and we use e for arrows. □

Definition 6 Let $\mathcal{U}$ be a set. By a **behaviour algebra** over $(C, u, \mathcal{U})$ we mean a functor $A\colon C \to \mathbf{Set}$ such that $Au = \mathcal{U}$. A homomorphism of these algebras is a natural transformation such that its component at u is the identity function on $\mathcal{U}$. These algebras and their homomorphisms form a category, $\mathrm{BALG}(C, u, \mathcal{U})$. □

From now on we fix a behaviour signature (C, u) and a set $\mathcal{U}$; also, we call a behaviour algebra over these simply an algebra. We now construct a terminal object, $\mathbf{B}$ for this category:

1. for each object h different from u, define $\mathbf{B}h$ to be the set of functions which take arrows $h \to u$ to an element of $\mathcal{U}$, that is $\mathcal{U}^{C[h,u]}$, and

2. for an arrow $e \in C[h, h']$, define $\mathbf{B}e$ to be $\mathcal{U}^{C[e,u]}$, the function $\psi\colon \mathcal{U}^{C[h,u]} \to \mathcal{U}^{C[h',u]}$ given by $(\psi f)e' = f(e; e')$ where $f \in \mathcal{U}^{C[h,u]}$ and $e' \in C[h', u]$.

Note that the definition of $\mathbf{B}$ on arrows $e \in C[h, u]$ makes sense under the canonical identification of $\mathcal{U}$ with $\mathcal{U}^{C[u,u]}$ (since $C[u, u]$ is a singleton set because no arrows go out of u except the identity).

Proposition 7 $\mathbf{B}$ is the terminal algebra over $(C, u, \mathcal{U})$.

Proof: Let A be any algebra over $(C, u, \mathcal{U})$. Fix any object h. If $m\colon A \to \mathbf{B}$ is a homorphism, then for any $e \in C[h, h']$ it satisfies $m_h; \mathbf{B}e = Ae; m_{h'}$ and hence for any $p \in C[h, u]$, $m_h; \mathbf{B}p = Ap; m_u$. But m_u is the identity, so this is $m_h; \mathbf{B}p = Ap$.

Observe that for any arrow $e \in C[h, u]$, $\mathbf{B}e$ is the projection $\mathcal{U}^{C[h,u]} \to \mathcal{U}$ on the e-th component. By the universal property of products there is a unique function $m_h\colon Ah \to \mathbf{B}h$ such that $m_h; \mathbf{B}e = Ae$ for any arrow $e \in C[h, u]$. Thus, there is at most one algebra homomorphism $m\colon A \to \mathbf{B}$.

All we still have to prove is that the unique function m defined above is indeed an algebra homomorphism, that is, $m_h; \mathbf{B}e = Ae; m_{h'}$ for any objects h and h' and for any arrow $e \in C[h, h']$. Pick an arbitrary arrow $e' \in C[h', u]$. Then:

$$m_h; \mathbf{B}e; \mathbf{B}e'$$

$$= \quad m_h; \mathbf{B}(e; e')$$

$$= \quad A(e; e') \qquad \text{(by definition of } m\text{)}$$

$$= \quad Ae; Ae'$$

$$= \quad Ae; m_{h'}; \mathbf{B}e' \quad \text{(by definition of } m\text{)}$$

By the universal property of the product $\mathcal{U}^{C[h',u]}$ we get the desired equality $m_h; \mathbf{B}e = Ae; m_{h'}$. $\square$

We now turn to the definition of quotient behaviour algebra using a rather abstract formulation, the notion of *image factorisation system* as defined in [1].

Fact 8 The category of algebras over $(C, u, \mathcal{U})$ has a canonical image factorisation system $(\mathcal{E}_C, \mathcal{M}_C)$ with $\mathcal{E}_C = \{e$ morphism of behaviour algebras $\mid e_h$ surjective for any $h\}$ and $\mathcal{M}_C = \{m$ morphism of behaviour algebras $\mid m_h$ injective for any $h\}$.

Proof: Each component of a morphism of behaviour algebras factors in **Set**, then we use the Diagonal Fill-in Property for image factorisation systems to define the image behaviour algebra on arrows.

More specifically, suppose $f\colon A \to B$ is a homomorphism of algebras and $k\colon s \to t$ in C, so that $A_k\colon A_s \to A_t$ and $\mathbf{B}_k\colon \mathbf{B}_s \to \mathbf{B}_t$. Then we factorise $f_s\colon A_s \to \mathbf{B}_s$ to get an intermediate I_s, similarly for t. We then use the fill in property to get $I_k\colon I_s \to I_t$. This gives the factorisation of f with image algebra I. $\square$

Any morphism $\phi\colon (C, u) \to (C', u)$ of behaviour signatures determines a functor $\mathrm{BALG}(\phi)\colon \mathrm{BALG}(C', u', \mathcal{U}) \to \mathrm{BALG}(C, u, \mathcal{U})$ mapping a behaviour algebra A' to $\phi; A'$ and any morphism f' of category algebras to $\phi f'$ (i.e., the vertical composition between ϕ as a functor and f' as a natural transformation).

Corollary 9 For any morphism $\phi\colon (C, u) \to (C', u)$ of behaviour signatures, $\mathrm{BALG}(\phi)$ is a morphism of factorisation systems $(\mathcal{E}_{C'}, \mathcal{M}_{C'}) \to (\mathcal{E}_C, \mathcal{M}_C)$, i.e., $\mathrm{BALG}(\phi)\mathcal{E}_{C'} \subseteq \mathcal{E}_C$ and $\mathrm{BALG}(\phi)\mathcal{M}_{C'} \subseteq \mathcal{M}_C$. $\square$

Lemma 10 Let $\phi\colon (C, u) \to (C', u)$ be a morphism of behaviour signatures with $\phi[h, u]\colon C[h, u] \to C'[\phi h, u]$ surjective for any h. Let $\mathbf{B}$ be the terminal behaviour algebra over $(C, u, \mathcal{U})$ and $\mathbf{B}'$ be the terminal algebra over $(C', u, \mathcal{U})$. Then the unique homomorphism of category algebras $m\colon \mathrm{BALG}(\phi)\mathbf{B}' \to \mathbf{B}$ is injective in all components, i.e., it belongs to $\mathcal{M}_C$.

Proof: Fix h object of C. $(\mathrm{BALG}(\phi)\mathbf{B}')h = \mathbf{B}'(\phi h) = \mathcal{U}^{C'[\phi h, u]}$. For any $f\colon C'[\phi h, u] \to \mathcal{U}$, $m_h(f) = \phi[h, u]; f$. Since surjective functions are epis, $m_h(f) = m_h(g)$ implies $f = g$ which proves the injectivity of m_h. $\square$

5.4   Hidden Many Sorted Signatures and Models

In [3], Goguen introduces the institution of hidden many sorted equational logic as a logical support for an algebraic semantics for object oriented programming. His definition of hidden many sorted signatures emphasize the *monadic* nature of observations. Furthermore, by forcing the Satisfaction Condition to hold, Goguen obtained the right notion of hidden many sorted signature. The restrictions imposed on morphisms of hidden many sorted signatures correspond exactly to the methodological principle of encapsulation from the practice of object oriented programming (see [3] for further details).

Here are his definitions for hidden many sorted signatures, morphisms of signatures and models:

Definition 11 Fix a set V of visible sorts, a many sorted signature (V, Ψ) and an algebra $\mathcal{U}$ over (V, Ψ). A **hidden many sorted signature** (H, V, Σ) is a many sorted signature $(H \cup V, \Sigma)$ with H the set of hidden sorts, V the set of visible sorts and satisfying the following conditions:

(S1) if $\sigma \in \Sigma_{w,v}$ with $w \in V^*$ and $v \in V$, then $\sigma \in \Psi_{w,v}$; and
(S2) if $\sigma \in \Sigma_{w,v}$ then at most one element of w lies in H.

A **hidden many sorted signature morphism** $\phi \colon (H, V, \Sigma) \to (H', V, \Sigma')$, is a many sorted signature morphism $\phi \colon (H \cup V, \Sigma) \to (H' \cup V, \Sigma')$ such that:

(M1) $\phi v = v$ for all $v \in V$ and $\phi \sigma = \sigma$ for all $\sigma \in \Psi$,
(M2) $\phi(H) \subseteq H'$, and
(M3) if $\sigma' \in \Sigma'_{w',s'}$ and some sort in w' lies in $\phi(H)$, then $\sigma' = \phi(\sigma)$ for some $\sigma \in \Sigma$.

A **hidden many sorted model** over (H, V, Σ) is a many sorted algebra M over $(H \cup V, \Sigma)$ such that $M \mid_\Psi = \mathcal{U}$ and a **homomorphism of hidden many sorted models** $h \colon M \to M'$ is a homomorphism of many sorted algebras such that $h \mid_\Psi = 1_\mathcal{U}$. □

Consider a hidden many sorted signature (H, V, Σ), with H as the set of hidden sorts, V as the set of visible sorts and $\mathcal{U}_v$ the fixed sets of "data values" for the visible sorts $v \in V$. Let now v and v' denote strings of visible sorts, i.e., elements of V^*. For each $v \in V^*$ we denote by $\mathcal{U}_v$ the cartesian product of all sets of data values corresponding to the elements of v.

The hidden many sorted signature (H, V, Σ) canonically determines a pointed graph (G, u) in the following way:

1. the nodes are all elements of H plus a distinguished node u,
2. for any nodes h, n with $h \in H$,
    $G[h, n]$ is the set $\{\langle a, \sigma, a' \rangle \colon v, v' \in V^*, \sigma \in \Sigma_{vhv',n}, a \in \mathcal{U}_v, a' \in \mathcal{U}_{v'}\}$, and
3. $G[u, u]$ is empty.

Let $C = G^*$ be the path category of G, i.e., the category freely generated by the graph G. Notice that the category C does not have any arrows out of u except the identity.

We will now define the behaviour algebras underlying hidden many sorted models. Since there is no danger of confusion, we denote by $\mathcal{U}$ be the disjoint union of the sets $\mathcal{U}_v$ for all $v \in V$.

Definition 12   There is a forgetful functor δ from the category of hidden many sorted models, $\text{HALG}(H, V, \Sigma)$, to the category of behaviour algebras, $\text{BALG}(C, u, \mathcal{U})$, defined by:

1. for any hidden many sorted model A, $\delta(A)h = A_h$ for $h \in H$ and each edge $\langle a, \sigma, a' \rangle \in G[h, n]$ is interpreted as $A_\sigma(a, \_, a') \colon A_h \to A_n$; now since C is the path category of G, this extends uniquely to an interpretation of all path, i.e., all morphisms of C, and
2. any homomorphism of hidden many sorted models $m \colon A \to B$ is mapped into the homomorphism of behaviour algebras $\delta(m)$ with $\delta(m)_h = m_h$ for $h \in H$.

□

The forgetful functor from hidden many sorted models to behaviour algebras has a lifting property which enables us to take advantage of working at the level of behaviour algebras rather than at the level of hidden many sorted models.

Lemma 13 Let A be a hidden many sorted model and $m \colon \delta(A) \to B$ be a homomorphism of behaviour algebras. There is a unique homomorphism of hidden many sorted models $m^\sharp \colon A \to B^\sharp$ such that $\delta(m^\sharp) = m$.

Proof: Because $\delta(m^\sharp)$ should be m, for any $h \in H$ we take $B_h^\sharp$ to be Bh and $m_h^\sharp$ to be m_h. If $\sigma \in \Sigma_{vhv',h'}$, then, for all $a \in \mathcal{U}_v$, $a' \in \mathcal{U}_{v'}$, $b \in Bh$, $B_\sigma^\sharp(a, b, a')$ is $(B\langle a, \sigma, a' \rangle)(b)$. If $\sigma \in \Sigma_{v,h}$, $v \in V^*$, $h \in H$, then, for all $a \in \mathcal{U}_v$, $B_\sigma^\sharp(a)$ is defined as $m_h(A_\sigma(a))$. These define a hidden sorted model $B^\sharp$ and a homomorphism $m^\sharp \colon A \to B^\sharp$. Notice that $m^\sharp$ is indeed a homomorphism of hidden sorted models because of the naturality of m and of the definition of the interpretations of the operations $\sigma \in \Sigma_{v,h}$, $v \in V^*$, $h \in H$, in $B^\sharp$. □

Fact 14 Any morphism of hidden many sorted signatures $\phi \colon (H, V, \Sigma) \to (H', V', \Sigma')$ determines a full morphism of behaviour signatures $\phi^* \colon (C, u) \to (C', u)$.

Proof: Let (G, u) and (G', u) be the pointed graphs determined by (H, V, Σ) and (H', V', Σ') respectively. The morphism of pointed graphs determined by ϕ maps edges $\langle a, \sigma, a' \rangle$ to edges $\langle a, \phi(\sigma), a' \rangle$. It is full because any edge $\langle a, \sigma', a' \rangle$ in G' is an image of an edge $\langle a, \sigma, a' \rangle$ in G, where $\phi(\sigma) = \sigma'$. Its unique extension to a functor ϕ^* between the path categories of G and G' is thus full. □

5.5 Hiding Sorts in Institutions

This section is devoted to the main result of this paper. The following theorem gives an abstract model theoretical construction of a "behavioural" (or "hidden") institution over any institution satisfying some mild and natural conditions. This method of constructing a behavioural satisfaction relation on the top of an ordinary satisfaction relation is totally independent of the form of the sentences and it contrasts with the more syntactical way of defining the behavioural satisfaction in the particular case of equational logic by using the concept of *context* (see [11] or [3]).

Let $\mathcal{I} = (\text{SIGN}, \text{MOD}, Sen, \models)$ be an institution and suppose that the following data is given:

- a subcategory of "hidden sorted" signatures $\text{HSIGN} \hookrightarrow \text{SIGN}$, and
- a subfunctor of "hidden sorted" models $\text{HMOD} \subseteq (\text{HSIGN} \hookrightarrow \text{SIGN}; \text{MOD})$.

Theorem 15 Given a functor $\text{BMOD} \colon \text{HSIGN} \to \mathbf{Cat}^{op}$ and a natural transformation $\delta \colon \text{HMOD} \to \text{BMOD}$ such that

- for each $\Sigma \in |\text{HSIGN}|$, $\text{BMOD}(\Sigma)$ has a terminal object $\mathbf{B}_\Sigma$ and an image factorisation system $(\mathcal{E}_\Sigma, \mathcal{M}_\Sigma)$,
- for each $\sigma \colon \Sigma \to \Sigma'$ in HSIGN, the unique map $\text{BMOD}(\sigma)(\mathbf{B}_{\Sigma'}) \to \mathbf{B}_\Sigma$ is in $\mathcal{M}_\Sigma$ and $\text{BMOD}(\sigma)$ preserves the image factorisation systems, and
- $\delta_\Sigma \colon M/\text{HMOD}(\Sigma) \simeq \delta_\Sigma(M)/\text{BMOD}(\Sigma)$ is a natural isomorphism of slice categories

then these canonically determine a "hidden sorted" institution

$$\mathbf{H}(\mathcal{I}) = (\text{HSIGN}, \text{HMOD}, Sen \mid_{\text{HSIGN}}, \models^b)$$

and a morphism of institutions $\langle \text{HSIGN} \hookrightarrow \text{SIGN}, \beta, 1_{Sen\mid_{\text{HSIGN}}} \rangle \colon \mathbf{H}(\mathcal{I}) \to \mathcal{I}$.

Proof: We first define the natural transformation $\beta \colon \text{HMOD} \to \text{MOD} \mid_{\text{HSIGN}}$ translating the models. Fix a signature $\Sigma \in |\text{HSIGN}|$.

For any model $M \in |\text{HMOD}(\Sigma)|$, let the 'observation map' obs_Σ^M be the unique arrow $\delta_\Sigma(M) \to \mathbf{B}_\Sigma$. Let $obs_\Sigma^M = e_M; m_M$ be its image factorisation and consider $e_M^\sharp \colon M \to \beta_\Sigma(M)$ the unique map of hidden sorted models such that $\delta_\Sigma(e_M^\sharp) = e_M$. For the definition of β_Σ on model morphisms, consider a morphisms of models $f \colon M \to N$. By the Diagonal Fill-in Property of image factorisation systems, $\delta_\Sigma(f)$ induces a canonical map f' such that $e_M; f' = \delta_\Sigma(f); e_N$ and $f'; m_N = m_M$. Define $\beta_\Sigma(f)$ to be $f'^\sharp$, i.e., the unique model morphism such that $\delta_\Sigma(f'^\sharp) = f'$. The functoriality of β_Σ follows from the uniqueness in the Diagonal Fill-in Property.

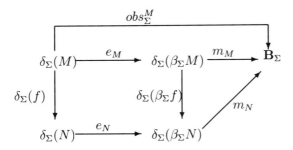

For proving the naturality of β we pick any morphism of hidden sorted signatures $\phi \in \mathrm{HSIGN}(\Sigma, \Sigma')$. Let M' be any Σ'-model. Let $obs_{\Sigma'}^{M'} = e_{M'}; m_{M'}$ be the image factorisation of the observation map of M'. Because $\mathrm{BMOD}(\phi)$ preserves the factorisation system, $\mathrm{BMOD}(\phi)(e_{M'}); \mathrm{BMOD}(\phi)(m_{M'})$ is an image factorisation for $\mathrm{BMOD}(\phi)(obs_{\Sigma'}^{M'})$. $\mathrm{BMOD}(\phi)(\delta_{\Sigma'}(M')) = \delta_\Sigma(M'\mid_\phi)$ by the naturality of δ. We know that the unique map $m \colon \mathrm{BMOD}(\phi)\mathbf{B}_{\Sigma'} \to \mathbf{B}_\Sigma$ is in $\mathcal{M}_\Sigma$. This shows that $\mathrm{BMOD}(\phi)(e_{M'}); (\mathrm{BMOD}(\phi)(m_{M'}); m)$ is an image factorisation for $\mathrm{BMOD}(\phi)(obs_{\Sigma'}^{M'}); m$ which is equal to $obs_\Sigma^{M'\mid_\phi}$ by the universal property of the terminal object. Then $\mathrm{BMOD}(\phi)(e_{M'}) = e_{M'\mid_\phi}$ which proves that $\beta_{\Sigma'}^{M'}\mid_\phi = \beta_\Sigma(M'\mid_\phi)$. The naturality of β on model morphisms follows in a similar way.

The "behavioural satisfaction" relation is the only possible choice for a satisfaction relation in $\mathbf{H}(\mathcal{I})$ which makes $\langle \mathrm{HSIGN} \hookrightarrow \mathrm{SIGN}, \beta, 1_{Sen\mid_{\mathrm{HSIGN}}} \rangle \colon \mathbf{H}(\mathcal{I}) \to \mathcal{I}$ into a morphism of institutions. More precisely, given a hidden sorted signature Σ, a hidden sorted model $M \in |\mathrm{HMOD}(\Sigma)|$ and a Σ-sentence e,

$$M \models_\Sigma^b e \quad \text{iff} \quad \beta_\Sigma(M) \models_\Sigma e \ .$$

All we still have to prove is that the behavioural satisfaction $\models^b$ verifies the Satisfaction Condition for the institution $\mathbf{H}(\mathcal{I})$.

Let $\phi \in \mathrm{HSIGN}(\Sigma, \Sigma')$ be any morphism of hidden sorted signatures and consider any hidden sorted model $M' \in |\mathrm{MOD}(\Sigma')|$ and any Σ-sentence e. Then $M' \models_{\Sigma'}^b (Sen\phi)(e)$ iff $\beta_{\Sigma'}(M') \models_{\Sigma'} (Sen\phi)(e)$ iff (by the Satisfaction Condition in $\mathcal{I}$) $\beta_{\Sigma'}(M')\mid_\phi \models_\Sigma e$. But $\beta_{\Sigma'}(M')\mid_\phi = \beta_\Sigma(M'\mid_\phi)$ by the naturality of β. It follows that $M' \models_{\Sigma'}^b (Sen\phi)(e)$ iff $\beta_\Sigma(M'\mid_\phi) \models_\Sigma e$ iff $M'\mid_\phi \models_\Sigma^b e$. $\square$

Turning to the example of hidden many sorted logic we have:

Corollary 16 Hidden many sorted equational logic with the behavioural satisfaction of equations by algebras is an institution. Moreover, there is a canonical morphism from the institution of hidden many sorted equational logic to the institution of many sorted equational logic.

Proof: Let $\mathcal{I}$ of the previous theorem be the institution of many sorted equational logic. Consider HSIGN to be the category of hidden sorted signatures for a fixed signature and a fixed algebra of data values, and let $\mathcal{U}$ be the disjoint union of the carriers of the algebra of data values. Let HMOD be the functor constructing the category of hidden many sorted models for any hidden many sorted signature.

Consider the forgetful functor $\mathcal{B} \colon$ HSIGN $\to$ $\mathbf{Cat}_u$ mapping hidden many sorted signatures to their underlying behaviour signatures (see Section 5.4) and morphisms of hidden many sorted signatures to morphisms of behaviour signatures. Consider the functor BALG $\colon$ $\mathbf{Cat}_u \to \mathbf{Cat}^{op}$ mapping any behaviour signature (C, u) to the category of behaviour algebras over $(C, u, \mathcal{U})$. The composition $\mathcal{B}$; BALG gives us the functor BMOD and Definition 12 parameterised by signatures defines a natural transformation $\delta \colon$ HMOD $\to \mathcal{B}$; BALG.

The existence of terminal objects for the categories BALG$(\mathcal{B}(H, V, \Sigma))$, where (H, V, Σ) is a hidden sorted many sorted signature, is assured by Proposition 7.

For any morphism of hidden sorted many sorted signatures ϕ, BALG$(\mathcal{B}(\phi))$ maps the terminal behaviour algebra over $(\mathcal{B}(H', V, \Sigma'), \mathcal{U})$ to a subalgebra of the terminal behaviour algebra over $(\mathcal{B}(H, V, \Sigma), \mathcal{U})$ by Lemma 10 and Fact 14.

Lemma 13 proves that the components of δ satisfy the lifting property expressed by the isomorphism of slice categories in the statement of the previous theorem.

Corollary 9 proves that the reduct functors between categories of behaviour algebras preserve the image factorisation systems. $\Box$

5.6   Hidden Order Sorted Logics

In this section we build the institution of hidden order sorted equational logic where the satisfaction relation between order sorted algebras and order sorted equations is behavioural. The notion of order-sortedness we use is due to Goguen and Meseguer [8] and it is the basis for the OBJ family languages, including the object oriented language FOOPS [7]. A comparison between different types of order-sortedness could be found in the survey [9] (where the Goguen-Meseguer approach has been referred as *overloaded* order sorted algebra).

Here is the definition of hidden order sorted signatures, signature morphisms and models, by adapting Definition 11 to the order sorted case:

Definition 17 Fix a set V of visible sorts, an order sorted signature $(V, \leq, \Psi)$ and an order sorted algebra U over $(V, \leq, \Psi)$. A **hidden order sorted signature** $(H, V, \leq, \Sigma)$ is an order sorted signature $(H \cup V, \leq, \Sigma)$ with $(H, \leq)$ the partially ordered set of hidden sorts, $(V, \leq)$ the partially ordered set of visible sorts such that no visible sort is related to any hidden sort and such that (H, V, Σ) is a hidden many sorted signature.

A **hidden order sorted signature morphism** $\phi \colon (H, V, \leq, \Sigma) \to (H', V, \leq, \Sigma')$ is both a morphism of order sorted signatures $(H \cup V, \leq, \Sigma) \to (H' \cup V, \leq, \Sigma')$ and a morphism of hidden many sorted signature $(H, V, \Sigma) \to (H', V, \Sigma')$ such that for any hidden sorts h, h', $\phi h \ < \phi h'$ implies $h \leq h'$.

A **hidden order sorted model** over $(H, V, \le, \Sigma)$ is an order sorted algebra M over $(H \cup V, \le, \Sigma)$ such that $M \mid_\Psi = U$ and a homomorphism of hidden sorted models $h: M \to M'$ is a homomorphism of order sorted algebras such that $h \mid_\Psi = 1_U$. $\square$

Let $(H, V, \le, \Sigma)$ be a hidden order sorted signature. Then the hidden many sorted signature (H, V, Σ) determines a pointed graph (G_0, u) as described in Section 5.4. Then $(H, V, \le, \Sigma)$ determines another pointed graph (G, u) thus:

- the nodes of G are the same as those of G_0 together with a new node 1,
- $G[1, 1]$ is empty,
- for each $h \in H$, $G[1, h]$ is $\{\perp_h\}$, and
- if $h < h'$ then $G[h, h'] = G_0[h, h'] \cup \{i_{h,h'}\}$ and $G[h', h] = G_0[h', h] \cup \{r_{h',h}\}$.

The intuitive understanding of these new edges is that $\perp_h$ stands for the undefined element of sort h, $i_{h,h'}$ stands for the inclusion between subsorts and $r_{h',h}$ stands for the right inverse to $i_{h,h'}$.

Now, we form a category $C = G^*/Q$, where Q is the congruence generated by the following identities:

- $i_{h,h'}; r_{h',h} = 1_h$ for all pairs h, h' with $h < h'$,
- $i_{h,h'}; i_{h',h''} = i_{h,h''}$ and $r_{h'',h'}; r_{h',h} = r_{h'',h}$ for all triples h, h', h'' with $h < h' < h''$,
- for all nodes n, n' and $f \in G^*[n, n']$, $\perp_n; f = \perp_{n'}$, and
- for all $\sigma \in \Sigma_{vhv',h'} \cap \Sigma_{v_0 h_0 v_0', h_0'}$ with $h_0' < h'$ and $a \in U_{v_0}$, $a' \in U_{v_0'}$, $i_{h_0,h}; \langle a, \sigma, a' \rangle = \langle a, \sigma, a' \rangle; i_{h_0',h'}$.

Let $\mathcal{U}_v$ be a fixed set of data values for the visible sort v and let $\mathcal{U}$ be the set obtained by adding a new element $\perp_u$ to the colimit of all these sets. There is a forgetful functor $\delta: \text{HALG}(H, V, \le, \Sigma) \to \text{BALG}(C, u, \mathcal{U})$ defined as follows for a hidden order sorted model A:

- $\delta(A)h = A_h \cup \{\perp_h\}$,
- $\delta(A)1$ is a singleton set and $\perp_h$ evaluates its element as $\perp_h$,
- for all pairs h, h' with $h < h'$, $i_{h,h'}$ is interpreted as the expansion of the inclusion $A_h \subseteq A_{h'}$ mapping $\perp_h$ to $\perp_{h'}$ and $r_{h',h}$ is interpreted as its right inverse which maps all elements of $A_{h'}$ that are not in A_h to $\perp_h$, and
- the interpretation of edges $\langle a, \sigma, a' \rangle$ is the same as in Definition 12.

The definition of δ on homomorphisms of hidden order sorted models m expands each component m_h by preserving $\perp_h$. By similarity with Lemma 13, we have the following lifting property:

Fact 18 For any hidden order sorted model M and any behaviour algebra morphism $f: \delta(M) \to N$ there is a unique morphism of hidden order sorted models $f^\sharp: M \to N^\sharp$ such that $\delta(f^\sharp) = f$. $\square$

Corollary 19 Hidden order sorted equational logic is an institution. Moreover, there is a canonical morphism of institutions from hidden order sorted equational logic to order sorted equational logic.

Proof: Let $\mathcal{I}$ of the previous theorem be the institution of order sorted equational logic. Consider HSIGN to be the category of hidden order sorted signatures for a fixed signature and a fixed algebra of data values, and let $\mathcal{U}$ be the colimit of the carriers of the algebra of data values. Let HMOD be the functor constructing the category of hidden order sorted models for any hidden order sorted signature.

Consider the forgetful functor $\mathcal{B}\colon$ HSIGN $\to$ **Cat**$_u$ mapping hidden order sorted signatures to their underlying behaviour signatures as described above and mapping morphisms of hidden order sorted signatures to morphisms of behaviour signatures in the canonical way. Consider the functor BALG: **Cat**$_u$ $\to$ **Cat**^{op} mapping any behaviour signature (C, u) to the category of behaviour algebras over $(C, u, \mathcal{U})$. The definition of forgetful functors from categories of hidden order sorted models to behaviour algebras described above gives a natural transformation $\delta\colon$ HMOD $\to \mathcal{B}; $BALG.

The existence of terminal objects for the categories $\mathrm{BALG}(\mathcal{B}(H, V, \leq, \Sigma))$, where $(H, V, \leq, \Sigma)$ is a hidden order sorted signature, is assured by Proposition 7.

For any morphism of hidden order sorted signatures ϕ, $\mathrm{BALG}(\mathcal{B}(\phi))$ maps the terminal behaviour algebra over $(\mathcal{B}(H', V', \Sigma'), \mathcal{U})$ to a subalgebra of the terminal category algebra over $(\mathcal{B}(H, V, \Sigma), \mathcal{U})$ by Lemma 10 and Fact 14.

Lemma 13 proves that the components of δ satisfy the lifting property expressed by the isomorphism of slice categories in the statement of the previous theorem.

The reduct functors between categories of behaviour algebras preserve image factorisation systems by Corollary 9. $\square$

5.7 Conclusions

We showed how abstract model theory could be used to define a behavioural satisfaction relation on top of any satisfaction relation. An important consequence of this construction is that it is totally independent of syntax (i.e., the shape of the sentences of the institution involved) and it could therefore be applied to institutions like Horn clause logics, first order logics, modal logics etc.

As a corollary we have proved that hidden order sorted equational logic is an institution, this institution underlying the algebraic foundations of object oriented programming.

An obvious step forward would be a proof theory for the behavioural satisfaction in connection with the quotienting of hidden sorted models through the image factorisation of the canonical morphisms to the terminal behaviour algebra.

References

[1] Michael Arbib and Ernest Manes. *Arrows, Structures and Functors*. Academic, 1975.

[2] Hartmut Ehrig and Bernd Mahr. *Fundamentals of Algebraic Specification 1: Equations and Initial Semantics*. Springer, 1985. EATCS Monographs on Theoretical Computer Science, Volume 6.

[3] Joseph Goguen. Types as theories. In George Michael Reed, Andrew William Roscoe, and Ralph F. Wachter, editors, *Topology and Category Theory in Computer Science*, pages 357–390. Oxford, 1991.

[4] Joseph Goguen. *Theorem Proving and Algebra*. MIT (?), to appear.

[5] Joseph Goguen and Rod Burstall. Institutions: Abstract model theory for specification and programming. *Journal of the Association for Computing Machinery*, 39(1):95–146, January 1992. Draft, as Report ECS-LFCS-90-106, Computer Science Department, University of Edinburgh, January 1990; an ancestor is "Introducing Institutions," in *Proceedings, Logics of Programming Workshop*, Edward Clarke and Dexter Kozen, editors, Springer Lecture Notes in Computer Science, Volume 164, pages 221–256, 1984.

[6] Joseph Goguen and Răzvan Diaconescu. Towards an algebraic semantics for the object paradigm. In *Proceedings, Tenth Workshop on Abstract Data Types*. Springer, to appear 1993.

[7] Joseph Goguen and José Meseguer. Unifying functional, object-oriented and relational programming, with logical semantics. In Bruce Shriver and Peter Wegner, editors, *Research Directions in Object-Oriented Programming*, pages 417–477. MIT, 1987. Preliminary version in *SIGPLAN Notices*, Volume 21, Number 10, pages 153–162, October 1986.

[8] Joseph Goguen and José Meseguer. Order-sorted algebra I: Equational deduction for multiple inheritance, overloading, exceptions and partial operations. *Theoretical Computer Science*, to appear 1992. Also, Programming Research Group Technical Monograph PRG–80, Oxford University, December 1989; earlier version, Technical Report SRI-CSL-89-10, SRI International, Computer Science Lab, July 1988.

[9] Joseph Goguen and Răzvan Diaconescu. A survey of order sorted algebra, 1992. Submitted for publication.

[10] Joseph Goguen, James Thatcher, Eric Wagner, and Jesse Wright. Initial algebra semantics and continuous algebras. *Journal of the Association for Computing Machinery*, 24(1):68–95, January 1977. An early version is "Initial Algebra Semantics", with James Thatcher, IBM T.J. Watson Research Center, Report RC 4865, May 1974.

[11] Horst Reichel. Behavioural equivalence – a unifying concept for initial and final specifications. In *Proceedings, Third Hungarian Computer Science Conference*. Akademiai Kiado, 1981. Budapest.

[12] Alfred Tarski. The semantic conception of truth. *Philos. Phenomenological Research*, 4:13–47, 1944.

Chapter 6

Monitors Revisited

Ole-Johan Dahl

6.1 Introduction

One of the most influential papers of Computer Science to appear during the late 1960's undoubtedly was Tony's "An Axiomatic Basis for Computer Programming" [1], introducing a special purpose logic, now called "Hoare logic", for reasoning about the behaviour of imperative programs. That paper and its many followers, notably [2], have induced a change of attitude to the art of programming, in focusing on verifiability as an essential aspect of program quality, and on program development as a mathematical activity.

A concept of *monitors* important for the design of interacting concurrent processes took form a few years later, based on ideas from various sources: critical regions, [5], shared variables and mechanisms for the sequencing of critical regions, [3], [6], and object classes, [7]. The concept received its final, convincing form in [4], where a monitor is an object in the role of a shared variable, whose operators are critical regions with respect to the object, and where the internal sequencing is by *wait* and *signal* operations, which are primitives comparable to (semi-) coroutine calls. Rules are given for the reasoning about partial correctness with respect to a local invariant. It is fitting in the present context to return to the application of Hoare logic to monitors in order to look at some useful extensions compared to the logic of [4].

6.2 Monitors Redefined

The main purpose of our redefinition is to impose a LIFO discipline on signallers, so that when a signalled process gives up the critical region, it is given to the last signaller waiting. This enables stronger state assertions at the time when a signaller regains control. We provide access to the length of process queues (using the convenient ad-hoc notation $\#c$ for *condition* variable c), not only a test for empty/non-empty. We also drop the notion of priority *condition* queues in favour of more explicit sequencing. Notice that the access to queue lengths does not enable access to individual processes in a multi-process queue, which implies that one can leave the queuing discipline undefined if desired (possibly to be defined at higher levels of abstraction for the purpose of system tuning).

We formulate the concept of monitor as such as a class to be used as a "prefix", in the style of Simula, to user defined monitor classes, thereby making them subclasses of the class *monitor*. We also extend the prefixing mechanism analogously to procedures, providing a "procedure prefix" *mon* as one of the components of the monitor concept, to be applied to user defined monitor procedures for turning their bodies into critical regions. The class concept as used below is supposed to give rise to named objects, i.e. (shared) program variables. The definition is given in terms of binary semaphores. N stands for a sufficiently large natural number.

class *monitor* {prefix to monitor classes} ==
begin var $s : Nat = 0$ {no. of signallers}, $m : $ **array** $0..N$ **of** $semaphore(0)$
$\qquad\qquad$ {$m[0]$ is an exclusion semaphore, $m[1..N]$ contain the stack of signallers};
$\qquad$ **invar** $m[0] \leq 1 \wedge m[1..N] = 0{\uparrow}N \wedge (m[0] = 1 \Rightarrow s = 0)$
$\qquad\qquad \wedge\ m[1..s]$ have queues of length $1 \wedge m[s+1..N]$ have empty queues;
$\qquad$ **proc** *mon* { "prefix" to monitor procedures } ==
$\qquad\qquad$ **begin** $P(m[0]);$ {grabs critical region}
$\qquad\qquad\qquad$ **inner;** {represents the body of a user defined monitor procedure}
$\qquad\qquad\qquad$ $V(m[s])$ {frees critical region or gives it to the last signaller}
$\qquad\qquad$ **end**;
$\qquad$ **class** *condition* {gives rise to named waiting queues} ==
$\qquad$ **begin var** $k : Nat = 0$ {no. of waiting processes}
$\qquad\qquad\qquad$ $w : semaphore(0)$ {the process queue};
$\qquad\qquad$ **invar** $w = 0 \wedge w$ has k processes waiting;
$\qquad\qquad$ **proc** *wait* == **begin**
$\qquad\qquad\qquad$ $k := k+1;\ V(m[s]);\ P(w)$ {$k \neq 0$} $k := k-1$ **end**;
$\qquad\qquad$ **proc** *signal* == **if** $k \neq 0$ **then**
$\qquad\qquad\qquad$ $s := s+1;$ **var** $t := s;$
$\qquad\qquad\qquad$ $V(w)$ {$t \neq 0$} $P(m[t])$ {$s \neq 0$} $s := s-1$ **fi**;
$\qquad\qquad$ **func** $\#^{\hat{}} : Nat == k;$
$\qquad$ **end**;
$\qquad$ $V(m[0])$ {frees critical region initially}
end

It is assumed that *mon* and *condition*, as well as the operators *wait*, *signal* and $\#^{\hat{}}$ of the latter (where the $\hat{}$ indicates an argument position), are the only declared items accessible within subclasses of *monitor*, and that no items local to user subclasses, other than *mon* procedures, are accessible from the outside, except possibly in state assertions. Thereby the *monitor* class is protected from outside interference.

Although monitor objects are shared, the above coding, together with the access rules, ensure that the internal activity is essentially sequential. Thus, at any time all *mon* procedure activations, except at most one, are in (or directly in front of) a *P*-operation on a semaphore with the value 0. (The exceptional one may stand in front of a *P*-operation on a semaphore equal to 1, thus temporarily violating the invariant specified for one of the *m* or *w* semaphores.) It follows that Hoare logic applies to the contents of monitors, when augmented with special rules for *wait* and *signal* operations.

The postcondition $s \neq 0$ of the operation $P(m[t])$ of *wait* deserves a comment. By the precondition, the process in question has queued up on an *m*-semaphore with positive index, and the exit must be from the same queue. Inspection shows that all *V*-operations on *m*-semaphores have the form $V(m[s])$, so s must be positive at the time of the exit.

In the following sections we show and exemplify reasoning and programming strategies. We assume throughout that references to non-local variables do not occur within monitor objects. Although LIFO signalling may be assumed for the purpose of reasoning, it makes no difference to the logic if a more efficient implementation is chosen for a *signal* immediately prior to *mon* procedure **end**, as in [4].

6.3   Strategy 1

Here we review shortly the reasoning strategy identified in [4]. The central idea is to postulate an invariant I for the set $\mathcal{D}$ of variables local to the monitor, excluding *condition* variables. The invariant is to hold whenever the monitor object is at rest. It is also assumed that the programmer specifies an "await" condition Bc associated with each *condition* variable c, specifying the expected state of $\mathcal{D}$-variables at the time when a *c.wait* is terminated. The following rules of thought were given in [4]. The syntactic function $\mathcal{V}$ computes the set of variables occurring free in the argument expression.

$$\{I\}\, c.wait\, \{I \wedge Bc\} \quad \text{and} \quad \{I \wedge Bc\}\, c.signal\, \{I\}, \quad \text{where} \quad \mathcal{V}[I, Bc] \subseteq \mathcal{D}.$$

Clearly, if Bc holds prior to all operations *c.signal*, it must hold after any *c.wait*. The requirement I in the precondition of *c.signal* caters for the case that c is empty (the *signal* having no effect).

Technically, the above rules play the role of *assumptions* in a set of rules which involves all *mon* procedures, as well as the initializing class block tail.

$$\vdash \{P_0\}S_0\{I\};$$
$$\frac{\{I\}c_i.wait\{I \wedge Bc_i\},\ \{I \wedge Bc_i\}c_i.signal\{I\},\ i=1..m \vdash \{P_j \wedge I\}S_j\{I\};\ j=1..n}{\vdash \{P_k\}S_k\{I\}}$$

   for $k = 1..n$

The deduction rules pertain to a *monitor* class containing m *condition* variables $c_1, \ldots, c_m$, n **mon** procedures with the bodies $S_1, \ldots, S_n$, and the initializing block tail S_0. The preconditions $P_0, P_1, \ldots, P_n$ express possible requirements for the correct usage of the monitor.

Example 1: (high level) semaphores

> *monitor* **class** $Sema(s_0: Int)$ $\{P_0: s_0 \geq 0\}$ ==
> **begin var** $s: Int = s_0$;
>   **var** $c: condition$ $\{Bc: s \neq 0\}$;
>   **invar** $I: s \geq 0$;
> *mon* **proc** P ==
> $\{I\}$**begin if** $s = 0$ **then** $\{I\}$ $c.wait$ $\{I \wedge Bc\}$ **fi**; $s := s-1$ **end**$\{I\}$;
> *mon* **proc** V == $\{I\}$**begin** $s := s+1$; $\{I \wedge Bc\}$ $c.signal\{I\}$ **end**$\{I\}$;
> $\{I\}$ **end**

A partial correctness verification of *Sema* consists in applying Hoare logic to the decorated program, where the inserted state assertions are those indicated in the inference rule. (The predicates P_0 and I might alternatively have been expressed by declaring s_0 and s to be of the subtype *Nat* of natural numbers.) Then, for any given semaphore object, say **var** $X: Sema(k)$, where $k \geq 0$, we may conclude that the invariant $X.s \geq 0$ holds throughout the scope of X.

A binary semaphore would be described by a specialized version of the *Sema* class, in which the predicates P_0 and I are strengthened accordingly, and the procedure V has the (added) precondition $s = 0$.

6.4   Strategy 2

Unfortunately, the class *Sema* would remain partially correct with respect to I even if the *signal* operation of the V procedure were omitted. In complicated cases forgetting a *signal* could be an error easy to make and difficult to locate. The difficulty would arise from the kind of incorrect program behaviour that would be observed: nothing "wrong" would happen, but actions which ought to take place would not. For instance, the system as a whole might stop prematurely without error indications. This indicates that partiality of correctness might be a more dangerous notion in the context of concurrency than for sequential programs.

It turns out, however, that errors of this kind can in fact be combatted within the framework of Hoare logic, provided invariants refer to a sufficient amount of "historic" data, such as sequences of records of past actions, say accumulated in "mythical" auxiliary variables. In order to prove sufficient signalling in a monitor, *condition* queue lengths together with ordinary $\mathcal{D}$-variables usually contain enough historic information. For instance, the monitor invariant of *Sema* strengthened by conjoining $\#c = 0 \vee s = 0$ asserts that waiting occurs only as long as necessary for the program logic.

In order to see the consequences of having an invariant, as well as await conditions, referring to queue lengths, it is useful to look at the details involved in *wait* operations. (In the present context it may be natural to drop the requirement that the monitor invariant should hold before a *signal*; it may not hold unaltered after the corresponding *wait* anyway):

$$\{I^{\#c}_{\#c+1}\} <\text{enters } c> \{I\} <\text{sleeps}> \{\#c\neq0 \wedge Bc^{\#c}_{\#c-1}\} <\text{leaves } c> \{Bc\}$$

Clearly, entering and leaving the c-queue have the effect of changing the value of $\#c$, seen as a program variable. It is at the moment of falling asleep that the critical region is relinquished, and that is when the invariant must be required to hold. Furthermore, it is after having completed the entire *wait* operation that the await condition will be expected to hold. Left construction now shows what must be required in the preconditions of *c.wait* and *c.signal*. Notice that $\#c\neq0$ holds until the process leaves c. Thus, the assumptions about waits and signals should be as follows:

$$\{I^{\#c}_{\#c+1}\}c.wait\{Bc\} \quad \text{and} \quad \{\#c\neq0 \wedge Bc^{\#c}_{\#c-1}\}c.signal\{I\} \quad \text{for } \mathcal{V}[I, Bc] \subseteq \mathcal{C} \cup \mathcal{D}$$

where $\mathcal{C}$ is the set of *condition* variables declared in the monitor. The following axiom schema will cater for signals to empty *condition* queues:

$$\vdash \{\#c=0 \wedge P\}c.signal\{P\} \qquad \text{for arbitrary predicate } P$$

With this reasoning strategy it is easy to verify that the class *Sema* is partially correct with respect to an invariant strengthened as indicated above, $I: s\geq0 \wedge (s=0 \vee \#c=0)$, but only if a proper *signal* operation occurs in the V procedure. An adequate await predicate may be found by left construction, $Bc: I^s_{s-1}$.

The new strategy can provide the same kind of guarantee for the following, possibly more efficient semaphore implementation:

Example 2

> $monitor$ **class** $Sema'(s_0: Int) \{s_0 \geq 0\}$ ==
> **begin var** $s: Int = s_0$;
>   **var** $c: condition \{Bc: I\}$;
>   **invar** $I: s\geq0 \wedge (\#c=0 \vee s=0)$;
> mon **proc** P ==
> $\{I\}$ **begin if** $s=0$ **then** $\{I^{\#c}_{\#c+1}\}$ $c.wait$ $\{Bc\}$ **else** $s := s-1$ **fi** $\{I\}$;
> mon **proc** V ==
> $\{I\}$ **begin if** $\#c\neq0$ **then** $\{\#c\neq0 \wedge Bc\}$ $c.signal\{I\}$
>   **else** $s := s+1$ **fi** $\{I\}$;
> $\{I\}$**end**

In order to verify *Sema'* we must prove the following verification conditions: $I \wedge s = 0 \Rightarrow I^{\#c}_{\#c+1}$, $I \wedge s \neq 0 \Rightarrow I^s_{s-1}$, $I \wedge \#c \neq 0 \Rightarrow I^{\#c}_{\#c-1}$, and $I \wedge \#c = 0 \Rightarrow I^s_{s+1}$, all of which hold trivially, and prove that the invariant holds initially.

It should be noted that, although *Sema* and *Sema'* have been proven partially correct with respect to the same monitor invariant, it has not been proved formally that objects of both kinds have similar external behaviour, or indeed that they behave according to the standard definition of semaphores. (Actually, adding a *c.signal* after the *c.wait* would not harm the proof of *Sema'*!)

6.5   Strategy 3

It is sometimes practical to use *signal* operations not immediately followed by *mon* procedure **end**. In the reasoning about such occurrences of *signal* we cannot in general require a postcondition describing monitor resting states. In order to improve our formal system we introduce a mythical variable $\mathcal{S}$: *Stack(condition)*, modelling the LIFO stack of signallers by (references to) the targets of the unfinished *signal* operations.

Let I be a monitor invariant containing $\mathcal{S}$. Then $I \wedge \mathcal{S} = \varepsilon$, where ε is the empty stack, describes resting states, whereas $I \wedge \mathcal{S}\,\textbf{top}\,c$, where the second conjunct states that $\mathcal{S}$ is non-empty and its top element is a reference to c, specifies states such that control is about to return to a c signaller.

Permitting $\mathcal{S}$ to occur in the monitor invariant, as well as in await conditions, we must take into account the fact that $\mathcal{S}$ changes within *signal* operations. If also references to queue lengths are allowed, a decorated model of *c.signal* for $\#c \neq 0$ must be as follows:

$$\{\#c \neq 0 \wedge Bc^{\#c,\ \mathcal{S}}_{\#c-1,push(c,\mathcal{S})}\}\ \mathcal{S} := push(c, \mathcal{S})$$
$$\{\#c \neq 0 \wedge Bc^{\#c}_{\#c-1}\} < \text{wake up and wait} > \{I\}\ \mathcal{S} := pop(\mathcal{S})\ \{I^{\mathcal{S}}_{push(c,\mathcal{S})}\}$$

We have to assume that the monitor invariant holds whenever a process gives up critical region; it follows that it will hold when a signaller regains control. The decoration of the model determines the form of assumptions about *signal* operations. The assumption about *c.wait* is as for strategy 2, but the fact that the waking up is caused by a *signal* on c is now expressible:

$$\{I^{\#c}_{\#c+1}\}c.wait\{Bc \wedge \mathcal{S}\,\textbf{top}\,c\} \quad \text{and} \quad \{\#c \neq 0 \wedge Bc^{\#c,\ \mathcal{S}}_{\#c-1,push(c,\mathcal{S})}\}c.signal\{I^{\mathcal{S}}_{push(c,\mathcal{S})}\}$$

The axiom for signalling on an empty *condition* remains unaltered. In addition we may state axioms expressing the fact that local variables remain unchanged over *wait* and *signal* operations:

$$\vdash \{P\}c.wait\{P\} \quad \text{for } \mathcal{V}[P] \cap (\mathcal{C} \cup \mathcal{D} \cup \{\mathcal{S}\}) = \emptyset$$
$$\vdash \{P\}c.signal\{P\} \quad \text{for } \mathcal{V}[P] \cap (\mathcal{C} \cup \mathcal{D}) = \emptyset$$

Notice that $\mathcal{S}$ also remains unchanged over *signals*. Obviously $I \wedge \mathcal{S} = \varepsilon$ may be assumed in the precondition of any *mon* procedure.

Example 3

We show a decorated version of a readers-and-writers monitor class, conforming to that of [4] in that it is fair to both sides. The variables r and w count the number of active readers, resp. writers, and the *condition* variables cr and cw are the queues of waiting readers and writers. The monitor invariant is in the form of four conjuncts: I_1 expresses the obvious exclusion conditions, I_2 and I_3 are the conditions that writers, resp. readers, may be waiting, and I_4 states that there are active readers and none waiting when control returns to a cr signaller. The second and third conjuncts are sufficient to prove adequate signalling. The last one makes it possible to prove the postcondition $r \neq 0$ of the *startread* procedure. Thus, the post- and preconditions of the *startread* and *endread* procedures express a requirement for parenthetic usage, which is also the case for *startwrite* and *endwrite*.

monitor **class** *Readers-and-Writers* $==$
begin var $r, w \colon Nat = 0$,
$\qquad\qquad cr, cw \colon condition \ \{Bcr \colon w = 0, \ Bcw \colon r + w = 0\}$
$\qquad$ **invar** $I \colon (I_1 \colon ((r = 0 \lor w = 0) \land w \le 1) \land$
$\qquad\qquad\qquad I_2 \colon (\#cw \neq 0 \Rightarrow r + w \neq 0) \land$
$\qquad\qquad\qquad I_3 \colon (\#cr \neq 0 \Rightarrow w + \#cw \neq 0) \land$
$\qquad\qquad\qquad I_4 \colon (\mathcal{S} \, \mathbf{top} \, cr \Rightarrow r \neq 0 \land \#cr = 0))$
$\quad mon$ **proc** *startread* $==$ **begin if** $w + \#cw \neq 0$ **then** $cr.wait$ **fi** $\{w = 0\}$
$\qquad\qquad\qquad r := r + 1 \, \{w = 0 \land r \neq 0\} \, cr.signal$ **end** $\{I \land r \neq 0\}$;
$\quad mon$ **proc** *endread* $== \{r \neq 0\}$ **begin** $r := r - 1 \, \{I_3 \land w = 0 \land \mathcal{S} = \varepsilon\}$
$\qquad\qquad$ **if** $r = 0$ **then** $\{I_3 \land r + w = 0 \land \mathcal{S} = \varepsilon\} \, cw.signal$ **fi end** $\{I\}$;
$\quad mon$ **proc** *startwrite* $==$ **begin if** $r + w \neq 0$ **then** $cw.wait$ **fi**
$\qquad\qquad\qquad \{r + w = 0 \land \neg \mathcal{S} \, \mathbf{top} \, cr\} \, w := w + 1$ **end** $\{I \land w = 1\}$;
$\quad mon$ **proc** *endwrite* $== \{w = 1\}$ **begin** $w := w - 1 \, \{r + w = 0 \land \mathcal{S} = \varepsilon\}$
$\qquad\qquad$ **if** $\#cr \neq 0$ **then** $cr.signal$ **else** $cw.signal$ **fi end** $\{I\}$;
$\{I\}$**end**

The procedure preconditions I and $\mathcal{S} = \varepsilon$ have been omitted in the text. The decorations are otherwise sufficient for proving all verification conditions. Actually, a stronger postcondition is provable for *startread*: the postcondition of the *signal* operation on cr is $I^{\mathcal{S}}_{push(cr,\mathcal{S})}$ by assumption in the case $\#cr \neq 0$, which implies $I \land r \neq 0 \land \#cr = 0$, and the latter condition also holds in the case $\#cr = 0$. Thus, whenever a reader is allowed to become active, all of them are.

It is possible to let the *endwrite* procedure do all necessary signalling to readers, by removing the (recursive) $cr.signal$ of *startread* and replacing that of *endwrite* by the loop: **while** $\#cr \neq 0$ **do** $cr.signal$ **od**. Since a return to *endwrite* will now occur after every $cr.signal$, the monitor invariant must be adjusted by weakening I_3 and I_4:

$$I'_3 \colon \neg \mathcal{S} \, \mathbf{top} \, cr \Rightarrow I_3 \quad \text{and} \quad I'_4 \colon \mathcal{S} \, \mathbf{top} \, cr \Rightarrow r \neq 0$$

Using the loop invariant $w = 0 \wedge r + \#cr \neq 0$, the required precondition of $cr.signal$ is implied, and its postcondition is $(I')^{S}_{push(cr,S)}$, which implies $r \neq 0$ by the fourth conjunct and then $w = 0$ by the first conjunct. The postcondition of the loop implies the original postcondition of $startread$, $I \wedge r \neq 0 \wedge \#cr = 0$, as it should.

6.6   Strategy 4

Sometimes the await predicate Bc associated with a *condition* variable c must depend on local variables, e.g. procedure parameters. Then Bc cannot be expressed outside that particular procedure instance without remodelling the programming language. In [4] a number of such cases have been elegantly treated by defining *condition* variables to be priority queues. Here we mention another, more explicit scheduling technique.

Let Bc depend on a local variable $t : T$ (possibly a tuple), $t \in \mathcal{V}[Bc]$. One way of communicating the required await predicate to other procedure instances is to include in the monitor a data structure implementing a function

$c: \; T \longrightarrow$ *condition* variable, such that
$\forall t : T \bullet$ the *condition* variable $c(t)$ has the associated await predicate Bc.

c will usually have to be a one-to-one function, so that $c(t_1)$ and $c(t_2)$ are distinct variables for $t_1 \neq t_2$, associated with distinct await predicates, $Bc^{t}_{t_1}$ and $Bc^{t}_{t_2}$ respectively.

A simple reasoning strategy which caters for this programming technique may be characterized by sequencing assumptions of the following form:

$$\{I\}c(e).wait\{Bc^{t}_{e}\} \quad \text{and} \quad \{\#c(d) \neq 0 \wedge Bc^{t}_{d}\}c(d).signal\{I\}$$
$$\text{for } \mathcal{V}[I] \subseteq \mathcal{D}, \; \mathcal{V}[Bc] \subseteq \mathcal{D} \cup \{t\}, \text{ and } \mathcal{V}[e] \cap (\mathcal{C} \cup \mathcal{D}) = \emptyset,$$

where $c \in \mathcal{C}$. The requirement on the argument expression e, that it should depend only on local variables, ensures that its value remains unchanged over the *wait* operation.

Example 4

We formulate a concept of "generalized semaphore", where an operation $GP(n)$, $1 \leq n \leq N$, is defined as n P operations on an ordinary semaphore, but executed as a single atomic operation not violating the semaphore invariant, and similarly for $GV(n)$.

monitor **class** $Gsema(s_0 : Nat)\{s_0 \leq N\} ==$
begin var $s : Nat = s_0$;
    var $c :$ **array** $1..N$ **of** *condition* $\{Bc[i : 1..N] : i \leq s \leq N\}$;

```
        invar s ≤ N;
  mon proc GP(k : Nat){k ≤ N} ==
            begin if k > s then c[k].wait fi {k ≤ s} s := s − k end;
  mon proc GV(k : Nat){k ≤ N − s} ==
            begin var j : Nat1 = s+1; s := s+k; while j ≤ s do
            if #c[j] ≠ 0 then c[j].signal else j := j+1 fi od end;
  end
```

The reasoning strategy 4 is sufficient for a verification with respect to the stated invariant. (The monitor invariant may in this case serve as the loop invariant as well.) It may, however, be combined with strategy 2 or 3 in order to provide for more powerful reasoning. Thus, the combination of strategies 3 and 4 enables the verification of the following monitor invariant:

$$s \le N \wedge \forall i, j : Nat1 \bullet i \le s \wedge (\mathcal{S} = \varepsilon \vee (i < j \le N \wedge \mathcal{S} \text{ top } c[j])) \Rightarrow$$
$$\#c[i] = 0,$$

with await predicates $Bc[t : 1..N] : t \le s \le N \wedge \forall u : Nat1 \bullet u < t \Rightarrow$
$$\#c[u] = 0,$$
and loop invariant $\qquad s \le N \wedge j \le N+1 \wedge \forall i : Nat1 \bullet i < j \Rightarrow \#c[i] = 0.$

The monitor invariant expresses sufficient signalling for the scheduling principle "cheapest need first" (the second disjunct of the parenthesis is needed in order to verify the signalling loop). Programming according to the combination of strategies 2 and 4 leads to a simpler monitor invariant for adequate signalling (without the disjunction), but to a more complicated program. We leave it to the reader to program and verify according to such a strategy.

In the example we have implemented the function c as an array. For large N it would be better to use a more dynamic data structure, in which only the non-empty *condition* variables were represented at any time.

6.7   External Specification of Monitors

It is an old idea (see e.g. [8]) that any variable, including an arbitrary class object, of a sequential program can be abstractly represented by the sequence of updates, parameter values included, since its declaration. This provides an entirely black box representation, since only aspects visible from the outside occur. As far as monitor variables are concerned, a more detailed representation is needed in order to cater for the internal delays which may occur.

It is sufficient, however, to distinguish between events corresponding to operation initiation and operation termination, as in [8]. Let a monitor procedure be of the form

$$mon \textbf{ proc } p(\textbf{in } x:T_x, \textbf{ out } y:T_y) == \ldots \ldots$$

where x and y are (lists of) input and output parameters. Then we may represent the events of initiating and terminating a p operation by structures of the form $p^i(x:T_x)$ and $p^t(y:T_y)$, respectively, where p^i and p^t are record classes.

Let a *monitor* class with *mon* procedures $p_1,\ldots,p_n$ be decorated by introducing a mythical history variable $H: Sequence(p_1^i \cup p_1^t \cup \ldots \cup p_n^i \cup p_n^t)$ and let the **begin** and **end** of *mon* **proc** p_k, $k=1,2,\ldots,n$, have the mythical effects of updating H by appending respectively $p_k^i(x_k)$ and $p_k^t(y_k)$, where x_k and y_k are the values of the input and output parameters.

Now an external specification of a monitor class M is a predicate *Spec* on the history variable H and the formal parameters of M. A verification of that specification requires a monitor invariant I such that $\vdash I \wedge \mathcal{S} = \varepsilon \Rightarrow Spec$. Notice that I may refer to variables hidden from the external specification.

Example 5

A semaphore class   *monitor* **class** $Sema(s_0 : Int)\{s_0 \geq 0\} == \ldots \ldots$ could have the following external specification:

$$s_0 \geq 0 \Rightarrow \#H/P^t = \min(\#H/P^i, \#H/V^i + s_0) \wedge \#H/V^t = \#H/V^i$$

where H/C stands for that subsequence of H which consists of all the elements of class C, and $\#\hat{\ }$ is the length operator. The specification states that the number of terminated P operations is equal to either the number of initiated P's or the number of initiated V's plus s_0, whichever is smaller. Thereby the delaying of P operations is specified up to an arbitrary queuing discipline. V operations are terminated immediately.

The monitor classes of examples 1 and 2 both satisfy that specification. This fact can be proved by choosing the following monitor invariant, which requires strategy 3 reasoning for its proof:

$$s \geq 0 \wedge (s = 0 \vee \#c = 0) \wedge s = s_0 + \#H/V^i - \#H/P^t \wedge$$
$$\#c = \#H/P^i - \#H/P^t \wedge \#H/V^i = \#H/V^t + \#\mathcal{S}$$

6.8   Conclusion

We have demonstrated reasoning techniques within the framework of Hoare logic for proving adequate signalling, arbitrary use of signal operations, and dealing with await predicates depending on local variables. In some cases ad-hoc preconditions have been prescribed for monitor procedures, indicating restrictions on the intended usage. If so, it has been tacitly assumed that any user would correctly observe these restrictions. An alternative could be to check such preconditions explicitly, possibly reacting by introducing necessary delays using waits (and signals). Another possibility is to replace monitor objects by processes deciding when and what kind of external calls to accept, thereby introducing implicit delays for unwanted calls. The internal logic would be similar, and so would the technique of external specification.

The reasoning about concurrent processes interacting through monitors can be in two steps: local reasoning according to Hoare logic, each process having a mythical history variable accumulating monitor calls, and a rule for parallel composition which requires compatibility in a certain sense of the history variables occurring in the system. See e.g. [9]. Although the results are restricted to partial correctness, the use of historic sequence variables implies that many aspects of behaviour, usually classified as liveness properties, can be reasoned about.

References

[1] C.A.R. Hoare: An Axiomatic Basis for Computer Programming. *Comm. ACM* **12**(10)(1969), pp. 576–580.

[2] C.A.R. Hoare: Proof of Correctness of Data Representations. *Acta Informatica* **1**(1972), pp. 271–281.

[3] C.A.R. Hoare: Towards a Theory of Parallel Programming. In C.A.R. Hoare and R.H. Perrott, eds.: *Operating System Techniques* (Academic Press 1972) pp. 61–71.

[4] C.A.R. Hoare: Monitors: an Operating System Structuring Concept. *Comm. ACM* **17**(10)(1974) pp. 549–557.

[5] E.W. Dijkstra: Co-operating Sequential Processes. In F. Genuys, ed.: *Programming Languages*, (Academic Press 1968), pp. 43–113.

[6] P. Brinch Hansen: *Operating System Principles* (Prentice Hall 1973).

[7] O.-J. Dahl and C.A.R. Hoare: Hierarchical Program Structures. In O.-J. Dahl, E.W. Dijkstra and C.A.R. Hoare: *Structured Programming* (Academic Press 1972) pp. 175–220.

[8] O.-J. Dahl: Can Program Proving be made Practical? In M. Amirchahy and D. Neel, eds.: *Les Fondements de la Programmation*, (IRIA 1978), pp. 57–113.

[9] N. Soundararajan: A Proof Technique for Parallel Programs. *Theoretical Computer Science 31.* (1984) pp.13–29.

Chapter 7

On the Design of Calculational Proofs

Edsger W. Dijkstra

§ **0.** By their brevity and unexpected turns, calculational proofs often strike the reader as being very ingenious constructions. Far be it from us to belittle the ingenuity of their inventors, but that should not prevent us from studying a number of representative proofs in the hope of learning why those proofs have the structure they have. This paper reports on such a study.

Among the things that will emerge, I already mention a few.

Firstly, many steps that may seem surprising at first sight, are, in fact, (almost) dictated, as they are the only (or by far the simplest) transformation that will enable us to exploit one of the givens that has to be taken into account. In this connection I recommend that we maintain as fine-grained a bookkeeping as possible of what of the givens we have used: what has not been used yet often indicates the direction in which the proof should be completed.

Secondly, when faced with an antisymmetric and reflexive relation, i.e. a relation $\leqslant$ (with transpose $\geqslant$) such that

$$x = y \ \equiv \ x \leqslant y \wedge x \geqslant y \qquad \text{for all } x, y \quad ,$$

we must be prepared for a proof with a possibly subtle interplay between calculating with equalities and with inequalities: any hints we can extract as to when to stress which of the two approaches will obviously be most welcome.

§ **1.** Let me show you, as a first indication of the kind of considerations I would like to highlight, a calculational proof of which each step is forced (as a result of which the proof is very well known, not to say canonical).

About predicate transformers f and g is given

$$(0) \qquad [f.x \Rightarrow y] \ \equiv \ [x \Rightarrow g.y] \qquad \text{for all } x, y \quad ;$$

we are asked to show that g is universally conjunctive, i.e.

(1) $[g.\langle \forall\, y : y \in W : y\rangle \;\equiv\; \langle \forall\, y : y \in W : g.y\rangle]$

for any bag W of predicates.

Remark We indicate function application not implicitly by juxtaposition but explicitly by an infix period of high syntactic binding power. With the square brackets we denote the "everywhere operator", a function from "predicates" to the "boolean scalars" *true* and *false*. For further elaboration we refer the reader for instance to [0]. *End of Remark.*

For brevity's sake, the range "$y \in W$" is omitted in the following calculation; we should remember that it is a scalar range. We shall first give the proof and then discuss it.

Proof We observe that for any x

$\qquad [x \Rightarrow g.\langle \forall\, y :: y\rangle]$

$=\qquad \{(0)$ with $y := \langle \forall\, y :: y\rangle\}$

$\qquad [f.x \Rightarrow \langle \forall\, y :: y\rangle]$

$=\qquad \{$pred. calc.: $Q \Rightarrow$ over $\forall\}$

$\qquad [\langle \forall\, y :: f.x \Rightarrow y\rangle]$

$=\qquad \{$pred. calc.: interchange (N.B. range is scalar)$\}$

$\qquad \langle \forall\, y :: [f.x \Rightarrow y]\rangle$

$=\qquad \{(0)\}$

$\qquad \langle \forall\, y :: [x \Rightarrow g.y]\rangle$

$=\qquad \{$pred. calc.: interchange (N.B. range is scalar)$\}$

$\qquad [\langle \forall\, y :: x \Rightarrow g.y\rangle]$

$=\qquad \{$pred. calc.: $Q \Rightarrow$ over $\forall\}$

$\qquad [x \Rightarrow \langle \forall\, y :: g.y\rangle]\quad ;$

having thus established

$\qquad [x \Rightarrow g.\langle \forall\, y :: y\rangle] \;\equiv\; [x \Rightarrow \langle \forall\, y :: g.y\rangle]\qquad$ for all $x\quad,$

we conclude (1) on account of

(2) $\langle \forall\, x : true : [x \Rightarrow P] \equiv [x \Rightarrow Q]\rangle \;\equiv\; [P \equiv Q]\quad,$

which is a well-known lemma that follows from implication's reflexivity and anti-symmetry. *End of Proof.*

Let us now analyse the extent to which the structure of the above proof has been forced upon us.

Firstly, do we need (0) in order to show (1)? Yes, we do, because (with $W := \{\}$) a consequence of (1) is $[g.true \equiv true]$, and that definitely does not hold for any g, for instance not for the predicate transformer g defined by $[g.x \equiv false]$ for all x.

Next, being obliged to use (0), we observe that our *only* way of exploiting that the g in the left-hand side $g.\langle \forall y :: y \rangle$ of (1) satisfies (0), is to instantiate the latter by $y := \langle \forall y :: y \rangle$; this *forces* us to explore $[x \Rightarrow g.\langle \forall y :: y \rangle]$, this now being the smallest expression that contains the left-hand side of (1) and can be rewritten using (0). The first step then applies (0) with that instantiation.

In view of the right-hand side of (1), it is from here on our duty to eliminate f and to reintroduce g, which can *only* be done by a second appeal to (0). Because there is no point in undoing the first step, we *must* apply (0) to a subexpression of the form $[f.x \Rightarrow ?]$ with a consequent different from $\langle \forall y :: y \rangle$. The next two steps of the predicate calculus form such a subexpression, and then our second appeal to (0) reintroduces g.

Our final task is to form $\langle \forall y :: g.y \rangle$, the right-hand side of (1), as subexpression; the next two steps of the predicate calculus form $\langle \forall y :: g.y \rangle$ as consequent, and, on account of (2), we are done.

The moral of the story is that, apart from the choice of syntax for proof presentation, we had no choice.

§ **2.**   The full-blown principle of Leibniz states (to the best of my knowledge) that for x and y of some type, and f ranging over the functions on that type

$$(3) \qquad x = y \; \equiv \; \langle \forall f :: f.x = f.y \rangle \quad .$$

Reading the above equivalence as a mutual implication, we observe that "$\Leftarrow$" follows by instantiating the right-hand side with for f the identity function. For this conclusion, even the existence of other functions is irrelevant. For the general function it is the implication in the other direction that is relevant:

$$(4) \qquad x = y \; \Rightarrow \; f.x = f.y \quad ,$$

and this is what is usually referred to as "Leibniz's Principle".

Remark   Appealing to

$$q \Rightarrow \langle \forall x :: x \rangle \; \equiv \; \langle \forall x :: q \Rightarrow x \rangle$$

– itself an immediate consequent of "$\lor$ distributes over $\forall$" – , we have taken the universal quantification over f outside. The possibility of thus removing a universal quantification from a consequent often provides the incentive to split up an equivalence involving a universally quantified equivalent into a mutual implication. *End of Remark.*

The connection between function application and equality is very tight: function application preserves equality and, conversely, – besides the two constant relations *true* and *false* – equality is the *only* relation that is preserved by function application. In Section 0, we referred to the interplay between calculating with equalities and with inequalities; the above observation tells us that when we have to capture the essence of function application, i.e. when we have to apply Leibniz's Principle, we may be forced to introduce an equality so as to be able to do so. The next section gives two examples of the phenomenon.

§ **3.**   In a wider context, Jamey Leifer had to deal with two functions f and g whose domains and ranges are all the same, and whose applications commute, i.e.

$$(5) \qquad f.(g.x) = g.(f.x) \qquad \text{for "all" } x \quad .$$

In order to appeal to (5), we have to apply – say – g to an f-value, say $f.x$. In order to appeal to Leibniz's Principle, that f-value has to equal something else, say y, for the time being. So we observe for any x, y

$$f.x = y$$
$$\Rightarrow \qquad \{\text{Leibniz's Principle}\}$$
$$g.(f.x) = g.y$$
$$= \qquad \{(5)\}$$
$$f.(g.x) = g.y \quad .$$

The last line tells us that a nice choice for y is x, and thus we have proved

$$f.x = x \;\Rightarrow\; f.(g.x) = g.x \quad ,$$

or, in words: if x is a fixed point of f, so is $g.x$. After the above observation, Jamey Leifer conducted all the rest of his (beautiful) argument in terms of fixed points, a concept that did not occur at all in the theorem he had set out to prove.

§ **4.**   The other example I would like to show is the proof of Perry Moerland's lemma. (Also this came up in a wider context.) About predicate transformer f we are given that it is monotonic and has a left-inverse g, i.e.

$$(6) \qquad [x \Rightarrow y] \;\Rightarrow\; [f.x \Rightarrow f.y] \qquad \text{for all } x, y$$
$$(7) \qquad [g.(f.x) \equiv x] \qquad\qquad\quad \text{for all } x \quad ;$$

we have to show that as a consequence

$$(8) \qquad [x] \;\Leftarrow\; [f.x] \qquad \text{for all } x \quad .$$

We are looking for a strengthening chain of booleans starting at $[x]$ and ending with $[f.x]$. Along the way we have to introduce f; for doing so, (6) is not a good candidate, but (7) is. The advantage of introducing f with the aid of (7) is that then g is introduced as well. (Note that (6) by itself does not suffice for the demonstration of (8), i.e. that (7) has to be exploited, but that exploitation obviously requires that g enters the picture.)

Having introduced g and still aiming for $[f.x]$, we have to get rid of g again. Since the *only* other thing known about g is that it is a function, the proper candidate for the removal of g is Leibniz's Principle. Since an appeal to the latter requires equalities, the introduction of an equality was Perry Moerland's first concern; one observes for any x

$$
\begin{aligned}
& [x] \\
=\ & \quad \{\text{predicate calculus}\} \\
& [x \equiv true] \\
=\ & \quad\quad \{(7) \,;\, (7) \,;\, \text{with } x := true\} \\
& [g.(f.x) \equiv g.(f.true)] \\
\Leftarrow\ & \quad\quad \{\text{Leibniz's Principle}\} \\
& [f.x \equiv f.true] \\
=\ & \quad\quad \{\text{predicate calculus}\} \\
& [f.x \Leftarrow f.true] \wedge [f.x \Rightarrow f.true] \\
=\ & \quad\quad\quad \{[x \Rightarrow true] \text{ and } (6) \text{ with } y := true\} \\
& [f.x \Leftarrow f.true] \\
\Leftarrow\ & \quad\quad \{\text{predicate calculus}\} \\
& [f.x] \quad .
\end{aligned}
$$

§ **5.**   With a relation like $\geqslant$ (and its transpose $\leqslant$) comes the notion of monotonicity with respect to it, i.e. "preserving it": "f is monotonic with respect to $\geqslant$" means

$$
(9) \quad x \geqslant y \ \Rightarrow\ f.x \geqslant f.y \qquad \text{for all } x, y
$$

(note that in this terminology, Leibniz's Principle states that each function is "monotonic with respect to $=$").

We now restrict ourselves to such domains and relations $\geqslant$ such that for any set of values the lowest higher bound "$\uparrow$" – and similarly the highest lower bound "$\downarrow$" – exists, i.e. we assume that for any range of the dummy x and any function t of the appropriate type we can define $\langle \uparrow x :: t.x \rangle$ by

$$
(10) \quad w \geqslant \langle \uparrow x :: t.x \rangle \ \equiv\ \langle \forall x :: w \geqslant t.x \rangle \qquad \text{for all } w \quad .
$$

The important theorem is that, for any f that is monotonic with respect to $\geqslant$,

(11) $f.\langle\uparrow x :: t.x\rangle \;\geqslant\; \langle\uparrow x :: f.(t.x)\rangle$;

its proof is another example of "there is only one thing you can do".

Proof   We observe for any monotonic f, etc.

$$f.\langle\uparrow x :: t.x\rangle \geqslant \langle\uparrow x :: f.(t.x)\rangle$$

$=$ $\{(10)$ with $w, t := f.\langle\uparrow x :: t.x\rangle, f \circ t\}$

$$\langle\forall x :: f.\langle\uparrow x :: t.x\rangle \geqslant f.(t.x)\rangle$$

$\Leftarrow$ $\{f$ monotonic with respect to $\geqslant$,
             $\forall$ monotonic with respect to $\Leftarrow\}$

$$\langle\forall x :: \langle\uparrow x :: t.x\rangle \geqslant t.x\rangle$$

$=$ $\{(10)$ with $w := \langle\uparrow x :: t.x\rangle\}$

$$\langle\uparrow x :: t.x\rangle \geqslant \langle\uparrow x :: t.x\rangle$$

$=$ $\{\geqslant$ is reflexive$\}$

true   .

Note that (10), when viewed as mutual implication, is used in either direction. *End of Proof.*

The above proof is so simple, and so completely forced by the definitions, that the usefulness of the theorem may come as a surprise. Predicate transformers that are monotonic with respect to implication are very common, and for such an f, which satisfies (6), we have

(12) $[f.\langle\forall x :: x\rangle \Rightarrow \langle\forall x :: f.x\rangle]$ for all ranges
(13) $[f.\langle\exists x :: x\rangle \Leftarrow \langle\exists x :: f.x\rangle]$ for all ranges   ,

with the special cases

(14) $[f.(x \wedge y) \Rightarrow f.x \wedge f.y]$ for all x, y
(15) $[f.(x \vee y) \Leftarrow f.x \vee f.y]$ for all x, y .

In fact, (12) through (15) are more than useful consequences of f's monotonicity, they are restatements of it.

§ **6.**   In Section 1 we proved – in our appeal to (2) – $[P \equiv Q]$ by showing that for any x

$$[x \Rightarrow P] \;\equiv\; [x \Rightarrow Q]   .$$

We may well ask what has been gained by the introduction of the dummy x. A possible answer is given by the observation that, in order to derive $[P \equiv Q]$ from the above, the latter has to be instantiated twice, viz. with $x := P$ and with $x := Q$. This double instantiation strongly suggests that the introduction of dummy x has enabled us to avoid a ping-pong argument (i.e a twofold case analysis).

But this is not the whole story, for, analogously to (2), we have, for instance,

$$(16) \qquad \langle \forall x :: [P \Rightarrow x] \Leftarrow [Q \Rightarrow x] \rangle \;\equiv\; [P \Rightarrow Q] \quad .$$

This authorizes us to conclude $[P \Rightarrow Q]$ by showing that for any x

$$(17) \qquad [P \Rightarrow x] \;\Leftarrow\; [Q \Rightarrow x] \quad ;$$

the conclusion, however, requires a single instantiation only, viz. $x := Q$. Yet, the introduction of dummy x as in (17) is justifiable in more than one way. We can (i) prove (17) for arbitrary x, and then instantiate (17) with $x := Q$, or (ii) carry out the argument not for arbitrary x, but right from the start for Q, thus deriving, instead of (17)

$$(18) \qquad [P \Rightarrow Q] \;\Leftarrow\; [Q \Leftarrow Q] \quad .$$

Here (i) is to be preferred above (ii) for more than one reason:

- The dummy x is shorter than the expression Q, hence (i) saves ink and paper.

- Argument (ii) obscures the existence of demonstrandum (17), obscures the fact that the internal structure of the first Q and of the last Q in (18) is totally irrelevant for the latter's demonstration; argument (i) is clearer than (ii) in that it heads for (17), which clearly states that the first and the last Q's in (18) could be "anything", provided that they are the same. In the jargon: argument (i) is better disentangled than argument (ii).

- The full force of this disentanglement manifests itself when, besides the proof, we design the theorem as well and Q emerges as the result of our calculations.

We shall illustrate the findings of the last two sections (and a little bit more) in the next section.

§ **7.** In this section, we are looking, by way of example, for a nontrivial theorem about relational composition. Composition will be denoted by an infix ";" with a syntactic binding power higher than that of the logical infix operators but lower than that of the unary operators "¬" and "∼".

We shall use that the transposition "∼" distributes over the logical operators, that composition is monotonic in both its arguments, and that composition and transposition are coupled by the "right-exchange", for which we choose here the formulation that for all x, y, z

$$(19) \qquad [x \,;\, y \wedge z \Rightarrow false] \;\equiv\; [\sim x \,;\, z \wedge y \Rightarrow false] \quad .$$

The exchange rules enable us to manipulate a composition that occurs as antecedent, but there are *no* analogous manipulative opportunities for a composition that occurs as consequent, and we may therefore expect a problem when trying to prove a theorem of the form

$$(20) \qquad [a \Rightarrow b \,;\, c] \quad .$$

This problem, however, can be overcome with the aid of (16), which states that we can demonstrate (20) by proving – in a variation of (17) – for arbitrary z

$$(21) \qquad [b \,;\, c \wedge z \Rightarrow false] \;\Rightarrow\; [a \wedge z \Rightarrow false] \quad ,$$

and in this formulation of our proof obligation, the composition "b;c" occurs as (conjunct in an) antecedent, and is thus amenable to manipulation via an exchange rule!

We shall now first give our calculation that transforms $[b \,;\, c \wedge z \Rightarrow false]$ without strengthening into $[a \wedge z \Rightarrow false]$ and shall discuss the proof later. In the course of the calculation, suitable values for c and a will be chosen. We observe that for any z

$$[b \,;\, c \wedge z \Rightarrow false]$$
$$= \quad \{\text{right-exchange}\} \tag{A}$$
$$[\sim b \,;\, z \wedge c \Rightarrow false]$$
$$= \quad \{\text{choose } c\colon \; [c \equiv \sim d \,;\, e \wedge f]\} \tag{B}$$
$$[\sim b \,;\, z \wedge \sim d \,;\, e \wedge f \Rightarrow false]$$
$$\Rightarrow \quad \{\text{monotonicities}\} \tag{C}$$
$$[(\sim b \wedge \sim d) \,;\, (z \wedge e) \wedge f \Rightarrow false]$$
$$= \quad \{\sim \text{ distributes over } \wedge\} \tag{D}$$
$$[\sim(b \wedge d) \,;\, (z \wedge e) \wedge f \Rightarrow false]$$
$$= \quad \{\text{right-exchange}\} \tag{E}$$
$$[(b \wedge d) \,;\, f \wedge e \wedge z \Rightarrow false]$$
$$= \quad \{\text{choose } a\colon \; [a \equiv (b \wedge d) \,;\, f \wedge e]\} \tag{F}$$
$$[a \wedge z \Rightarrow false] \quad ,$$

and thus we have proved (20) with the choices made in steps (B) and (F), i.e.

$$(22) \qquad [(b \wedge d) \,;\, f \wedge e \Rightarrow b \,;\, (\sim d \,;\, e \wedge f)] \quad ,$$

a theorem, even uglier than "the first ugly theorem" of [1].

Remark We have used (19) instead of the formulation of the right-exchange from [2]

(23) $\qquad [x \mathbin; y \Rightarrow z] \;\equiv\; [\sim x \mathbin; \neg z \Rightarrow \neg y]$

and (21) instead of what (17) would have given, viz.

$$[b \mathbin; c \Rightarrow z] \;\Rightarrow\; [a \Rightarrow z] \quad ,$$

thus avoiding the need of introducing negations and moving terms back and forth with the shunting rule

$$[x \Rightarrow y \lor z \;\equiv\; x \land \neg y \Rightarrow z] \quad .$$

In [1], this economy is achieved by the introduction of the "somewhere" operator. *End of Remark.*

Step (A) is not surprising because (21) was intentionally chosen so as to make the right-exchange applicable to its antecedent.

The purpose of step (B) is to apply the most general substitution for b or c that makes continued manipulation possible. For b, I could not find a productive substitution: after $b := d \lor e$, we can use composition's monotonicity as in (15) but that creates two occurrences of dummy z, and after $b := d \land e$, we are stuck because then composition's monotonicity as in (14) works in the wrong direction. If, however, we substitute a composition like $\sim d \mathbin; e$ for c, then monotonicity as in (14) works in the right direction. The inclusion of the additional "$\land f$" is, in a sense, obligatory if we wish to keep our options open: since c occurs as conjunct and conjunction is associative, the additional "$\land f$" does not hamper the combination of the two compositions, and, furthermore, omission of the conjunct "$\land f$" can be interpreted as a possibly premature instantiation of $f := true$. (The choice of "$\sim d \mathbin; e$" instead of "$d \mathbin; e$" is an irrelevant matter of elegance; it allows us to ignore that "$\sim$" is its own inverse.)

Step (C) exploits the monotonicity of ";" (plus the usual ones from predicate calculus), and, in view of our target, our remaining duty is to extricate dummy z from the composition.

Step (E) performs this extraction by – what else? – a second appeal to right-exchange after step (D) has prepared the ground. (Step (D) could have been postponed, but then later simplification would have needed that "$\sim$" is its own inverse.)

Our final step (F) embodies the recognition of what to choose for "a" and thus we have designed and proved theorem (22).

§ **8.** In [2], left- and right-conditions are defined by

(24a)	(p is a left-condition)	$\equiv$	$[p \mathbin; true \equiv p]$
(24b)	(q is a right-condition)	$\equiv$	$[true \mathbin; q \equiv q]$;

we now focus our attention on the right-condition.

In [2], Feijen & van Gasteren point out that – because $[true \; ; x \Leftarrow x]$ for all x – definition (24b) is equivalent to

(25) $(q$ is a right-condition$) \equiv [true \; ; q \Rightarrow q]$,

the right-hand side of which is formally weaker than that of (24b). Lincoln A. Wallen has taught us a greater awareness of monotonicity arguments and has urged us to notice when we used only one direction of a mutual implication. To prove that a relation is a right-condition, (25) is more convenient for the formulation of the demonstrandum than (24b).

When trying to use that a relation is a right-condition, formally stronger characterizations are, in general, to be preferred.   The stronger (24b) captures $[true \; ; x \Leftarrow x]$ – which follows from the existence of a neutral element of the composition and the latter's monotonicity – . Here I propose another strengthening of (25), one that captures composition's monotonicity (in its left argument):

(26) $(q$ is a right-condition$) \equiv \langle \forall x :: [x \; ; q \Rightarrow q] \rangle$.

We shall use this definition (twice) to prove the following theorem:

$(q$ is a right-condition$) \Rightarrow (\neg q$ is a right-condition$)$.

Proof   We observe for arbitrary relation q

$\qquad (\neg q$ is a right-condition$)$
$=\qquad \{(26)$ with $q := \neg q\}$
$\qquad \langle \forall x :: [x \; ; \neg q \Rightarrow \neg q] \rangle$
$=\qquad \{(23),$ i.e. right-exchange$\}$
$\qquad \langle \forall x :: [\sim x \; ; q \Rightarrow q] \rangle$
$\Leftarrow\qquad \{$instantiation $x := \sim x\}$
$\qquad \langle \forall x :: [x \; ; q \Rightarrow q] \rangle$
$=\qquad \{(26)\}$
$\qquad q$ is a right-condition

End of Proof.

In both [1] and [2], the proof of this theorem appeals to $[\sim true \equiv true]$, whereas the above proof does not use any properties of $\sim$ or *true*. The manipulative disadvantage of (25) is that it contains a constant whose properties we have to use.

The heuristic significance of formulation (26) is that it almost dictates monotonicity arguments because the fact that prefixing q by an arbitrary "x;" weakens it, fully captures that q is a right-condition. In other words, if, for instance, we set ourselves to prove that for a right-condition q

(27) $[q \; ; true \; ; \sim q \equiv q \; ; \sim q]$,

the implication sign in (26) tells us that a ping-pong argument is appropriate.

Remark   When faced with a demonstrandum of the form $[A \equiv B]$ we have a demonstrandum that *does not* depend (anti) monotonically on either A or B. Hence, proving this directly can *only* be done by appealing to Leibniz's Principle. i.e. by value-preserving transformations. (We have seen an example of this in Section 1.) Rewriting the demonstrandum as mutual implication $[A \Rightarrow B] \wedge [A \Leftarrow B]$ yields two conjuncts that *do* depend (anti) monotonically on both A and B! Because we like to avoid avoidable ping-pong arguments, it is nice to recognize circumstances under which they are indicated. *End of Remark.*

In proving (27) we observe that for ping:

$$[q \ ; \ true \ ; \sim q \Leftarrow q \ ; \sim q]$$
$$\Leftarrow \quad \{\text{monotonicity of } ;\}$$
$$[q \ ; \ true \Leftarrow q]$$
$$= \quad \{[x \ ; \ true \Leftarrow x]\}$$
$$true \quad ,$$

a demonstration in which we did not use that q is a right-condition. For pong we observe that we can strengthen the right-hand side:

$$[q \ ; \ true \ ; \sim q \Rightarrow q \ ; \sim q]$$
$$\Leftarrow \quad \{(26) \text{ with } x := q \ ; \ true \ ; \sim q\}$$
$$[q \ ; \ true \ ; \sim q \Rightarrow q \ ; \ true \ ; \sim q \ ; q \ ; \sim q]$$
$$\Leftarrow \quad \{\text{monotonicity of } ;\}$$
$$[\sim q \Rightarrow \sim q \ ; q \ ; \sim q]$$
$$= \quad \{(28) \text{ with } b := \sim q\}$$
$$true \quad ,$$

where the "seesaw lemma" – see [1] –

(28) $[b \Rightarrow b \ ; \sim b \ ; b]$

follows from (22) with $d, e, f := b, b, true$. (Knowledge of the seesaw lemma admittedly helps in the choice of how to instantiate x in (26).)

§ **9.**   In [1] "middle-conditions" are introduced by

(29) $(c$ is a middle-condition$) \equiv [c \Rightarrow J]$,

where "J" is the neutral element of "$;$". Also here the constant can be eliminated from the definition: we could have defined

(30) $(c$ is a middle-condition$) \equiv \langle \forall x :: [c \ ; x \Rightarrow x] \rangle$

or

$$(31) \qquad (c \text{ is a middle-condition}) \equiv \langle \forall x :: [x \; ; \; c \Rightarrow x] \rangle \quad .$$

In other words, c being a middle-condition is captured by the fact that the prefix operator "c;" and the postfix operator "; c" are strengthening operators. The implication signs in these definitions tell us that, for instance,

$$(32) \qquad [c \equiv \sim c] \qquad \text{for middle-condition } c$$

has to be proved by mutual implication. Since $[\sim x \Rightarrow x] \equiv [x \Rightarrow \sim x]$, it suffices to prove $[c \Rightarrow \sim c]$. We observe to this end

$$\sim c$$
$$\Leftarrow \qquad \{(30) \text{ with } x := \sim c\}$$
$$c \; ; \sim c$$
$$\Leftarrow \qquad \{(31) \text{ with } x := c \; ; \sim c\}$$
$$c \; ; \sim c \; ; c$$
$$\Leftarrow \qquad \{(28) \text{ with } b := c\}$$
$$c \quad .$$

Our wish to apply strengthening operators suggested to start at the consequent and the first two steps then followed. (And we were just lucky that we did not try to prove $[\sim c \Rightarrow c]$ according to the above scheme.)

§ **10.** Let me conclude. We set out to explore for antisymmetric and reflexive relations the interplay between calculating with equalities and inequalities, the latter drawing our attention to monotonicity arguments. In passing we encountered a number of instances – (2), (3), (16), (26), (30), (31) – where, sometimes to clear advantage, a formula or definition could be rewritten as a universally quantified expression.

A closely related topic is the design of calculational proofs of theorems about extreme solutions. Since this topic has been dealt with in [0] we shall not pursue it here. To close I shall borrow an example from [1] to show that also here universal quantification can be used to eliminate a constant. Instead of defining the reflexive transitive closure by

$$(s^* \text{ is the reflexive transitive closure of } s) \equiv$$
$$(s^* \text{ is the strongest solution of } x : [J \lor s \; ; x \Rightarrow x])$$

we can define s^* equivalently by

$$\langle \forall t :: s^* \; ; t \text{ is the strongest solution of } x : [t \lor s \; ; x \Rightarrow x] \rangle \quad .$$

We shall not repeat the standard proof here (which is, as is to be expected, a ping-pong argument). We do wish to point out that the instantiation $t := J$ returns the original definition.

Acknowledgements   Anyone familiar with their writings will realize that I am greatly endebted to Rutger M. Dijkstra, W. H. J. Feijen, and A. J. M. van Gasteren.

References

[0]   Predicate Calculus and Program Semantics, Edsger W. Dijkstra & Carel S. Scholten, Springer-Verlag, 1990.

[1]   Relational Calculus and Relational Program Semantics, Rutger M. Dijkstra, 1992.

[2]   An Introduction to the Relational Calculus, W. H. J. Feijen & A. J. M. van Gasteren. Appeared in: C. S. Scholten Dedicata: Van oude machines en nieuwe rekenwijzen, W. H. J. Feijen & A. J. M. van Gasteren (Eds.) Schoonhoven, Academic Service, 1991.

Chapter 8

Proof of Correctness of Object Representations

Joseph A. Goguen and Grant Malcolm

8.1 Introduction

This paper presents an algebraic account of implementation that is applicable to the object paradigm. The key to its applicability is the notion of state: objects have local states that are observable only through their outputs. That is, objects may be viewed as abstract machines with hidden local state (as in [9]). Consequently, a correct implementation need only have the required visible behaviour.

We use hidden order sorted algebra to formalise the object paradigm [4, 5, 8]. Advantages of an algebraic approach include a high level of intellectual rigour, a large body of supporting mathematics, and simple, efficient proofs using only equational logic. A wide variety of extensions to equational logic have been developed to treat various programming features, while preserving its essential simplicity. For example, order sorted equational logic uses a notion of subsort to treat computations that may raise exceptions or fail to terminate.

Hidden sorted logic extends standard equational logic to capture an important distinction between *immutable data types*, such as booleans and integers, and *mutable objects*, such as program variables and database entities. The terms *abstract data types* and *abstract object classes* refer to these two kinds of entity. The former represent 'visible' data values; the latter represent data stored in a hidden state. In hidden sorted equational logic, an equation of hidden sort need not be satisfied in the usual sense, but only *up to observability*, in that only its visible consequences need hold. Thus, hidden sorted logic allows greater freedom in implementations.

The simplicity of the underlying logic is important, because we want a *tractable* approach in which implementations are as easily expressible and provable as possible. A specification is just a set of sentences in some logical system: that is, a *theory*. An algebraic specification is then a set of equations. An implementation is expressed by a *theory morphism*, which says how to interpret a theory into its implementation in such a way that each model of the concrete theory gives a model of the abstract theory. In this respect, our approach is similar to the seminal work of Hoare on data refinement [15], in which correctness of implementation is expressed by a mapping from concrete variables to the abstract objects which they represent.

The following section introduces notation for hidden order sorted specifications, and summarises the main algebraic notions and results used in this paper. Order sorted algebra is the basis for the semantics of the executable specification language OBJ [13], and hidden order sorted algebra is the basis for an algebraic semantics of the object oriented language FOOPS [16]. Our examples of implementations use the notation of these languages. Section 8.3 presents implementations of hidden order sorted specifications, and a technique for proving correctness. We believe that this technique leads to proofs that are simpler than those of other approaches. Subsection 8.3.3 applies this technique to the implementation of collections of objects.

This paper is dedicated with warm affection to Tony Hoare, whose work on data representation and on concurrency has been an inspiration to us.

8.2   Hidden Order Sorted Algebra

Many sorted algebra (hereafter, 'MSA') was developed by the ADJ group [12] into a form suitable for abstract data types in computer science. The logic of MSA is first order equational logic, which is relatively simple. The following subsection summarises the main definitions and results of MSA, while Subsections 8.2.2 and 8.2.3 describe order sorted specification and hidden order sorted specification.

8.2.1   Many sorted algebra

An unsorted algebra is a set with 'structure' described by some operations and equations. The set is referred to as the carrier of the algebra. MSA extends this traditional view by defining an algebra to have any number of carriers. For example, what we might call a 'list algebra' is a quadruple $(C, \eta, \oplus, e)$, where the carriers are $C_{\texttt{Elt}}$ and $C_{\texttt{List}}$, and $\eta : C_{\texttt{Elt}} \to C_{\texttt{List}}$ is a unary function, and $\oplus : C_{\texttt{List}} \times C_{\texttt{List}} \to C_{\texttt{List}}$ is an associative binary operation with neutral element $e \in C_{\texttt{List}}$; that is, the following equations are satisfied for all $x, y, z \in C_{\texttt{List}}$:

$$
\begin{aligned}
x \oplus (y \oplus z) &= (x \oplus y) \oplus z \\
e \oplus x &= x \\
x \oplus e &= x
\end{aligned}
$$

This specification of list algebras has three components: the carriers, named by the 'sorts' Elt and List; the operations η, $\oplus$ and e; and the three equations above. We address each of these aspects in turn.

Definition 1 Given a set S, an S-**sorted set** is a collection $(A_s)_{s \in S}$ of sets indexed by elements of S. All set theoretic operations can be extended to operations on

S-sorted sets; for example, if A and B are S-sorted sets, then $A \cup B$ is defined by $(A \cup B)_s = A_s \cup B_s$, and $A \subseteq B$ means that $A_s \subseteq B_s$ for each $s \in S$.

An S-**sorted function** $f : A \to B$ is a collection of functions indexed by S such that $f_s : A_s \to B_s$ for each $s \in S$. Similarly, an S-**sorted relation** R from A to B is a collection of relations indexed by S such that R_s is from A_s to B_s for each $s \in S$. We write the identity relation on an S-sorted set A as id_A.

For example, the carrier of a list algebra is an $\{\texttt{Elt}, \texttt{List}\}$-sorted set.

Definition 2 A **many sorted signature** is a pair (S, Σ), where S is a set of sorts and Σ is an $(S^* \times S)$-sorted set of operation names. Thus, if $l \in S^*$ and $s \in S$ then $\Sigma_{l,s}$ is a set of operation names. If Σ is clear from the context, we sometimes write $f : l \to s$ instead of $f \in \Sigma_{l,s}$ to emphasise that f is intended to denote an operation mapping the sorts denoted by l to the sort denoted by s. Usually we abbreviate (S, Σ) to Σ. Elements of $\Sigma_{[],s}$ are referred to as **constants** of sort s.

An operation can be declared to have more than one type, e.g., we might have $f \in \Sigma_{l,s} \cap \Sigma_{l',s'}$ where l, s is different from l', s'. In this case, f is said to be **overloaded**.

Signatures provide a uniform notation for specifying the carriers and operations of many sorted algebras. Later sections consider implementing one specification by another; in order to compare two specifications, we use *signature morphisms*, which view one algebraic structure in terms of another.

Definition 3 A **signature morphism** $\phi : (S, \Sigma) \to (S', \Sigma')$ is a pair (ϕ_1, ϕ_2), where $\phi_1 : S \to S'$ maps sorts in S to sorts in S', and ϕ_2 maps the operation names of Σ to operation names of Σ' in such a way that for each $f \in \Sigma_{l,s}$ we have $\phi_2(f) \in \Sigma'_{\phi_1^*(l), \phi_1(s)}$, where $\phi_1^*(l)$ denotes ϕ_1 applied component-wise to the list l; i.e., $\phi_1^*[] = []$ and $\phi_1^*(s\,l) = (\phi_1\,s)(\phi_1^*\,l)$.

A useful example of a signature morphism is the inclusion of one signature in another: if $S \subseteq S'$ and $\Sigma \subseteq \Sigma'$, then there is an inclusion $\iota : (S, \Sigma) \to (S', \Sigma')$.

Signatures may be thought of as specifying algebras with no equations, and so we may speak of the algebras of a signature. An algebra for a signature Σ is an S-sorted set with the structure specified by the operation names of Σ.

Definition 4 For a many sorted signature Σ, a Σ-**algebra** A is given by the following data: an S-sorted set, usually denoted A, called the **carrier** of the algebra; an element $A_f \in A_s$ for each $s \in S$ and $f \in \Sigma_{[],s}$; and for each non-empty list $l \in S^*$, and each $s \in S$ and $f \in \Sigma_{l,s}$, an operation $A_f : A_l \to A_s$, where if $l = s1 \ldots sn$ then $A_l = A_{s1} \times \cdots \times A_{sn}$.

Given Σ-algebras A and B, a Σ-**homomorphism** $h : A \to B$ is an S-sorted function $A \to B$ such that:

- given a constant $f \in \Sigma_{[],s}$, then $h_s(A_f) = B_f$;
- given a non-empty list $l = s1 \ldots sn$ and $f \in \Sigma_{l,s}$ and $ai \in A_{si}$ for $i = 1, \ldots, n$, then $h_s(A_f(a1, \ldots, an)) = B_f(h_{s1}(a1), \ldots, h_{sn}(an))$.

Thus, an algebra for a signature interprets the sort names as sets and the operation names as operations, while homomorphisms preserve the structure of the algebra in that they distribute over the operations of the algebra.

Given any signature, we can construct an algebra whose carriers are sets of terms built up from the given operation names viewed as symbols of an alphabet.

Definition 5 Given a many sorted signature Σ, the **term algebra** T_Σ is constructed as follows. Let $\cup\Sigma$ be the set of all operation names in Σ; T_Σ is the least S-sorted set of strings over the alphabet $(\cup\Sigma) \cup \{(,)\}$ such that:

* for each constant symbol $f \in \Sigma_{[],s}$, the string $f \in (T_\Sigma)_s$;
* for each non-empty list $l = s1 \ldots sn \in S^*$, and each $f \in \Sigma_{l,s}$, and all $ti \in (T_\Sigma)_{si}$ for $i = 1, \ldots, n$, the string $f(t1 \ldots tn) \in (T_\Sigma)_s$.

We show that T_Σ is a Σ-algebra by showing how the operation names of Σ are interpreted: for each constant $f \in \Sigma_{[],s}$, the constant $(T_\Sigma)_f$ is the string $f \in (T_\Sigma)_s$; for each non-empty list $l = s1 \ldots sn \in S^*$ and operation name $f \in \Sigma_{l,s}$, the operation $(T_\Sigma)_f : (T_\Sigma)_l \to (T_\Sigma)_s$ maps a tuple of strings $t1 \ldots tn$ to the string $f(t1 \ldots tn)$. The special symbols '(' and ')' are used to emphasise that the carriers of T_Σ are sets of strings; from now on we write '$f(t1, \ldots, tn)$' for '$f(t1 \ldots tn)$'.

This shows that T_Σ is a Σ-algebra. In fact, if Σ contains no overloaded symbols, it has the special property of being an *initial* Σ-algebra.

Definition 6 An **initial Σ-algebra** is a Σ-algebra A such that for each Σ-algebra B there is exactly one Σ-homomorphism $A \to B$.

Proposition 7 If Σ contains no overloaded operation names, then T_Σ is an initial Σ-algebra. For any Σ-algebra A, the unique Σ-homomorphism $h : T_\Sigma \to A$ is defined recursively as follows:

* for each constant symbol $f \in \Sigma_{[],s}$, let $h_s(f) = A_f$;
* for each non-empty list $l = s1 \ldots sn$ and $f \in \Sigma_{l,s}$ and $ti \in (T_\Sigma)_{si}$ for $i = 1, \ldots, n$, let $h_s(f(t1, \ldots, tn)) = (A_f)(h_{s1}(t1), \ldots, h_{sn}(tn))$.

The homomorphism h assigns a value in A to terms by interpreting the operation names of Σ as the corresponding operations on A. If Σ contains overloaded operations, an initial algebra can still be constructed as a term algebra where the operation names are distinguished by 'tagging' them with their result sorts [7].

Let us now consider algebras with equations. An equation is usually presented as two terms (the left- and right-hand sides) which contain variables. For example, one of the equations for list algebras was $(x \oplus y) \oplus z = x \oplus (y \oplus z)$, where x, y and z are variables that range over $C_{\texttt{List}}$. Because variables only serve as placeholders for values of the sorts that they range over, any signature of constant symbols can be used to provide variables.

Definition 8 A **ground signature** is a signature (S, Σ) such that for all $l \in S^*$ and $s \in S$, if $l \neq [\,]$ then $\Sigma_{l,s} = \emptyset$, and such that the $\Sigma_{l,s}$ are disjoint; i.e., the operation names of ground signatures are distinct constants.

We assume disjointness so that distinct variables cannot be identified.

Ground signatures are essentially the same thing as S-sorted sets, because any S-sorted set X can be viewed as a ground signature by taking $X_{l,s}$ to be X_s if $l = [\,]$ and the empty set otherwise. Moreover, a ground signature Σ can be viewed as the S-sorted set $(\Sigma_{[\,],s})_{s \in S}$. This determines a bijection between ground signatures and S-sorted sets; we take advantage of this by sometimes treating ground signatures as S-sorted sets. Now it is a simple matter to characterise terms containing variables:

Definition 9 Given a many sorted signature (S, Σ) and a ground signature (S, X) such that Σ and X are disjoint, **terms with variables from** X are elements of $T_{\Sigma \cup X}$. Now $T_{\Sigma \cup X}$ can be viewed as a Σ-algebra if we forget about the constants in X: when we view $T_{\Sigma \cup X}$ as a Σ-algebra, we write it as $T_\Sigma(X)$.

A Σ-**equation** is a triple (X, l, r), where (S, X) is a ground signature, and l and r are terms in $T_\Sigma(X)$ of the same sort; i.e., $l, r \in T_\Sigma(X)_s$ for some $s \in S$. We write such an equation in the form $(\forall X)\, l = r$.

A **specification** is a triple (S, Σ, E), where (S, Σ) is a signature and E is a set of Σ-equations. We usually abbreviate (S, Σ, E) to (Σ, E).

Algebras of a specification are Σ-algebras that satisfy the equations; we turn now to what it means for an algebra to satisfy an equation. The first issue is how to interpret the left- and right-hand sides of an equation in an arbitrary Σ-algebra. Because $T_\Sigma(X)$ is a Σ-algebra, there is a homomorphism $T_\Sigma \to T_\Sigma(X)$, which is the inclusion of variable-free terms into terms with variables. However, T_Σ is not in general a $(\Sigma \cup X)$-algebra, because we do not know how to interpret the variables in X. If we can assign values to those variables, then we can assign values to terms containing those variables.

Proposition 10 Given a Σ-algebra A and an S-sorted function $\theta : X \to A$ (often called an 'interpretation of variables'), there is a unique Σ-homomorphism $\bar\theta : T_\Sigma(X) \to A$ such that $\bar\theta(\iota(x)) = \theta(x)$ for all variables x, where $\iota : X \to T_\Sigma(X)$ maps $x \in X_s$ to the string $x \in T_\Sigma(X)_s$. The homomorphism is defined as follows:

- for each $x \in X_s$, let $\bar\theta_s(x) = \theta_s(x)$;
- for each constant symbol $f \in \Sigma_{[\,],s}$, let $\bar\theta_s(f) = A_f$;
- for each non-empty list $l = s1 \ldots sn$, $f \in \Sigma_{l,s}$, and all $ti \in T_\Sigma(X)_{si}$ for $i = 1, \ldots, n$, let $\bar\theta_s(f(t1, \ldots, tn)) = A_f(\bar\theta_{s1}(t1), \ldots, \bar\theta_{sn}(tn))$.

Equations have an implicit universal quantification over the variables. An algebra satisfies a given equation iff the left- and right-hand sides of the equation are equal under all interpretations of the variables:

Definition 11 A Σ-algebra A **satisfies** a Σ-equation $(\forall X)\ l = r$ iff $\bar{\theta}(l) = \bar{\theta}(r)$ for all $\theta : X \to A$. We write $A \models e$ to indicate that A satisfies the equation e. For a set E of equations, we write $A \models E$ iff $A \models e$ for each $e \in E$. Given a specification (Σ, E), a (Σ, E)-**algebra** is a Σ-algebra A such that $A \models E$.

Just as each signature has an initial algebra, each specification has an initial algebra. The initial algebra is constructed from the term algebra by identifying terms that are 'equal' as a consequence of the given equations. This identification is achieved using the notion of *congruence*.

Each equation gives rise to a relation in the following way: given a Σ-algebra A let e be a Σ-equation $(\forall X)\ l = r$, and define the relation $\mathsf{R}(e) : A \sim A$ by $a\ \mathsf{R}(e)\ b$ iff $a = \bar{\theta}(l)$ and $b = \bar{\theta}(r)$ for some $\theta : X \to A$. In other words, a is related to b iff a is an instance of the left-hand side and b is an instance of the right-hand side, under some interpretation of the variables. We seek an equivalence relation that contains all the relations derived from the equations of a specification, and that allows the substitution of equals for equals.

Definition 12 Given a signature Σ and a Σ-algebra A, a Σ-**congruence** is an S-sorted equivalence relation R such that the following **substitutivity property** holds: for all $f \in \Sigma_{l,s}$ and $x, y \in A_l$, if $x\ R_l\ y$ then $A_f(x)\ R_s\ A_f(y)$, where if $l = s1 \ldots sn$, then $x \in A_l$ means $x = x1 \ldots xn$ with $xi \in A_{si}$, and $x\ R_l\ y$ means $xi\ R_{si}\ yi$ for $i = 1, \ldots, n$.

If E is a set of Σ-equations and A is a Σ-algebra, then $\equiv_{A,E}$ denotes the least Σ-congruence on A which contains each equation in E; that is, for each $e \in E$, $\mathsf{R}(e) \subseteq \equiv_{A,E}$. We usually write $=_E$ instead of $\equiv_{T_\Sigma, E}$.

The Σ-congruence $=_E$ allows the identification of terms which are equal as a result of the equations E.

Proposition 13 Given a specification (Σ, E) where Σ contains no overloaded operations, the initial (Σ, E)-algebra is the **quotient term algebra** $T_{\Sigma,E} = T_\Sigma/=_E$. That is, the carriers of $T_{\Sigma,E}$ are sets of equivalence classes under $=_E$; specifically, $(T_{\Sigma,E})_s = \{[t] \mid t \in (T_\Sigma)_s\}$, where $[t]$ denotes the equivalence class of t under $=_E$. The structure of $T_{\Sigma,E}$ as a Σ-algebra is given by:

- for each constant symbol $f \in \Sigma_{[],s}$, let $(T_{\Sigma,E})_f = [f]$;
- for each non-empty list $l = s1 \ldots sn$, $f \in \Sigma_{l,s}$, and $[ti] \in (T_{\Sigma,E})_{si}$ for $i = 1, \ldots, n$, let $(T_{\Sigma,E})_f([t1], \ldots, [tn]) = [(T_\Sigma)_f(t1, \ldots, tn)]$.

The last equation is well-defined by the substitutivity property of the congruence $=_E$. By construction, $T_{\Sigma,E}$ satisfies the equations E.

The above proposition refers to 'the' initial (Σ, E)-algebra, but a specification may have more than one initial algebra. However, any two initial (Σ, E)-algebras are isomorphic, because the unique homomorphisms from each algebra to the other are inverses. Thus all initial algebras are 'abstractly the same'. ADJ [12] define an abstract data type to be the collection of initial algebras of a specification. Such a collection is an equivalence class, since being isomorphic is an equivalence relation, and this equivalence class may be represented by $T_{\Sigma,E}$. The importance of initiality is that it gives a canonical interpretation of a specification as an abstract data type. Moreover, completeness results state that a Σ-equation is satisfied by all (Σ, E)-algebras iff it can be proved using the equations E and the standard properties of equality: reflexivity, symmetry, transitivity and substitutivity. This allows the use of equational deduction in prototyping and proving properties of specifications, for example, using OBJ [13].

8.2.2   Order sorted algebra

Partial operations and error handling play an important rôle in many computer science applications. A partial operation produces well-defined values only on some subsort of its domain. For example, division in a field produces a well-defined value only when the denominator is not zero. Order sorted algebra (hereafter, 'OSA') is a variation on MSA that allows algebras with partial operations. It also provides a model of inheritance that is useful in formalising the object paradigm. This subsection summarises definitions and results of OSA that are relevant to this paper. A comprehensive survey is given by Goguen and Diaconescu in [7].

Both OSA and MSA are based on the notion of S-sorted sets, but whereas in MSA S is a set, in OSA S is a partially ordered set. If S is a set of sort names, the partial order indicates the subsort relations between the carriers of algebras. For a partially ordered set $(S, \leq)$, we refer to $\leq$ as **the subsort ordering**. We sometimes extend this ordering to lists over S of equal length by $s1 \ldots sn \leq s1' \ldots sn'$ iff $si \leq si'$ for $i = 0, \ldots, n$.

Definition 14 Given a partial order $(S, \leq)$, an equivalence class of the transitive symmetric closure of $\leq$ is called a **connected component**, and two elements of the same connected component are said to be **connected**. A partial order $(S, \leq)$ is **locally filtered** iff any two connected sorts have a common supersort, that is, iff whenever s and s' are connected, there is an s'' such that $s, s' \leq s''$.

The notion of local filtering allows many results of MSA to extend to OSA [7].

Definition 15 An $(S, \leq)$-**sorted set** is an S-sorted set A such that whenever $s \leq s'$ then $A_s \subseteq A_{s'}$. An $(S, \leq)$-**sorted function** $f : A \to B$ is an S-sorted function such that whenever $s \leq s'$ then $f_s \subseteq f_{s'}$. An $(S, \leq)$-**sorted relation** R from A to B is an S-sorted relation such that if $s \leq s'$ and $x \in A_s$ and $y \in B_s$, then $x\, R_s\, y$ iff $x\, R_{s'}\, y$. We sometimes abbreviate '$(S, \leq)$-sorted' to 'S-sorted'.

Most definitions of MSA apply, *mutatis mutandis*, to OSA; the main differences concern monotonicity.

Definition 16 An **order sorted signature** is a triple $(S, \leq, \Sigma)$ where $(S, \leq)$ is a locally filtered partial order and (S, Σ) is a many sorted signature which satisfies the **monotonicity requirement**: if $f \in \Sigma_{l,s} \cap \Sigma_{l',s'}$ and $l \leq l'$ then $s \leq s'$. We usually abbreviate $(S, \leq, \Sigma)$ to just Σ.

An **order sorted signature morphism** $\phi : (S, \leq, \Sigma) \to (S', \leq', \Sigma')$ is a many sorted signature morphism such that $\phi_1 : (S, \leq) \to (S', \leq')$ is monotonic. A signature morphism ϕ **preserves overloading** iff whenever $f \in \Sigma_{l,s} \cap \Sigma_{l',s'}$ then ϕ_2 applied to $f \in \Sigma_{l,s}$ gives the same result as ϕ_2 applied to $f \in \Sigma_{l',s'}$.

Monotonicity is also needed for the algebras of an order sorted signature.

Definition 17 Given an order sorted signature $(S, \leq, \Sigma)$, an **order sorted Σ-algebra** is a many sorted Σ-algebra A such that A is an $(S, \leq)$-sorted set and A is **monotonic**, in the sense that for all $f \in \Sigma_{l,s} \cap \Sigma_{l',s'}$ if $l \leq l'$ and $s \leq s'$ then $A_f : A_l \to A_s$ is equal to $A_f : A_{l'} \to A_{s'}$ on A_l.

For order sorted Σ-algebras A and B, an **order sorted Σ-homomorphism** $h : A \to B$ is a many sorted Σ-homomorphism which satisfies the **restriction condition**: if $s \leq s'$ then $h_s = h_{s'}|_{A_s}$ where $h_{s'}|_{A_s}$ denotes the restriction of $h_{s'} : A_{s'} \to B_{s'}$ to A_s.

The construction of the term algebra is as in MSA, but requires the carrier of T_Σ to be $(S, \leq)$-sorted, so that $(T_\Sigma)_s \subseteq (T_\Sigma)_{s'}$ whenever $s \leq s'$. In general, T_Σ is not an initial Σ-algebra unless Σ satisfies a regularity condition [11]:

Definition 18 An order sorted signature Σ is **regular** iff for any $f \in \Sigma_{l1,s1}$ and $l0 \leq l1$ there is a least pair (l, s) such that $l0 \leq l$ and $f \in \Sigma_{l,s}$.

The importance of regularity is that terms can be parsed as having a least sort. Goguen and Diaconescu [7] note that regularity is not essential, in that OSA can be developed in greater generality under the assumption only of local filtering. The construction of an initial algebra is then more complicated, and we do not give details here, as all specifications in this paper are regular.

Unlike in MSA, the left- and right-hand sides of an equation need not have the same sort; their sorts need only be connected.

Definition 19 Given an order sorted signature $(S, \leq, \Sigma)$, a **Σ-equation** is a triple (X, l, r), where X is a ground signature disjoint from Σ with $l \in T_\Sigma(X)_s$ and $r \in T_\Sigma(X)_{s'}$ for some connected $s, s' \in S$. We use the notation $(\forall X)\, l = r$.

The definitions of satisfaction of equations and congruence in OSA are as in MSA, but with 'S-sorted' everywhere changed to '$(S, \leq)$-sorted'. An **order sorted specification** is an order sorted signature together with a set E of Σ-equations, and a **(Σ, E)-algebra** is a Σ-algebra which satisfies all equations in E. The quotient term algebra $T_{\Sigma,E}$ is constructed as in MSA, dividing by the least $(S, \leq)$-sorted Σ-congruence which extends the equations of the specification. If the signature is regular, this gives an initial (Σ, E)-algebra.

We end our summary of OSA with 'retract' specifications, which allow operations to be applied to arguments which may lie outside their domain of definition, possibly resulting in values that are 'ill-defined' in the sense that they involve the special 'retract' operations. This allows order sorted specifications to model partial operations (see [11, 7] for a full treatment).

Definition 20 Given an order sorted specification $P = (S, \leq, \Sigma, E)$, we write $P^{\otimes}$ for its **retract extension** $(S, \leq, \Sigma^{\otimes}, E^{\otimes})$, where $\Sigma^{\otimes}$ is Σ extended with an operation $r_{s1,s2} : s1 \to s2$ for each $s1, s2 \in S$ such that $s2 \leq s1$, and $E^{\otimes}$ is E extended with an equation $(\forall S : s2)\, r_{s1,s2}(S) = S$ for each $s2 \leq s1$ as above.

We wish the result of adding retracts to be a conservative extension of the given specification; that is, for all $t1, t2 \in T_{\Sigma}$, $t1 =_E t2$ iff $t1 =_{E^{\otimes}} t2$, i.e., the new equations added by the introduction of retracts do not cause distinct terms of T_{Σ} to become identified. Goguen and Meseguer [11] give sufficient conditions on specifications for adding retracts to be conservative. These conditions go beyond the scope of the present paper, but we note that all our example specifications are such that their retract extensions are conservative.

8.2.3   Hidden order sorted algebra

Hidden sorted algebra was developed as a variation on MSA for objects with local states [5, 8]. In a hidden sorted specification, the set of sort names is partitioned into 'visible' and 'hidden' sorts. Operations which return hidden sorted values correspond to the internal operations of an object, while visible sorted values correspond to an object's inputs and outputs. This subsection summarises the basic definitions of hidden sorted algebra, and then combines it with OSA to give hidden order sorted algebra (hereafter, 'HOSA').

Definition 21 A **hidden sorted signature** is a triple (S, V, Σ), where (S, Σ) is a many sorted signature and $V \subseteq S$. The elements of V are referred to as **visible sorts**, and elements of $S - V$ as **hidden sorts**.

A **hidden sorted signature morphism** $\phi : (S, V, \Sigma) \to (S', V', \Sigma')$ is a many sorted signature morphism which maps visible sorts to visible sorts and hidden sorts to hidden sorts, i.e., $s \in V$ iff $\phi_1(s) \in V'$.

A **hidden sorted specification** is a hidden sorted signature together with a set E of Σ-equations (in the sense of MSA).

We might refer to the above as 'pre-signature' and 'pre-signature morphism' (and similarly for the HOSA definitions below), since Goguen and Diaconescu [8] give extra restrictions on signatures which correspond to aspects of object oriented computation and make hidden sorted algebra an institution [1]. We do not make these extra restrictions here as they are not necessary for our results. However, we note that in [8] a hidden sorted specification includes a fixed 'data algebra' D for the visible sorts such that for any Σ-algebra A, $D_v = A_v$ for all visible sorts v.

The definition of satisfaction differs from MSA in that only the visible consequences of an equation need hold. The notion of 'visible consequence' is made
precise by defining *contexts* for terms:

Definition 22 Given a term $t \in (T_\Sigma)_s$, a **context for** t **of sort** s' is a term
$c \in T_\Sigma(\{z\})_{s'}$ where z is a new variable of sort s, i.e., a context is just a term
which contains a distinguished variable. We write $T_\Sigma[z]$ instead of $T_\Sigma(\{z\})$, and
if c is a context for t, we write $c[t]$ for the result of substituting t for z in c.

Contexts of visible sort can be considered experiments which, applied to an
object's hidden state, give visible outputs. The definition of satisfaction for HSA
says that two states are distinguished iff they give different results for some experiment, and an equation is behaviourally satisfied if its left- and right-hand sides
always instantiate to states that cannot be distinguished by any experiment.

Definition 23 A Σ-algebra A **behaviourally satisfies** a Σ-equation e of the
form $(\forall X)\, l = r$ (denoted $A \models_b e$) iff $A \models (\forall X)\, c[l] = c[r]$ for all $v \in V$ and
$c \in T_\Sigma[z]_v$. Implicitly, the variable z has the same sort as l and r. For a set E
of Σ-equations, we write $A \models_b E$ iff $A \models_b e$ for all $e \in E$.

If an equation has visible sort, then behavioural satisfaction is the same as
satisfaction in MSA, because for c we can always choose the 'empty context'
$z \in T_\Sigma[z]_v$. Behavioural satisfaction of equations can also be expressed more
abstractly:

Proposition 24 $A \models_b E$ iff $(\equiv_{A,E})|_V \subseteq id_A|_V$ where $R|_V$ is the restriction of an
S-sorted relation R to the visible sorts of V i.e., $R|_V$ is the V-sorted relation
$(R_v)_{v \in V}$.

This can be read as saying that E does not identify distinct elements of A of
visible sort, which we might summarise by saying there is 'no confusion'.

A **behavioural (Σ, E)-algebra** is a Σ-algebra A such that $A \models_b E$. The
notion of implementation that we use in the following sections is based on the idea
that an object is implemented by a behavioural algebra of its specification.

We now give the hidden sorted version of OSA.

Definition 25 An **HOSA signature** is a quadruple $(S, V, \leq, \Sigma)$ where $(S, \leq, \Sigma)$
is an order sorted signature, and the visible sorts $V \subseteq S$ partition the partially
ordered set S in the sense that whenever $s \leq s'$ then $s \in V$ iff $s' \in V$.

An **HOS signature morphism** $\phi : (S, V, \leq, \Sigma) \to (S', V', \leq', \Sigma')$ is an order
sorted signature morphism which maps visible sorts to visible sorts and hidden
sorts to hidden sorts in the sense that $s \in V$ iff $\phi_1(s) \in V'$.

The definitions of algebra, equation, specification and retract are as in OSA,
but satisfaction of equations in HOSA only requires that the visible consequences
of an equation hold. Because of the order-sortedness of HOSA signatures, defining satisfaction in terms of contexts would require contexts that contain retracts.

Burstall and Diaconescu [1] give an abstract categorical definition of behavioural satisfaction for OSA, which is beyond the scope of the present paper. Moreover, their definitions of HOSA signature, etc., are different from those given here; for example, they require that the visible sorts have a fixed interpretation (cf. the comments after Definition 21). Because of these differences, we say instead that a Σ-algebra A **behaviourally satisfies** E iff there is no confusion in the sense of Proposition 24 (i.e., $(\equiv_{A,E})|_V \subseteq id_A|_V$). A **behavioural** (Σ, E)-**algebra** is a Σ-algebra A such that A behaviourally satisfies E.

This definition of satisfaction generalises the definition for OSA, in that given an order sorted specification $(S, \leq, \Sigma, E)$, we can construct the HOSA specification $(S, S, \leq, \Sigma, E)$ where all sorts are visible; then for any $(S, \leq, \Sigma)$-algebra A, we have $A \models E$ iff $A \models_b E$.

Section 8.3 considers implementations using a translation from terms of the abstract specification to terms of the concrete specification; this states how programs of the abstract specification are to be 'compiled'. The simplest way to achieve such a translation is by a signature morphism: if we know how to translate operations of the abstract specification, then we can translate terms built from those operations. Often the abstract signature is contained in the concrete; that is, all the sorts and operations of the abstract specification are available in the concrete one. In that case all terms over the abstract signature are also terms over the concrete signature. However, non-inclusion translations are sometimes useful (see Subsection 8.3.2). The following states how an arbitrary signature morphism extends to a translation of terms.

Proposition 26 Every signature morphism $\phi : \Sigma \to \Sigma'$ which preserves overloading can be extended to a function ϕ such that $\phi : (T_\Sigma)_s \to (T_{\Sigma'})_{\phi_1(s)}$ for all $s \in S$. This extension is defined as follows:

- for each constant symbol $f \in \Sigma_{[],s}$, let $\phi(f) = \phi_2(f)$;
- for each non-empty list $l = s1 \dots sn$, $f \in \Sigma_{l,s}$, and all $ti \in (T_\Sigma)_{si}$ for $i = 1, \dots, n$, let $\phi(f(t1, \dots, tn)) = (\phi_2(f))(\phi(t1), \dots, \phi(tn))$.

If ϕ_1 is an inclusion of S into S' then ϕ is an S-sorted function $T_\Sigma \to T_{\Sigma'}$ and if $\Sigma \subseteq \Sigma'$ then ϕ is the unique inclusion homomorphism $T_\Sigma \to T_{\Sigma'}$, so that terms of T_Σ are also terms of $T_{\Sigma'}$.

Moreover, ϕ extends to $\phi^\otimes : T_{\Sigma^\otimes} \to T_{\Sigma'^\otimes}$ by setting $\phi_2^\otimes(r_{s1,s2}) = r_{\phi_1(s1),\phi_1(s2)}$. Finally, ϕ extends to $\phi_s : T_\Sigma(X)_s \to T_{\Sigma'}(X')_{\phi_1(s)}$ for each $s \in S$, where $X'_{s'} = \{x \in X_s \mid \phi_1(s) = s'\}$; thus, ϕ may change the sort but not the name of a variable. Note that because all the variables of X are distinct (cf. Definition 8), ϕ cannot identify distinct variables.

8.3   Implementation

This section defines implementation for HOSA specifications and presents a technique for proving correctness of implementation that is illustrated in two examples.

Let us now fix two HOSA specifications, $A = (SA, \leq_A, VA, \Sigma A, EA)$ and $C = (SC, \leq_C, VC, \Sigma C, EC)$, where A is for 'abstract' and C is for 'concrete', plus a signature morphism $\phi : \Sigma A \to \Sigma C$ which preserves overloading. We also use the following abbreviations:

Notation 27 Write TA for the carrier of the term algebra $T_{\Sigma A}$; $TA^\otimes$ for that of $T_{\Sigma A^\otimes}$ (cf. Definition 20); $TA[z]$ for the contexts in $T_{\Sigma A}[z]$ and $TA[z]^\otimes$ for $T_{\Sigma A^\otimes}[z]$ (cf. Definition 22); TA_s for the terms of sort s, etc., and similarly for C; and ϕ for $\phi : TA \to TC$ as well as for $\phi^\otimes : TA^\otimes \to TC^\otimes$ (cf. Proposition 26).

What do we mean by 'A is implemented by C'? If we ignore hidden and order sortedness, the answer is straightforward: all ground equalities in A, when translated by ϕ, should hold in C; i.e.,

(8.1) $t_1 =_{EA} t_2$ implies $\phi(t_1) =_{EC} \phi(t_2)$ for all $t_1, t_2 \in TA$.

The intuitive meaning is that if t_1 is some program that gives result t_2 in the abstract specification, then its translation should give the corresponding result in the implementation. More formally, (8.1) states that the ϕ-translations of the ground consequences of the equations EA are entailed by EC. It can be shown that this is equivalent to requiring the ϕ-translations of ground instances of the equations in EA to be entailed by EC, i.e., that

(8.2) $\phi(\bar{\theta}(lhs)) =_{EC} \phi(\bar{\theta}(rhs))$ for each $(\forall X)\, lhs{=}rhs \in EA$ and $\theta : X \to TA$.

This is equivalent to (8.1), but has a form that is generally easier to prove.

If we take hidden sortedness into account, we need only consider equalities of visible sort, so that the requirement (8.1) for implementation becomes

(8.3) $t_1 =_{EA} t_2$ implies $\phi(t_1) =_{EC} \phi(t_2)$ for all $v \in VA$ and $t_1, t_2 \in TA_v$.

This is the definition given by Henniker in [14], though only for signature inclusions. Henniker also proposes a method for proving implementation correctness based on induction over the structure of contexts, by restating this condition in terms of behavioural equivalence.

Definition 28 $t, t' \in TC$ are A-**behaviourally equivalent**, written $t \sim t'$, iff for all $v \in VA$ and $c \in TA[z]_v$, we have $\phi(c)[t] =_{EC} \phi(c)[t']$, where $\phi(c)[t]$ denotes the ϕ-translation of c with the term t substituted for z. Implicitly, if the variable z has sort s, then t and t' have sort $\phi_1(s)$.

It can be shown that (8.3) is equivalent to:

(8.4) $t_1 =_{EA} t_2$ implies $\phi(t_1) \sim \phi(t_2)$ for all $s \in SA$ and $t_1, t_2 \in TA_s$.

Henniker shows that (8.3), and therefore (8.4), is equivalent to:

(8.5) $\phi(\bar{\theta}(lhs)) \sim \phi(\bar{\theta}(rhs))$ for each $(\forall X)\, lhs{=}rhs \in EA$ and $\theta : X \to TA$.

The equivalence of (8.1) and (8.2) is mirrored in that of (8.4) and (8.5). Both (8.2) and (8.5) have a form that simplifies the proof obligations. However, proofs of (8.5) can still be surprisingly complicated (e.g., see [14]).

The situation is more complex for OSA because the definition of implementation has to consider well-definedness of terms, which may amount to termination of programs. Schoett [17] defines implementation for partial algebras, and gives a necessary and sufficient condition in terms of a congruence between models of the abstract and concrete specifications. Schoett's definition is stronger than that given below: he restricts attention to terms all of whose subterms are equal to a well-defined value (in our setting this means that they contain no retract operations). For example, consider an abstract specification of stacks with operations `top`, `pop`, `empty` and `push` (as in Subsection 8.3.2 below), where `top` requires a non-empty stack as argument, and should satisfy the equation $(\forall X : \text{Nat}, S : \text{Stack})$ `top push`$(X,S) = X$. The term `top push(0, pop empty)` can be viewed in two ways: it either gives the value 0, or else is undefined. The first view corresponds to lazy evaluation, where terms with ill-defined subterms can still have well-defined values; the second view, implicit in Schoett's definition, corresponds to call-by-value, where any term with an undefined subterm is itself undefined. In Schoett's call-by-value approach, an implementation of stacks may allow `top push(0, pop empty)` to take any value at all. We consider 'lazy' implementation important because many programming languages either have lazy evaluation or else facilities for error handling.

Our definition of implementation in HOSA is that C implements A iff whenever a visible sorted term of $TA^\otimes$ gives a well-defined value (i.e., a term of TA), then the ϕ-translation of that term gives the corresponding value in TC.

Definition 29 A specification C is a **partial behavioural implementation** of a specification A via the signature morphism ϕ (we write $\phi : A \sqsubseteq C$) iff $t =_{EA^\otimes} t'$ implies $\phi(t) =_{EC^\otimes} \phi(t')$ for all $v \in VA$, $t \in TA_v^\otimes$ and $t' \in TA_v$. We say that C **behaviourally implements** A iff the above implication is an equivalence.

This definition of partial implementation generalises (8.3) to the order sorted case. The difference between partial implementation and implementation is that in the latter the mapping ϕ from $TA^\otimes$ to $TC^\otimes$, or more properly from $T_{\Sigma A^\otimes, EA^\otimes}$ to $T_{\Sigma C^\otimes, EC^\otimes}$, is injective on the visible sorts in the sense that it doesn't confuse distinct data values. Consequently, 'trivial' implementations, in which all equations are satisfied, are not allowed. If our definitions for HOSA had followed [8], in particular by requiring a fixed interpretation for visible data sorts, then $\phi : A \sqsubseteq C$ would imply that ϕ is injective on visible sorts because of their fixed interpretation. In the following, we concentrate on proofs of partial implementation, i.e., on showing that terms equal in the abstract specification are equal in the concrete.

We note that if ϕ is a signature inclusion and $\phi : A \sqsubseteq C$ then any behavioural algebra of C is also a behavioural algebra of A.

8.3.1   Proofs of partial implementation

One way to show that C implements A is to construct an intermediate relation R on C terms such that (a) if $t =_{EA^\otimes} t'$ then the ϕ-translations of t and t' are related by R, and (b) the restriction of R to visible sorted ϕ-translations is contained in $=_{EC^\otimes}$. Such a relation bridges the gap between the antecedent and consequent in Definition 29. If R is also a $\Sigma A^\otimes$-congruence, then (a) holds iff R extends the ground instances of the equations in $EA^\otimes$. This is the intuition behind Proposition 31 below, which is our main technical result. Its statement uses the following:

Notation 30 If R is a relation on $TC^\otimes$, then the relation R^ϕ on $TA^\otimes$ is defined for $t, t' \in TA^\otimes$ by: $t\ R^\phi\ t'$ iff $\phi(t)\ R\ \phi(t')$.

Proposition 31 $\phi : A \sqsubseteq C$ if there exists an equivalence relation R on $TC^\otimes$ such that R^ϕ is a $\Sigma A^\otimes$-congruence and

(8.6) $\bar{\theta}(lhs)\ R^\phi\ \bar{\theta}(rhs)$ for each $(\forall X)\ lhs{=}rhs \in EA^\otimes$ and $\theta : X \to TA^\otimes$,

(8.7)   if $t\ R^\phi t'$ then $\phi(t) =_{EC^\otimes} \phi(t')$ for all $v \in VA$, $t \in TA^\otimes_v$ and $t' \in TA_v$.

Proof: The relation $=_{EA^\otimes}$ is by definition the least $\Sigma A^\otimes$-congruence satisfying (8.6), so $=_{EA^\otimes} \subseteq R^\phi$. To show that $\phi : A \sqsubseteq C$, fix $v \in VA$, $t \in TA^\otimes_v$, $t' \in TA_v$; if $t =_{EA^\otimes} t'$ then because $=_{EA^\otimes} \subseteq R^\phi$, we have $t\ R^\phi\ t'$, and since t and t' are of visible sort, (8.7) gives $\phi(t) =_{EC^\otimes} \phi(t')$ as desired.

A weaker, but very useful version of this result is obtained by strengthening (8.6):

Proposition 32 For any relation R on $TC^\otimes$, condition (8.6) of Proposition 31 follows from

(8.8) $=_{EC^\otimes}\ \subseteq\ R$,

(8.9) $\bar{\theta}(lhs)\ R^\phi\ \bar{\theta}(rhs)$ for each $(\forall X)\ lhs{=}rhs \in EA$ and $\theta : X \to TA^\otimes$.

Proof: $EA^\otimes$ consists of EA plus equations of the form $(\forall S : s2)\ r_{s1,s2}(S) = S$. By construction, $EC^\otimes$ contains the equation $(\forall S' : \phi_1(s2))\ r_{\phi_1(s1),\phi_1(s2)}(S') = S'$, so for any $\theta : \{S\} \to TA^\otimes$, we have $\phi(\bar{\theta}(r_{s1,s2}(S))) = r_{\phi_1(s1),\phi_1(s2)}(\phi(\bar{\theta}(S))) =_{EC^\otimes} \phi(\bar{\theta}(S))$. Therefore by (8.8), $\bar{\theta}(r_{s1,s2}(S))\ R^\phi\ \bar{\theta}(S)$, and combining this with (8.9) gives (8.6).

The weakening of Proposition 31 by replacing (8.6) with (8.8) and (8.9) is useful because with (8.8), in proving that two terms are related by R we may freely rewrite those terms using the equations of $EC^\otimes$; moreover, the example relations R that we use below satisfy (8.8), so that in proving partial implementation, we may concentrate on proving (8.9), ignoring the retract equations.

To use these results, we need a suitable relation R. A likely candidate is behavioural equivalence, which we could define as in Definition 28; but the following relation is more general:

Definition 33 For $t, t' \in TC^{\otimes}$, **equivalence up to definition**, denoted $t \simeq t'$, is defined by: $t =_{EC^{\otimes}} t'' \Leftrightarrow t' =_{EC^{\otimes}} t''$ for all $t'' \in TC$.

Note that if $t, t' \in TC$, then $t \simeq t'$ iff $t =_{EC^{\otimes}} t'$.

Definition 34 For any relation R on $TC^{\otimes}$, **behavioural R-equivalence** is defined for $t, t' \in TC^{\otimes}$ by $t \, \tilde{R} \, t'$ iff $\phi(c)[t] \, R \, \phi(c)[t']$ for all $v \in VA$ and $c \in TA[z]_v^{\otimes}$.

Two natural choices for R in this definition are $=_{EC^{\otimes}}$ and $\simeq$. The first is sufficient for the examples given below, but the second is more general. Each choice satisfies condition (8.8):

Proposition 35 When R is $=_{EC^{\otimes}}$ or $\simeq$, then $=_{EC^{\otimes}} \subseteq \tilde{R}$.

We note that behavioural $=_{EC^{\otimes}}$-equivalence is the same as $=_{EC^{\otimes}}$ for visible sorts, because if t and t' are of visible sort, then we may take c to be the empty context, that is, $c = z$, so that $t =_{EC^{\otimes}} t'$.

In the sequel, we use only behavioural $\simeq$-equivalence, which we denote $\approx$, and refer to simply as **behavioural equivalence** i.e.,

(8.10) $t \approx t'$ iff $(\forall v \in V)(\forall c \in TA[z]_v^{\otimes}) \, \phi(c)[t] \simeq \phi(c)[t']$.

However, the results of this section can equally well be developed for behavioural $=_{EC^{\otimes}}$-equivalence.

The reader may check that $\approx$ satisfies all requirements of Proposition 31 except (8.6). From Propositions 32 and 35, we obtain:

Corollary 36 $\phi : A \sqsubseteq C$ if all equations of EA are behaviourally satisfied by C, i.e., if $\bar{\theta}(lhs) \approx^{\phi} \bar{\theta}(rhs)$ for each $(\forall X) lhs = rhs$ in EA and $\theta : X \to TA^{\otimes}$.

This result can still lead to complicated proofs by context induction. A simpler proof method is obtained by splitting the signature of $A^{\otimes}$ in two: suppose that $\Sigma A^{\otimes} = G \cup D$. (The letters stand for '**G**enerators' and '**D**efined functions' to suggest the decomposition that we have in mind; however, we make no assumptions about G or D.) Typically, in proving that an equation is behaviourally satisfied, we wish to show that it holds in contexts made from defined functions only. This agrees with the intuition behind behavioural equivalence, that two terms are behaviourally equivalent if the same visible information can be extracted from each of them. Extracting information corresponds to applying a defined function, whereas constructors may be thought of as adding new information. This gives a notion of behavioural equivalence that is easier to check:

Definition 37 For $t, t' \in TC^{\otimes}$, we define $t \smile t'$ iff $\phi(c)[t] \simeq \phi(c)[t']$ for all $v \in VA$ and $c \in TD[z]_v$, where $TD[z]_v$ denotes the set $T_D[z]_v$ of contexts built from the operations of D.

A useful consequence of this definition is that terms of hidden sort are behaviourally equivalent iff their images under each operation of D are behaviourally equivalent. This is used in Subsections 8.3.2 and 8.3.3, in examples where all derived functions are unary, an assumption that allows us to state the property concisely:

Proposition 38 If all the operations of D have only one argument, then for $h \in SA - VA$ and $t, t' \in TC_h^\otimes$, we have $t \smile t'$ iff $(\phi_2 f)(t) \smile (\phi_2 f)(t')$ for each $r \in SA$ and $f \in D_{h,r}$.

The relation $\smile$ is an equivalence relation, it contains $=_{EC^\otimes}$, and its restriction to visible sorts is the same as behavioural equivalence; moreover, $\smile^\phi$ is a D-congruence, so to use Proposition 32, we need only show that it is also a G-congruence. In fact, there is a nice relationship between our two notions of behavioural equivalence: from $D \subseteq \Sigma A^\otimes$, it follows that $\approx \subseteq \smile$; moreover, if $\smile$ is also a G-congruence then the following proposition shows that $\smile \subseteq \approx$, and so $\smile = \approx$.

Proposition 39 $\smile = \approx$ if $t \smile t'$ implies $(\phi_2 f)(x) \smile (\phi_2 f)(y)$ for all $f \in G_{l,s}$ and $t, t' \in TC_{\phi_1^*(l)}^\otimes$.

Proof: We have already noted that $\smile \supseteq \approx$, so it suffices to show that $\smile \subseteq \approx$. Now $\smile^\phi$ is a D-congruence, so if it is also a G-congruence (as stated in the condition above), then because $\Sigma A^\otimes = G \cup D$, it is a $\Sigma A^\otimes$-congruence. So:

$$t \smile t'$$
$$\Rightarrow \quad \{ \smile^\phi \text{ is a congruence } \}$$
$$(\forall v \in VA)(\forall c \in TA[z]_v^\otimes) \ \phi(c)[t] \smile \phi(c)[t']$$
$$\Rightarrow \quad \{ \smile|_{VA} \subseteq \simeq \}$$
$$(\forall v \in VA)(\forall c \in TA[z]_v^\otimes) \ \phi(c)[t] \simeq \phi(c)[t']$$
$$\Leftrightarrow \quad \{ (8.10) \}$$
$$t \approx t'$$

Corollary 36 and Proposition 39 together give the following sufficient condition for implementation:

Proposition 40 $\phi : A \sqsubseteq C$ if $\bar{\theta}(lhs) \smile^\phi \bar{\theta}(rhs)$ for each $(\forall X) lhs{=}rhs$ in EA and $\theta : X \to TA^\otimes$, and if $t \smile t'$ implies $(\phi_2 f)(t) \smile (\phi_2 f)(t')$ for all $f \in G_{l,s}$ and $t, t' \in TC_{\phi_1^*(l)}^\otimes$.

The following subsection shows that this proposition is especially useful when the operations of D are defined by structural induction over terms of G, because the second condition of the proposition then follows straightforwardly from the first.

8.3.2 A stack object

We now give an example proof of partial implementation using the technique developed in the previous subsection. The abstract specification defines a sort of stacks; a subsort relation makes operations **top** and **pop** defined only on non-empty stacks. The concrete specification implements stacks by means of arrays and pointers. This example, adapted from [4], is well-known, but we present it here to demonstrate that the proof we give is every bit as trivial as one could hope (cf. the statement in [3] that 'putting context induction into practise was less straightforward than expected').

The OBJ code which defines the abstract specification of stacks is given in the following two modules:

```
obj NAT is                       obj STACK is pr NAT .
  sort Nat .                       sorts  NeStack Stack .
  op  0 : -> Nat .                 subsort  NeStack < Stack .
  op  s : Nat -> Nat .             op  empty : -> Stack .
  op  p : Nat -> Nat .             op  push : Nat Stack -> NeStack .
  var N : Nat .                    op  top_ : NeStack -> Stack .
  eq  p(0)  =  0 .                 op  pop_ : NeStack -> Stack .
  eq  p(s(N))  =  N .              var S : Stack .   var I : Nat .
endo                               eq  top push(I,S)  =  I .
                                   eq  pop push(I,S)  =  S .
                                 endo
```

The OBJ keyword **sort** precedes the declaration of a sort name, and the keyword **op** precedes the declaration of an operation name; these declarations define the signature of the module. Equations are preceded by the keyword **eq**; these and the signature constitute the specification of the module. The keyword **pr** (for 'protecting') indicates that one module inherits the declarations of another; thus the module **STACK** contains all the declarations of the module **NAT**.

In order to demonstrate the use of signature morphisms in implementation, we give a concrete implementation of stacks using arrays and pointers that does not distinguish a subsort of non-empty stacks. The OBJ code for the concrete specification is given below:

```
obj ARR is pr NAT .
  sort  Arr .
  op  nil : -> Arr .
  op  put : Nat Arr Nat -> Arr .
  op  _[_] : Arr Nat -> Nat .
  var I M N : Nat .   var A : Arr .
  eq  nil[N]  =  0 .
  eq  put(I,A,M)[N]  =  if M == N then I else A[N] fi .
endo

obj STACK is pr ARR .
```

```
sort Stack .
op  <<_;_>> : Nat Arr -> Stack .
op  1st_ : Stack -> Nat .
op  2nd_ : Stack -> Arr .
op  empty : -> Stack .
op  push : Nat Stack -> Stack .
op  top_ : Stack -> Nat .
op  pop_ : Stack -> Stack .
var I N : Nat .   var S : Stack .   var A : Arr .
eq  1st << N ; A >>  =  N .
eq  2nd << N ; A >>  =  A .
eq  empty  =  << 0 ; nil >> .
eq  push(I,S)  =  << s(1st S) ; put(I, 2nd S, s(1st S)) >> .
eq  top S  =  (2nd S)[ 1st S ] .
eq  pop S  =  << p(1st S) ; 2nd S >> .
endo
```

The signature morphism ϕ from the abstract to the concrete specification maps both **NeStack** and **Stack** to the single sort **Stack**, and leaves the names of the operations unchanged. Note that the types of the operations *are* changed, because ϕ identifies **NeStack** and **Stack**. Specifically, ϕ is defined as follows.

$$
\begin{array}{rcl}
\texttt{Nat} & \mapsto & \texttt{Nat} \\
\texttt{Stack, NeStack} & \mapsto & \texttt{Stack} \\
\texttt{empty : -> Stack} & \mapsto & \texttt{empty : -> Stack} \\
\texttt{push : Nat Stack -> NeStack} & \mapsto & \texttt{push : Nat Stack -> Stack} \\
\texttt{top : NeStack -> Nat} & \mapsto & \texttt{top : Stack -> Nat} \\
\texttt{pop : NeStack -> Stack} & \mapsto & \texttt{pop : Stack -> Stack}
\end{array}
$$

If we let ΣA denote the signature of the abstract module, then $\Sigma A^{\otimes}$ also contains the retract operation

$$r_{\texttt{NeStack,Stack}} : \texttt{Stack -> NeStack} .$$

Because ϕ identifies **Stack** and **NeStack**, this operation is mapped to (cf. Proposition 26) the operation

$$r_{\texttt{Stack,Stack}} : \texttt{Stack -> Stack} .$$

But by Definition 20, the retract extension of the concrete specification includes the equation $(\forall S : \texttt{Stack})\ r_{\texttt{Stack,Stack}}(S) = S$, which means that $r_{\texttt{Stack,Stack}}$ is the identity function in the concrete specification, so we may safely ignore retracts in what follows. Moreover, since the names of the operations are unchanged by this mapping, we can denote the ϕ-translation of a term by the term itself.

We now prove that the implementation of **STACK** is a partial behavioural implementation, where the set of visible sorts is $\{\texttt{Nat}\}$. For G, the set of generators, we take $\{\texttt{empty}, \texttt{push}\}$; for D, the set of defined functions, we take $\{\texttt{top}, \texttt{pop}\}$.

By Proposition 40, there are two proof obligations. The first is that the left- and right-hand sides of each equation are related by ⌣ :

(8.11) top push(I, S) ⌣ I
(8.12) pop push(I, S) ⌣ S

The second proof obligation is that ⌣ is preserved by the operations of G. Since empty is a constant and ⌣ is reflexive, we need only consider push:

(8.13) x1 ⌣ x2 and s1 ⌣ s2 imply push(x1, s1) ⌣ push(x2, s2).

Requirement (8.11) is trivial, since the left-hand side is equal, in the concrete specification, to I. To show (8.12) and (8.13), we use the following:

Lemma 41 << 1st s ; put(x, 2nd s, n) >> ⌣ s if for all $i \geq 0$ it is not the case that $\mathbf{p}^i(\texttt{1st s}) =_{EC\otimes} \texttt{n}$ (i.e., if n > 1st s).

This can be proved by induction on the structure of contexts; only contexts built from top and pop need be considered.

Now, to show (8.12): note that pop push(I, S) is equal in the concrete specification to << 1st S ; put(I, 2nd S, s(1st S)) >> and by Lemma 41, this is related to S.

Similarly, (8.13) is demonstrated as follows:

$$
\begin{aligned}
& \texttt{push(x1,s1)} ⌣ \texttt{push(x2,s2)} \\
\Leftrightarrow \quad & \{\text{ Proposition 38 }\} \\
& \texttt{top push(x1,s1)} ⌣ \texttt{top push(x2,s2)} \ \wedge \\
& \texttt{pop push(x1,s1)} ⌣ \texttt{pop push(x2,s2)} \\
\Leftrightarrow \quad & \{\ \texttt{top push(X,S)}\ \text{reduces to}\ \texttt{X}\ \} \\
& \texttt{x1} ⌣ \texttt{x2} \ \wedge \ \texttt{pop push(x1,s1)} ⌣ \texttt{pop push(x2,s2)} \\
\Leftarrow \quad & \{\ (8.12)\ \} \\
& \texttt{x1} ⌣ \texttt{x2} \ \wedge \ \texttt{s1} ⌣ \texttt{s2}
\end{aligned}
$$

This concludes the proof of partial implementation. Lemma 41, which relates pop push(I, S) to S, is the only part of the proof that is not extremely trivial: the remainder of the proof consists of rewriting terms by using equations.

8.3.3 Several stack objects

Hidden sorted specification is well suited to the object paradigm because objects may be thought of as automata with hidden local states, whose behaviour is observable only through their visible inputs and outputs. The object oriented language FOOPS [10] distinguishes between sorts and classes: the former refer to abstract data types; the latter to abstract object classes. Thus, a FOOPS specification

distinguishes between hidden sorts for classes, and visible data sorts. A class of
objects is specified by declaring some *methods*, operations that modify the state
of an object, and some *attributes*, which give access to parts of an object's state.
A method is typically defined by equations which state how that method modifies
an object's attributes. Our proof technique is particularly useful in this context
because the operations in a FOOPS specification are divided into methods and
attributes, which correspond to generators and defined functions. In the following
example, we do not give all formal details, but rather the broad outlines of the
proof. In particular, we do not consider order sortedness.

The abstract specification (adapted from [10]) describes a class `Stackvar` of stack
variables. The signature comprises that of `NAT`, as in the previous subsection, the
class `Stackvar`, and the following operations:

```
me   push : Nat Stackvar -> Stackvar .
me   pop  : Stackvar -> Stackvar .
at   top  : Stackvar -> Nat .
at   rest : Stackvar -> Stackvar .
```

The FOOPS keyword 'me' declares a method; 'at' an attribute. The attribute `rest`
is intended to represent the 'tail' of a stack variable. Note that this attribute has
object values: one may think of stack variables as linked lists, whose state consists
of a natural number (its `top`), and a pointer to another stack variable (its `rest`).

The methods `push` and `pop` are defined by the following equations, where `N` is a
variable ranging over `Nat`, and `SV` is a variable ranging over `Stackvar`:

```
top pop SV  = top rest SV .
rest pop SV  =  rest rest SV .
top push(N,SV)  = N .
rest push(N,SV)  =  SV ! .
```

The postfix operation ! in the last equation is a polymorphic operation that exists
for all FOOPS classes. Its operational semantics is that `SV !` creates a copy of
the object `SV` that has the same attributes. That is, for any attribute `a` and object
`o`, we have `a(o !) = a(o)` .

We show that this specification is implemented by a concrete specification which
uses the abstract data type of stacks as defined in the previous subsection (though,
for the sake of simplicity, we ignore its order sorted aspects). The concrete specification comprises the class name `Stackvar`, and two operations, one which assigns
a value to a stack variable, and one which gives the value held by a stack variable:

```
me   _:=_ : Stackvar Stack -> Stackvar .
at   val_ : Stackvar -> Stack .
```

The assignment method (`:=`) is defined by the following equation, where `SV` is a
variable ranging over `Stackvar`, and `S` is a variable ranging over the sort `Stack`:

```
val (SV := S)  =  S .
```

Thus stack variables in the concrete specification may be thought of as cells which hold values of sort `Stack`.

The concrete implementation of the methods `push` and `pop`, and attributes `top` and `rest`, is defined by the following equations:

```
push(N,SV)  =  SV := push(N, val SV) .
pop SV  =  SV := pop val SV .
top SV  =  top val SV .
rest SV  =  SV ! := pop val SV .
```

The operations `push`, etc., in the right-hand sides of these equations are the operations from `STACK`. The last equation perhaps requires some explanation. In the abstract specification, the attribute `rest` returns an object that is different from its argument (hence '!'), with value the 'tail' of its argument (hence 'pop').

The visible equations of the abstract specification hold in the concrete as a result of these equations, so a proof of partial implementation need only consider the hidden equations:

```
rest pop SV  =  rest rest SV .
rest push(N,SV)  =  SV ! .
```

We use Proposition 40, with generators $G = \{\mathsf{push}, \mathsf{pop}\}$ and defined functions $D = \{\mathsf{top}, \mathsf{rest}\}$. This division is natural, because G contains all the methods of the abstract specification, and D all the attributes. The proof obligations are:

(8.14)   `rest pop SV` $\smile$ `rest rest SV`

(8.15)   `rest push(N,SV)` $\smile$ `SV !`

(8.16)   `SV1` $\smile$ `SV2` $\Rightarrow$ $\mathsf{push}(\mathsf{N}, \mathsf{SV1}) \smile \mathsf{push}(\mathsf{N}, \mathsf{SV2})$

(8.17)   `SV1` $\smile$ `SV2` $\Rightarrow$ `pop SV1` $\smile$ `pop SV2`

We use the following lemma.

Lemma 42 If `val SV1 = val SV2` then `SV1` $\smile$ `SV2`.

This lemma can be proved by induction on the structure of contexts built from D: since D contains only two operations, there are only two cases to consider.

Now (8.14) and (8.15) are easy consequences. To show (8.16):

$$\mathsf{push}(\mathsf{N}, \mathsf{SV1}) \smile \mathsf{push}(\mathsf{N}, \mathsf{SV2})$$

$\Leftrightarrow$ { Proposition 38 }

```
         top push(N,SV1) ⌣ top push(N,SV2)  ∧
         rest push(N,SV1) ⌣ rest push(N,SV2)
```

$\Leftrightarrow$ { first conjunct trivial, definition of push }

```
         rest (SV1 := push(N, val SV1)) ⌣
         rest (SV2 := push(N, val SV2))
```

$$\Leftrightarrow \qquad \{ \text{ definition of } \texttt{rest} \ \}$$

```
      (SV1:= push(N,val SV1))!   := val SV1  ⌣
      (SV2:= push(N,val SV2))!   := val SV2
```

$$\Leftarrow \qquad \{ \text{ see below } \}$$

```
      SV1 ⌣ SV2
```

The last step uses the fact that `SV := val SV′ ⌣ SV′`, which is a consequence of Lemma 42. Finally, (8.17) follows straightforwardly from Proposition 38 and (8.14); we conclude that the partial implementation is correct.

8.4   Conclusion

We have given a definition of implementation for hidden order sorted specifications, and a technique for proving correctness of partial implementation by proving behavioural satisfaction of equations in the concrete specification. This technique leads to proofs based on term rewriting which seem much simpler than other proofs in the literature. Our approach is directly applicable to the object paradigm by associating visible sorts with data types, and hidden sorts with object classes.

Hidden sorted algebra leads to an abstract treatment of states of objects, and to a similarly abstract treatment of object implementation. The treatment of object implementation given by Costa *et al.* [2] uses a concrete description of state in object specifications. Showing correctness of object implementation then requires a mapping from the states of the one object to the states of the other. In contrast, hidden sorted algebra provides a unified treatment of states, abstract data types and behaviour, abstracting away from details of how states are represented.

One question not addressed in this paper is concurrency. Hidden sorted specifications can be thought of as specifying networks of concurrent, interacting objects. Our approach to implementation is obviously applicable to serial evaluation by term rewriting (as in OBJ), but less obviously to concurrent models of computation. Goguen and Diaconescu [8] give a construction for the concurrent interconnection of collections of objects, and show how such interconnections can be enriched with interactions between component objects. We hope to develop a sheaf-theoretic semantics for FOOPS objects (as in [6]) which addresses such issues and extends our notion of implementation to concurrent, interacting systems.

Acknowledgements

The research reported in this paper has been supported in part by grants from the Science and Engineering Research Council, ESPRIT Working Group 6071, IS-CORE, and Fujitsu Laboratories Limited, and a contract with the Information Technology Promotion Agency, Japan, as part of the R & D of Basic Technology for Future Industries "New Models for Software Architecture" project sponsored by NEDO (New Energy and Industrial Technology Development Organization).

References

[1] Rod Burstall and Răzvan Diaconescu. Hiding and Behaviour: an institutional approach. This volume.

[2] José Felix Costa, Amilcar Sernadas, and Cristina Sernadas. Inductive objects. INESC, Lisbon, 1992.

[3] Marie Claude Gaudel and I. Privara. Context induction: an exercise. Technical Report 687, LRI, Univ. Paris Sud, 1991.

[4] Joseph Goguen. An algebraic approach to refinement. In Dines Bjorner, C.A.R. Hoare, and Hans Langmaack, editors, *Proceedings, VDM'90: VDM and Z – Formal Methods in Software Development*, pages 12–28. Springer, 1990. Lecture Notes in Computer Science, Volume 428.

[5] Joseph Goguen. Types as theories. In George Michael Reed, Andrew William Roscoe, and Ralph F. Wachter, editors, *Topology and Category Theory in Computer Science*, pages 357–390. Oxford, 1991. Proceedings of a Conference held at Oxford, June 1989.

[6] Joseph Goguen. Sheaf semantics for concurrent interacting objects. *Mathematical Structures in Computer Science*, 11:159–191, 1992. Given as lecture at Engeler Festschrift, Zürich, 7 March 1989, and at U.K.-Japan Symposium on Concurrency, Oxford, September 1989; draft as Report CSLI-91-155, Center for the Study of Language and Information, Stanford University, June 1991.

[7] Joseph Goguen and Răzvan Diaconescu. A survey of order sorted algebra, 1992. Submitted to *Mathematical Structures in Computer Science*.

[8] Joseph Goguen and Răzvan Diaconescu. Towards an algebraic semantics for the object paradigm. In *Proceedings, Tenth Workshop on Abstract Data Types*. Springer, to appear 1993.

[9] Joseph Goguen and José Meseguer. Universal realization, persistent interconnection and implementation of abstract modules. In M. Nielsen and E.M. Schmidt, editors, *Proceedings, 9th International Conference on Automata, Languages and Programming*, pages 265–281. Springer, 1982. Lecture Notes in Computer Science, Volume 140.

[10] Joseph Goguen and José Meseguer. Unifying functional, object-oriented and relational programming, with logical semantics. In Bruce Shriver and Peter Wegner, editors, *Research Directions in Object-Oriented Programming*, pages 417–477. MIT, 1987.

[11] Joseph Goguen and José Meseguer. Order-sorted algebra I: Equational deduction for multiple inheritance, overloading, exceptions and partial operations. *Theoretical Computer Science*, 105(2):217–273, 1992.

[12] Joseph Goguen, James Thatcher, and Eric Wagner. An initial algebra approach to the specification, correctness and implementation of abstract data types. Technical Report RC 6487, IBM T.J. Watson Research Center, October 1976. In *Current Trends in Programming Methodology, IV*, Raymond Yeh, editor, Prentice-Hall, 1978, pages 80–149.

[13] Joseph Goguen, Timothy Winkler, José Meseguer, Kokichi Futatsugi, and Jean-Pierre Jouannaud. Introducing OBJ. In Joseph Goguen, editor, *Applications of Algebraic Specification using OBJ*. Cambridge, to appear 1993. Also to appear as Technical Report from SRI International.

[14] Rolf Henniker. Context induction: a proof principle for behavioural abstractions. In A. Miola, editor, *Design and Implementation of Symbolic Computation Systems*. Springer-Verlag Lecture Notes in Computer Science 429, 1990.

[15] C.A.R. Hoare. Proof of correctness of data representations. *Acta Informatica*, 1:271–281, 1972.

[16] Lucia Rapanotti and Adolfo Socorro. Introducing FOOPS. Oxford University Computing Laboratory, 1992.

[17] Oliver Schoett. Behavioural correctness of data representations. *Science of Computer Programming*, pages 43–57, 1990.

Chapter 9

A Mechanized Hoare Logic of State Transitions

Mike Gordon

The field of programming logics stands on the foundation laid by C.A.R. Hoare in his seminal paper 'An axiomatic basis for computer programming' [8]. In that paper Hoare presented a calculus of formulae $P\{C\}Q$ meaning "If assertion P is true before initiation of a program C, then the assertion Q will be true on its completion." [1] Since 1969, research into Hoare logics has been a major topic in the theory of programming. Numerous variations and extensions of Hoare's original ideas have been developed. These have both been studied theoretically [1] and put into practice [3, 9]. This tradition is continued here. An interpretation of Hoare logic is described that is intended for the analysis of programs implementing real-time reactive systems. Versions of Hoare's original rules have been derived and form the basis for a prototype computer assisted program verifier. The aim has been to produce an automated system that uses 'Hoare-style' reasoning to establish both total correctness and 'fine grain' timing properties of programs. There already exist extensions of Hoare logic that enable the running time of programs to be analysed [11]. The work here extends and automates these. Formulae of the form $\{P\}$ C $\{Q\}$ $[I]$ $\langle t \rangle$ are introduced where P, Q and I are assertions, C is a command (i.e. a program) and t is a number. The meaning of such formulae is "If P is true and the instructions compiled from C are executed, then in at most t machine cycles the execution of C will terminate in a state satisfying Q and all intermediate states will satisfy I."

9.1 An Introductory Example

The simple example given in this section aims to convey the 'look and feel' of the verification method presented in subsequent sections. Some notations and concepts appear before they are properly introduced and as a result some of the details may be obscure.

---

[1]From now on $\{P\}$ C $\{Q\}$ will written instead of Hoare's original $P\{C\}Q$.

Consider the specification of the form $\{P\}\,\mathcal{C}\,\{Q\}\,[I]$ shown in box 1 below. $\mathcal{C}$ is an annotated command and P, Q, I are conditions on the values of program variables. The condition I is intended to hold throughout the computation (i.e. in the final state and all intermediate states), whereas Q is only intended to hold in the final state. The annotations in the command are an assertion after the first assignment and a variant [x] and invariant for the **while**-loop. Each time around the loop the invariant holds and the value of the variant decreases (values are assumed to be positive integers). Variables like x in teletype font are program variables; variables like x in italics are logical variables (also called 'ghost' or 'auxiliary' variables).

```
                                                              ┌─┐
  {x  =  x ∧ y  =  y}                                         │1│
    out  := 0;  {out  =  0   ∧   x = x   ∧   y = y}
    if  ¬(x = 0 ∨ y = 0)
      then  while   x > 0
              do  [x] {out  +  (x × y)  =  x × y   ∧   y = y}
                  out  := out + y;
                  x  := x − 1
  {out  =  x × y }
  [y  =  y]
```

The verifier initially generates eleven verification conditions. Ten of these are solved by the currently implemented simplifier leaving the following one for the user:

```
                                                              ┌─┐
  (out  +  (x × y)  = x × y)  ⇒                               │2│
  ¬(x  =  0)  ⇒
  ((out  + y)  + ((x  −  1) × y)  =  x × y)
```

This is proved manually and then the verifier generates the theorem shown in box 3 below, which has the form $\vdash \{P\}\,\mathcal{C}\,\{Q\}\,[I]\,\langle t\rangle$, where $\mathcal{C}$ is the un-annotated multiplication program, MultProg, say. Such augmented Hoare specifications mean that $\{P\}\,\mathcal{C}\,\{Q\}$ holds (interpreted as a total correctness specification), the execution of $\mathcal{C}$ requires at most t cycles and all intermediate states satisfy I.

```
                                                              ┌─┐
  ⊢ {x  =  x ∧ y  =  y}                                       │3│
      out  := 0;
      if  ¬(x = 0 ∨ y = 0)
        then  while   x > 0
                do
                    out  := out + y;
                    x  := x − 1
  {out  =  x × y }
  [y  =  y]
  ⟨15 + (13×x)⟩
```

Thus the multiplication takes at most $15 + (13 \times x)$ machine cycles, where x is the initial value of x and the value of program variable y remains stable throughout the computation. This bound on the number of cycles is computed (and verified) automatically. The semantics of $\{P\}\ \mathcal{C}\ \{Q\}\ [I]\ \langle t\rangle$ is formulated directly in terms of state transitions made by machine instructions compiled from $\mathcal{C}$. The machine MultMachine in box 4 is defined by the sequence of instructions obtained by compiling MultProg (see 9.4). The instruction numbers %n% are comments.

```
                                                               4
MultMachine  =  Machine  [OP0 0;        %0 %
                          PUT out;      %1 %
                          GET x;        %2 %
                          OP1 ¬;        %3 %
                          GET y;        %4 %
                          OP1 ¬;        %5 %
                          OP2 ∨;        %6 %
                          OP1 ¬;        %7 %
                          JMZ 22;       %8 %
                          GET x;        %9 %
                          OP0 0;        %10%
                          OP2 >;        %11%
                          JMZ 22;       %12%
                          GET out;      %13%
                          GET y;        %14%
                          OP2 +;        %15%
                          PUT out;      %16%
                          GET x;        %17%
                          OP0 1;        %18%
                          OP2 −;        %19%
                          PUT x;        %20%
                          JMP 9]        %21%
```

Expanding the theorem of the form $\{P\}\ \mathcal{C}\ \{Q\}\ [I]\ \langle t\rangle$ into its semantics yields the state transition assertion (or STA) [6] in box 5. State transition assertions are defined in 9.7. They are formulae of the form:

$$\mathcal{M} \models A \xrightarrow{\mathcal{I}} B$$

which means "If machine $\mathcal{M}$ is in a state satisfying A then a state satisfying B will be reached and the sequence of intermediate states will satisfy $\mathcal{I}$."

In the STA in box 5, vertical stacking means conjunction, At m is true when the program counter is m, $[I]$ is true of a sequence if I is true of all elements in the sequence and By m is true of any sequence of length less than m.

```
                                                               5
                              By(15 + (13 × x))
                     At 0     [y = y]
MultMachine  ⊨       x = x    ─────────────────→   At 22
                     y = y                          out = x × y
```

This says that if control is at instruction number 0 and the values in locations x and y are x and y, respectively, then within $15 + (13 \times x)$ cycles control will reach instruction 22 and the value of out will then be $x \times y$ and the value of y will have remained stable throughout the computation. A similar state transition assertion going from instruction n to instruction $n + 22$ could be deduced if the compiled instructions from MultProg were loaded at position n in memory.

This result is a worst case analysis. If further information is known about the starting state, then a tighter time bound may be provable. For example, in the following annotated specification the precondition has the extra assumption $x = 0$ and the conditional has been annotated with [F] (which is necessary for the verification condition generator – see 9.6).

```
{x = x ∧ y = y ∧ x = 0}                                              6
  out := 0;  {out = 0  ∧  x = x  ∧  y = y ∧ x = 0}
  if ¬(x = 0 ∨ y = 0) [F]
    then while  x > 0
            do [x] {out + (x × y) = x × y  ∧  y = y}
               out := out + y;
               x := x − 1
{out = x × y }
[y  =  y]
```

The five verification conditions (see 9.6.5) from this are all solved automatically and the resulting STA follows:

```
                                                                     7

                        At 0      By 11
                        x = x     [y = y]      At 22
MultMachine  ⊨          y = y   ───────────→   out = x × y
                        x = 0
```

This shows that if x is initially 0 then the computation takes at most 11 cycles. The STAs in boxes 5 and 7 can be combined into a single STA covering both cases:

```
                                                                     8

                               By(x = 0  →  11 | 15 + (13 × x))
                        At 0      [y = y]
MultMachine  ⊨          x = x   ─────────────────────────────→   At 22
                        y = y                                    out = x × y
```

where $b \rightarrow p \mid q$ is the conditional *if b then p else q*.

9.2   Overview

The verifier illustrated in the previous section is built on top of a version of Hoare logic for judgements of the form $\{P\}\ \mathcal{C}\ \{Q\}\ [I]\ \langle t \rangle$. This, in turn, is built on top of the theory of state transition assertions and a compiler for a simple programming language. Finally, these are defined directly in higher order logic. Here's a diagram:

Verification conditions	
Hoare logic of STAs	
Theory of STAs	Compiler
Higher order logic	

The approach is purely definitional in that each layer is defined in terms of the concepts of a lower one. The theory of STAs and their use in reasoning about machine instructions is described elsewhere [6]. To make this paper self-contained, a simplified version of the theory is outlined in 9.7. The general idea of mechanising Hoare logics by generating verification conditions and then feeding them to a theorem prover is standard [3, 5, 13]. The particular approach used here was originally developed for non-timed Hoare logics [4]. Verification conditions are described in 9.6. The main contribution of this paper is to make the use of STAs for reasoning about data-processing algorithms much easier by defining a Hoare logic on top of them.

9.3 Timed Hoare Specifications

The syntax of expressions $\mathcal{E}$ and commands $\mathcal{C}$ is given by the following BNF, where $\mathcal{N}$ ranges over the natural numbers, $\mathcal{V}$ ranges over the set *Var* of program variables, $\mathcal{U}$ ranges over unary operators and $\mathcal{B}$ ranges over binary operators.

$$\mathcal{E} \ ::= \ \mathcal{N} \ | \ \mathcal{V} \ | \ \mathcal{U} \, \mathcal{E} \ | \ \mathcal{E}_1 \, \mathcal{B} \, \mathcal{E}_2$$

$$
\begin{aligned}
\mathcal{C} \ ::= \ & \mathcal{V} := \mathcal{E} \\
| \ & \mathcal{C}_1 \ ; \ \mathcal{C}_2 \\
| \ & \textbf{if } \mathcal{E} \textbf{ then } \mathcal{C} \\
| \ & \textbf{if } \mathcal{E} \textbf{ then } \mathcal{C}_1 \textbf{ else } \mathcal{C}_2 \\
| \ & \textbf{while } \mathcal{E} \textbf{ do } \mathcal{C}
\end{aligned}
$$

This BNF syntax is ambiguous; if necessary, brackets will be used to disambiguate particular examples.

Expressions and commands are executed by translating them to sequences of instructions for a simple stack machine and then running the resulting machine code programs. The state of the target machine is a triple (pc, stk, mem) consisting of a program counter $pc : \mathbb{N}$, a stack $stk : \text{seq} \, \mathbb{N}$ and a memory $mem : Var \rightarrow \mathbb{N}$.

The meaning of timed Hoare specifications $\{P\} \, \mathcal{C} \, \{Q\} \, [I] \, \langle t \rangle$ is defined in terms of the execution of instructions compiled from $\mathcal{C}$.

The specification $\{P\} \, \mathcal{C} \, \{Q\} \, [I] \, \langle t \rangle$ is true iff [2] whenever the program counter points to the beginning of the instructions compiled from C and P is true then the target machine goes through a sequence of states satisfying I and reaches within t steps a state in which Q is true and the program counter points to the end of instructions compiled from C.

This informal definition is refined and formalised in 9.7 using state transition assertions.

---

[2] "iff" abbreviates "if and only if".

9.4   A Simple Machine and Compiler

Programs are compiled to sequences of instructions from the following instruction set:

JMP n	unconditional jump to instruction n
JMZ n	pop stack then jump to instruction n if the result is zero
JMN n	pop stack then jump to instruction n if the result is non-zero
POP	pop the top of the stack
OP0 v	push v onto the stack
OP1 $\mathcal{U}$	pop one value from stack, perform unary operation $\mathcal{U}$, push result
OP2 $\mathcal{B}$	pop two values from stack, perform binary operation $\mathcal{B}$, push result
GET x	push the contents of memory location x onto the stack
INP i	push the input from i onto the stack
PUT x	pop the top of the stack and store the result in memory location x

Let $[\![\mathcal{E}]\!]$ denote the instructions that expression $\mathcal{E}$ compiles to and let $s_1 \frown s_2$ denote the concatenation of sequences s_1 and s_2, then:

$$
\begin{aligned}
[\![\mathcal{N}]\!] &= \text{OP0 } \mathcal{N} \\
[\![\mathcal{V}]\!] &= \text{GET } \mathcal{V} \\
[\![\mathcal{U}\ \mathcal{E}]\!] &= [\![\mathcal{E}]\!] \frown \text{OP1 } \mathcal{U} \\
[\![\mathcal{E}_1\ \mathcal{B}\ \mathcal{E}_2]\!] &= [\![\mathcal{E}_1]\!] \frown [\![\mathcal{E}_2]\!] \frown \text{OP2 } \mathcal{B}
\end{aligned}
$$

It is easy to prove that if $|\mathcal{E}|$ is the number of instructions in $[\![\mathcal{E}]\!]$ then:

$$
\begin{aligned}
|\mathcal{N}| &= 1 \\
|\mathcal{V}| &= 1 \\
|\mathcal{U}\ \mathcal{E}| &= |\mathcal{E}| + 1 \\
|\mathcal{E}_1\ \mathcal{B}\ \mathcal{E}_2| &= |\mathcal{E}_1| + |\mathcal{E}_2| + 1
\end{aligned}
$$

Let $[\![\mathcal{C}]\!]\ n$ be the sequence of instructions that command $\mathcal{C}$ compiles to if the first instruction is placed at position n. Let $|\mathcal{C}|$ be the number of instructions in $[\![\mathcal{C}]\!]$, then:

$$
\begin{aligned}
|\mathcal{V} := \mathcal{E}| &= |\mathcal{E}| + 1 \\
|\mathcal{C}_1\ ;\ \mathcal{C}_2| &= |\mathcal{C}_1| + |\mathcal{C}_2| \\
|\textbf{if } \mathcal{E} \textbf{ then } \mathcal{C}| &= |\mathcal{E}| + |\mathcal{C}| + 1 \\
|\textbf{if } \mathcal{E} \textbf{ then } \mathcal{C}_1 \textbf{ else } \mathcal{C}_2| &= |\mathcal{E}| + |\mathcal{C}_1| + |\mathcal{C}_2| + 2 \\
|\textbf{while } \mathcal{E} \textbf{ do } \mathcal{C}| &= |\mathcal{E}| + |\mathcal{C}| + 2
\end{aligned}
$$

and

$$[\![\mathcal{V} := \mathcal{E}]\!]\ n \qquad\qquad = \ [\![\mathcal{E}]\!] \frown \mathrm{PUT}\ \mathcal{V}$$

$$[\![\mathcal{C}_1\ ;\ \mathcal{C}_2]\!]\ n \qquad\qquad = \ [\![\mathcal{C}_1]\!]\ n \frown [\![\mathcal{C}_2]\!](n+|\mathcal{C}_1|)$$

$$[\![\textbf{if }\mathcal{E}\textbf{ then }\mathcal{C}]\!]\ n \qquad = \ [\![\mathcal{E}]\!] \frown \mathrm{JMZ}(n+|\mathcal{E}|+|\mathcal{C}|+1) \frown [\![\mathcal{C}]\!](n+|\mathcal{E}|+1)$$

$$[\![\textbf{if }\mathcal{E}\textbf{ then }\mathcal{C}_1\textbf{ else }\mathcal{C}_2]\!]\ n \ = \ [\![\mathcal{E}]\!] \frown \mathrm{JMZ}(n+|\mathcal{E}|+|\mathcal{C}_1|+2) \frown [\![\mathcal{C}_1]\!](n+|\mathcal{E}|+1)$$
$$\frown \mathrm{JMP}(n+|\mathcal{E}|+|\mathcal{C}_1|+|\mathcal{C}_2|+2) \frown [\![\mathcal{C}_2]\!](n+|\mathcal{E}|+|\mathcal{C}_1|+2)$$

$$[\![\textbf{while }\mathcal{E}\textbf{ do }\mathcal{C}]\!]\ n \qquad = \ [\![\mathcal{E}]\!] \frown \mathrm{JMZ}(n+|\mathcal{E}|+|\mathcal{C}|+2) \frown [\![\mathcal{C}]\!](n+|\mathcal{E}|+1) \frown \mathrm{JMP}\ n$$

9.5   A Timed Hoare Logic

The axioms and rules in this section can all be derived from the definition of $\{P\}\ C\ \{Q\}\ [I]\ \langle t\rangle$ given in 9.7 below.

9.5.1   The assignment axiom

The notation $P[\mathcal{E}/\mathcal{V}]$ denotes the result of substituting $\mathcal{E}$ for $\mathcal{V}$ in P. The assignment axiom states:

$$\vdash \{P[\mathcal{E}/\mathcal{V}]\}\ \mathcal{V}\text{:=}\mathcal{E}\ \{P\}\ [P \vee P[\mathcal{E}/\mathcal{V}]]\ \langle|\mathcal{E}|+1\rangle$$

The assignment takes one more cycle than the evaluation of $\mathcal{E}$ and during its execution the value of $\mathcal{V}$ is either its initial value or the value of $\mathcal{E}$.

9.5.2   The sequencing rule

$$\frac{\vdash \{P\}\ C_1\ \{Q\}\ [I_1]\ \langle t_1\rangle \qquad \vdash \{Q\}\ C_2\ \{R\}\ [I_2]\ \langle t_2\rangle}{\vdash \{P\}\ C_1;\ C_2\ \{R\}\ [I_1 \vee I_2]\ \langle t_1 + t_2\rangle}$$

The time taken to execute $C_1;C_2$ is the sum of the times taken by C_1 and C_2 and throughout the combined computation either I_1 or I_2 holds of the memory. The invariant could probably be strengthened to say that first I_1 and then I_2 holds; this could be expressed with a 'chop' operator from interval temporal logic [10]. So far this strengthening has not been needed and the rule above has been sufficient.

9.5.3   The conditional rules

The one-armed conditional rule is:

$$\frac{\vdash \{P \wedge \mathcal{E}\}\, \mathcal{C}\, \{Q\}\, [I]\, \langle t \rangle \qquad \vdash P \wedge \neg \mathcal{E} \Rightarrow Q \qquad \vdash P \Rightarrow I}{\vdash \{P\}\, \textbf{if } \mathcal{E}\, \textbf{then}\, \mathcal{C}\, \{Q\}\, [I]\, \langle |\mathcal{E}| + t + 1 \rangle}$$

The time taken by **if** $\mathcal{E}$ **then** $\mathcal{C}$ is at most the time taken to evaluate $\mathcal{E}$ plus the time taken to execute $\mathcal{C}$ plus 1. If the invariant I is initially true and its truth is maintained by $\mathcal{C}$, then it is true throughout the entire computation of the conditional.

If it is known that the test $\mathcal{E}$ is false, then the time bound can be improved and the invariant strengthened to the precondition (since expression evaluations cannot change the memory).

$$\frac{\vdash P \Rightarrow \neg \mathcal{E}}{\vdash \{P\}\, \textbf{if } \mathcal{E}\, \textbf{then}\, \mathcal{C}\, \{P\}\, [P]\, \langle |\mathcal{E}| + 1 \rangle}$$

The two-armed conditional rule is:

$$\frac{\begin{array}{c} \vdash \{P \wedge \mathcal{E}\}\, \mathcal{C}_1\, \{Q\}\, [I_1]\, \langle t_1 \rangle \\ \vdash \{P \wedge \neg \mathcal{E}\}\, \mathcal{C}_2\, \{Q\}\, [I_2]\, \langle t_2 \rangle \\ \vdash P \wedge \mathcal{E} \Rightarrow I_1 \\ \vdash P \wedge \neg \mathcal{E} \Rightarrow I_2 \end{array}}{\vdash \{P\}\, \textbf{if } \mathcal{E}\, \textbf{then}\, \mathcal{C}_1\, \textbf{else}\, \mathcal{C}_2\, \{Q\}\, [I_1 \vee I_2]\, \langle |\mathcal{E}| + \mathsf{Max}(t_1, t_2) + 2 \rangle}$$

The time taken to execute **if** $\mathcal{E}$ **then** $\mathcal{C}_1$ **else** $\mathcal{C}_2$ is at most the time taken to evaluate $\mathcal{E}$ plus the maximum of the times taken to execute $\mathcal{C}_1$ and $\mathcal{C}_2$ plus 2. If when $\mathcal{C}_1$ is executed then I_1 holds throughout the computation and when $\mathcal{C}_2$ is executed I_2 holds, then $I_1 \vee I_2$ holds no matter what arm of the conditional is taken.

If the precondition P determines the value of $\mathcal{E}$, then a tighter time bound can be derived. In the case that P forces $\mathcal{E}$ to be true:

$$\frac{\vdash \{P\}\, \mathcal{C}_1\, \{Q\}\, [I]\, \langle t \rangle \qquad \vdash P \Rightarrow \mathcal{E} \qquad \vdash P \Rightarrow I}{\vdash \{P\}\, \textbf{if } \mathcal{E}\, \textbf{then}\, \mathcal{C}_1\, \textbf{else}\, \mathcal{C}_2\, \{Q\}\, [I]\, \langle |\mathcal{E}| + t + 2 \rangle}$$

In the case that P forces $\mathcal{E}$ to be false:

$$\frac{\vdash \{P\}\, \mathcal{C}_2\, \{Q\}\, [I]\, \langle t \rangle \qquad \vdash P \Rightarrow \neg \mathcal{E} \qquad \vdash P \Rightarrow I}{\vdash \{P\}\, \textbf{if } \mathcal{E}\, \textbf{then}\, \mathcal{C}_1\, \textbf{else}\, \mathcal{C}_2\, \{Q\}\, [I]\, \langle |\mathcal{E}| + t + 1 \rangle}$$

The reason for "2" in the time bound when $\mathcal{E}$ is true, but "1" when it is false is that the compiler generates a jump instruction from after the code for $\mathcal{C}_1$ to the end of the conditional. This jump is not executed if the **else**-arm is taken.

9.5.4   The while rule

In the rule that follows $\mathcal{V}$ is a variant, i.e. a variable whose value strictly decreases each time around the loop; note that all values are natural numbers, so the value of $\mathcal{V}$ cannot be negative. The function WhileTime is defined by:

$$\mathsf{WhileTime}(e, t, n) \quad =_{def} \quad e \; + \; 1 \; + \; n \times (e + t + 2)$$

$\mathsf{WhileTime}(e, t, n)$ is an upper bound on the number of cycles taken to execute n iterations of **while** $\mathcal{E}$ **do** $\mathcal{C}$, where e is an upper bound on the number of cycles to evaluate $\mathcal{E}$ and t is an upper bound on the number of cycles to execute $\mathcal{C}$.

$$\frac{\vdash \; \forall v. \; \{P \wedge \mathcal{E} \wedge \mathcal{V} = v\} \; \mathcal{C} \; \{P \wedge \mathcal{V} < v\} \; [I] \; \langle t \rangle \qquad\qquad \vdash \; P \Rightarrow I}{\vdash \; \forall v. \; \{P \wedge \mathcal{V} = v\} \; \textbf{while } \mathcal{E} \textbf{ do } \mathcal{C} \; \{P \wedge \neg \mathcal{E}\} \; [I] \; \langle \mathsf{WhileTime}(|\mathcal{E}|, t, v) \rangle}$$

If it is known that $\mathcal{E}$ is false, then the body of the while loop is never executed. This is reflected in the following rule.

$$\frac{\vdash \; P \Rightarrow \neg \mathcal{E}}{\vdash \; \{P\} \textbf{ while } \mathcal{E} \textbf{ do } \mathcal{C} \; \{P\} \; [P] \; \langle |\mathcal{E}| + 1 \rangle}$$

9.5.5   The consequence rule

Preconditions can be strengthened and postconditions, invariants and time-bounds weakened:

$$\frac{\begin{array}{c} \vdash \; \{P\} \; \mathcal{C} \; \{Q\} \; [I] \; \langle t \rangle \\ \vdash \; P' \Rightarrow P \\ \vdash \; Q \Rightarrow Q' \\ \vdash \; I \Rightarrow I' \\ \vdash \; t \leq t' \end{array}}{\vdash \; \{P'\} \; \mathcal{C} \; \{Q'\} \; [I'] \; \langle t' \rangle}$$

9.5.6   The cases rule

$$\frac{\begin{array}{c} \vdash \; \{P_1\} \; \mathcal{C} \; \{Q\} \; [I] \; \langle t \rangle \\ \vdash \; \{P_2\} \; \mathcal{C} \; \{Q\} \; [I] \; \langle t \rangle \end{array}}{\vdash \; \{P_1 \vee P_2\} \; \mathcal{C} \; \{Q\} \; [I] \; \langle t \rangle}$$

9.5.7   An example proof

The following proof establishes the specification in box 6 on page 146.

1. By the assignment axiom:

$$\vdash \{\mathsf{x} = x \wedge \mathsf{y} = y \wedge x = 0 \wedge 0 = 0\}$$
  out := 0
$$\{\mathsf{x} = x \wedge \mathsf{y} = y \wedge x = 0 \wedge \mathsf{out} = 0\}$$
$$[(\mathsf{x} = x \wedge \mathsf{y} = y \wedge x = 0 \wedge \mathsf{out} = 0) \vee (\mathsf{x} = x \wedge \mathsf{y} = y \wedge x = 0 \wedge 0 = 0)]$$
$$\langle 2 \rangle$$

2. By the consequence rule this entails:

$$\vdash \{\mathsf{x} = x \wedge \mathsf{y} = y \wedge x = 0\}$$
  out := 0
$$\{\mathsf{x} = x \wedge \mathsf{y} = y \wedge x = 0 \wedge \mathsf{out} = 0\}$$
$$[\mathsf{y} = y]$$
$$\langle 2 \rangle$$

3. Since $(\mathsf{x} = x \wedge \mathsf{y} = y \wedge x = 0 \wedge \mathsf{out} = 0) \Rightarrow \neg(\neg(\mathsf{x} = 0 \vee \mathsf{y} = 0))$ and $|\neg(\mathsf{x} = 0 \vee \mathsf{y} = 0)| = 8$, it follows by the second one-armed conditional rule (the one for when the test is false) that:

$$\vdash \{\mathsf{x} = x \wedge \mathsf{y} = y \wedge x = 0 \wedge \mathsf{out} = 0\}$$
  if $\neg(\mathsf{x} = 0 \vee \mathsf{y} = 0)$ then $\mathcal{C}$
$$\{\mathsf{x} = x \wedge \mathsf{y} = y \wedge x = 0 \wedge \mathsf{out} = 0\}$$
$$[\mathsf{x} = x \wedge \mathsf{y} = y \wedge x = 0 \wedge \mathsf{out} = 0]$$
$$\langle 9 \rangle$$

4. This simplifies by the consequence rule to:

$$\vdash \{\mathsf{x} = x \wedge \mathsf{y} = y \wedge x = 0 \wedge \mathsf{out} = 0\}$$
  if $\neg(\mathsf{x} = 0 \vee \mathsf{y} = 0)$ then $\mathcal{C}$
$$\{\mathsf{out} = x \times y\}$$
$$[\mathsf{y} = y]$$
$$\langle 9 \rangle$$

5. Applying the sequencing rule to 2 and 4 yields:

$$\vdash \{\mathsf{x} = x \wedge \mathsf{y} = y \wedge x = 0 \wedge \mathsf{out} = 0\}$$
  out := 0;
   if $\neg(\mathsf{x} = 0 \vee \mathsf{y} = 0)$
    then $\mathcal{C}$
$$\{\mathsf{out} = x \times y\}$$
$$[\mathsf{y} = y]$$
$$\langle 11 \rangle$$

9.6   Verification Conditions

The proof in the previous section was a sequence of lines each of which was an axiom or followed from earlier lines by a rule of inference. Such forward proofs are tedious to produce. An alternative is to proceed backwards, by starting from the goal to be proved and then splitting this into subgoals, subsubgoals, etc., until instances of axioms are reached. A traditional way of organizing such goal-directed proofs is to use verification conditions [3, 13]. The idea is to generate from a goal $\{P\}\ C\ \{Q\}$ a set of purely logical formulae – the verification conditions – that have the property that if they are true then the Hoare specification from which they were generated is also true. To enable verification conditions to be easily generated, the command C needs to be annotated with hints; in particular the variant and invariants for while loops need to be supplied (though attempts have been made to generate this information automatically [14]). The verification conditions are generated by a straightforward recursion on the structure of C.

Verification conditions are related to Dijkstra's weakest preconditions [2], though they predate it. Dijkstra's idea was to replace $\{P\}\ C\ \{Q\}$ by the purely logical formula $P \Rightarrow \mathsf{wp}(C, Q)$, where $\mathsf{wp}(C, Q)$ is the weakest precondition for C to establish Q. The rules for calculating $P \Rightarrow \mathsf{wp}(C, Q)$ are similar to the rules for generating verification conditions from $\{P\}\ C\ \{Q\}$.

The verifier described here requires the variant and invariant of all while loops to be supplied, as well as an assertion before each command in a sequence that is not an assignment. These assertions should be statements that are true when control reaches the point at which they occur. Additional optional assertions of the form [T] or [F] may also be added after the test in conditional and while commands; these indicate the truth value of the test.

A goal has the form $\{P\}\ C\ \{Q\}\ [I]$, where C is an annotated command. It is assumed that each while command has a distinct variant v (and associated auxiliary variable v) and that for each such variant there is a conjunct $\mathsf{v} = v$ in P. The annotations in C enable an expression $\mathsf{Time}\ C$ to be computed syntactically that gives a bound on the running time of C in terms of the initial values of the variants.

$$
\begin{aligned}
\mathsf{Time}(\mathcal{V} := \mathcal{E}) &= |\mathcal{E}| + 1 \\
\mathsf{Time}(\mathcal{C}_1\ ;\ \mathcal{C}_2) &= \mathsf{Time}\ \mathcal{C}_1 + \mathsf{Time}\ \mathcal{C}_2 \\
\mathsf{Time}(\mathcal{C}_1\ ;\ \{R\}\ \mathcal{C}_2) &= \mathsf{Time}\ \mathcal{C}_1 + \mathsf{Time}\ \mathcal{C}_2 \\
\mathsf{Time}(\textbf{if}\ \mathcal{E}\ \textbf{then}\ \mathcal{C}) &= |\mathcal{E}| + \mathsf{Time}\ \mathcal{C} + 1 \\
\mathsf{Time}(\textbf{if}\ \mathcal{E}\ [\mathsf{F}]\ \textbf{then}\ \mathcal{C}) &= |\mathcal{E}| + 1 \\
\mathsf{Time}(\textbf{if}\ \mathcal{E}\ \textbf{then}\ \mathcal{C}_1\ \textbf{else}\ \mathcal{C}_2) &= \mathsf{Time}\ \mathcal{E} + \mathsf{Max}(\mathsf{Time}\ \mathcal{C}_1, \mathsf{Time}\ \mathcal{C}_2) + 2 \\
\mathsf{Time}(\textbf{if}\ \mathcal{E}\ [\mathsf{T}]\ \textbf{then}\ \mathcal{C}_1\ \textbf{else}\ \mathcal{C}_2) &= \mathsf{Time}\ \mathcal{E} + \mathsf{Time}\ \mathcal{C}_1 + 2 \\
\mathsf{Time}(\textbf{if}\ \mathcal{E}\ [\mathsf{F}]\ \textbf{then}\ \mathcal{C}_1\ \textbf{else}\ \mathcal{C}_2) &= \mathsf{Time}\ \mathcal{E} + \mathsf{Time}\ \mathcal{C}_2 + 1 \\
\mathsf{Time}(\textbf{while}\ \mathcal{E}\ \textbf{do}\ [\mathsf{v}]\ \{R\}\ \mathcal{C}) &= \mathsf{WhileTime}\ (|\mathcal{E}|, \mathsf{Time}\ \mathcal{C}, v) \\
\mathsf{Time}(\textbf{while}\ \mathcal{E}\ [\mathsf{F}]\ \textbf{do}\ [\mathsf{v}]\ \{R\}\ \mathcal{C}) &= |\mathcal{E}| + 1
\end{aligned}
$$

For example, $\mathsf{Time}(\mathsf{out} := \mathsf{out} + \mathsf{y};\ \ \mathsf{x} := \mathsf{x} - 1)$ simplifies to 8 and $\mathsf{Time}\ \mathsf{MultProg}$ (where $\mathsf{MultProg}$ is the command in box 1 on page 144) simplifies to $15 + (13 \times x)$.

When the verifier is invoked with a goal $\{P\}\, \mathcal{C}\, \{Q\}\, [I]$, it tries to prove the specification $\{P\}\, \mathcal{C}\, \{Q\}\, [I]\, \langle \mathsf{Time}\, \mathcal{C} \rangle$ using a set of derived rules 'backwards'. It matches the specification with the conclusions of these rules (which are given below) and then generates subgoals consisting of the hypotheses of the (unique) rule that matched. [3] This process is repeated on the subgoals until they are all reduced to purely logical formulae. These formulae are then mechanically simplified and those that do not reduce to true are returned as the verification conditions. It is clear that if the verification conditions are proved then the rules may be applied in the 'forward' direction to establish the original goal. A more detailed discussion of this process can be found elsewhere [4, 5].

The following rules generate the verification conditions; they can be derived from the axioms and rules given in 9.5.

9.6.1   Assignments

$$\frac{\vdash\, P\, \Rightarrow\, Q[\mathcal{E}/\mathcal{V}] \qquad Q \lor Q[\mathcal{E}/\mathcal{V}]\, \Rightarrow\, I}{\vdash\, \{P\}\, \mathcal{V} := \mathcal{E}\, \{Q\}\, [I]\, \langle \mathsf{Time}(\mathcal{V} := \mathcal{E}) \rangle}$$

9.6.2   Sequencing

$$\frac{\vdash\, \{P\}\, \mathcal{C}_1\, \{R\}\, [I]\, \langle \mathsf{Time}\, \mathcal{C}_1 \rangle \qquad \vdash\, \{R\}\, \mathcal{C}_2\, \{Q\}\, [I]\, \langle \mathsf{Time}\, \mathcal{C}_2 \rangle}{\vdash\, \{P\}\, \mathcal{C}_1;\, \{R\}\, \mathcal{C}_2\, \{Q\}\, [I]\, \langle \mathsf{Time}(\mathcal{C}_1\, ;\, \mathcal{C}_2) \rangle}$$

$$\frac{\vdash\, \{P\}\, \mathcal{C}\, \{Q[\mathcal{E}/\mathcal{V}]\}\, [I]\, \langle \mathsf{Time}\, \mathcal{C} \rangle}{\vdash\, \{P\}\, \mathcal{C};\, \mathcal{V} := \mathcal{E}\, \{Q\}\, [I]\, \langle \mathsf{Time}(\mathcal{C}\, ;\, \mathcal{V} := \mathcal{E}) \rangle}$$

9.6.3   Conditionals

$$\frac{\vdash\, \{P \land \mathcal{E}\}\, \mathcal{C}\, \{Q\}\, [I]\, \langle \mathsf{Time}\, \mathcal{C} \rangle \qquad \vdash\, P \land \neg\mathcal{E}\, \Rightarrow\, Q \qquad \vdash\, P \Rightarrow I}{\vdash\, \{P\}\, \mathbf{if}\, \mathcal{E}\, \mathbf{then}\, \mathcal{C}\, \{Q\}\, [I]\, \langle \mathsf{Time}(\mathbf{if}\, \mathcal{E}\, \mathbf{then}\, \mathcal{C}) \rangle}$$

$$\frac{\vdash\, P \Rightarrow \neg\mathcal{E} \qquad \vdash\, P \Rightarrow Q \qquad \vdash\, P \Rightarrow I}{\vdash\, \{P\}\, \mathbf{if}\, \mathcal{E}\, [\mathsf{F}]\, \mathbf{then}\, \mathcal{C}\, \{Q\}\, [I]\, \langle \mathsf{Time}(\mathbf{if}\, \mathcal{E}\, [\mathsf{F}]\, \mathbf{then}\, \mathcal{C}) \rangle}$$

---

[3]Matching is currently done by an *ad hoc* procedure which has the definition of Time built in. A more general approach would use Prolog-style metavariables to synthesize running times by unification. Theorem provers such as Isabelle [12] provide built-in facilities to support this.

$$\vdash \{P \wedge \mathcal{E}\} \, C_1 \, \{Q\} \, [I] \, \langle \mathsf{Time} \, C_1 \rangle$$
$$\vdash \{P \wedge \neg \mathcal{E}\} \, C_2 \, \{Q\} \, [I] \, \langle \mathsf{Time} \, C_2 \rangle$$
$$\vdash P \Rightarrow I$$

$$\overline{\vdash \{P\} \text{ if } \mathcal{E} \text{ then } C_1 \text{ else } C_2 \, \{Q\} \, [I] \, \langle \mathsf{Time}(\text{if } \mathcal{E} \text{ then } C_1 \text{ else } C_2) \rangle}$$

$$\frac{\vdash \{P \wedge \mathcal{E}\} \, C_1 \, \{Q\} \, [I] \, \langle \mathsf{Time} \, C_1 \rangle \qquad \vdash P \Rightarrow \mathcal{E} \qquad \vdash P \Rightarrow I}{\vdash \{P\} \text{ if } \mathcal{E} \text{ [T] then } C_1 \text{ else } C_2 \, \{Q\} \, [I] \, \langle \mathsf{Time}(\text{if } \mathcal{E} \text{ [T] then } C_1 \text{ else } C_2) \rangle}$$

$$\frac{\vdash \{P \wedge \neg \mathcal{E}\} \, C_2 \, \{Q\} \, [I] \, \langle \mathsf{Time} \, C_2 \rangle \qquad \vdash P \Rightarrow \neg \mathcal{E} \qquad \vdash P \Rightarrow I}{\vdash \{P\} \text{ if } \mathcal{E} \text{ [F] then } C_1 \text{ else } C_2 \, \{Q\} \, [I] \, \langle \mathsf{Time}(\text{if } \mathcal{E} \text{ [F] then } C_1 \text{ else } C_2) \rangle}$$

9.6.4 While loops

$$\vdash \forall v. \, \{R(v) \wedge \mathcal{E} \wedge \mathtt{v} = v\} \text{ while } \mathcal{E} \text{ do } [\mathtt{v}] \, \{R(v)\} \, C \, \{R(v) \wedge \mathtt{v} < v\} \, [I] \, \langle \mathsf{Time} \, C \rangle$$
$$\vdash \forall v. \, P(v) \Rightarrow R(v) \wedge \mathtt{v} = v$$
$$\vdash \forall v. \, R(v) \Rightarrow I$$

$$\overline{\vdash \forall v. \, \{P(v)\} \text{ while } \mathcal{E} \text{ do } [\mathtt{v}] \, \{R(v)\} \, C \, \{Q\} \, [I] \, \langle \mathsf{Time}(\text{while } \mathcal{E} \text{ do } [\mathtt{v}] \, \{R(v)\} \, C) \rangle}$$

$$\frac{\vdash P \Rightarrow \neg \mathcal{E} \qquad \vdash P \Rightarrow Q \qquad \vdash P \Rightarrow I}{\vdash \{P\} \text{ while } \mathcal{E} \text{ [F] do } [\mathtt{v}] \, \{R\} \, C \, \{Q\} \, [I] \, \langle \mathsf{Time}(\text{while } \mathcal{E} \text{ [F] do } [\mathtt{v}] \, \{R\} \, C) \rangle}$$

9.6.5 Example

Consider the goal in box 6 on page 146. Using the definition of Time the verifier computes that 11 cycles are needed. It thus tries to show:

```
{x = x ∧ y = y ∧ x = 0}
out := 0;  {out = 0 ∧  x = x  ∧  y = y ∧ x = 0}
 if ¬(x = 0 ∨ y = 0) [F]
   then while  x > 0
           do [x] {out + (x × y) = x × y  ∧  y = y}
              out := out + y;
              x := x − 1
{out = x × y }
[y  =  y]
⟨11⟩
```

Backchaining with the first rule in 9.6.2 yields two subgoals:

(1) $\{\mathbf{x} = x \wedge \mathbf{y} = y \wedge x = 0\}$
    out := 0
    $\{\text{out} = 0 \ \wedge \ \mathbf{x} = x \ \wedge \ \mathbf{y} = y \wedge x = 0\}$
    $[\mathbf{y} = y]$
    $\langle 2 \rangle$

(2) $\{\text{out} = 0 \ \wedge \ \mathbf{x} = x \ \wedge \ \mathbf{y} = y \wedge x = 0\}$
    if $\neg(\mathbf{x} = 0 \vee \mathbf{y} = 0)$ [F]
      then while $\mathbf{x} > 0$
          do [x] $\{\text{out} + (\mathbf{x} \times \mathbf{y}) = x \times y \ \wedge \ \mathbf{y} = y\}$
          out := out + y;
          x := x − 1
    $\{\text{out} = x \times y \}$
    $[\mathbf{y} = y]$
    $\langle 9 \rangle$

The assignment rule in 9.6.1 reduces (1) to two purely logical verification conditions; both are trivial.

(3) $(\mathbf{x} = x \wedge \mathbf{y} = y \wedge x = 0) \ \Rightarrow$
    $(0 = 0 \wedge \mathbf{x} = x \wedge \mathbf{y} = y \wedge x = 0)$

(4) $(0 = 0 \wedge \mathbf{x} = x \wedge \mathbf{y} = y \wedge x = 0) \vee$
    $(\text{out} = 0 \wedge \mathbf{x} = x \wedge \mathbf{y} = y \wedge x = 0) \Rightarrow$
    $(\mathbf{y} = y)$

The second conditional rule 9.6.3 reduces (2) to three purely logical verification conditions; all three are trivial.

(5) $(\text{out} = 0 \ \wedge \ \mathbf{x} = x \ \wedge \ \mathbf{y} = y \wedge x = 0) \Rightarrow$
    $\neg(\neg(\mathbf{x} = 0 \vee \mathbf{y} = 0))$

(6) $(\text{out} = 0 \ \wedge \ \mathbf{x} = x \ \wedge \ \mathbf{y} = y \wedge x = 0) \Rightarrow$
    $(\text{out} = x \times y)$

(7) $(\text{out} = 0 \ \wedge \ \mathbf{x} = x \ \wedge \ \mathbf{y} = y \wedge x = 0) \Rightarrow$
    $(\mathbf{y} = y)$

The verification conditions from the original goal are (3), (4), (5), (6) and (7). They can all be solved automatically.

9.7 State Transition Assertions

A state transition assertion (STA) has the form:

$$\mathcal{M} \models A \xrightarrow{\mathcal{I}} B$$

where $\mathcal{M}$ is a machine, A and B are predicates on states and $\mathcal{I}$ is a predicate on sequences of states. In general, a machine is a function from states and inputs to states [6], but as inputs are not considered here, a machine will be represented by a function from states to states. If $\mathcal{M} : state \rightarrow state$ is such a machine, then one cycle is a step $s \mapsto \mathcal{M}\ s$. A trace of $\mathcal{M}$ is a sequence:

$$s \frown (\mathcal{M}\ s) \frown (\mathcal{M}(\mathcal{M}\ s)) \frown (\mathcal{M}(\mathcal{M}(\mathcal{M}\ s))) \dots$$

The STA above is true iff for all traces $s_0 \frown s_1 \frown \dots$ of $\mathcal{M}$, if A is true of s_i then there is a later state s_j (where $i < j$) for which B is true and $\mathcal{I}$ is true of all subsequences $s_{i+1} \frown \dots \frown s_k$, where $k \leq j$.

A machine code program $\mathcal{O}$ determines a machine Machine $\mathcal{O}$ that maps a state (pc, stk, mem) to the state resulting from executing the instruction pointed to by the program counter pc. For example, the program in box 4 on page 145 determines a machine that maps the state $(8, stk, mem)$ to the successor state $(22, stk, mem)$, since the program counter (viz. 8) points to the instruction JMP 22 (the program counter starts at 0, so 8 points to the 9th instruction).

The predicate At n is true of a state (pc, stk, mem) iff $pc = n$. The predicate By t is true of a sequence of states iff its length is at most t.

If the object code for a command $\mathcal{C}$ is loaded into program memory starting at location n, then the resulting machine code program, $\mathcal{O}$ say, will contain instructions $[\![\mathcal{C}]\!]n$ from position n to position $n + |\mathcal{C}|$. The notation Loaded$(\mathcal{O}, \mathcal{C}, n)$ means that this is the case.

If $\mathcal{F}$ is a formula then $\{\mathcal{F}\}$ is the predicate on states defined by:

$$\{\mathcal{F}\}(pc, stk, mem) = \mathcal{F}[mem\ \mathbf{x}_1, \dots, mem\ \mathbf{x}_n / \mathbf{x}_1, \dots, \mathbf{x}_n]$$

where $\mathbf{x}_1, \dots, \mathbf{x}_n$ are the teletype font variables in $\mathcal{F}$ and $\mathcal{F}[v_1, \dots, v_n / \mathbf{x}_1, \dots, \mathbf{x}_n]$ denotes the result of textually substituting v_i for $\mathbf{x}_i$ (for $1 \leq i \leq n$) in $\mathcal{F}$. For example:

$$\{\text{out} + (\mathbf{x} \times \mathbf{y}) = x \times y \ \wedge \ \mathbf{y} = y\}(pc, stk, mem) =$$
$$(mem\ \text{out}) + ((mem\ \mathbf{x}) \times (mem\ \mathbf{y})) = x \times y \ \wedge \ (mem\ \mathbf{y}) = y$$

This notation formalizes the convention that teletype font variables are program variables (i.e. names bound by the memory) and italic variables are logical (or auxiliary) variables.

If $\mathcal{P}$ is a predicate on states then $[\mathcal{P}]$ is the predicate on sequences of states that is true iff $\mathcal{P}$ is true of each individual state in the sequence.

The conjunction of predicates on states and sequences of states will be indicated by vertical stacking.

Armed with all this notation, the timed Hoare formula $\{P\}\ \mathcal{C}\ \{Q\}\ [I]\ \langle t\rangle$ can now be defined to mean:

$$\forall\mathcal{O}\ n.\ \mathsf{Loaded}(\mathcal{O},\mathcal{C},n)\quad\Rightarrow\quad\mathsf{Machine}\ \mathcal{O}\models\ \begin{array}{c}\mathsf{At}\ n\\\{P\}\end{array}\ \xrightarrow[\textstyle\{Q\}]{\begin{array}{c}\mathsf{By}\ t\\[-2pt][\![\{I\}]\!]\end{array}\ \mathsf{At}(n+|\mathcal{C}|)}$$

In practice, the curley brackets $\{\ \}$ are omitted. For example, if $\mathcal{O}$ is the sequence of instructions in box 4 on page 145 and $\mathsf{Loaded}(\mathcal{O},\mathsf{Multiprog},0)$, then the meaning of the timed Hoare formula in box 3 on page 144 entails the STA in box 5 on page 145.

9.8   Mechanisation

The prototype verifier is implemented in HOL [7]. First STAs are defined and various derived rules for them are proved. Next the stack machine, programming language and compiler are defined. Timed Hoare formulæ are then defined in terms of STAs and the various laws in 9.5 are proved. Finally, tactics are programmed to generate verification conditions from goals; the justification part of these tactics is the derived rules [4].

9.9   Conclusions

The work described here is just the beginning of an attempt to provide theorem proving support for specifying and verifying timed reactive systems. Such systems alternate between waiting for input events in the environment and processing the data associated with these events. This paper concentrates on the data processing aspects (another paper [6] discusses waiting states and reaction times). Although some theorem-proving technology has been developed for reasoning about STAs, it is still not clear how useful the STA formalism is as a specification method for 'real' real-time systems.

9.10   Acknowledgements

This work was carried out as part of the **safemos** project; a SERC/DTI funded collaboration between **inmos**, SRI International, the Oxford University Programming Research Group and the Cambridge University Computer Laboratory. I am grateful to my collaborators on this project: Jonathan Bowen, Juanito Camilleri, Rachel Cardell-Oliver, Roger Hale, John Herbert and David Shepherd. In addition, I have had useful feedback on STAs from Victor Carreno, Nancy Day and Neil Viljoen.

References

[1] Apt, K.R., 'Ten years of Hoare's logic: a survey – part 1', ACM *Trans. on Programming Languages and Systems*, **3**, pp. 431-483, 1981.

[2] Dijkstra, E.W., *A Discipline of Programming*, Prentice-Hall, 1976.

[3] Good, D.I., 'Mechanical proofs about computer programs', in Hoare, C.A.R. and Shepherdson, J.C. (Eds), *Mathematical Logic and Programming Languages*, Prentice Hall, 1985.

[4] Gordon, M.J.C., 'Mechanizing Programming Logics in Higher Order Logic', G. Birtwistle and P.A. Subrahmanyam, (Eds), *Current Trends in Hardware Verification and Automated Theorem Proving*, Springer-Verlag, 1989.

[5] Gordon, M.J.C., *Programming Language Theory and its Implementation*, Prentice-Hall International Series in Computer Science, 1988.

[6] Gordon, M.J.C., 'State transition assertions: a case study', in Jonathan Bowen (Ed.), *Towards System Verification*, Real-Time Safety-Critical Systems series, Elsevier, 1993.

[7] Gordon, M.J.C. and Melham, T.F., *Introduction to HOL: a theorem-proving environment for higher-order logic*, Cambridge University Press, 1993.

[8] Hoare, C.A.R., 'An axiomatic basis for computer programming', *Communications of the ACM*, **12**, pp. 576-583, October 1969.

[9] Jones, C.B., *Systematic Software Development Using VDM*, Prentice Hall, 1986.

[10] J. Halpern, Z. Manna and B. Moszkowski., 'A Hardware Semantics based on Temporal Intervals', In the proceedings of the *10-th International Colloquium on Automata, Languages and Programming*, Barcelona, Spain, 1983.

[11] Nielson, H.R., 'A Hoare-like proof system for run-time analysis of programs', *Science of Computer Programming*, **9**, 1987.

[12] Paulson, L.C., 'Isabelle: The Next 700 Theorem Provers', in Odifreddi, P. (Ed) *Logic and Computer Science*, pp. 361–386, Academic Press, 1990.

[13] von Henke, F.W. and Luckham, 'Automatic Program Verification III: A Methodology for Verifying Programs', Stanford University Computer Science Department, Report No. STAN-CS-74-474, 1974.

[14] Wegbreit, B., 'The synthesis of loop predicates', *Comm. ACM*, **17**, pp 102–112, 1974.

Chapter 10

Constant-space Quicksort

David Gries

10.1 Introduction

It is a pleasure to write a paper that deals with algorithm *Quicksort*, which was invented by Tony Hoare [4], and that presents a version of *Quicksort* in terms of its correctness proof, a method of presentation that owes its existence to fundamental work by Tony Hoare. This paper is a response to [1] and [2], which attempt to describe a constant-space *Quicksort*. In [1], Durian presents his algorithm in a traditional operational fashion. The inadequacy of this approach is exemplified by the fact that his algorithm *IQS* does not work correctly for arrays of size less than 10. In [2], Wegner does provide some form of proof of correctness, but, as far as I could tell, the invariants he proposed were not invariants, and I had great difficulty understanding his algorithm.

Based on what I gleaned from [1] and [2], I developed my own version of constant-space *Quicksort*. The presentation given below is in two parts. First, I present a *Quicksort* algorithm in which variables explicitly contain the bounds of segments of the array still to be sorted. Second, I give a *coordinate transformation* to eliminate these variables, thus eliminating the extra space. This separates nicely the basic understanding of *Quicksort* from the change in data structures needed to force constant space. It also allowed me to see that a binary search could be used, and on a segment of the array that is not sorted!

Let me offer a frustration of mine. I can explain the idea behind constant-space *Quicksort* on a whiteboard in less than five minutes. However, to write a correct and understandable algorithm that incorporates that idea is not so easy, as the results of two earlier papers show. Unfortunately, ideas and their implementation in algorithms are two different things.

Experiments with constant-space *Quicksort* by Brandon Dixon found it to be about 5% slower than our best *Quicksort* on arrays of 1K to 100K elements. Since the best *Quicksort* requires only $O(log.n)$ space to sort an n-element array, it remains the algorithm of choice in most instances.

In the interests of brevity and clarity, our algorithm is only for arrays with distinct elements; the extension to arrays with duplicates is left to the reader. Finally, we take extreme care with parts of the proof, giving many details, so that the reader not too well versed in presentation-by-correctness-proof can see what really is necessary in proving a program correct.

10.2   Quicksort as a Preprocessor for Insertionsort

Integer array $b[0..n-1]$, where $0 \le n$ and all elements are distinct, can be sorted by algorithm *Insertionsort* (which appears in most introductory texts) in expected and worst-case time $O(n^2)$. However, by suitably preprocessing b in expected time $O(n \cdot log.n)$, *Insertionsort* will take only linear time, so the total expected time will be $O(n \cdot log.n)$. This preprocessing is the subject of this paper.

An integer i is called a *pivot* of b if everything to the left of $b.i$ is less than $b.i$ and everything to the right is greater:

$$pivot.i = b[..i-1] < b.i < b[i+1..] \quad . \tag{10.1}$$

We assume virtual elements $b.(-1) = -\infty$ and $b.n = \infty$, so that b has at least the pivots -1 and n. Suppose i and j are pivots satisfying $i < j \le i + H$ for some constant $H > 1$, so that

$$b[..i] < b[i+1..j-1] < b[j..] \quad .$$

Then, when sorting b, *Insertionsort* requires at most time $O(H)$ to place one element of $b[i+1..j-1]$ in its final position and time $O(H \cdot (j-i-1))$ to place them all. Also, all pivots are in their final positions and require only constant-time processing. Hence, if successive pivots of b are at most H apart, *Insertionsort* requires at most time $O(H \cdot n)$ to sort b. Thus, we seek preprocessing that creates such successive pivots.

10.3   Linear-space Preprocessing

We now present an algorithm for permuting $b[0..n-1]$ so that its successive pivots are at most H apart. With B denoting the initial value of b, and remembering the two virtual elements $b.(-1)$ and $b.n$, the precondition is

$$\begin{aligned} Q: \ & 0 \le n \wedge b[-1..n] = B \ \wedge \\ & b.-1 = -\infty \wedge b.n = \infty \ \wedge \\ & (\forall i,j \mid -1 \le i < j \le n : b.i \ne b.j) \quad . \end{aligned}$$

In presenting the postcondition, we use the following notation and terminology on sequences. Juxtaposition denotes catenation of sequences and elements. When they are not explicitly typed, capital letters denote elements and small letters sequences. Function *first.x* yields the first element of sequence x and *last.x* its last, and function *tail.x* is defined by $x = first.x \ tail.x$. Finally, for sequences x and y we define

$$x \ \mathbf{seg} \ y = (\exists w, z \mid : w \ x \ z = y) \quad .$$

The postcondition of the preprocessing algorithm consists of the conjuncts $R0$, $R1$, $R2$, and $R3$, given below, which use two variables u and v of type $seq(int)$ to contain sequences of pivots. Two variables are used instead of one to ease the later exposition.

$R0$ states that b is a permutation of its initial value. $R1$ states that sequence $u \ v$ is in strictly ascending order ($increasing(u \ v)$) and defines the first element of u and last element of v as the virtual pivots of b. $R2$ indicates that all elements of $u \ v$ are pivots. Finally, $R3$ indicates that successive elements of $u \ v$ are at most H apart.

$$
\begin{aligned}
&R0 : \ perm(b, B) \\
&R1 : \ increasing(u \ v) \wedge first.u = -1 \wedge last.v = n \\
&R2 : \ (\forall I \mid I \in (u \ v) : pivot.I) \\
&R3 : \ (\forall I, J \mid (I \ J) \ \mathbf{seg} \ (u \ v) : J - I \leq H)
\end{aligned}
$$

Algorithm (10.2) below truthifies this postcondition.

$$u, v := \langle -1 \rangle, \langle n \rangle; \tag{10.2}$$
$\{\text{Invariant} : R0 \wedge R1 \wedge R2 \wedge P3 \text{ (see below)}\}$
$\mathbf{do} \ first.v - last.u > H \rightarrow$
$\qquad \mathbf{var} \ k : int;$
$\qquad Partition(b, last.u + 1, first.v - 1, k);$
$\qquad \{R0 \wedge R1 \wedge R2 \wedge P3 \wedge P4 \text{ (see below)}\}$
$\qquad v := k \ v$
$[\!] \ first.v - last.u \leq H \wedge first.v \neq n \rightarrow u, v := u \ first.v, tail.v$
$\mathbf{od}$

The invariant is similar to postcondition R, except that $R3$ has been weakened to $P3$, which says that successive pivots in u (and not $u \ v$) are at most H apart).

$$P3 : \ (\forall I, J \mid (I \ J) \ \mathbf{seg} \ u : J - I \leq H) \tag{10.3}$$

$$P4 : \ last.u < k < first.v \wedge b[..k-1] < b.k < b[k+1..] \tag{10.4}$$

Statement $Partition(\ldots)$ of the algorithm is the standard partition algorithm, which permutes nonempty segment $b[last.u + 1..first.v - 1]$ and sets k to truthify

$$last.u < k < first.v \wedge \tag{10.5}$$
$$b[last.u + 1..k - 1] < b.k < b[k + 1..first.v - 1] \quad .$$

Partition does not falsify the invariants $R0$, $R1$, $R2$, and $P3$. Predicate $P4$ in the postcondition of *Partition* follows from (10.5) and $R2$. Thus, execution of *Partition*($\ldots$) creates a new pivot k. We shall not deal further with *Partition*($\ldots$).

We now deal with the initial truth and the invariance of $R0$, $R1$, $R2$, and $P3$. $R0$ is initially true, since initially $b = B$. The only statement that changes b is *Partition*($\ldots$), and it is guaranteed only to permute b, so $R0$ remains true.

Consider $R1$. With $u = [-1]$ and $v = [n]$, and with $n \geq 0$, $R1$ is initially true. We now show the invariance of $R1$ with regard to the statement $v := k\ v$ of the first guarded command. We have,

$$wp(`v := k\ v`,\ R1)$$
$$= \quad \langle \text{Definition of } wp \text{ and } R1 \rangle$$
$$increasing(u\ k\ v) \wedge first.u = -1 \wedge last.(k\ v) = n \quad .$$

The first conjunct follows from $P4$ and $R1$, and the last two conjuncts follow from $R1$. Hence, $R1$ is true after execution of the first guarded command.

Consider the invariance of $R1$ over the second guarded command. We have

$$wp(`u, v := u\ first.v, tail.v`,\ R1)$$
$$= \quad \langle \text{Definition of } wp \text{ and } R1 \rangle$$
$$increasing(u\ first.v\ tail.v) \wedge$$
$$first.(u\ first.v) = -1 \wedge last.(tail.v) = n$$
$$= \quad \langle \text{Definition of } first \text{ and } tail \rangle$$
$$increasing(u\ v) \wedge first.(u\ first.v) = -1 \wedge last.(tail.v) = n$$

The first two conjuncts are implied by $R1$. The last conjunct holds from $R1$ provided that $tail.v$ is not empty, which follows from the guard $first.v \neq n$ and conjunct $last.v = n$ of $R1$.

The proofs of invariance of $R2$ and $P3$ are just as simple and can be easily verified informally as well as formally. Hence, they are left to the reader.

So, $R0$, $R1$, $R2$, and $P3$ are loop invariants and are true upon termination. We now prove that upon termination $R3$ holds.

$$P3 \wedge \text{falsity of the loop guards}$$
$$= \quad \langle \text{Predicate calculus} \rangle$$
$$P3 \wedge first.v - last.u \leq H \wedge first.v = n$$
$$= \quad \langle R1 \rangle$$
$$P3 \wedge first.v - last.u \leq H \wedge v = [n]$$
$$= \quad \langle \text{Predicate calculus; One-point rule, } (\forall x \mid x = e : P) \equiv P[x := e] \rangle$$
$$P3 \wedge (\forall I, J \mid (I\ J)\ \mathbf{seg}\ (last.u\ v) : J - I \leq H)$$
$$= \quad \langle \text{Range-split; Definition of } R3 \rangle$$
$$R3$$

To prove termination of the loop, consider the expression $(\#u + \#v) + \#u$. By $R1$, it is bounded above by $2 \cdot n + 3$. Its initial value is 3. Each iteration increases it by 1. Hence, there are at most $2 \cdot n$ iterations.

Algorithm (10.2) is a version of *Quicksort*, as a preprocessor for *Insertionsort*, in which the sequence of generated pivots is maintained explicitly and the segments of b delimited by those pivots are processed in left-to-right order. The analysis of its expected and worst-case execution times is the same as that of other versions of *Quicksort* and is left to the reader. Our next step is to provide a coordinate transformation that eliminates variables u and v, leaving a constant-space *Quicksort*.

10.4   A Coordinate Transformation

Our coordinate transformation replaces variables b, u, v by an array c and integer variables i, j, h. Initially, we assume that $b = c$, and we prove that, upon termination of the transformed algorithm, again $b = c$. Thus, the final algorithm *Quicksorts* c and not b. The relationship between b, u, v and c, i, j, h is given by three coupling invariants $C0$, $C1$, and $C2$. The first coupling invariant defines i, j and h in terms of u and v:

$$C0 :\ \ i = last.u \ \wedge\ j = first.v \ \wedge\ (h\ n)\ \mathbf{seg}\ (u\ v)$$

$C0$ allows replacement expressions $last.u$ and $first.v$ of algorithm (10.2) by i and j. Variable h is the penultimate pivot in sequence $u\ v$. It is needed because the segment $b[h + 1..n - 1]$ has to be handled specially because its delimiting pivot n references the virtual array element $b.n$ instead of a real array element.

The second coupling invariant indicates the segments of b and c that are equal:

$$C1 :\ \ c[..j] = b[..j] \ \wedge\ c[h + 1..] = b[h + 1..] \quad .$$

It remains to define $c.t$ for $j < t \le h$. This definition is the key to achieving a constant-space *Quicksort*. Suppose $\#v > 2$, and introduce V and $\bar{v}$ satisfying $v = j\ V\ \bar{v}$. Note that $V \le h$. Consider the second guarded command of algorithm (10.2), which sets v to $tail.v$. In order to maintain $C0$ when $v := tail.v$ is executed, j has to be set to V, but without referring to v! We make this possible by defining $c[j + 1..V]$ appropriately. Suppose $b[j + 1..V]$ has the following form:

where $X < x < Y$

where x is a sequence and X and Y are elements. Then, $c[j + 1..V]$ has the value shown below:

where $X < x < Y$

Thus, $c[j + 1..V]$ is $b[j + 1..V]$ with its first and last elements swapped. Since $b[k] \le b.V$ for $j < k \le V$, we have $c[j + 1..V] \le c.(j + 1)$. Since $b.V < b[V + 1..]$, we have $c.(j + 1) < c[V + 1..]$. Hence, given j, we can determine V using a linear search (or as we shall see later, a binary search), as the single integer satisfying

$$j < V \le h \ \wedge\ c[j + 1..V] \le c.(j + 1) < c[V + 1..] \quad .$$

The above analysis gives the main idea behind constant-space *Quicksort*, and
if that is all the reader wants they may stop here.

The above analysis, with the pictures, deals poorly with the case $j+1 = V$. We
now introduce notation to deal rigorously with the definition of $c[j+1..V]$. Define
function $sw(b, p, q)$, for b an array (segment) and p, q integers, to be

$$sw(b, p, q) = \text{``}b \text{ with } b.p \text{ and } b.q \text{ swapped''} \quad .$$

Then define $c[j+1..V]$ to be $b[j+1..V]$ with its first and last elements swapped:

$$c[j+1..V] = sw(b[j+1..V], j+1, V) \quad .$$

Using this notation, we define all segments of c that are delimited by pivots in v,
except the last:

$$C2: \ (\forall I, J \mid (I\ J)\ \textbf{seg}\ v \wedge J \neq n : c[I+1..J] = sw(b[I+1..J], I+1, J) \quad .$$

With this definition of $c[j+1..V]$, the following theorem shows how to find the
follower of j in v.

Theorem 0. Given $R1$, $R2$, $C0$, $C1$, $C2$, and $j < h$, the follower of j in v is
the unique solution of $f.t$ defined by

$$f.t \ \equiv \ j < t \leq h \wedge c.t \leq c.(j+1) < c.(t+1) \quad . \tag{10.6}$$

Proof. First, we prove that $f.V$ holds for the follower V of j in v. Since $j < V \leq h$, by the definition of c there exists a value p, $V < p$, such that $b.p = c.(V+1)$.
Using this value p, we prove that the second conjunct of $f.V$ holds:

$$
\begin{aligned}
& c.V \\
=\ & \langle \text{Definition of } c \rangle \\
& b.(j+1) \\
\leq\ & \langle V \text{ is a pivot and } j+1 \leq V \rangle \\
& b.V \\
=\ & \langle \text{Definition of } c \rangle \\
& c.(j+1) \qquad - \text{ hence, } c.V \leq c.(j+1) \\
=\ & \langle \text{Definition of } c \rangle \\
& b.V \\
<\ & \langle V \text{ is a pivot of } b \text{ and } V < p \rangle \\
& b.p \\
<\ & \langle \text{Definition of } c \rangle \\
& c.(V+1) \qquad - \text{ hence, } c.V \leq c.(j+1) < c.(V+1)
\end{aligned}
$$

Hence, $f.V$ is true. Now consider any value t, $j+1 \leq t < V$. Since $b[j+1..V] \leq b.V$, we have $c[j+1..V] \leq c.(j+1)$. Hence, $c(t+1) \leq c.(j+1)$, so $f.t$ is false.

Finally, consider a value t satisfying $V < t \leq h$. Since V is a pivot, $b.V < b.t$.
By the definition of c, $c.(j+1) < c.t$, so $f.t$ is false.

Thus, the follower of j in v is the only solution of f defined by the equation of the theorem. Q.E.D.

We now provide translations of expressions and statements of (10.2). For each expression in u, v, b, we provide an equal expression in i, j, h, c, with the coupling invariants being used to prove equality. For the initialization of u, v we provide initialization for i, j, h such that the simultaneous execution of the initializations truthifies the coupling invariants. Finally, for each other statement of (10.2) that involves u, v, b, we provide an equivalent statement that involves i, j, h, c, such that the coupling invariants are invariantly true over the simultaneous execution of the two statements.

The translation of *last.u* is i (by $C0$).

The translation of *first.v* is j (by $C0$).

The translation of $u, v := [-1], [n]$ is $i, j, h := -1, n, -1$. That the two together truthify $C0$ is trivial. $C1$ is truthified because initially $b = c$ is assumed. $C2$ is truthified, with the range of quantification empty.

The translation of *Partition*$(b,\ last.u + 1,\ first.v - 1,\ k)$ is *Partition*$(c, i + 1, j - 1, k)$. By $C0$ and $C1$, the two segments of b and c that are being partitioned have the same value, so that executing the two calls leaves the segments still equal; further the two calls store the same value in k.

The translation of $v := k\ v$ is

> **if** $i = h \to j, h := k, k$
> $[\!]\ i < h \to$ Swap $c.(k+1), c.j;\ j := k$
> **fi**

We prove that this translation is correct. First, $C0 \Rightarrow i \leq h$, so the statement does not abort. We handle the cases $i = h$ and $i < h$ separately. Assume $i = h$, i.e. we deal with the guarded command $j, h := k, k$. We prove that $C0$, $C1$, and $C2$ are maintained by it.

> $\quad wp('v := k\ v; j, h := k, k', C0)$
> $= \quad$ ⟨Definition of wp and $C0$⟩
> $\quad i = last.u\ \wedge\ k = first.(k\ v)\ \wedge\ (k\ n)\ \textbf{seg}\ (u\ k\ v)$

The first conjunct is true by $R1$; the second by the definition of *first*. Consider the third. From $i = h$, $C0$, and $R1$, we have $v = [n]$, from which the third conjunct follows.

> $\quad wp('v := k\ v; j, h := k, k', C1)$
> $= \quad$ ⟨Definition of wp and $C1$⟩
> $\quad c[..k] = b[..k]\ \wedge\ c[k+1..] = b[k+1..]$
> $= \quad$ ⟨Property of arrays⟩
> $\quad c = b$

From $C0$, $i = h$, and $R1$, we have $j = n$. Together with $C1$, this implies $b = c$. Hence, $C1$ is maintained by the first guarded command. Similarly, $C2$ remains true – with its range of quantification empty.

Now consider the case $i < h$, i.e. consider the second guarded command.

$$wp(\text{'}v := k\ v;\ \text{Swap } c.(k+1), c.j;\ j := k\text{'}, C0)$$
$$= \quad i = last.u \wedge k = first.(k\ v) \wedge (h\ n)\ \mathbf{seg}\ (u\ k\ v)$$

The first conjunct is in $R1$, the second is true by the definition of *first*, and the third follows from $R1$ and $i < h$.

$$wp(\text{'}v := k\ v;\ \text{Swap } c.(k+1), c.j;\ j := k\text{'}, C1)$$
$$= \quad \langle \text{Definition of } wp \text{ and } C1 \rangle$$
$$sw(c, k+1, j)[..k] = b[..k] \wedge sw(c, k+1, j)[h+1..] = b[h+1..]$$
$$= \quad \langle \text{By } P4 \text{ and } C0,\ i < k < j \le h \rangle$$
$$c[..k] = b[..k] \wedge c[h+1..] = b[h+1..]$$

This follows from $k < j$ and $C1$.

$$wp(\text{'}v := k\ v;\ \text{Swap } c.(k+1), c.j;\ j := k\text{'}, C2)$$
$$= \quad \langle \text{Definition of } wp \text{ and } C2 \rangle$$
$$(\forall I, J \mid (I\ J)\ \mathbf{seg}\ (k\ v) \wedge J \ne n : sw(c, k+1, j)[I+1..J] =$$
$$sw(b[I+1..J], I+1, J))$$
$$= \quad \langle \text{Range split: One-point rule; } j = first.v \rangle$$
$$sw(c, k+1, j)[k+1..j] = sw(b[k+1..j], k+1, j) \wedge C2$$
$$= \quad \langle \text{Interchange of swapping and referencing a subsegment} \rangle$$
$$sw(c[k+1..j], k+1, j) = sw(b[k+1..j], k+1, j) \wedge C2$$
$$= \quad \langle \text{Property of swap} \rangle$$
$$c[k+1..j] = b[k+1..j] \wedge C2$$

The first conjunct follows from $C1$.

The translation of $u, v := u\ first.v, tail.v$ is

```
i := j;
if i = h → j := n
▯ i < h → j := V, where V satisfies f.V (see (10.6));
           Swap c.(i+1), c.j
fi
```

The proof of correctness of this replacement is similar to that of the previous replacement and is left to the reader. The key, of course, is Theorem 0.

10.5   Using Binary Search

Even though $c[j+1..h+1]$ is not sorted, binary search can be used to find V that satisfies $f.V$ (see (10.6)), as required in the translation of $u, v := u\ first.v, tail.v$.

Here, without much explanation, is a binary search algorithm due to E.W. Dijkstra, written as a procedure:

{Let initially $p = P$ and $q = Q$. Given is $c.p \leq x < c.q$. Set p to
truthify the following, while referencing only elements of $c[P + 1..Q - 1]$:
$$P \leq p < Q \wedge c.p \leq x < c.(p + 1)\}$$
procedure *bsearch*(**var** b:**array** ; **var** p:*int*; q, x:*int*);
{invariant: $P \leq p < q \leq Q \wedge c.p \leq x < c.q$}
do $p + 1 \neq q \rightarrow$ **var** $e := (p + q) \div 2$;
$$\{P \leq p < e < q \leq Q\}$$
    if $c.e \leq x \rightarrow p := e$
    [] $c.e > x \rightarrow q := e$
    fi
od

This algorithm is readily seen to satisfy its specification, though $c[P..Q]$ need not be ordered. Since the value V that satisfies (10.6) is unique, the following statement stores the desired value V in j:

$$j := i + 1; \ bsearch(c, j, h + 1, c.(i + 1)) \quad . \tag{10.7}$$

10.6   The Final Algorithm

Making the replacements in algorithm (10.2) that are described in the previous section yields the following algorithm. It would be nice to have a program construct to perform such a coordinate transformation automatically, given the statements and expressions to be replaced and their replacements.

var $i, j, h := -1, n, -1$;
do $j - i > H \rightarrow$ **var** k;
            $Partition(c, i + 1, j - 1, k)$;
            if $i = h \rightarrow j, h := k, k$
            [] $i < h \rightarrow$ Swap $c.(k + 1), c.j$; $j := k$
            fi
[] $j - i \leq H \wedge j \neq n \rightarrow i := j$;
            if $i = h \rightarrow j := n$
            [] $i < h \rightarrow j := i + 1$; $bsearch(c, j, h + 1, c.(i + 1))$;
                        Swap $c.(i + 1), c.j$
            fi
od

Note that, from the falsity of the guards of the loop, we have $j = n$; together with $C1$, this implies $b = c$.

This algorithm requires only constant extra space. In return, for each pivot created it requires two swaps and a binary search of $b[j..h]$, which takes at most logarithmic time. Since there are at most $n + 2$ pivots, the algorithm remains $O(n \cdot log.n)$.

10.7 Acknowledgements

This work was supported by NSF under grant IRI-8804801 and by NSF and Darpa under grant ASC-8800465. Brandon Dixon spent some time analysing constant-space *Quicksort* under the NSF program Research Experience for Undergraduates. Thanks go to Edsger W. Dijkstra for advising me to make the presentation rigorous.

References

[1] B. Durian. Quicksort without a stack. *Proceedings of the Mathematical Foundations of Computer Science*, LNCS 233, August 1986, 283–289.

[2] L. M. Wegner. A generalized, one-way, stackless quicksort. *BIT 27* (1987), 44–48.

[3] D. Gries. *The Science of Programming*. Springer Verlag, New York, 1981.

[4] C. A. R. Hoare. Quicksort. *BCS, Computer Journal* 5(1), 10–15 (1962). Also appears in C. A. R. Hoare and C.B. Jones. *Essays in Computing Science*. Prentice Hall International Series in Computer Science, 1989.

Chapter 11

From CSP to Hybrid Systems

He Jifeng

11.1 Introduction

Hybrid systems are interactive systems of continuous devices and digital control programs. Typical examples are digital modules that control a physical environment evolving over time. The principal problem of the subject is to model them so that given a specification for the continuous component of the system, we can extract, if this is possible, from the description of the total system and the specification of the continuous component, the specification of the control program which will force the continuous device to meet its specification. For hybrid systems a variety of formal models have been developed, among them phase transition system [9], declarative control [3], *extended state-transition graph* [10], and the extended duration calculus [14]. However, it remains a difficult task to design a correct computing device from the specification of the whole system.

This paper presents a formal description language for hybrid systems, which is an extension of CSP, as invented by Hoare in [5], and defined by a specification-oriented semantics [11]. The advantage of model-oriented specifications is that they describe as directly as possible, using the full expressive power of mathematics, the observable and testable properties of the desired system. These properties can be specified in independent modules, which are assembled by simple combinators. Because design notation and programming language are also given model-oriented semantics, correctness can be proved by simple deduction.

This paper also outlines an algebraic approach for the design and analysis of hybrid systems. Algebra is the branch of mathematics most suitable for practical use by engineers. Furthermore, it offers the prospect of rigorous derivation of solutions from specifications, achieving correctness by construction rather than proof, and also amenable to efficient implementation by computer [6, 13].

The continuous component of a hybrid system is regarded as an abstract representation of a physical device, and is often represented by a continuous function of time. Its change is assumed always visible, and often described by differential equations. Our model presents the concept of *abstract time* to relate the state of a system to a *global clock* where time passes at the same rate in all components of a system. In this paper, the time domain *TIME* is simply a set of non-negative reals.

A hybrid system continuously reacts to stimuli from its environment. To this end, such a system can be seen as a communicating process equipped with directed channels. Similar to TCSP [12], our model adopts the following view of the nature of communicating processes:

- The execution of discrete events may take a certain amount of time, which is represented by a delay command.
- All communication events are synchronised, i.e., they can occur if both sender and receiver are willing to cooperate [2]. As a result, once a system is prepared to communicate with its environment, it will wait indefinitely until either it can engage in a synchronisation or it runs out the time.
- Systems are assumed not to have infinite behaviour, in other words, only a finite sequence of discrete events can be recorded over any finite interval of time.

As advocated by Hoare in [6], a reactive system can be identified by the set of all observations which could in any circumstances be made of that system, which is represented by a *description predicate* with the same name as the system for convenience. As usual, an alphabet is attached to a system P (and its behaviours predicate as well), including the following parts:

1. **state**(P): a set of the continuous component names, whose change is governed by P. For convenience it is arranged into a list s.
2. **inchan**(P): the set of input channel names used to interact with its users.
3. **outchan**(P): the set of output channel names. We define

$$\textbf{chan}(P) \stackrel{def}{=} \textbf{inchan}(P) \cup \textbf{outchan}(P)$$

4. **var**(P): the set of program variable names used to specify the state of the embedded computing device. It is arranged into a list v.
5. **readvar**(P): a subset of **var**(P) which contains all program variables whose values are never modified by P.

Given an alphabet of a hybrid system, we are now ready to represent its timed observation by a tuple

$$(\overrightarrow{time}, \overleftarrow{time}, s, tr, ref, v, \grave{v}, st)$$

where

- $\overrightarrow{time}$ and $\overleftarrow{time}$ are the start point and the end point of a time interval over which an observation is recorded. We use $\delta(time)$ to represent the length of the time interval

$$\delta(time) \stackrel{def}{=} (\overleftarrow{time} - \overrightarrow{time})$$

- s is a real-valued function of time, used to describe the physical state of the system. We use $\dot{s}$ to stand for its derivative, and $\vec{s}$ and $\overleftarrow{s}$ the values of s at the start and the end of the time interval.

- tr, standing for trace, specifies the communication events a system has engaged over the time interval along the channels in **Chan**(P). It is a function over the interval $[\overrightarrow{time}, \overleftarrow{time}]$ assigning a sequence of communications to the time at which they occur. Except on a finite set of times, tr always yields an empty sequence $\langle\rangle$.

- ref, standing for refusal, describes the state of channels, which is a step function associating a set of channel names with the time interval over which they may become idle.

- v represents the initial values of program variables v, and $\dot{v}$ the final values at termination.

- st is the status of the system at the end of the time interval. It assumes the value **stable** if the system is inactive except for the evolution of its continuous components; the value **term** if the system is terminated; and the value **div** when the system is preoccupied with indefinite internal computation.

Later in this paper we will give a predicate semantics to a CSP-like description language, and pursue an algebraic approach to the design of hybrid systems. The next section provides a set of prerequisite notations for the construction of a predicate model. Section 3 is devoted to composite systems and their algebraic properties. Section 4 introduces some operators relating to the continuous components. Section 5 studies the Cat and Mouse problem and the Water Tank Controller, and illustrates how to use our formalism to analyse systems.

11.2 Preliminaries

In the rest of this paper we need the following definitions:

- Let ch be a channel name and m a message. The notation $ch.m$ represents a communication event. We use **Comm**(P) to denote the set of all communication events P may engage in its life time.

- Let α, β be sequences of communication events. The notation $\alpha \cdot \beta$ denotes the concatenation of α and β. $\alpha \preceq \beta$ indicates there is a sequence γ such that $\beta = \alpha \cdot \gamma$, in other words, α is a *prefix* of β. Let *Comm* be a set of communication events. The projector $\downarrow$ *Comm* maps a sequence α to its subsequence containing only elements of *Comm*.

- Let f be a function. **domain**(f) and **range**(f) represent the domain and the range of f respectively. The notation $f \odot g$ stands for the overriding of f by the function g.

- Let f be a time function with as its range the set of finite sequences of communication events. The notation $\mathbf{begin}(f)$ denotes the *earliest time* at which f yields a nonempty sequence:

$$\mathbf{begin}(f) \ = \ \mathbf{min}\,\{\, t \mid f(t) \neq \langle\rangle \,\}$$

with the convention $\mathbf{min}\{\} = \infty$. The notation $f \downarrow Comm$ stands for the composition of functions f and $\downarrow Comm$.

- We will use $\langle\rangle$ to represent the constant trace function which always yields the empty sequence. We will also use CH to represent a constant refusal function which takes the set CH as its value.

As in Temporal Logic [8], we introduce a binary "chop" operator to describe the composite behaviour of description predicates.

$$
P^\frown Q \ \overset{def}{=} \ \begin{aligned}[t]
& P \wedge st = \mathbf{stable} \vee P[\mathbf{div}/st] \vee \\
& \exists\, t,\, tr_P,\, tr_Q,\, ref_P,\, ref_Q \bullet \\
& \quad tr = tr_P \cdot tr_Q \wedge ref = ref_P \odot ref_Q \wedge \\
& \quad P[tr_P/tr,\, ref_P/ref,\, \mathbf{term}/st,\, t/\overleftarrow{time}] \wedge \\
& \quad Q[t/\overrightarrow{time},\, tr_Q/tr,\, ref_Q/ref]
\end{aligned}
$$

where the binary operator $\cdot$, defined over time functions tr, is a lift version of sequence concatenation. A lift version of $\preceq$ over time functions tr is defined by

$$tr_2 \preceq tr_1 \ \overset{def}{=} \ \exists\, tr_3 \bullet tr_1 = tr_2 \cdot tr_3$$

The chop operator is associative and disjunctive.

Another useful binary operator is "product": $P \times Q$ specifies the parallel system with components described by P and Q separately.

$$
P \times Q \ \overset{def}{=} \ \begin{aligned}[t]
& \exists\, tr_P,\, tr_Q,\, ref_P,\, ref_Q \bullet \\
& \quad tr_P = tr \downarrow \mathbf{Comm}(P) \wedge tr_Q = tr \downarrow \mathbf{Comm}(Q) \wedge \\
& \quad ref = ref_P \cup ref_Q \wedge \\
& \quad P[tr_P/tr,\, ref_P/ref] \wedge Q[tr_Q/tr,\, ref_Q/ref]
\end{aligned}
$$

The product operator is symmetric, associative and disjunctive.

11.3   Primitive Systems

This section discusses some simple systems, which serve as primitive components and need to be connected together and used in combination to exhibit more complex behaviour. For simplicity we will leave the alphabet of the systems unspecified.

As the worst system, $\perp$ is totally unpredictable and uncontrollable. It is identified by the predicate **true**:

$$\perp \overset{def}{=} \mathbf{true}$$

With an invisible continuous state, the system STOP does nothing, and remains stable forever.

$$\text{STOP} \overset{def}{=} st = \mathbf{stable} \wedge tr = \langle \rangle$$

The system SKIP terminates immediately having no effect on its program variables.

$$\text{SKIP} \overset{def}{=} \delta(time) = 0 \wedge st = \mathbf{term} \wedge tr = \langle \rangle \wedge \grave{v} = v$$

The notation $ch.m$ stands for a system which has an invisible continuous component, and is willing to perform the communication event $ch.m$ and then terminates.

$$\begin{aligned}
ch.m \overset{def}{=} \quad & ch \notin \mathbf{range}(ref) \wedge \\
& (st = \mathbf{stable} \wedge tr = \langle \rangle \vee \\
& \quad st = \mathbf{term} \wedge \grave{v} = v \wedge tr = \langle \rangle \odot \{\overleftarrow{time} \mapsto ch.m\})
\end{aligned}$$

11.4   Composite Systems

This section deals with system combinators. In order to ensure in advance a composite system will work as intended, we are required to formalise mathematical definition of the various combinators by which components can be combined into larger assemblies or can be adopted for a new purpose. In our case, such system combinators are simply defined as description predicate operators. Except where mentioned explicitly, each construct defined below has the same alphabet as its individual components.

11.4.1   Nondeterministic choice

If P and Q are systems, the notation $P \sqcap Q$ represents a composite system which behaves either like P or like Q, where the selection between them is made arbitrary, without the control of the system designers and users.

$$P \sqcap Q \overset{def}{=} P \vee Q$$

$\sqcap$ is idempotent, symmetric and associative.

11.4.2   Sequence

The system $(P \ ; \ Q)$ behaves like P before it terminates, and then behaves like Q afterwards.

$$P \ ; \ Q \ \stackrel{def}{=} \ P^\frown Q$$

Sequential composition is associative, and distributes over nondeterministic choice. It has STOP and $\bot$ as its left zero.

11.4.3   Prefix

Let $ch \in \mathbf{chan}(P)$. The notation $ch.m \longrightarrow P$ describes a system which performs the communication event $ch.m$ then behaves like the system P.

$$ch.m \longrightarrow P \ \stackrel{def}{=} \ (ch.m \ ; \ P)$$

11.4.4   Guarded choice

Let P and Q be prefix constructs. The notation $P \ \square \ Q$ stands for the system which behaves either like P or like Q, where the selection between alternatives is decided by the environment when it undertakes one of the first actions offered by P and Q.

$$P \ \square \ Q \ \stackrel{def}{=} \ (P \vee Q) \wedge \mathbf{agree}(\{P, \ Q\})$$

where

$$\mathbf{agree}(\{P, \ Q\}) \ \stackrel{def}{=} \ (\exists \ st_P, \ st_Q \bullet P[st_P/st] \wedge Q[st_Q/st] \wedge st = \mathbf{term})^\frown$$
$$(\delta(time) = 0 \vee \mathbf{begin}(tr) = \overrightarrow{time})$$

The first component of the chop operator in the definition of **agree** states that the observation is agreed by both P and Q before the choice is made. The second one describes the case where the selection is made at the very beginning of the time interval. Like $\sqcap$, the guarded choice operator $\square$ is idempotent and symmetric.

We can define the external choice on any set of prefix constructs.

$$\square \ \{\} \ \stackrel{def}{=} \ \text{STOP}$$
$$\square \ \mathcal{S} \ \stackrel{def}{=} \ (\bigvee \mathcal{S}) \wedge \mathbf{agree}(\mathcal{S})$$

where **agree** has a nonempty set of processes as its argument:

$$\mathbf{agree}(\mathcal{S}) \ \stackrel{def}{=} \ (\bigwedge \{P : P \in \mathcal{S} : \exists \ st \bullet P\} \wedge st = \mathbf{term})^\frown$$
$$(\delta(time) = 0 \vee \mathbf{begin}(tr) = \overrightarrow{time})$$

11.4.5 Synchronisation

Let P and Q be systems satisfying

$$
\begin{aligned}
\mathbf{state}(P) \cap \mathbf{state}(Q) &= \{\} \\
\mathbf{inchan}(P) \cap \mathbf{inchan}(Q) &= \{\} \\
\mathbf{outchan}(P) \cap \mathbf{outchan}(Q) &= \{\} \\
\mathbf{var}(P) \cap \mathbf{var}(Q) &= \mathbf{readvar}(P) \cap \mathbf{readvar}(Q)
\end{aligned}
$$

The notation P **sync** Q represents a system which behaves as if P and Q are running independently except that all the communications between P and Q have to be synchronised. Such a system terminates only when both of its components do so. P **sync** Q is attached with the following alphabet

$$
\begin{aligned}
\mathbf{state}(P\ \mathbf{sync}\ Q) &\overset{def}{=} \mathbf{state}(P) \cup \mathbf{state}(Q) \\
\mathbf{inchan}(P\ \mathbf{sync}\ Q) &\overset{def}{=} \mathbf{inchan}(P) \cup \mathbf{inchan}(Q) \\
\mathbf{outchan}(P\ \mathbf{sync}\ Q) &\overset{def}{=} \mathbf{outchan}(P) \cup \mathbf{outchan}(Q) \\
\mathbf{var}(P\ \mathbf{sync}\ Q) &\overset{def}{=} \mathbf{var}(P) \cup \mathbf{var}(Q) \\
\mathbf{readvar}(P\ \mathbf{sync}\ Q) &\overset{def}{=} \mathbf{readvar}(P) \cup \mathbf{readvar}(Q)
\end{aligned}
$$

and its behaviour is identified by the predicate

$$
P\ \mathbf{sync}\ Q \overset{def}{=} \mathbf{Synch}(P,\ Q) \vee \mathbf{Diverge}(P,\ Q)
$$

where $\mathbf{Synch}(P,\ Q)$ specifies the case where neither P nor Q diverges, and all communications between them are synchronised.

$$
\mathbf{Synch}(P,\ Q) \overset{def}{=} P \times (Q\ ;\ \Theta) \vee (P\ ;\ \Theta) \times Q
$$

and the predicate $\mathbf{Diverge}(P,\ Q)$ deals with the case when either P or Q becomes uncontrollable eventually:

$$
\mathbf{Diverge}(P,\ Q) \overset{def}{=} (\exists\, st \bullet (P[\mathbf{div}/st] \times (Q\ ;\ \Theta) \vee (P\ ;\ \Theta) \times Q[\mathbf{div}/st]))^\frown \bot
$$

Here Θ behaves like `STOP`, but it may terminate at any time.

$$
\Upsilon \overset{def}{=} tr = \langle\rangle \wedge (st = \mathbf{stable} \vee st = \mathbf{term} \wedge \grave{v} = v)
$$

The operator **sync** is symmetric and associative. It distributes over $\sqcap$, and has $\bot$ as its zero.

11.4.6   Hiding

Let P be a system with $CH \subseteq \mathbf{chan}(P)$, and suppose that the channels in CH connect components of P. We wish to hide from the environment of P all communications along the channels in CH. In this case, any message passing these channels is intended to be transferred automatically and instantaneously as soon as all components connected are ready for it. The resulting system is denoted $P \setminus CH$, and defined by

$$\mathbf{state}(P \setminus CH) \stackrel{def}{=} \mathbf{state}(P)$$
$$\mathbf{inchan}(P \setminus CH) \stackrel{def}{=} \mathbf{inchan}(P) - CH$$
$$\mathbf{outchan}(P \setminus CH) \stackrel{def}{=} \mathbf{outchan}(P) - CH$$
$$\mathbf{var}(P \setminus CH) \stackrel{def}{=} \mathbf{var}(P)$$
$$\mathbf{readvar}(P \setminus CH) \stackrel{def}{=} \mathbf{readvar}(P)$$

$$P \setminus CH \stackrel{def}{=}$$
$$\exists\, tr_P \bullet (tr = tr_P \downarrow \mathbf{Comm}(P \setminus CH) \wedge P[tr_P/tr, (ref \cup CH)/ref])$$

The hiding operator is strict, and distributes through nondeterministic choice and sequential composition. It also satisfies the following laws:

(hiding-1) (1) $(ch.m \longrightarrow P) \setminus CH = P \setminus CH$ if $ch \in CH$
                (2) $(ch.m \longrightarrow P) \setminus CH = ch.m \longrightarrow (P \setminus CH)$ if $ch \notin CH$

(hiding-2) $(P\ \mathbf{sync}\ Q) \setminus CH = (P \setminus CH)\ \mathbf{sync}\ Q$
                if $CH \subseteq (\mathbf{chan}(P) \setminus \mathbf{chan}(Q))$.

11.4.7   Conditional

Let P and Q be systems with the same alphabet, and b a Boolean expression only containing program variables. The system $P \lhd b \rhd Q$ works like P if b is true at the initial state, otherwise it looks like Q.

$$P \lhd b \rhd Q \stackrel{def}{=} (b \wedge P) \vee (\neg b \wedge Q)$$

11.4.8   Timeout

Let $d \in TIME \cup \{\infty\}$. The notation $P\ \rhd_d\ Q$ represents a system which operates like P if P engages a communication within the first d time units, otherwise turns to run system Q after it runs out d time units.

$$P \ \rhd_d \ Q \stackrel{def}{=}$$
$$P \wedge (\delta(time) \leq d \vee \mathbf{begin}(tr) \leq (\overrightarrow{time} + d)) \vee$$
$$\exists st_P \bullet (\exists \dot{v} \bullet P[st_P/st] \wedge tr = \langle \rangle \wedge \delta(time) = d \wedge st = \mathbf{term})^\frown Q$$

Timeout distributes through $\sqcap$, and a conditional in its first component. The nested timeout can be eliminated by using the following law.

(timeout-1) $\qquad (P \ \rhd_{d+\delta} \ Q) \ \rhd_d \ R \ = \ P \ \rhd_d \ R$

provided that $\delta > 0$. Define

$$\mathbf{delay} \ d \stackrel{def}{=} (\text{STOP} \ \rhd_d \ \text{SKIP})$$

which specifies a silent system terminating after d time units elapse. We also define

$$\mathbf{delay} \ \leq d \stackrel{def}{=} \bigvee_{t \leq d} \mathbf{delay} \ t$$

11.4.9 Assignment

Let x be a program variable, and e an expression with only the program variables. The notation $(x := e)_{\leq d}$ represents a computing device which assigns the value of the expression e to x, and claims no more than d units execution time.

$$(x := e)_{\leq d} = (\mathbf{delay} \ \leq d)[e/x]$$

11.4.10 Input and output

Let ch be a channel name and $d \geq 0$. The notation $(ch?x)_{\leq d}$ represents an input device which is willing to accept a message from the channel ch and assigns it to the program variable x. The execution of the input event takes at most d time units.

$$(ch?x)_{\leq d} \stackrel{def}{=} \square\{m \ : \ m \in Mes \ : \ ch.m \longrightarrow (x := m)_{\leq d}\}$$

where Mes is the set of all messages transferred by the channel ch.

The output device $(ch!e)_{\leq d}$ delivers the value of the expression e to the channel ch, and the output event claims no more than d time units.

$$(ch!e)_{\leq d} \stackrel{def}{=} ch.e \longrightarrow \mathbf{delay} \ \leq d$$

11.4.11   Alternation

The constructor **alt** takes as arguments guarded systems $g\, P$, where P is a system and the guard g can be either an input, or an output, or a delay.

An alternation without argument behaves like the system STOP.

$$\mathbf{alt}\,(\,) \stackrel{def}{=} \text{STOP}$$

In general, an alternation can be defined as a time-out construct.

$$\mathbf{alt}\,(io_1\, P_1,\, ...,\, io_n\, P_n,\, \mathbf{delay}\; d_1\, Q_1,\, ... \mathbf{delay}\; d_k\, Q_k) \stackrel{def}{=}$$
$$(\square\{i\,:\, 1 \leq i \leq n\,:\, io_i\,;\, P_i\})\; \trianglerighteq_d\; Q$$

where all io_i are communication guards, and $d \stackrel{def}{=} \mathbf{min}\,\{d_1,\, ...,\, d_n\}$ and

$$Q \stackrel{def}{=} \bigvee \{j\,:\, 1 \leq j \leq k\, \&\, d_j = d\,:\, Q_j\}$$

11.4.12   Parallel

Let P and Q be systems such that

$$\begin{aligned}
\mathbf{state}(P) \cap \mathbf{state}(Q) &= \{\} \\
\mathbf{inchan}(P) \cap \mathbf{inchan}(Q) &= \{\} \\
\mathbf{outchan}(P) \cap \mathbf{outchan}(Q) &= \{\} \\
\mathbf{var}(P) \cap \mathbf{var}(Q) &\models \mathbf{readvar}(P) \cap \mathbf{readvar}(Q)
\end{aligned}$$

The system $P \parallel Q$ behaves as if P and Q are working independently except that all communications along those channels connecting P and Q are to be synchronised and concealed.

$$P \parallel Q \stackrel{def}{=} (P\; \mathbf{sync}\; Q) \setminus \mathbf{Link}(P,\, Q)$$

where

$$\mathbf{Link}(P,\, Q) \stackrel{def}{=} (\mathbf{inchan}(P) \cap \mathbf{outchan}(Q)) \cup (\mathbf{inchan}(Q) \cap \mathbf{outchan}(P))$$

11.4.13   Recursion

Let $F(X)$ be a system description where X is a system variable. The notation $\mu\, X.F(X)$ stands for the least fixed point of the equation $X = F(X)$.

11.5 Operators for Continuous Components

This section examines the combinators for continuously evolving components of the systems. We will present a set of algebraic laws which can be used for the analysis and implementation of hybrid systems.

11.5.1 Differential equations

A continuous component s of a hybrid system is usually described by a differential equation

$$\mathcal{F}(s, \dot{s}) = 0$$

which generates the following observations:

$$\mathcal{F}(s, \dot{s})_a \stackrel{def}{=} st = \mathbf{stable} \wedge tr = \langle\rangle \wedge \vec{s} = a \wedge \lceil \mathcal{F} = 0 \rceil^*$$

where a stands for the initial value of the continuous state s, and the duration $\lceil P \rceil^*$ [14] is defined

$$\lceil P \rceil^* \stackrel{def}{=} \delta(time) > 0 \Rightarrow \forall \, time \in [\overrightarrow{time}, \overleftarrow{time}) \bullet P$$

In general a different equation $\mathcal{E}\mathcal{Q}(s)$ with an initial value constraint $C(s)$ can be defined by

$$\mathcal{E}\mathcal{Q}(s)_C \stackrel{def}{=} \bigvee_{a \in \{a | C(a)\}} \mathcal{E}\mathcal{Q}(s)_a$$

Since a differential equation describes a non-terminating process, it is thus a left unit of sequential composition.

$$(\text{equ-1}) \qquad \mathcal{E}\mathcal{Q}_a \, ; \, Q = \mathcal{E}\mathcal{Q}_a$$

When both components of a timeout construct are specified by the same equation, then the timeout becomes vacuous.

$$(\text{equ-2}) \qquad (\mathcal{E}\mathcal{Q}_a \, \trianglerighteq_d \mathcal{E}\mathcal{Q}) = \mathcal{E}\mathcal{Q}_a$$

The timeout commutes the parallel operator whenever all components involved are equations.

$$(\text{equ-3}) \qquad (\mathcal{E}\mathcal{Q}\mathcal{A} \, \trianglerighteq_d \mathcal{E}\mathcal{Q}\mathcal{B}) \parallel (\mathcal{E}\mathcal{Q}\mathcal{C} \, \trianglerighteq_d \mathcal{E}\mathcal{Q}\mathcal{D}) = $$
$$(\mathcal{E}\mathcal{Q}\mathcal{A} \parallel \mathcal{E}\mathcal{Q}\mathcal{C}) \, \trianglerighteq_d (\mathcal{E}\mathcal{Q}\mathcal{B} \parallel \mathcal{E}\mathcal{Q}\mathcal{D})$$

11.5.2   Preemption

Let B be a Boolean expression containing the continuous state s. The notation $P\,[B]\,Q$ represents a system which operates like P before B becomes true, and then operates like Q afterwards.

$$P\,[B]\,Q \;\stackrel{def}{=}\; (Q \lhd B[\vec{s}/s] \rhd (P \wedge \lceil \neg B \rceil^*)) \vee$$
$$(\lceil \neg B \rceil^* \wedge B[\vec{s}/s] \wedge st = \textbf{term} \wedge \exists\, st \bullet P)^\frown Q$$

When B holds initially, Q will proceed immediately.

([ ]-1) $P\,[\textbf{true}]\,Q \;=\; Q$

If B is unsatisfied, then Q will never be activated.

([ ]-2) $P\,[\textbf{false}]\,Q \;=\; P$

The next two laws show how to eliminate the nested preemption.

([ ]-3) $P\,[B]\,(Q\,[B \vee C]\,R) \;=\; P\,[B]\,R$

([ ]-4) $(P\,[B]\,Q)\,[B \vee C]\,R \;=\; P\,[B \vee C]\,R$

The preemption operator "runs" both of its operands at most once, so it distributes through nondeterministic choice

([ ]-5a) $(P_1 \sqcap P_2)\,[B]\,Q \;=\; (P_1\,[B]\,Q) \sqcap (P_2\,[B]\,Q)$

([ ]-5b) $P\,[B]\,(Q_1 \sqcap Q_2) \;=\; (P\,[B]\,Q_1) \sqcap (P\,[B]\,Q_2)$

The parallel operator commutes the preemption.

([ ]-6) $(P_1\,[B]\,Q_1) \parallel (P_2\,[B]\,Q_2) \;=\; (P_1 \parallel P_2)\,[B]\,(Q_1 \parallel Q_2)$

Sequential composition distributes over a preemption if the preempting condition is determined by its first component.

([ ]-7) $(\mathcal{E}\mathcal{Q}(s)\,[B(s)]\,Q)\;;\;R \;=\; \mathcal{E}\mathcal{Q}(s)\,[B(s)]\,(Q\;;\;R)$

If the second component of a preemption operator is an equation, then its initial value must be consistent with the preempting condition.

([ ]-8) $P\,[B(s)]\,\mathcal{E}\mathcal{Q}(s)_C \;=\; P\,[B(s)]\,\mathcal{E}\mathcal{Q}(s)_{(B \wedge C)}$

The next law describes the case when the timeout operator can commute the preemption.

([ ]-9) $(\mathcal{E}\mathcal{Q}_a \trianglerighteq_d P)\,[B]\,Q \;=\; \mathcal{E}\mathcal{Q}_a \trianglerighteq_d (P\,[B]\,Q)$

provided that $\neg B[a/s]$ and $(\vec{s} = a \wedge \lceil \mathcal{EQ} \rceil^* \wedge \delta(time) \leq d) \Rightarrow \lceil \neg B \rceil^*$. If the first component of a timeout operator can establish the preempting condition, then the second component can be ignored.

$([\,]\text{-}10)$ $(\mathcal{EQ}_a \trianglerighteq_d P)[B]\,Q = \mathcal{EQ}_a\,[B]\,Q$

provided that $(\vec{s} = a \wedge \lceil \mathcal{EQ} \rceil^* \wedge \delta(time) = d) \Rightarrow \neg \lceil \neg B \rceil^*$. A preempting condition can be simplified by the next law

$([\,]\text{-}11)$ $\mathcal{EQ}_a\,[B \vee C]\,Q = \mathcal{EQ}_a\,[B]\,Q$

provided that $\neg C[a/s]$ and $(\vec{s} = a \wedge \lceil \mathcal{EQ} \rceil^* \wedge \lceil \neg B \rceil^*) \Rightarrow \lceil \neg C \rceil^*$. The next law shows how to transform a preemption construct into a timeout one.

$([\,]\text{-}12)$ $\mathcal{EQ}_a\,[B]\,Q = \mathcal{EQ}_a \trianglerighteq_d Q$

provided that $\neg B[a/s]$ and

$$(\neg B[a/s] \wedge \lceil \mathcal{EQ} \rceil^* \wedge \delta(time) = d) \Rightarrow (\lceil \neg B \rceil^* \wedge B[\overleftarrow{s}/s])$$

11.5.3 Await

Let B be a Boolean expression with continuous states, and Q a system. The notation **await** B **do** Q specifies a system which keeps silent until B becomes true, and then works like Q.

$$\textbf{await } B \textbf{ do } Q \stackrel{def}{=} \text{STOP}\,[B]\,Q$$

The nested awaits can be eliminated when the inner preempting condition implies the outer one.

(await-1)   **await** $(B \vee C)$ **do** (**await** B **do** Q) = **await** B **do** Q

11.5.4 Choice of awaits

The notation (**await** B_1 **do** Q_1) $\oplus$ (**await** B_2 **do** Q_2) specifies a system which proceeds to execute one of its alternatives Q_i once its guard B_i turns to be true. When both B_1 and B_2 become true simultaneously, the selection between Q_1 and Q_2 is nondeterministic.

$$(\textbf{await } B_1 \textbf{ do } Q_1) \oplus (\textbf{await } B_2 \textbf{ do } Q_2) \stackrel{def}{=}$$
$$B_1[\vec{s}/s] \wedge Q_1 \vee B_2[\vec{s}/s] \wedge Q_2 \vee$$
$$\text{STOP} \wedge \lceil \neg(B_1 \vee B_2) \rceil^* \vee$$
$$(\lceil \neg(B_1 \vee B_2) \rceil^* \wedge (B_1 \vee B_2)[\overleftarrow{s}/s] \wedge st = \textbf{term} \wedge \exists st \bullet \text{STOP})$$
$$\frown(B_1[\vec{s}/s] \wedge Q_1 \vee B_2[\vec{s}/s] \wedge Q_2)$$

In general, the choice operator $\oplus$ can be extended by having a set of awaits as its operands, and its definition is very similar to the previous one, and omitted.

Two awaits with the same guarded system can be combined.

($\oplus$-1) $(\textbf{await } B \textbf{ do } Q) \oplus (\textbf{await } C \textbf{ do } Q) = \textbf{await } (B \vee C) \textbf{ do } Q$

The choice among awaits can be resolved when the initial state is known in advance.

($\oplus$-2) $P\,[B \wedge \neg C]\,((\textbf{await } B \textbf{ do } Q) \oplus (\textbf{await } C \textbf{ do } R)) = P\,[B \wedge \neg C]\,Q$

The final law describes the case where a parallel construct can be reduced to a choice on awaits.

($\oplus$-3)   Let $P = \Box_{i \in \mathcal{I}}\,(c_i?x_i \longrightarrow P_i(x_i)$
and $Q = \oplus_{j \in \mathcal{J}}\textbf{await } B_j \textbf{ do } (c_j!e_j \longrightarrow Q_j)$
Assume that all c_i are internal link between P and Q, then
$(P \parallel Q) = \oplus_{k \in \mathcal{I} \cap \mathcal{J}} \textbf{ await } B_k \textbf{ do } (P_k(e_k) \parallel Q_k)$

11.5.5   Interrupt by communication

Let P be a non-terminating process, and $Q = \Box_{i \in \mathcal{I}}\,(c_i?x_i \longrightarrow Q_i)$. The notation $P \trianglelefteq Q$ specifies a system which initially proceeds like P, and is interrupted on occurrence of the first communication event of Q.

$$P \trianglelefteq Q \stackrel{def}{=} \; P \wedge \forall i \in \mathcal{I} \bullet c_i \notin \textbf{range}(ref) \vee$$
$$(st = \textbf{term} \wedge \forall i \in \mathcal{I} \bullet c_i \notin \textbf{range}(ref) \wedge \exists st \bullet P)^\frown$$
$$(\textbf{begin}(tr) = \overrightarrow{time} \wedge Q)$$

It is the environment which decides when the interrupt occurs.

($\trianglelefteq$-1)   Let $P = d?(x) \longrightarrow P(x)$
Then $P \trianglelefteq Q = (Q \,\Box\, (d?(x) \longrightarrow (P(x) \trianglelefteq Q)))$

STOP is interruptible only when the first communication of Q actually happens.

($\trianglelefteq$-2)   STOP $\trianglelefteq Q = Q$

Sequential composition distributes backwards through the interrupt construct since the first operand of the interrupt never terminates.

($\trianglelefteq$-3) $(P \trianglelefteq Q)\,;\,R = P \trianglelefteq (Q\,;\,R)$

The next two laws show how to reduce the parallel construct to preemption and timeout constructs.

($\trianglelefteq$-4)   Let $P = \oplus_{j \in \mathcal{J}}(\textbf{await } B_j \textbf{ do } (c_j!e_j \longrightarrow P_j)$
and $Q = \Box_{i \in \mathcal{I}}\,(c_i?x_i \longrightarrow Q_i(x_i))$.
If all channels c_i are internal links between P and Q, and all Boolean expressions B_j refer only to a continuous state s, then
$(\mathcal{E}Q(s)_a \trianglelefteq Q) \parallel P = (\mathcal{E}Q(s)_a\,[\bigvee_{k \in \mathcal{I} \cap \mathcal{J}} B_k]\,(Q \parallel P)$

($\lhd$-5)   Let $Q = \square_{i \in \mathcal{I}}\, c_i?x_i \longrightarrow Q(x_i)$. Then

$$(\mathcal{E}\mathcal{Q}(s)_a \lhd Q) \parallel (\mathbf{delay}\; d\; ;\; P) = (\mathcal{E}\mathcal{Q}(s)_a \unrhd_d (\mathcal{E}\mathcal{Q}(s) \lhd Q) \parallel P)$$

provided that all c_i are internal links between Q and P

11.6   Examples

11.6.1   Cat and mouse

This is a variation of the example presented in [9]. Briefly the description is the following: at $time = 0$ a mouse starts running on the floor in a straight line to the hole in the wall, at a constant velocity $v_m > 0$. After a delay of L time units, a cat is released, and chases the mouse along the same straight line at a constant velocity $v_c > 0$. They stop running when either the mouse reaches sanctuary or the cat overtakes the mouse before it enters into the hole. It is assumed that initially they are distance sm and sc from a hole in a wall. Their movement can be described by the following hybrid systems.

$$M \stackrel{def}{=} (\dot{m} = -v_m)_{sm}\, [m = 0 \vee a = m > 0]\, (\dot{m} = 0)$$
$$C \stackrel{def}{=} ((\dot{a} = 0)_{sc} \unrhd_L (\dot{a} = -v_c))\, [m = 0 \vee a = m > 0]\, (\dot{a} = 0)$$

where the continuous states m and a measure the distance of the mouse and the cat to the hole respectively. We can explore all possible termination scenarios by putting M and C in parallel and sending the final outcome of the game to the channel c.

$$MC \stackrel{def}{=} (M \parallel C)\, [m = 0 \vee a = m > 0]\, R$$

where

$$R \stackrel{def}{=} (\mathbf{await}\; m = 0\; \mathbf{do}\; c!Mouse - wins) \oplus$$
$$(\mathbf{await}\; a = m > 0\; \mathbf{do}\; c!Cat - wins)$$

First, the parallel system $(M \parallel C)$ can be simplified:

$$M \parallel C$$
$$= \quad \{\text{law ([]-6)}\}$$
$$((\dot{m} = -v_m)_{sm} \parallel ((\dot{a} = 0)_{sc} \unrhd_L (\dot{a} = -v_a)))$$
$$[m = 0 \vee a = m > 0]\, (\dot{m} = 0 \parallel \dot{a} = 0)$$
$$= \quad \{\text{law (equ-2)}\}$$
$$(((\dot{m} = -v_m)_{sm} \unrhd_L (\dot{m} = -v_m)) \parallel ((\dot{a} = 0)_{sc} \unrhd_L (\dot{a} = -v_a)))$$
$$[m = 0 \vee a = m > 0]\, (\dot{m} = 0 \parallel \dot{a} = 0)$$
$$= \quad \{\text{law (equ-3)}\}$$
$$((\dot{m} = -v_m)_{sm} \parallel (\dot{a} = 0)_{sc}) \unrhd_L (\dot{m} = -v_m \parallel \dot{a} = -v_c))$$
$$[m = 0 \vee a = m > 0]\, ((\dot{m} = 0) \parallel (\dot{a} = 0))$$

from which and law ([]-4) one ends with

$$MC = ((\dot{m} = -v_m)_{sm} \ \| \ (\dot{a} = 0)_{sc}) \ \unrhd_L ((\dot{m} = -v_m) \ \| \ (\dot{a} = -v_c))$$
$$[m = 0 \vee a = m > 0] \, R$$

Let us consider three cases.

Case 1: $sm \le L \times v_m$.

$$MC$$
$$= \{\text{laws ([]-10) and ([]-11)}\}$$
$$((\dot{m} = -v_m)_{sm} \ \| \ (\dot{a} = 0)_{sc}) \, [m = 0 \vee \neg(a = m > 0)] \, R$$
$$= \{\text{law } (\oplus\text{-2})\}$$
$$((\dot{m} = -v_m)_{sm} \ \| \ (\dot{a} = 0)_{sc}) \, [m = 0 \vee \neg(a = m > 0)] \, c! \, Mouse - wins$$
$$= \{\text{law ([]-12}\}$$
$$((\dot{m} = -v_m)_{sm} \ \| \ (\dot{a} = 0)_{sc}) \ \unrhd_{sm/v_m} \ c! \, Mouse - wins$$

which predicts that the mouse will safely enter into the hole after sm/v_m time units.

Case 2: $(L \times v_m) < sm \le ((L \times v_m) + (v_m \times sc/v_c))$.

$$MC$$
$$= \{\text{laws ([]-9) and ([]-11)}\}$$
$$((\dot{m} = -v_m)_{sm} \ \| \ (\dot{a} = 0)_{sc}) \ \unrhd_L ((\dot{m} = -v_m)_{sm-L\times v_m} \ \| \ (\dot{a} = -v_c)_{sc})$$
$$[m = 0 \wedge \neg(a = m > 0)] \, R$$
$$= \{\text{law } (\oplus\text{-2})\}$$
$$((\dot{m} = -v_m)_{sm} \ \| \ (\dot{a} = 0)_{sc}) \ \unrhd_L (((\dot{m} = -v_m)_{sm-L\times v_m} \ \| \ (\dot{a} = -v_c)_{sc})$$
$$[m = 0 \wedge \neg(a = m > 0)] \, c! \, Mouse - wins)$$
$$= \{\text{law ([]-12)}\}$$
$$((\dot{m} = -v_m)_{sm} \ \| \ (\dot{a} = 0)_{sc}) \ \unrhd_L$$
$$(((\dot{m} = -v_m)_{sm-L\times v_m} \ \| \ (\dot{a} = -v_c)_{sc}) \ \unrhd_{(sm/v_m)-L} \ c! \, Mouse - wins)$$

which indicates that the cat is unable to catch the mouse.

Case 3: $((L \times v_m) + (v_m \times sc/v_c)) < sm$ and $v_c > v_m$.

$$MC$$
$$= \{\text{laws ([]-9) and ([]-11)}\}$$
$$((\dot{m} = -v_m)_{sm} \ \| \ (\dot{a} = 0)_{sc}) \ \unrhd_L$$
$$((\dot{m} = -v_m)_{sm-L\times v_m} \ \| \ (\dot{a} = -v_c)_{sc}) \, [(a = m > 0)] \, R$$

$$= \{\text{law } (\oplus\text{-2})\}$$
$$((\dot{m} = -v_m)_{sm} \parallel (\dot{a} = 0)_{sc}) \trianglerighteq_L$$
$$(((\dot{m} = -v_m)_{sm-L\times v_m} \parallel (\dot{a} = -v_c)_{sc})[(a = m > 0)] \, c! \, Cat - wins)$$
$$= \{\text{law } ([\,]\text{-12})\}$$
$$((\dot{m} = -v_m)_{sm} \parallel (\dot{a} = 0)_{sc}) \trianglerighteq_L (((\dot{m} = -v_m)_{sm-L\times v_m} \parallel (\dot{a} = -v_c)_{sc})$$
$$\trianglerighteq_{(sc-sm+L\times v_m)/(v_c-v_m)} \, c! \, Cat - wins)$$

which says that the cat will eventually overtake the mouse.

11.6.2 A water tank controller

The system is used to control the water level in a tank by switching on a control valve. The goal is to maintain the water level between 30 and 60 units. At *time* $= 0$ the valve is open, and the water level is 40 units high, and rising at speed 0.1. Once the valve is closed, the water level will drop at speed -0.2 until the valve is reopened. The following shows the hybrid system *WL* of the water level, where the continuous state h represents the water level in the tank, and the channel c links the controller with the actuator of the valve.

$$WL \ \stackrel{def}{=} \ (\dot{h} = 0.2)_{40} \trianglelefteq (c?x \longrightarrow W(x))$$

$$W(\textbf{off}) \ \stackrel{def}{=} \ (\dot{h} = -0.1) \trianglelefteq (c?x \longrightarrow W(x))$$

$$W(\textbf{on}) \ \stackrel{def}{=} \ (\dot{h} = 0.2) \trianglelefteq (c?x \longrightarrow W(x))$$

The controller C opens the valve when the water level drops to 30 units, and closes the valve once the water level rises to 60 units.

$$C \ \stackrel{def}{=} \ (\textbf{await } h = 30 \textbf{ do } (c!\, \textbf{on} \longrightarrow (\textbf{delay } 1 \ ; \ C))) \oplus$$
$$(\textbf{await } h = 60 \textbf{ do } (c!\, \textbf{off} \longrightarrow (\textbf{delay } 1 \ ; \ C)))$$

Now we want to show that the controller maintains the water level within the proposed range.

$$(WL \parallel C) \Rightarrow \lceil 30 \le h \le 60 \rceil^*$$

First one has

$$WL \parallel C$$
$$= \{\text{laws } (\trianglelefteq\text{-4}) \text{ and } (\oplus\text{-3})\}$$
$$(\dot{h} = 0.2)_{40} [h = 30 \vee h = 60]$$
$$((\textbf{await } h = 30 \textbf{ do } (W(\textbf{on}) \parallel (\textbf{delay } 1 \ ; \ C)) \oplus$$
$$(\textbf{await } h = 60 \textbf{ do } (W(\textbf{off}) \parallel (\textbf{delay } 1 \ ; \ C)))$$

$$= \{\text{laws ([]-11) and ($\oplus$-2)}\}$$
$$(\dot{h} = 0.2)_{40}\,[h = 60]$$
$$(((\dot{h} = -0.1)_{60} \trianglelefteq (c?x \longrightarrow W(x)) \parallel (\textbf{delay } 1 \,;\, C))$$
$$= \{\text{law ([]-12)}\}$$
$$(\dot{h} = 0.2)_{40} \; \trianglerighteq_{100}$$
$$((\dot{h} = -0.1)_{60} \trianglelefteq (c?x \longrightarrow W(x)) \parallel (\textbf{delay } 1 \,;\, C))$$

Following a similar argument one can show that

$$((\dot{h} = -0.1)_{60} \trianglelefteq (c?x \longrightarrow W(x)) \parallel (\textbf{delay } 1 \,;\, C)$$
$$= (\dot{h} = -0.1)_{60} \; \trianglerighteq_{300}$$
$$(((\dot{h} = 0.2)_{30} \trianglelefteq (c?x \longrightarrow W(x))) \parallel (\textbf{delay } 1 \,;\, C))$$
$$= (\dot{h} = -0.1)_{60} \; \trianglerighteq_{300} ((\dot{h} = 0.2)_{30} \; \trianglerighteq_{150}$$
$$(((\dot{h} == -0.1)_{60} \trianglelefteq (c?x \longrightarrow W(x)) \parallel (\textbf{delay } 1 \,;\, C))$$

The above analysis shows

- Within the first 100 time units the water level is rising, and finally reaches 60 units.
- Later the dropping and rising periods are interleaved with 150 and 300 time units respectively.
- The water level always lies between 30 and 60 units as required.

References

[1] J. C. M. Baeten and J. A. Bergstra. *Discrete time process algebra*. Technical Report P9208, University of Amsterdam, 1992.

[2] S. D. Brookes, C. A. R. Hoare and A. W. Roscoe. *A Theory of Communicating Sequential Processes*. JACM, 1984.

[3] W. Kohn. *A Declarative Theory for Rational Controllers*. Proc. 27th CDC, 130–136, 1988.

[4] R. Gerth and A. Boucher. *A timed failure model for extended communicating processes*. LNCS 267, 95–114, 1987.

[5] C. A. R. Hoare. *Communicating Sequential Processes*. Prentice-Hall International, London, 1984.

[6] C. A. R. Hoare. *Algebra and Models*. ProCoS Technical Report, 1990.

[7] C. Huizing and others. *Full Abstraction of a Denotational Semantics for Real-Time Concurrency*. Proc. 14th ACM Symposium on Principles of Programming Languages, 223–237, 1987.

[8] Z. Manna and A. Pnueli. *The Temporal Logic of Reactive and Concurrent Systems – Specification.* Springer-Verlag, 1991.

[9] O. Maler, Z. Manna and A. Pnueli. *From timed to hybrid systems* LNCS 600, Springer-Verlag, 1992.

[10] X. Nicolin, J. Richier, J. Sifakis and J. Voiron. *An approach to the Description and Analysis of Hybrid Systems* presented at the Workshop on Theory of Hybrid Systems, Lyngby, Denmark, 1992.

[11] E. R. Olderog and C. A. R. Hoare. *Specification-oriented Semantics for Communicating Processes.* Acta Informatica 23, 9–66, 1986.

[12] G. M. Reed and A. W. Roscoe. *A Timed Model for Communicating Sequential Processes.* LNCS 226, 314–323, 1986.

[13] A. W. Roscoe and C. A. R. Hoare. *Laws of occam Programming.* Theoretical Computer Science, 60, 177–229, 1988.

[14] Zhou Chao Chen, A. P. Ravn and M. R. Hansen. *Extended Duration Calculus for Hybrid Systems,* presented at the Workshop on Theory of Hybrid Systems, Lyngby, Denmark, 1992

Chapter 12

Abstractions of Time

Eric C. R. Hehner

The first usable theory of programming is due to C. A. R. Hoare in 1969 [4]. That work is so important that no-one ever needs to look in the references to see what paper it might be, and all work on the subject since then builds on that work. The kind of semantics used in the present paper, a single boolean expression, was developed in discussion with Tony Hoare during a fruitful term I spent at Oxford in 1981, and presented in a joint paper [1]. For those and many other inspirations, I thank Tony Hoare.

12.1 Introduction

The execution time of programs has been modeled, or measured, or calculated, in a variety of ways. This paper is concerned with measurements of time that are part of a formal semantics of programs. A semantics can enable us to calculate the execution time of programs quite precisely. This is necessary for applications known as real-time. For other applications, a more abstract measure of time, called recursive time, is both sufficient and convenient. More abstract still is the measure of time used in a total correctness semantics; time is reduced to a single bit that distinguishes between finite and infinite execution time. Continuing to the extreme, we find partial correctness, where time has been eliminated. Between the extremes of real-time and partial correctness there are other points of interest, such as the quantified time of temporal logic, and the timed processes of ATP.

It is reasonable to retain several theories with different abstractions of time if they allow us to trade simplicity against accuracy. We use a simple theory whenever we can, moving to a more complex theory when more accuracy is required. But if one theory is both simpler and more accurate than another, requiring less formal labor to obtain more timing information, then the other theory should be discarded. As we shall see, that is indeed the case.

Different abstractions of time can best be compared if they are all presented, as much as possible, within one semantic framework. The framework used in this paper is characterized by the following principles:

- We first decide what quantities are of interest, and introduce a variable for each such quantity. A variable may represent input to a computation, or output from a computation.
- A specification is a boolean expression whose variables represent the quantities of interest. A specification is implemented on a computer when, for any values of the input variables, the computer generates (computes) values of the output variables to satisfy the specification. In other words, we have an implementation when the specification is true of every computation. (Note that we are specifying computations, not programs.)
- A program is a specification that has been implemented.

Suppose we are given specification S. If S is a program, we can execute it. If not, we have some programming to do. That means finding a program P such that $S \Leftarrow P$ is a theorem; this is called refinement. Since S is implied by P, all computer behavior satisfying P also satisfies S. We might refine in steps, finding specifications R, Q,... such that $S \Leftarrow R \Leftarrow Q \Leftarrow \ldots P$.

12.2   Notation

Here are all the notations used in this paper, arranged by precedence level:

0. *true*   *false*   ( )   numbers   names
1. juxtaposition
2. superscript   subscript   underscore   ::
3. $\times$ /   **div**   ! $\downarrow$
4. $+$ $-$
5. $=$ $\neq$ $<$ $>$ $\leqslant$ $\geqslant$
6. $\neg$
7. $\wedge$
8. $\vee$
9. $\Rightarrow$ $\Leftarrow$
10. :=   **if then else**   **while do**
11. $\lambda \bullet$ $\forall \bullet$ $\exists \bullet$ $\Sigma \bullet$ $\Pi \bullet$; $\|$ $\square$ $\Diamond$ $\circ$
12. $=$ $\Rightarrow$ $\Leftarrow$

On level 2, superscripting, subscripting, and underscoring serve to bracket all operations within them. Juxtaposition associates from left to right, so that $a\ b\ c$ means $(a\ b)\ c$. The infix operators / and $-$ associate from left to right. The infix operators $\times$ $+$ $\wedge$ $\vee$; and $\|$ are associative (they associate in both directions). On levels 5, 9, and 12 the operators are continuing; for example, $a = b = c$ neither associates to the left nor associates to the right, but means $a = b \wedge b = c$. On any one of these levels, a mixture of continuing operators can be used. For example, $a \leqslant b < c$ means $a \leqslant b \wedge b < c$. On level 10, the precedence does not apply to operands that are surrounded by the operator. On level 11, the function notation $\lambda v : D \bullet b$ surrounds D, so the precedence does not apply to D; it applies to b. Similarly for $\forall \bullet \ \exists \bullet \ \Sigma \bullet$ and $\Pi \bullet$. The operators $\ = \ \Rightarrow$ and $\ \Leftarrow$ are identical to $= \Rightarrow$ and $\Leftarrow$ except for precedence.

12.3   Partial Correctness

For simplicity, we'll start with partial correctness, which ignores time. We can observe the initial state of memory, represented by variables x, y, ..., whose values are provided as input. We can also observe the final state of memory, represented by variables x', y', ..., whose values are the result of a computation. Specification S is implementable if and only if $\forall\, x, y, \dots \bullet \exists\, x', y', \dots \bullet S$.

As specification language, we allow ordinary logic, arithmetic, notations that are specific to the application, and any other well-defined notations that the specifier considers convenient, including notations invented on the spot for the purpose. We also include in our specification language the following notations:

$$
\begin{aligned}
ok \ &= x' = x \wedge y' = y \wedge \dots \\
x := e \ &= x' = e \wedge y' = y \wedge \dots \\
\textbf{if } b \textbf{ then } P \textbf{ else } Q &= b \wedge P \vee \neg b \wedge Q \\
&= (b \Rightarrow P) \wedge (\neg b \Rightarrow Q) \\
P\,;Q \ &= \exists\, x'', y'', \dots \bullet \quad (\text{substitute } x'', y'', \dots \text{ for } x', y', \dots \text{ in } P) \\
&\qquad\qquad\qquad\ \wedge (\text{substitute } x'', y'', \dots \text{ for } x, y, \dots \text{ in } Q\,)
\end{aligned}
$$

The notation ok specifies that the final values of all variables equal the corresponding initial values. A computer can satisfy this specification by doing nothing. Let us take ok to be a program. In the assignment notation, x is any state variable and e is any expression in the domain of x. Let us take assignments in which expression e does not use primed variables, and uses only those operators that are implemented, to be programs. In the **if** notation, if b does not use primed variables, and uses only those operators that are implemented, and P and Q are programs, then let us take **if** b **then** P **else** Q to be a program. The specification $P\,;Q$ can be implemented by a computer that first behaves according to P, then behaves according to Q, with the final values from P serving as initial values for Q. It therefore describes sequential execution. If P and Q are programs, let us take $P\,;Q$ to be a program.

From these definitions, many useful laws of programming can be proved. Here are a few. Note that P, Q, R, and S can be any specifications, not just programs.

$ok\,;P\ =P\,;ok\ =P$	Identity Law
$P\,;(Q\,;R)\ =(P\,;Q)\,;R$	Associative Law
if b **then** P **else** $P\ =P$	Idempotent Law
if b **then** P **else** $Q\ =$ **if** $\neg b$ **then** Q **else** P	Case Reversal Law
$P\ =$ **if** b **then** $b\Rightarrow P$ **else** $\neg b\Rightarrow P$	Case Creation Law
$P\vee Q\,;R\vee S\ =$	Distributive Law
$\qquad(P\,;R)\vee(P\,;S)\vee(Q\,;R)\vee(Q\,;S)$	
(**if** b **then** P **else** Q) $\wedge R\ =$	Distributive Law
$\qquad$ **if** b **then** $P\wedge R$ **else** $Q\wedge R$	

and all other operators in place of $\wedge$ including sequential execution:

(**if** b **then** P **else** Q)$\,;R\ =$
$\qquad$ **if** b **then** $(P\,;R)$ **else** $(Q\,;R)$

$x:=$ **if** b **then** e **else** $f\ =$	Functional-Imperative Law
$\qquad$ **if** b **then** $x:=e$ **else** $x:=f$	
$x:=e\,;P\ =$	Substitution Law
$\qquad$ (for x substitute e in P)	

For this paper, we need only the four programming notations we have introduced, but we need one more way to create programs. Any implementable specification S is a program if a program P is provided such that $S\Leftarrow P$ is a theorem. To execute S, just execute P. One can imagine a library of specifications that have become programs by being provided with implementations. Furthermore, recursion is allowed: within P, we can use specification S as a program. A computer executes S by behaving according to program P, and whenever S is encountered again, the behavior is again according to P.

To illustrate, here is a small problem.   If ! is the factorial function, then $(a+b)!/(a!\times b!)$ is the number of ways to partition $a+b$ things into a things and b things. In natural variables x, a, and b, the specification is

$$x'=(a+b)!/(a!\times b!)$$

There are many ways to refine this specification. One of them is

$$x'=(a+b)!/(a!\times b!)\ \Leftarrow\ x:=1\,;x'=x\times(a+b)!/(a!\times b!)$$

which is proved by one application of the Substitution Law. The right side uses a new specification that requires refinement:

$x'=x\times(a+b)!/(a!\times b!)\ \Leftarrow$
$\qquad$ **if** $a=0\vee b=0$ **then** ok
$\qquad$ **else** $(x:=x/a/b\times(a+b-1)\times(a+b);$
$\qquad\qquad a:=a-1\,;b:=b-1\,;x'=x\times(a+b)!/(a!\times b!))$

The proof uses three applications of the Substitution Law and some simplification. The right side uses the specification we are refining recursively. We have not used any new, unrefined specifications, so we are done.

If ! is not an implemented operator, then $x := (a+b)!/(a! \times b!)$ is not a program. Whether it is or not, we may still refine it, to obtain the following solution:

$$x := (a + b)!/(a! \times b!) \quad \Longleftarrow$$
$$\textbf{if } a = 0 \vee b = 0 \textbf{ then } x := 1$$
$$\textbf{else } (a := a - 1 \; ; b := b - 1 \; ; x := (a + b)!/(a! \times b!));$$
$$a := a + 1 \; ; b := b + 1 \; ; x := x/a/b \times (a + b - 1) \times (a + b))$$

The occurrence of $x := (a + b)!/(a! \times b!)$ on the right side is a recursive call.

Note that we have loops in the refinement structure, but no looping construct in our programming notations. This avoids a lot of semantic complications.

12.4   Real-time

To talk about time, we just add a time variable t. We do not change the theory at all; the time variable is treated just like any other variable, as part of the state. The interpretation of t as time is justified by the way we use it. In an implementation, the other variables $x, y, \ldots$ require space in the computer's memory, but the time variable t does not; it simply represents the time at which execution occurs.

We use t for the initial time, the time at which execution starts, and t' for the final time, the time at which execution ends. To allow for nontermination we take the domain of time to be a number system extended with an infinite number ∞.

Time cannot decrease, therefore a specification S with time is implementable if and only if

$$\forall x, y, \ldots, t \bullet \exists x', y', \ldots, t' \bullet S \wedge t' \geqslant t$$

For each initial state, there must be at least one satisfactory final state in which time has not decreased.

To obtain the real execution time, just insert time increments as appropriate. Of course, this requires intimate knowledge of the implementation, both hardware and software; there's no way to avoid it. Before each assignment $x := e$ insert $t := t + u$ where u is the time required to evaluate and store e. Before each conditional **if** b **then** P **else** Q insert $t := t + v$ where v is the time required to evaluate b and branch. Before each call S insert $t := t + w$ where w is the time required for the call and return. For a call that is implemented in-line, this time will be zero. For a call that is executed last in a refinement, it may be just the time for a branch. Sometimes it will be the time required to push a return address onto a stack and branch, plus the time to pop the return address and branch back. We could place the time increase after each of the programming notations instead of before; by placing it before, we make it easier to use the Substitution Law.

Any specification can talk about time: $t' = t + e$ specifies that e is the execution time; $t' \leqslant t + e$ specifies that e is an upper bound on the execution time; and $t' \geqslant t + e$ specifies that e is a lower bound on the execution time.

In the partition example, suppose that the **if**, the assignment, and the call each take time *1*. Let $\downarrow$ be the *minimum* operator. Inserting time increments, we can easily prove

$$t' = t + 5 \times (a \downarrow b) + 3 \ \Longleftarrow$$
$$\qquad t := t + 1 \,;\, x := 1 \,;\, t := t + 1 \,;\, t' = t + 5 \times (a \downarrow b) + 1$$
$$t' = t + 5 \times (a \downarrow b) + 1 \ \Longleftarrow$$
$$\qquad t := t + 1;$$
$$\qquad \textbf{if } a = 0 \vee b = 0 \textbf{ then } ok$$
$$\qquad \textbf{else } (t := t + 1 \,;\, x := x/a/b \times (a + b - 1) \times (a + b);$$
$$\qquad\qquad t := t + 1 \,;\, a := a - 1 \,;\, t := t + 1 \,;\, b := b - 1;$$
$$\qquad\qquad t := t + 1 \,;\, t' = t + 5 \times (a \downarrow b) + 1)$$

So the execution time is $5 \times (a \downarrow b) + 3$. The Law of Refinement by Parts says that we can conjoin specifications that have similar refinements, so without any further proof we have

$$x' = (a + b)!/(a! \times b!) \wedge t' = t + 5 \times (a \downarrow b) + 3 \ \Longleftarrow$$
$$\qquad t := t + 1 \,;\, x := 1 \,;\, t := t + 1;$$
$$\qquad x' = x \times (a + b)!/(a! \times b!) \wedge t' = t + 5 \times (a \downarrow b) + 1$$

$$x' = x \times (a + b)!/(a! \times b!) \wedge t' = t + 5 \times (a \downarrow b) + 1 \ \Longleftarrow$$
$$\qquad t := t + 1;$$
$$\qquad \textbf{if } a = 0 \vee b = 0 \textbf{ then } ok$$
$$\qquad \textbf{else } (t := t + 1 \,;\, x := x/a/b \times (a + b - 1) \times (a + b);$$
$$\qquad\qquad t := t + 1 \,;\, a := a - 1 \,;\, t := t + 1 \,;\, b := b - 1 \,;\, t := t + 1;$$
$$\qquad\qquad x' = x \times (a + b)!/(a! \times b!) \wedge t' = t + 5 \times (a \downarrow b) + 1)$$

When we place a time increment $t := t + e$ in a program, the expression e can depend on the values of variables; it doesn't have to be a constant. If we cannot say precisely what the time increment is, perhaps we can say what its bounds are: $a \leqslant t' - t \leqslant b$.

12.5   Recursive Time

To free ourselves from having to know implementation details, we allow any arbitrary scheme for inserting time increments $t := t + u$ into programs. Each scheme defines a new measure of time. In the recursive time measure, each recursive call costs time *1*, and all else is free. This measure neglects the time for straight-line and branching programs, charging only for loops.

In the recursive measure, our earlier example becomes

$$t' = t + a \downarrow b \iff x := 1 \; ; \; t' = t + a \downarrow b$$

$$t' = t + a \downarrow b \iff$$
$$\quad \text{if } a = 0 \lor b = 0 \text{ then } ok$$
$$\quad \text{else } (x := x/a/b \times (a + b - 1) \times (a + b);$$
$$\qquad\qquad a := a - 1 \; ; \; b := b - 1 \; ; \; t := t + 1 \; ; \; t' = t + a \downarrow b)$$

Since implication is reflexive, we can refine any specification by itself. For example,

$$x' = 2 \iff x' = 2$$

With this refinement, $x' = 2$ is a program that claims x will have the final value 2, but it doesn't say when. Now let's add time. If we specify that execution time is finite, say $t' = t + n$, and insert the time increment before the recursive call we find that

$$x' = 2 \land t' = t + n \iff t := t + 1 \; ; \; x' = 2 \land t' = t + n$$

is not a theorem. The only implementable specification we can refine this way is $t' = \infty$:

$$x' = 2 \land t' = \infty \iff t := t + 1 \; ; \; x' = 2 \land t' = \infty$$

This specification says that execution takes forever.

In the partition example, suppose now that a and b are integer variables. We can prove the following specification of execution time:

$$(0 \leqslant a \leqslant b \lor b < 0 \leqslant a \Rightarrow t' = t + a)$$
$$\land \, (0 \leqslant b \leqslant a \lor a < 0 \leqslant b \Rightarrow t' = t + b)$$
$$\land \, (a < 0 \land b < 0 \Rightarrow t' = \infty)$$

12.6   Total Correctness

In a total correctness semantics, the only question asked about time is whether it is finite or infinite. Since we only want to know one bit of information about time, we might consider using a boolean abstraction. Let s mean "execution starts at a finite time" and s' mean "execution ends at a finite time". The programming notations can remain as they were, satisfying the same axioms and laws, except that s replaces t. This sort of total correctness semantics has been suggested in [2] and in [7]. But there's a problem: we can no longer insert a time increment into a recursion. We have nothing to correspond to the tick of a clock. So we cannot account for the passage of time in a recursive refinement.

One solution to the problem is to abandon recursive refinement, and to invent a loop construct; a well-known syntax is **while** b **do** S. If we are to make use of our theory for programming (and surely that is its purpose), we must define **while** b **do** S for arbitrary specifications S, not just for programs. That is necessary so that we can introduce a loop and show that we have done so correctly, separately from the refinement of its body. There are essentially two ways to do it: as a limit of a sequence of approximations, or as a least (pre)fixed-point.

The limit of approximations works like this. Define

$$W_0 \;=\; true$$
$$W_{n+1} \;=\; \textbf{if } b \textbf{ then } (S \,;\, W_n) \textbf{ else } ok$$

Then

$$\textbf{while } b \textbf{ do } S \;\;=\;\; \forall\, n \bullet W_n$$

As an example, we will find the semantics of

$$\textbf{while } x \neq 1 \textbf{ do } x := x \textbf{ div } 2$$

in one integer variable x. We find

$$W_0 \;=\; true$$
$$W_1 \;=\; \textbf{if } x \neq 1 \textbf{ then } (x := x \textbf{ div } 2 \,;\, true) \textbf{ else } ok$$
$$\;=\; x = 1 \Rightarrow x' = 1$$
$$W_2 \;=\; \textbf{if } x \neq 1 \textbf{ then } (x := x \textbf{ div } 2 \,;\, x = 1 \Rightarrow x' = 1) \textbf{ else } ok$$
$$\;=\; 1 \leqslant x < 4 \Rightarrow x' = 1$$

Jumping to the general case, which we could prove by induction,

$$W_n \;=\; 1 \leqslant x < 2^n \Rightarrow x' = 1$$

And so

$$\textbf{while } x \neq 1 \textbf{ do } x := x \textbf{ div } 2$$
$$=\; \forall\, n \bullet 1 \leqslant x < 2^n \Rightarrow x' = 1$$
$$=\; 1 \leqslant x \Rightarrow x' = 1$$

In effect, we are introducing recursive time in disguise. W_n is the strongest specification of behavior that can be observed before time n, measured recursively.

The other way to define while-loops is as a least fixed-point. There are two axioms. The first

$$\textbf{while } b \textbf{ do } S \;\;=\;\; \textbf{if } b \textbf{ then } (S;\, \textbf{while } b \textbf{ do } S) \textbf{ else } ok$$

says that a **while**-loop equals its first unrolling. Stated differently, **while** b **do** S is a solution of the fixed-point equation (in unknown W)

$$W \quad = \quad \textbf{if } b \textbf{ then } (S \,;\, W) \textbf{ else } ok$$

The other axiom

$$\forall \, \sigma, \sigma' \bullet (W \; = \textbf{if } b \textbf{ then } (S \,;\, W) \textbf{ else } ok) \implies$$
$$\forall \, \sigma, \sigma' \bullet (W \implies \textbf{while } b \textbf{ do } S)$$

(where σ is the state variables) says that **while** b **do** S is as weak as any fixed-point, so it is the weakest (least strong) fixed-point.

The two axioms we have just seen are equivalent to the following two axioms:

$$\textbf{while } b \textbf{ do } S \implies \textbf{if } b \textbf{ then } (S; \textbf{while } b \textbf{ do } S) \textbf{ else } ok$$

$$\forall \, \sigma, \sigma' \bullet (W \implies \textbf{if } b \textbf{ then } (S \,;\, W) \textbf{ else } ok) \implies$$
$$\forall \, \sigma, \sigma' \bullet (W \implies \textbf{while } b \textbf{ do } S)$$

The first of these says that a **while**-loop refines (implements) its first unrolling; it is a prefixed-point. The second says that **while** b **do** S is as weak as any prefixed-point, so it is the weakest prefixed-point. Though equivalent to the former definition, this definition has an advantage. From the prefixed-point definition it is easy to prove the fixed-point formulas, but the reverse proof is quite difficult. These (pre)fixed-point definitions introduce a form of induction especially for **while**-loops, a kind of **while**-loop arithmetic, in place of the arithmetic of a time variable.

The limit of approximations definition and the (pre)fixed-point definition agree when the body of a loop uses only programming notations, but they sometimes disagree when the body is an arbitrary specification. A famous example, in one integer variable x, is

$$\textbf{while } x \neq 0 \textbf{ do if } x > 0 \textbf{ then } x := x - 1 \textbf{ else } x' \geqslant 0$$

According to the limit of approximations, this **while**-loop equals

$$x \geqslant 0 \Rightarrow x' = 0$$

According to the (pre)fixed-point, it equals

$$x' = 0$$

They differ on whether we should consider a computation to be terminating in the absence of any time bound.

A total correctness semantics makes the proof of invariance properties difficult, or even impossible. For example, we cannot prove

$$x' \geqslant x \; \Longleftarrow \textbf{while } b \textbf{ do } x' \geqslant x$$

which says, quite reasonably, that if the body of a loop doesn't decrease x, then the loop doesn't decrease x. The problem is that the semantics does not allow us to separate such invariance properties from the question of termination. In the recursive time semantics, in place of

$$S \ \Leftarrow \textbf{while } b \textbf{ do } P$$

we write

$$S \ \Leftarrow \textbf{if } b \textbf{ then } (P \ ; \ t := t + 1 \ ; \ S) \textbf{ else } ok$$

and the proof of the invariance property

$$x' \geqslant x \ \Leftarrow \textbf{if } b \textbf{ then } (x' \geqslant x \ ; \ t := t + 1 \ ; \ x' \geqslant x) \textbf{ else } ok$$

is easy.

In practice, neither the limit of approximations nor the (pre)fixed-point definition is usable for programming. Instead, programming is split into partial correctness and termination argument. To prove

$$x \geqslant 1 \Rightarrow x' = 1 \ \Leftarrow \textbf{while } x \neq 1 \textbf{ do } x := x \textbf{ div } 2$$

we prove partial correctness, which is

$$x \geqslant 1 \Rightarrow x' = 1 \ \Leftarrow \textbf{if } x \neq 1 \textbf{ then } (x := x \textbf{ div } 2 \ ; \ x \geqslant 1 \Rightarrow x' = 1)$$
$$\textbf{else } ok$$

For termination we use a 'variant' or 'bound function' or 'well-founded set'. In this example, we show that for $x > 1$, x is decreased but not below 0 by the body $x := x \textbf{ div } 2$ of the loop. The bound function is again recursive time in disguise. We are showing that execution time is bounded by x. Then we throw away the bound, retaining only the one bit of information that there is a bound, so there is no incentive to find a tight bound. In the example, showing that x is a variant corresponds to the proof of

$$x \geqslant 1 \Rightarrow t' - t \leqslant x \ \Leftarrow$$
$$\textbf{if } x \neq 1 \textbf{ then } (x := x \textbf{ div } 2 \ ; \ t := t + 1 \ ; \ x \geqslant 1 \Rightarrow t' - t \leqslant x)$$
$$\textbf{else } ok$$

This linear time bound is rather loose; for about the same effort, we can prove a logarithmic time bound:

$$x \geqslant 1 \Rightarrow t' \leqslant t + \log x \ \Leftarrow$$
$$\textbf{if } x \neq 1 \textbf{ then } (x := x \textbf{ div } 2 \ ; \ t := t + 1 \ ; \ x \geqslant 1 \Rightarrow t' \leqslant t + \log x)$$
$$\textbf{else } ok$$

In any case, we can express the termination proof in exactly the same form as the partial correctness proof (though occasionally time must be measured by a tuple of numbers, rather than just a single number).

A total correctness formalism introduces all the formal machinery necessary to calculate time bounds, but in a disguised and unusable way. A proof of total correctness necessarily requires finding a time bound, then throws it away. Of all the abstractions of time, total correctness gives least benefit for effort.

Furthermore, from Gödel and Turing we know that a complete and consistent theory in which termination can be expressed is impossible. Any total correctness theory will therefore be incomplete in its treatment of termination.

12.7   Temporal Logic

An interesting abstraction of time is offered by temporal operators such as $\Box$ (always), $\Diamond$ (sometime, eventually), and $\bigcirc$ (next). We want $\Box P$ to mean that P is true at all times during a computation, and $\Diamond P$ to mean that P is true at some time during a computation. Until now, we have assumed that only the initial and final states are observable, but for temporal operators we want intermediate states to be observable, too. We keep t and t' for the initial and final execution time, but state variables x, $y,\ldots$, are now functions of time. The value of x at time t is xt. An expression such as $x + y$ is also a function of time; its argument is distributed to its variable operands as follows: $(x+y)t = xt + yt$. The programming notations are redefined as follows:

$$ok \;=\; t' = t$$

$$x := e \;=\; t' = t + 1 \wedge xt' = et \wedge yt' = yt \wedge \ldots$$

$$P;Q \;=\; \exists\, t'' : t \leqslant t'' \leqslant t' \bullet (\text{substitute } t'' \text{ for } t' \text{ in } P) \wedge (\text{substitute } t'' \text{ for } t \text{ in } Q \,)$$

$$\textbf{if } b \textbf{ then } P \textbf{ else } Q \;=\; bt \wedge P \vee \neg bt \wedge Q$$

We can now talk about intermediate states. For example,

$$x := x + 3 \,;\, x := x + 4$$
$$=\; t' = t + 2 \wedge x(t + 1) = xt + 3 \wedge x(t + 2) = xt + 7 \wedge$$
$$yt = y(t + 1) = y(t + 2)$$

As before, any implementable specification S is a program if a program P is provided such that $S \Leftarrow P$ is a theorem. Recursion is allowed if it is preceded by the passage of time. An assignment is assumed to take time *1*, but that is easily changed if one wants a different measure of time.

Before defining the temporal operators, here is a nice way to look at quantifiers. A quantifier is an operator that applies to functions. The quantifiers Σ and Π apply to functions that have a numeric result, and the quantifiers $\forall$ and $\exists$ apply to functions that have a boolean result (a function with a boolean result is called a predicate). If f is a function with numeric result, then Σf is the numeric result of applying f to all its domain elements and adding up all the results. Similarly Πf is the numeric result of applying f to all its domain elements and multiplying all the results. If p is a predicate, then $\forall p$ is the boolean result of applying p to all its domain elements and conjoining all the results. Similarly $\exists p$ is the boolean result of applying p to all its domain elements and disjoining all the results. For the sake of tradition, when a quantifier is applied to a function written as a λ-expression, the λ is omitted. For example, the application of Σ to $\lambda n : nat \bullet 1/2^n$ is written $\Sigma n : nat \bullet 1/2^n$, and the application of $\forall$ to $\lambda r : rat \bullet r < 0 \vee r = 0 \vee r > 0$ is written $\forall r : rat \bullet r < 0 \vee r = 0 \vee r > 0$.

This treatment of quantifiers allows us to write the Generalization and Specialization Laws as follows: if x is in the domain of p, then

$$\forall p \implies px \implies \exists p$$

A quantification such as $\forall x \bullet lost\ x$ can be written more briefly as $\forall lost$. With composition of operators, we can write deMorgan's Laws this way:

$$\neg \forall p \;=\; \exists \neg p$$
$$\neg \exists p \;=\; \forall \neg p$$

or even this way:

$$\neg \forall \;=\; \exists \neg$$
$$\neg \exists \;=\; \forall \neg$$

Let S be a specification. The extension of S, written $\underline{S}$ and pronounced "S extended", is defined as follows:

$$\underline{S} \;=\; \lambda t'' : t \leqslant t'' \leqslant t' \bullet (\text{substitute } t'' \text{ for } t \text{ in } S)$$

Whatever S may say about time t, $\underline{S}$ extends it to all times from t to t'. Now we define

$$\Box S \;=\; \forall \underline{S}$$
$$\Diamond S \;=\; \exists \underline{S}$$
$$\circ S \;=\; \underline{S}(t+1)$$

These definitions give us something close to Interval Temporal Logic [9]. We can prove deMorgan's Laws

$$\neg \Box S \;=\; \Diamond \neg S$$
$$\neg \Diamond S \;=\; \Box \neg S$$

and other identities of ITL, such as

$$\Diamond S \;=\; true \,;\, S$$

But we still have a time variable. We can say that x is constant like this: $\Box\, xt = xt'$. We can prove

$$\bigcirc S \;=\; t' = t + 1 \,;\, S \;=\; t' \geqslant t + 1 \,\wedge\, (\text{substitute } t + 1 \text{ for } t \text{ in } S)$$

In Interval Temporal Logic, time is discrete. With the definitions of $\Box$ and $\Diamond$ given above, time can be discrete or continuous. If it is continuous, we might like to strengthen assignment as follows:

$$x := e \;=\; t' = t + 1 \,\wedge\, xt' = et \,\wedge\, (\Box\, yt' = yt) \,\wedge\, \ldots$$

so that unaffected variables remain continuously constant, while x is unknown during the assignment and known to have its newly assigned value only at the end. With continuous time, the $\bigcirc$ operator no longer means "next", and is not particularly useful. If time is discrete, we can say that x never decreases like this: $\Box\, x(t + 1) \geqslant xt$. If time is discrete and $t' = \infty$, we can prove the fixed-point equations

$$\Box\, S \;=\; S \wedge \Box \bigcirc S$$
$$\Diamond\, S \;=\; S \vee \Diamond \bigcirc S$$

Temporal logic considers time to be too holy to speak its name; it replaces $\forall\, t$, $\exists\, t$, and $t + 1$ by $\Box$, $\Diamond$, and $\bigcirc$. We need quantifiers for many purposes, and we quantify over many things. The temporal operators $\Box$ and $\Diamond$ replace the usual quantifiers $\forall$ and $\exists$ only for quantifications over time, and then only in some cases. We needed $\exists$ over time to define sequential execution (chop in Interval Temporal Logic). With two sets of symbols to do similar jobs, we are burdened with learning two sets of similar laws. By treating quantifiers as operators, and by defining extensions, we make the usual quantifiers just as convenient for time as the temporal operators. On the other hand, if extensions are used only in combination with quantifiers, we might still prefer to write $\Box\, S$ and $\Diamond\, S$ than to write $\forall\, \underline{S}$ and $\exists\, \underline{S}$. (Underscore is a poor notation anyway.)

As noted already, the "next" operator is useless for continuous time; in a practical sense, it is also inadequate for discrete time. Arithmetic operations on the time variable are a convenient and familiar way to express specifications concerning quantities of time. To be limited to a successor operator is too constraining.

12.8   Concurrency

A computation is sometimes modeled as a sequence of states, or state transitions. The index (or position) of a state (or transition) in a sequence is an abstraction of the time of its occurrence. In some models, an increasing index means increasing time; in others, it means nondecreasing time. A sequence of computations is easily composed into a single computation just by catenation. But composition of parallel computations is not so obvious.

Suppose computation is a sequence of actions, and an increasing index represents nondecreasing time. Then two adjacent actions in the sequence may perhaps occur at the same time. So it seems we have a possibility to represent concurrency. But how do we distinguish concurrent actions from sequential adjacent actions? An answer that has often been given is the following: if a specification allows two actions to occur adjacently in either order, then they are concurrent. This answer has been well criticised for confusing nondeterminacy (disjunction) with concurrency. Saying that two actions occur sequentially in either order is not the same as saying they occur concurrently.

This abstraction of time, as an index in a sequence, leads to another well-known problem. If parallel processes are represented as an interleaving of actions, we stretch time; a longer sequence is needed to represent the same time. Perhaps we do not mind, but many people have been concerned to say that time must not be stretched too far: a finite time (for one process) must not require an infinite sequence. This is the issue of fairness, and it suffers the same criticisms as a total correctness formalism.

Concurrency is basically conjunction. To say that P and Q are concurrent is to say that P and Q both describe the computation. In [5], parallelism is distinguished from communication between processes; the parallelism is disjoint, and it is exactly conjunction. When memory is shared, there is a problem: conjunction is not always implementable, even when both conjuncts are. For example, $x := 2 \parallel x := 3$ asks for two contradictory actions at the same time (it does not ask for two actions sequentially in either order). We may dismiss this example, saying that anyone who asks for the impossible should not expect to get it. But here is a less easily dismissed example: $x := x+1 \parallel y := y+1$. The left process says not only that x is increased, but also that y is unchanged. The right process says that y is increased and x is unchanged. Again, they contradict each other. What we want, of course, is that x and y are increased, and all other variables are unchanged.

In a semantics that does not measure time, and hides intermediate states, such as the partial correctness and total correctness semantics shown earlier, there is another problem. In such a semantics,

$$x := x + 1 \; ; x := x - 1 \quad = \quad ok$$

And so, with no escape,

$$(x := x + 1 \; ; x := x - 1) \parallel y := x$$
$$= \quad ok \parallel y := x$$

According to the first line, it may seem that $y' = x + 1$ is a possibility: the right process $y := x$ may be executed in between the two assignments $x := x + 1$ and

$x := x - 1$ in the left process. According to the last line, this does not happen; the final value of y is the initial value of x. No process may see or affect the intermediate states of another process. Intermediate state arises in the definition of sequential execution; it is the means by which information is passed from one program to a sequentially later program. It was not invented for passing information between parallel processes, and cannot be used for that purpose.

Useful concurrency is still possible in a semantics that does not measure time and hides intermediate states. Information can be passed between processes by communication primitives designed for the purpose. For one such definition, see [3].

For parallel processes to co-operate through shared memory, they must make their intermediate states visible to each other, and make their times explicit. The semantics in the section on temporal logic does exactly that. We need two more auxiliary ideas. First, we define *wait* as an easily implemented specification whose execution takes an arbitrary amount of time, and leaves all other variables unchanged during that time.

$$wait \quad = \quad t' \geqslant t \wedge \Box\, xt = xt' \wedge yt = yt' \wedge \ldots$$

As in the definition of assignment, we must know what the state variables are in order to write the right side of this equation. We have been assuming throughout this paper that we always know what our state variables are in any specification. To make it explicit, we can adopt a notation similar to that used in [8]. Let $\alpha :: P$ be specification P with state variables α and t. For example,

$$x, y :: (x := y + z) \quad = \quad t' = t + 1 \wedge xt' = (y + z)t \wedge yt' = y$$

Here, x, y and t are the state variables; z is an ordinary variable, or parameter of the specification. That was the second auxiliary idea. Now we define parallel composition as follows:

$$\alpha :: P \parallel \beta :: Q \quad = \quad \alpha :: P \wedge \beta :: (Q\,;\, wait) \vee \alpha :: (P\,;\, wait) \wedge \beta :: Q$$

If P and Q are programs, we do not need to state α and β because they can be determined syntactically from the variables that appear on the left of assignments. Of course, to make use of $\parallel$ for programming, we must define it for more than just program operands.

Here is a simple example in variables x and y just to see that it works.

$$
\begin{aligned}
&(x := 2\,;\, x := x + y\,;\, x := x + y) \parallel (y := 3\,;\, y := x + y)\\
=\quad & (t' = t + 1 \wedge xt' = 2\,;\, t' = t + 1 \wedge xt' = xt + yt;\\
&\qquad t' = t + 1 \wedge xt' = xt + yt)\\
&\wedge (t' = t + 1 \wedge yt' = 3\,;\, t' = t + 1 \wedge yt' = xt + yt;\\
&\qquad t' \geqslant t \wedge \Box\, yt' = yt)\\
\vee\quad & (t' = t + 1 \wedge xt' = 2;\\
&\qquad t' = t + 1 \wedge xt' = xt + yt\,;\, t' = t + 1 \wedge\\
&\qquad xt' = xt + yt\,;\, t' \geqslant t \wedge \Box\, xt' = xt)\\
&\wedge (t' = t + 1 \wedge yt' = 3\,;\, t' = t + 1 \wedge yt' = xt + yt)
\end{aligned}
$$

$$= \quad (t' = t + 3 \wedge x(t+1) = 2 \wedge x(t+2) = x(t+1) + y(t+1) \wedge$$
$$x(t+3) = x(t+2) + y(t+2))$$
$$\wedge \, (t' \geqslant t + 2 \wedge y(t+1) = 3 \wedge y(t+2) = x(t+1) + y(t+1) \wedge$$
$$\Box y t' = y(t+2))$$
$$\vee \quad (t' \geqslant t + 3 \wedge \text{other conjuncts})$$
$$\wedge \, (t' = t + 2 \wedge \text{other conjuncts})$$
$$= \quad t' = t + 3 \wedge x(t+1) = 2 \wedge y(t+1) = 3 \wedge x(t+2) = 5 \wedge$$
$$y(t+2) = 5 \wedge x(t+3) = 10 \wedge y(t+3) = 5$$

In that example, for ease of calculation, we made the unrealistic assumption that every assignment takes exactly one time unit. To be more realistic, we could suppose that assignment time depends on the operators within the assignment's expression, and possibly on the values of the operands. We could also allow time to be nondeterministic, perhaps with lower and upper bounds, by writing $a \leqslant t' - t < b$. Whatever timing policy we decide on, whether deterministic or nondeterministic, whether discrete or continuous, the definitions and theory remain unchanged. Of course, complicated timing leads quickly to very complicated semantic expressions that describe all possible interactions. If we want to know only something, not everything, about the possible behaviors, we can proceed by implications instead of equations, weakening for the purpose of simplifying. Programming goes the other way: we start with a specification of desired behavior, and strengthen as necessary to obtain a program.

Here are some useful laws that can be proved from the definition of concurrent composition just given. Let b be a boolean expression and let P, Q, R, and S be specifications. Then

$$P \parallel Q \; = \; Q \parallel P \qquad\qquad\qquad \text{symmetry}$$
$$P \parallel (Q \parallel R) \; = \; (P \parallel Q) \parallel R \qquad \text{associativity}$$
$$P \parallel ok \; = \; ok \parallel P \; = \; P \qquad\quad \text{identity}$$
$$P \parallel Q \vee R \; = \; (P \parallel Q) \vee (P \parallel R) \quad \text{distributivity}$$
$$P \parallel \textbf{if } b \textbf{ then } Q \textbf{ else } R \qquad\qquad \text{distributivity}$$
$$= \textbf{if } b \textbf{ then } (P \parallel Q) \textbf{ else } (P \parallel R)$$
$$\textbf{if } b \textbf{ then } (P \parallel Q) \textbf{ else } (R \parallel S) \qquad \text{distributivity}$$
$$= \textbf{if } b \textbf{ then } P \textbf{ else } R \parallel \textbf{if } b \textbf{ then } Q \textbf{ else } S$$

12.9   A Caution Concerning Synchronization

In FORTRAN (prior to 1977) we could have a sequential composition of **if**-statements, but we could not have an **if**-statement containing a sequential composition. In ALGOL the syntax was fully recursive; sequential and conditional compositions could be nested, each within the other. Did we learn a lesson? Apparently we did not learn a very general one: we now seem happy to have a parallel composition of sequential compositions, but very reluctant to have a sequential composition of parallel compositions.

Suppose, for example, that we decide to have two processes, as follows:

$$(x := x + y \ ; x := x \times y) \ \| \ (y := x - y \ ; y := x/y)$$

The first modifies x twice, and the second modifies y twice. Suppose we want to synchronize the two processes at their mid-points, between the two assignments, forcing the faster process to wait for the slower one, and then to allow the two processes to continue with the new, updated values of x and y. The usual solution is to invent synchronization primitives to control the rate of execution of processes. But synchronization is sequencing, and we already have an adequate sequencing primitive. The solution should be

$$(x := x + y \ \| \ y := x - y) \ ; (x := x \times y \ \| \ y := x/y)$$

We just allow a sequential composition of parallel compositions.

12.10   An Aside Concerning Specification

The specifications in this paper are boolean expressions. Traditionally, the presence or possibility of quantifiers turns a boolean expression into a predicate; in this paper, a predicate is a function with boolean range, and the quantifiers $\forall$ and $\exists$ apply to predicates to produce booleans. Thus $\forall x : int \bullet x \leqslant y$ is a boolean expression.

We could have used predicate expressions rather than boolean expressions for specifications; the difference is language level. A predicate expression takes arguments by position, or address, whereas a boolean expression is supplied values for variables by their names. For example, in the predicate expression $\lambda x, y : int \bullet x \leqslant y$, the names x and y are local (bound) and of no global significance (not free). We can supply 3 as first argument and 5 as second argument, as follows:

$$(\lambda x, y : int \bullet x \leqslant y) \ 3 \ 5$$

In the boolean expression $x \leqslant y$, the names x and y are global (free), and we can supply value 3 for x and 5 for y as follows:

$$x := 3 \ ; y := 5 \ ; x \leqslant y$$

according to the Substitution Law. For the convenience of using variables' names rather than addresses, we have used boolean expressions rather than predicates for specifications.

In the well-known theory called Hoare Logic, a specification is a pair of boolean expressions. We specify that variable x is to be increased as follows:

$$\{x = X\} \ S \ \{x > X\}$$

(The parentheses were originally around S, but no matter.) In Dijkstra's theory of weakest preconditions, it is similar:

$$x = X \Rightarrow wp\ S\ (x > X)$$

There are two problems with these notations: X and S. They do not provide any way of relating the prestate and the poststate, hence the introduction of X. We ought to write $\forall X$, making X local, but customarily the quantifier is omitted. This problem is solved in the Vienna Development Method, in which the same specification is

$$\{true\}\ S\ \{x' > x\}$$

The other problem is that the programming language and specification language are disjoint, hence the introduction of S. Again, S should be local, but the appropriate quantifier is not obvious, and it is customarily omitted. In [2, 7, 3], the programming language is a sublanguage of the specification language. The specification that x is to be increased is

$$x' > x$$

The same single-expression double-state specifications are used in Z, but refinement is rather complicated. In Z, S is refined by P if and only if

$$\forall \sigma \bullet (\exists \sigma' \bullet S) \Rightarrow (\exists \sigma' \bullet P) \wedge (\forall \sigma' \bullet S \Leftarrow P)$$

where σ is the state variables. In Hoare Logic, $\{P\}\ S\ \{Q\}$ is refined by $\{R\}\ S\ \{U\}$ if and only if

$$\forall \sigma \bullet P \Rightarrow R \wedge (Q \Leftarrow U)$$

In this paper, S is refined by P if and only if

$$\forall \sigma, \sigma' \bullet S \Leftarrow P$$

Since refinement is what we must prove when programming, it is best to make refinement as simple as possible.

One might suppose that any type of mathematical expression can be used as a specification: whatever works. A specification of something, whether cars or computations, distinguishes those things that satisfy it from those that don't. Observation of something provides values for certain variables, and on the basis of those values we must be able to determine whether the something satisfies the specification. Thus we have a specification, some values for variables, and two possible outcomes. That is exactly the job of a boolean expression: a specification (of anything) really is a boolean expression. If instead we use a pair of predicates, or a function from predicates to predicates, or anything else, we make our specifications in an indirect way, and we make the task of determining satisfaction more difficult.

One might suppose that any boolean expression can be used to specify any computer behavior: whatever correspondence works. In Z, the expression *true* is used to specify (describe) terminating computations, and *false* is used to specify (describe) nonterminating computations. The reasoning is something like this: *false* is the specification for which there is no satisfactory final state; an infinite computation is behavior for which there is no final state; hence *false* represents infinite computation. Although we cannot observe a "final" state of an infinite computation, we can observe, simply by waiting *10* time units, that it satisfies $t' \geqslant t + 10$, and it does not satisfy $t' < t + 10$. Thus it ought to satisfy any specification implied by $t' \geqslant t + 10$, including *true* , and it ought not to satisfy any specification that implies $t' < t + 10$, including *false*. Since *false* is not true of anything, it does not (truly) describe anything. A specification is a description, and *false* is not satisfiable, not even by nonterminating computations. Since *true* is true of everything, it (truly) describes everything, even nonterminating computations. To say that P refines Q is to say that all behavior satisfying P also satisfies Q, which is just implication. The correspondence between specifications and computer behavior is not arbitrary.

12.11   Conclusions

The most striking conclusion of this paper is that a total correctness semantics is not worth its trouble. It is a considerable complication over a partial correctness semantics in order to gain one bit of information of dubious value (since nontermination cannot be observed, a promise of termination without a time bound is worthless). Partial correctness, with a time variable, provides more information at less cost. (The pejorative term "partial correctness" should not be used, and was not used in [4].)

Another contribution of this paper is a new semantics for Interval Temporal Logic, based on a boolean semantics of visible intermediate states, and using extensions. This semantics allows arbitrary arithmetic on a time variable, using the temporal operators as convenient quantifications.

And finally, a compositional semantics of concurrency with shared variables is presented.

Acknowledgment

I thank Theo Norvell, Andrew Malton, and IFIP Working Group 2.3 for many good ideas, and helpful discussion.

References

[1] E. C. R. Hehner, C. A. R. Hoare: "A More Complete Model of Communicating Processes", *Theoretical Computer Science* v26 p105–120, 1983.

[2] E. C. R. Hehner: "Predicative Programming", *CACM* v27 n2 p134–151, 1984 February. See p142.

[3] E. C. R. Hehner: *A Practical Theory of Programming*, Springer, New York, 1993.

[4] C. A. R. Hoare: "an Axiomatic Basis for Computer Programming", *CACM* v12 n10 p567–580, 583, 1969 October.

[5] C. A. R. Hoare: "a Calculus of Total Correctness of Communicating Processes", *The Science of Computer Programming* v1 n1–2 p49–72, 1981 October, and in C. A. R. Hoare, C. B. Jones: *Essays in Computing Science*, p289–314, Prentice-Hall International Series in Computer Science, London, 1989.

[6] C. A. R. Hoare: "Programs are Predicates", in C. A. R. Hoare, J. C. Shepherdson: *Mathematical Logic and Programming Languages*, p141–154, Prentice-Hall International, London, 1985, and in C. A. R. Hoare, C. B. Jones: *Essays in Computing Science*, p333–349, Prentice-Hall International, London, 1989.

[7] C. A. R. Hoare: lectures given at the NATO Advanced Study Institute, International Summer School on Program Design Calculi, Marktobedorf, 1992 July 28–August 9.

[8] C. C. Morgan: *Programming from Specifications*, Prentice-Hall International, London, 1990.

[9] B. C. Moszkowski: *Executing Temporal Logic Programs*, Cambridge University Press, 1986.

[10] X. Nicollin, J. Richier, J. Sifakis, J. Voiron: "ATP: an Algebra for Timed Processes", *Programming Concepts and Methods*, p414–443, Galilee, 1990.

Chapter 13

Software Development Method

M. A. Jackson

It is a great pleasure to be able to contribute to a Festschrift in Tony Hoare's honour. I have known him since we were both undergraduates nearly forty years ago, and have found continually renewed reason to admire his rare combination of an open mind with the highest standards of clarity and precision. Unlike many computer scientists, he is receptive to ideas painted on a broader canvas than that of a mathematical formalism. Knowing that, I have dared to take the whole of software development as my subject.

13.1 Introduction

Software development is a human activity. Like any human activity, it has many facets, and can be analysed from many points of view. Social scientists and experts in human relations examine the interactions among developers and between the development group and its customers. Lawyers and trades unionists see software systems as a means of changing working practices. Business theorists analyse development projects for their profitability, and measure return on investment. Quality control experts see the need for process optimisation based on statistical evidence. Some software developers see themselves as engineers, and want to be judged by the canons of such established disciplines as aeronautical, civil, or electrical engineering. Many say that programs are mathematical objects whose creation and study is a legitimate branch – some would say, the most challenging branch – of mathematics.

Each of these views is valid, at least for some parts of some projects. But when all the experts have claimed the substance of their different disciplines, is there any particular substance left that belongs peculiarly to software development? Or are we left only with the grin of the Cheshire Cat when its body has departed?

Software development does have a substance all of its own that gives it its special character. Software development is about the structure and technique of description. The task of the developer is to create transparently clear descriptions of complex systems in which many domains meet and interact – computing machinery and many other things too. Mathematics is an essential tool in software development, and in many parts of a large development proofs and calculi must be brought to bear. But software development is not mathematics any more than bridge building is mathematics. The central emphasis is on description more than on invention, on structure more than on calculation, on achieving self-evident clarity more than on constructing proofs of unobvious truths. Some properties of complex systems will demand and admit formal proof. But most will require a transparent clarity of description, and a separation of concerns by which clarity may be attained.

Development method, therefore, must concentrate on the separation of concerns and on their description once they have been separated: the central questions are what to describe, and how to describe it. Because the systems we develop are complex, there will be many things to describe, and their descriptions will be of many kinds. The relationships among descriptions will form non-trivial structures, and we will be concerned to keep intellectual control of these structures and to know clearly what each description describes and how it is related to the other descriptions. These concerns are not always well served by our present culture of software development.

13.2   Our Product Is a Machine

Software development is description. Yet the goal of our description activity is the construction of a machine. At the heart of every system we build is a machine – or, in a distributed system, several machines. The machine is our central artifact, the chief domain that we must describe: a tangible machine, not a mathematical abstraction. Of course, abstraction may be a necessary tool in arriving at the machine's description; but in the final analysis we must produce a machine with a certain behaviour appropriate to supporting the administration of a library, or to switching telephone messages, manipulating documents, or controlling a motor car or washing machine. Our products will usually be far more complex than a motor car or a washing machine, but must always be just as tangible.

Although our artifact is tangible, we make it merely by describing it. A general-purpose machine – a Universal Turing Machine – accepts our description of the special-purpose machine we wish to construct – a Turing Machine – and converts itself into that machine. It does not only compute about our description; it does not only translate it or analyse it. It actually adopts the properties and behaviour of the machine we have described, and itself becomes that machine. This relationship between our descriptions and the material world allows us, if anything does, to claim that software development is engineering.

The power of the special-purpose machines we construct by our descriptions is, ultimately, limited by the power of the general-purpose machines that clothe themselves in those descriptions. We can specialise the behaviour of the general-purpose machine, and we can understand its specialised behaviour in terms of our own choosing. But we cannot enlarge its behaviour – we can neither extend its state space nor add to its alphabet of events. We can only reduce it to meet our special needs, and we must take care to understand the extent of that reduction.

If, for example, our need is for a machine specially adapted to evaluating pure function applications, we may implement a pure functional language by describing the machine that interprets that language. The implementation provides us with a machine that operates in a Read-Eval-Print loop, each iteration of the loop reading a description of a function and its arguments and computing and printing the resulting value. The functional language itself rigorously eschews side-effects and abstracts from the order of function evaluation, this abstraction being a key advantage of such a language for its declared purpose. The resulting machine is ideally suited to its special purpose; but it is not at all suited to controlling a motor car, or to switching messages, or to word processing. Although the behaviours necessary to such purposes could be *described* in the functional language, and the function-evaluation machine could *compute about* them, it cannot itself *adopt* such behaviours. Its behaviour has been specialised to the Read-Eval-Print loop. The fact that it can compute – without side-effects – about motor car control, message switching, and word processing does not make it useful for performing those tasks. And the goal of software development is building useful machines.

13.3   The Machine and Other Domains

A fundamental rule of methodology is the rule of proportionate method: the scale of the method must be proportionate to the scale of the problem. For a trivial problem of software development, we just write the program in an available programming language. For a slightly less trivial problem we devote some effort to structuring the program. As the problem becomes more difficult we must begin to pay serious attention to its subject matter.

Even a trivial problem is about something. It has some subject matter, some real world, some domain of discourse other than the machine itself. A payroll system is about the employees and their work and pay; a process control system is about the plant and its vessels, valves, and pipes; a system for producing a Shakespeare concordance is about the texts of Shakespeare's plays and sonnets. Even when the subject matter is abstract – a graph to be traversed or a number to be tested for primality – it still furnishes a domain distinct from the machine itself.

The subject matter domain invites description in its own right. But for a small or fairly simple problem we often neglect to make such a description. And often we do so with impunity, because the description of the subject matter can be inferred from a reading of the program texts. A Pascal program, carefully constructed, shows clearly the structures of its inputs and outputs, and, if it is conversational, how its behaviour is interleaved with that of its user. The COBOL text of a payroll program exhibits the rules for calculating gross pay, and also the format of the printed payslips. Indeed, the originators of COBOL and some other programming languages wanted them to be 'problem-oriented languages', in which the program text would be itself a clear description of the subject matter of the program and the problem that it solved.

This view can be vigorously justified. The machine interacts with its environment, where the problem is located. The interaction can be viewed as an interface of shared phenomena. State is shared because the environment contains sensors that the machine can interrogate, and vice versa; events are shared because both environment and machine must participate in each event occurrence. It follows that an event trace of the machine behaviour at the interface is also a trace of the environment behaviour there; and the same is true of a trace of interface states. By describing one we also necessarily describe the other. Separate descriptions would be otiose.

Another, related, justification rests on the modelling relationship between the machine and the problem domain. In many systems the machine must incorporate a model of the problem domain; in an object-oriented system, for example, the objects are models of real-world objects of interest. This means that there are certain aspects of the machine's properties and behaviour, and certain aspects of the problem domain's properties and behaviour, that are both described by the same description. We may trust that these are the only aspects of the domain that are of interest. By describing the corresponding aspects of the machine we discharge any obligation to describe the problem domain.

13.4   Requirements, Specifications and Programs

In serious development, these justifications break down. The interface between a machine and its environment is rarely transparent. In a data processing or administrative system the interface is usually an elaborate structure of hardware and software, meriting careful attention in its own right. Events and states of the domain are not shared with the machine, but are transmitted unreliably and often with considerable delay; even reordering of messages is not excluded. In a control system, or an embedded system, the interface is usually more reliable, but still often imperfect.

The modelling justification is no more robust. The domain may have important properties that the system relies on but the machine does not model explicitly. One important property of a lift mechanism is that when the motor is set to 'up' and turned on, the lift will start to rise: the control system relies on this property, but it does not appear in the description of the control machine. More significantly, the machine will have many properties that are not shared with the problem domain or environment. If we are restricted to one description for both we can have no way of separating the properties they share from those that they do not.

There are many positive reasons for making separate explicit descriptions of domains other than the machine. Separation of concerns is more effective when it is accompanied by a separation of descriptions: no compiler writer would argue that a separate description of the grammar of the language to be compiled is unnecessary. Nor is the grammar thrown away or put on the shelf once it has been written down; in one way or another it provides a foundation for describing the parsing behaviour of the machine. The commonly heard plea that we should describe *what* the machine does before we describe *how* it does it is, in effect, a plea for a separate description of the problem domain. A brief thought experiment will show why. Ask yourself *what* a motor car does, and try to answer purely in terms of the car itself. The task is impossible. To say *what* a car does, we must talk of roads and passengers and drivers and fuel and baggage. They are not parts of the car.

Here we may draw a useful distinction between Requirements, Specifications, and Programs. A Requirement is located in the problem domain. Whatever the problem domain may be, it is certainly distinct from the machine domain. It is where the customer for the software will experience, interpret, and evaluate the effects brought about by the machine. A Requirement is not an informal or vague Specification. It can be as formal as we wish, even if the domain itself is informal. But it is about the problem domain, and not about the machine.

A Specification, by contrast, is a description of the machine itself. It describes those properties that the machine must have to satisfy the Requirement. Usually we expect a Specification to be a more abstract description of the machine than a Program: for example, it may describe the machine only implicitly. But it is still a description of the machine.

13.5   The Idea of a Problem Frame

The distinctions between *what* and *how*, between Requirement and Specification, and between Specification and Program, are too general to serve as the foundations of a method. It is not good enough to speak vaguely – as I have done – of the 'problem domain' or the 'environment'. To get a sufficient grip on a problem we must fit it into a tighter conceptual framework. Such a framework may be called a Problem Frame. It provides a structure into which we can fit the problem so that it can be worked on, almost as a mechanical part may be fitted into a jig for machining or welding.

The essential idea of a problem frame – though not by that name – is explained by Polya in his monograph *How To Solve It*. A problem can be analysed into its 'principal parts'. The idea is due to the ancient Greek mathematicians, and Polya illustrates it with problems in elementary Euclidean geometry. He distinguishes 'problems to prove' from 'problems to find'. An example of a problem to find is:

construct a triangle whose sides have the lengths a, b, and c. The principal parts of a problem to find are the Unknown, the Data, and the Condition. The task for the solver is to find an Unknown of the required kind that satisfies the Condition. Here the Unknown is a triangle; the Data are the lengths a, b, and c; and the Condition is that the triangle should have sides of the lengths given in the Data.

A problem to prove has different principal parts: it has a Hypothesis and a Conclusion. The task for the solver is to deduce the Conclusion from the Hypothesis, or else to show that the deduction is impossible. We recognise the different kinds of problem because they have different principal parts. More exactly, we choose to treat a given problem as a problem of one kind or the other because we can fit it comfortably into the prescribed structure of principal parts. But this choice is not objective, and is not always clear. A problem to prove, whose statement begins 'prove that there is at least one integer such that ... ', may obviously be treated as a problem to find; a problem to find, whose statement begins 'find an integer such that ... ', may sometimes be solved by guessing the integer and proving that it has the required property.

Having identified the principal parts of the problem, Polya proceeds to recommend a method. The method consists largely of heuristics: Split the Condition into parts; Check that you are using all the Data; Vary the Unknown to bring it closer to the Data; Think of a familiar problem having a similar Unknown. Only the establishment of the problem frame makes it possible to discuss method in this way. The recommendations are cast in terms of the defined problem frame, of the named principal parts and their distinctly identifiable roles, and in terms of their relationships to one another.

13.6   Problem Frames for Describing Machines

This is the essence of any problem-solving method, and methods for solving software development problems are no exception. Each method offers a particular problem frame, a characterisation of its principal parts, and a prescription for solving the problem by building a particular sequence of descriptions of its parts, culminating in a description of the desired machine. Usually certain languages are stipulated for describing particular parts, because they can capture and exploit the characteristic properties of those parts. Certain operations may also be stipulated for constructing the descriptions, exploiting the properties of their stipulated languages and thus again, indirectly, the characteristic properties of the principal parts.

Here, for example, is the traditional problem frame for Top-Down Functional Decomposition:

Machine The machine that is to be described. It autonomously executes one procedure.

Function What the Machine is to do: that is, the procedure it is to execute.

The solution task is to find a Machine that can execute the Function. A typical prescription for solution is to describe the Function in a succession of procedural descriptions. The first describes it at a single procedural level in natural language. Later descriptions introduce additional levels of invoked procedures, and rely less on natural language and more on the programming language. At each step the current set of descriptions forms a hierarchy of procedures. The final set, expressed entirely in the programming language, is interpretable by the general-purpose computer. It describes the desired Machine, and so solves the problem.

This problem frame, and hence inevitably any method that uses it, is extremely weak. The principal parts are so general that it is impossible to imagine a software development problem that they could not fit. But they fit no problem well. The only specific aspect is the characterisation of the Machine as a hierarchy of executable procedures. This would no doubt frustrate a developer resolved or required to use Prolog: but the characterisation is more one of the solution than of the problem or its parts. It is therefore impossible for Top-Down Functional Decomposition to be regarded as a serious method: it simply provides no grip on the problem.

Here is another problem frame, associated with Model-Oriented Specification methods:

Machine The machine that is to be described. It does nothing autonomously, but responds to user requests.

Operations Operations, atomic from the user's point of view, that the Machine performs at the user's request.

Model The state space of the Machine, as constrained by certain invariants and traversed by performance of the requested Operations.

The multiplicity of Operations, their atomic nature, and their relationship to the state space and its invariants, make this a stronger problem frame. The solution task is to find a Machine that can perform the requested Operations while maintaining the invariants of the Model. A number of different prescriptions are offered for solution. Various languages are prescribed for describing the Model structure and invariants, and for describing the Operations by relations on Model states. Eventually the Model is to be transformed into a data structure within the Machine, and the Operations into executable procedures. In a data-processing problem the Model data structure may be implemented in a relational database. In a different kind of problem it may be the representation of an abstract data type instance.

A related, but different, problem frame is used by Property-Oriented Specification methods. There is no Model principal part, and the Operations are described entirely in terms of their relationships to one another. For problems of a certain class this provides a simplification, and a release from suspicions that the Model is biased towards its eventual implementation.

13.7   Richer Problem Frames

These problem frames are relatively impoverished by their exclusive focus on the machine. Development of more demanding systems needs richer problem frames in which some of the principal parts are explicitly devoted to other domains.

The problem frame for the basic version of Structured Analysis and Specification has these parts:

System The machine that is to be described, including the computing machinery and possibly some clerical operations. It transforms input data flows to output data flows.

External Entities Entities, such as customers, suppliers, and other systems, that supply flows of input data to the System and receive its output data flows.

Function What the System must do to transform and process its inputs to produce its outputs.

Data Stores What the System must remember to perform the Function.

The solution task is to find a System that will perform the Function, interacting appropriately with the External Entities. The basis of the method is to describe the System as a process communicating by data flows with its External Entities, and maintaining and using the Data Stores. The resulting data flow diagram is then elaborated by replacing the System process symbol by a more detailed diagram showing two or more processes communicating by data flows, and so on successively until finally every process represented is simple enough to be directly described in a procedural 'mini-specification'.

This method is far less rich than it may appear at first sight, and far less rich than its problem frame would allow. The External Entities, which may be regarded as embodying the problem domain or environment, are not directly described. The input and output data flows of each Entity are separately described (but not the relationship of an Entity's inputs to its outputs), and a part of its state may be indirectly modelled in the Data Stores; but nothing more.

JSD is richer as a method. The principal parts of its problem frame are:

System The machine to be described. It runs a simulation and produces information about it both autonomously and on request.

Real World The problem domain about which the Machine is to compute, and of which it is to embody a model. The Real World has an autonomous behaviour over time, which is the subject matter of the simulation.

Function The production of output messages and reports by the Machine, containing information about the Real World obtained from the simulation.

The solution task is to find a System that models or simulates the Real World and performs the Function by extracting information from its Real World model. The first step of the method describes the Real World as a set of sequential processes in which events are represented abstractly. The same descriptions are then used to define the model within the System, the event representations now denoting receipt of messages about Real World events. The Function is described in terms of output operations embedded in model processes, and additional processes that communicate with the model and produce outputs reflecting its state. Finally, an executable description of the System is obtained by transforming the resulting process network so that it may be composed with the description of a scheduling scheme.

Another problem frame may be called the Workpiece problem frame. It may be suitable for such applications as word-processing. Its principal parts are:

Machine The machine to be described. It creates, manipulates, displays and exports objects at the user's request.

Workpieces The objects, often textual and graphic documents, that are to be worked on with the help of the Machine. The objects are inert: that is, they have no autonomous behaviour.

Worker The user – the person operating the Machine and working autonomously on the Workpieces.

Operations The operations that the Worker can ask the Machine to perform on the Workpieces.

The solution task is to find a Machine that allows the Worker to work on the Workpieces by performing the Operations on them. The first prescribed step may be to describe the type of the Workpiece as a data object with invariants. Then to describe the permitted sequences of Operations on a Workpiece, and the effect of each Operation. Next, to describe the behaviour of the Worker in terms of permitted sequences of Operations on a set of Workpieces. And finally to describe the Machine behaviour in response to the Worker behaviour, the Machine invoking appropriate Operations on the selected Workpiece objects or engaging in a diagnostic dialogue when the Worker has made a mistake.

Our last example may be called the Environment-Effect frame: some recent work by Parnas uses a version of this problem frame. It is a richer frame, and the associated method is more elaborate. It may be suitable for an embedded system that controls an external domain. Its principal parts are:

Machine The machine to be described. Its behaviour may be partly autonomous and partly responsive.

Environment The domain to be controlled by the Machine. It has state, and a behaviour that is partly autonomous and partly responsive.

Requirement The domain properties and behaviour – relationships among domain phenomena – that the Machine is to bring about.

Connection The connection between the Machine and the Environment by which the Machine can sense and affect states and events in the Environment.

The solution task is to construct a Machine that senses and controls the Environment through the Connection, and brings about the Requirement. In doing so, the Machine must take proper account, and proper advantage, of the properties that the Environment possesses independently of the Machine's behaviour.

A method adopting the Environment-Effect problem frame might prescribe that the first description should be of the Environment, stating the properties and behaviour that it possesses independently of the Machine. Then the Requirement should be described, stating the additional behaviour and properties that we desire the Environment to have. In general, the Requirement will be expressed at least partly in terms of phenomena that the Machine cannot control directly, and perhaps cannot even sense through the Connection.

The Requirement description should therefore then be refined, using relationships stated in the Environment description, so that it becomes feasible. That is, it must require only such Environment states to hold, and only such Environment events to occur, as the Machine can cause through the Connection; it must forbid only such Environment states and events as the Machine can inhibit through the Connection; and the conditions for causation and inhibition must be expressed only in terms of Environment states and events that the Machine can sense through the Connection.

Then the Connection should be described, to make explicit the association between phenomena it shares with the Environment at one end, and phenomena it shares with the Machine at the other end. Finally, the refined Requirement should be further modified, using this Connection description, into a Specification: that is, a description of the desired Machine expressed entirely in terms of Machine phenomena.

A simpler version of the Environment-Effects frame omits the Connection, assuming it to be reliable and effectively transparent.

13.8   Fitting the Frame to the Problem

Even from these cursory, disputable, and greatly simplified accounts of some methods and their associated problem frames, it is apparent that many different problem frames are possible, and that the choice of an appropriate problem frame is a matter of serious concern. An ill-fitting problem frame will be as irksome as an ill-fitting pair of shoes. Progress is not impossible, but it is painful; and as the journey proceeds the pain may eventually become crippling. Developers who, for whatever reason, find themselves using an unsuitable problem frame can resort to various unsatisfactory expedients. Like Procrustes they can force the problem into the frame whether it fits or not. More intelligently, they can bend the frame to accommodate the problem, or add parts to the frame structure to accommodate problem parts that would otherwise be neglected. Of course, there is a price to be paid. The accompanying method becomes progressively less useful as the problem frame becomes more distorted.

The fitness of a frame to a problem may be checked by some simple informal tests. They should be applied consciously at the outset of a development, while the shoe has not yet started to pinch, and a reasonably unconstrained choice may still be made.

The *separability test* requires that the problem can indeed be teased apart so that the principal parts are properly separated. The Model-Oriented Specification frame would fail this test for the problem of specifying a program that conducts a typical interactive dialogue with the user. The dialogue would have to be viewed as a series of user inputs, alternating with machine responses. Each user input would be regarded as an atomic Operation request, and the program's response as the Machine's performance of the requested Operation. But a dialogue cannot usually be separated into request–response pairs in this way. The interaction is more complex, the initiative passing to and fro between the user and the program. Separating the dialogue into a succession of pairs, each consisting of one user request and one corresponding program response, would be very difficult and entirely inappropriate.

The *completeness test* requires that every part of the problem should be accommodated in a natural way in some principal part of the frame. The JSD frame would fail this test for certain kinds of control problem. The Real World model part of the JSD frame accommodates a description of the real world as it actually is at any point in the history of the system. But it provides no accommodation for a description of what in the Environment-Effect frame is called the Requirement – that is, of the real world as it is supposed to be but will not be unless the system ensures that it is so. To take a trivial illustration, consider the requirement in a library system that no borrower may have more than six books out on loan at any time. Clearly, the limit of six books is not a part of the Real World model: in the absence of a properly functioning system borrowers will no doubt borrow as many books as they wish. Nor can it be regarded as a part of the Function: the System may produce a suitable warning output when a borrower threatens to exceed the limit, but the description of such a warning is not itself a statement of the Requirement. There is simply nowhere in the JSD frame to state the Requirement.

The *proportionality test* requires that the parts of the problem frame should be filled approximately equally: no principal part should be filled to overflowing while another is almost empty. The Structured Analysis and Specification frame would fail this test for the problem of printing the Nth prime number. The External Entities are the anonymous source of the input number N and the anonymous recipient of the computed prime. The sole input data flow is just one integer, and so is the sole output data flow. The Function accommodates almost the whole of the problem, while every other principal part is empty or nearly so.

The *part-characteristics test* requires the identified principal parts to exhibit the characteristics expected of them. The Workpiece frame would fail this test for a process control problem. If the plant to be controlled were identified as the

Workpiece, it would lack an essential characteristic expected of that principal part. The Workpiece is expected to be inert: it does nothing of its own initiative, but only waits to be operated upon at the Worker's request. But the plant in a process control system, if left to its own devices, is not inert; it is replete with vessels overflowing and emptying, with liquids reaching critical temperatures and gases reaching critical pressures.

The tests are, unsurprisingly, far from orthogonal. A frame that fails to fit on one test can usually be judged to fail on another, too. And if we stretch a point to pass one test we will usually aggravate the misfit elsewhere.

13.9   Problem Frame Complexity

In applying these tests, we must always bear in mind the rule of proportionate method. Even with a large repertoire of problem frames we should not expect to fit every problem perfectly. Where the misfit is not too serious, and the project admits of some compromise, we must be willing to bend the frame a little, or perhaps to defer a small and non-critical part of the problem until a later stage when it can be dealt with *ad hoc*. The pass mark in the frame fitness tests is less than 100%. But even when we lower the pass mark we will often find problems that simply do not fit any frame.

Such problems may need more than one frame. This is a form of problem complexity, to be measured, not by an absolute measure, but by the power of the problem frames and methods we have available. We tackle it by analysing a problem into subproblems, each with its own appropriately chosen problem frame.

Consider this small mathematical problem: Given a point p and three lengths a, b, and c, construct the circle centred at p and circumscribing a square whose area is equal to that of a triangle whose sides are of lengths a, b, and c. Polya's simple Unknown-Data-Condition frame does not fit this problem: it fails the proportionality test, because the Condition that relates the Data (p, a, b, and c) to the Unknown (a circle) is disproportionately elaborate. The problem may be structured into three subproblems, each fitting Polya's frame:

Subproblem-1

> **Unknown-1** A triangle.
>
> **Data-1** The lengths a, b, and c.
>
> **Condition-1** The triangle sides are equal to the lengths.

Subproblem-2

> **Unknown-2** A square.
>
> **Data-2** A triangle.
>
> **Condition-2** The square and triangle have equal areas.

Subproblem-3

> **Unknown-3** A circle.
>
> **Data-3** A point p and a square.
>
> **Condition-3** The circle is centred at p and circumscribes the square.

This little complexity is of an obvious kind, and its solution is obvious. There is only one problem frame to be applied, and the problem is solved by applying it three times. The subproblems are linked together in a chain, the Unknown of one subproblem serving as the Data of the next. This chain structuring of subproblems occurs also in the design of sequential processes. Starting with a problem that we expect will fit a frame whose parts are Input, Process, and Output, we find that the problem does not fit the frame. Perhaps it fails the proportionality test, or perhaps the method insists on some mapping between Input and Output that cannot be achieved within one simple sequential process. We then form a structure of subproblems, the Output of one furnishing the Input of the next.

Top-Down Functional Decomposition can be viewed in a similar light. Instead of a chain of subproblems there is a tree or hierarchy. Criteria for decomposition may be mere rules of thumb: no procedure text may be more than 50 lines long. Or they may attempt to capture some required characteristic of procedures, which are the chief constituents of the principal parts in the Top-Down problem frame: for example, by defining measures such as those of coupling and cohesion.

13.10   Heterogeneous Complexity

But the weakness of the Top-Down problem frame allows only very weak criteria for problem decomposition. Nor is it usual to find that one problem frame will suffice for a problem, even if it is applied more than once. Just as a richer problem frame allows a more helpful method at the level of solving individual problems – the problem can be fitted with more confidence into a frame whose parts have stronger characteristics, and the prescriptions of the method can be more specific and more detailed – so a repertoire of several different richer and stronger problem frames makes it easier to structure a complex problem into subproblems. The aspects or parts of the problem that should be identified as individual subproblems and fitted into separate frames are more easily identified because the frames themselves are more tightly constraining.

Consider, for example, the problem of constructing a simple CASE tool. The Workpiece problem frame would be obviously appropriate, the Workpieces here being the software descriptions whose construction and manipulation the tool is to support. But if the tool is also to provide some information for the management of the development project, this frame is clearly not enough. For the problem of providing the managment information the JSD problem frame may be suitable. The principal parts of the two subproblems are then:

Workpiece Frame-1

> **Machine-1** The machine supporting substantive development work.
>
> **Workpieces-1** The software descriptions being developed.
>
> **Worker-1** The software developer.
>
> **Operations-1** The development operations on the software descriptions.

JSD Frame-2

> **System-2** The machine providing management information about the development.
>
> **Real-World-2** The development products (**Workpieces-1**) and the work done on them (**Operations-1**).
>
> **Function-2** The reports and messages containing management information about the development.

The problem decomposition is uncontentious, given the small repertoire of problem frames we have made available to ourselves in our discussion, and the relative strength of those frames. The two problem frames are linked together by their common parts: the Workpieces-1 and Operations-1 parts of the first frame furnish the Real-World-2 part of the second. Machine-1 and System-2 need not be realised by the same general-purpose computer, although that will often be a convenient choice.

Here are some other examples of such complexities and possible solutions:

- In a problem for which the Environment-Effect frame has been chosen, the connection is not provided ready-made, but must be built by the developers.

Environment-Effect Frame-1

> **Machine-1** The machine of the substantive system.
>
> **Environment-1** The environment of the substantive system.
>
> **Requirement-1** The substantive requirement, not including the behaviour of the connection.
>
> **Connection-1** The connection to be constructed.

Environment-Effect Frame-2

> **Machine-2** This is **Connection-1**.
>
> **Environment-2** This is **Machine-1** and **Environment-1**.
>
> **Requirement-2** This is the behaviour required of **Connection-1**, connecting phenomena of **Machine-1** to phenomena of **Environment-1**.

The second subproblem also uses the Environment-Effect frame, but this time without the Connection part. In the second subproblem the connection is presumed to be reliable and transparent, comprising just the interfaces between Connection-1 and Machine-1 and between Connection-1 and Environment-1. These, of course, we must indeed regard as interfaces of shared phenomena: if we did not, we would have an infinite regress of connections.

- A substantive system is to be developed with significant security and access control properties.

    Environment-Effect Frame-1

    Machine-1 The machine of the substantive system.

    Environment-1 The environment of the substantive system.

    Requirement-1 The substantive requirement, not including access restrictions.

    Connection-1 The connection of the substantive system, perhaps including terminals at which users can interact with the system, and at which access is to be restricted.

    Environment-Effect Frame-2

    Machine-2 This is the machine that implements the access control rules.

    Environment-2 This is **Connection-1**, the terminals and interactions whose use is to be restricted, together with other phenomena (such as passwords) associated with access control.

    Requirement-2 This is the constraint on **Environment-2** (that is, on **Connection-1**), by which access to interaction with the substantive system is restricted.

    Again, the Environment-Effect frame is used for each of two subproblems. The terminals and interaction procedures for the substantive system appear as part of Connection-1 in the first subproblem. In the second subproblem they appear as the part of the Environment that is to be controlled.

- A CASE tool is to support a software development activity, and also to impose constraints reflecting management or methodological considerations.

    Workpiece Frame-1

    Machine-1 The machine supporting substantive development work.

    Workpieces-1 The software descriptions being developed.

    Worker-1 The software developer.

    Operations-1 The development operations on the software descriptions.

Environment-Effect Frame-2

> **Machine-2** The machine providing management and methodological control of the development activity.
>
> **Environment-2** The products of development (**Workpieces-1**), the work done on them (**Operations-1**), and possibly also the software developer **Worker-1**.
>
> **Requirement-2** The constraints to be imposed on the software development activity.

The development activity domains of the first subproblem furnish the environment to be controlled in the second subproblem. The behaviour of Worker-1, regarded as essentially autonomous in the first subproblem, is to be brought under the control of the machine in the second subproblem.

Decomposition into subproblems often suggests a natural order of proceeding with the development. For example, where a domain common to two subproblems appears as the Machine in one of them, it may well be desirable to solve that subproblem first, at least to the point at which the domain has been described well enough for its use in the other subproblem. Such ordering constraints can sometimes be circumvented by suitable abstractions: the outcome of the first subproblem can be prejudged well enough for the purposes of the second. Sometimes the constraints cannot be overcome in this way. Sometimes, what is even worse, there is a circularity in the natural ordering – in essence, a high-level failure of separability in the problem.

13.11   Languages for Descriptions

The use of richer problem frames, and of more than one for a single problem, demands descriptive techniques outside the main stream of the traditional culture of software development.

The traditional culture has grown from its origins in programming. Programming languages – even those of the rococo school – aim at relatively simple computational models: that is, they adopt simple problem frames. Elegance is achieved by economy and simplicity of principal parts. This elegance is so highly valued that some language designers even banished the vital but inconvenient complexities of input and output from the scope of the programming language itself, so that what remains could be captured in a few simple concepts, or – even better – in just one. If the frame cannot be reduced to a single principal part, it may still be possible to give all the principal parts the same characteristics. Everything is an S-expression; or everything is an object; or everything is a goal that can succeed or fail. We expect to write each program in a single language, in which such qualities as uniformity and referential transparency are highly prized.

This approach led to notable success in the design and definition of programming languages, and in the construction of compilers. So it is natural to persist in the same tradition in the larger work of systems requirements, specification, analysis, and design. We still hope to express our descriptions in a single language that shares the prized qualities of traditional programming languages.

But the tradition, for all its virtues, constrains us too tightly when we want to step outside the bounds of programming. The world is not homogeneous like the computational model of an elegant programming language. We need to describe many diverse domains, possessing many different characteristics. Some domains are inert, changing only by force of externally applied operations. Some have autonomous behaviour, with events and state changes occurring spontaneously – that is, for reasons that we choose to leave unexplained and unexplored. In some domains nothing ever changes: there is no time dimension at all. We need to describe diverse relationships – especially causal and control relationships – among the parts of one problem frame. And we must also describe causality within a domain, distinguishing events and state changes we regard as spontaneous from those we regard as being caused by mechanisms within the domain.

These descriptive needs cannot be met by a single language. Just as engineers choose the most appropriate material for each physical part of their products, so we must choose the most appropriate language for each description. The idea of a universal formal language, a raw material suitable for every description, is a chimera; and the use of an informal or unsuitable language is a serious obstacle to success.

13.12   Designating Domain Phenomena

The essence of the mathematical approach to description is to forget what our symbols mean in the physical world and consider only their formal significance. But the forgetfulness must be very temporary, lasting only for individual bouts of concentrated reasoning. Both before and after each bout we must be very clear indeed what reality we are talking about. Where there is a modelling relationship between a machine and a problem domain, we will apply some of our descriptions to both, some to one only, and some to the other. Where there is a non-transparent connection between the machine and its environment, we will need to describe event occurrences in each domain separately. Where a domain phenomenon appears in more than one principal part, in the same or in different problem frames, we will refer to it in more than one description: an action of the CASE tool user on a Workpiece will need to be described in Workpieces-1, in Operations-1, in Worker-1, in Environment-2, and in Requirement-2. In each description we must always be able to say very exactly what we are talking about: as John von Neumann pointed out, there is no sense in being precise if you don't know what you are talking about.

Saying what we are talking about means explicitly *designating* the *phenomena* of interest in the domain, explaining how they may be recognised, and associating them with terms that we can then use in precise descriptions.

Here is an example of a designation:

"At time t the count of
parts contained in the $\triangleright$ $\text{NetContent}(b, q, t)$
warehouse bin b is q"

The LHS of the designation is an informal narrative from which the designated phenomenon can be recognised reliably enough for the purposes of the system. The RHS is a formal term – here it is a predicate – that can be used in a description to refer to the designated phenomenon.

A designation is created for some phenomenon of a particular domain, which may be anything in the world that we wish to describe. We apply a description to a domain by associating it explicitly with a set of designations. The designated terms appearing in the description then have the meanings given in the LHSs of their designations. The meaning of the whole description, as associated with the designation set, is bounded by the designated phenomena: it can refer to nothing else.

As well as describing an actual or desired state of affairs in a domain, a description can also define new terms. These new terms do not refer to new phenomena: a description cannot create phenomena, but can only describe their relationships. The new terms merely provide convenient ways of referring to expressions involving already designated phenomena of the described domain.

Explicit designation of phenomena has several advantages. Most notably, it allows clear criteria of correctness for descriptions of non-abstract domains. A designation set tells us how to identify the domain phenomena about whose relationships the formal descriptions make their assertions, and hence how to check whether those assertions are true or false. The designated phenomena relate descriptions to domains, just as triangulation points relate Ordnance Survey maps to the terrain they describe. When the designations of terms are merely implicit in their names, or diffused in an informal narrative accompanying the formal descriptions, it is impossible to check the truth of a domain description. If the description appears false, that may be due to errors in our assumed designations: perhaps we mistook one bridge for another and misaligned the map and the terrain. And if the description appears true, we are in no better case.

Another advantage of this phenomenological approach is that it can help to resolve, or at least to mitigate, the difficulty of using many languages in one development. Formal semantics may provide us with radically different models for different languages, and hence lead us to treat those languages as if they were completely incommensurable. The semantics of Z is based on sets; the semantics of JSD is based on regular languages over events: therefore, we may think, there is no possibility of combining the two in a formal or rigorous development. But clearly there is something seriously wrong here. Evidently many of the same real phenomena might be referred to, and the same real relationships among phenomena might be asserted, in both languages. Any apparent incommensurability reflects only the limitations of the formal semantics, and its inability to capture meaning in the phenomenological sense.

13.13   Structures of Descriptions

Richer problem frames, and the richer descriptive techniques we need to deal with them, lead inevitably to richer structures of descriptions. There will be many more descriptions, related in many ways. In the Environment-Effect frame the Environment description is in the indicative mood, while the Requirement is in the optative mood, although it is about the same phenomena. We can rely on the truth of the Environment description in refining the Requirement, but not vice versa. In modelling we apply one description to different domains by using it with different designation sets. In incremental and partial description we apply different descriptions to one domain by using them with the same designation set. Different designation sets may have designations in common: descriptions used with those designation sets then have intersecting subject matter and their conjunction is potentially non-trivial. A description may be applied directly to a domain by a designation set, or indirectly by referring to terms defined in another description, or by a combination of the two. The definition of terms may itself rely on terms defined in yet another description.

In these and other ways description set structures become elaborate enough to demand systematic control within a development. It is not enough to formalise syntax and semantics of individual descriptions; we must also formalise – or at least systematise – the relationships among descriptions and between descriptions and the domains they describe. These relationships are the links in a multi-dimensional structure of descriptions. They cannot be captured in a single linguistic framework. Evidently, richer problem frames, richer descriptive techniques, and richer descriptive structures will need mechanised support. There are simply too many descriptions, and too many relationships, to be managed by hand. Today, most development support tools are still designed to mechanise old and inadequate manual methods. This will not continue long. New tools will not only support ideas already waiting for a practical vehicle; they will also stimulate new ideas about method that today we cannot readily imagine.

13.14   Acknowledgements

Many of the ideas put forward here have been explored and put to the test during several years' cooperation with Pamela Zave of AT&T Bell Laboratories, Murray Hill, New Jersey. They have also been discussed on many occasions with Daniel

Jackson of Carnegie-Mellon University. Both of them kindly read earlier drafts of this paper and made many helpful comments. Cliff Jones and Jeff Kramer have also helped me. If this paper has virtues some of the credit is theirs; its defects are all my own work.

Chapter 14

Process Algebra Arguments about an Object-based Design Notation

C. B. Jones

The research reported in this paper is intended to contribute to the quest for compositional development methods for concurrent programs: the use of some notions from object-oriented languages is a means to tame interference rather than a (fashionable) end in itself. Two earlier papers give examples of the use of an object-based design notation and a third gives a semantics to that notation by mapping it to a process algebra; the current paper indicates how arguments about the design notation might be based on that semantics.

Tony Hoare has had a major impact on program development methods which is partly traced in [10]. More personally, the current author's initial research on rely and guarantee-conditions [16] was conducted in Oxford at a time of intensive research on CSP: the current paper might be seen as a belated acceptance of process calculi.

14.1 Introduction

Development methods which are *compositional* make it possible to justify one step of development before proceeding to subsequent design activity: specifications need to isolate the sub-components introduced in a development step. Compositional development methods offer scope for improving the productivity of the design process by minimizing the 'scrap and rework' inherent in the late detection of early design errors. Relatively simple specification ideas (e.g. pre- and post-conditions) suffice for the compositional development of sequential programs; *interference* makes it difficult to find useful compositional approaches for concurrent programs (some trace of this quest is contained in [6, 8]). Two papers – [18, 20] – indicate that selected features from object-oriented languages might further the quest for compositional development methods (they also provide references which trace the evolution of the ideas). Interference is an issue for both shared-variable and communication-based concurrency; object-based languages offer a compromise between the two extremes by placing control of access to state (i.e. instance variables) in the hands of the developer and supporting ways of controlling the activation of methods.

A way of limiting interference in object-based languages is exploited in [18] to show how concurrency can be introduced by transformations. Central to the justification of observational equivalence is the use of invariants on the *object graphs* which can arise. Interference cannot always be controlled in this way and [20] shows how a logic notation discussed in [17] can be used to reason about interference over complex object graphs. The design notation used in both of these papers is currently known as $\pi o\beta\lambda$. Rather than being viewed as a contending programming language, it is hoped that $\pi o\beta\lambda$ will be used as a design notation for the development of programs in languages like POOL [1], ABCL [34], Beta [21], Modula-3 [27] or UFO [29]. But – if sound development methods are required – design notations have to be given semantics. For example, the transformation rules used in [18] have to be shown to preserve observational equivalence. The semantics of $\pi o\beta\lambda$ is fixed in [19] by mapping it to the process algebra known as the π-calculus [26]. The current paper investigates the task of basing arguments on that semantics. One of the conclusions is that the familiar notions of *bi-simulation* etc. are not appropriate for the proofs needed here. Although the arguments given below are hopefully convincing, they are not completely formal and the current paper might be viewed as a challenge which could stimulate the development of new approaches to equivalence proofs.

In order to make the current paper relatively self-contained, an example of the final form of a $\pi o\beta\lambda$ program is shown in Figure 14.1: this is the outcome of a development in [18] from a simple specification describing an *abstract machine* for handling symbol tables which associate *Key/Data* pairs: the associations are created or modified by the *insert* method and used by the *search* method. The representation used in Figure 14.1 is a binary tree whose nodes are instances of the *Symtab* class. Each such instance – as well as storing a local *Key* (k) and *Data* (d) pair – has references to two sub-trees. These (l and r) references are marked **private** to indicate that they cannot be be copied. This immediately ensures that the object-graph has no sharing: it is a tree. (It is interesting to compare this with [11].)

The semantics of $\pi o\beta\lambda$ require that at most one method can be active in each (object) instance at any one time. An interesting question is how this restriction admits concurrency (see [1] for a review of the options). The intention of the conditional statement in the *insert* method should be obvious. But notice that this is preceded by a return statement. The effect of the return is to release the invoking code from the *rendezvous* and to permit execution of statements following the method call to overlap with that of the body of the *insert* method. Given the restriction on only one method being active per instance, a further invocation might be somewhat delayed. But notice that once the nested invocation (e.g. $l!insert(k', d')$) is released from its *rendezvous*, the first method can complete. In this way, a whole series of *insert* methods can be rippling down a (binary tree

Symtab class
vars k: *Key* ← nil; d: *Data* ← nil;
                l: private ref(*Symtab*) ← nil; r: private ref(*Symtab*) ← nil
insert(k': *Key*, d': *Data*) method
  return
  if k = nil then (k ← k'; d ← d')
  elif k' = k then d ← d'
  elif $k' < k$ then (if l = nil then l ← new *Symtab* fi ; l!*insert*(k', d'))
  else (if r = nil then r ← new *Symtab* fi ; r!*insert*(k', d'))
  fi
search(k': *Key*) method *Data*
  if k = k' then return d
  elif $k' < k$ then yield l!*search*(k')
  else yield r!*search*(k')
  fi

Figure 14.1 Example program *Symtab* (concurrent)

Symtab class
vars k: *Key* ← nil; d: *Data* ← nil;
                l: private ref(*Symtab*) ← nil; r: private ref(*Symtab*) ← nil
insert(k': *Key*, d': *Data*) method
  if k = nil then (k ← k'; d ← d')
  elif k' = k then d ← d'
  elif $k' < k$ then (if l = nil then l ← new *Symtab* fi ; l!*insert*(k', d'))
  else (if r = nil then r ← new *Symtab* fi ; r!*insert*(k', d'))
  fi
  return
search(k': *Key*) method *Data*
  if k = k' then return d
  elif $k' < k$ then return l!*search*(k')
  else return r!*search*(k')
  fi

Figure 14.2 Example program *Symtab* (sequential)

representation of a) symbol table. Achieving a similar effect for *search* (and an intermingling of the two activities) requires noticing that the invoking code must be held up until a value can be returned but that – if the task of returning that value is delegated – the instance first called can be made dormant and thus available for other method calls. This is the semantics chosen for the yield statement of $\pi o \beta \lambda$.

The class in Figure 14.1 is actually developed via the sequential version shown in Figure 14.2; the final step of the design process in [18] is to apply given $\pi o\beta\lambda$ transformation rules. One reason for introducing concurrency at the end of the development becomes obvious if the task of specifying – for example – the *insert* method of Figure 14.1 is considered: a post-condition alone will not suffice unless some form of auxiliary variable is used to fix the methods which are active on sub-trees when the method itself begins execution.[1] In contrast, the design in [18] is not only based on a simple pre/post–condition specification, but even the initial design steps use standard sequential data reification and operation decomposition proofs.

The next section of this paper introduces the process algebra used to give a semantics to $\pi o\beta\lambda$; Section 14.3 outlines the mapping to that notation; the correctness of two transformations[2] which affect the degree of concurrency is discussed in Sections 14.4 and 14.5; the paper concludes with a discussion in Section 14.6.

14.2   The π-calculus

Since the pioneering publications on CSP [12] and CCS [22], many process algebras have been studied (e.g. [9, 3, 13, 23]). However, the treatment of names in the π-calculus [26] makes it an obvious candidate as a semantic base for object-oriented languages. The version of the π-calculus used here is a minor variant of the (first-order) polyadic π-calculus proposed in [25]: the only difference is that the decision to identify abstractions and concretions as separate phrases of the language has not been followed.[3] Unlike [32, 24], (binary) sums are employed here – the summands are always prefixed so normal processes are identified as a separate class.

The syntax of the calculus is very simple. Processes (typical elements P, Q) can be

$$P ::= N \ \Big| \ P \mid Q \ \Big| \ !P \ \Big| \ (\boldsymbol{\nu}x)P$$

Normal processes (typical elements M, N) can be

$$N ::= \pi.P \ \Big| \ \mathbf{0} \ \Big| \ M + N$$

Prefixes (typical element π) are

$$\pi ::= x(\widetilde{y}) \ \Big| \ \overline{x}\widetilde{y}$$

---

[1] It would, of course, be possible to define the task in terms of streams in the style of [2].

[2] There are, of course, many simpler transformation rules than those considered here: for example, rules can be given to insert assignment of expressions to local instance variables.

[3] The symmetry in [25] is pleasing but here there is little benefit in separating concretions; even for abstractions, it appears to fit better with object-oriented thinking to locate everything by name. This would be reconsidered if a move were made to the higher-order π-calculus.

Typical elements for names here are x, y (names more closely linked to the objects being mapped are used below). Prefix and ν bind more strongly than composition; sum binds weakest of all.

A number of abbreviations are useful. Trailing stop processes are omitted, so $\pi.\mathbf{0}$ can be written π. Multiple new names are combined, so $(\nu x)(\nu y)$ is written (νxy). A sequence of names such as α_1, α_2 is sometimes abbreviated to $\tilde{\alpha}$. Recursive definitions are written with an obvious meaning; they can be viewed as an abbreviation of a 'baton' passing trick with replication. The parentheses on the input prefix $(x(\tilde{y}))$ should remind the reader that this – and of course ν – serve to bind names whereas the basic output prefix $(\overline{x}\tilde{y})$ does not. There is however a convenient abbreviation with a binding form of the output prefix.[4]

$$\overline{x}(\tilde{y}).P \stackrel{\text{def}}{=} (\nu\tilde{y})(\overline{x}\tilde{y}.P)$$

Structural equivalences can be defined. Alpha-convertible terms are taken to be structurally equivalent. Structural equivalence laws include the following (the first three rules for $+$ ($|$) can be summarized by saying that $M/+/\mathbf{0}$ ($P/\mid/\mathbf{0}$) are symmetric monoids):

$$
\begin{aligned}
M + \mathbf{0} &\equiv M \\
M + N &\equiv N + M \\
M_1 + (M_2 + M_3) &\equiv (M_1 + M_2) + M_3 \\
M + M &\equiv M \\
P \mid \mathbf{0} &\equiv P \\
P \mid Q &\equiv Q \mid P \\
P \mid (Q \mid R) &\equiv (P \mid Q) \mid R \\
!P &\equiv P \mid !P \\
(\nu x)\mathbf{0} &\equiv \mathbf{0} \\
(\nu x)(\nu y)P &\equiv (\nu y)(\nu x)P
\end{aligned}
$$

A function (fn) which yields the free names of a process can be defined:

$$
\begin{aligned}
fn(P \mid Q) &= fn(P) \cup fn(Q) \\
fn(\,!P) &= fn(P) \\
fn((\nu x)P) &= fn(P) - \{x\} \\
fn(\mathbf{0}) &= \{\,\}
\end{aligned}
$$

---

[4]This is not used in [19]. In fact, it would make the mapping easier to employ finer binding distinctions as in [31].

$$
\begin{aligned}
fn(M + N) &= fn(M) \cup fn(N) \\
fn(x(\widetilde{y}).P) &= \{x\} \cup (fn(P) - \{\widetilde{y}\}) \\
fn(\overline{x}\widetilde{y}.P) &= \{x\} \cup \{\widetilde{y}\} \cup fn(P) \\
fn(\overline{x}(\widetilde{y}).P) &= \{x\} \cup (fn(P) - \{\widetilde{y}\})
\end{aligned}
$$

A similar function (bn) for bound names can be defined and $P\{\widetilde{x}/\widetilde{y}\}$ is the obvious syntactic substitution (with avoidance of accidental capture). The following equivalences also hold:

$$
\begin{aligned}
(\boldsymbol{\nu}x)(P \mid Q) &\equiv P \mid (\boldsymbol{\nu}x)Q \text{ if } x \notin fn(P) \\
(\boldsymbol{\nu}x)y(\widetilde{z}).P &\equiv y(\widetilde{z}).(\boldsymbol{\nu}x)P \text{ where } x \neq y, x \notin \widetilde{z} \\
(\boldsymbol{\nu}x)\overline{y}\widetilde{z}.P &\equiv \overline{y}\widetilde{z}.(\boldsymbol{\nu}x)P \text{ where } x \neq y, x \notin \widetilde{z} \\
(\boldsymbol{\nu}x)\pi.P &\equiv \mathbf{0} \text{ if } \pi \text{ is } x(\widetilde{y}) \text{ or } \overline{x}\widetilde{y}
\end{aligned}
$$

The notion of *reduction* is key to the understanding of further equivalences. Reading $P \to Q$ as P can immediately reduce to Q, the following rules are taken from [25]:

$$
\boxed{COMM} \frac{}{(\cdots + \overline{x}\widetilde{y}.P) \mid (x(\widetilde{z}).Q + \cdots) \to P \mid Q\{\widetilde{y}/\widetilde{z}\}}
$$

$$
\boxed{PAR} \frac{P \to P'}{P \mid Q \to P' \mid Q}
$$

$$
\boxed{RES} \frac{P \to P'}{(\boldsymbol{\nu}x)P \to (\boldsymbol{\nu}x)P'}
$$

$$
\boxed{STRUCT} \frac{Q \equiv P \quad P \to P' \quad P' \equiv Q'}{Q \to Q'}
$$

Notice that reduction is invalid under prefix or sum; there is also no rule given for reduction under replication but its effect can be simulated.

As in CCS, *bi-simulation* can be defined. But it is argued below that this does not hold for the examples in Sections 14.4 and 14.5. In arguments there, the reflexive, transitive closure of $\to$ is discussed: this is written $\twoheadrightarrow$. One rule for this can already be given: from *COMM* and *STRUCT* it follows that

$$
\boxed{COMM'} \frac{}{(\cdots + \overline{x}(\widetilde{y}).P) \mid (x(\widetilde{z}).Q + \cdots) \twoheadrightarrow (\boldsymbol{\nu}\widetilde{y})(P \mid Q\{\widetilde{y}/\widetilde{z}\})}
$$

Bit class
vars $v: \mathbb{B} \leftarrow$ false
$w(x: \mathbb{B})$ method $v \leftarrow x$; return
$r()$ method return v

Figure 14.3 Example program *Bit*

14.3 Mapping

A detailed mapping from $\pi o\beta\lambda$ to the π-calculus is given in Appendix B of [19]; this section sketches enough of the mapping to support the discussion in Sections 14.4 and 14.5 below.

Like the λ-calculus, the π-calculus provides no basic values: Booleans and integers have to be constructed. A process which makes available two names (b_t, b_f) for the two Boolean values is as follows:

$$Bool \stackrel{\text{def}}{=} \; ! \, b_t(tf).\overline{t} \; | \; ! \, b_f(tf).\overline{f}$$

This process is composed with the processes generated by the translation of classes. It is important in the arguments below to notice that this process is *immutable* in that it does not change with use (essentially, replication provides any number of identical values).

The easiest way to understand the main points of the mapping is to study the simple example given in Figure 14.3 and the following π-calculus equivalent:

$$[\![Bit]\!] = \; ! \, I_{Bit}$$
$$I_{Bit} = \overline{bit}(u).(\boldsymbol{\nu} s_v a_v)(V_{b_f} \mid B_u)$$
$$V_y = (\overline{a_v}y. V_y + s_v(z). V_z)$$
$$B_u = \overline{u}(\tilde{\alpha}).M_u$$
$$M_u = (\alpha_w(\omega_w x).\overline{s_v}x.\overline{\omega_w}.B_u + \alpha_r(\omega_r).a_v(y).\overline{\omega_r}y.B_u)$$

The mapping function is $[\![\_]\!]$; its result – $! \, I_{Bit}$ – represents the semantics of *Bit* by requiring a particular behaviour over its interface (bit, u, α, ω); the replication provides any number of instances of the class; each such instance is identical (again, this fact is important in the following arguments) but has a unique name associated with it by the binding output $(\overline{bit}(u))$. The result of mapping a class has a process like V_y for each instance variable and one (B_u) for the body of the class; these communicate via strictly local names s_v to set and a_v to access the variable; variables are initialized. The body of the process B_u has one summand per method. Private names for the methods are communicated by $\overline{u}(\tilde{\alpha})$ from the u instance. The ordering of the statements within each summand of M_u is shown here by prefixing; the mapping in Appendix B of [19] has to cope with statements whose mapping can yield a composition (the familiar baton passing trick is used); both forms of sequencing are subsumed below under P before Q. The *rendezvous* with a method terminates when the relevant ω prefix occurs as the mapping of the return statement. The fact that only one method can be active in any instance of *Bit* is regulated by the way the recursion on B_u works.

Code which invokes **new** *Bit* is mapped to

$$bit(u). \cdots u \cdots$$

Code to invoke $w(e)$ is mapped to prefixes which firstly obtain (private) names for both methods then select α_w and pass a private name for termination indication as well as a mapping of the parameter:

$$u(\widetilde{\alpha}).(\boldsymbol{\nu}\omega_w)(\overline{\alpha_w}\omega_w\, e.\omega_w())$$

The mapping of an invocation of $r()$ reflects the fact that there is no parameter but there is a value to be returned:

$$u(\widetilde{\alpha}).(\boldsymbol{\nu}\omega_r)(\overline{\alpha_r}\omega_r.\omega_r(y))$$

The way in which instance variables which contain references are mapped can be understood by comparing Figure 14.2 with the following:

$$
\begin{aligned}
[\![Symtab]\!] &= \,!\, I_{Symtab} \\
I_{Symtab} &= \overline{symtab}(u).(\boldsymbol{\nu}\widetilde{s}\widetilde{a})(K_{\mathsf{nil}} \mid D_{\mathsf{nil}} \mid (\boldsymbol{\nu}n)(L_n) \mid (\boldsymbol{\nu}n)(R_n) \mid B_u) \\
K_y &= (\overline{a_k}y.K_y + s_k(z).K_z) \\
D_y &= (\overline{a_d}y.D_y + s_d(z).D_z) \\
L_y &= (\overline{a_l}y.L_y + s_l(z).L_z) \\
R_y &= (\overline{a_r}y.R_y + s_r(z).R_z) \\
B_u &= \overline{u}(\widetilde{\alpha}).M_u \\
M_u &= \left(\begin{array}{l} \alpha_i(\omega_i k' d'). \cdots. a_l(u').u'(\widetilde{\alpha'}).(\boldsymbol{\nu}\omega_i')(\overline{\alpha_i'}\omega_i'k'd'.\omega_i'()).\overline{\omega_i}.B_u \\ + \\ \alpha_s(\omega_s k'). \cdots. a_l(u').u'(\widetilde{\alpha'}).(\boldsymbol{\nu}\omega_s')(\overline{\alpha_s'}\omega_s'k'.\omega_s'(d')).\overline{\omega_s}d'.B_u \end{array} \right)
\end{aligned}
$$

14.4   Moving Return Statements

The issue addressed in this section is the conditions under which it is valid to commute return statements with statements which invoke methods via (private) references. In order to see that the restriction to private references is crucial, consider the following example (with *Bit* as in Figure 14.3).

```
Flipflop class
vars l: private ref ← new Bit
      v: 𝔹
f() method v ← l!r(); l!w(¬ v); return
r() method return l!r()
```

In this case the reference l is marked private and, if the return statement were moved to the beginning of method f, no invocation would detect the difference: e.g.

$$c \leftarrow \text{new } \textit{Flipflop}; \; c!f(); \; x \leftarrow c!r()$$

If, however, a new method e were added which exposes the l reference, the situation is entirely different:

> $\textit{Flipflop2}$ class
> vars l: shared ref $\leftarrow$ new $\textit{Bit}$
> $v : \mathbb{B}$
> $f()$ method $v \leftarrow l!r(); \; l!w(\neg v); \;$ return
> $r()$ method return $l!r()$
> $e()$ method return (l)

Notice that the fact that the reference l is copied forces it to be marked shared. Now, consider

$$c \leftarrow \text{new } \textit{Flipflop2}; \; l \leftarrow c!e(); \; c!f(); \; x \leftarrow l!r()$$

If the return statement is moved to the beginning of method f in $\textit{Flipflop2}$, the value of x would depend on the relative progress of the invoking and method code. It is therefore necessary to be precise about the conditions under which concurrency can be introduced by repositioning a return statement.

The relevant transformation rule is

$$S; \text{return } e \quad \text{can be replaced by} \quad \text{return } e; S \tag{14.1}$$

providing

1. S always terminates;[5]
2. e is not affected by S; and
3. S only invokes methods reachable by private references.

An example of a specific transformation (akin to $\textit{Bit}$) is proved to give observational equivalence in [19] by showing that the reductions of the mapped forms of both versions of the class eventually reduce to equivalent processes. The argument which follows is more general but employs essentially the same idea which is that certain reductions cannot interfere with each other. Notice however that this property is more delicate in the π-calculus than, for example, CCS because it is not sufficient to know that $fn(P) \cap fn(Q) = \{\,\}$ to conclude that P and Q cannot affect each other's reductions: consider

$$\overline{x}y.y(z).\mathbf{0} \mid x'(y'').\overline{y''}z'$$

---

[5]Termination is not, of course, a syntactically checkable property but it is in the spirit of the development method envisaged here that termination would anyway be proved.

Although their free name sets are respectively $\{x, y\}$ and $\{x', z'\}$, these two terms interact if composed with the additional term

$$\cdots \mid x(y').\overline{x'}y'$$

As a basis for general argument, consider the following class:

D class
vars $\cdots$
$m_1(x)$ method S_1; S; return y; S_2
$m_2(x)$ method $\cdots$

There is no loss of generality in showing a return with a variable (rather than an expression e) because a simple transformation rule could be used to assign e to y. The interest is in (non-trivial) activity in S.

The class D is mapped as follows:

$$[\![D]\!] = \; ! \, \overline{d}(u).(\boldsymbol{\nu}\widetilde{s}\widetilde{a})(\cdots \mid B_u)$$
$$B_u = \overline{u}(\widetilde{\alpha}).M_u$$
$$M_u = (\alpha_1(\omega_1 x).[\![S_1]\!] \text{ before } [\![S]\!] \text{ before } a_y(y).\overline{\omega_1}y.[\![S_2]\!] \text{ before } B_u + \cdots)$$

Notice that communication with any instance variables (shown by $\cdots$ in $[\![D]\!]$) is hidden by $(\boldsymbol{\nu}\widetilde{s}\widetilde{a})$; in fact, $fn([\![D]\!]) = \{d\}$.

It is a key point of arguments about observational equivalence at the $\pi o\beta\lambda$ level that methods are only invoked by π-calculus expressions which also result from the mapping $[\![\_]\!]$. Consider some context C which invokes methods of class D (assume, without loss of generality, that Q has no use of u):

$$C = d(u).P_1.Q \text{ before } P_i$$

where

$$P_i = u(\widetilde{\alpha}).(\boldsymbol{\nu}\omega_i)(\overline{\alpha_i}\omega_i x.\omega_i(y))$$

The effect of **new** D is to obtain a unique name $d(u)$ which by $COMM'$ becomes hidden from any other R:

$$C \mid [\![D]\!] \mid R \twoheadrightarrow (\boldsymbol{\nu}u)(P_1.Q \text{ before } P_i \mid (\boldsymbol{\nu}\widetilde{s}\widetilde{a})(\cdots \mid B_u)) \mid R$$

The invocation of m_1 causes further reduction to

$$\twoheadrightarrow (\boldsymbol{\nu}u)(\boldsymbol{\nu}\omega_1)(\omega_1(y).Q \text{ before } P_i \mid$$
$$(\boldsymbol{\nu}\widetilde{s}\widetilde{a})(\cdots \mid [\![S_1]\!] \text{ before } [\![S]\!] \text{ before } a_y(y).\overline{\omega_1}y.[\![S_2]\!])) \mid R$$

Now $[\![S_1]\!]$ can change R (and local variables elided by $\cdots$) but so far the distinction between the two versions of D has not come into play; therefore the reduction is to

$$\twoheadrightarrow (\boldsymbol{\nu}u)(\boldsymbol{\nu}\omega_1)(\omega_1(y).Q \text{ before } P_i \mid$$
$$(\boldsymbol{\nu}\widetilde{s}\widetilde{a})(\cdots \mid [\![S]\!] \text{ before } a_y(y).\overline{\omega_1}y.[\![S_2]\!])) \mid R'$$

Even if new instances are created and their references stored in instance variables of D, their names are kept local.

At this point, the distinction which comes from commuting $[\![S]\!]$ and return (e) becomes important. The alternative to the preceding equation is as follows:

$$\twoheadrightarrow (\boldsymbol{\nu} u)(\boldsymbol{\nu} \omega_1)(\omega_1(y).Q \text{ before } P_i \mid$$
$$(\boldsymbol{\nu} \widetilde{s}\widetilde{a})(\cdots \mid a_y(y).\overline{\omega_1}y.[\![S]\!] \text{ before } [\![S_2]\!])) \mid R'$$

Now, the second side condition on Rule 14.1 ensures that S cannot affect y; therefore $[\![S]\!]$ cannot use $\overline{s_y}z$. The only other possible source of $\overline{s_y}z$ – since s_y and a_y are hidden – is another summand of B_u; but these are not available until a negative u is encountered after B_u recurses. Therefore, y is bound to the same name in Q before P_i whichever version of D is used provided $\overline{\omega_1}y$ occurs. The first side condition of Rule 14.1 requires that S terminates so the termination prefix will occur.

The other – more interesting – effect of commuting the return statement is that whereas $[\![S]\!]$ had to complete before Q before P_i, the repositioning of $\overline{\omega_1}y$ allows them to run concurrently. Firstly, notice that $[\![S]\!]$ actually only overlaps with Q since P_i cannot begin until a negative u is available and this only happens after B_u recurses. Secondly, note that the transformation allows all of the earlier reductions: if

$$([\![S]\!] \mid R') \twoheadrightarrow (\mathbf{0} \mid R'')$$

then

$$([\![S]\!] \text{ before } Q \mid R') \twoheadrightarrow (Q \mid R'')$$

but a possible reduction in the concurrent case is

$$([\![S]\!] \mid Q \mid R') \twoheadrightarrow (Q \mid R'')$$

What needs to be checked, of course, is whether any of the extra reductions of $[\![S]\!] \mid Q$ produce different $\pi o \beta \lambda$ behaviour. Several things prevent an argument by bi-simulation here. Firstly, there is a technical problem in that $[\![S]\!]$ and Q do share names. This can be circumvented since the only names that they can share are those for constants (e.g. b_t) and class models. These are all immutable so there would appear to be no problem. Formally, it is a property of the π-calculus that

$$!P = !P \mid !P$$

The split replications can then be commuted and re-bracketed so that $(\boldsymbol{\nu} b_t)$ etc. can be inserted to localize the communication. Notice this should be done for all class models because of possible indirect calls.

But there are still further steps in $[\![S]\!]$ which get merged with those of Q. As observed above, the names $\widetilde{s}, \widetilde{a}$ are local; these can however be used to access names of other processes (e.g. u') stored as references in instance variables. The third side condition of Rule 14.1 ensures that no such name is shared. Therefore the u' remains local to the $(\boldsymbol{\nu}u')$ which created it: u' is not passed as an object name. The only name which affects the reduction of both invocation and D is then ω_1 and that serves to re-synchronize the reductions.

14.5   Using Yield Statements

The transformation rule for the introduction of yield statements is

$$\textsf{return } l!m(x) \quad \text{can be replaced by} \quad \textsf{yield } l!m(x) \tag{14.2}$$

provided

1. $l!m()$ terminates; and
2. l is a private reference and m only invokes methods reachable by private references.

Consider the following class:

E class
vars l: private ref
$m_1()$ method S_1; return $l!m_i()$; S_2
$m_2()$ method $\cdots$

This translates to

$$\llbracket E \rrbracket = !\,\overline{e}(u).(\boldsymbol{\nu}s_l a_l)((\boldsymbol{\nu}n)L_n \mid B_u)$$
$$L_y = (\overline{a_l}y.L_y + s_l(z).L_z)$$
$$B_u = \overline{u}(\widetilde{\alpha}).M_u$$
$$M_u = (\alpha_1(\omega_1).\llbracket S_1 \rrbracket \textsf{ before } a_l(u').u'(\widetilde{\alpha'}).\overline{\alpha'_i}(\omega'_i).\omega'_i(y).\overline{\omega_1}y.\llbracket S_2 \rrbracket \textsf{ before } B_u + \cdots)$$

Whereas the translation when a yield statement is substituted for the return is

$$M'_u = (\alpha_1(\omega_1).\llbracket S_1 \rrbracket \textsf{ before } a_l(u').u'(\widetilde{\alpha'}).\overline{\alpha'_i}(\omega_1).\llbracket S_2 \rrbracket \textsf{ before } B'_u + \cdots)$$

The value which is returned over ω_1 is the same in both cases because the privacy of the references prevents any interference. This would be formalized as in the previous section by arguing that $\boldsymbol{\nu}$ localizes the immutable references.

Here again, the more interesting effect is that the process invoked by α'_i now runs concurrently with $\llbracket S_2 \rrbracket$. But it can again be shown that they cannot interfere. It is also the case that the recursion on B'_u occurs earlier than that on B_u because in the former case the delegation of the task of returning on ω_1 completes the m_1 method. This allows further negative occurrences of u and thus invocations of either m_1 or m_2. The privacy of names again removes the risk of interference.

14.6 Discussion

There is a significant corpus of related work that tackles the relationship between object-oriented languages and various process calculi. References in general – and specific acknowledgements to those which have influenced the results in the $\pi o\beta\lambda$ research – are given in [19]. More recently, Davide Sangiorgi's work on the Higher-Order π-calculus [28] provides arguments for using a non-first-order calculus; furthermore [33] actually provides a mapping from $\pi o\beta\lambda$ to the Higher-Order π-calculus. It is still a research issue to establish whether the extra power actually makes the sort of proof considered in the current paper easier or not: [33] only uses second-order processes and these appear to do little more than economize on the notation to pass values. As indicated in Section 14.2, it is a tenet of object-oriented thinking that everything is passed as a name.

Further developments by the group at Keio University (e.g. [14]) on the ν-calculus could influence the approach to the required formalization of the proofs; furthermore [30] considers the problem of *principal types* in the π-calculus.

Much more work remains to be done. Although the arguments in Sections 14.4 and 14.5 are hopefully convincing, more formality would permit the use of mechanical proof tools which might be worth while as more proofs are needed. Moreover, the challenge of such formalization could yield new insights into notions of behavioural equivalences. As the logic used in [20] stabilizes, it will be necessary to undertake justification of its interference rules and this will require proofs about the relationship between logical expressions and $\pi o\beta\lambda$ statements.

Furthermore, continuing work on general properties of rely/guarantee specifications (notably [5, 4]) could force reconsideration of the approach taken in [20].

Acknowledgements

It is a pleasure to be able to acknowledge not only the stimulus of his scientific publications but also the more personal effect that Tony Hoare has had on my own work: he has been both an inspiration and a friend.

The presentation in this paper has been influenced by comments on an earlier version by David Walker and by discussions with Samson Abramsky and Colin Stirling (in Tokyo!). My research is supported by a Senior Fellowship from SERC.

References

[1] Pierre America. Issues in the design of a parallel object-oriented language. *Formal Aspects of Computing*, 1(4), 1989.

[2] Manfred Broy. On bounded buffers: Modularity, robustness, and reliability in reactive systems. Technical Report MIP-8920, Universitat Passau, Fakultat fur mathe-

matik und Informatik, June 1989.

[3] J. C. M. Baeten and W. P. Weijland, editors. *Process Algebra*. Cambridge University Press, 1990.

[4] Pierre Collette and Antonio Cau. Parallel composition of assumption-commitment specifications, 1993. private communication.

[5] Pierre Collette. Application of the composition principle to Unity-like specifications. In *[7]*, pages 230–242, 1993.

[6] W. P. de Roever. The quest for compositionality: A survey of assertion-based proof systems for concurrent programs: Part I: Concurrency based on shared variables. In E. J. Neuhold and G. Chroust, editors, *Formal Models in Programming*. North-Holland, 1985.

[7] M-C. Gaudel and J-P. Jouannaud, editors. *TAPSOFT'93: Theory and Practice of Software Development*, volume 668 of *Lecture Notes in Computer Science*. Springer-Verlag, 1993.

[8] J. Hooman and W. P. de Roever. The quest goes on: a survey of proof systems for partial correctness of CSP. In J.W. de Bakker, W. P. de Roever, and G. Rozenberg, editors, *Current Trends in Concurrency*, pages 343–395. Springer-Verlag, 1986. LNCS 224.

[9] M. Hennessy. *The Semantics of Programming Languages*. John Wiley, 1990.

[10] C. A. R. Hoare and C. B. Jones. *Essays in Computing Science*. Prentice Hall International, 1989.

[11] C. A. R. Hoare. Recursive data structures. *International Journal of Computer & Information Sciences*, 4(2):105–132, June 1975. see also, Chapter 14 of [10].

[12] C. A. R. Hoare. Communicating sequential processes. *Communications of the ACM*, 21(8):666–677, August 1978. see also, Chapter 16 of [10].

[13] C. A. R. Hoare. *Communicating Sequential Processes*. Prentice-Hall, 1985.

[14] Kohei Honda and Nobuko Yoshida. On reduction-based process semantics, 1993. private communication.

[15] T. Ito and A. R. Meyer, editors. *TACS'91 – Proceedings of the International Conference on Theoretical Aspects of Computer Science, Sendai, Japan*, volume 526 of *Lecture Notes in Computer Science*. Springer-Verlag, 1991.

[16] C. B. Jones. *Development Methods for Computer Programs including a Notion of Interference*. PhD thesis, Oxford University, June 1981. Printed as: Programming Research Group, Technical Monograph 25.

[17] C. B. Jones. Interference resumed. In P. Bailes, editor, *Engineering Safe Software*, pages 31–56. Australian Computer Society, 1991.

[18] C. B. Jones. Constraining interference in an object-based design method. In *[7]*, pages 136–150, 1993.

[19] C. B. Jones. A pi-calculus semantics for an object-based design notation. In *CONCUR'93*, Lecture Notes in Computer Science. Springer-Verlag, 1993.

[20] C. B. Jones. Reasoning about interference in an object-based design method. In *FME'93: Industrial-Strength Formal Methods*, volume 670 of *Lecture Notes in Computer Science*, pages 1–18. Springer-Verlag, 1993.

[21] B. B. Kristensen, O. L. Madsen, B. Møller-Pedersen, and K. Nygaard. Object oriented programming in the Beta programming language. Technical report, University of Oslo, September 1991.

[22] R. Milner. *A Calculus for Communicating Systems*, volume 92 of *Lecture Notes in Computer Science*. Springer Verlag, 1980.

[23] R. Milner. *Communication and Concurrency*. Prentice Hall, 1989.

[24] R. Milner. Functions as processes. *Mathematical Structures in Computer Science*, 2(2):119–141, 1992.

[25] R. Milner. The polyadic π-calculus: A tutorial. In M. Broy, editor, *Logic and Algebra of Specification*. Springer-Verlag, 1992.

[26] R. Milner, J. Parrow, and D. Walker. A calculus of mobile processes. *Information and Computation*, 100:1–77, 1992.

[27] G. Nelson, editor. *Systems Programming with Modula-3*. Prentice Hall, 1991.

[28] D. Sangiorgi. From pi-calculus to higher-order pi-calculus – and back. In *[7]*, pages 151–166, 1993.

[29] J. Sargeant. UFO – united functions and objects draft language description. Technical Report UMCS-92-4-3, Manchester University, 1992.

[30] V. T. Vasconcelos and K. Honda. Principal typing schemes in a polyadic π-calculus. In *CONCUR'93*, Lecture Notes in Computer Science. Springer-Verlag, 1993.

[31] D. Walker. π-Calculus semantics of object-oriented programming languages. In *[15]*, pages 532–547, 1991.

[32] D. Walker. Objects in the π-calculus. *Information and Computation*, 1993. (to appear).

[33] D. Walker. Process calculus and parallel object-oriented programming languages. In *International Summer Institute Parallel Computer Architectures, Languages, and Algorithms, Prague*, 1993.

[34] Akinori Yonezawa, editor. *ABCL: An Object-Oriented Concurrent System*. MIT Press, 1990.

Chapter 15

Bracket Notation for the 'Coefficient of' Operator

Donald E. Knuth

When $G(z)$ is a power series in z, many authors now write '$[z^n]\,G(z)$' for the coefficient of z^n in $G(z)$, using a notation introduced by Goulden and Jackson in [5, p. 1]. More controversial, however, is the proposal of the same authors [5, p. 160] to let '$[z^n/n!]\,G(z)$' denote the coefficient of $z^n/n!$, i.e., $n!$ times the coefficient of z^n. An alternative generalization of $[z^n]\,G(z)$, in which we define $[F(z)]\,G(z)$ to be a linear function of both F and G, seems to be more useful because it facilitates algebraic manipulations. The purpose of this paper is to explore some of the properties of such a definition. The remarks are dedicated to Tony Hoare because of his lifelong interest in the improvement of notations that facilitate manipulation.

Informal introduction. In this paper '$[z^2 + 2z^3]\,G(z)$' will stand for the coefficient of z^2 plus twice the coefficient of z^3 in $G(z)$, when $G(z)$ is a function of z for which such coefficients are well defined. More generally, if $F(z) = f_0 + f_1 z + f_2 z^2 + \cdots$ and $G(z) = g_0 + g_1 z + g_2 z^2 + \cdots$, we will let

$$[F(z)]\,G(z) = f_0 g_0 + f_1 g_1 + f_2 g_2 + \cdots$$

be the "dot product" of the vectors $(f_0, f_1, f_2, \ldots)$ and $(g_0, g_1, g_2, \ldots)$, assuming that the infinite sum exists. Still more generally, if $F(z) = \cdots + f_{-2} z^{-2} + f_{-1} z^- + f_0 + f_1 z + f_2 z^2 + \cdots$ and $G(z) = \cdots + g_{-2} z^{-2} + g_{-1} z^- + g_0 + g_1 z + g_2 z^2 + \cdots$ are doubly infinite series, we will write

$$[F(z)]\,G(z) = \cdots + f_{-2} g_{-2} + f_{-1} g_{-1} + f_0 g_0 + f_1 g_1 + f_2 g_2 + \cdots, \qquad (1)$$

again assuming convergence. (It is convenient to write 'z^-' for $1/z$, as in [8].) The right side of (1) is symmetric in F and G, so we have a commutative law:

$$[F(z)]\,G(z) = [G(z)]\,F(z). \qquad (2)$$

There also is symmetry between positive and negative powers:

$$[F(z)]\,G(z) = [F(z^-)]\,G(z^-). \qquad (3)$$

247

In particular, we will write $[1]\, G(z)$ for the constant term g_0 of a given doubly infinite power series $G(z) = \sum_n g_n z^n$. Notice that $[z^n]\, G(z) = [1]\, z^{-n} G(z)$ and in fact

$$[F(z)]\, G(z) = [1]\, F(z^-)G(z)\,, \tag{4}$$

when the product of series is defined in the usual way:

$$\sum_n h_n z^n = \left(\sum_n f_n z^n\right)\left(\sum_n g_n z^n\right) \quad\Longleftrightarrow\quad h_n = \sum_{j+k=n} f_j g_k\,. \tag{5}$$

Relation (4) gives us a useful rule for moving factors in and out of brackets:

$$[F(z)]\, G(z)H(z) = [F(z)G(z^-)]\, H(z)\,. \tag{6}$$

Both sides reduce to $[1]\, F(z^-)G(z)H(z)$, so they must be equal. This rule is most often applied in a simple form such as

$$[z^n]\, z^3 H(z) = [z^{n-3}]\, H(z)\,,$$

but it is helpful to remember the general principle (6). Similarly,

$$[F(z)G(z)]\, H(z) = [F(z)]\, G(z^-)H(z)\,. \tag{7}$$

A paradox.   So far the extended bracket notation seems straightforward and innocuous, but if we start to play with it in an undisciplined fashion we can easily get into trouble. For example, one of the first uses we might wish to make of relation (1) is

$$\left[\frac{z^n}{1-z}\right]\, G(z) = g_n + g_{n+1} + g_{n+2} + \cdots\,, \tag{8}$$

because $z^n/(1-z) = z^n + z^{n+1} + z^{n+2} + \cdots$. This, unfortunately, turns out to be dangerous, if not outright fallacious.

The danger is sometimes muted and we might be lucky. For example, if we try combining (8) with (7) in the case $G(z) = 1/(1-z)$ and $H(z) = (1-z)^2 = 1-2z+z^2$, we get

$$\left[\frac{z^n}{1-z}\right] (1-z)^2 = [z^n]\, \frac{(1-z)^2}{1-z^-} = [z^n]\, (z^2 - z)\,. \tag{9}$$

Sure enough, the sum $h_n + h_{n+1} + h_{n+2} + \cdots$ is nonzero in this case only when $n = 2$ and $n = 1$, and (9) gives the correct answer. So far so good.

But (7) and (8) lead to a contradiction when we apply them to the trivial case $F(z) = H(z) = 1$ and $G(z) = 1/(1-z)$:

$$1 = \left[\frac{1}{1-z}\right] 1 = [1]\, \frac{1}{1-z^-} = [1]\, \frac{-z}{1-z} = 0\,. \tag{10}$$

What went wrong?

Formal analysis. To understand the root of the paradox (10), and to learn when (6) and (7) are indeed valid rules of transformation, we need to know the basic properties of double power series $\sum_n g_n z^n$. The general theory can be found in Henrici [6, §4.4]; we will merely sketch it here.

If $G(z)$ is analytic in an annulus $\alpha < |z| < \beta$, it has a unique double series representation $G(z) = \sum_n g_n z^n$. Conversely, any double power series that converges in an annulus defines an analytic function there. The proof is based on the contour integral formula

$$G(z) = \frac{1}{2\pi i} \oint_{|t|=\beta'} \frac{G(t)\,dt}{(t-z)} - \frac{1}{2\pi i} \oint_{|t|=\alpha'} \frac{G(t)\,dt}{(t-z)} , \qquad (11)$$

where α' is between $|z|$ and α while β' is between $|z|$ and β. The quantity $1/(t-z)$ can be expanded as $t^-(1 + z/t + z^2/t^2 + \cdots)$ when $|t| > |z|$ and as $-z^-(1 + t/z + t^2/z^2 + \cdots)$ when $|t| < |z|$.

If $F(z)$ and $G(z)$ are both analytic for $\alpha < |z| < \beta$, their product $H(z)$ is an analytic function whose coefficients are given by (5). Moreover, the infinite sum over all j and k with $j + k = n$ in (5) is absolutely convergent: The terms are $O((\alpha'/\beta')^k)$ as $k \to +\infty$ and $O((\beta'/\alpha')^k)$ as $k \to -\infty$.

The coefficients of $G(z)$ in its double power series depend on α and β. For example, suppose $G(z) = 1/(2-z)$; we have

$$\frac{1}{2-z} = \begin{cases} \frac{1}{2} + \frac{1}{4}z + \frac{1}{8}z^2 + \cdots , & \text{when } |z| < 2; \\ -z^- - 2z^{-2} - 4z^{-3} - \cdots , & \text{when } |z| > 2. \end{cases} \qquad (12)$$

Thus if $F(z) = 1/(2-z) + 1/(2-z^-)$, there are three expansions

$$F(z) = \begin{cases} \frac{1}{2} + (\frac{1}{4} - 1)z + (\frac{1}{8} - 2)z^2 + (\frac{1}{16} - 4)z^3 + \cdots , & |z| < \frac{1}{2}; \\ \cdots + \frac{1}{8}z^{-2} + \frac{1}{4}z^- + 1 + \frac{1}{4}z + \frac{1}{8}z^2 + \cdots , & \frac{1}{2} < |z| < 2; \\ \cdots + (\frac{1}{16} - 4)z^{-3} + (\frac{1}{8} - 2)z^{-2} + (\frac{1}{4} - 1)z^- + \frac{1}{2}, & |z| > 2. \end{cases} \qquad (13)$$

Here's another example, this time involving a function that has an essential singularity instead of a pole:

$$e^{z/(1-z)} = \begin{cases} 1 + z + \frac{3}{2}z^2 + \frac{13}{6}z^3 + \frac{73}{24}z^4 + \cdots , & |z| < 1; \\ e^- - e^- z^- - \frac{e^-}{2} z^{-2} - \frac{e^-}{6} z^{-3} + \frac{e^-}{24} z^{-4} + \cdots , & |z| > 1. \end{cases} \qquad (14)$$

The coefficients when $|z| < 1$ are $P_n/n!$, where P_n is the number of "sets of lists" of order n [9].

Explaining the paradox. The dependency of coefficients on α and β makes our notation $[F(z)]\,G(z)$ ambiguous; that is why we ran into trouble in the paradoxical "equation" (10). We can legitimately use bracket notation only when the context specifies a family of "safe" functions – functions with well defined coefficients.

The basic definition of $[F(z)]\,G(z)$ in (4) should be used only if the product $F(z^-)G(z)$ is safe. Operation (6), which moves a factor $G(z)$ into the bracket, should be used only if $F(z^-)G(z)H(z)$ is safe. Operation (7), which removes a factor $G(z)$ from the bracket, should be used only if $F(z^-)G(z^-)H(z)$ is safe.

The root of our problem in (10) begins in (8), where we used the expansion $F(z) = z^n/(1-z) = z^n + z^{n+1} + z^{n+2} + \cdots$; in other words, $F(z^-) = z^{-n}/(1-z^-) = z^{-n} + z^{-n-1} + z^{-n-2} + \cdots$. The latter expansion is valid only when $|z| > 1$, so the bracket notation of (8) refers to coefficients in the region $1 < |z| < \infty$. In the last step of (10), however, we said that $[1]\,(-z/(1-z)) = 0$, using coefficients from the region $|z| < 1$. The correct result for $|z| > 1$ is

$$[1]\,\frac{-z}{1-z} = [1]\,\frac{1}{1-z^-} = [1]\,(\cdots + z^{-2} + z^- + 1) = 1\,.$$

Bracket notation is most often used when $|z|$ is small, so we should actually forget the "rightward sum" appearing in equation (8); it hardly ever yields the formula we want. The "leftward sum" rule

$$\left[\frac{z^n}{1-z^-}\right]\,G(z) = \cdots + g_{n-2} + g_{n-1} + g_n \tag{15}$$

should be used instead, because $z^n/(1-z^-) = \cdots + z^{n-2} + z^{n-1} + z^n$ is valid for $|z^-| < 1$. *When the bracket notation $[F(z)]\,G(z)$ is being used in the annulus (α,β), the functions $F(z^-)$ and $G(z)$ should be analytic in (α,β).* Note that $f(z^-)$ is analytic in (α,β) if and only if $f(z)$ is analytic in (β^-,α^-).

Formal series.   Manipulations of generating functions are often done on formal power series, when the coefficients are arbitrary and convergence is disregarded. However, formal power series are not allowed to be infinite in both directions; a formal series $G(z) = \sum_n g_n z^n$ is generally required to be a "formal Laurent series" – a series in which $g_n = 0$ for all sufficiently negative values of n. We shall call such series *L-series* for short. Similarly, we shall say that a reverse formal Laurent series, in which $g_n = 0$ for all sufficiently *positive* values of n, is an *R-series*. A power series is both an *L*-series and an *R*-series if and only if it is a polynomial in z and z^-.

Henrici [6, §1.2–1.8] shows that the normal operations on power series – addition, subtraction, multiplication, division by nonzero, differentiation, composition – can all be done rigorously on *L*-series without regard to convergence. Thus *L*-series are "safe" functions: *We can define bracket notation $[F(z)]\,G(z)$ by rule (4) whenever $F(z)$ is an R-series and $G(z)$ is an L-series.* Convergence is not then an issue. This definition provides the default meaning of bracket notation, whenever no other context is specified. The transformations in (7) and (8) are valid when the functions inside brackets are *R*-series and the functions outside brackets are *L*-series. Equations (2) and (3) should not be used unless F and G are both *L*-series and *R*-series.

In such cases paradoxes do not rear their ugly heads. The ill-fated equation (8) may fail, but equation (15) is always true.

Additional properties.   The bracket notation satisfies several identities in addition to (2), (3), (6), and (7), hence we can often transform formulas in which it appears. In the first place, the operation is linear in both operands:

$$[a\,F(z) + b\,G(z)]\,H(z) = a[F(z)]\,H(z) + b[G(z)]\,H(z)\,;\tag{16}$$

$$[F(z)](a\,G(z) + b\,H(z)) = a[F(z)]\,G(z) + b[F(z)]\,H(z)\,.\tag{17}$$

In the second place, there is a general multiplication law

$$[F_1(z)\,F_2(z)]\,G_1(z)\,G_2(z) = \sum_k ([F_1(z)z^k]\,G_1(z))([F_2(z)z^{-k}]\,G_2(z))\,.\tag{18}$$

If $F_1(z) = F_2(z) = 1$, this equation is simply the special case $n = 0$ of (5), and for general F_1 and F_2 it follows from the special case because we can replace $G_1(z)$ and $G_2(z)$ by $F_1(z^-)G_1(z)$ and $F_2(z^-)G_2(z)$ using (7).

We also have

$$[F(z^m)]\,G(z^m) = [F(z)]\,G(z)\tag{19}$$

for any nonzero integer m; this equation, which includes (3) as the special case $m = -1$, follows immediately from (4) because $[1]\,H(z) = [1]\,H(z^m)$. Equation (19) suggests that we generalize bracket notation to functions that are sums over non-integral powers, in which case m would not need to be an integer. Then we could write (19) as

$$[F(z)]\,G(z^m) = [F(z^{1/m})]\,G(z)\,,\quad m \neq 0\,.\tag{19'}$$

Such generalizations, extending perhaps to integrals as well as to sums, may prove to be quite interesting, but they will not be pursued further here.

If a is any nonzero constant, we have $[1]\,H(az) = [1]\,H(z)$. This rule implies that $[1]\,F(z^-)G(az) = [1]\,F(az^-)G(z)$, and (4) yields

$$[F(z)]\,G(az) = [F(az)]\,G(z)\,.\tag{20}$$

The special case where $F(z)$ is simply z^m is, of course, already familiar:

$$[z^m]\,G(az) = [(az)^m]\,G(z) = a^m[z^m]\,G(z)\,.$$

Bracket notation also interacts with differentiation in interesting ways. We have, for instance,

$$[z^-]\,G'(z) = 0\tag{21}$$

for any function $G(z) = \sum_{n=-\infty}^{\infty} g_n z^n$. More significantly,

$$[F(z)]\,z\,G'(z) = [z\,F'(z)]\,G(z)\,.\tag{22}$$

Equation (21) is essentially the special case $F(z) = 1$ of (22), but we can also derive (22) from (21): Let $H(z) = F(z^-)G(z)$; then $0 = [1]\, z\, H'(z) = [1]\, z\, (F(z^-)G'(z) - z^{-2}F'(z)G(z))$, hence $[1]\, F(z^-)\, z\, G'(z) = [1]\, z^- F'(z^-)G(z)$, which is (22).

Let ϑ be the operator $z\frac{d}{dz}$. Then (22) implies by induction on m that

$$[F(z)]\, \vartheta^m\, G(z) = [\vartheta^m\, F(z)]\, G(z)$$

for all integers $m \geq 0$, and we have

$$[F(z)]\, P(\vartheta)\, G(z) = [P(\vartheta)\, F(z)]\, G(z) \tag{23}$$

for any polynomial P. If $F(z) = \sum_n f_n z^n$ and $G(z) = \sum_n g_n z^n$, both sides of (23) evaluate to $\sum_n P(n) f_n g_n$.

Additional variables.   When $G(w, z)$ is a bivariate generating function we also wish to write $[w^m z^n]$ for the coefficient of $w^m z^n$ in G. In general we can define

$$[F(w, z)]\, G(w, z) = [1]\, F(w^-, z^-)\, G(w, z)\,, \tag{24}$$

extending (4).

Variables must be clearly distinguished from constants. If w and z are both variables, we have for instance $[z]\, wz = 0$, while if w is constant we have $[z]\, wz = w$. If the set of variables is not clear from the context, we can specify it by writing its elements as subscripts on the brackets. For example,

$$[F(w)\, G(z)]_{w,z}\, H(w, z) = [G(z)]_z([F(w)]_w\, H(w, z)) \tag{25}$$

because the former is $[1]_{w,z}\, F(w^-)G(z^-)H(w, z)$ while the latter is

$$[1]_z(G(z^-)\, [1]_w(F(w^-)H(w, z))) = [1]_z[1]_w\, G(z^-)\, F(w^-)\, H(w, z)$$

and $[1]_{w,z} = [1]_w[1]_z$.

After we have evaluated the parenthesis on the right side of (25), the ambiguity disappears, because w is no longer present. For example, if $m \geq 0$ we have

$$[w^m z^n]\, \frac{1}{1 - wF(z)} = [z^n]\left([w^m]_w\, \frac{1}{1 - wF(z)}\right) = [z^n]\, F(z)^m\,, \tag{26}$$

where brackets without subscripts assume that both w and z are variables. Similarly

$$[w^m z^n]\, e^{wF(z)} = [z^n]\, \frac{F(z)^m}{m!}\,, \tag{27}$$

$$[w^m z^n]\, G(w\, F(z))\, H(z) = [z^n]\, F(z)^m\, H(z)\, [w^m]\, G(w)\,. \tag{28}$$

Suppose w and z are variables. Then laws (19) and (20) extend to

$$[F(w, z)]\, G(aw, z) = [F(aw, z)]\, G(w, z)\,, \qquad a \neq 0\,; \tag{29}$$

$$[F(w^m, z)]\, G(w^m, z) = [F(w, z)]\, G(w, z)\,, \qquad \text{integer } m \neq 0\,; \tag{30}$$

$$[F(w, w^m z)]\, G(w, w^m z) = [F(w, z)]\, G(w, z)\,; \tag{31}$$

and we have indeed the general rule

$$[F(a^- w^k z^l, b^- w^m z^n)] \, G(aw^k z^l, bw^m z^n) = [F(w, z)] \, G(w, z) \tag{32}$$

when $a \neq 0$, $b \neq 0$, and $\begin{vmatrix} k & l \\ m & n \end{vmatrix} \neq 0$, i.e., $kn \neq lm$. A similar formula applies with respect to any number of variables.

The following example from the theory of random graphs [3, (10.10) and (10.14)] illustrates how these rules are typically applied. Suppose we want to evaluate the coefficient of $[w^m z^n]$ in the expression $e^{U(wz)/w+V(wz)}$, where U and V are known functions with $U(0) = 0$. The two-variable problem is reduced to a one-variable problem as follows:

$$
\begin{aligned}
[w^m z^n] \, e^{U(wz)/w+V(wz)} &= [(w^-)^{n-m} (wz)^n] \, e^{U(wz)w^- + V(wz)} \\
&= [w^{n-m} z^n] \, e^{U(z)w+V(z)} \\
&= \frac{1}{(n-m)!} \, [z^n] \, U(z)^{n-m} e^{V(z)},
\end{aligned}
\tag{33}
$$

by (32) with $F(w, z) = w^{n-m} z^n$, $G(w, z) = e^{U(z)w+V(z)}$, $a = b = 1$, $k = -1$, $l = 0$, $m = n = 1$. The final step uses (28) with $F(z) = U(z)$, $G(w) = e^w$, and $H(z) = e^{V(z)}$.

As before, we need to check that the functions are safe before we can guarantee that such manipulations are legitimate. For formal power series, the functions inside brackets should be R-series and the functions outside should be L-series. This condition holds in each step of (33) because $U(0) = 0$.

Additional identities. The bracket notation also obeys more complex laws that deserve further study. For example, Gessel and Stanton [4, Eq. (3)] have shown among other things that

$$[F(w, z)] \, \frac{G(w, z)}{1 - wz} = [F(w(1 + z^-), z(1 + w^-))] \, G\left(\frac{w}{1+z}, \frac{z}{1+w}\right). \tag{34}$$

If we set $F(w, z) = w^k z^l$ and $G(w, z) = (1 + w)^m (1 + z)^n / (1 - wz)^{m+n}$, Gessel and Stanton observe that we obtain Saalschütz's identity after some remarkable cancellation:

$$
\begin{aligned}
\sum_r \binom{m}{k-r} \binom{n}{l-r} \binom{m+n+r}{r} &= [w^k (1 + z^-)^k z^l (1 + w^-)^l] \, (1 + w)^m (1 + z)^n \\
&= [w^k z^l] \, (1 + w)^{m+l} (1 + z)^{n+k} \\
&= \binom{m+l}{k} \binom{n+k}{l}.
\end{aligned}
\tag{35}
$$

And if we set $F(w, z) = w^{l+n} z^{m+n}$, $G(w, z) = (w - z)^{l+m}/(1 - wz)^{l+m}$, the left side of (34) reduces to

$$[w^{l+n} z^{m+n}] \, \frac{(w - z)^{l+m}}{(1 - wz)^{l+m+1}} = (-1)^m \, \frac{(l+m+n)!}{l! \, m! \, n!}; \tag{36}$$

the right side is

$$[w^{l+n}(1+z^-)^{l+n}z^{m+n}(1+w^-)^{m+n}] (w-z)^{l+m}$$
$$= [w^{l+n}z^{m+n}] (w-z)^{l+m}(1+w)^{m+n}(1+z)^{l+n}$$
$$= \sum_k (-1)^{k+m} \binom{l+m}{k+m}\binom{m+n}{k+n}\binom{n+l}{k+l}. \tag{37}$$

The fact that (36) = (37) is Dixon's identity [7, exercise 1.2.6–62].

Equation (34) can be generalized to n variables, and we can replace the '1' on the right by any nonzero constant a:

$$[F(z_1,\ldots,z_n)] \frac{G(z_1,\ldots,z_n)}{1-z_1\ldots z_n}$$
$$= [F(z_1(a+z_2^-),\ldots,z_n(a+z_1^-))] \, G\left(\frac{z_1}{a+z_2},\ldots,\frac{z_n}{a+z_1}\right). \tag{38}$$

It suffices to prove this when $F(z_1,\ldots,z_n) = 1$ and $G(z_1,\ldots,z_n) = z_1^{m_1}\ldots z_n^{m_n}$, in which case both sides are 0 unless $m_1 = \cdots = m_n \le 0$, when both sides are 1. Equation (38) holds in particular when $n = 1$:

$$[F(z)] \frac{G(z)}{1-z} = [F(1+az)] \, G\left(\frac{z}{a+z}\right), \qquad a \ne 0. \tag{39}$$

Returning to the case of a single variable, we should also state the general rule for composition of series:

$$G(F(z)) = \sum_n F(z)^n \, [z^n] \, G(z). \tag{40}$$

Special conditions are needed to ensure that this infinite sum is well defined.

Lagrange's inversion formula.   Let $F(z) = f_1 z + f_2 z^2 + f_3 z^3 + \cdots$, with $f_1 \ne 0$, and let $G(z)$ be the inverse function so that

$$F(G(z)) = G(F(z)) = z. \tag{41}$$

Lagrange's celebrated formula for the coefficients of G can be expressed in bracket notation in several ways; for example, we have

$$n[z^n] \, G(z)^m = m \, [z^{-m}] \, F(z)^{-n}, \tag{42}$$

for all integers m and n.

One way to derive (42), following Paule [10], is to note first that (40) implies

$$z^m = G(F(z))^m = \sum_k F(z)^k \, [z^k] \, G(z)^m. \tag{43}$$

Differentiating with the ϑ operator and dividing by $F(z)^n$ yields

$$\frac{mz^m}{F(z)^n} = \sum_k kF(z)^{k-1-n}\vartheta F(z)\,[z^k]\,G(z)^m. \tag{44}$$

Now we will study the constant terms of (44). If $k \neq n$,

$$[1]\,F(z)^{k-1-n}\vartheta F(z) = [1]\,\frac{\vartheta(F(z)^{k-n})}{k-n} = 0\,, \tag{45}$$

by (22). And if $k = n$,

$$[1]\,\frac{\vartheta F(z)}{F(z)} = [1]\,\frac{f_1 + 2f_2 z + 3f_3 z^2 + \cdots}{f_1 + f_2 z + f_3 z^2 + \cdots} = 1\,, \tag{46}$$

because $f_1 \neq 0$. Therefore the constant terms of (44) are

$$[1]\,\frac{mz^m}{F(z)^n} = n\,[z^n]\,G(z)^m\,;$$

this is Lagrange's formula (42).

Conclusions.   Many years of experience have confirmed the great importance of generating functions in the analysis of algorithms, and we can reasonably expect that some fluency in manipulating the "coefficient-of" operator will therefore be rewarding.

If, for example, we are faced with the task of simplifying a formula such as

$$\sum_k \binom{m}{k}[z^{n-k}]\,F(z)^k\,,$$

a rudimentary acquaintance with the properties of brackets will tell us that it can be written as $\sum_k \binom{m}{k}[z^n]\,z^k\,F(z)^k$ and then summed to yield

$$[z^n](1 + z\,F(z))^m\,.$$

We have seen several examples above in which formulas that are far less obvious can be derived rapidly by bracket manipulation, when we use quantities more general than monomials inside the brackets.

In most applications we use bracket notation in connection with formal Laurent series, in which case it is important to remember that our identities for $[F(z)]\,G(z)$ require $G(z)$ to have only finitely many *negative* powers of z while $F(z)$ must have only finitely many *positive* powers. If we write, for example,

$$\left[\frac{z^n}{z-1}\right]G(z)\,, \tag{47}$$

we should think of the quantity in brackets as an infinite series

$$z^{n-1} + z^{n-2} + z^{n-3} + \cdots$$

that descends to arbitrarily *negative* powers of z; the bracket notation then denotes the sum $g_{n-1} + g_{n-2} + g_{n-3} + \cdots$, which will be finite. We have seen that other interpretations of bracket notation are possible for functions analytic in an annulus; but great care must be taken to avoid paradoxes in such cases, hence the extra effort might not be worth while.

Bracket notation, like all notations, is "dispensable," in the sense that we can prove the same theorems without it as with it. But the use of a good notation can shorten proofs and help us see patterns that would otherwise be difficult to perceive.

Let us close with one more example, illustrating that the notation (47) helps to simplify some of the formulas in [2]. The *coupon collector's problem* asks for the expected number of trials needed to obtain n distinct coupons from a set C of m given coupons, where each trial independently produces coupon c with probability $p(c)$. Theorem 2 of [2] says, when rewritten in the notation discussed above, that this expected number is

$$\int_0^\infty \left[\frac{z^n}{z-1} \right] \prod_{c \in C} \left(1 + z(e^{p(c)t} - 1) \right) e^{-t}\, dt \,. \tag{48}$$

We can evaluate (48) by expanding the integrand as follows:

$$\left[\frac{z^n}{z-1} \right] \prod_{c \in C} \left(1 + z(e^{p(c)t} - 1) \right) = \sum_{\substack{B \subseteq C \\ |B| < n}} \prod_{c \in B} \left(e^{p(c)t} - 1 \right)$$

$$= \sum_{\substack{A \subseteq B \subseteq C \\ |B| < n}} (-1)^{|B|-|A|} e^{p(A)t}$$

$$= \sum_{\substack{A \subseteq C \\ |A| < n}} e^{p(A)t} \sum_{|A| \leq k < n} (-1)^{k-|A|} \binom{|C| - |A|}{k - |A|}$$

$$= \sum_{\substack{A \subseteq C \\ |A| < n}} e^{p(A)t} (-1)^{n-1-|A|} \binom{|C| - |A| - 1}{|C| - n} ,$$

where $p(A)$ denotes $\sum_{a \in A} p(a)$. The integral (48) is therefore

$$\sum_{\substack{A \subseteq C \\ |A| < n}} (-1)^{n-1-|A|} \binom{|C| - |A| - 1}{|C| - n} \Big/ \left(1 - p(A) \right) . \tag{49}$$

(This is Corollary 3 of [2], which was stated without proof.)

Related work. Steven Roman's book on umbral calculus [11] develops extensive properties of his notation $\langle G(t) \mid F(x) \rangle$, which equals $\sum_{n \geq 0} f_n g_n$ when $F(x) = \sum_{n \geq 0} f_n x^n$ and $G(t) = \sum_{n \geq 0} g_n t^n / n!$; the function $F(x)$ in these formulas must be a polynomial. Thus, if D is the operator d/dx, Roman's $\langle G(t) \mid F(x) \rangle$ is the constant term of the polynomial $G(D) F(x)$. Chapter 6 of [11] considers generalizations in which $\langle G(t) \mid F(x) \rangle$ is defined to be $\sum_{n \geq 0} f_n g_n$ when $G(t) = \sum_{n \geq 0} g_n t^n / c_n$ and c_n is an arbitrary sequence of constants; the case $c_n = 1$ corresponds to the special case of bracket notation $[F(z)] \, G(z)$ when F and G involve no negative powers of z. Roman traces the theory back to a paper by Morgan Ward [12].

G. P. Egorychev's book [1] includes a great many examples that demonstrate the value of coefficient extraction in the midst of formulas.

Open problems. One reason formal power series are usually restricted to *L*-series is that certain doubly infinite power series are divisions of zero. For example, $\sum_{n=-\infty}^{\infty} z^n$ is a divisor of zero because multiplication by $1 - z$ annihilates it. (This series causes no problem in the theory of non-formal power series because it does not converge for any value of z.) All double series having the form $\sum_n n^m \alpha^n z^n$ for $\alpha \neq 0$ and integer $m \geq 0$ can also be shown to be divisors of zero. Question: Do there exist divisors of zero besides finite linear combinations of the double series just mentioned? Conjecture: There is no nonzero double series $F(z)$ such that $e^z F(z) = 0$. (A counterexample would necessarily be divergent.)*

It may be possible and interesting to extend the theory of formal Laurent series to arbitrary functions of the form $F(z) \sum_n g_n z^n$, where g_n is zero for all sufficiently negative n and where $F(z)$ is analytic for $0 < |z| < \infty$.

Acknowledgments. I wish to thank Edsger and Ria Dijkstra for the splendid opportunity to write this paper in the guest room of their Texas home, and Peter Paule for his penetrating comments on the first draft.

* Note added in proof: An interesting family of counterexamples has just been discovered by Philippe Jacquet and Philippe Flajolet.

References

[1] G. P. Egorychev, *Integral Representation and the Computation of Combinatorial Sums*, (Providence, Rhode Island: American Mathematical Society, 1984).

[2] Philippe Flajolet, Danièle Gardy, and Loÿs Thimonier, "Birthday paradox, coupon collectors, caching algorithms and self-organizing search," *Discrete Applied Mathematics* **39** (1992), 207–229.

[3] Philippe Flajolet, Donald E. Knuth, and Boris Pittel, "The first cycles in an evolving graph," *Discrete Mathematics* **75** (1989), 167–215.

[4] Ira Gessel and Dennis Stanton, "Short proofs of Saalschütz's and Dixon's theorems," *Journal of Combinatorial Theory* **A38** (1985), 87–90.

[5] I. P. Goulden and D. M. Jackson, *Combinatorial Enumeration* (New York: Wiley, 1983).

[6] Peter Henrici, *Applied and Computational Complex Analysis*, Volume 1 (New York: Wiley, 1974).

[7] Donald E. Knuth, *Fundamental Algorithms*, Volume 1 of *The Art of Computer Programming* (Reading, Massachusetts: Addison–Wesley, 1968).

[8] Donald E. Knuth, "Efficient representation of perm groups," *Combinatorica* **11** (1991), 33–43.

[9] T. S. Motzkin, "Sorting numbers for cylinders and other classification numbers," *Proceedings of Symposia in Pure Mathematics* **19** (1971), 167–176.

[10] P. Paule, "Ein neuer Weg zur q-Lagrange Inversion", *Bayreuther Mathematische Schriften* **18** (1985), 1–37.

[11] Steven Roman, *The Umbral Calculus* (Orlando, Florida: Academic Press, 1984).

[12] Morgan Ward, "A calculus of sequences," *American Journal of Mathematics* **58** (1936), 255–266.

Chapter 16

Implementing Coherent Memory

Butler W. Lampson

In the design of a shared-memory multiprocessor, there is a conflict between the need for a *coherent* memory in which every write done by one processor is immediately visible to all the others, and the fact that a memory read or write that uses only a cache local to the processor can be done more quickly than one that communicates with a global memory or another processor. Coherent memory is good because we know how to program with it; the *incoherent* memory that results from minimizing communication is good because it is fast.

In this paper we show how to write precise specifications for coherent and incoherent memory, and how to implement coherent memory in several ways, one of which is on top of incoherent memory. Our technique for showing the correctness of the implementations is the abstraction function introduced by Hoare [8] to handle abstract data types. A decade later, Lamport [1] and Lynch [10] extended Hoare's methods to concurrent systems like the ones we treat.

We begin by giving a careful specification for the coherent memory S that we really want; it is just a function from addresses to data values. We also specify an incoherent memory T that has fast implementations. After a brief explanation of what it means to implement a specification and how to prove the correctness of an implementation using abstraction functions, we explore how to change T so that it implements coherent memory with as little communication as possible. Our first step is a simple idealized implementation U derived from T by strengthening the guards. Unfortunately U is extremely non-local and therefore impractical. We describe two ways to make U local enough to be practical. Both are based on the idea of using locks on memory locations.

First we show how to use reader/writer locks to get a practical version of U called a coherent cache. We do this in two stages: an ideal cache B and a concrete cache C. The cache changes the guards on internal actions of T as well as on the external read and write actions, so it can't be implemented simply by adding a test before each read or write of T, but instead requires changes to the insides of T. We complete our treatment of caches by sketching several implementations of C that are used in commercial multiprocessors.

Then we show how to use locks in a different way to get another practical version of U, called E. The advantage of E is that the locking is separate from the internal actions of the memory system, and hence E can be implemented entirely in software on top of an incoherent memory system that only implements T. In other words, E is a practical way to program coherent memory on a machine whose hardware provides only incoherent memory.

All our implementations make use of a global memory that is modelled as a function from addresses to data values; in other words, the specification for the global memory is simply S. This means that an actual implementation may have a recursive structure, in which the top-level implementation of S using one of our algorithms contains a global memory that is implemented with another algorithm and contains another global memory, etc. This recursion terminates only when we lose interest in another level of virtualization. For example,

> a processor's memory may be made up of a first level cache plus
> > a global memory made up of a second level cache plus
> > > a global memory made up of a main memory plus
> > > > a global memory made up of a local swapping disk plus
> > > > > a global memory made up of a file server ....

16.0.1   Notation

We write our specifications and implementations using *state machines* [9]. As usual, a state machine consists of

- a state space, which we represent by the values of a set of named variables,
- a set of initial states, and
- a set of transitions or *actions*. Each action consists of:
  - a *name*, which may include some parameters,
  - a *guard*, a predicate on the state that must be true for the action to happen, and
  - a *state change*, which we represent by a set of assignments of new values to the state variables.

We write an action in the form

$$name \qquad = guard \qquad \rightarrow \quad state\ change$$

Actions are atomic: each action completes before the next one is started. To express concurrency we introduce more actions. Some of these actions may be *internal*, that is, they may not involve any interaction with the client of the memory. Internal actions usually make the state machine non-deterministic, since they can happen whenever their guards are satisfied, unlike external actions, which require some interaction with the environment.

To make our state machines easier to understand we give types for the variables, either scalar or function types. We also give names to some *state functions* on the variables. For instance, we define $clean = (\forall p \,.\, \neg\, new_p)$ and then use $clean$ in expressions exactly like a variable. Finally, we write down useful invariants of each state machine, predicates that are true in every reachable state.

16.1   S: Coherent memory specification

This is just what you expect. The memory is modeled as a function m from addresses to data values, and the *Read* and *Write* actions give direct access to the function. We write the spec in this rather fussy form only for compatibility with the more complicated versions that follow. The actions take a processor p as a parameter so that they have the same names as the *Read* and *Write* actions of later systems, but in this spec they don't depend on p:

type
A		Address
D		Data
P		Processor

variable
m	$: A \to D$	Memory

action
$Read(p, a, \textbf{var } d)$	$=$	$d := m(a)$
$Write(p, a, d)$	$=$	$m(a) := d$

From now on we reduce clutter in the text of the specs by:

- Dealing only with one address, dropping the a argument everywhere.
- Writing the p argument as a subscript.

With these conventions, the actions above look like this:

action
$Read_p(\textbf{var } d)$	$=$	$d := m$
$Write_p(d)$	$=$	$m := d$

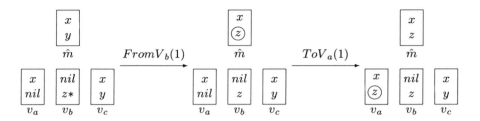

Figure 16.1 Some possible transitions of T with three processors

16.2   T: Incoherent memory specification

The idea of incoherent memory is that in addition to a global memory $\hat{m}$ there is a private *view* v_p for each processor; it contains data values for some subset of the addresses. Here is the state of T:

variable

$\hat{m}$	$: A \to D$
v	$: P \to A \to (D \mid nil)$
new	$: P \to A \to Bool$

state function

$live_p$	$\equiv (v_p \neq nil)$

invariant

new_p	$\Rightarrow live_p$

Processor p uses v_p to do its $Read_p$ and $Write_p$ actions. Internal actions ToV_p and $FromV_p$ copy data back and forth between p's view and the global memory $\hat{m}$. An address is *live* in p if p's view has a value for it. To do a $Read_p$ a processor may have to wait for a ToV_p to make the address live; a processor can do a $Write_p$ at any time. Each view also keeps track in *new* of the addresses for which it has new data that hasn't yet been copied to $\hat{m}$. An internal $Drop_p$ action removes a datum that isn't new from p's view. An external $Barrier_p$ action waits until an address is not live; this ensures that the value written by any earlier $Write$ has been copied to $\hat{m}$ and that any later $Read$ sees a value from $\hat{m}$.

There are commercial machines whose memory systems have essentially this specification [3]. Others have explored similar specifications [4, 5].

Figure 16.1 is a simple example which shows the contents of two addresses 0 and 1 in $\hat{m}$ and in three processors a, b, and c. A new value is marked with a *, and circles mark values that have changed. Initially $Read_b(1)$ yields the new value z, $Read_c(1)$ yields y, and $Read_a(1)$ blocks because $v_a(1)$ is nil. After the $FromV_b$ the global location $\hat{m}(1)$ has been updated with z. After the ToV_a, $Read_a(1)$ yields z.

One way to ensure that the $FromV_b$ and ToV_a actions happen before the $Read_a(1)$ is to do $Barrier_b$ followed by $Barrier_a$ between the $Write_b(1)$ that makes z new in v_b and the $Read_a(1)$.

Here are the possible transitions of T for a given address:

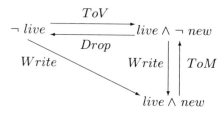

Finally, here are the actions of the specification for incoherent memory:

action

$Read_p(\mathbf{var}\ d)$	$= live_p$	$\rightarrow$	$d := v_p$
$Write_p(d)$	$=$		$v_p := d,\ new_p := true$
$Barrier_p$	$= \neg\ live_p$	$\rightarrow$	**skip**

internal action

ToV_p	$= \neg\ new_p$	$\rightarrow$	$v_p := \hat{m}$
$FromV_p$	$= new_p$	$\rightarrow$	$\hat{m} := v_p,\ new_p := false$
$Drop_p$	$= \neg\ new_p$	$\rightarrow$	$v_p := nil$

After a $Barrier_p$, v_p is guaranteed to agree with $\hat{m}$ until the next time $\hat{m}$ changes.[1]

Note that in general a ToV action is needed to establish the guard on $Read$, and a $Drop$ action to establish the guard on $Barrier$. This means that an implementation will do something that has the effect of ToV when it's trying to do a $Read$, and similarly for $Drop$ and $Write$. A $Drop$ in turn may require a $FromV$ to establish its guard.

This is the weakest shared-memory spec that seems likely to be useful in practice. But perhaps it is too weak. Why do we introduce this messy incoherent memory T? Wouldn't we be much better off with the simple and familiar coherent memory S? There are two reasons to prefer T to S.

1. An implementation of T can run faster – there is more locality and less communication. As we will see in implementation E, software can batch the communication that is needed to make a coherent memory out of E.

---

[1] An alternative version of $Barrier$ has the guard $\neg\ live_p \lor (v_p = \hat{m})$; this is equivalent to the current $Barrier$ followed by an optional ToV_p. You might think that it's better because it avoids a copy from $\hat{m}$ to v_p in case they already agree. But this is a spec, not an implementation, and the change doesn't affect its external behavior.

2. Even S is tricky to use when there are concurrent clients. Experience has shown that it's necessary to have wizards to package it so that ordinary programmers can use it safely. This packaging takes the form of rules for writing concurrent programs, and procedures that encapsulate references to shared memory. The two most common examples are:

- Mutual exclusion / critical sections / monitors, which ensure that a number of references to shared memory can be done without interference, just as in a sequential program. Reader/writer locks are an important variation.

- Producer–consumer buffers.

For the ordinary programmer only the simplicity of the package is important, not the subtlety of its implementation. As we shall see, we need a smarter wizard to package T, but the result is as simple to use as the packaged S. The implementation E below shows how to use T to obtain critical sections.

16.2.1   Specifying legal histories directly

It's common in the literature to write the specifications S and T explicitly in terms of legal sequences of references at each processor, rather than as state machines [3, 4]. We digress briefly to explain this approach.

For S, there must be a total ordering of the $Read_p(a, d)$ or $Write_p(a, d)$ actions done by the processors that

- respects the order at each p, and
- such that for each $Read_p(a, d)$ and latest preceding $Write_p(a, d')$, $d = d'$.

For T, there must be a total ordering of the $Read_p(a, d)$, $Write_p(a, d)$, and $Barrier_p(a)$ actions done by the processors that

- respects the order of $Read_p(a, -)$, $Write_p(a, -)$, and $Barrier_p(a)$ at each p for each a, and
- such that *Read* reads the data written by the latest preceding *Write*, as in S.

The T spec is weaker than S because it allows references to different addresses to be ordered differently. Usually the barrier operation actually provided does a *Barrier* for every address, and thus forces all the references preceding it at a given processor to precede all the references following it.

It's not hard to show that these specs written in terms of ordering are almost equivalent to S and T. Actually they are somewhat more permissive. For example, the T spec allows the following history:

- Initially $x = 1, y = 1$.

- Processor a reads 4 from x, then writes 8 to y.
- Processor b reads 8 from y, then writes 4 to x.

We can rule out this kind of predicting the future by observing that the processors make their references in some total order in real time, and requiring that a suitable ordering exist for the references in each prefix of this real time order, not just for the entire set of references. With this restriction, the two versions of the T spec are equivalent.

16.3   Implementations

Having seen the specs for coherent and incoherent memory, we are ready to study some implementations. We begin with a precise statement of what it means for an implementation Y to satisfy a specification X [1, 10].

X and Y are state machines. We partition their actions into *external* and *internal* actions. A history of a machine M is a sequence of actions that M can take starting in an initial state, and an *external history* of M is the subsequence of a history that contains only the external actions.

We say Y *implements* X iff every external history of Y is an external history of X.[2] This expresses the idea that what it means for Y to implement X is that the externally observable behavior of Y is a subset of the externally observable behavior of X; thus you can't tell by observing Y that you are not observing X.

The set of all external histories is a rather complicated object and difficult to reason about. Fortunately, there is a general method for proving that Y implements X without reasoning explicitly about histories in each case. It works as follows. First, define an *abstraction function* f from the state of Y to the state of X. Then show that Y *simulates* X:

1. f maps an initial state of Y to an initial state of X.
2. For each Y-action and each state y there is a sequence of X-actions that is the same externally, such that the diagram below commutes.

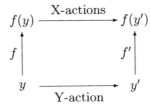

---

[2]Actually this definition only deals with the implementation of *safety* properties. Roughly speaking, a safety property is an assertion that nothing bad happens; it is a generalization of the notion of partial correctness for sequential programs. Specifications may also include *liveness* properties, which roughly assert that something good eventually happens; these generalize the notion of termination for sequential programs [1]. Liveness is beyond the scope of this paper.

A sequence of X-actions is the same externally as a Y-action if they are the same after all internal actions are discarded. So if the Y-action is internal, all the X-actions must be internal (there might be none at all). If the Y-action is external, all the X-actions must be internal except one, which must be the same as the Y-action.

Then by a straightforward induction Y implements X, because for any Y-history we can construct an X-history that is the same externally, by using (2) to map each Y-action into a sequence of X-actions that is the same externally. Then the sequence of Y-actions will be the same externally as the corresponding sequence of X-actions.

In order to prove that Y simulates X we usually need to know what the reachable states of Y are, because it won't be true that every action of Y from an arbitrary state of Y simulates a sequence of X actions. The most convenient way to characterize the reachable states of Y is by an *invariant*, a predicate that is true of every reachable state. Often it's helpful to write the invariant as a conjunction, and to refer to each conjunct as an invariant.

So the structure of a proof goes like this:

- Establish invariants to characterize the reachable states, by showing that the invariants are true in each initial state and that each action maintains the invariants.
- Define an abstraction function.
- Establish the simulation, by showing that each Y action simulates a sequence of X actions that is the same externally.

This method works only with actions and does not require any reasoning about histories. Furthermore, it deals with each action independently; only the invariants connect the actions. So if we change (or add) an action, we only need to verify that the new action maintains the invariants and simulates a sequence of S-actions that is the same externally. In particular, strengthening a guard preserves the "implements" relation. We will exploit this observation to evolve an obviously correct implementation of S into some more efficient ones.

In what follows we give only the abstraction function and the invariants; the actual proofs of invariants and simulations are routine.

16.4   U: An impractical implementation of S

We begin by giving an implementation called U which is identical to T except that some of the guards are stronger, in fact, strong enough that U implements S. Therefore there's no need for *Barrier* in U. Unfortunately, U can't be directly implemented itself because a practical implementation must look only at local state, and U has variables cur_p and *clean* that are not local. However, U is easy to understand, and it gives us a basis from which to develop a number of different implementations that are practical.

For the sake of brevity, in describing U we leave out most of the actions that are the same in T. In order to make it easy for the reader to compare T and U, we mark the changes by striking out text that is only in T and boxing text that is only in U.

For this and all our other implementations of S, we use the same abstraction function:

$$m = \textbf{if } clean \textbf{ then } \hat{m} \textbf{ else } (v_p \text{ for some } p \text{ such that } new_p)$$

This is only well-defined if v_p is the same for every p for which $new_p = true$. All of our implementations maintain the invariant that new_p is exclusive, that is, true for at most one p, which ensures that the abstraction function is well-defined.

variable

$\hat{m}$	$: A \to D$
v	$: P \to A \to (D \mid nil)$
new	$: P \to A \to Bool$

state function

$live_p$	$\equiv (v_p \neq nil)$
cur_p	$\equiv (v_p = m)$
$clean$	$\equiv \forall\, p\,.\, \neg\, new_p$

invariant

new_p	$\Rightarrow live_p$

$\boxed{new \text{ is exclusive, that is, it's true for at most one processor}}$

action

$Read_p(\textbf{var } d)$	$= \cancel{live_p}$	$\boxed{cur_p}$	$\to\quad d := v_p$
$Write_p(d)$	$= \boxed{clean \lor new_p}$		$\to\quad v_p := d,\ new_p := true$

Barrier is uninteresting because every p is always current when it does a *Read*.

U implements S because:

- *new* is exclusive, so m is well-defined;
- *Read* returns m as required, *Write* changes m as required;
- Other actions leave m unchanged.

16.5   B and C: A cache implementation of U

We take two steps to get from U to a generic cache implementation. The first step is B, which still uses non-local state functions *clean* and $only_p$, but gets rid of cur_p by maintaining a new invariant, $live_p \Rightarrow cur_p$ and strengthening the guard on *Read* from cur_p to $live_p$. To maintain the new invariant we also need to strengthen the guards on $Write_p$ and ToV_p.

variable

$\hat{m}$	$: A \to D$
v_p	$: A \to (D \mid nil)$
new_p	$: A \to Bool$

state function

$live_p$	$\equiv (v_p \neq nil)$
cur_p	$\equiv v_p = m)$
$clean$	$\equiv \forall\, p\,.\, \neg\, new_p$
$\boxed{only_p}$	$\equiv \forall\, q \neq p\,.\, \neg\, live_q$

invariant

new_p	$\Rightarrow live_p$
new is exclusive	
$\boxed{live_p}$	$\Rightarrow cur_p$

action

$Read_p(\textbf{var } d)$	$= \cancel{cur_p}$	$\boxed{live_p}$	$\to$ $d := v_p$
$Write_p(d)$	$= \cancel{clean \vee new_p}$	$\boxed{only_p}$	$\to$ $v_p := d,\ new_p := true$

internal action

ToV_p	$= \cancel{\neg\ new_p}$	$\boxed{clean}$	$\to$ $v_p := \hat{m}$

$\cdots$

As in U, *Barrier* is uninteresting because every p is always current when it does a *Read*.

Now we can give C, a practical implementation of *Read*, *Write*, and *ToV* which pushes the non-locality into an action *Acquire* that acquires a write lock, and the state function *free*. The invariants imply that the new guards are as strong as the old ones.

variable

$\hat{m}$	$: A \to D$
v	$: P \to A \to (D \mid nil)$
new	$: P \to A \to Bool$
$\boxed{lock}$	$: P \to A \to Bool$

state function

$live_p$	$\equiv (v_p \neq nil)$
cur_p	$\equiv (v_p = m)$
$clean$	$\equiv \forall\, p\,.\, \neg\, new_p$
$only_p$	$\equiv \forall\, q \neq p\,.\, \neg\, live_q$
$\boxed{free}$	$\equiv \forall\, p\,.\, \neg\, lock_p$

invariant

$$new_p \Rightarrow live_p$$

new is exclusive

$$live_p \Rightarrow cur_p$$

new_p	$\Rightarrow lock_p$
$lock_p$	$\Rightarrow only_p$
$lock$ is exclusive	

action

$Read_p(\textbf{var } d)$	$= live_p$	$\rightarrow$	$d := v_p$
$Write_p(d)$	$= \cancel{only_p}\ \boxed{lock_p}$	$\rightarrow$	$v_p := d,\ new_p := true$

internal action

ToV_p	$= \cancel{clean}\ \boxed{\begin{array}{l}\neg\ new_p\ \wedge \\ (lock_p \vee\ free)\end{array}}$	$\rightarrow$	$v_p := \hat{m}$

. . .

$Acquire_p$	$= free \wedge only_p$	$\rightarrow$	$lock_p := true$
$Release_p$	$= \neg\ new_p$	$\rightarrow$	$lock_p := false$

16.5.1   Implementing *Acquire*

Now all we have to do is implement the guard of *Acquire*. To establish $free \wedge only_p$, we need:

- a way to test it, and
- a way to progress toward it by suitable $Release_p$ and $Drop_p$ operations.

There are three general approaches to solving these problems. All three have been used in commercial multiprocessors [2, 7].

1. *Directory*, usually in conjunction with a switch-based processor-memory interconnect [11]:

   - Keep centrally a set $\{p : live_p \vee lock_p\}$ for each address or set of addresses or "cache block". Usually this directory information is kept with the $\hat{m}$ data.
   - Ask each p that holds data or a lock to give it up (by doing $Drop_p$ or $Release_p$) in order to ensure progress.

2. *Snoopy*, usually in conjunction with a bus-based processor-memory interconnect [6]:

   - If you don't hold the necessary lock, broadcast a request for progress to all processors.

- Each processor q responds with the value of $lock_q$; "or" all the responses, often using a "wired-or" electrical signalling scheme.

3. *Hierarchical*, which handles problems of scale by subdividing the problem; either method (1) or method (2) can be used at each level of the hierarchy.

  - Partition the ps into $pSets$
  - Keep $live_{ps}$ and $lock_{ps}$ variables for each $pSet$
  - Maintain $\bigvee_{p \in ps} live_p \Rightarrow live_{ps}$ and $\bigvee_{p \in ps} lock_p \Rightarrow lock_{ps}$.
  - Deal with each $pSet$ separately. Use any of (1)–(3) to handle each $pSet$ and to handle the set of $pSets$. It's not necessary to use the same method in each case.

16.5.2   Update protocols

There is a popular variation of the caches described by B and C called an "update protocol". It allows data to be copied directly from one cache to another without going through $\hat{m}$. Here is B-update; it simply adds one action to B:

internal action

$VtoV_{pq}$	$= live_q$	$\rightarrow \quad v_p := v_q$

$VtoV_{pq}$ maintains the invariants because of the invariant $live_p \Rightarrow cur_p$, and it doesn't change m.

And here is C-update; we mark the changes from C, except that we show how the guards of ToV and $VtoV$ are changed from B-update. The invariant is weaker than C's, and the guards on ToV correspondingly stronger. The idea is that p can release the lock, so that copies are allowed in other processors' views, without updating $\hat{m}$ and making new_p false. So the guard on ToV is quite non-local, and only a snoopy implementation is attractive. Actual implementations usually broadcast writes to shared locations; this corresponds to doing $Drop_q; Write_p; VtoV_{pq}$ more or less atomically, and ensuring this atomicity can be tricky.

invariant

$\quad \overline{new_p} \qquad \overline{\Rightarrow lock_p}$

action

ToV_p	$= clean \; \boxed{\wedge\; \textit{free}}$	$\rightarrow \quad v_p := \hat{m}$
$VtoV_{pq}$	$= live_q \; \boxed{\wedge\; \textit{free}}$	$\rightarrow \quad v_p := v_q$

16.6   E: Programming with incoherent memory

Now for a different modification of U that gets us to a different practical implementation, similar to C but not identical. We call this E, and we show changes from U by the outer boxes and strikeouts, and the differences from C inside. The latter are:

- The invariant relating *live* and *cur* is weaker:
  - C: $live \Rightarrow cur$
  - E: $live \wedge lock \Rightarrow cur$

  This is the crucial difference.
- *Read* has a stronger guard that includes a *lock* conjunct.
- *ToV* has a weaker guard, just $\neg\ new$ without the $lock \vee free$ conjunct.
- *Acquire* has a weaker guard without *only*; in fact, E doesn't use *only* at all.
- *Acquire* and *Release* have added *Barrier* actions.

The critical difference between E and C is that the internal actions of E are the same as those of T. This means that we can use an unmodified T as the basis of E. The *Read* and *Write* actions of E are the *Read* and *Write* actions of T preceded by tests that *lock* is true. Usually this is done by confining all occurrences of *Read* and *Write* to critical sections within which *lock* is known to be true. The *Acquire* and *Release* operations are done at the start and end of a critical section in the usual way. In other words, E shows how to build coherent memory on top of incoherent memory.

Note: it's not actually necessary for *Acquire* and *Release* to be fully atomic; the *Barrier*s can be done separately.

variable

$\hat{m}$	$: A \to D$
v	$: P \to A \to (D \mid nil)$
new	$: P \to A \to Bool$
$\boxed{lock \qquad\qquad : P \to A \to Bool}$	

state function

$live_p$	$\equiv (v_p \neq nil)$
cur_p	$\equiv (v_p = m)$
clean	$\equiv \forall\ p\ .\ \neg\ new_p$
~~$only_p$~~	~~$\equiv \forall\ q \neq p\ .\ \neg\ live_q$~~
free	$\equiv \forall\ p\ .\ \neg\ lock_p$

invariant

new_p	$\Rightarrow live_p$

new is exclusive

$$
\begin{array}{ll}
live_p\ \boxed{\wedge\ lock_p} & \Rightarrow cur_p \\
new_p & \Rightarrow lock_p \\
\sout{lock_p} & \Rightarrow \sout{only_p} \\
\end{array}
$$
lock is exclusive

action

$$
\begin{array}{llll}
Read_p(\textbf{var } d) & = \sout{cur_p}\ \boxed{lock_p\ \wedge}\ \boxed{live_p} & \rightarrow & d := v_p \\
Write_p(d) & = \sout{clean \vee new_p}\ \boxed{lock_p} & \rightarrow & v_p := d,\ new_p := true \\
\end{array}
$$

internal action

$$
\begin{array}{llll}
ToV_p & = \neg\ new_p\ \boxed{\sout{\wedge\ lock_p}\ \vee\ \sout{free}} & \rightarrow & v_p := \hat{m} \\
\end{array}
$$

$$
\begin{array}{llll}
Acquire_p & = free \wedge \sout{only_p} & \rightarrow & lock_p := true\ \boxed{;\ Barrier} \\
Release_p & = \neg\ new_p & \rightarrow & \boxed{Barrier\ ;}\ lock_p := false \\
\end{array}
$$

We have written E with an exclusive lock, which is the most common way to do critical sections. It works just as well with reader/writer locks; the guard for *Read* is $rlock_p \wedge live_p$, the guard for *Write* is $wlock_p$, and there are separate *Acquire* and *Release* actions for the two kinds of locks.

16.6.1   Remarks

The T spec allows a multiprocessor shared memory to respond to *Read* and *Write* actions without any interprocessor communication. Furthermore, these actions only require communication between a processor and the global memory when a processor reads from an address that isn't in its view. The expensive operation in this spec is *Barrier*, since the sequence $Write_a$; $Barrier_a$; $Barrier_b$; $Read_b$ requires the value written by a to be communicated to b. In current implementations $Barrier_p$ is even more expensive because it acts on all addresses at once. This means that, roughly speaking, there must be at least enough communication to record globally every address that p wrote before the $Barrier_p$ and to drop from p's view every address that is globally recorded as new.

Although this isn't strictly necessary, all current implementations have additional external actions that make it easier to program mutual exclusion. These usually take the form of some kind of atomic read-modify-write operation, for example an atomic swap of a register value and a memory value. A currently popular scheme is two actions: $ReadLinked(a)$ and $WriteConditional(a)$, with the property that if any other processor writes to a between a $ReadLinked_p(a)$ and the next $WriteConditional_p(a)$, the $WriteConditional$ leaves the memory unchanged and returns a failure indication. The effect is that once the $WriteConditional$ succeeds, the entire sequence is an atomic read-modify-write from the viewpoint of another processor [3]. Of course these operations also incur communication costs, at least if the address a is shared.

We have shown that a program that touches shared memory only inside a critical section cannot distinguish memory that satisfies T from memory that satisfies the serial specification S. This is not the only way to use T, however. It is possible to program other standard idioms, such as producer-consumer buffers, without relying on mutual exclusion. We leave these progams as an exercise for the reader.

16.7   Conclusion

The lesson of this paper is twofold:

- It is possible to give simple but precise specifications for several kinds of shared memory that do not depend on the intended implementations. Furthermore, the essential ideas of the implementations can also be described precisely, and it is fairly straightforward to prove that the implementations satisfy the specifications. Standard methods for reasoning about concurrent programs and their specifications work very well.
- Techniques for implementing serial shared memory have much more in common than you might think, even though they may use very different combinations of hardware and software to realize the common idea.

References

[1] Abadi, M. and Lamport, L., The existence of refinement mappings, *Theoretical Computer Science* 82 (2), 1991, 253-284.

[2] Archibald, J. and Baer, J-L., Cache coherence protocols: Evaluation using a multiprocessor simulation model, *ACM Trans. Computer Systems* 4 (4), Nov. 1986, 273-298.

[3] Digital Equipment Corporation, *Alpha Architecture Handbook*, 1992.

[4] Gharachorloo, K., et al., Memory consistency and event ordering in scalable shared-memory multiprocessors, *Proc. 17th Symposium on Computer Architecture*, 1990, 15-26.

[5] Gibbons, P. and Merritt, M., Specifying nonblocking shared memories, Proc. 4th ACM Symposium on Parallel Algorithms and Architectures, 1992, 158-168.

[6] Goodman, J., Using cache memory to reduce processor-memory traffic. *Proc. 10th Symposium on Computer Architecture*, 1983, 124-131.

[7] Hennessy, J. and Patterson, D., *Computer Architecture: A Quantitative Approach*, Morgan Kaufann, 1990.

[8] Hoare, C. A. R., Proof of Correctness of Data Representation, *Acta Informatica* 4, 1972, 271-281.

[9] Lamport, L., A simple approach to specifying concurrent systems, *Communications of the ACM*, 32 (1), 1989, 32-47.

[10] Lynch, N. and Tuttle, M., Hierarchical correctness proofs for distributed algorithms, *Proc. ACM Symposium on Principles of Distributed Computing*, 1987, 137-151.

[11] Tang, C., Cache system design in the tightly coupled multiprocessor system. *Proc. AFIPS National Computer Conference*, 1976, 749-753.

Chapter 17

How to Design a Parallel Computer

David May

This paper is dedicated to Tony Hoare, whose outstanding work on CSP has had a profound influence both on the theory of concurrency, and on the design of concurrent programming languages and parallel computers.

17.1 Introduction

A central problem for contemporary computer science is the development of a standard architecture for parallel computers. This would allow the development of re-usable parallel algorithms and software, and enable mass-production of standard parallel computers. Further, it would allow parallel software to be used on successive generations of parallel computers, exploiting new technologies to deliver increasing levels of performance.

One of the most important components of a parallel computer is its interprocessor communication network. The VLSI technology of the 1990s will allow the construction of the high-throughput, low-delay communication networks. These can be used to build general purpose message-passing machines, based on a scalable architecture and supporting scalable re-usable software. Enhancements to the networks and processors will extend the capabilities of these machines to support a wide variety of programming styles. The resulting machines will combine the capabilities of message-passing and shared-memory architectures: they will be *general purpose* parallel computers.

17.2 Parallel Computers

Over the last decade, many different parallel computers have been developed; these have been used in a wide range of applications. Increasing levels of component integration, coupled with difficulties in further increasing clock speed, make parallel

275

processing technically attractive. By the late 1990s, chips with 10^8 transistors will be in use, but design and production will continue to be most effective when applied to volume manufacture. A general purpose parallel architecture would allow cheap, standard multiprocessors to become pervasive, in much the same way that the Von Neumann architecture has allowed standard uniprocessors to take over from specialised electronics in many application areas.

One of the major challenges for general purpose parallel architecture is to allow performance to scale with the number of processors. There are obvious limits to scalability:

- For a given problem size, there will be a limit to the number of processors which can be used efficiently. However, we would expect it to be easy to increase the problem size to exploit more processors.
- There will in practice be technological limits to the number of processors used. These will include physical size, power consumption, thermal density and reliability. However, as we expect performance/chip to achieve 10^8-10^9 Mflops during the 1990s, the most significant markets will be served by machines with less than 10^3 processors.

Another major challenge for a general purpose parallel architecture is to eliminate the need to design algorithms to match the details of specific machines. Algorithms must be based on features common to a large number of machines, and which can be expected to remain common to a large number of machines as technology evolves. Both programmer and computer designer have much to gain from identifying the essential features of a general purpose parallel architecture:

- the programmer because his or her programs will work on a variety of machines – and will continue to work on future machines.
- the computer designer because he or she will be able to introduce new designs which make best use of technology to increase performance of the software already in use.

Most parallel computers are based either on a message-passing architecture or on a shared-memory architecture. There are signs of convergence between these two different architectures. In order to simplify programming, message-passing architectures are being extended to support shared-memory programming styles. At the same time, to support large numbers of processors, *virtual* shared-memory architectures are being developed; these use message-passing networks and special protocols to provide the appearance of a single shared memory.

17.3   General Purpose Message-passing Machines

A general purpose message-passing machine consists of a number of computing nodes connected via a communications network. Each processing node contains a processor, memory and a communications system. Programs for message-passing machines can be expressed as a collection of concurrent processes which compute values and periodically communicate with each other. In writing *portable* message-passing programs, we do not want to be concerned about the structural details of the communications network. In addition, we do not want give the programmer, compiler or operating system the problems of optimising communications by careful allocation of processes to processing nodes. Consequently, the network must be able to support efficient system-wide communication.

For high efficiency, the processing nodes must be able to communicate information to and from the network at the same time as processing, and they must communicate information at the same *rate* that they process it. Equally, the network as a whole must be able to support a communication rate similar to the processing rate of the whole machine. Failure to achieve an adequate rate of communication will impose practical limitations on the use of the machine; typically machines with low communication rates are suitable only for solving large problems, rather than for solving small problems quickly.

An inevitable property of the network is that there will be a delay as data passes through it. Indeed, practical networks connecting a large number of processing nodes will be sparse, so that, in a network connecting p processing nodes, the delay will grow as $log(p)$. Fortunately, there are a number of techniques which can be used to minimise the effects of network delay. One of these is *hiding*, which can be achieved by making each processing node execute a small collection of processes. In this case, a simple scheduling system can be used to de-schedule processes which are waiting for communication to complete.

A general purpose message-passing machine can therefore be constructed from:

- p processing nodes with concurrent processing and communication, and process scheduling.
- interconnection networks with scalable throughput (linear in p) and low delay (scaling as $log(p)$).

Programs must take into account the relationship between the computation throughput and the communication throughput of the machine. We will call this ratio the *grain* (g) of the architecture, and measure it as operations/operand. For simplicity, we will assume that a processor performs a single operation in one clock *tick*, so that we can measure the grain in ticks/operand. Ideally, we would like to fix the grain to about $g = 1$; this is consistent with the rate at which operands are moved between processor and memory in uniprocessors. For general purpose message-passing machines, we will require that this ratio is maintained for system-wide inter-processor communication. It turns out that this can be achieved using 1990s VLSI technology.

Some machines operate with small g only when large data items are being manipulated. For example, there may be high overheads in setting up a communication, so that only large vectors can be communicated efficiently. We will assume that a general purpose machine with low g will also provide a rate of processing small (scalar) operands similar to the rate of initiating communications of them. This will require a high rate of process scheduling in the processing nodes, which can be achieved by providing a set of registers for each process, or by pipelining processes through the processor.

Programs will either be written as a collection of processes, or will be written in terms of array operations or parallel FOR-statements which can be converted by a compiler into a collection of processes. The programmer or compiler will use the grain parameter g, and will produce a collection of v virtual processors (processes) of grain $> g$. The resulting processes can be thought of as executing in a sequence of steps, with each step of length s ticks. In s ticks, each process will communicate s/g operands and perform s operations. Notice that we want to keep the grain of the software as low as possible so as to exploit all possible parallelism for a given problem size, but at least g to avoid processor idling.

The output of the compiler is a program suitable for use on all general purpose machines of grain g. We expect to keep the program in this form, and perhaps distribute it in this form. We note that g is fixed for a range of machines based on the same components, and further that there is likely to be little variation in g even for machines based on different components. This means that the compiled program is likely to be re-usable.

To load a compiled program for execution, we make use of a loader which takes as parameter the latency of communication: l (ticks). This will vary from machine to machine and will scale as $log(p)$ for realisable networks. The loader will allocate at least l/s virtual processors to at most $(v \times s)/l$ processors. There would be no point in using more processors than this, as this would result in processors idling some of the time; it would be better instead to leave some processors available for allocation to another program. Thus the program will run at optimal efficiency on a p-processor machine provided that $(v \times s) > (l \times p)$.

Notice that our loader ensures that there will always be enough processes on each processor to ensure that (at least) one is executable; the others will be waiting for communication to complete. This means that we will need to use at least $log(p)$ times as many processes as processors. Another way to think of this is that we could use a specialised machine exactly matched to the algorithm in which each processor executes only one process; this would offer $log(p)$ more performance. Specialised parallel computers will still be needed for maximising performance where the problem size is limited!

We note that our proposal for universal message-passing is closely related to Valiant's proposal for Universal PRAMs [12] in which $l = log(p)$ and $s = 1$.

17.4   Processing Components for Universal Machines

VLSI technology enables a complete computer to be constructed on a single silicon chip. One example is the T9000 transputer [5] which contains a processor, memory and communications links; peak performance is about 200 Mips and 25 (scalar) Mflops. Each link provides simultaneous transfer of data in both directions at about 10Mbytes/second. Thus the T9000 can supply data from its four links at about 40Mbytes/second, whilst simultaneously receiving data at 40Mbytes/second. Internally, the T9000 is designed to maintain high communication rates whilst also processing data, and supports a grain $g = 1$ for single length floating point programs communicating data through all four links.

Transputers have the ability to communicate directly with each other via their communication links; this enables transputers to be connected together to construct multiprocessor systems to tackle specific problems. For the construction of general purpose machines, the links will be used to connect the transputers into a communications network constructed from communication components.

Transputer

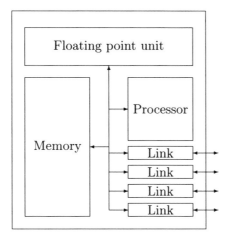

Each transputer includes a hardware kernel with the ability to execute many software processes at the same time, to create new processes rapidly, and to perform communication both between processes within a transputer and between processes in different transputers. All of these capabilities are integrated into the hardware of the transputers, and are very efficient. Kernel operations such as process scheduling and communication take about 1 microsecond, in contrast to the 100 microsecond overheads typical of software kernels. The close integration of the processor and links within the T9000 transputers provides high-throughput, low-delay interprocess communication via the links, with hardware being used to multiplex many interprocess communication channels along a single physical link.

The parallel processing capabilities of the transputers directly implement the constructs of the occam programming language [3], itself based on CSP [2]. The occam language allows an application to be expressed as a collection of concurrent processes which communicate via channels. Each channel is a point-to-point connection between two processes; one process always inputs from the channel and the other always outputs to it. Communication is synchronised; the first process ready to communicate waits until the second is also ready, then the data is copied from the outputting process to the inputting process and both processes continue. A description of the implementation of occam on the transputer can be found in [6].

17.5   Communication Components for Universal Machines

During the 1990s, VLSI will be applied to the development of components for communication networks. One example is the the Inmos C104 packet routing chip, designed to connect 32 links of the kind used on the T9000 transputer. The C104 contains a 32-way crossbar switch, through which all of the 32 inputs can be routed simultaneously to the 32 outputs. Routing delays are minimised by the use of wormhole routing, in which a packet can start to be output from a switch whilst it is still being input.

A packet arriving at a switch is routed according to its header. If the required outbound link is available, the packet starts to be output immediately. However, if the link required is in use, the packet will be temporarily blocked, and will start to be taken into a buffer. The C104 provides one packet of inbound buffering and one packet of outbound buffering on each link, so it is possible for a whole packet to be taken into a buffer, waiting for its required output. Therefore if the network is very busy, the performance will approximate to the performance of a store-and-forward network.

The C104 can support a number of network routing schemes. The simplest of these is *deterministic* routing, in which the route is determined only by the choice of source and destination nodes. Another scheme, used to avoid network hot-spots, is *universal routing* [13] in which a packet is first sent to a randomly chosen intermediate node before it travels to its final destination. Any of the links on the C104 can be set to create a random header for each inbound packet on that link. At the intermediate node, this random header is deleted, leaving the original header to route the message to its real destination. The C104 can also be used to construct networks in which packets use the first-available of a group of outputs, or to construct randomly-wired networks [4].

There is no shared resource within the C104. All routing, header creation and deletion is performed on a per-link basis. This has the effect of making the links of the network the shared resources, rather than the nodes of the network. A full description of the C104, and of its use in networks is given in [7].

17.6   Networks for Universal Message-passing Machines

In a communication network connecting p terminals, we can realistically expect the distance a packet will travel to increase with $log(p)$. Consequently, in order to maintain throughput per terminal, the number of packets in flight from each terminal will scale with $log(p)$. Therefore network capacity required for each terminal will scale with $log(p)$, and the total capacity of a network with p terminals must scale as $p \times log(p)$. One structure which achieves this is the hypercube or binary n-cube, with a processor at each node. Another structure is the butterfly network, with a processor at each terminal. In contrast, the two-dimensional grid does not maintain throughput per node as the network scales.

17.6.1   Network Performance

In order to demonstrate that devices such as the C104 can support the communication requirements of general purpose parallel computers, we summarise recent simulation results. A more complete study can be found in [1].

The simulations examine hypercubes and two-dimensional grids; for both of these, three network sizes are measured for three traffic patterns. The simplest of traffic pattern, *random* traffic, operates by continuously supplying packets at every node of the network. The destination of this packet is chosen at random from all possible destination addresses. This traffic pattern spreads traffic over the network, in a similar manner to that of universal routing.

A more interesting pattern is *systematic* traffic, in which each source sends all of its packets to a specific destination. The pattern chosen is a permutation, so that no two source nodes send to the same destination. The patterns represent an operation which we could reasonably expect an algorithm to perform. However, in each case the pattern chosen will create severe hot-spots in the network. We show that universal routing eliminates these hot-spots.

On the hypercube, the random traffic shows the throughput to scale, as predicted. On the other hand, the systematic permutation shows a large decrease in throughput/node for an increase in network size. Universal routing has the effect of bringing the performance of the systematic traffic towards that of the random traffic. The small variations of throughput with network size are attributable to properties of the random number generator.

For contrast, we show the throughput of a two-dimensional grid. In this case, the random traffic shows that throughput per node degrades with increasing network size. This is to be expected, as the grid capacity does not increase fast enough. Systematic traffic shows that the throughput and scalability on a grid can both be

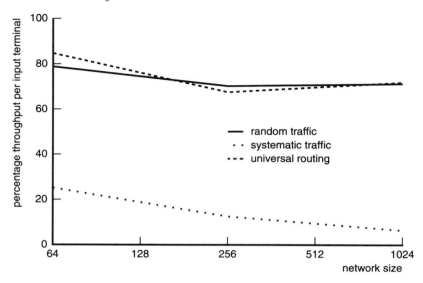

Figure 17.1 Throughput varying with network size on a hypercube.

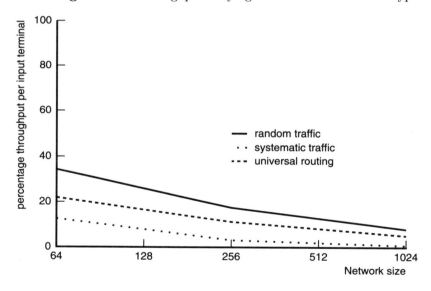

Figure 17.2 Throughput varying with network size on a grid.

affected considerably by the traffic pattern. Universal routing pulls the behaviour back towards the random traffic, providing similar scalability in throughput which is now still limited by the overall capacity of the network. It would be possible to use several grids in parallel to deliver throughput comparable to the hypercube or

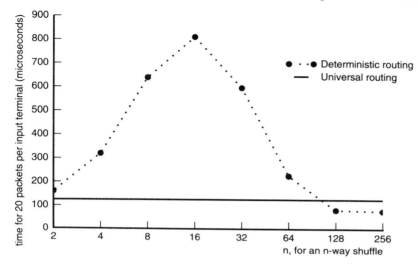

Figure 17.3 The variation of time taken to finish with the degree of shuffle.

butterfly. However, grids have a relatively high latency because packets typically pass through a large number of intermediate nodes.

17.6.2 Performance Predictability

The previous results show that universal routing will improve the throughput and the scalability of a network. In this section, universal routing is shown to improve the predictability of the network also.

The cube is the structure investigated. Each node in the network sends to a distinct destination node. This traffic pattern is a permutation. Each node creates twenty packets to this destination, and the time taken for all of the packets to reach their destination is noted. The underlying permutation is the perfect shuffle; the basis of many fast parallel sorting algorithms. This corresponds to deriving the destination node number by rotating the bits of the source node number by a particular amount. A rotate of 1 gives a 2-way shuffle, the rotate of 2 gives a 4-way shuffle, and so on. The rotation is varied from 0 to the cube dimension. The time is measured for both deterministic and universal routing.

The results for the 8d cube are shown in the graph of Figure 17.3. This shows that the deterministic routing gives a wide variation in run-time. For instance, changing a program to be an 8-way shuffle rather than a 4-way shuffle would increase the network delivery time by a factor of 2. With universal routing the time taken remains approximately constant; a representative value is shown. This is a major advantage, since calculating a bound on the run-time requires that the worst case must be taken into account.

17.7   Is All This Reasonable?

To show that the programming process outlined earlier can be applied to realistic problems for realisable machines, we consider a simple image smoothing example. Each processing node will store and process a small portion of the image. This kind of problem can easily be implemented by a two-dimensional grid of nodes, as the image is two-dimensional; in this case communication is between adjacent processors. However, here we will use a general purpose machine, and distribute the image arbitrarily among the processors.

We first have to produce an algorithm matched to the grain of the general purpose machine. The machine we will consider will be a collection of T9000s each connected via a single link to a hypercube network of C104s. Our simulations have shown that hypercubes operate at about 80% of peak throughput/link. This gives a grain g of about 5, for a T9000 which sustains about 10 Mflops.

For image smoothing, which consists of 5 operations per point (4 additions and one division), we can split a picture into 4 pixel by 4 pixel squares. This provides 16×5 floating point operations and 16 communications – a grain of exactly 5 and a step of 80.

We know that for a 64 processor machines, the probability of any message being delayed by more than 800 is very small ($< 10^{-3}$). So if we load at least 10 processes on to each processor, we can be sure that the machine will run at high efficiency, achieving 64×10 Mflops on a $10 \times 64 \times 16$ point image. This is 640 Mflops on an image of 10 240 points. As this is well below the size of typical images, we might want to scale up the problem size and/or the machine. Scaling up is possible without modifying the algorithm or adjusting its grain: all we need to do is to add more processes, and rely on the loader to load sufficient processes/processor.

17.8   Message-passing and Shared Memory

In message-passing machines, the data associated with the computation is localised within the same processing node as the processes which operate on it, and no provision is made for direct access to remote data. This has some disadvantages, as it is sometimes difficult or impossible to determine the data required by a process at the time that the process is initiated. This is one reason why it is desirable to combine the capabilities of message-passing and shared-memory programming.

Highly-parallel message-passing algorithms, like the image smoothing problem above, are closely related to a simple class of shared-memory algorithms. In message-passing algorithms, a collection of processes synchronise locally as they pass data to each other. In an equivalent shared-memory algorithm, each of the processes would modify a small partition of the shared memory, and periodically all of the processes would synchronise; the communication of data via message-passing is replaced by changes of the partitioning of the shared memory at each synchronisation.

We might expect that the same techniques used to construct general-purpose message-passing machines could also be used to build shared-memory machines. We start by using our scalable networks to support global *read* and *write* operations, instead of message-passing. Later we will combine the two architectures.

17.9   Shared-memory Machines

We will concentrate on supporting a simple form of shared-memory programming, captured by the occam parallel construct. This follows simple rules which allow operations on many variables to be performed in parallel. For example:

```
VAR sum, prod, a, b:
SEQ
  ...
  PAR
    sum := a + b
    prod := a * b
```

Here global state which is updated by the components of the parallel construct (the variables `sum` and `prod`) is partitioned between the components. The variables `a` and `b` which are not modified by either component can be used in both of them. Apart from eliminating time-dependent errors, these principles allow a number of implementations of the parallel construct.

When a parallel construct initiates one of its components on another (remote) processing node P, the global variables used by the component can be copied to the memory of P. When the component terminates, values of any updated variables can be copied back again. It is *never* necessary for the value of any variable to be transferred to P more than once, nor to be transferred from P more than once. Notice, however, that any variable used in many components (but not updated) will need to be transferred to *all* of these components.

We note in passing that these simple rules for parallel *disjointness* are very similar to the rules to prevent *aliasing* in sequential programming. Aliasing rules have similar benefits both in eliminating troublesome programming errors and in allowing copying to be used to eliminate repeated accesses to the same variable. The widespread adoption of alias and disjointness checkers for programming languages would improve the reliability of programs and also improve their efficiency!

17.10   Parallel Random Access Machines (PRAMs)

Many theoretical studies of highly-parallel shared-memory algorithms over the past decade have been based on Parallel Random Access Machines (PRAMs). A substantial collection of PRAM algorithms has built up, and there would be great advantages in machines which can execute these algorithms efficiently.

PRAM programs make use of simple programming style, representable as a set of parallel processes which operate on components of the shared global state, here represented by **g**:

```
VAR g:
SEQ i = 0 FOR n
  PAR j = 0 FOR m
    P(i, j, g)
```

As it is not likely to be efficient to initiate and terminate a large collection of processes, we expect to implement these programs by converting them to:

```
VAR g:
PAR j = 0 FOR m
  SEQ i = 0 FOR n
    P(i, j, g); SYNC
```

Here **SYNC** represents a synchronisation between the **m** processes. Effectively, we have replaced a large number of process creations and terminations (*forks* and *joins*) with synchronising operations. We expect **n** to be large, so that the time to initiate the parallel processes will be small in relation to the time for the main body of the algorithm. Following our approach to message-passing programs, we expect **m** to be at least $kp \times log(p)$ (k an architectural constant and p the maximum number of processors ever to be used).

A number of optimisations are possible. We may exploit an optimising compiler (a *serialising* compiler!) to combine processes executed on the same processor into a single sequential process in which global memory requests are initiated as early as possible and replies used as late as possible. This is fairly easy if the component processes only perform global synchronisations, and do not interact in other ways (e.g. by message-passing). Indeed, it would be attractive to perform this operation in the loader, as it is the loader which determines the allocation of a group of processes to a processor. Such optimisations may reduce the number of global memory operations performed by each processor, effectively allowing local memory to be used as a cache. However, none of these optimisations are *necessary* for scalability or, nor will they work in general; they simply improve performance for specific algorithms.

17.11   Architectures for Shared-memory Machines

To support PRAM algorithms, we must support a combination of shared memory access and synchronisation. We expect that each processing node will have a local memory module, and a shared-memory module (which all processors will access via the network). Alternatively, we could make dedicated processing nodes, connected via an interconnection network to dedicated shared-memory modules.

We want to extend the capabilities of our processing nodes in several ways, for example:

- The processor must deschedule processes which are performing accesses to remote shared-memory locations, so that delays in the network are hidden.
- Except for simple problems where allocation of memory can be performed by compiler, it must be possible to operate the local memory as a cache.
- Efficient support for synchronisation between a group of processes distributed among many processors must be provided.

We expect program and process workspaces to normally reside in the local caches. Shared (remote) data will make use of the cache also, but for best results this must be controlled by compiler. In particular, we want to be able to use the cache to reduce the amount of global network traffic to match the grain g which can be supported by the network. Compiling a process so that it tries to use more cache capacity to go below this g will not necessarily provide any performance advantage, and may actually reduce performance by causing too much competition for available cache space.

The instructions needed to control a cache in this way are:

- *load using cache*
- *load directly from global memory*
- *store using cache*
- *store directly to global memory*
- *discard from cache*

Discarding items from the cache is useful to prevent unnecessary write operations for variables which have gone out of scope.

17.12   Shared-memory Access

It is useful to consider the different types of traffic pattern which will arise in a communication network when a shared-memory algorithm is executed. The traffic patterns which cause most congestion are those in which all of the processors make requests at the same time. This usually occurs immediately after a synchronisation, for example. Three different patterns can easily be identified:

- In a *seclusive* access, each processor will access a different memory module, so that the accesses are evenly distributed
- In an *exclusive* access, several processors may access the same module, but no two processors will access the same memory location

- In a *concurrent* access, many processors may access the same memory location at the same time

As with the message-passing programs, we will execute v/p processes on each processor. For seclusive accesses, when all of the processes make a request, every processor will issue v/p requests and every memory will receive v/p requests. The network therefore implements a *permutation*-routing operation. The ability of (e.g.) a hypercube to support permutation routing among the v processes in $log(p)$ time is demonstrated by the theoretical studies of Valiant [13], and of Upfal [10]. These studies are supported by our simulations.

It is clear that the grain g and latency l will be similar to that of a message-passing machine.

17.13   Exclusive Access

We can now extend our machine to permit exclusive access. Exclusive access patterns arise when data-structures are mapped into the memory modules in such a way that accesses are not evenly spread across the modules. For example, if a two-dimensional array is stored with one column in each module, then a parallel access to every element in a column will cause all of the processors to try to access the same module.

To overcome this problem, we hash the address space (by providing a local hashing function in the addressing system of each processing node), with the result that data again becomes spread fairly evenly between the memory modules. It has been demonstrated theoretically [8] that using certain hash functions, if each processor issues $log(p)$ access requests at the same time, at most $3log(p)$ will arrive together at the same memory module.

The factor of 3 affects throughput and delay, so we must allow for it in the grain g and latency l. (In a machine designed to support exclusive operation, we might provide a three-ported memory module, and leave g and l unchanged!)

We note that it is very difficult to generate access patterns which exhibit the factor of 3 and it is widely believed that very simple hash functions (much simpler than those proposed in [8]) would be adequate [9]. It may also be possible to choose these hash functions so as to eliminate hot-spots in the network, removing the need for randomisation.

17.14   Concurrent Access

For the data which is used by the many components of a parallel construct (but not updated by any of them), we must ensure that collisions in accessing the memory locations where this data is held do not adversely affect performance. One possibility is to enhance the communications network using *combining* routers. Provided that we restrict combining to *read* operations only, it is possible to perform combining within each router as follows:

- Maintain an associative store of the requests which have been output by the router, and for which no response has yet been received.
- As each request arrives, compare it with the stored requests and only output requests which do not match stored requests.
- As each response arrives, copy it to all of the requestors (and remove the requests from the store).

Notice that this technique will not support *concurrent write* operations of the kind proposed for some of the more complex forms of PRAM. Some of these (for example *fetch-and-add*) are used to optimise certain control structures, but they require a more complex (and slower) implementation in hardware. They are probably best supported in the processing nodes. Similar remarks apply to *reducing* operations such as forming the sum of the results from many processes. Here it is important that the full range of operations available in the programming language is provided, so that these operations must be implemented by the processing nodes.

Even for simple *read*-combining, the major disadvantage of building a network from combining routers is that it is difficult to avoid the extra hardware increasing the message delay through the router. An additional problem is that the router needs to contain enough memory to hold the requests, and the size of this memory will depend on the network delay (which cannot be predicted when the router is built). An alternative possibility is to use the communications processors in the processing nodes to perform combining operations, and optimise the network routers for non-combining operation. A suitable technique for distributing the combining operations across the processing nodes so as to ensure that no bottlenecks are created can be found in [11].

Our shared-memory machine is now complete, except for the ability to bring all of the processes into synchronisation after each step of the computation.

17.15 Synchronisation

We assume the existence of a binary synchronisation which brings two processes into synchronisation. In a network supporting synchronised message-passing, this is easily achieved by transmission of a null message. In a network supporting shared-memory operations, we must add the ability for a processing node to send and receive requests to schedule processes. These *run* requests will specify a process identifier. In addition, we must provide at least an indivisible *exchange* request which exchanges data d with the contents of address a, producing the contents as reply r:

$$exchange(a, d, r) : mem[a], r := d, mem[a]$$

The SYNC operation for a process with identifier p can now be defined as:

$$SYNC(a,p): \quad exchange(a,p,r);$$
$$\qquad if\ r = empty \qquad then\ deschedule(p)$$
$$\qquad\qquad\qquad\qquad else\ run(r);\ mem[a] := empty$$

We can now implement global synchronisation between v processes executed on p processors as follows:

- Locally synchronise the v/p processes on each processor at a cost of 1 local synchronisation/process (constant cost/process).
- Perform a global synchronisation between the p processors at cost $< 2log(p)$ global communications (constant cost/process).
- Locally synchronise the v/p processes on each processor again at a cost of 1 local synchronisation/process (constant cost/process).

We can implement global synchronisation in time $2log(p)$ using a minimum-depth spanning tree connecting p processors. However, if $p = 2^n$ for some n, we can reduce this to exactly $log(p)$ using a virtual hypercube, and performing the binary synchronisations along the edges. In a message-passing network, this would consist of a set of virtual communication channels arranged to form a hypercube; in a shared-memory network, it might consist of an array of synchronising locations.

Suppose that each process performs a sequence of SYNC operations, synchronising along the edges of the virtual hypercube in sequence, starting with the highest dimension and ending with the lowest. We want to prove that *no process finishes its final synchronisation until all of the processes have started their initial synchronisation.*

We construct an order-n hypercube by connecting corresponding nodes of two order-$(n-1)$ hypercubes, H and J. We now assume that the algorithm works for an order-$(n-1)$ hypercube. Now no process in H can start synchronisation within H until it has synchronised with the corresponding processes within J. So (by assumption) synchronisation within H cannot complete until every process within H has synchronised with the corresponding process within J. So no process within H can complete its final synchronisation until every process within J has started its initial synchronisation.

By symmetry, no process within J can complete its final synchronisation until every process within H has started its initial synchronisation. We conclude (by induction) that the synchronisation algorithm works, and clearly takes exactly $log(p)$ steps.

Synchronisation has added to the fixed processing cost per process, and again can be taken into account in calculating g. We can take two approaches to delay:

- We can rely on *hiding*.
- We can provide a separate network for synchronisation.

Hiding can be expected to work well unless each node is only executing a collection of similar processes which form part of the same parallel construct, so that they will all start synchronising at the same time. However, if the processes *do* all start to synchronise at the same time, the network will be relatively empty (it will only contain the small amount of synchronisation traffic), so the delay will be small (wormhole routing allows the short messages to travel very quickly through the network).

17.16   Load-distribution

We have assumed so far that processes will be pre-distributed by a loader. We now consider programs which dynamically generate new processes which must be evenly distributed among the processors. We will try to ensure that each processor will have a large enough collection of processes for it to operate optimally; the size of this collection will be determined from the latency l by the loader.

We can use a virtual hypercube to redistribute processes in time $klog(p)$ for some constant k which depends on the cost of initiating a new task. This represents a constant cost of k/process. In practice, k may be very small if (for example) the code to be executed is already available at the destination.

Our hypercube-based algorithm is similar to the synchronisation algorithm. It makes use of a 2-way balancing operation. In a 2-way balancing operation, two processors P and Q start with p processes and q processes respectively. P transmits p to Q, and simultaneously Q transmits q to P. If $p > q$, P transmits $(p - q)/2$ processes to Q, otherwise Q transmits $(q - p)/2$ processes to P.

Suppose that each processor performs a sequence of 2-way balancing operations, balancing along the edges in sequence, starting with the highest dimension and ending with the lowest. We want to prove that after every processor has performed $log(p)$ 2-way balancing operations, every processor will have the same number of processes.

We construct an order-n hypercube by connecting corresponding nodes of two order-$(n - 1)$ hypercubes H and J. We will assume that the algorithm works for an order-$(n - 1)$ hypercube. After every processor has performed the first 2-way balancing operation, J and H will have the same number of processes. Balancing then proceeds within J and H separately, and (by assumption) results in even distribution.

As, in practice, we are not interested in fractions of a process, we sometimes introduce a unit imbalance. The result is that after $log(p)$ steps, the imbalance will be at most $log(p)$ processes. The whole balancing operation takes exactly $log(p)$ steps, and therefore adds to the fixed processing cost per process.

This method can be expected to produce good results for a large collection of processes which can execute at a similar rate, as in PRAM programs. If this is not the case, it is probably better to use hashing to distribute the processes among the processors.

17.17   Integrating Message-passing and Shared Memory

It is now possible to combine our message-passing and shared-memory architectures. There are several ways to so this. One is to construct a protocol for the interconnection network which includes both the message-passing and the shared memory operations. This would have the following messages:

read(address, process)	readreply(process, data)
write(address, data, process)	writereply(process)
send(channel, data)	acknowledge(channel)

An alternative scheme is to implement all of the message-passing operations in terms of the read, write, exchange and run operations. In this case, the protocol would be:

read(address, process)	readreply(process, data)
write(address, data, process)	writereply(process)
exchange(address, data, process)	exchangereply(process, data)
run(process)	

For each channel C, we allocate a small collection of store locations consisting of a synchronising location $C.S$ and a buffer $C.B$. An output command $C!x$ for a process p can be implemented by:

$$C.B := x;\ SYNC(C.S, p);\ SYNC(C.S, p) \quad \text{and an input command } C?y \text{ by:}$$

$$SYNC(C.S, p);\ y := C.B;\ SYNC(C.S, p)$$

In addition to the parallel construct, shared memory and message-passing, many parallel programming styles include some form of mutual exclusion. One example is the occam alternative construct which selects one of a number of channels for communication. To implement such constructs we must provide a means of arbitrating between a number of processes and descheduling those which become blocked. It turns out that this can be achieved using the *exchange* and *run* operations we have already introduced.

For the implementation of synchronisations and arbitrations, the exchange operations require that at most two processes access the same store location. The store locations used can form part of the normal hashed address space and do not give rise to a need for combining. We note in passing, however, that exchanges can be combined with the same efficiency as reads.

17.18 Summary

We have taken advantage of several results from contemporary computer science:

- the ability of randomised interconnection networks to support scalable throughput and low delay for large numbers of processing nodes.
- the existence of hash functions and combining techniques which reduce memory contention.
- simple algorithms to perform synchronisation and load-balancing

These techniques can be used to design scalable machines supporting scalable programs. The use of a programming language supporting structured parallel programming helps both in reliable programming and in runtime efficiency. One such language is occam, which is the basis for the concurrent processing system used in the transputers, and is itself based on CSP. Message-passing and shared-memory techniques can be used in combination.

We have outlined how 1990s technology can be used to construct these scalable machines. The most important components are:

- Processing nodes, preferably with efficient process scheduling, in which processing throughput and communication throughput is balanced.
- Routing nodes which can be used to construct networks with scalable throughput and low delay.

Continuous enhancements to processing and communications nodes can be expected to improve efficiency and scalability, especially of the shared memory operations. The resulting machines will combine the capabilities of message-passing and common-memory operations: they will be *general purpose* parallel computers.

References

[1] C. Barnaby, M. D. May, *Performance of C104 networks*, in *Networks, Routers and Transputers*, IOS press, 1993.

[2] C. A. R. Hoare, *Communicating Sequential Processes*, Communications of the ACM, 21(8), pp. 666-677.

[3] Inmos Limited, *occam2 reference manual*, Prentice Hall 1988.

[4] T. Leighton, B. Maggs, *The role of randomness in the design of interconnection networks*, Information Processing 92, p. 291, IFIP 1992.

[5] M. D. May, R. M. Shepherd, *The T9000 Transputer*, Proceedings of the International Conference on Computer Design, IEEE, 1992.

[6] M. D. May, R. M. Shepherd, *The Transputer Implementation of occam*, Proceedings of the Second International Conference on Fifth Generation Computers, Tokyo 1985.

[7] M. D. May, P. Thompson, *Transputers and Routers: Components for Concurrent Machines*, Proceedings of the Third Transputer/Occam International Conference, Tokyo, IOS press 1990.

[8] K. Melhorn, U. Vishkin, *Randomised and Deterministic simulations of PRAMs*, Acta Informatica 21, 1984, pp. 339-374.

[9] A. G. Ranade, S. N. Bhatt, S. L. Johnson, *The Fluent Abstract Machine*, Fifth MIT Conference on Advanced Research in VLSI, pp. 71-93, 1988.

[10] E. Upfal, *Efficient Schemes for parallel communication*, JACM 31, 3(1984) pp. 507-517.

[11] L. G. Valiant, *A combining mechanism for parallel computers*, TR-24-92, Aiken Computation Laboratory, Harvard University, 1992.

[12] L. G. Valiant, *General Purpose Parallel Architectures*, Handbook of theoretical Computer Science, North Holland, 1990.

[13] L. G. Valiant, G, J. Brebner, *Universal Schemes for Parallel Communication*, ACM STOC (1981) pp. 263-277.

Chapter 18

Powerlist: A structure for parallel recursion

Jayadev Misra

(Preliminary version)

Dedicated, on his 60th birthday, to C. A. R. Hoare who taught me to step without fear wherever there is a firm theoretical foundation.

18.1 Parallelism and Recursion

Many important synchronous parallel algorithms – Fast Fourier Transform, routing and permutation, Batcher Merge, solving tridiagonal linear systems by odd-even reduction, prefix-sum algorithms – are best formulated in a recursive fashion. The network structures on which parallel algorithms are typically implemented – Butterfly, Sorting Networks, hypercube, complete binary tree – are, also, recursive in nature. However, parallelism, an implementation technique, is awkward to combine with recursion. Therefore, parallel recursive algorithms are typically described iteratively, one parallel step at a time[1]. Similarly, the connection structures are often explained pictorially, by displaying the connections between one "level" and the next. The mathematical properties of the algorithms and connection structures are rarely evident from these descriptions.

A data structure, *powerlist*, is proposed in this paper that highlights the role of both parallelism and recursion. Many of the known parallel algorithms – FFT, Batcher Merge, Prefix Sum, embedding arrays in hypercubes, etc. – have surprisingly concise descriptions using powerlists. A variety of data structures and connection networks can also be conveniently represented; see Misra[10]. Simple algebraic properties of powerlists permit us to deduce properties of these algorithms and connection networks employing structural induction on powerlists. The proposal promises to be useful in implementing parallel algorithms on specific connection structures.

---
[1]A notable exception is the recursive description of a prefix sum algorithm in Karp and Ramachandran[5].

18.2   Powerlist

The basic data structure on which recursion is employed (in LISP[8] or ML[9]) is a *list*. A list is either empty or it is constructed by concatenating an element to a list. (We restrict ourselves to finite lists throughout this paper.) We call such a list *linear* (because the list length grows by 1 as a result of applying the basic constructor). Such a list structure seems unsuitable for expressing parallel algorithms succinctly; an algorithm that processes the list elements has to describe how successive elements of the list are processed.

We propose *powerlist* as a data structure that is more suitable for describing parallel algorithms. The base – corresponding to the empty list for the linear case – is a list of one element. (Clearly, there are many bases, depending on the specific element in the list.) A larger powerlist is constructed from the elements of two powerlists of the same length (as described below). Thus, powerlist is multiplicative in nature; its length doubles by applying the basic constructor.

There are two different ways in which powerlists are joined to create a larger powerlist. If p, q are powerlists of the same length then

$p \mid q$ is the powerlist formed by concatenating p and q

$p \bowtie q$ is the powerlist formed by successively taking alternate items from p and q, starting with p.

Further, we restrict p, q to contain similar elements (defined in Section 18.2.1).

In the following examples the sequence of elements of a powerlist are enclosed within angular brackets.

$\langle 0 \rangle \mid \langle 1 \rangle = \langle 0\ 1 \rangle$
$\langle 0 \rangle \bowtie \langle 1 \rangle = \langle 0\ 1 \rangle$
$\langle 0\ 1 \rangle \mid \langle 2\ 3 \rangle = \langle 0\ 1\ 2\ 3 \rangle$
$\langle 0\ 1 \rangle \bowtie \langle 2\ 3 \rangle = \langle 0\ 2\ 1\ 3 \rangle$

The operation $\mid$ is called *tie* and $\bowtie$ is *zip*.

18.2.1   Definitions

A data item from the linear list theory will be called a *scalar*. (Typical scalars are the items of base types – integer, boolean, etc. – tuples of scalars, functions from scalars to scalars and linear lists of scalars.) Scalars are uninterpreted in our theory. We merely assume that scalars can be checked for type compatibility. We will use several standard operations on scalars for purposes of illustration.

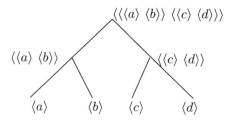

Figure 18.1 Representation of a complete binary tree where the data are at the leaves. For leaf nodes, the powerlist has one element. For nonleaf nodes, the powerlist has two elements, namely, the powerlists for the left and right subtrees.

Notational convention: Linear lists will be enclosed within square brackets, [ ].

A *powerlist* is a list of length 2^n, for some n, $n \geq 0$, all of whose elements are similar.

Two scalars are *similar* if they are of the same type. Two powerlists are *similar* if they have the same length and any element of one is similar to any element of the other. (Observe that *similar* is an equivalence relation.)

A recursive definition of a powerlist is as follows; here, S denotes an arbitrary scalar, P a powerlist and u, v similar powerlists. A powerlist is,

$$\langle S \rangle \quad \text{or} \quad \langle P \rangle \quad \text{or} \quad u \mid v \quad \text{or} \quad u \bowtie v$$

Examples

$\langle 2 \rangle$ powerlist of length 1 containing a scalar

$\langle \langle 2 \rangle \rangle$ powerlist of length 1 containing a powerlist of length 1 of scalar

$\langle \, \rangle$ not a powerlist

$\langle [\,] \rangle$ powerlist of length 1 containing the empty linear list

$\langle \, \langle [2] \, [3 \, 4 \, 7] \rangle \, \langle [4] \, [\,] \rangle \, \rangle$

     powerlist of length 2, each element of which is a powerlist of length 2, whose elements are linear lists of numbers

$\langle \, \langle 0 \, 4 \rangle \, \langle 1 \, 5 \rangle \, \langle 2 \, 6 \rangle \, \langle 3 \, 7 \rangle \rangle$

     a representation of the matrix $\begin{bmatrix} 0 \, 1 \, 2 \, 3 \\ 4 \, 5 \, 6 \, 7 \end{bmatrix}$ where each column is an element of the outer powerlist.

$\langle \, \langle 0 \, 1 \, 2 \, 3 \rangle \, \langle 4 \, 5 \, 6 \, 7 \rangle \, \rangle$

     another representation of the above matrix where each row is an element of the outer powerlist.

$\langle \langle \langle a \rangle \, \langle b \rangle \rangle \, \langle \langle c \rangle \, \langle d \rangle \rangle \rangle$

     representation of the tree in Figure 18.1. The powerlist contains two elements, for the left and right subtrees.

18.2.2   Functions over powerlists

Notation: We write function application without parentheses where no confusion is possible. Thus, we write "$f\ x$" instead of "$f(x)$" and "$g\ x\ y$" instead of "$g(x,y)$". The constructors | and $\bowtie$ have the same binding power and their binding power is lower than function application.

Throughout this paper, S denotes a scalar, P a powerlist and x,y either scalar or powerlist. Typical names for powerlist variables are p,q,r,s,t,u,v.   □

Functions over linear lists are, typically, defined by case analysis – a function is defined over the empty list, and, recursively, over nonempty lists. Functions over powerlists are defined analogously. For instance, the following function, *rev*, reverses the order of the elements of the argument powerlist:

$$rev\ \langle x \rangle = \langle x \rangle$$
$$rev\ (p \mid q) = (rev\ q) \mid (rev\ p)$$

The case analysis, as for linear lists, is based on the length of the argument powerlist. We adopt the pattern matching scheme of ML[9] and Miranda[11][2] to *deconstruct* the argument list into its components, p and q, in the recursive case. Deconstruction, in general, uses the operators | and $\bowtie$; see Section 18.3. In the definition of *rev*, we have used | for deconstruction though we could have used $\bowtie$ and defined *rev* in the recursive case by

$$rev(p \bowtie q) = (rev\ q) \bowtie (rev\ p)$$

It can be shown, using the laws in Section 18.3, that the two proposed definitions of *rev* are equivalent and that

$$rev(rev\ P) = P$$

for any powerlist P.

Scalar functions
Operations on scalars are outside our theory. Some of the examples in this paper, however, use scalar functions, particularly, addition and multiplication (over complex numbers) and *cons* over linear lists. A scalar function, f, has zero or more scalars as arguments and its value is a scalar. We coerce the application of f to a powerlist by applying f "pointwise" to elements of the powerlist; we define

$$f\langle x \rangle = \langle f\ x \rangle$$
$$f(p \mid q) = (f\ p) \mid (f\ q)$$

---

[2]Miranda is a trademark of Research Software Ltd.

It can be shown that

$$f(p \bowtie q) = (f\ p) \bowtie (f\ q)$$

A scalar function that operates on two arguments will often be written as an infix operator. For any such function $\oplus$, we have

$$\langle x \rangle \oplus \langle y \rangle = \langle x \oplus y \rangle$$
$$(p \mid q) \oplus (u \mid v) = (p \oplus u) \mid (q \oplus v)$$
$$(p \bowtie q) \oplus (u \bowtie v) = (p \oplus u) \bowtie (q \oplus v)$$

Thus, scalar functions commute with both $\mid$ and $\bowtie$.

Note: Since a scalar function is applied recursively to each element of a powerlist, its effect propagates through all "levels". Thus, $+$ applied to matrices forms their elementwise sum.   □

18.2.3   Discussion

The base case of a powerlist is a singleton list, not an empty list. We believe that empty lists (or, equivalent data structures) do not arise in parallel programming. For instance, in matrix algorithms the base case is a 1×1 matrix rather than an empty matrix, Fourier Transform is defined for a singleton list (not the empty list) and the smallest hypercube has one node.

The recursive definition of a powerlist says that a powerlist is either of the form $u \bowtie v$ or $u \mid v$. In fact, every non-singleton powerlist can be written in either form in a unique manner (see Laws in Section 18.3). A simple way to view $p \mid q = L$ is that if the elements of L are indexed by n-bit strings in increasing numerical order (where the length of L is 2^n) then p is the sublist of elements whose highest bit of the index is 0 and q is the sublist with 1 in the highest bit of the index. Similarly, if $u \bowtie v = L$ then u is the sublist of elements whose lowest bit of the index is 0 and v's elements have 1 as the lowest bit of the index.

It may, at first, seem strange to allow two different ways of constructing the same list – using tie or zip. As we see in this paper, this causes no difficulty, and further, this flexibility is essential because many parallel algorithms – the Fast Fourier Transform being the most prominent – exploit both forms of construction.

We have restricted u, v in $u \mid v$ and $u \bowtie v$ to be similar. This restriction allows us to process a powerlist by recursive divide and conquer, where each division yields two halves that can be processed in parallel, by employing the same algorithm. (Square matrices, for instance, are often processed by quartering them. We will show how quartering, or quadrupling, can be expressed in our theory.) The similarity restriction allows us to define complete binary trees, hypercubes and square matrices that are not "free" structures.

The length of a powerlist is a power of 2. This restricts our theory somewhat. It is possible to design a more general theory eliminating this constraint; we sketch an outline in Section 18.6.

18.3   Laws

L0. For singleton powerlists, $\langle x \rangle, \langle y \rangle$
   $$\langle x \rangle \mid \langle y \rangle = \langle x \rangle \bowtie \langle y \rangle$$

L1. (Dual Deconstruction)
   For any non-singleton powerlist, P, there exist similar powerlists r, s, u, v such that
   $$P = r \mid s \text{ and } P = u \bowtie v$$

L2. (Unique Deconstruction)
   $$(\langle x \rangle = \langle y \rangle) \equiv (x = y)$$
   $$(p \mid q = u \mid v) \equiv (p = u \land q = v)$$
   $$(p \bowtie q = u \bowtie v) \equiv (p = u \land q = v)$$

L3. (Commutativity of $\mid$ and $\bowtie$)
   $$(p \mid q) \bowtie (u \mid v) = (p \bowtie u) \mid (q \bowtie v)$$

These laws can be derived by suitably defining tie and zip, using the standard functions from the linear list theory. One possible strategy is to define tie as the concatenation of two equal length lists and then, use Laws L0 and L3 as the definition of zip; Laws L1, L2 can be derived next. Alternatively, these laws may be regarded as axioms relating tie and zip.

Law L0 is often used in proving base cases of algebraic identities. Laws L1, L2 allow us to uniquely deconstruct a non-singleton powerlist using either $\mid$ or $\bowtie$. Law L3 is crucial. It is the only law relating the two construction operators, $\mid$ and $\bowtie$, in the general case. Hence, it is invariably applied in proofs by structural induction where both constructors play a role.

Inductive proofs

Most proofs on powerlists are by induction on the length, depth or shape of the list. The length, *len*, of a powerlist is the number of elements in it. Since the length of a powerlist is a power of 2, the logarithmic length, *lgl*, is a more useful measure. Formally,

$$lgl\langle x \rangle = 0$$
$$lgl(u \mid v) = 1 + (lgl\ u)$$

The *depth* of a powerlist is the number of "levels" in it.

$depth \langle S \rangle = 0$
$depth \langle P \rangle = 1 + (depth\ P)$
$depth\ (u \mid v) = depth\ u$

(In the last case, powerlists u, v have the same depth, since they are similar.) Most inductive proofs on powerlists order them lexicographically on the pair (depth, logarithmic length). For instance, to prove that a property Π holds for all powerlists, it is sufficient to prove

$\Pi \langle S \rangle$, and
$\Pi\ P \Rightarrow \Pi \langle P \rangle$, and
$(\Pi\ u) \wedge (\Pi\ v) \wedge (u, v)$ similar $\Rightarrow \Pi(u \mid v)$

The last proof step could be replaced by

$(\Pi\ u) \wedge (\Pi\ v) \wedge (u, v)$ similar $\Rightarrow \Pi(u \bowtie v)$

The *shape* of a powerlist P is a sequence of natural numbers $n_0, n_1, \ldots, n_d$ where d is the depth of P and

n_0 is the logarithmic length of P,
n_1 is the logarithmic length of (any) element of P, say r
n_2 is the logarithmic length of any element of $r, \ldots$
$\vdots$

A formal definition of shape is similar to that of depth. The shape is a linear sequence because all elements, at any level, are similar. The shape and the type of the scalar elements define the structure of a powerlist completely. For inductive proofs, the powerlists may be ordered lexicographically by the pair (depth, shape), where the shapes are, again, compared lexicographically.

18.4   Examples

We show a few small examples of algorithms on powerlists. The examples include such famous ones as the Fast Fourier Transform and Batcher Merge. We have restricted ourselves to simple powerlists (where the depth is 0); higher dimensional lists (and algorithms for matrices and hypercubes) are taken up in a later section. Since the powerlists are simple, induction based on length is sufficient to prove properties of these algorithms.

18.4.1   Permutations

We define a few functions that permute the elements of powerlists. The function *rev*, defined in Section 18.2.2, is a permutation function. These functions appear as components of many parallel algorithms.

Rotate

Function *rr* rotates a powerlist to the right by one; thus, $rr\langle a\ b\ c\ d\rangle = \langle d\ a\ b\ c\rangle$. Function *rl* rotates to the left; $rl\langle a\ b\ c\ d\rangle = \langle b\ c\ d\ a\rangle$.

$$rr\langle x\rangle = \langle x\rangle \qquad , \qquad rl\langle x\rangle = \langle x\rangle$$
$$rr(u \bowtie v) = (rr\ v) \bowtie u \quad , \quad rl(u \bowtie v) = v \bowtie (rl\ u)$$

There does not seem to be any simple definition of *rr* or *rl* using | as the deconstruction operator. It is easy to show, using structural induction, that *rr*,*rl* are inverses. An amusing identity is $rev(rr(rev(rr\ P))) = P$.

Rotate index

A class of permutation functions can be defined by the transformations on the element indices. Imagine that each element of a powerlist, having 2^n elements, has associated with it an *n*-bit index, where the indices are in increasing numerical order. (For a powerlist $u \mid v$, indices for the elements in *u* have "0" as the highest bit and in *v* have "1" as the highest bit. In $u \bowtie v$, similar remarks apply for the lowest bit.) Any bijection, *h*, mapping indices to indices defines a permutation of the powerlist: the element with index *i* is moved to the position where it has index $(h\ i)$. Below, we consider two simple index mapping functions; the corresponding permutations of powerlists are useful in describing the shuffle-exchange network; see Leighton[7, Section 3.31]. Note that indices are not part of our theory.

A function that rotates an index to the right (by one position) has the permutation function *rs* (for *r*ight *s*huffle) associated with it. The definition of *rs* may be understood as follows. The effect of rotating an index to the right is that the lowest bit of an index becomes the highest bit; therefore, if *rs* is applied to $u \bowtie v$, the elements of *u* – those having 0 as the lowest bit – will occupy the first half of the resulting powerlist (because their indices have "0" as the highest bit, after rotation); similarly, *v* will occupy the second half. Analogously, the function that rotates an index to the left (by one position) induces the permutation defined by *ls* (for *l*eft *s*huffle), below. Figure 18.2 shows the effects of index rotations on an 8-element list.

$$rs\langle x\rangle = \langle x\rangle \qquad , \qquad ls\langle x\rangle = \langle x\rangle$$
$$rs(u \bowtie v) = u \mid v \quad , \quad ls(u \mid v) = u \bowtie v$$

It is trivial to see that *rs*, *ls* are inverses.

$$
\begin{aligned}
P\text{'s indices} &= (000 \quad 001 \quad 010 \quad 011 \quad 100 \quad 101 \quad 110 \quad 111) \\
\text{List } P &= \langle a \quad\;\; b \quad\;\; c \quad\;\; d \quad\;\; e \quad\;\; f \quad\;\; g \quad\;\; h \rangle
\end{aligned}
$$

$$
\begin{aligned}
P\text{'s indices rotated right} &= (000 \quad 100 \quad 001 \quad 101 \quad 010 \quad 110 \quad 011 \quad 111) \\
rs\ P &= \langle a \quad\;\; c \quad\;\; e \quad\;\; g \quad\;\; b \quad\;\; d \quad\;\; f \quad\;\; h \rangle
\end{aligned}
$$

$$
\begin{aligned}
P\text{'s indices rotated left} &= (000 \quad 010 \quad 100 \quad 110 \quad 001 \quad 011 \quad 101 \quad 111) \\
ls\ P &= \langle a \quad\;\; e \quad\;\; b \quad\;\; f \quad\;\; c \quad\;\; g \quad\;\; d \quad\;\; h \rangle
\end{aligned}
$$

Figure 18.2 Permutation functions *rs*, *ls* defined in Section 18.4.1.

Inversion

The function *inv* is defined by the following function on indices. An element with index b in P has index $REV(b)$ in *inv* P, where $REV(b)$ is the reversal of the bit string b. Thus,

$$
inv\langle \overset{00}{a}\ \overset{01}{b}\ \overset{10}{c}\ \overset{11}{d} \rangle = \langle \overset{00}{a}\ \overset{01}{c}\ \overset{10}{b}\ \overset{11}{d} \rangle
$$

The definition of *inv* is

$$
inv\langle x \rangle = \langle x \rangle
$$
$$
inv(p \mid q) = (inv\ p) \bowtie (inv\ q)
$$

This function arises in a variety of contexts. In particular, *inv* is used to permute the output of a Fast Fourier Transform network into the correct order.

The following proof shows a typical application of structural induction:

INV1. $inv(p \bowtie q) = (inv\ p) \mid (inv\ q)$

Proof : By structural induction on p and q.

Base : $inv(\langle x \rangle \bowtie \langle y \rangle)$
$=$ {From Law L0 : $\langle x \rangle \bowtie \langle y \rangle = \langle x \rangle \mid \langle y \rangle$}
$\quad inv(\langle x \rangle \mid \langle y \rangle)$
$=$ {definition of *inv*}
$\quad inv\langle x \rangle \bowtie inv\langle y \rangle$
$=$ {$inv\langle x \rangle = \langle x \rangle$, $inv\langle y \rangle = \langle y \rangle$. From Law L0}
$\quad inv\langle x \rangle \mid inv\langle y \rangle$

Induction :
$\quad inv((r \mid s) \bowtie (u \mid v))$
$=$ {commutativity of $\mid$, $\bowtie$}
$\quad inv((r \bowtie u) \mid (s \bowtie v))$
$=$ {definition of *inv*}
$\quad inv(r \bowtie u) \bowtie inv(s \bowtie v)$
$=$ {induction}
$\quad (inv\ r \mid inv\ u) \bowtie (inv\ s \mid inv\ v)$

$$= \quad \{|, \bowtie \text{ commute}\}$$
$$(inv \ r \bowtie inv \ s) \mid (inv \ u \bowtie inv \ v)$$
$$= \quad \{\text{apply definition of } inv \text{ to both sides of } |\}$$
$$inv(r \mid s) \mid inv(u \mid v) \hspace{4cm} \square$$

Using INV1 and structural induction, it is easy to establish

$$inv \ (inv \ P) = P$$

$$inv \ (rev \ P) = rev \ (inv \ P)$$

and for any scalar operator $\oplus$

$$inv \ (P \oplus Q) = (inv \ P) \oplus (inv \ Q)$$

The last result holds for any permutation function in place of *inv*.

18.4.2   Reduction

In the linear list theory[2], reduction is a higher order function of two arguments, an associative binary operator and a list. Reduction applied to $\oplus$ and $[a_0 a_1 \ldots a_n]$ yields $(a_0 \oplus a_1 \oplus \ldots \oplus a_n)$. This function over powerlists is defined by

$$red \oplus \langle x \rangle = x$$
$$red \oplus (p \mid q) = (red \oplus p) \ \oplus \ (red \oplus q)$$

18.4.3   Gray code

Gray code sequence for n, $n \geq 0$, is a sequence of 2^n n-bit strings where the consecutive strings in the sequence differ in exactly one bit position. (The last and the first strings in the sequence are considered consecutive.) Standard Gray code sequences for $n = 0, 1, 2, 3$ are shown in Figure 18.3. We represent the n-bit strings by linear lists of length n and a Gray code sequence by a powerlist whose elements are these linear lists. The standard Gray code sequence may be computed by function G, for any n:

$$G \ 0 = \langle [\ ] \rangle$$
$$G \ (n+1) = (0 \ : \ P) \mid (1 \ : \ (rev \ P))$$
$$\text{where } P = (G \ n)$$

Here, $0 :$ is a scalar function that takes a linear list as an argument and appends 0 as its prefix. According to the coercion rule, $0 \ : \ P$ is the powerlist obtained by prefixing every element of P by 0. Similarly, $1 : (rev \ P)$ is defined, where the function *rev* is from Section 18.2.2.

$$n = 0 \quad \langle [\ ] \rangle$$
$$n = 1 \quad \langle [0]\ [1] \rangle$$
$$n = 2 \quad \langle [00]\ [01]\ [11]\ [10] \rangle$$
$$n = 3 \quad \langle [000]\ [001]\ [011]\ [010]\ [110]\ [111]\ [101]\ [100] \rangle$$

Figure 18.3 Standard Gray code sequence for n, $n = 0, 1, 2, 3$

18.4.4 Polynomial

The polynomial $\sum\limits_{0 \le i < 2^n} p_i \times \omega^i$, where $n \ge 0$, p_is are the coefficients and ω is the variable, may be represented by a powerlist, p, whose i^{th} element is p_i. The polynomial can be evaluated for a specific value of ω by the function *ep*:

$$ep\ \langle x \rangle\ \omega = x$$
$$ep\ (p \bowtie q)\ \omega = b + c$$
$$\text{where } b = ep\ p\ \omega^2$$
$$c = \omega \times (ep\ q\ w^2)$$

The definition of *ep* in the recursive case is obtained by grouping the terms of the polynomial into two groups – coefficients with even indices and those with odd indices.

The function *ep* is used in defining and deriving properties of Fourier Transform (Section 18.4.5). In that section, we will also need a function *poly* that creates a powerlist of the successive powers of an argument:

For a complex number, ω, and a natural number n, *poly* ω n is the powerlist $\langle \omega^0, \omega^1\ \dots\ \omega^{2^n-1} \rangle$. The definition of *poly* is analogous to that of *ep*:

$$poly\ \omega\ 0 = \langle 1 \rangle$$
$$poly\ \omega\ (n+1) = p \bowtie q$$
$$\text{where } p = poly\ \omega^2\ n$$
$$q = (\omega \times)\ p$$

Here, $(\omega \times)$ is a unary scalar function that multiplies its scalar argument by ω. (Applied to the powerlist p it multiplies each element of p by ω.)

18.4.5 Fast Fourier Transform

For a powerlist, P, of complex numbers, its Fourier Transform, Q, is a powerlist of the same length where

$$Q_i = ep\ P\ \omega^i\ \ ,\ 0 \le i < N$$

where N is the length of P (and Q), ω is the Nth principal root of 1 and *ep* is the function (defined in Section 18.4.4) that evaluates a polynomial at a given point.

Here, Q_i is the ith element of Q. (The elements of Q are indexed consecutively starting at 0. The indexing notation is not a part of our theory.)

The straightforward computation of Q_i requires $O(N)$ additions and $O(N)$ multiplications; therefore, the computation of Q takes $O(N^2)$ steps. The Fast Fourier Transform (*FFT*), given in [4], reduces the number of steps to $O(N \log N)$. It also admits of efficient parallel implementation taking $O(\log N)$ steps on $O(N)$ processors.

The strategy employed in *FFT* is to deconstruct P using $\bowtie$, into u and v. Let U, V be the Fourier transforms of u, v (these can be computed recursively). It can be shown, see[3, Section 6.13], that

$$
\begin{aligned}
Q_i &= U_i + \omega^i \times V_i && , \ 0 \le i < (len\ u) \\
Q_{i+(len\ u)} &= U_i - \omega^i \times V_i && , \ 0 \le i < (len\ u)
\end{aligned}
$$

Thus, Q can be obtained from the three powerlists – U, V, W (W is *poly* ω (*lgl u*); see Section 18.4.4 for the definition of *poly*). The left half of Q is $U + V \times W$ and the right half is $U - V \times W$. Specifically (with $+$ and $\times$ denoting pointwise addition and multiplication of powerlists, and $\times$ having higher binding power than $+$),

$$
\begin{aligned}
FFT\ &\langle x \rangle = \langle x \rangle \\
FFT\ &(u \bowtie v) = (U + V \times W) \mid (U - V \times W) \\
&\text{where} \quad U = FFT\ u \\
&\qquad\qquad\ V = FFT\ v \\
&\qquad\qquad\ W = \ poly\ \omega\ (lgl\ u)
\end{aligned}
$$

Recall that ω is the Nth principal root of 1 where N is the length of $u \bowtie v$.

It is clear that $FFT\ (u \bowtie v)$ can be computed from $(FFT\ u)$ and $(FFT\ v)$ in $O(N)$ sequential steps or $O(1)$ parallel steps using $O(N)$ processors. Therefore, $FFT\ (u \bowtie v)$ can be computed in $O(N \log N)$ sequential steps or $O(\log N)$ parallel steps using $O(N)$ processors.

The compactness of this description of *FFT* is in striking contrast to the usual descriptions; see, for instance, Chandy and Misra[3, Section 6.13]. The compactness can be attributed to the use of recursion and the avoidance of explicit indexing (of the elements), by employing $\mid$ and $\bowtie$. *FFT* illustrates the need for including both $\mid$ and $\bowtie$ as constructors for powerlists. (Another function that employs both $\mid$ and $\bowtie$ is *inv* of Section 18.4.1.) *FFT* can be implemented efficiently on a Butterfly network. That implementation shows the connection between *FFT* and *inv*.

Inverse Fourier Transform

The inverse of the Fourier Transform, *IFT*, can be defined similarly to the *FFT*. In fact, the definition of *IFT* can be derived from that of the *FFT* by pattern matching.

For a singleton powerlist, $\langle x \rangle$, we compute

$$IFT \ \langle x \rangle$$
$$= \quad \{\langle x \rangle = FFT \ \langle x \rangle\}$$
$$IFT \ (FFT \ \langle x \rangle)$$
$$= \quad \{IFT, FFT \ \text{are inverses}\}$$
$$\langle x \rangle$$

For the general case, we have to compute u, v given p, q such that

$$IFT \ (p \mid q) = u \bowtie v$$

(These forms of deconstructions are chosen so that we can easily solve the equations we generate, next.)

Taking FFT of both sides,

$$FFT \ (IFT \ (p \mid q)) = FFT \ (u \bowtie v)$$

The left side is, simply, $p \mid q$ because IFT, FFT are inverses. Replacing the right side by the definition of $FFT \ (u \bowtie v)$ yields the following equations:

$$p \mid q = (U + V \times W) \mid (U - V \times W)$$
$$U = FFT \ u$$
$$V = FFT \ v$$
$$W = \ poly \ \omega \ (lgl \ u)$$

These equations are easily solved for the unknowns U, V, W, u, v. (Note that the law of unique deconstruction, L2, is used to deduce from the first equation that $p = U + V \times W$ and $q = U - V \times W$.) The solutions of these equations yield the following definition for IFT. Here, $/2$ divides each element of the given powerlist by 2.

$$IFT \ \langle x \rangle = \langle x \rangle$$
$$IFT \ (p \mid q) = u \bowtie v$$
$$\text{where} \quad U = (p + q)/2$$
$$W = poly \ \omega \ (lgl \ p)$$
$$V = ((p - q)/2)/W$$
$$u = IFT \ U$$
$$v = IFT \ V$$

As before, ω is the Nth principal root of 1 where N is the length of $(p \mid q)$.

Note: The division by W (in the definition of V) may be replaced by a multiplication by W' where $W' = poly \ \omega^{-1} \ (lgl \ p)$. □

As in the FFT, the definition of IFT includes both constructors, $\mid$ and $\bowtie$. It can be implemented efficiently on a Butterfly network. The complexity of IFT is the same as that of the FFT.

18.4.6   Batcher Merge

In this section, we develop some elementary results about sorting and discuss a remarkable sorting method due to Batcher[1]. We find it interesting that $\bowtie$ (not $|$) is the preferred operator in discussing the principles of parallel sorting.

A merge algorithm creates a sorted powerlist from the data items of two sorted powerlists. By applying merge to successively longer segments, any powerlist can be sorted. In this section, we consider a specific merge scheme due to Batcher.

Basic to this merge scheme is a comparison operation, $\updownarrow$, that is applied to a pair of powerlists.

$$p \updownarrow q = (p \ \text{min} \ q) \bowtie (p \ \text{max} \ q)$$

That is, the $2i^{th}$ and $(2i+1)^{th}$ items of $p \updownarrow q$ are $(p_i \ \text{min} \ q_i)$ and $(p_i \ \text{max} \ q_i)$, respectively. The expression $p \updownarrow q$ can be computed in constant time using $O(len \ p)$ processors.

The merge scheme of Batcher, bm, is defined as an infix operator below:

$$\langle x \rangle \ bm \ \langle y \rangle = \langle x \rangle \updownarrow \langle y \rangle$$
$$(r \bowtie s) \ bm \ (u \bowtie v) = (r \ bm \ v) \updownarrow (s \ bm \ u)$$

The function bm is well suited for parallel implementation. The recursive form suggests that $(r \ bm \ v)$ and $(s \ bm \ u)$ can be computed in parallel. Since $\updownarrow$ can be applied in $O(1)$ parallel steps using $O(N)$ processors, where N is the length of the argument powerlists, the function bm can be evaluated in $O(\log N)$ parallel steps. In the rest of this section, we develop certain elementary facts about sorting and prove the correctness of bm.

Elementary facts about sorting
We consider only "compare and swap" type sorting methods. It is known (see Knuth[6]) that such a sorting scheme is correct iff it sorts lists containing 0's and 1's only. Therefore, we restrict our discussion to powerlists containing 0's and 1's, only.

For a powerlist p, let $z \ p$ be the number of 0's in it. To simplify notation, we omit the space and write zp. Clearly,

(A0) $z(p \bowtie q) = zp + zq$

Powerlists containing 0's and 1's are sorted under the following conditions:

(A1) $\langle x \rangle$ sorted
(A2) $(p \bowtie q)$ sorted $\equiv p$ sorted $\wedge q$ sorted $\wedge 0 \le zp - zq \le 1$

Note: The analogous condition under which $p \mid q$ is sorted is,

(A2′) $(p \mid q)$ sorted $\equiv$ p sorted $\wedge$ q sorted $\wedge$ $(zp < (len\ p) \Rightarrow zq = 0)$

The simplicity of (A2), compared with (A2′), may suggest why $\bowtie$ is the primary operator in parallel sorting.   □
    The following results are easy to prove:

B1. p sorted, q sorted, $zp \geq zq$ $\Rightarrow$ $(p\ min\ q) = p \wedge (p\ max\ q) = q$ □

B2. $z(p \updownarrow q) = zp + zq$ □

   We show,

B3. p sorted, q sorted, $|zp - zq| \leq 1$ $\Rightarrow$ $(p \updownarrow q)$ sorted

Proof: Since all operations on p, q are symmetric in the statement of the theorem, assume $zp \geq zq$.

> p sorted, q sorted, $|zp - zq| \leq 1$
> $\Rightarrow$ {assumption: $zp \geq zq$}
> p sorted, q sorted, $0 \leq zp - zq \leq 1$
> $\Rightarrow$ {A2 and B1}
> $p \bowtie q$ sorted, $(p\ min\ q) = p, (p\ max\ q) = q$
> $\Rightarrow$ {replace p, q in $p \bowtie q$ by $(p\ min\ q), (p\ max\ q)$}
> $(p\ min\ q) \bowtie (p\ max\ q)$ sorted
> $\Rightarrow$ {definition of $p \updownarrow q$}
> $p \updownarrow q$ sorted   □

From (A1), singleton powerlists are sorted. Therefore, using B3, and that $|z\langle x \rangle - z\langle y \rangle| \leq 1$,

Corollary: $\langle x \rangle \updownarrow \langle y \rangle$ sorted.

Correctness of Batcher Merge
We show that bm indeed merges two sorted powerlists: B4 states that bm preserves the number of zeros of its argument lists (i.e., it loses no data) and B5 states that the resulting list is sorted.

B4. $z(p\ bm\ q) = zp + zq$

Proof: By structural induction, using B2.   □

B5. p sorted, q sorted $\Rightarrow$ $(p\ bm\ q)$ sorted

Proof: By structural induction.

Base:
$$\langle x \rangle \; bm \; \langle y \rangle$$
$$= \quad \{\text{definition of } bm\}$$
$$\langle x \rangle \updownarrow \langle y \rangle$$

From Corollary to B3, $\langle x \rangle \updownarrow \langle y \rangle$ sorted.

Induction:
$$r \bowtie s \text{ sorted, } u \bowtie v \text{ sorted}$$

$\Rightarrow$ {A2}
r sorted, s sorted, $0 \le zr - zs \le 1$, u sorted, v sorted, $0 \le zu - zv \le 1$

$\Rightarrow$ {induction on (r, v) and (s, u)}
$(r \; bm \; v)$ sorted, $(s \; bm \; u)$ sorted, $0 \le zr - zs \le 1, 0 \le zu - zv \le 1$

$\Rightarrow$ {The inequalities imply}
$(r \; bm \; v)$ sorted, $(s \; bm \; u)$ sorted, $|(zr + zv) - (zs + zu)| \le 1$

$\Rightarrow$ {Applying B4 twice.}
$(r \; bm \; v)$ sorted, $(s \; bm \; u)$ sorted, $|z(r \; bm \; v) - z(s \; bm \; u)| \le 1$

$\Rightarrow$ {Apply B3 with $(r \; bm \; v), (s \; bm \; u)$ for p, q}
$((r \; bm \; v) \updownarrow (s \; bm \; u))$ sorted

$\Rightarrow$ {definition of bm}
$((r \bowtie s) \; bm \; (u \bowtie v))$ sorted $\square$

The compactness of the description of Batcher Merge and the simplicity of its correctness proof, again, demonstrate the importance of treating recursion and parallelism simultaneously.

18.5   Higher Dimensional Arrays

A major part of parallel computing involves arrays of one or more dimensions. An array of m dimensions (dimensions are numbered 0 through $m - 1$) is represented by a powerlist of depth $(m - 1)$. Conversely, since powerlist elements are similar, a powerlist of depth $(m - 1)$ may be regarded as an array of dimension m. For instance, a matrix of r rows and c columns may be represented as a powerlist of c elements, each element being a powerlist of length r storing the items of a column;

conversely, the same matrix may be represented by a powerlist of r elements, each element being a powerlist of c elements.

In manipulating higher dimensional arrays we prefer to think in terms of array operations rather than operations on nested powerlists. Therefore, we introduce construction operators, analogous to $|$ and $\bowtie$, for tie and zip along any specified dimension. We use $|', \bowtie'$ for the corresponding operators in dimension 1, $|'', \bowtie''$ for dimension 2, etc. The definitions of these operators are in Section 18.5.1; for the moment it is sufficient to regard $|'$ as the pointwise application of $|$ to the argument powerlists (and similarly, $\bowtie'$). Thus, for similar (power) matrices A, B that are stored columnwise (i.e., each element is a column), $A \mid B$ is the concatenation of A, B by rows and $A \mid' B$ is their concatenation by columns. Given these constructors we may define a matrix to be either

a singleton matrix $\langle\langle x \rangle\rangle$, or
$p \mid q$ where p, q are (similar) matrices, or
$u \mid' v$ where u, v are (similar) matrices.

Analogous definitions can be given for n-dimensional arrays. Observe that the length of each dimension is a power of 2. As we had in the case of a powerlist, the same matrix can be constructed in several different ways, say, first by constructing the rows and then the columns, or vice versa. We will show, in Section 18.5.1, that

$$(p \mid q) \mid' (u \mid v) = (p \mid' u) \mid (q \mid' v)$$

i.e., $|, |'$ commute.

Note: We could have defined a matrix using $\bowtie$ and $\bowtie'$ instead of $|$ and $|'$. As $|$ and $\bowtie$ are duals in the sense that either can be used to construct (or uniquely deconstruct) a powerlist, $|'$ and $\bowtie'$ are also duals, as we show in Section 18.5.1. Therefore, we will freely use all four construction operators for matrices. □

Example: matrix transposition
Let τ be a function that transposes matrices. From the definition of a matrix, we have to consider three cases in defining τ:

$$\tau\langle\langle x \rangle\rangle = \langle\langle x \rangle\rangle$$
$$\tau(p \mid q) = (\tau\ p) \mid' (\tau\ q)$$
$$\tau(u \mid' v) = (\tau\ u) \mid (\tau\ v)$$

The definition of function τ, though straightforward, has introduced the possibility of an inconsistent definition. For a 2×2 matrix, for instance, either of the last two deconstructions apply. Using the fact that $|$ and $|'$ commute, we can show that the same result is obtained no matter in which order the deconstructions are applied, i.e., τ, as defined above, is indeed a function.

It is easy to show that

$$\tau\ (p \bowtie q) = (\tau\ p) \bowtie' (\tau\ q) \text{ and}$$
$$\tau\ (u \bowtie' v) = (\tau\ u) \bowtie (\tau\ v)$$

18.5.1   Derivative

Let g be a function mapping items of type α to type β. Then g', which we call the *derivative* of g, maps a powerlist of α-items to a powerlist of β-items.

$$g'\langle x\rangle = \langle g\ x\rangle$$
$$g'(r \mid s) = (g'\ r) \mid (g'\ s)$$

Similarly, for a binary operator *op*

$$\langle x\rangle\ op'\ \langle y\rangle = \langle x\ op\ y\rangle$$
$$(r \mid s)\ op'\ (u \mid v) = (r\ op'\ u) \mid (s\ op'\ v)$$

We have defined these two forms explicitly because we use one or the other in all our examples; f' for a function f of arbitrary arity is similarly defined. Observe that f' applied to a powerlist of length N yields a powerlist of length N. The number of primes over f determines the dimension at which f is applied (the outermost dimension is numbered 0; therefore writing $\bowtie$, for instance, without primes, simply zips two lists).

Common special cases for the binary operator, *op*, are $\mid$ and $\bowtie$ and their derivatives. In particular, writing $\bowtie^m$ to denote $\bowtie \overbrace{''\cdots'}^{m}$, we have, $\bowtie^0 = \bowtie$ and for $m > 0$,

$$\langle x\rangle \bowtie^m \langle y\rangle = \langle x \bowtie^{m-1} y\rangle$$
$$(r \mid s) \bowtie^m (u \mid v) = (r \bowtie^m u) \mid (s \bowtie^m v)$$

The definition of derivative states that f' and $\mid$ commute. We have the same result for f' and $\bowtie$, because f' is a pointwise application of f to the outer powerlist.

Theorem 1: $f', \bowtie$ commute.

Proof: Omitted.

Theorem 2:   For a scalar function f, $f' = f$.

Proof: Proof by structural induction is straightforward.   □

Theorem 3:   If f, g commute then so do f', g'.

Proof: By structural induction.   □

The following results about commutativity can be derived from Theorems 1, 2, and 3. In the following, m, n are natural numbers.

C1. For any f and $m > n$
$f^m, |^n$ commute , and
$f^m, \bowtie^n$ commute.

C2. For $m \neq n$,
$|^m, |^n$ commute , and
$\bowtie^m, \bowtie^n$ commute.

C3. For all m, n, $|^m, \bowtie^n$ commute.

C4. For any scalar function, f
$f, |^m$ commute , and
$f, \bowtie^n$ commute.

C1 follows by applying induction on Theorems 1 and 3 (and the fact that $f', |$ commute). C2 follows from C1; C3 from C1, Law L3 and Theorem 3; C4 from C1 and Theorem 2.

18.5.2 Deconstruction with derivatives

In this section we show that any powerlist that can be written as $p \mid^m q$ for some p, q can also be written as $u \bowtie^m v$ for some u, v and vice versa; this is analogous to Law L1, for dual deconstruction. Analogous to Law L2, we show that deconstruction using any of the derivatives is unique.

Theorem 4 (dual deconstruction): For any p, q and $m \geq 0$, if $p \mid^m q$ is defined then there exist u, v such that

$$u \bowtie^m v = p \mid^m q$$

Conversely, for any u, v and $m \geq 0$, if $u \bowtie^m v$ is defined then there exist some p, q such that

$$p \mid^m q = u \bowtie^m v \qquad \qquad \qquad \square$$

We do not prove this theorem; its proof is similar to the theorem given below.

Theorem 5 (unique deconstruction): Let $\oplus$ be $\mid$ or $\bowtie$. For any natural number m,

$$(p \oplus^m q = u \oplus^m v) \equiv (p = u \ \wedge \ q = v)$$

Proof: Proof is by induction on m.

$m = 0$:   The result follows from Law L2.
$m = n + 1$: Assume that $\oplus = |$. The proof is similar for $\oplus = \bowtie$. We prove
           the result by structural induction on p.

Base: $p = \langle a \rangle$, $q = \langle b \rangle$, $u = \langle c \rangle$, $v = \langle d \rangle$
       $\langle a \rangle \mid^{n+1} \langle b \rangle = \langle c \rangle \mid^{n+1} \langle d \rangle$
   $\equiv$ {definition of $\mid^{n+1}$}
       $\langle a \mid^n b \rangle = \langle c \mid^n d \rangle$
   $\equiv$ {Law L2}
       $a \mid^n b = c \mid^n d$
   $\equiv$ {induction on n}
       $(a = c) \wedge (b = d)$
   $\equiv$ {Law L2}
       $(\langle a \rangle = \langle c \rangle) \wedge (\langle b \rangle = \langle d \rangle)$

Induction: $p = p_0 \mid p_1$, $q = q_0 \mid q_1$, $u = u_0 \mid u_1$, $v = v_0 \mid v_1$
       $(p_0 \mid p_1) \mid^{n+1} (q_0 \mid q_1) = (u_0 \mid u_1) \mid^{n+1} (v_0 \mid v_1)$
   $\equiv$ {definition of $\mid^{n+1}$}
       $(p_0 \mid^{n+1} q_0) \mid (p_1 \mid^{n+1} q_1) = (u_0 \mid^{n+1} v_0) \mid (u_1 \mid^{n+1} v_1)$
   $\equiv$ {unique deconstruction using $\mid$}
       $(p_0 \mid^{n+1} q_0) = (u_0 \mid^{n+1} v_0) \wedge (p_1 \mid^{n+1} q_1) = (u_1 \mid^{n+1} v_1)$
   $\equiv$ {induction on the length of p_0, q_0, p_1, q_1}
       $(p_0 = u_0) \wedge (q_0 = v_0) \wedge (p_1 = u_1) \wedge (q_1 = v_1)$
   $\equiv$ {Law L2}
       $(p_0 \mid p_1) = (u_0 \mid u_1) \wedge (q_0 \mid q_1) = (v_0 \mid v_1)$ $\square$

Theorems 4 and 5 allow a richer variety of pattern matching in function definitions, as we did for matrix transposition. We may employ $\mid, \bowtie$ or any of their derivatives to construct a pattern over which a function can be defined.

18.6   Remarks

Powerlists seem to combine parallelism and recursion effectively. Functions defined in this manner may be easier to compile for executions on specific connection structures, or for implementations as hardware circuits. The forms of the equations – as in *FFT*, where both $\mid$ and $\bowtie$ are used – often suggest the connection structure on which a particular function may be efficiently implemented. Additionally, the effectiveness of the manipulation rules give us hope that certain aspects of circuit verifications could be made simpler by employing this formalism.

   The various combinations of linear and powerlists suggest a variety of ways in which sequential and parallel computing can be combined. We take linear list as the paradigm for sequential computing and powerlist for parallel computing. A powerlist consisting of linear lists as components admits of parallel processing in which each component is processed sequentially. A linear list consisting of powerlists suggests a computation strategy where the parallel computations are performed in sequence. Such is the case, for instance, with a matrix whose different columns have to be processed sequentially while each column may be processed in parallel; the matrix is best represented by a linear list of columns where each column is represented by a powerlist. Powerlists of powerlists allow multidimensional parallel computations and linear lists of linear lists suggest a hierarchy of sequential computations.

The lengths of the powerlists have been restricted to be of the form 2^n, $n \geq 0$, because we could, then, develop a simple theory. We can admit powerlists of arbitrary positive length by observing that a positive integer can be defined, recursively, as 1, or $2 \times m$, for some positive integer m, or $2 \times m + 1$ for some positive integer m. This suggests that a powerlist be defined as either a singleton list or the tie (or zip) of two powerlists with, optionally, an additional element. The generalization, however, requires reformulations of the deconstruction and commutativity laws (L1, L2, L3). Also, it, typically, introduces asymmetry in function definitions, in order to treat arguments of even and odd lengths, separately.

Acknowledgement: This paper has been enriched by comments and suggestions from several colleagues, in particular, Will Adams, Bob Boyer, Al Carruth (who suggested the term powerlist), Jorge Cobb, Edsger W. Dijkstra, Rajeev Joshi, Markus Kaltenbach, Jacob Kornerup, Scott Page, Vijaya Ramachandran, Alex Tomlinson, and Evelyn Tumlin. Ernie Cohen was singularly helpful at an early stage of this research. I am grateful to the Austin Tuesday Afternoon Club which read and commented on a draft of this manuscript. This material is based in part upon work supported by the Texas Advanced Research Program under Grant No. 003658–219 and by the National Science Foundation Award CCR–9111912.

References

[1] K. Batcher. Sorting networks and their applications. In *Proc. AFIPS Spring Joint Computer Conference*, volume 32, pages 307–314, 1968.

[2] R. S. Bird. Lectures on constructive functional programming. In Manfred Broy, editor, *Constructive Methods in Computing Science*, NATO ASI Series F: Computer and Systems Sciences, pages 151–216. Springer-Verlag, 1989.

[3] K. Mani Chandy and Jayadev Misra. *Parallel Program Design: A Foundation*. Addison Wesley, 1988.

[4] J. M. Cooley and J. W. Tukey. An algorithm for the machine calculation of complex Fourier series. *Math. Comp.*, 19:297–301, 1965.

[5] Richard M. Karp and Vijaya Ramachandran. Parallel algorithms for shared memory machines. In J. van Leeuwen, editor, *Handbook of Theoretical Computer Science*. Elsevier and the MIT Press, 1990.

[6] D. E. Knuth. *Sorting and Searching*, volume 3 of *The Art of Computer Programming*. Addison-Wesley, Reading, Massachusetts, 1973.

[7] F. Thompson Leighton. *Introduction to Parallel Algorithms and Architectures*. Morgan Kaufmann Publishers, San Mateo, California, 1992.

[8] John McCarthy, Paul W. Abrahams, Daniel J. Edwards, Timothy P. Hart, and Michael I. Levin. *LISP 1.5 Programmer's Manual*. MIT Press, 1962.

[9] Robin Milner, Mads Tofte, and Robert Harper. *The Definition of Standard ML*. MIT Press, 1990.

[10] J. Misra. Powerlist: A structure for parallel recursion. Report, The University of Texas at Austin, May 1993.

[11] David Turner. An overview of Miranda. *ACM SIGPLAN Notices*, 21:156–166, December 1986.

Chapter 19

The Cuppest Capjunctive Capping, and Galois

Carroll Morgan

Tony Hoare visited the University of Wollongong, in 1980, to give a series of lectures on CSP. It was as usual evident that a hazard facing overseas computer scientists at the time was the swarm of buzzing students that would follow their every step, settling instantly around the visitor whenever he chose to sit. (A similar problem continues to dog bushwalkers.) On one of those occasions a student asked "Which do you consider to be your most important contribution to computer science?"

What an awful question; but it evoked what I now know to have been a typical answer. Tony replied that he was glad to have been one of those who had advocated type checking in high-level programming languages.

The student was puzzled. Perhaps he had expected "quicksort" – but I'm convinced his surprise was simply that things hadn't *always* been that way.

Tony Hoare is also, among others, an advocate of algebraic reasoning in computer science, and that is the theme of this note. The target is a slightly out-of-the-way problem in the theory of imperative program development, which is to find the 'least-refined conjunctive refinement' of a given predicate transformer. We will look at an elegant solution involving algebraic reasoning over Galois connections, weakest pre- and post-specifications and relations. Some small liberties are taken with notation and terminology.

19.1 The Problem

Predicate transformers [4] can be regarded as total functions, to sets of (suitable) initial states from sets of (desired) final states; those that model executable imperative programs are monotonic and distribute intersection, at least. Taking I to be the set of possible initial states and F to be the set of possible final states, if p is such a transformer (to $\mathbb{P}\,I$ from $\mathbb{P}\,F$ thus) then by those terms we mean

- *Monotonic*: For F' and F'' subsets of F , whenever $F' \subseteq F''$ we have $p.F' \subseteq p.F''$ also. (We denote function application by an infix dot.)
- *Distribute intersection*: For F' and F'' as above, $p.(F' \cap F'') = p.F' \cap p.F''$.

Although the second property implies the first, more-recent work in the *refinement calculus* [2, 13, 10] has considered transformers that satisfy the first alone.

For example, consider an operator $\|$ on transformers (introduced as $\ddagger$ in [5]), defined

$$(p \parallel q).F' := p.F' \cup q.F' .$$

(We write $:=$ for "is defined to be equal to".) It is the dual of the more familiar $[\![$ operator used for nondeterministic choice [9, 14]: whereas the program $p [\![q$ behaves like p or like q , the program $p \parallel q$ could be said to behave like p *and* like q .

Alas, but not quite: for A a subset of F let the transformer **choose** A be defined

$$i \in (\textbf{choose}\, A).F' := A \subseteq F' ,$$

for i in I and F' any subset of F .

We see that **choose** A is insensitive to its initial state (because i does not appear on the right-hand side): it simply selects a final state nondeterministically from the set A .

Now consider the program **choose** $A \parallel$ **choose** B ; we have

$$\begin{aligned}
(\textbf{choose}\, A \parallel \textbf{choose}\, B).A &= I \\
(\textbf{choose}\, A \parallel \textbf{choose}\, B).B &= I \\
\text{yet}\quad (\textbf{choose}\, A \parallel \textbf{choose}\, B).(A \cap B) &\neq I \cap I ,
\end{aligned}$$

unless $A \subseteq B$ or $B \subseteq A$.

Thus **choose** $A \parallel$ **choose** B does not distribute intersection in general; in particular, it is not equal to **choose** $(A \cap B)$, which does.

Since 'real' programs *do* distribute intersection, it seems a shame that $p \parallel q$ does not. If we are using transformers to construct real programs from their specifications then, given some s as a starting point, ultimately we are interested only in intersection-distributing r that are at least s in the so-called *refinement* order:

$$s \sqsubseteq r := \text{for all subsets } F' \text{ of } F , s.F' \subseteq r.F' .$$

Thus if s does not distribute intersection, it is 'not refined enough' [3, 11]: the only *real* programs that refine **choose** $A \parallel$ **choose** B refine **choose** $(A \cap B)$ also. Why then aren't they equal?

The sections that follow concern the discovery of an operator $\Box$ on transformers such that $\Box.p$ is the least-refined transformer that both distributes intersection and refines p : one can think of it as the least step up the refinement order that regains intersection distribution.

Perhaps $\Box$ itself is not that interesting. But its discovery certainly is: the first encounter with $\Box$ yielded a putative definition, but over a period of months neither of us[1] managed to show that it had the properties necessary. More than a year later, after exposure to the notion of adjoints, I redefined the operator – and established its properties – in an evening [11].

Later still, using the mathematical tools below (all of them invented by other people), I found the operator in only a few minutes (Section 19.10). The real point of this paper, then, is just to introduce those tools.

19.2   Notation

Function application is denoted by infix dot, and associates to the left: thus $f.g.x$ means $f(g)$ applied to x , and $f.(g.x)$ means f applied to $g(x)$. Application binds most-tightly, in expressions.

Function spaces are written *to* left *from* right (backwards, in other words): thus a function in $B \leftarrow A$ delivers an element of B , given an element of A .

Relation spaces are written $B \leftrightarrow A$, as usual – but where we use them to model (nondeterministic) programs, we shall in agreement with functions think of them as acting to left from right: *to* final *from* initial.

Functional or relational composition is denoted by infix $\circ$.

We write $:=$ for "is defined here, and is equal to", with the newly-introduced symbol or concept on the left. (Using $=:$, we could put the new symbol in the right.) Similarly, when introducing a new symbol that is an *element* of, or a *subset* of some set, we use $:\in$ and $:\subseteq$ respectively. Thus in all three cases the colon : indicates the distinction between a definition, which introduces, and a statement, which describes.

Finally, the title. We shall be using at least three order symbols, $\leq$, $\subseteq$ and $\sqsubseteq$, and their associated meets and joins, and in many respects we will be treating them all in the same way. So we *pronounce* each of $x \leq y$, $x \subseteq y$ and $x \sqsubseteq y$ in the same way too: " x cups y "; similarly $x \geq y$, $x \supseteq y$ and $x \sqsupseteq y$ are pronounced " x caps y ". Conjunction, intersection and $\|$ are all "cap"; disjunction, union and $\|$ are all "cup". Distributing conjunction, intersection or $\|$ is "being capjunctive", and distributing disjunction, union or $\|$ is "being cupjunctive".

19.3   An Inventory of Tools

In finding the operator $\square$ we'll use three mathematical tools: the power transpose of relations, weakest pre- and post-specifications and Galois connections. We look first at the power transpose [8].

---

[1]Paul Gardiner and me; the definition was Paul's.

19.3.1   Power transpose

Given a relation $r :\in F \leftrightarrow I$, the *power transpose* of r is written $\Lambda.r$, and is defined for $i :\in I$

$$\Lambda.r.i := \{f :\in F \mid f\langle r\rangle i\} , \tag{19.1}$$

where $f\langle r\rangle i$ means " f is related by r to i ".

The power transpose Λ is itself a function, to $\mathbb{P}F \leftarrow I$ from $F \leftrightarrow I$, that for a given domain element collects into a single set all the range elements related to it. Thus, for example, $\Lambda.(\geq).0$ is just the set of all non-negative numbers. As shown later, power transposes have a number of nice properties. One of them (Lemma 19.9.1) is that composition with a total function distributes on the right: for total function f ,

$$\Lambda.r \circ f = \Lambda.(r \circ f) . \tag{19.2}$$

(Note the tighter binding of application on the left-hand side: we mean $(\Lambda.r) \circ f$ there.)

19.3.2   Weakest specifications

The second tool is the weakest pre- and post-specification [6]. Given two relations $l :\in F \leftrightarrow M$ and $r :\in M \leftrightarrow I$, their relational composition $l \circ r$ is an element of $F \leftrightarrow I$. When such relations model (possibly) nondeterministic programs, say to final states in F from initial states in I , the composition models "first do r , then do l ". The natural notion of refinement when relations are used that way is $\supseteq$, and thus one might well ask how to refine a given relation $s :\in F \leftrightarrow I$ into a relational composition $l \circ r$ of two others.

In particular, one might wish to solve for l in the inequation

$$s \supseteq l \circ r ,$$

given r and s . In turns out that, while there is not a unique solution in general, there is nevertheless a weakest (largest) one. We call it here the *weakest left-specification*, write it s/r , and define it by the equivalence

$$s/r \supseteq l \quad \text{iff} \quad s \supseteq l \circ r . \tag{19.3}$$

Similarly we can define the *weakest right-specification* by

$$l\backslash s \supseteq r \quad \text{iff} \quad s \supseteq l \circ r . \tag{19.4}$$

(For the curious, the set-theoretic definitions of / and \ are given by (19.23) and (19.24) in Section 19.11, allowing for example (19.5) below to be checked directly. Here however we will rely only on the defining properties.)

The two relational operators / and \ allow us effectively to 'divide' a given relation s (think of it as a specification), either on the left by l or on the right by r (think of them as proposed design steps), so making progress towards finding the other component. And again, there are many interesting properties of those operators. One is that, just as for the power transpose, composition on the right with a total function f distributes through weakest right-specification (Lemma 19.9.2):

$$(l \backslash s) \circ f = l \backslash (s \circ f) \ . \tag{19.5}$$

The third tool, more substantial than the others, is the Galois connection.

19.4   Galois Connections

A *Galois connection* between two partially-ordered sets $(A, \leq_A)$ and $(B, \leq_B)$ is a pair of functions between them, say

$$
\begin{aligned}
f &:\in \ B \leftarrow A \\
g &:\in \ A \leftarrow B \ ,
\end{aligned}
$$

with the property that, for all $a :\in A$ and $b :\in B$,

$$f.a \leq_B b \ \text{ iff } \ a \leq_A g.b \ . \tag{19.6}$$

(In fact (19.6) is just one of many equivalent formulations of the Galois property, and we shall see others below.) As in [1], we call f the *lower adjoint* and g the *upper adjoint*.

The simplicity of (19.6) nevertheless accounts for a number of properties of the functions f and g . For example,

Lemma 19.4.1 Lower adjoints distribute cup $\vee$. (We write 'pointy' $\vee$ for cup with respect to (pointy) $\leq$; and we are thus assuming further that A is a semilattice.)

Proof: Let f be the lower, and g the upper, adjoint of a Galois connection. Given $a, a' :\in A$, we have for arbitrary $b :\in B$

$$
\begin{array}{ll}
& f.(a \vee a') \leq b \\
\text{iff} & \text{``Galois property (19.6)''} \\
& a \vee a' \leq g.b \\
\text{iff} & \text{``definition } \vee \text{''} \\
& a \leq g.b \ \text{ and } \ a' \leq g.b \\
\text{iff} & \text{``Galois property (19.6)''} \\
& f.a \leq b \ \text{ and } \ f.a' \leq b \ .
\end{array}
$$

Thus $f.(a \vee a')$ satisfies the defining equation for $f.a \vee f.a'$, establishing both the existence of the latter and the desired equality with it.   ◁

Other properties include these:

Lemma 19.4.2 Upper adjoints distribute cap $\wedge$.   ◁

Lemma 19.4.3 Both adjoints are monotonic (they distribute cups $\leq$).   ◁

Lemma 19.4.4 For f and g as above, and for all $a :\in A$, we have $a \leq g.(f.a)$.

Proof: Immediate from (19.6), starting from $f.a \leq f.a$.   ◁

In Lemma 19.4.4 we can, by lifting cups $\leq$ pointwise to cups $\leq°$ at the function level, rewrite the inequality as

$$1 \leq° g \circ f ,$$

where 1 is the appropriate identity function (on A in this case). Similarly,

Lemma 19.4.5 For f and g as above, we have $f \circ g \leq° 1$.   ◁

In fact, Lemmas 19.4.3, 19.4.4 and 19.4.5 together offer an equivalent presentation of the Galois relationship, for

$$f.a \leq b$$
implies   "Lemma 19.4.3"
$$g.(f.a) \leq g.b$$
implies   "Lemma 19.4.4"
$$a \leq g.b$$

   etc.

Galois connections abound; for now, we consider two examples that we shall use later on. First, the weakest (left- or right-) specification is an adjoint. For the weakest right-specification in particular, think of "divide by l on the left" and "compose with l on the left" both as functions (written $(l\backslash)$ and $(l\circ)$ respectively), and rewrite (19.4) as

$$(l\backslash).s \supseteq r \quad \text{iff} \quad s \supseteq (l\circ).r .$$

That exposes $(l\backslash)$ as the lower- and $(l\circ)$ as the upper adjoint respectively of a Galois connection (in the 'reversed' order $\supseteq$), and the other properties above are available immediately.

The second example is the power transpose: it is an adjoint of a 'double' Galois connection whose other adjoint is $(\in\circ)$ (compose on the left with the relation $\in$). Given $r :\in F \leftrightarrow I$ and $f :\in \mathbb{P}F \leftarrow I$, we have

$$\Lambda.r \subseteq° f \quad \text{iff} \quad r \subseteq \in \circ f \tag{19.7}$$
$$\Lambda.r \supseteq° f \quad \text{iff} \quad r \supseteq \in \circ f . \tag{19.8}$$

Note that (19.7) and (19.8) together establish an (order) isomorphism between $F \leftrightarrow I$ and $\mathbb{P}F \leftarrow I$:

$$\Lambda.r = f \quad \text{iff} \quad r = \in \circ f . \tag{19.9}$$

To show (19.7), we argue

	$\Lambda.r \subseteq^{\circ} f$
iff	"definition of $\subseteq^{\circ}$ "
	$(\forall i :\in I \cdot \Lambda.r.i \subseteq f.i)$
iff	"Definition 19.1 of Λ "
	$(\forall i :\in I \cdot \{x :\in F \mid x\langle r\rangle i\} \subseteq f.i)$
iff	"set theory"
	$(\forall i :\in I; x :\in F \cdot x\langle r\rangle i \Rightarrow x \in f.i)$
iff	"taking f as a relation"
	$(\forall i :\in I; x :\in F \cdot x\langle r\rangle i \Rightarrow x\langle \in \circ f\rangle i)$
iff	"set theory"
	$r \subseteq \in \circ f$.

In fact we could have taken (19.7) to define Λ , for the above argument shows (19.1) to be derivable from it. Either way, for (19.8) one simply reverses the inequalities in the argument.

Now we leave our investigation of Galois connections, temporarily, and return to the original problem. There we will see that the key turns out to be a Galois connection between relations and predicate transformers.

19.5 Embedding Relations Within Predicate Transformers

Both predicate transformers $\mathbb{P} I \leftarrow \mathbb{P} F$ and relations $F \leftrightarrow I$ model programs that begin in an initial state drawn from I and finish in a final state drawn from F .

In fact $\mathbb{P} I \leftarrow \mathbb{P} F$, the predicate transformers, are strictly more general. For each relation $r :\in F \leftrightarrow I$ there can be found a corresponding predicate transformer as follows: for all $F' :\subseteq F$, the predicate transformer p corresponding to r is defined

$$ p.F' := \{i :\in I \mid (\forall f :\in F \cdot f\langle r\rangle i \Rightarrow f \in F')\} \ . $$

If we give $F \leftrightarrow I$ the name $\mathcal{R}$ (for *relation*) and $\mathbb{P} I \leftarrow \mathbb{P} F$ the name $\mathcal{T}$ (for *transformer*), then the above embedding – call it $\overline{A}$ – goes to $\mathcal{T}$ from $\mathcal{R}$, and is illustrated in Fig. 19.1 for two three-element state spaces.

One reason for our interest in the embedding $\overline{A}$ is that embedded relations (predicate transformers of the form $\overline{A}.r$ for some r) distribute cap: they are *capjunctive*[2]. (That will be obvious at (19.16), somewhat later.) Thus, in looking for a capjunctive refinement of a given predicate transformer p , we might look at relations r that satisfy $p \sqsubseteq \overline{A}.r$.

The second reason – further encouragement – is that *every* capjunctive predicate transformer p is the embedding of some relation. (That will be obvious at (19.26), later still.) Those two facts together allow us to reformulate our problem in the following way:

---

[2] By that we mean *universally* capjunctive, distributing all caps, even empty and infinite.

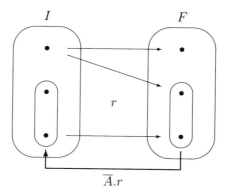

Figure 19.1 The predicate transformer $\overline{A}.r$ corresponding to the relation r.

Find a function $\square :\in \mathcal{T} \leftarrow \mathcal{T}$ such that for all $p :\in \mathcal{T}$ and $r :\in \mathcal{R}$ we have

$$\square.p \text{ is capjunctive} \tag{19.10}$$
$$\text{and} \quad p \sqsubseteq \overline{A}.r \text{ iff } \square.p \sqsubseteq \overline{A}.r . \tag{19.11}$$

That reformulation is the key to the solution.

Property (19.11) states clearly that $\square.p$ cups all capjunctive cappings of p . And here is the reason that (19.10) and (19.11) ensure that $\square.p$ itself caps p :

$$\square.p \text{ is capjunctive}$$
implies "(19.26) referred to above"
$$\square.p \text{ is } \overline{A}.r \text{ for some } r$$
implies "(19.11)"
$$p \sqsubseteq \square.p \text{ iff } \square.p \sqsubseteq \square.p$$
implies $p \sqsubseteq \square.p$.

Now Property (19.11) looks familiar, but is not quite Galois – or is it?

19.6   The Galois-connection Connection

One of the consequences of our Galois definitions is the following, which instantiates to (19.11) above:

Lemma 19.6.1 (Continuing our established naming conventions and types.) We have

$$a \leq g.b \text{ iff } (g \circ f).a \leq g.b .$$

Proof:

	$a \le g.b$
iff	"Galois property (19.6)"
	$f.a \le b$
implies	"Lemma 19.4.3"
	$g.(f.a) \le g.b$
implies	"Lemma 19.4.4"
	$a \le g.b$.

$\triangleleft$

With (19.11) in mind, we instantiate Lemma 19.6.1 to

$$p \sqsubseteq \overline{A}.r \ \text{ iff } \ (\overline{A} \circ \underline{A}).p \sqsubseteq \overline{A}.r \ ,$$

supposing as we do so that we can find a lower adjoint $\underline{A}$ to the upper adjoint $\overline{A}$. Specifically, if

$$\underline{A} :\in \ \mathcal{R} \leftarrow \mathcal{T}$$
$$\overline{A} :\in \ \mathcal{T} \leftarrow \mathcal{R}$$

form a Galois connection, then $\square$ will be given by the simple composition

$$\overline{A} \circ \underline{A} \ . \tag{19.12}$$

That $\square.p$ is capjunctive (our first requirement, at (19.10) above) now follows immediately from its being an $\overline{A}$-image.

Drawing all the above together, we have now reduced our problem simply to finding an $\underline{A}$ that is lower-adjoint to $\overline{A}$. But to *calculate* $\underline{A}$ we shall need a nice formulation of $\overline{A}$ itself. In fact $\overline{A}.r$ will turn out to act like a weakest precondition; since we are using relations, however, we first look at the relationally-simpler notion of strongest postcondition.

19.7 Strongest Postconditions

Perhaps the most straightforward link between relations and predicate transformers is the relational image: given $r :\in F \leftrightarrow I$, define $E.r$ to be the function to F from I that maps subsets of I to their image under r . Thus for $I' :\subseteq I$

$$E.r.I' := \{f :\in F \mid (\exists i :\in I' \cdot f \langle r \rangle i)\} \ , \tag{19.13}$$

and E itself is an element of $(\mathbb{P} F \leftarrow \mathbb{P} I) \leftarrow (F \leftrightarrow I)$. In fact $E.r.I'$ can be seen as the 'strongest postcondition' of 'program' r with respect to 'precondition' I' : it is the smallest set of final states within which the 'result' of r is guaranteed to lie.

For calculation, however, there are more convenient formulations of E than (19.13). For example, we have

$$E.r.I'$$
$$= \quad \text{"Definition (19.13) of } E \text{ "}$$
$$\{f :\in F \mid (\exists i :\in I' \cdot f\langle r\rangle i)\}$$
$$= \quad \text{"logic"}$$
$$\{f :\in F \mid (\exists i \cdot f\langle r\rangle i \wedge i \in I')\}$$
$$= \quad \text{"relational composition"}$$
$$\{f :\in F \mid f\langle r \circ \in\rangle I'\}$$
$$= \quad \text{"Definition (19.1) of power transpose"}$$
$$\Lambda.(r \circ \in).I'$$

and, since I' was arbitrary, we conclude that

$$E.r = \Lambda.(r \circ \in) . \tag{19.14}$$

We use (19.14) henceforth, and turn now to weakest preconditions.

19.8   Weakest Preconditions

Given a set of initial states $I' :\subseteq I$, a set of final states $F' :\subseteq F$ and a relational program r , there are two popular ways of expressing the notion " r is correct with respect to precondition I' and postcondition F' ". One is

The strongest postcondition of r with respect to I' is contained in F' ,

and the other is

I' is contained in the weakest precondition of r with respect to F' .

Thus we have the equivalence

$$E.r.I' \subseteq F' \text{ iff } I' \subseteq \overline{A}.r.F' , \tag{19.15}$$

showing clearly that $E.r$ and $\overline{A}.r$ are Galois-connected, with $E.r$ the lower- and $\overline{A}.r$ the upper adjoint. The latter gives us immediately that

$$\overline{A}.r \text{ is capjunctive,} \tag{19.16}$$

which deals with the first of our undischarged requirements for approaching the problem via (19.10) and (19.11). (The second, still to come at (19.26), was that *every* capjunctive predicate transformer is expressible that way.)

We can use the Galois connection to calculate $\overline{A}$ from E ; in particular, we lift[3] (19.15) to

$$E.r \circ i \subseteq^\circ f \text{ iff } i \subseteq^\circ \overline{A}.r \circ f , \tag{19.17}$$

where i and f are *functions* to I and F respectively, from some arbitrary set. Then to calculate $\overline{A}.r$, we start with the left-hand side of (19.17) above:

---

[3]This lifting and the immediately-following calculation are due to Chritiene Aarts.

$$E.r \circ i \subseteq^\circ f$$
iff   "(19.14)"
$$\Lambda.(r \circ \in) \circ i \subseteq^\circ f$$
iff   "(19.2)"
$$\Lambda.(r \circ \in \circ i) \subseteq^\circ f$$
iff   "Galois connection (19.7)"
$$r \circ \in \circ i \subseteq \in \circ f$$
iff   "weakest right-specification (19.4)"
$$\in \circ i \subseteq r \backslash (\in \circ f)$$
iff   "Galois connection (19.8)"
$$i \subseteq^\circ \Lambda.(r \backslash (\in \circ f))$$
iff   "(19.2) and (19.5)"
$$i \subseteq^\circ \Lambda.(r \backslash \in) \circ f \ ,$$

thus, given the right-hand side of (19.17), establishing that

$$\overline{A}.r := \Lambda.(r \backslash \in) \tag{19.18}$$

is the definition we are looking for.

Along the way, however, we appealed to two properties concerning distribution of composition with total functions. We justify them in the next section.

19.9   Total Functions

Functions, say to B from A , are relations $B \leftrightarrow A$ of a special kind: for each value $a :\in A$ there is at most one corresponding value $b :\in B$. If a function is *total* then for each value $a :\in A$ there is exactly one corresponding value $b :\in B$.

For our first deferred lemma we need very little in the way of specific properties of functions. We have

Lemma 19.9.1 For appropriately-typed relation r and total function f ,

$$\Lambda.r \circ f = \Lambda.(r \circ f) \ .$$

(That was introduced as Property (19.2) of Λ .)

Proof: We use the special properties of f only indirectly, exploiting the isomorphism (19.9) between relations and total functions:

$$\Lambda.r \circ f$$
=   "$\Lambda.r \circ f$ a total function; isomorphism (19.9)"
$$\Lambda.(\in \circ \Lambda.r \circ f)$$
=   "isomorphism (19.9)"
$$\Lambda.(r \circ f) \ .$$

$\triangleleft$

Our second lemma distributes composition with a total function into a weakest right-specification, and for that we need more-specific properties of functions and their converses (also called inverses).

A function is possibly 'one from many' but certainly is not 'many from one'. The *converse* of a function is the relation that takes the result of the function back to the possible arguments, and it has precisely the converse properties – it's possibly 'many from one' but certainly is not 'one from many':

> For relation $r :\in B \leftrightarrow A$, the converse relation $\check{r}$ is an element of $A \leftrightarrow B$ and is defined
>
> $$a\langle \check{r} \rangle b := b\langle r \rangle a .$$
>
> For function $f :\in B \leftarrow A$, the converse *relation* $\check{f}$ is an element of $A \leftrightarrow B$ and is defined
>
> $$a\langle \check{f} \rangle b := b = f.a .$$

Total functions and their converses together satisfy the following two properties, where 1 is the identity relation: for any total function f ,

$$1 \subseteq \check{f} \circ f \tag{19.19}$$
$$f \circ \check{f} \subseteq 1 . \tag{19.20}$$

That looks sufficiently like Lemmas 19.4.4 and 19.4.5 to suggest yet another Galois connection. It is in fact between these two functions: "compose with f " (the upper adjoint); and "compose with $\check{f}$ " (the lower adjoint). Thus we have from (19.6), choosing composition on the right in particular,

$$l \circ \check{f} \subseteq r \text{ iff } l \subseteq r \circ f , \tag{19.21}$$

for suitably-typed relations l and r . (Actually (19.19) for example would be better written $1 \subseteq^{\circ} (\circ f) \circ (\circ \check{f})$ to make the connection clear.)

Now we return to Property (19.5), of weakest right-specifications:

Lemma 19.9.2 For any relations s and l and total function f of appropriate types,

$$(l \backslash s) \circ f = l \backslash (s \circ f) .$$

Proof: For arbitrary relation r ,

$$r \subseteq (l \backslash s) \circ f$$
iff   "(19.21)"
$$r \circ \check{f} \subseteq l \backslash s$$
iff   "weakest right-specification (19.4)"
$$l \circ r \circ \check{f} \subseteq s$$
iff   "(19.21)"
$$l \circ r \subseteq s \circ f$$
iff   "weakest right-specification (19.4)"
$$r \subseteq l \backslash (s \circ f) .$$

◁

19.10   Calculating □ – finally

One could be forgiven for having forgotten, by now, what originally we wanted to calculate. It was □ , which we discovered could be given by $\overline{A} \circ \underline{A}$ (19.12). We began with a set-theoretic formulation of strongest postcondition $E.r$ (19.13), from which immediately we calculated a more compact formulation (19.14). From that, via a Galois connection, we arrived at a definition (19.18) of $\overline{A}.r$.

Galois connections will now lead us from $\overline{A}$ directly to $\underline{A}$. We merely instantiate (19.6) yet again,

$$\underline{A}.p \supseteq r \ \text{ iff } \ p \sqsubseteq \overline{A}.r \ ,$$

and calculate

$$
\begin{array}{ll}
& p \sqsubseteq \overline{A}.r \\
\text{iff} & \text{“Definition (19.18) of } \overline{A} \text{ ”} \\
& p \sqsubseteq \Lambda.(r \backslash \in) \\
\text{iff} & \text{“ } (\sqsubseteq) = (\subseteq^{\circ}) \text{ ”} \\
& p \subseteq^{\circ} \Lambda.(r \backslash \in) \\
\text{iff} & \text{“Galois connection (19.8)”} \\
& \in \circ p \subseteq r \backslash \in \\
\text{iff} & \text{“weakest right-specification (19.4)”} \\
& r \circ \in \circ p \subseteq \in \\
\text{iff} & \text{“weakest left-specification (19.3)”} \\
& r \subseteq \in / (\in \circ p) \ .
\end{array}
$$

Thus we have immediately that we should define

$$\underline{A}.p := \in / (\in \circ p) \ ,$$

whence □ is given to us by (19.12):

$$\square.p := \Lambda.((\in / (\in \circ p)) \backslash \in) \ . \tag{19.22}$$

And that's the end of the story.

19.11   Epilogue

Well, almost. Masochists would write $\square = \Lambda \circ (\backslash \in) \circ (\in /) \circ (\in \circ)$, but (19.22) can be put into a more familiar form by appealing to the set-theoretic definitions of the operators concerned: the power transpose Λ , and the weakest specifications $/$ and $\backslash$. The first we have already at (19.1); for the weakest left-specification, we calculate

$$(\forall f, m \cdot f\langle l\rangle m \Rightarrow f\langle s/r\rangle m)$$
iff "set theory"
$$l \subseteq s/r$$
iff "weakest left-specification (19.3)"
$$l \circ r \subseteq s$$
iff "set theory"
$$(\forall f, i \cdot f\langle l \circ r\rangle i \Rightarrow f\langle s\rangle i)$$
iff "relational composition"
$$(\forall f, i \cdot (\exists m \cdot f\langle l\rangle m \wedge m\langle r\rangle i) \Rightarrow f\langle s\rangle i)$$
iff "predicate calculus"
$$(\forall f, m \cdot f\langle l\rangle m \Rightarrow (\forall i \cdot m\langle r\rangle i \Rightarrow f\langle s\rangle i)) \ .$$

Since l is arbitrary, we define

$$f\langle s/r\rangle m := (\forall i \cdot m\langle r\rangle i \Rightarrow f\langle s\rangle i) \ . \tag{19.23}$$

Notice that the reasoning above not only gives us the definition (19.23) that we were looking for, but establishes as well that it has the required property (19.3). Similarly we can determine for the weakest right-specification

$$m\langle l\backslash s\rangle i := (\forall f \cdot f\langle l\rangle m \Rightarrow f\langle s\rangle i) \ . \tag{19.24}$$

With those, some further routine predicate calculation then reveals the following, when $\Box.p$ is applied to a particular set F' of states:

$$\Box.p.F' = (\bigcap f :\in F \mid f \notin F' \cdot p.\bar{f}) \ , \tag{19.25}$$

where we write $\bar{f}$ for the set $\{f' :\in F \mid f' \neq f\}$. (Recall we are considering only monotonic transformers.)

Formulation (19.25) is useful not only for working out $\Box.p$ in practical cases, but meets our last reservation outstanding about approaching $\Box$ via (19.10) and (19.11):

> every (universally) capjunctive p is the $\overline{A}$-image of some r . $\tag{19.26}$

That is because (19.25) shows $\Box$ to act as the identity on capjunctive p :

$$\Box.p.F'$$
= "(19.25)"
$$(\bigcap f :\in F \mid f \notin F' \cdot p.\bar{f})$$
= "assuming p capjunctive"
$$p.(\bigcap f :\in F \mid f \notin F' \cdot \bar{f})$$
= "set theory"
$$p.F' \ .$$

That, in turn, means that every capjunctive p is the $\overline{A}$-image of $\underline{A}.p$, as required.

Finally, we give two examples of $\Box$ in specific cases. Note for the first that **abort** is not capjunctive, because it does not distribute the empty capjunction F . Thus, for any $F' :\subseteq F$, we have

$$i \in \square.\textbf{abort}.F'$$
iff $\quad i \in (\bigcap f :\in F \mid f \notin F' \cdot \textbf{abort}.\bar{f})$
iff $\quad (\forall f :\in F \cdot f \notin F' \Rightarrow i \in \{\})$
iff $\quad F \subseteq F'$
iff $\quad i \in (\textbf{choose}\,F).F'$.

Hence $\square.\textbf{abort}$ is $\textbf{choose}\,F$, which is unpredictable except that it terminates. For our other example, we return to $\textbf{choose}\,A \parallel \textbf{choose}\,B$:

$$i \in \square.(\textbf{choose}\,A \parallel \textbf{choose}\,B).F'$$
iff $\quad i \in (\bigcap f :\in F \mid f \notin F' \cdot (\textbf{choose}\,A \parallel \textbf{choose}\,B).\bar{f})$
iff $\quad (\forall f :\in F \cdot f \notin F' \Rightarrow f \notin A \vee f \notin B)$
iff $\quad A \cap B \subseteq F'$.

Thus $\square.(\textbf{choose}\,A \parallel \textbf{choose}\,B)$ is $\textbf{choose}\,(A \cap B)$, after all.

Acknowledgements

I'm grateful for the attentions of IFIP 2.1, *ofac*, and the second Australian Refinement Workshop, and for the extensive suggestions of Chritiene Aarts, whose more-elegant calculations in Section 19.8 and Lemma 19.9.2 appear in place of my own.

The work of Hoare and He, Oege de Moor, and the organisers and lecturers of the International Summer Schools on Constructive Algorithmics [7] form collectively the inspiration for most of what is here.

References

[1] C. Aarts, R. Backhouse, P. Hoogendijk, E. Voermans, and J. van der Woude. A relational theory of datatypes, December 1992. An *FTP* document, available at ftp.win.tue.nl in /pub/math.prog.construction/book.dvi.Z.

[2] R.-J.R. Back. A calculus of refinements for program derivations. *Acta Informatica*, 25:593–624, 1988.

[3] A. Bijlsma, P.A. Matthews, and J.G. Wiltink. A sharp proof rule for procedures in wp semantics. *Acta Informatica*, 26:409–419, 1989.

[4] E.W. Dijkstra. *A Discipline of Programming*. Prentice-Hall, Englewood Cliffs, 1976.

[5] P.H.B. Gardiner and C.C. Morgan. Data refinement of predicate transformers. *Theoretical Computer Science*, 87:143–162, 1991. Reprinted in [12].

[6] C.A.R. Hoare and J.F. He. The weakest prespecification. *Fundamenta Informaticae*, IX:51–84, 1986.

[7] International summer schools on constructive algorithmics. For information, contact prof. dr. S.D. Swierstra, Vakgroep Informatica, Rijksuniversiteit Utrecht, Padualaan 14, 3584 CH Utrecht, The Netherlands.

[8] O. de Moor. *Categories, Relations and Dynamic Programming*. DPhil thesis, Programming Research Group, Oxford University, 1992.

[9] C.C. Morgan. The specification statement. *ACM Transactions on Programming Languages and Systems*, 10(3), July 1988. Reprinted in [12].

[10] C.C. Morgan. *Programming from Specifications*. Prentice-Hall, 1990.

[11] C.C. Morgan. Sharpness without procedures. Talk given at Technische Universiteit Eindhoven, September 1990.

[12] C.C. Morgan and T.N. Vickers, editors. *On the Refinement Calculus*. FACIT Series in Computer Science. Springer, 1993. To appear.

[13] J.M. Morris. Programs from specifications. In E.W. Dijkstra, editor, *Formal Development of Programs and Proofs*. Addison-Wesley, 1989.

[14] G. Nelson. A generalization of Dijkstra's calculus. *ACM Transactions on Programming Languages and Systems*, 11(4):517–561, October 1989.

Chapter 20

The Advantages of Free Choice: a symmetric and fully distributed solution for the dining philosophers problem

Michael O. Rabin and Daniel Lehmann

Dedicated to Tony Hoare with admiration

20.1 Introduction

Since randomized algorithms have been introduced in [12] and [13], they have been used in different fields to provide algorithms that are more efficient than the deterministic algorithms known to solve the same problem. In [14] and [15], the first author has used randomization to solve some questions of concurrency control and interprocess cooperation in distributed systems. We present here an application of this idea to the dining philosophers problem and exhibit a randomized solution for it which guarantees, with probability one, that every hungry philosopher eventually gets to eat. We feel that this application is interesting in many ways.

Concurrent programming seems to be a field particularly well suited to probabilistic algorithms. The idea of building an operating system out of probabilistic processes and proving that it performs correctly with a very high probability, under all possible external circumstances, is an attractive alternative to the common practice of writing operating systems that perform correctly only under 'most' external circumstances.

For the first time, it provides an example of a problem that can be solved by probabilistic processes but cannot be solved by deterministic processes.

As we shall see later, our system of probabilistic processes may be proved to behave correctly with probability one and not just with a probability that is as close to one as one likes.

Our analysis of the interplay between probabilistic ideas and the area of large systems of simple processes suggests an application to the theory of biological systems where all three features of randomness, large number of components and simplicity of those components appear.

It is only recently that efforts have been made to devise really distributed solutions to the dining philosophers problem and the protocols presented here are one of the first really distributed solutions to the dining philosophers problem (N. Francez and M. Rodeh [4] have, concurrently, also proposed such a solution; their solution is written in the language CSP [6] and does not use random draws). We feel that our protocols provide an elegant solution to the problem and that the ideas presented here should be useful to solve other problems in the area of concurrency control and cooperation between asynchronous processes.

The present paper is the full version, including proofs, of the extended abstract [10]. Since the appearance of [10] and the papers cited there, many authors in well over a hundred papers have used the method of randomization to solve problems dealing with synchronization, coordination and agreement in distributed computing. We did not attempt to collect this extensive bibliography in the present paper.

20.2   The Dining Philosophers Problem

In [3] E. Dijkstra proposed a concurrent programming exercise that has, since then, been considered classical, the dining philosophers problem. It is interesting, not so much on account of its practical importance, but because it is a paradigm for a large class of concurrency control problems.

The reader may find in [3] an entertaining description of the dilemma of a group of spaghetti eating philosophers and much background information. The system of interest comprises n processes (the philosophers, P_1 to P_n, indexed by the elements of the cyclic group of order n) and n resources (the chopsticks, C_1 to C_n, indexed in the same way). We shall say that P_{k+1} is seated next and to the right of P_k and that C_{k+1} is located between P_k and P_{k+1}. Remember that $n + 1 = 1$.

A philosopher's behaviour may be described by a program looping indefinitely over the sequential composition of a *thinking* section, a *trying* section, an *eating* section and an *exiting* section (while true do think; try; eat; exit od). The trying and exiting sections are for us to specify and they may use variables that are not accessible to the thinking and eating sections. Even though we are free to specify the protocols for the trying and exiting sections, we have no control over or knowledge of the timing of the execution of those sections. The thinking and eating sections are out of our control. We may assume that, if a philosopher enters his eating section, he will eventually leave it and move to the first statement of the exiting section. We may not assume that, if a philosopher enters his thinking section, he will eventually leave it. In other words, the eating section always terminates, but the thinking section does not always terminate. A philosopher who entered his thinking section never to leave it, is said to have *died.*

The protocols for the trying and exiting sections must ensure that, while he is in his eating section, P_k has exclusive access to C_k and C_{k+1} and that, with varying degrees of strength, philosophers wishing to do so will be able to eat. Thus, we will be talking, not of one, but of several problems and solutions.

20.3   Constraints and Properties of the Solution

We shall now describe the class of solutions we are willing to consider. The constraints we are imposing upon the solutions will be justified both by aesthetic and practical considerations.

Our first constraint is that we are interested only in truly distributed systems, i.e., systems in which there is no central memory, or central process, every other process may have access to. We are considering only systems in which there are no active agents other than the philosophers. The philosophers do not communicate directly with each other and chopsticks are represented by passive cells (memories) that may be accessed only by the two adjacent philosophers (C_i may be accessed only by P_i and P_{i-1}). N. Francez and M. Rodeh have considered this constraint and remarked that none of the solutions published so far (e.g., [2]–[3], [5]–[7], [8]) satisfied this criterion. Indeed they all use some kind of central scheduler that regulates the meals of the philosophers. Francez and Rodeh [4] propose a solution that is truly distributed, in the language CSP [6].

The reason for such a constraint is that we are thinking of the dining philosophers problem as an exercise in distributed programming. The main challenge, therefore, arises for systems of a very large number of processes, in which case it would not be reasonable to assume that they all have access to the same memory or that they may all communicate with the same process. Thus, we assume that every pair of adjacent philosophers shares a variable. This shared variable may take only a finite (independent of the number of philosophers present around the table) number of different values. By use of this shared variable, two adjacent philosophers try to agree on the use of their shared chopstick. Other than those variables shared by neighbours, the protocols make use only of variables that are strictly private to each philosopher's protocol.

A second constraint which we impose, is that all philosophers be identical. This is a natural assumption for a very large number of simple philosophers, so simple, in fact, that they could not even remember an identification number, personal to each one of them (assume we have more than n philosophers, each of whom can hold in memory fewer than $\log n$ bits). It follows that P_k cannot be aware that his index is k. We also restrict our attention to initial configurations that are symmetric: we assume that, in the beginning, all philosophers are in the same state and all shared variables hold the same value. Were it not for such an assumption, it would be easy to code different protocols for the different philosophers in the initial values of the shared variables (or the initial states of the different philosophers); protocols similar to those described in Section 6 would also do the job if the initial values of the shared variables are favourable. In short, we are interested in large distributed systems of simple identical processes.

Our goal is to find protocols that satisfy our two constraints and allow the philosophers to eat. If every hungry philosopher (i.e., a philosopher who has entered his trying section) eventually gets to eat, then we shall say the system is *lockout-free*. We shall exhibit such a system. But as a first step, we will build a system that enjoys only a weaker non-starvation property: if at any time, there is a hungry philosopher, say Plato, then at some later time some philosopher (not necessarily Plato) will eat. A system that enjoys this property will be said to be *deadlock-free*.

A word on our assumptions concerning the underlying computation model and the synchronization of the different processes. We are assuming that every process (philosopher) proceeds at his own pace, atomic operation after atomic operation. The exact definition of the atomic operations that deal with variables that are private to each philosopher is of no importance here. The only available atomic operations to deal with the shared variables is a '*test and set*' operation, in which a philosopher, in one indivisible step, reads the current value of the variable, and assigns it a new value, which is a function of the old value and the philosopher's current internal state (of which there is only a fixed, independent of n, number). Since the status of C_i will be represented by the value of a variable shared by P_{i-1} and P_i, a philosopher may, in one move and without risk of being disturbed by or of disturbing a neighbour, check that a chopstick is down on the table and pick it up. In a run of the system, the atomic operations performed by different philosophers are interleaved in a totally arbitrary way. We may not, therefore, exclude the possibility of an adversary scheduler who would, for example, do his best to keep Plato from eating, by activating him (i.e., letting him perform an atomic operation) only when one of his neighbours is eating. We allow this adversary scheduler to make use of all information about the system, including the result of *past* random draws performed by processes, the values of shared variables and the value of the private variables of each philosopher. This is an extremely severe assumption, which ensures that the protocols presented here have very strong correctness properties. In other works ([4] and [14]), in different situations, less severe assumptions have been made. This adversary scheduler, though, is not allowed to use information about the results of *future* random draws. We allow for the possibility of an *adversary* scheduler, since we assume that the interactions we describe between philosophers are only the visible part of an iceberg of complex relations about which we do not know and that we are not willing to study. We are to assume that the worst is certain to happen, which is a very sound principle of system design.

20.4   Deterministic Solutions

A simple argument will now show there is no solution to the problem, satisfying the constraints mentioned above, in which the philosophers are deterministic processes. After the completion of a preliminary version of this paper, the authors became aware that this statement may be found in [11], together with references to unpublished works on the subject of distributed control.

Theorem 1. *There is no deterministic, deadlock-free, truly distributed and symmetric solution to the dining philosophers problem.*

Proof. Suppose there is a deterministic, truly distributed and symmetric solution. We shall define a scheduler that will allow no philosopher to eat, showing in this manner that no such solution may be deadlock-free. The scheduler will activate each philosopher, for a single atomic operation, in the order 1 to n, then repeat another similar round in the course of which the philosophers 1 to n are activated in turn, and so on. The claim is that, if the configuration is symmetric with respect to all philosophers at the beginning of a round, then the configuration will again be symmetric at the end of the round.

Since the philosophers are deterministic processes, the next operation of each philosopher is completely determined by his present internal state and the value of the variable he is about to test and set. Consider the start of a round of atomic operations, when, by assumption, all processes and variables are in the same state. There are three cases to consider: every philosopher is, at the beginning of the round, in a state in which his next atomic operation is some internal operation not involving the variables he shares with his neighbours, every philosopher is in a state in which his next atomic operation involves the variable he shares with his right neighbour, or every philosopher is in a state in which his next atomic operation involves the variable he shares with his left neighbour. Recall that an atomic operation by a processor may address at most one shared variable. In the first case, since all philosophers start the round in the same state, they will, independently of one another, perform the same internal atomic operation and the configuration will be again symmetric at the end of the round. In the other two cases, since the values of all the shared variables are the same at the start of the round, and since there is a one-to-one correspondence between philosophers and the variable they are about to test and set, the philosophers will not interfere with one another and will perform the same atomic operation on that variable. Since every shared variable was acted upon, at the end of the round the configuration will again be symmetric. We may therefore conclude that, if the initial configuration is symmetric, then the scheduler described above will leave a symmetric configuration at the end of each round. An important role in this argument is played by the symmetry assumption that the philosophers' Left and Right sides are coherent around the table.

Assume, now, that some philosopher succeeds in picking up his second chopstick, while he still has the first one in hand. At the end of this atomic operation he will have two chopsticks in his hands. By symmetry then, at the end of the round, each philosopher would have two chopsticks in his hands and we have a contradiction. We have shown that the scheduler described above will cause a deadlock, whatever deterministic protocols are chosen for the philosophers. Thus no deterministic, truly distributed and symmetric solution may be deadlock-free. Q.E.D.

The deterministic solution proposed by Francez and Rodeh in [4] seems to contradict the claim we just made. The solution to this apparent contradiction is that there is no truly distributed deterministic implementation of CSP. L. Lamport [9] seems to have been the first to notice this fact, and Theorem 1 above, together with the CSP protocols proposed in [4], constitutes a formal proof of this fact. Thus any truly distributed implementation of CSP must be probabilistic and, in such an implementation, even terminating programs (for the semantics of CSP) terminate only with probability one. Such a probabilistic implementation of CSP is proposed in [4].

After having shown the impossibility of a deterministic solution satisfying our constraints, let us proceed to give a solution using probabilistic processes. We shall first formulate a solution which is deadlock-free and later upgrade it to a lockout-free solution.

20.5   The Free Philosopher's Algorithm

The gist of our idea is the following: since the problem with any deterministic solution is the symmetry that could keep recurring, we need a way to break this symmetry. We shall incorporate random choices into the protocols of the individual philosophers, letting the laws of probability ensure that, with probability one, the symmetry will be broken. Informally, when a philosopher becomes hungry he will randomly draw a side (Right or Left) and try first to pick up the corresponding chopstick. He will wait until he is able to pick up this first chopstick and then turn to the other side and look for his second chopstick. At this point, if his second chopstick is not available he will not wait for it but place back on the table the chopstick he has in hand and draw again a random side. If his second chopstick is available, then he will pick it up and eat.

A formal definition of this behaviour, in terms of a flowchart, may be found in Fig. 20.1. The boxes of the flowchart have been labeled for identification purposes only. The function R is the reflection function on {Right, Left}. The fork below box THINK has to be understood as a non-deterministic choice: after thinking a philosopher may either become hungry and move to box CHOOSE or die (i.e., enter an infinite loop). The sub-diagram consisting of boxes CHOOSE, FIRST and SECOND is our protocol for the trying section and boxes PUT1 and PUT2 our exit section. The reader should note that the operations of checking whether the $R(s)$ chopstick is available (box SECOND) and of releasing the first chopstick (box RELEASE) are different atomic operations and could not be implemented as a single atomic operation, since they deal with different chopsticks. An arbitrary amount of time may therefore elapse between the moment a philosopher finds in box SECOND that his second chopstick is in the hand of his neighbour and the moment he releases the chopstick he had already grabbed. The random draw appearing in

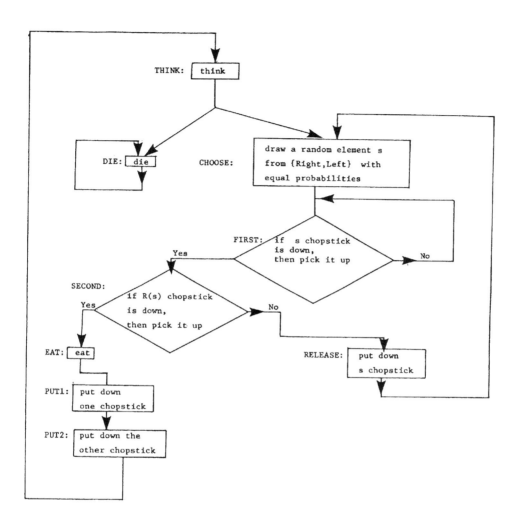

Figure 20.1 Protocol for the free philosopher.

box CHOOSE is performed with equal probabilities, but Theorem 2 below holds even if the random draw is performed with unequal, positive probabilities.

Boxes FIRST, SECOND, RELEASE, PUT1 and PUT2 contain atomic operations. Boxes THINK, DIE, CHOOSE and EAT are composed of a linear finite sequence of atomic operations. We assume that all basic operations terminate. It follows that, if P_i performs an infinite number of atomic operations, he will eventually leave every box he enters.

We intend to formulate and prove results of the form that computations according to protocols have certain properties with probability one (or zero). To this end we must specify the probability space with respect to which these statements are made. The next definition captures the idea of a schedule, i.e., the behaviour of the system under all possible circumstances.

Definition. A schedule S, for n philosophers, is a function that assigns to every past behaviour of the system of philosophers, the philosopher P_i whose turn is next to perform an atomic operation. Under past behaviour up to any given time, we mean the complete sequence of atomic operations (we assume that the description of an atomic operation includes the index of its author) and random draws with their results, up to that time.

Following [14], a schedule is not merely a fixed sequence of activations but, rather, a mapping which makes the process that is next to perform an atomic operation depend on the whole past behaviour. This captures the idea that, for any specific system, what will happen next depends on the whole history of past successes and failures of the processes to gain access to shared resources, as well as on what has happened internally with the processes. Unlike [14], we also include under past history the results of random draws already made.

For a given schedule S and specific outcomes of the random draws D (D is an infinite sequence of elements of the set {Right, Left}), we get a particular computation $C = COM(S, D)$, which is an infinite sequence of atomic operations. Note that a computation is unending and embodies the total life-span of the system. We shall use the term finite computation to denote a finite sequence of atomic operations. The ith element of a computation C is the atomic operation that takes place at time i. Note that we assume that no two atomic operations take place at exactly the same time in C; this restriction could be easily lifted to allow atomic operations of different processes, as long as they do not address the same shared variable, to take place exactly at the same time.

Definition. A computation C is *proper* if, in C, every philosopher performs an infinite number of atomic operations. A schedule S is called *proper* if, for every sequence D of outcomes of the random draws, the computation $COM(S, D)$ is proper.

It follows from the above explanations that if a schedule S is proper then, in every possible computation $C = COM(S, D)$, a philosopher who enters a box eventually leaves it (possibly returning to it right away, in the case of DIE or FIRST).

On the space of all possible outcomes of random draws D we impose the uniform probability distribution. The function COM then associates with every schedule S a probability distribution on the space of all computations, the probability of a set E of computations being defined as the probability of the set of sequences of random draws D such that $COM(S, D)$ is in E.

In the sequel we shall make no assumption on S, *except that it is proper.* Our theorems, thus, ensure that certain properties hold for every individual proper schedule. We do not assume a probability distribution on the space of schedules.

Our goal is to show that, in the system of the free philosophers, for every proper schedule, a deadlock may occur only with probability zero. We shall first define precisely the events in question.

Definition. A *deadlocked* computation C is a computation for which there exists a point t in time, at which at least one philosopher is trying to eat, but after which no philosopher eats. A philosopher P_i is *locked-out* (or starving) in a computation C, if there exists a time t at which P_i is trying to eat, and after which P_i never eats.

Note that P_i may starve in C in one of two ways, either there is a last time at which he picks up a chopstick, or he picks up a chopstick an infinite number of times, but gets to hold two chopsticks simultaneously just a finite number of times.

For a fixed proper schedule S, the event of being a deadlocked computation has a well-defined probability (the proof is left to the reader). Denote $DL(S) = Pr(\{D|C = COM(S,D)$ is deadlocked$\})$. We want to prove that, for every proper schedule S, $DL(S) = 0$.

The following lemmas refer to two philosophers, Plato and Aristotle, where Plato is seated next and to the *left* of Aristotle (see Fig. 20.2). Our convention for Left and Right in Fig. 20.2 is set up so that the common chopstick is on Plato's Right and on Aristotle's Left.

Lemma 1. *If Plato picks up a chopstick an infinite number of times (in box FIRST) but Aristotle picks up a chopstick only a finite number of times (in box FIRST), then with probability one, Plato eats an infinite number of times.*

Proof. The precise meaning of the lemma is that the event of Plato eating an infinite number of times has probability one relative to the event described in the hypotheses. The claim is meaningful only for those schedules that attach a positive probability to the hypotheses (that probability is clearly well defined), and it should be understood that the lemma applies only to those schedules.

We start by noting that if in a proper computation C a philosopher picks up a chopstick, then he must eventually release that chopstick. Hence, there must be a moment t in time after which Aristotle does not hold a chopstick any more. If Plato picks up a chopstick an infinite number of times, he must perform an infinite number of random draws and, with probability one, he draws Left an infinite number of times. Each time Plato draws Left he waits for his left chopstick (box FIRST) and eventually obtains it (otherwise he would not be able to pick up a chopstick an infinite number of times). He then looks for his right chopstick and finds it on the table, since Aristotle does not pick it up any more. Therefore Plato eats each time he draws Left after Aristotle has held the common chopstick for the last time. Q.E.D.

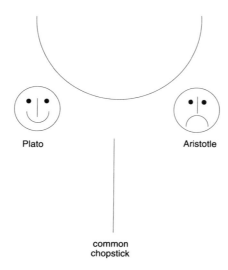

Figure 20.2

Lemma 2. *In a deadlocked computation, every philosopher picks up a chopstick an infinite number of times (in box FIRST), with (relative) probability one.*

Proof.   In line with our explanation at the start of the proof of Lemma 1, we assume that $DL(S) > 0$. Let C be a deadlocked computation. By Lemma 1, with probability one, either every philosopher picks up a chopstick an infinite number of times or every philosopher picks up a chopstick a finite number of times (the case where the probability of the event described in the hypotheses of Lemma 1 is zero is dealt with easily). The possibility that every philosopher picks up a chopstick only a finite number of times stands in direct contradiction with C being deadlocked. Q.E.D.

Lemma 3. *Let F be a finite computation consisting of t steps, such that, at time t, both Plato and Aristotle are trying to eat, Plato's last random draw was Left and Aristotle's last random draw was Right. Consider all (infinite) computations C that are continuations of F. Then, with probability at least one half: at least*

*one of Plato or Aristotle picks up a chopstick just a finite number of times in C,
or at least one of them gets to eat in C, after his last random draw in F and no
later than two random draws after his last random draw in F.*

Proof. The chopstick located between Plato and Aristotle will be referred to as
the common chopstick. Neither Plato nor Aristotle drew the side of the common
chopstick in their respective last random draws in F. For the proof it is sufficient
to consider continuations C of F in which both Plato and Aristotle pick up a
chopstick an infinite number of times. We shall distinguish three cases concerning
the time intervals from the respective last random draws of Plato and Aristotle in
F, to the end t of F.

Case 1. None of Plato or Aristotle has looked for the common chopstick (box
SECOND) between his last random draw in F and time t. Then, in C, both Plato
and Aristotle will look for the common chopstick after time t, because they lift a
chopstick an infinite number of times in C, and the first one to look for it after t
will, with certainty, pick it up and eat, before he draws even a next random draw.

Case 2. Both Plato and Aristotle have looked for the common chopstick (box
SECOND) between their respective last random draws and time t. If the first one
to look for it has picked it up, he has begun a meal after his last random draw in
F and before t, and the conclusion holds. If he has not found it on the table (box
SECOND), then he will not look for any chopstick again before his next random
draw and certainly not before time t. Thus, the second one of Plato and Aristotle
to look for the common chopstick (after his last draw in F and before time t) found
it on the table and has begun a meal before time t.

Case 3. One of Plato or Aristotle, say Plato, has not looked for the common
chopstick (box SECOND) between his last random draw and time t, while the
other one, Aristotle, has looked for the common chopstick (box SECOND) between
his last random draw and time t. We must consider three subcases:

Subcase a. Aristotle did find the common chopstick on the table. Then, with
certainty, he begun a meal since his last random draw and before time t.

Subcase b. Aristotle did not find the common chopstick on the table, and his
next random draw in C is at a time s that is posterior to t, but before Plato has
looked for the common chopstick. At time s, with probability one half, Aristotle
will again draw Right. Then, for the finite subcomputation F' of C up to time
s, Case 1 holds and one of the two philosophers will eat with certainty, before he
draws a new random draw.

Subcase c. Aristotle did not find the common chopstick (box SECOND), and his
next random draw takes place, in C, at time s, only after Plato has looked for
the common chopstick. In this case, since Aristotle did not pick up the common
chopstick between times t and s, Plato must have found the common chopstick on
the table and begun a meal between t and his next random draw. Q.E.D.

To each time instant there corresponds a *configuration* of the latest random draws by all the (live) philosophers. We shall say that a configuration, A, and a later configuration B, are *disjoint* if each (live) philosopher has, between A and B, performed a random draw.

Lemma 4. *If every philosopher picks up a chopstick an infinite number of times, and if, at time t, the configuration of last random draws is A, then there will arise, with probability one, a later configuration B, disjoint from A, in which some philosopher's last random draw is Left while his right neighbour's last random draw is Right.*

Proof. Starting in configuration A, each philosopher will eventually draw a new random side (since each philosopher picks up a chopstick an infinite number of times he performs an infinite number of random draws). A configuration G disjoint from A will therefore certainly be obtained, and all configurations thereafter will be disjoint from A. If G satisfies the condition of the lemma we are through. If not, it must be the case that, in G, all philosophers' last random draws are Left, or that, in G, all philosophers' last random draws are Right. The first philosopher to perform a new random draw will, with probability one half, change the side he last drew and create a configuration satisfying the condition of the lemma. The conclusion of the lemma follows because the probability that all subsequent independent random draws give Left (or Right) is zero. Q.E.D.

We now get to the main theorem concerning the free philosophers.

Theorem 2. *For every proper schedule S, $DL(S) = 0$.*

Proof. We shall prove the theorem by contradiction. Assume that $DL(S) > 0$. We may then talk about the probability of events relative to a deadlock. By Lemma 2, with probability one (relative to the event of a deadlocked computation), every philosopher performs an infinite number of random draws. By Lemma 4, there will arise, with probability one, an infinite sequence of disjoint configurations of last random draws satisfying the hypotheses of Lemma 3: say $A_0, A_1, \ldots, A_k, \ldots$. By Lemma 3, some philosopher eats between the time of A_k and the time of A_{k+2}, for every k, with probability one half. But the random draws occurring in disjoint configurations are independent, and hence some philosopher will eat with probability one. We have shown that, relative to the event of deadlocked computations, non-deadlocked computations have probability one. We conclude that deadlocks may occur with probability zero. Q.E.D.

Corollary 1. *Consider a system of n free philosophers $P_1, P_2, \ldots, P_n$ sitting in a row (they are numbered from left to right, the chopstick placed at the left of P_1 may be used only by P_1, and the chopstick located at the right of P_n may be used only by P_n). Assume that, at time t, some philosopher P_k, $1 \leq k \leq n$, is trying to eat then, with probability one, some philosopher P_i, $1 \leq i \leq n$, will eat after time t.*

Proof. Consider the system of $n+1$ free philosophers sitting around a table. To any schedule S for the row of n philosophers there corresponds a schedule S' for the circle of $n+1$ philosophers, in the following way: at time t, S' sends philosopher $n+1$ to his death and thereafter, at time $t+1$, schedule S' behaves as schedule S would behave at time t. By Theorem 2, with probability one, S' causes no deadlock and therefore, with probability one, S causes no deadlock. Q.E.D.

20.6   Lockouts Are Possible

As indicated in the introduction, one would like to have a lockout-free system. It can be shown that the system proposed above is not lockout-free.

Theorem 3. *The system of the free philosophers is not lockout-free.*

Proof. We shall show here that even when there are only two philosophers, one of them may be starved. A stronger property concerning systems of an arbitrary number of philosophers will be proved thereafter. Assume that there are only two philosophers around the table: Plato and Aristotle. The schedule may make them hungry and let Plato draw a random side. It could then, before Plato had a chance to look for his first chopstick, let Aristotle draw a random side, pick his first chopstick up, pick his second chopstick up and eat. While Aristotle is eating Plato gets to look for his first chopstick but does not find it on the table. He keeps waiting for it, but before he may have another look, Aristotle finishes his meal, becomes hungry again, draws a random side and picks up both his chopsticks. It is possible, then for a schedule to arrange, with certainty, that each time Plato looks for his first chopstick, Aristotle has it in hand and is eating. Q.E.D.

In the proof above Plato was starving, waiting indefinitely for his first chopstick. The proof of the next theorem will show that the scheduler could also manage to starve Plato while he lifts a chopstick an infinite number of times.

C.A.R. Hoare [5] has proposed a measure of the quality of a solution to the dining philosophers problem: the size of the longest chain of starving philosophers that may occur. Though it is possible that the protocols proposed above are quite satisfactory in practice, we shall show that a schedule may, with probability one, starve all but one philosopher.

Theorem 4. *For this system of n free philosophers, there is a schedule that starves, with probability one, $n-1$ philosophers.*

Proof. Assume all philosophers are hungry but none of them has yet drawn a random s. A schedule can easily arrange for this to happen. It will be shown that a schedule can guarantee that, with probability one, only Plato will eat an infinite number of times and all other philosophers will starve while lifting a chopstick an infinite number of times. At first the schedule will activate only Plato and let him eat a number of times until he draws Left (this happens with probability one). Then, before Plato picks up his left chopstick, it activates Plato's right neighbour. He will draw Right a number of times and be able to eat and eventually he will draw Left (with probability one). The schedule will then send him to sleep before he has a chance to look for his left chopstick. Now the schedule will move around the table counterclockwise and activate each philosopher, possibly letting him eat a few times, until he has randomly drawn Left. Then the schedule will let every philosopher pick up his left chopstick. Now every philosopher has drawn Left and has picked up his first chopstick, but none of them has looked for his right chopstick yet. From now on, only Plato will eat. Plato's right neighbour is now activated and finds his right chopstick in the hand of his neighbour. He puts down his left chopstick, draws a random s, and, if he drew Left he goes through the same routine without being able to eat, until he eventually draws Right. The schedule leaves him at this point, before he had a chance to look for his right chopstick, and moves counterclockwise, performing the same trick on each philosopher including Plato's left neighbour. Now Plato is activated, looks on his right (he still has his left chopstick in hand), eats, puts down his chopsticks, goes a number of times through the same routine having each time a meal, until he draws Right. Now, all philosophers have drawn Right but none of them has looked for his right chopstick yet. We are back to a situation that is symmetric to a situation already encountered. Q.E.D.

It should be noted that the schedule S used in the above proof is *not* proper in the sense of our definition. There are sequences D of random draws for which the computation $C = COM(S, D)$ is not proper, but the probability for this to happen is zero.

The previous theorem sheds light on why the Proof of Theorem 2 had to be delicate. No local reasoning would succeed in showing that one of a chain of *fixed* (independent of n) length of philosophers sitting next to each other will get to eat.

We shall now offer another solution which guarantees that, with probability one, there will be no lockout, i.e., nobody will starve.

20.7   The Courteous Philosopher's Algorithm

The possibility for lockouts demonstrated in Section 6 is due to the fact that a philosopher P_i may be discourteous enough to pick up his neighbour's chopstick (box FIRST), even if that neighbour is trying to eat and P_i has already eaten after his neighbour's most recent meal. By using additional values for the variables shared by neighbouring philosophers, we can ensure courteous behaviour and obtain a lockout-free system.

Informally, when a courteous philosopher becomes hungry, he first signals to both his neighbours that he is trying to eat, and then draws a side at random. He turns to the side he drew and waits until the corresponding chopstick is available and, if he has already eaten at least one meal, until the corresponding neighbour either is not trying to eat or has eaten more recently than himself. If such a situation occurs (and the philosopher is lucky enough to be activated while this situation holds) he picks up the chopstick and turns around to the other side. Then, if he finds his second chopstick available, he picks it up and eats. But if the chopstick is not available, he replaces his first chopstick on the table and draws another random side. After having eaten, he signals to both his neighbours that he was the latest to have a meal and that he is not trying to eat. He then replaces his chopsticks on the table. The flowchart of Fig. 20.3 is a formal definition of the behaviour of a courteous philosopher.

As was indicated in Section 3, two neighbouring philosophers share a single variable that may take on only a finite number of different values independent of the number of philosophers (in fact $2 \cdot 2 \cdot 2 \cdot 3 = 24$ different values). In Fig. 20.3, we look at this single shared variable as being composed of four different fields: *chopstick* (which may take the values Down or Up), *signal* (Off or On), *neighbour-hungry* (Off or ON), and *last* (Neutral, Right or Left). Those fields are prefixed by Right or Left to indicate whether they are part of the variable shared with the right or the left neighbour. If Plato is seated next and to the left of Aristotle (Fig. 20.2) Plato's Right-chopstick and Right-last are Aristotle's Left-chopstick and Left-last, respectively, but Plato's Right-signal and Right-neighbour-hungry are Aristotle's Left-neighbour-hungry and Left-signal, respectively. The initial values of those fields are Down, Off and Neutral. A philosopher has read-write permission on his chopstick, signal and last fields, but only read permission on his neighbour-hungry fields. Figure 20.4 pictures the initial configuration; a full line indicates read-write permission and a broken line indicates read permission only.

The notions of a schedule, proper schedule, and the probability distribution on the space of all computations are defined as in Section 5. Our statements about something occurring with probability one (or zero) have then a meaning similar to that of the propositions in Section 5. As in Section 5, we shall suppose that Plato is seated next and to the left of Aristotle. We shall first show that, in a system of courteous philosophers, with probability one, no philosopher is locked-out (starves) before he has eaten at least once. Then, we shall prove that, with probability one, no philosopher is locked-out.

Lemma 5. *Let S be a proper schedule for a system of courteous philosophers. The probability of Plato being locked-out, in a computation $C = COM(S, D)$, without eating a single meal in C, is zero.*

Proof. It is evident from the protocol for the courteous philosophers that, as long as a philosopher has not eaten, his Left-last variable may only have value Neutral or Left, and his Right-last variable may only have value Neutral or Right. Thus, as long as no philosopher has eaten, the condition CON in box FIRST will be true and the wait condition (box FIRST) will be equivalent to the wait condition of the free philosopher (box FIRST of the free philosopher's algorithm). We conclude that, as

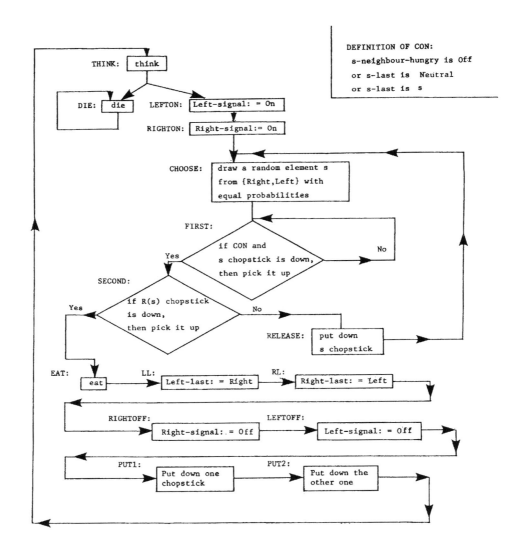

Figure 20.3 Protocol for the courteous philosopher.

long as no philosopher has eaten yet, a system of courteous philosophers behaves exactly as a system of free philosophers and that, by Theorem 2, a deadlock has probability zero. Hence, with probability one, *some* philosopher will eat at least once in C.

Assume now that Plato is locked-out (and consequently is alive) and does not eat a single meal in C. He must be part of a maximal row of philosophers who are all

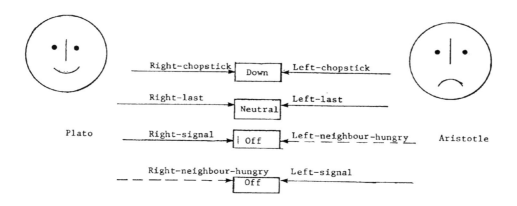

Figure 20.4

locked-out and do not eat a single meal: P_i, P_{i+1}, ..., P_j. By the previous remark, with probability one, P_i is not P_{j+1} (recall that the indices of the philosophers are defined only modulo n, i.e., P_{i+n} is the same as P_i). Then, P_{i-1} and P_{j+1} (who could be the same) either die or eat at least one meal in C.

Assume that P_{i-1} does not die in C. (The case that P_{i-1} dies is even simpler.) By our assumptions, there will be a moment t in C when P_{i-1} has already eaten (and has released his chopstick), and P_i is hungry. At that moment we shall have for P_{i-1} the values: Right-last = Left, Right-neighbour-hungry = On. Similarly for some moment s for P_j and P_{j+1}.

We claim that, with probability one, after moment t philosopher P_{i-1} will pick up the chopstick C_i common to him and P_i just a finite number of times. This is because P_{i-1} can pick up C_i only as his *second* chopstick. Also, if P_{i-1} draws Right after t then he remains waiting for C_i forever. Thus, in order to pick up C_i infinitely often, P_i must from moment t onwards always draw left, an event that has probability zero.

Thus with probability one there is a moment t_1 in C after which the chopsticks C_i and C_{j+1} (between P_j and P_{j+1}) are always down and the shared variables between P_{i-1} and P_i as well as between P_j and P_{j+1} will show that P_i and P_j were the last ones to eat. From moment t_1 onwards, row P_i, ..., P_j behaves as the one described in Corollary 1 and we conclude that, with probability one, one of P_i, ..., P_j eats a meal, contradicting the assumption. We conclude that a philosopher may be locked-out without eating a single meal only with probability zero. Q.E.D.

The following proof requires an ordering in time of the meals of the philosophers. It turns out that while there is no natural way to define a total order on the meals, we are able to say when a philosopher's meal preceded or followed his neighbour's meal. This local ordering suffices for our proof.

When a philosopher eats he goes through the following sequence of actions: picking up a first chopstick (box FIRST), picking up a second chopstick (box SECOND), setting his Left-last variable to Right (box LL), setting his Right-last variable to Left (box RL), and putting down both his chopsticks (boxes PUT1 and PUT2). If, while performing the sequence described above, a philosopher picks up his second chopstick (box SECOND) at time t_1 and puts down the first of the chopsticks he releases at time t_2 (box PUT1), we shall say that his corresponding *meal-interval* is $[t_1, t_2]$ (this implies $t_1 < t_2$).

Definition. We shall say that meal-interval $[t_1, t_2]$ *precedes* meal-interval $[t_3, t_4]$ ($[t_1, t_2] < [t_3, t_4]$) if $t_2 < t_3$.

Remark 1: The relation 'precedes' is antireflexive and transitive.

Remark 2: If $[t_1, t_2]$ is a meal-interval of Plato, then between time t_1 and t_2, Plato is the only philosopher who can change Plato's Left-last and Right-last variables (since Plato holds both his chopsticks during this interval of time and no philosopher ever changes his 'last' variables unless he holds both his chopsticks) and therefore at time t_2 Plato's Left-last variable has value Right and his Right-last variable has value Left.

Remark 3: If, in a computation C, $[t_1, t_2]$ is a meal-interval of Plato and $[t_3, t_4]$ is a meal-interval of Aristotle, then either $[t_1, t_2] < [t_3, t_4]$ or $[t_3, t_4] < [t_1, t_2]$ (since a philosopher has both his chopsticks in hand during any meal-interval of his and no two neighbors may each have both their chopsticks in hand at the same time).

Theorem 5. *If S is a proper schedule for a system of courteous philosophers, then with probability one, a computation $C = COM(S, D)$ is lockout-free.*

Proof. By lemma 5, with probability one, all philosophers who are locked-out in C eat at least one meal in C. Assume that some philosophers are locked-out in C. Then, with probability one, each of them has a last meal in C, and let $[t_1, s_1], [t_2, s_2], \ldots, [t_k, s_k]$ be the respective meal-intervals corresponding to the last meals of the locked-out philosophers. Among those meal-intervals, there must be one that is not preceded by any of them, i.e. a minimal one for the relation 'preceds.' Suppose $[t_1, s_1]$ is such a meal-interval and it corresponds to a meal of Plato. We want to show that, with probability one, after a certain time, Plato's both chopsticks will be permanently on the table and the condition of box FIRST permanently true for Plato. Let us concentrate our attention on Aristotle (a symmetric reasoning will take care of Plato's left neighbour).
Case 1: If Aristotle dies in C then, after a certain time, Plato's right chopstick will be permanently on the table and his Right-neighbour-hungry permanently Off.
Case 2: If Aristotle has an infinite number of meals in C or is locked-out in C then, he must have a meal in C whose meal-interval $[a, b]$ is preceded by $[t_1, s_1]$ (by Remark 3) and, by Remark 2, after time b, Aristotle's Left-last variable, which is Plato's Right-last variable, will permanently be equal to Right. If follows that,

after a certain time, as soon as Aristotle draws Left, he will wait indefinitely for this (first) chopstick. Therefore, with probability one, Aristotle will pick up a chopstick only a finite number of times (end of Case 2).

But if, after a certain time, Plato's both chopsticks are permanently on the table and the condition of box FIRST permanently true for Plato, then Plato will certainly eat a meal after his last meal. We conclude that Plato is locked-out only with probability zero and that, with probability one, no philosopher is locked out. Q.E.D.

20.8   Conclusions

The solution to the dining philosophers problem presented here suggests an approach to the general question of programming methodology that seems to be opposed to the prevalent one, as illustrated in particular in [1] There, the reproducible behaviour of programs is advocated as a necessary condition for debugging and it is claimed that for systems to be reliable, they must be built out of components that have, themselves, a reproducible behaviour. Here the reliability of the system is guaranteed even though the component processes may have a totally irreproducible behaviour, which makes debugging impossible.

Acknowledgements

We are grateful to Nissim Francez, Michael Rodeh, Amir Pnueli and Michael Ben-Or for fruitful discussions.

References

[1] Brinch, Hansen P. *Operating Systems Principles*. Prentice-Hall 1973.

[2] Brinch, Hansen P. Distributed processes, a concurrent programming concept. CACM 21, 11 (November 1978).

[3] Dijkstra, E.W. Hierarchical ordering of sequential processes, in *Operating Systems Techniques* (C.A.R. Hoare and R.H. Perrot, eds.). Academic Press 1972.

[4] Francez, N. and Rodeh, M. A distributed abstract data type implemented by a probabilistic communication scheme, IEEE 21st Annual Symposium on *Foundations of Computer Science* (October 1980), pp. 372–379.

[5] Hoare, C.A.R. Towards a theory of parallel programming, in *Operating Systems Techniques*, quoted above.

[6] Hoare, C.A.R. Communicating sequential processes. CACM 21, 8 (August 1978).

[7] Holt, R.C., Graham, G.S., Lazowska, E.D., and Scott, M.A. *Structured Concurrent Programming with Operating Systems Applications*. Addison-Wesley 1978.

[8] Kaubisch, W.H., Perrot, R.H., and Hoare, C.A.R. Quasiparallel programming, *Software and Experience*, Vol. 6 1976, pp. 341–356.

[9] Lamport, L. Private communication, 1978.

[10] Lehmann, D. and Rabin, M.O. A symmetric and fully distributed solution to the dining philosophers problem (extended abstract), 8th ACM Symp. on Principles of Programming Languages (1981), pp. 133–138.

[11] Lynch, Nancy A. Fast allocation of nearby resources in a distributed system, Proc. of the 12th Annual ACM Symposium on the Theory of Computing, Los Angeles, April 1980, pp. 70–81.

[12] Rabin, M.O. Theoretical impediments to artificial intelligence, IFIP Congress (1974, Jack L. Rosenfeld, ed.), pp. 615–619.

[13] Rabin, M.O. Probabalistic algorithms, in *Algorithms and Complexity, New Directions and Recent Trends* (J.F. Traub, ed.), Academic Press, New York (1976), pp. 21–39.

[14] Rabin, M.O. N-process synchronization by $4\log_2 N$−valued shared variable, *Jour. Comp. Sys. Sc.*, vol. 25 (1982), pp. 66–75. (See also IEEE 21st Annual Symposium on *Foundations of Computer Science* (October 1980), pp. 407–410.)

[15] Rabin, M.O. The choice coordination problem, *Acta Informatica*, vol. 17 (1982), pp. 121–134.

Chapter 21

Model-checking CSP

A.W. Roscoe

21.1 Introduction

It is both inspiring and frustrating to work as closely with Tony Hoare as I have had the privilege to do over the past fifteen years. The source of the inspiration is obvious to all. The frustration comes from his ability to get things so right at the outset that the academic's usual meat and drink – refining and changing an idea, and exploring varieties of theories, until a consensus emerges – is often missing.

I believe this is true of the invention of his that I have spent longest working on, namely CSP [1]. The elegance and expressive power of the notation, and the simplicity of the standard semantic models, have the consequence that exploring other possibilities for these has been far less popular – and fruitful – than with other process algebras. Instead, theoretical work on CSP has concentrated on clear extensions, such as the inclusion of unbounded nondeterminism [2, 3], real time [4], probability [5] and similar. The basic ideas and notation have proved remarkably robust in these contexts.

One of the most stringent tests of a notation or idea is how it stands up to uses which the original designer never imagined. In this paper I describe work carried out over the last two years in building and using FDR[1], a model-checker/refinement-checker for CSP. Both CSP and its theories prove remarkably well-suited for this. Hoare's decisions which have proved helpful include

- basing the semantics, and equivalence, around the idea of refinement;
- separating the ideas of parallel composition and hiding, so that multiple processes can synchronise on events and enforce constraints, and hiding can be used as abstraction;
- the inclusion of a wide range of operators, both ones representing real modes of constructing processes and ones which, while pointless or difficult to implement, are useful in building specifications.

---

[1]FDR is a product of Formal Systems (Europe) Ltd.

These have meant that it has been possible to build a fast refinement checker which can be used for the great majority of correctness proofs one is likely to want, and that the language is able to represent complex systems succinctly and clearly.

21.2   Understanding Refinement

The greatest stylistic difference between CSP and most other process algebras, at least to a theoretician, is Hoare's decision to base its semantics on mathematical models remote from the language itself. In CSP, a process is identified with its set of possible behaviours chosen from some class, whereas other process *algebras* have either been exactly that – with their notion of equality defined by some set of algebraic laws – or based on operational semantics.

The model-based approach has a considerable influence on the design of a language, primarily because we can only use operators with respect to which the chosen model is a congruence. The clearest consequence of this in CSP is in its choice constructs: since internal actions (τ) are invisible to the model, they cannot, for example, be allowed to resolve alternatives. Thus, CSP has a pair of choice constructs: □ which is only resolved by external events and ⊓ where the choice is arbitrary, playing the role of the single operator + (afforced by τ) in CCS.

Arguably the greatest difference appears in the treatment of recursion, since we are obliged to have a fixed-point theory over the abstract model which corresponds to our understanding of how a recursively-defined process is meant to behave[2]. This contrasts with an operationally-based theory, for example, where recursion is trivial to define using an unwinding/re-writing rule. Getting recursion to 'work' in an abstract theory is often the hardest thing to get right and a place where plausible-seeming congruences break up. It is largely the problems of recursion that led to the severe treatment of divergence in CSP.

The model-based approach thus imposes additional constraints. Whether the effect of these is positive or negative depends on one's viewpoint. One direct benefit is that models of the sort described above automatically supply a theory of *refinement*. Given that each process is identified with the set of all behaviours that it is allowed to display, it is natural to say that reducing this set corresponds to refinement. The fact that the whole language is compositional, and almost certainly

---

[2]The correctness of the representation of recursion or any other language construct is usually judged via congruence with an operational semantics. Since the abstract model is based on the set of all possible behaviours of some type(s) of a process, the 'real' value of a process can be extracted by seeing which behaviours are possible for its operational semantics. This generates a natural *abstraction* map Φ from the operational model to the behavioural model. An abstract operator *op* and the corresponding concrete/operational version **op** are congruent if, for all operational processes **P**, we have $\Phi(\mathbf{op}(\mathbf{P})) = op(\Phi(\mathbf{P}))$. The operational and denotational semantics of a language are congruent if all constructs in the language have this property, which implies that the behaviours predicted for any term by the denotational semantics are always the same as those that can be observed of its operational semantics. That the standard semantics of CSP are congruent to a natural operational semantics is shown in, for example, [2].

monotone, with respect to the behavioural model means that the refinement order has the properties one might expect.

The standard model for (untimed) CSP is the *failures/divergences* model, where each process is represented by two sets of behaviours:

- *failures* are pairs (s, X) where s is a finite trace of the process and X is a set of events it can refuse after s;

- *divergences* are finite traces on which the process can perform an infinite sequence of consecutive actions.

For various technical reasons it is more difficult to model accurately the behaviour of a process after the possibility of divergence than on traces where no such possibility has arisen. Therefore, after each minimal (under the prefix order) divergence trace, the model identifies a process with $\perp$, the most nondeterministic process. The clearest way to understand accurately what the model represents is that

- the failures on non-divergent traces are precisely those (s, X) where the process can, after s, come into a *stable* state (one with no internal progress possible) that has no transition in X;

- the minimal divergences are the actual least traces after which the process can perform an infinite sequence of τs;

- all failures on divergent traces, and non-minimal divergences, are present because of our decision not to model this type of behaviour: the fact that they are there carries no information (positive or negative) about what the process can actually do. It is a deliberate obfuscation, introduced to get the theory to work better.

What this statement actually defines is the abstraction mapping Φ from the labelled transition-system operational semantics of CSP (or, indeed, any other labelled transition system where internal actions are labelled τ) to the model.

In this paper we will be considering largely this model, though the techniques in this paper can be closely related to recent work on seeing beyond the first divergence [6] and, perhaps less expectedly, to the extensions of the model [2] by infinite traces to handle unboundedly nondeterministic constructs and specifications. We will discuss these possibilities briefly in Section 21.5. We will also only deal with the case where the overall alphabet of possible actions is finite, since this makes the model a little more straightforward, and is an obvious prerequisite to model-checking.

Given the philosophy described above of what the failures and divergences mean, the following properties, which define the model, should be self-evident. The *failures/divergences model* $\mathcal{N}_\Sigma$ over a given finite alphabet Σ of communications is the set of all pairs (F, D), $F \subseteq \Sigma^* \times \mathcal{P}(\Sigma)$, $D \subseteq \Sigma^*$ satisfying

$(F1)$ $\qquad\qquad\qquad\quad (F \neq \{\}) \quad \wedge \quad ((st, \{\}) \in F \Rightarrow (s, \{\}) \in F)$

$(F2)$ $\qquad\quad (t, X) \in F \wedge Y \subseteq X \quad \Rightarrow \quad (t, Y) \in F$

$(F3)$ $\quad ((t, X) \in F \wedge (t\langle a \rangle, \{\})) \notin F \quad \Rightarrow \quad (t, X \cup \{a\}) \in F$

$(D1)$ $\qquad\qquad\qquad\qquad\quad s \in D \quad \Rightarrow \quad st \in D$

$(D2)$ $\qquad\qquad\qquad\qquad\quad s \in D \quad \Rightarrow \quad (st, X) \in F.$

The process $P = (F, D)$ *refines* $P' = (F', D')$, written $P' \sqsubseteq P$, if and only if

$$F \subseteq F' \qquad \text{and} \qquad D \subseteq D' \,.$$

The semantics of CSP over this model may be found in many places, including [7, 1]. Important facts that we will need in this paper include the following:

1. The least process under the refinement order, $\perp$, equates to any process that can diverge immediately (i.e., without performing any visible actions first). The refinement order, under the restrictions given, is complete and its maximal elements are the *deterministic* processes: divergence free and, after each trace s, only able to refuse those events that it cannot communicate after s.

2. Each standard CSP operator can be defined as an operator over $\mathcal{N}_\Sigma$; each is continuous with respect to the refinement order; using that order and least fixed points for the semantics of recursion gives a denotational semantics that is congruent to the operational semantics.

The congruence theorem is vital in underpinning the model checking work, since all of the computations we do to test refinement – a notion based on the abstract model – are in fact carried out over the operational semantics. The rest of this section develops the theory of how the question $P \sqsubseteq Q$? is decided.

Though there are possibilities for relaxing this at the specification (left-hand) side, we choose only to deal with processes whose operational semantics are *finite state*. This is defined to mean that, as the operational semantics is unfolded, only finitely many process terms are generated. Thus,

$$P = a \rightarrow ((b \rightarrow STOP) \,\square\, (c \rightarrow P))$$

is finite state – it has three or four states depending on whether one adopts the operational semantics in which a recursion is unfolded directly or guarded by a τ^3. On the other hand,

$$Q = a \rightarrow (Q \,\|\, (b \rightarrow STOP)$$

---

[3]Over the failures/divergences equivalence, a node N in a labelled transition system is indistinguishable from one whose only transition is τ to N. The full operational semantics of CSP requires that the rule for a recursive term be

$$\mu\, p.P \xrightarrow{\tau} P[\mu\, p.P/p]$$

in order to give a semantics to action-unguarded terms such as $\mu\, p.p$ (which the reader will is infinite-state, and fundamentally so since it is a process which can always communicate a, and will communicate b provided this will not make the number of bs so far exceed the number of as. There are some simple rules to help determine what classes of CSP process are likely to be finite state. These are discussed in Section 21.3.2. We will therefore, for the rest of this section, think of the decision question above as being one between finite directed graphs where all edges are labelled with an action, either τ or visible (finite labelled transition systems). It divides into two parts: normalising the specification, and then checking the implementation against the resulting normal form.

21.2.1   Normalising a transition system

The transition systems arising from CSP descriptions typically contain a high degree of nondeterminism, in the sense that after any trace s of visible actions there may be many states of a system which the process might be in. This can happen both because of the existence of invisible actions and because of the branching that occurs when a node has two identically-labelled actions, whether visible or invisible. Any method for deciding refinement between these systems will have to keep track of all the states reachable at the specification side on a given trace s, since it is merely necessary that every behaviour of the implementation on s is possible for one of these. And any method we devise will need a way of telling when a large enough set of traces have been tried to establish refinement.

Life would be easier if there were exactly one state corresponding to each possible trace. This can be achieved by transforming the original specification transition system to an equivalent *normal form*. The idea of a normal form for CSP processes has its origins in [8], where it is shown that each finite CSP term is equivalent to one in the following normal form:

- $\perp$ is a normal form;
- all others take the form

$$\sqcap\{(x : A \to P(x)) \mid A \in \mathcal{A}\}$$

  for $\mathcal{A}$ a *convex* subset of Σ such that $\bigcup \mathcal{A} \in \mathcal{A}$, and each $P(x)$ a normal form which depends only on x, not on A.

Except for trivial re-orderings (which are invisible in the above presentation in any case), two normal forms are equivalent semantically if and only if they are equivalent syntactically. Thus, except for the special case of $\perp$, each process is determined by

---

note is correctly given a divergent operational semantics). However, since terms like this are trivially detectable syntactically, and are always semantically equivalent to $\perp$, we actually choose to disregard them and *not* introduce the τ guard. This gives transition systems with the same abstract semantics and fewer states.

- its initial actions ($\bigcup \mathcal{A}$);
- its minimal acceptance sets, the minimal elements of $\mathcal{A}$, which are in direct correspondence with the maximal refusal sets;
- its behaviour after each initial action.

The most vital property, for us, of this normal form is that it branches uniquely and on visible actions only: given a starting normal form and one of its traces, we can follow this trace and get the unique normal form state the process is in after it.

The normal form was initially conceived as a target for algebraic transformation: if we can give enough laws so that any finite term can be transformed to normal form, then the laws can reasonably be said to be *complete*. However, since the normal form has a very clear relationship with behaviour, it is possible to compute it from the operational semantics, or indeed to find a normal form for any member of a labelled transition system: for any trace s of a process,

- if P can diverge on some proper prefix of s, there is no normal form node corresponding to s;
- if P can diverge after s but on no proper prefix, then the normal form node is $\bot$;
- otherwise, the initial actions are just the actions a such that $s\langle a \rangle$ is a trace of P (namely, there is some node of P that has trace s and can perform a); the minimal acceptances are the smallest sets of visible actions possible for stable nodes with trace s; the successor nodes are just those computed this way from the $s\langle a \rangle$.

For a process that has infinitely many traces, this formulation generates an infinite normal form. To be usable in our context we need to close the graph by re-using nodes that have identical behaviour (both on the first step and forever after). However, for finite-state processes there is a finite-state version of the normal form, computed using the following two-stage process.

Stage 1   Given a finite labelled transition system $L = (V, E, v_0)$, we form a graph $\mathcal{P}_L$ whose nodes are members of $\mathcal{P}(V)$ as follows

- The initial node is $\tau^*(v_0)$, where $\tau^*(v)$ is defined to be $\{w \mid v \xrightarrow{\tau} {}^* w\}$, the nodes reachable under some sequence of τs from v_0.
- For each node generated we have to decide whether it is divergent: this is true if and only if it contains a divergent node of L. A method for deciding this is described in Section 21.2.2. A divergent normal form node has no successors.
- If a node N is not divergent, we determine the set of non-τ actions possible for $v \in N$. For each such action a we form a new node, the set $\bigcup\{\tau^*(w) \mid \exists v \in N.v \xrightarrow{a} w\}$, the set of all nodes reachable after action a and any number of τs from members of N.

- The search is completed when all 'new' nodes generated are ones that have been previously expanded.

The resulting graph will be termed the *pre-normal* form of L.

This generates a transition system where there are only visible actions and where each node only has a single successor for each of its actions. What we produce by this process is the set of all the sets of nodes of L that are those reachable on any trace. Given any trace of v_0, the set of nodes of L that can be reached is one of the nodes of this new graph, except in the case of a divergence. The possible refusals of one of these nodes v are just the sets refused by the stable $v \in N$ (note that each non-divergent N must have such v).

As examples, we will normalise the processes B_3 and Q_0 defined:

$$B_3 = COPY \gg COPY \gg COPY$$

$$Q_i = (a \to STOP) \;\square\; (a \to Q_{i+1}) \quad \text{for } i = 0, 1$$
$$Q_2 = (a \to Q_0) \;\square\; (a \to Q_1)$$

where $COPY = left \to right \to COPY$. ($\gg$ is a parallel operator that connects the *right* channel of the left-hand argument to the *left* channel of the other, and hides the result.) The transition systems of each of these processes, and the corresponding pre-normal forms, are shown in Figure 21.1. B_3 has eight states, corresponding to each of the component processes being in state $COPY = C$ or $right \to COPY = F$. Its pre-normal form has four states, one of each possible number of 'items' this 'buffer' is holding (**0,1,2** or **3**). Though Q_0 has only four states and one possible action, its pre-normal form has six states. These are shown superimposed on the base transition system as sets of states: the numbers indicating how many a's are taken to reach it. The pre-normal form is also shown below, with the solid and empty circles respectively denoting states that can, and cannot, refuse a.

Stage 2   Examining the pre-normal forms generated by our two examples, there is a real sense in which the nodes from B_3's pre-normal form are all essentially different, for they allow different numbers of *left* events before this is refused. On the other hand, nodes **4** and **5** from Q_0's pre-normal form are actually indistinguishable: each of them can perform as many a's as it pleases, with the ability to $STOP$ (refuse everything) at any time. Thus the behaviour if this system is equivalent to one with five nodes, formed by identifying the last two in the pre-normal form. This is why we have termed $\mathcal{P}_L$ a pre-normal form rather than a normal form, for in a true normal form we would not expect there to be two essentially different representations of the same thing. To make it into a normal form we have to identify semantically identical nodes such as these.

The question of which nodes should be identified is easily determined by first marking each with *either* $\bot$ *or* its initial actions and maximal refusals, as appropriate, and then computing the fixed point $\sim$ of the following sequence of equivalence relations:

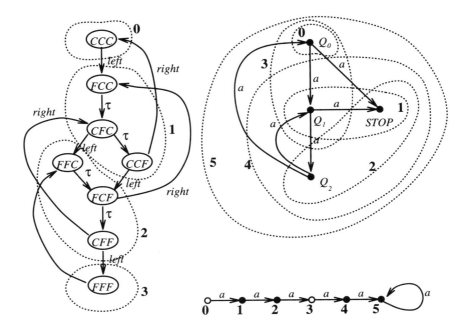

Figure 21.1 Pre-normalising two transition systems.

- $N \sim_0 M$ if, and only if, they have the same marking.
- $N \sim_{n+1} M \Leftrightarrow (N \sim_n M) \wedge \forall N', M'.(N \xrightarrow{a} N' \wedge M \xrightarrow{a} M' \Rightarrow N' \sim_n M')$.

Note that in the example above the initial marking corresponds to the 'full' or 'empty' marking in Figure 21.1. This equivalence over pre-normal form states is just a simple form of bisimulation with 'coloured' nodes. It is made particularly straightforward by the fact that two identically marked nodes have the same initial actions, and exactly one successor node for each such action.

The *normal form* of the labelled transition system L is thus its pre-normal form under the equivalence relation $\sim$, where the initial node is the equivalence class of $\tau^*(v_0)$, the transition relation is the obvious one and the only detail we record about each node is the marking as described above.

The complexity of normalisation
Given that the pre-normalisation process builds a transition system over the powerspace of the original one, there is the possibility that the normal form will be exponential in the size of the original system. This can indeed occur, as is shown by the example below. This possibility is to be expected given the result [9] that checking failures/divergence refinement of transition systems is PSPACE-hard. This result, which has been known for some time, can be blamed for the failure of the

tool-building community to tackle failures/divergence refinement hitherto.

Fortunately there are two mitigating factors that work in our favour, making this particular obstacle more-or-less disappear.

1. 'Real' process definitions simply do not behave as badly as the pathological example below. In practice it is rare for the normal form of a naturally-occurring process to have more states than the original transition system. Indeed, the normal form is frequently significantly *smaller*, offering scope for intermediate compression. It seems that, at least tackled using our algorithms, deciding failures/divergence refinement is one of that large class of NP-complete and similar problems where the hard cases are rare.

2. It is only the *specification* end of the refinement that we have to normalise. In practice the simpler process is usually that one rather than the implementation. Frequently, indeed, the specification is a representation of an abstract property such as two events alternating or deadlock-freedom, and has a trivial number of states.

    One would usually expect that a process playing the role of a 'specification' is reasonably clearly and cleanly constructed, with understandable behaviour. These aims are more-or-less inconsistent with the sort of nondeterminism that leads to an explosion in the normal form.

Example   The potential for state explosion on normalisation is shown in extreme form by the following pathological system, defined for any $n > 0$. We construct a transition system with $n + 1$ states and n events $\{1, \ldots n\} = B$. If the kth state is P_k we define

$$
\begin{aligned}
P_0 &= STOP \\
P_k &= r : B \to P_{k+1} \quad k \in \{1, \ldots, n-1\} \\
P_n &= r : B \to P_0 \\
    &\quad \Box\, r : B \to P_1 \\
    &\quad \Box\, r : B \to P_r
\end{aligned}
$$

This system is illustrated in Figure 21.2. The pre-normal and normal forms of this system (with initial state P_1) both have precisely $2^n - 1$ states (one for each nonempty subset A of the states $P_1, \ldots, P_n$ since, as can be proved by induction on the size of A, there is for each such subset a trace s_A such that the states reachable on s_A are A and perhaps P_0). The role of the state P_0 is to allow us to distinguish between these sets: if it is in the set reachable after a given trace then P_1 can deadlock after that trace, otherwise not. If the state P_0 is removed we get a system with the same number of pre-normal form states but only *one* normal form state, since every one is then semantically equal to

$$
RUN = x : B \to RUN
$$

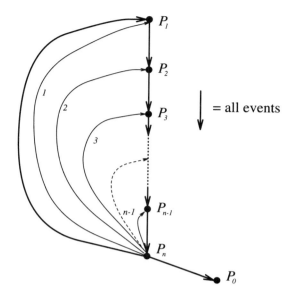

Figure 21.2 Transition system with pathological normalisation.

21.2.2   Checking refinement

Once the specification end of a refinement check has been normalised, the following two phases are necessary to establish failures/divergence refinement.

- Establish which states of the implementation transition system are divergent, marking them as such.
- Model-check the implementation, thus marked, against the normal form.

A state P is divergent if, and only if, the directed graph formed by considering only τ actions has a cycle reachable from P. There are two standard algorithmic approaches to this problem: computing the transitive closure of the graph or taking advantage of the properties of depth-first search (DFS). The latter is more efficient, since it offers an essentially linear (assuming constant-time set membership test) algorithm, based on the fact that in a DFS, the set of partially explored nodes (ones that have been visited, but not all nodes reachable from them) always forms a chain from the root of the search. The marking process[4] proceeds as follows:

- Perform DFSs rooted at successive nodes of the graph until each node has been visited at least once.

---

[4]This algorithm was devised by Michael Goldsmith.

- Any node can be marked non-divergent, divergent or unresolved, initially all being unresolved. During each individual search, only the successors of unresolved nodes are explored.
- If, during any DFS, either a node on the current partially explored chain or a marked divergent node is reached, then all of the nodes on the partially explored chain are marked divergent and this particular DFS is terminated.
- When a node leaves the partially explored chain because all its successors have been explored without the above occurring beneath it, then it is marked non-divergent (as must all its successors have been). For the root node this corresponds to the end of the DFS.

In the model checking phase we have to discover whether all the behaviours of each implementation state are allowable in all the normal form states such that they have a trace in common. This is done by exploring the cartesian product of the normal form and implementation state machines as follows.

We maintain a set of checked pairs and a set of *pending* pairs; initially the former is empty and the latter is the singleton set of the pair of initial states of the two systems. Until it is empty, we repeatedly inspect pairs from *pending*. The pair $\langle \nu, w \rangle$ checks if (i) the normal-form state ν is divergent *or* (ii) the implementation state w is non-divergent *and*

- the set of initial actions of w is a subset of those of ν *and*
- either w is unstable (has a τ-action) *or* the set of actions it refuses (the complement of its initials) is a subset of one of the maximal refusals of ν.

The set of all pairs reachable from $\langle \nu, w \rangle$ and not in *checked* is added to *pending*. A pair $\langle \nu', w' \rangle$ is *reachable* from $\langle \nu, w \rangle$ if either

(a) $w \overset{\tau}{\longrightarrow} w'$ and $\nu = \nu'$, or
(b) $w \overset{a}{\longrightarrow} w'$ and $\nu \overset{a}{\longrightarrow} \nu'$ for $a \neq \tau$; noting that whenever $w \overset{a}{\longrightarrow} w'$, then this ν' must exist and be unique.

If a pair is found which fails to check, then the proposed refinement does not hold. If the above process completes without finding such a pair, then refinement does hold.

The first case (failure of refinement) is easy to see: the implementation has a trace (the sequence of visible actions used to bring the cartesian product to the failing state-pair), which can bring it into a state with behaviours not possible for the normal form. This means there is a divergence, a trace or a refusal of the implementation that is not allowed in the specification. Provided we have a way of finding the trace that led to a specific pair $\langle \nu, w \rangle$ being considered, it is thus possible to report not only the failure of refinement but also a reason.

Conciseness being a virtue, it is as well to report the shortest possible sequence of actions that can lead to an error. This is achieved if we perform a breadth-first search (BFS) during the model-checking phase. We shall see later that this brings other advantages.

The case of successful proof is a little more subtle. One can justify the claim that refinement always holds in these circumstances either operationally or abstractly. Operationally, if refinement fails, then it must hold because the implementation has some behaviour that is banned by the normal form. There is therefore some sequence of actions which exhibit this, potentially bringing the implementation into some state w where it can (a) diverge illegally, (b) perform an event that takes the traces outside the set permitted by the normal form or (c) refuse a set not refused by the normal form. It is clear that the unique normal form state ν corresponding to this trace is such that $\langle \nu, w \rangle$ will be found in the search above, leading to a failure to check.

Abstractly, one can show that the refinement checking process is simultaneously formulating and proving a sort of mutual recursion induction over the state-space of the implementation. This style of proof is discussed in [10], though one also needs the result of [11] that a divergence-free component of a CSP mutual recursion is identical in any fixed point of the recursive function.

21.3   Implementation Issues

21.3.1   Machine-readable CSP

CSP has been, in the best tradition of 'blackboard' languages, a rather variable notation, with some parts being used differently in different schools and some parts being rather under-defined. Since it is written, essentially, as a series of algebraic expressions using a variety of peculiar-looking operators, it does not look like the sort of programming language one usually types into a computer.

FDR emerged as part of a general effort to make tools available for CSP. There was thus an obvious need for a standardised syntax, parser and type theory/checker for the language. The work[5] to develop these has been led by J.B. Scattergood [14], and has gone on hand-in-hand with that on FDR which, together with several other tools, uses them.

The objective of this work has been to preserve as much as possible of the form, spirit and flexibility of the blackboard language, while bringing in structure to allow for building the larger programs we can expect to see with the availability of tools and practical use. For portability, it was decided to do all of this within the confines of an ASCII syntax – where the chief compromise is in the representations of the operators – though this does not preclude the building of more elaborate display and printing facilities on top of it.

Aside from trivial issues such as the shapes of operators, most of the decisions in the design of the syntax revolved around the sub-process objects such as events, their atomic components and parameters to processes (which can be thought of as

---

[5]The CSP parser and typechecker were produced under an ONR-sponsored project, and are freely available to anyone interested in producing tools related to CSP.

process state). Unless we change the CSP semantics of termination and sequencing, the treatment of these objects is necessarily declarative: there is no assignment or similar construct that can change the value of an existing variable within its scope. This makes CSP unlike occam, which requires a more elaborate semantics of termination [12, 13], and also contrasts with Hoare's earlier 'CSP 1978' [15]. It also affects the style of CSP programs, which become *scripts* of definitions (of a mixture of processes and other objects) in the style of functional programming languages such as Haskell and that of [16].

More specific features of the machine-readable syntax include:

1. In [1], every process has an intrinsic alphabet, with these being important for the semantics of the parallel operator. A pair of processes must synchronise on events in the intersection of their alphabets. We have found it more convenient to supply either these alphabets directly when using the parallel operator or, more usually, to define the interface set of each parallel composition: $P \parallel_A Q$, written P [|A|] Q in ASCII, makes P and Q synchronise on elements of A. Thus, processes in our standard syntax *do not* have intrinsic alphabets.

2. Each event is made up from a constructor representing its name and a number of 'data' components from a fixed list of types (which may be empty). Each 'channel' thus has a possibly trivial cartesian product type. The events are formed using infix dots, sometimes by ? representing input and binding the identifiers to their right until the occurrence of a ! representing output. Thus the event a.1?x!y is a communication over channel a, whose first and last components are fixed and the middle one is open and will bind x to the value input. FDR demands that all channels used are specifically declared.

3. The syntax has specific support for booleans, numbers, sequences, tuples and sets. Any undefined identifiers (ones not bound to anything specific) are treated as tokens or constructors introduced by the user.

21.3.2   Implementing checking and debugging

The front end
FDR has a Standard ML front end (itself sometimes hidden by an X Windows interface) which calls on optimised routines in C to perform computationally-intensive tasks. The front end's main role is to compile the high-level CSP notation into a form that can be efficiently manipulated at the lower level, and to interpret the results.

FDR makes a distinction between *low-level* processes and *high-level* processes. The former are intended to be compiled into a raw state-machine representation by the ML. The latter are typically the composition of several low-level processes: FDR deals with these by compiling these components in the front end and using the back-end routines to combine them. At the time of writing this distinction is made by dividing the operators of CSP into two classes.

- Low-level operators are prefixing, the various forms of choice, conditional, sequencing and all parameterisation of processes.
- High-level operators are all forms of parallel, hiding and renaming.

No low-level construct may be used syntactically outside a high-level one, and the low-level components of a system are just the maximal components composed of low-level operators.

This hierarchy is generally consistent with the way CSP is used, and indeed what it in fact enforces is the notion of a CSP program as a system of *communicating sequential processes*! It is also close to the syntactic restriction necessary to enforce finite state spaces. Infinite state spaces can be created in CSP through the effects of parameterisation, and recursion through the left-hand argument of ; (sequencing) or through parallel, hiding and renaming in various combinations. Of these, only the first two remain possible in our restricted syntax. While not forbidden in FDR, use of recursion through the left-hand-side of sequencing should be used only with care for obvious reasons. Similarly, recursions parameterised by infinite data types need to be treated with care.

The back end

There are three main functions carried out by the back end in the current version of FDR: expanding and normalising the specification process, divergence-checking the implementation, and doing the model-checking of the two. The essential features of these algorithms have already been set out in an earlier section, so we will restrict attention to one important issue. This is how to deal efficiently with the problems that appear in managing the very large sets of states that typically appear in checking a large parallel system.

Because more elaborate computations are needed over the specification system, the simple enumeration of its states is typically not a limiting factor. Thus the size of state-space we can deal with at the implementation end of refinement is currently two to three orders of magnitude larger than that at the specification end. This has rarely proved a problem, for essentially the reasons discussed in Section 2.

The most interesting issue is the difference between the DFS used for divergence checking and the BFS used for model checking. Both of these algorithms rely on the maintenance of sets of which states have been visited before. In a DFS we need a constantly updated representation of this set so that we can discover whether the state we are looking at has been visited before (and in our case, whether it is on the current chain). Since we immediately look at the children of the most recently visited node, there is no potential for grouping these tests. Our preferred representation for the set in this case has thus been a hash table.

In performing a BFS there is a high latency between generating a pending state and actually visiting it, if it is new. The test of whether it is new can be performed at any time during this interval. A natural way of doing this is to look at all successor states generated during a particular 'layer' of the search. If the current list of visited states is stored as a sorted list, then we can find out which of the successors are new by sorting the successors (naturally, removing duplicates) and then merging them into the established list. Obviously the successors of each genuinely new state can be generated as it is merged in.

This latter method has been found to be faster and more memory-efficient than the former. The greatest benefit appears when the set of states becomes too large to fit within the physical memory of the computer. Hash table representations of sets map so badly onto virtual memory that they are effectively unusable at this level. The sorted list representation maps onto virtual memory extremely well: all access into the lists is sequential (depending on which sorting routine is used during that phase). We have found very little degradation in performance in checks when they are forced to use virtual memory.

This fact has meant that it is often significantly quicker to perform the model-checking phase than the divergence-checking, and indeed the former can frequently be performed on systems when the latter is not within reach. FDR thus provides the option of 'failures-only' checking, which establishes whether all the traces and stably-observable failures are allowed by the specification. Of course this proves full refinement on the assumption that the implementation is divergence-free, something which is frequently either obvious or can be established by other methods. The notion of failures-only checking also has independent interest in connection with [6].

Debugging

When a state-pair is found which fails to check, we would like to be able to help the user find why things went wrong. To do this, FDR discovers a shortest sequence of actions that bring the system into the errant state, and helps the user to see the state and actions each component process of the implementation contributed to the problem via its graphical interface.

The simplest way of reconstructing the path taken by the BFS to the error state is by storing, with each state, a record of its parent. Unfortunately this essentially doubles the storage requirement. It is more efficient (for the overall operation of the system) to store with each state-pair the level of the BFS on which it was generated. The path can then be reconstructed straightforwardly by essentially running the transition system backwards starting from the erroneous one: if we have currently got a state-pair at level $N + 1$, the next one is any pair at level N of the original BFS from which the $N + 1$ one can be reached.

As indicated above, it is possible for FDR to give a detailed analysis of why the implementation performed an illegal behaviour. An interesting problem that has arisen in practical use is that it is sometimes the *specification* that is 'wrong', not saying what was really intended. A 'missing' behaviour is, of course, output. But it is much harder to attribute blame within the specification for why it did *not* allow it, both because of the large transformation the specification has gone through on normalisation, and because the lack of a behaviour is a much harder thing to pin down than why one is there.

21.4   FDR in Practice

The title of this section could equally be 'CSP in practice', since the utility of FDR derives from the expressive power of the notation and of CSP refinement. The former is important in the effective way we can express a wide range of systems, the second because of the wide range of correctness questions that can be resolved using only one well-sharpened tool.

FDR actually has its origins in a real, practical problem: the specification and design of the VCP and other communications hardware of the Inmos T9000 transputer family [17, 18]. Inmos identified the need for a tool to support failures/divergence refinement on realistic-size problems (then of order 10^4–10^5 states) with debugging facilities.

Since those early prototypes both the algorithms, and in particular the interface, have become a great deal more sophisticated and the tool has been used in a variety of studies, both practical and academic. At the time of writing (June 1993) it is capable of dealing with implementation state-spaces of order 10^7 on a moderate-sized workstation (where a check of size 10^6 might take 20 to 60 minutes) and order 10^4 normal form states. We expect considerable improvements, by a variety of methods such as those detailed in the next section.

Two things about CSP work hand-in-hand to make FDR useful: the theory of refinement and the expressive power of its operators. Refinement both brings a theory of program development, through its transitivity and monotonicity, and also, since it is based on nondeterminism, gives a uniform way of expressing correctness conditions. Any condition R on processes that takes the form of specifying that each behaviour of a process satisfies some predicate (a *behavioural specification*) – and most practical conditions take this form – has a most nondeterministic process P_R that satisfies it. A general process Q then satisfies R if, and only if, $P_R \sqsubseteq Q$.

CSP is fortunately well-equipped with notation for expressing nondeterminism, so that it is usually possible to find a concise representation for P_R in the language. Such a representation may be finite or infinite state. 'Safety' and 'liveness' properties can both be written in this form, as can ones that mix these two ideas. For example,

$$P \underset{\{a,b\}}{\|} CHAOS(\Sigma) \qquad \text{where} \quad P = a \to b \to P$$

specifies that a and b alternate, without expressing any condition on other events. $CHAOS(A)$ is the most nondeterministic divergence-free process using the events in A:

$$CHAOS(A) = STOP \sqcap (x : A \to CHAOS(A))$$

This is a *safety* specification because it allows any refusal. *Liveness* specifications usually allow any trace, but put limitations on what can be refused. A typical – and the most commonly used – example is

$$DF = \bigcap_{a \in \Sigma} a \to DF$$

which states that the process is deadlock-free. Note that DF can perform any trace, and select any event at any time, but may not refuse all events.

Safety and liveness properties tend to represent desirable facets of a process, rather than attempting to capture the full essence of intended behaviour. One that does this is likely to contain both safety and liveness elements. A particularly simple example which might apply to a communications protocol is that it should behave like a one-place buffer:

$$COPY = left?x \to right!x \to COPY$$

(Note that this simply adds data to the version of $COPY$ seen earlier.) This will apply to most implementations of the alternating bit protocol, for example. $COPY$ is actually a *deterministic* process, so that $COPY \sqsubseteq P$ implies $COPY = P$: refining it makes a very precise statement indeed. In many protocols a certain amount of *buffering* is introduced, and we may well not care how much. We would therefore want to generalise the above specification to that of the most nondeterministic buffer:

$$
\begin{aligned}
B_{\langle\rangle} &= left?x \to B_{\langle x \rangle} \\
B_{s\langle y \rangle} &= ((left?x \to B_{\langle x \rangle s \langle y \rangle}) \sqcap STOP) \\
&\quad \square \; right!y \to B_s
\end{aligned}
$$

This process cannot refuse to input when empty, or to output when nonempty. It never loses any input and preserves output. The nondeterminism comes in because it *may*, but is not *obliged to* accept further input when non-empty. This specification is infinite-state, since the buffer can hold any number of items. In practical use it is thus necessary to introduce some maximum permitted buffering.

The ability of CSP to describe nondeterministic behaviour is also useful at the implementation side, both in cases when some part of the system (such as an unreliable communications medium) is outside the control of the programmer, and also in cases where it is desired to abstract away from the way decisions are made. The former was illustrated in [19], which describes how FDR can be used to verify communications protocols. It has also been used to good effect in the development of fault-tolerant systems. The latter can be valuable both by cutting down state-spaces and by proving more general results. These ideas are discussed in [20], for example.

CSP is unusual among process algebras in the way it makes multi-way synchronisation natural, Hoare pointing out that parallel composition acts like conjunction over trace specifications. A fascinating illustration of the power of this notion is the way FDR can be used to solve the well-known puzzle *peg solitaire*. A move in this game, illustrated in Figure 21.3, consists of a peg hopping up, down, left or right over one peg, which is removed, into an empty hole. Starting with 32 pegs and a hole in the centre, the objective is to have left only a single peg, in the centre hole. The reason why we have coloured eight pegs differently will become apparent shortly.

Thinking of each of the 33 squares as a separate process, each move becomes a three-way synchronisation (between the from-, over- and to-squares). A typical square, at co-ordinates (i,j) has two states (*Full* and *Empty*) and can be written:

$$
\begin{aligned}
Empty(i,j) \quad = \quad & left.i.j \to Full(i,j) \\
& \square \ down.i.j \to Full(i,j) \\
& \square \ up.i.j \to Full(i,j) \\
& \square \ right.i.j \to Full(i,j)
\end{aligned}
$$

$$
\begin{aligned}
Full(i,j) \quad = \quad & left.(i-2).j \to Empty(i,j) \\
& \square \ down.i.(j-2) \to Empty(i,j) \\
& \square \ up.i.(j+2) \to Empty(i,j) \\
& \square \ right.(i+2).j \to Empty(i,j) \\
& \square \ left.(i-1).j \to Empty(i,j) \\
& \square \ down.i.(j-1) \to Empty(i,j) \\
& \square \ up.i.(j+1) \to Empty(i,j) \\
& \square \ right.(i+1).j \to Empty(i,j)
\end{aligned}
$$

Note that there are four 'channels', corresponding to a move in any of the four directions. The move $direction.i.j$ represents the move *to* square (i,j) from the appropriate source.

We form the complete starting position from 32 *Full* squares and 1 *Empty* one, synchronising on appropriate events. Or nearly, since the use of the generic square process means that most (all but the nine middle ones) of the processes have non-real events possible: ones relating to squares off the edge of the board. This problem can be removed at once by putting the combination in parallel with the process *STOP*, synchronising on all these false events, thereby banning them. We then have a process, which we can call *BOARD*, which allows precisely the sequences of moves allowable in solitaire.

A solution to the puzzle is thus a trace of 31 moves, with the last one a jump to the centre square ($(3,3)$ in the co-ordinate system where the left and bottom squares have x and y co-ordinate 0). In principle we can find this by specifying it is impossible, checking the result (which will fail) and using the debugging information to find the winning sequence of moves. The specification for this is

$$
\begin{aligned}
TEST \quad &= \quad MOVE(30) \underset{\Sigma}{\parallel} CHAOS(\Sigma), \quad \text{where} \\
MOVE(0) \quad &= \quad x : (\Sigma \setminus Middle) \to STOP \\
MOVE(n+1) \quad &= \quad x : \Sigma \to MOVE(n)
\end{aligned}
$$

where *Middle* is the set of moves to (3,3).

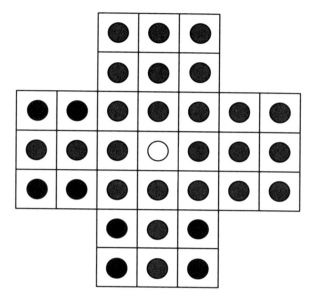

Figure 21.3 Peg solitaire showing tactically fixed pegs.

Unfortunately there are too many states in this pure version of the puzzle (order 10^9–10^{10}). Here, multi-way synchronisation comes to our rescue again, for we can put *BOARD* in parallel with processes that put restrictions (*tactics*) on the moves we allow. One simple one that works is to forbid eight specified pegs (shown in Figure 21.3) from moving until the 20th move. This finds a solution in 729 833 states.

A number of other similar puzzles have been solved similarly, including one example where FDR beat the best-known solution by some way!

This example is interesting because it shows both how CSP can be used to represent state-, and rule-based systems outside the domain one would at first expect, and how multi-way synchronisation can be used to carry out restricted tests in cases where a full check is either unnecessary or unacceptably slow.

21.5   Prospects

Even though FDR has already shown itself to be a practical tool, there are numerous ways in which it can be developed. These can be broken into the categories of improvements to the basic structure, and of widening its scope. All of the following possibilities have either been experimented with or are under consideration.

21.5.1   General improvements

Inference and infrastructure

The present tool provides a powerful calculator for deciding refinement questions. The properties of refinement (monotonicity, transitivity, etc.) mean that there are potentially many inferences one can make once one has established a few refinements between processes in a system. There is the potential to build a proof/development management system on top of the calculator to record what facts have been established in a session (or longer), record any assumptions that the user might wish to assert, and make appropriate deductions (perhaps by integrating an established logical inference tool).

Once one has such an infrastructure, it will be possible to build in other tools, such as algebraic transformations, and support for deadlock or divergence analysis using analytic rather than model-checking techniques (though probably supported by them). Tools for establishing divergence-freedom are particularly desirable, given the difficulties discussed in Section 21.3.2.

Compression

Currently FDR expands the state-spaces of its processes fully and *explicitly*. Since the state-spaces of parallel compositions typically grow exponentially with the number of processes involved, this limits the size of problem that can be dealt with: while we can deal with many realistic problems, there are also many which are too large and others where considerable ingenuity has to be exercised to keep the size manageable. Methods which do not exhaustively list all reachable states, rather proving results of the state space in blocks, are known as *implicit*.

Three general types of method are known to me: Binary Decision Diagrams (BDDs), exploiting compositionality, and the symbolic representation of state. The first of these has attracted a considerable amount of work, most notably from Clarke [21], and it is possible to 'cover' enormous state-spaces provided the problems have sufficient regularity. Since the usual problem-domain of this type of system (both in terms of the type of property proved and the type of system analysed) is somewhat remote from that of FDR we have no immediate plans to incorporate this type of technology, though in future, in a large integrated tool, there will almost certainly be a role for it.

Like BDDs, compressing state-spaces via compositionality is a technique which is likely to work well for some examples and badly for others. The basic idea is to attempt to compress the state-spaces of the intermediate syntactic components of a system as it is built up, rather than letting it just multiply. One would thus expand the states of a component, compress it, and then use the compressed version in building up the system from there on. What we need of the compressed version is that it should have the same semantics as the original (failures, or failures and divergences depending on the sort of check being done).

The obvious techniques for compression include direct forms of surgery on transition systems, cutting out sequences of internal actions for example, and normalisation, both discussed earlier and possibly also in 'failures-only' and 'traces-only' forms. In our experience, normalisation can be expected to reduce the size of a state space of a system if that system includes hiding of internal actions *provided* the system does not include explicit nondeterminism ($\sqcap$) or many nondeterministic arbitrations that are hidden. (In other words, the internal actions should essentially be 'making progress' rather than 'making choices'.)

Either of these will make it desirable that we extend the basic notation of labelled transition system to allow nodes to have sets of maximal refusals: any stable node must have at least one, and nodes with τ-actions may now have them. In other words, we want a notion of transition system which includes both the traditional one and the additional information contained in the normal form systems.

One of the most interesting and challenging things when incorporating these ideas will be preserving the debugging functionality of the system. The debugging process will become hierarchical: at the top level we will find erroneous behaviours of compressed parts of the system; we will then have to debug the pre-compressed forms for the appropriate behaviour, and so on down.

When doing failures-only checking (i.e., disregarding the possibility of divergence) it will be possible to hide any events which can be made irrelevant to the specification, greatly increasing the scope for compression of this sort. The most spectacular example of this is deadlock-freedom, where the whole alphabet can be hidden: a general process P can deadlock if and only if $P \setminus \Sigma$ can (necessarily on the empty trace).

Consider the case of the N dining philosophers (in a version, for simplicity, without a Butler process). A natural way of building this system up hierarchically is as progressively longer chains of the form

$$PHIL_0 \| FORK_0 \| PHIL_1 \| \ldots \| FORK_{m-1} \| PHIL_m$$

In analysing the whole system for deadlock, we can hide all those events of a subsystem that do not synchronise with any process outside the subsystem. Thus in this case we can hide all events other than the interactions between $PHIL_0$ and $FORK_{N-1}$, and between $PHIL_m$ and $FORK_m$. The failures normal form of the subsystem will have very few states (typically four, though the number may vary for small m and different versions of the system). Thus we can compute the failures normal form of the whole hidden system in time proportional to N, even though an explicit model-checker would find exponentially many states. (At a higher level, this particular example offers the possibility of inductive proof, proving results independent of N. This is a separate issue.)

A mode of state-space compression that is possible in the present system relates to systems of the form $C[P]$, where $C[\cdot]$ is a *context* and P is a subprocess whose states we wish to compress to allow reasoning with $C[P]$. If we can find a specification S with fewer states than P such that $S \sqsubseteq P$ and S either is equivalent to P or is thought to capture all the properties of P required by $C[\cdot]$, then it makes sense to analyse $C[S]$ rather than $C[P]$. An example of this might be where P is a communications protocol and S is an appropriate buffer specification.

This suggests a further possibility for compression in cases where the normal form of some subsystem is larger than we might wish (offering negative or little saving). A normal form where this occurs is likely to contain a number of (powerspace) nodes containing the initial node system being normalised. The process represented by any of these will be an approximation to the initial node, and the larger the set (i) the smaller the set of normal form states reachable from it and (ii) the worse approximation one gets. In the second example of Figure 21.1, apart from node **1**, with five normal form states, we could choose **3** or **4/5** with two and one states respectively. Clearly the use of such approximate compressions will sometimes give false negative results (assuming the compression occurs only on the implementation side), though these will be detected in attempting to debug the 'error'. Pragmatically, unless the context prevents the subprocess from performing any trace that would get it into the approximate state, one would normally expect such approximations to be valid. For otherwise the specification would be expecting less of the initial state of the system when it is returned to than at the beginning.

Symbolic manipulations

Though CSP is primarily a notation for describing and reasoning about how processes interact, it can also describe how the internal states of these processes evolve. In other words, CSP processes sometimes contain, and communicate, data. We have seen one fairly typical example of this in buffer processes.

At the time of writing, FDR deals with this data by expanding any input on a channel into an alternative choice with one communication for each element of the underlying type. Thus the version of $COPY$ with data has $N+1$ states where there are N members of the type of *left* and *right*. In the general case there seems no alternative to this approach, since conditional constructs, etc., allow one to create complex patterns of behaviour on a single channel. However it is frequently the case, as in the buffer case, that data (or at least most data) does not alter the control-flow of a process: it is treated as tokens, perhaps with operations carried out on it.

There appears to be considerable potential for reducing state explosion by recognising this fact and adding the capability for including symbolic representations of data in the transition systems used: inputs will not have to be expanded as above, and outputs will become abstract representations of the data they carry.

Specification operators

The CSP operators currently implemented are those that have a convenient operational semantics over standard transition systems. Though – as we have remarked – these include constructs whose main role is to allow us to construct specification-like processes, there are other constructs which it would be useful to have for specifications, that do not fit into this category.

Obvious ones include ⊔ (least upper bound), which can be thought of as *full* conjunction (as opposed to ‖ which acts as *trace* conjunction) and *P/s* (after). We have identified various others. These are characterised by being only, or most conveniently, implemented as direct transformations on normal forms. We propose to implement a variety of these in future versions of FDR. For them to be used at the implementation side (and there are good reasons for wanting this facility) it will be helpful to be using the extended form of transition systems identified above. This feature has many of the same needs as compression by normalisation.

A related issue is the possibility of creating finite-state representations of infinitary (typically *fairness*) specifications. The idea here is to create a system where we specify that all infinite traces must pass infinitely often though a specified set of nodes. It should be possible to present such infinitary specifications rather more compactly than most of their conventional finite approximations. This will require a revised form of normalisation.

21.5.2 Widening scope

Time and priority

The tool we have described deals only with the untimed version of CSP, where we are concerned with the relative order of events but not with exactly when they occur. Many concurrent systems developments are concerned with time: either real, continuous time or clocked time (in synchronous VLSI and similar applications). This has led to a variety of timed process algebras (including Timed CSP) and timed model-checking work.

Applications of Timed CSP have demonstrated the desirability of having mechanisms (such as Timewise Refinement [22]) for moving between the timed and untimed theories – either for different parts of a system, or during phases of a development. This creates the desire that FDR might be extended to deal with timed systems. One can identify three models of time such a version might operate.

- Real, continuous time as in Timed CSP.
- Clocked, or checkpointed, time where a special event is assumed to fire regularly, but where the relative order of events between checkpoints remains relevant.
- Discrete time, where there is a regular clock and process state only exists at the ticks, with multisets of events between them.

The first of these carries the obvious problem that there are infinitely many points in real time to worry about in any interval of non-zero length. It is not tractable in general, though results have been proved [23, 24] which show that, under certain conditions, a sufficiently fine finite granularity will do.

The second can be viewed as approximating the first. We have implemented a prototype system extended by a priority mechanism that makes this type of reasoning sensible. The basic principle we follow is that, at the highest level, most non-time events should have priority over time. A variety of examples have been studied.

The third is what is probably required for reasoning about synchronous VLSI at the cycle level. By treating the events between ticks as bags, and not recording intermediate state, one can expect to generate less states than in the asynchronous cases.

Non-CSP state machines
CSP specifications, and the theory of refinement we have developed, make as much sense for systems developed in other notations than CSP. Indeed the initial uses of the prototype system by Inmos used a variety of input formats for the state machines under consideration. We expect to deal with input derived from a number of non-CSP sources, including VHDL and LOTOS.

Acknowledgements

I have not written a single line of the code of FDR. Most of the credit, for implementing my ideas and many of their own, therefore goes to Dave Jackson, Michael Goldsmith, Bryan Scattergood and Jason Hulance. We owe much to the initial stimulus from Inmos, in particular Geoff Barrett and Victoria Griffiths, and to our various users and customers.

Partial funding for this work has come from ONR, ESPRIT and Inmos.

References

[1] C.A.R. Hoare, *Communicating Sequential Processes*, Prentice-Hall 1985.

[2] A.W. Roscoe, *Unbounded Nondeterminism in CSP*, in 'Two Papers on CSP', PRG Monograph PRG-67. Also Journal of Logic and Computation (1993).

[3] Barrett, G., *The fixed-point theory of unbounded nondeterminism*, Formal Aspects of Computing 3 pp110-128 (1991).

[4] G. M. Reed and A. W. Roscoe, *Metric spaces as models for real-time concurrency*, Proceedings of the Third Workshop on the Mathematical Foundations of Programming Language Semantics, Springer LNCS 298, 1987.

[5] G. Lowe, *Priorities and probabilities in Timed CSP*, Oxford University D.Phil thesis, 1993.

[6] L. Jategoankar, A Meyer and A.W. Roscoe, *Separating failures from divergence*, In preparation.

[7] S.D. Brookes and A.W. Roscoe, *An improved failures model for communicating processes*, in Proceedings of the Pittsburgh seminar on concurrency, Springer LNCS 197 (1985), 281-305.

[8] S.D. Brookes, *A model for communicating sequential processes*, Oxford University D.Phil thesis, 1983.

[9] P.C. Kanellakis and S.A. Smolka, *CCS expressions, Finite state processes and three problems of equivalence*, Information and Computation **86**, 43-68 (1990).

[10] A.W. Roscoe, *Topology, Computer Science and the Mathematics of Convergence*, in Topology and Category Theory in Computer Science (Reed, Roscoe, Wachter, eds) OUP 1991.

[11] A.W. Roscoe, *An alternative order for the failures model*, in 'Two papers on CSP', technical monograph PRG-67, Oxford University Computing Laboratory, July 1988. Also appeared in Journal of Logic and Computation **2**, 5 pp557-577.

[12] A.W. Roscoe, *Denotational semantics for occam*, in Proceedings of the Pittsburgh seminar on concurrency, Springer LNCS 197 (1985), 306-329.

[13] M.H. Goldsmith, A.W. Roscoe and B.G.O. Scott, *Denotational Semantics for Occam II*, Oxford University Computing Laboratory technical monograph PRG-108 (1993). Also submitted to Transputer Communications.

[14] J.B. Scattergood, *A basis for CSP tools*, To appear as Oxford University Computing Laboratory technical monograph, 1993.

[15] C.A.R. Hoare, *Communicating Sequential Processes*, CACM **21**, 666-677 (1978).

[16] R.S. Bird and P. Wadler, *An introduction to functional programming*, Prentice-Hall 1988.

[17] M.D. May, G. Barrett and D. Shepherd, *Designing chips that work*, in *Mechanised Reasoning and Hardware Design*, M.J.C. Gordon and C.A.R. Hoare, eds (Prentice-Hall, 1992).

[18] A.W. Roscoe, *Occam in the Specification and Verification of Microprocessors* Phil Trans R. Soc. Lond A (1992) **339**, 137-151. Also in *Mechanised Reasoning and Hardware Design*, M.J.C. Gordon and C.A.R. Hoare, eds (Prentice-Hall, 1992).

[19] A.W. Roscoe *Developing and verifying protocols in CSP*, Proceedings of Mierlo workshop on protocols, published by TU Eindhoven.

[20] A.W. Roscoe and Naiem Dathi *The pursuit of deadlock freedom*, Information and Computation **75**, 3 (December 1987), 289-327.

[21] J.R. Burch, E.M. Clarke, D.L. Dill and L.J. Hwang, *Symbolic model checking: 10^{20} states and beyond*, Proc. 5th IEEE Annual Symposium on Logic in Computer Science, IEEE Press (1990).

[22] S.A. Schneider, *Timewise refinement for communicating processes*, proceedings MFPS 9, LNCS to appear, 1993.

[23] R.Alur, C. Courcoubetis and D.L. Dill, *Model-Checking for real-time systems*, in Proceedings of Symposium on Logic in Computer Science, pp414-425.

[24] D. M. Jackson, *Logical verification of reactive software system*, Oxford University D.Phil Thesis, 1992.

Chapter 22

The Semantics of Id

J. E. Stoy

TONY HOARE was beginning his work on Communicating Sequential Processes [17, 18] at about the time of his move to Oxford, and it has been the basis of much fruitful work there, by himself and others, in the last fifteen years. During the same period the Programming Research Group, under his leadership, has continued and expanded its interest in Functional Programming, with the aim of making the use of computers simpler and more reliable. In this paper, dedicated to Tony, we use CSP to investigate the semantics of one particular functional programming language.

22.1 Introduction

Ever since John McCarthy [21] borrowed Alonzo Church's λ-notation [9], though not his calculus, for Lisp [22], and the Cuch [8] and ISWIM [20] appeared as the first really functional programming languages, interest in the area has steadily grown. The interest has been multi-faceted. On the one hand, functional languages provided a programming notation with simple and regular semantics: programs in these languages were more likely to do what they were supposed to do, and it was easier to prove that they did, or to perform formal transformations on them to produce more efficient versions. The textbook of Bird and Wadler [6] is just one of many possible exemplars of this approach. On the other hand, the same regular semantics caught the attention of those interested in parallel implementations: the Church-Rosser property [10] of these languages made them particularly susceptible to concurrent evaluation. Thus, for example, Jack Dennis, whose germinating interest in vehicles for parallelism [11] led to his work on dataflow [12], developed with his colleagues and students the functional language Val [1], which in turn inspired the development of Sisal [23, 7].

These two motivations have influenced the evolution of functional languages in different directions. A notable example is evaluation order. A concern for maximum parallelism suggests eager evaluation as the rule – this obtains in Val and Sisal, which have correspondingly strict semantics. Concern for semantic elegance, and in particular for the universal applicability of the β-substitution rule (which Landin had noted as crucial in his presentation of ISWIM), leads to non-strict semantics implemented by a lazy-evaluation rule. Haskell [19] is a leading modern example of this approach.   The tension between these two concerns has caused some languages to split: thus ML [14], originally conceived as a metalanguage for constructing proofs in a Logic of Computable Functions, now exists in both "standard" (strict) and "lazy" versions.

A similar tension may be found in the area of non-functional features. The concern for semantic simplicity leads to such features being rigorously eschewed, causing considerable extra work when trying to accommodate mechanisms, such as input-output, which naturally have to do with state: see, for example, Andrew Gordon's study of I/O in Haskell [13]. The seekers for parallel implementations, however, are much more likely simply to include non-functional features in order to permit the coding of important algorithms which would be impossible, or much less efficient, in purely functional languages.

22.1.1   The Id language

The Id language is an attempt to have the best of both worlds. It originated in 1978 [4] at the University of California at Irvine, and has run through several redesigns. It has been implemented on simulated and real dataflow hardware, and there are also implementations on several single-processor platforms. The current version of the language is described in Version 90.1 of the Reference Manual [28], which is taken as definitive for this paper.

The Id language is syntactically separable into three layers. The base layer is purely functional: it is claimed to combine non-strict semantics with eager evaluation. Superimposed on this is an "I-structures" (incremental structures) layer: this allows data structures with components for which no value need be specified when the structure is defined; they receive their values later, in separate "assignments". Attempts to read a value before it has been set are held up until it is available; attempts to set a particular component's value more than once lead to a catastrophic failure of the entire program. The result is a language which remains deterministic, but for which β-substitution is not universally valid – the duplication of a sub-expression might, for example, lead to multiple attempts to set the same I-structure component.

The third layer adds "M-structures" (mutable structures) to the mix. An M-structure component is initially "empty", but may be set by an assignment, which performs a "**put**" operation on the component thereby "filling" it with a value. Subsequent computations typically read the value with a "**take**" operation (thereby rendering the component empty again), and use it to compute a new value which they "**put**" back. Attempts to **take** from an empty component wait until a value is available – in the case of several attempts waiting it is unspecified which of them is satisfied first. Attempts to **put** to a full component result in catastrophic failure. The language is therefore now nondeterministic. Since it is now sometimes necessary to specify more precisely the order in which parts of the evaluation happen, a construct called a "barrier" is provided; its use is shown in examples below.

22.1.2 Our objectives

This paper represents the start of an investigation into how all these features interact. As we have noted, the layers of Id are syntactically separable, so that one can tell, for example, when one is working in the purely functional subset of the language. We would like to know whether we can use standard functional programming techniques when working within this subset. To that end, we present first a formal semantics for a large subset of the language (including I-structures and M-structures). Then we present classical denotational semantics for the functional layer; and we prove that the two definitions agree for complete purely functional programs. We reserve to later work the question of how to deal with parts of programs: a functional fragment within a non-functional program or *vice versa*.

We ignore many of the details of Id when they are irrelevant to our particular focus[1]. For example, Id is strongly typed, and comes equipped with a Hindley-Milner type inference system [16, 26]: we shall simply assume that all our programs are fully typed. It also uses pattern-matching to select clauses of expressions and to bind local variables: we assume that all this has successfully been translated into conditionals and selector functions.

22.1.3 The syntax of Id

In this paper we shall deal with the following subset of Id.

$$
\text{E} ::= \text{C} \mid \text{I} \mid \textbf{if } \text{E}_1 \textbf{ then } \text{E}_2 \textbf{ else } \text{E}_3 \mid \text{E}_1\Omega\text{E}_2 \mid \text{E}_1[\text{E}_2] \mid \text{E}_1![\text{E}_2] \mid \text{E}_1!![\text{E}_2] \mid (\text{E}_1,\text{E}_2)
$$

$$
\mid \textbf{fun } (\text{I}_1,\ldots,\text{I}_n) \bullet \text{E} \mid \text{E}_f(\text{E}_1,\ldots,\text{E}_n) \mid \text{S in E} \mid
\begin{array}{l} \{\text{S}_1 \\ \vdots \\ \text{S}_n \\ \textbf{in E}\} \end{array}
\mid
\begin{array}{l} \{\text{S}_1 \\ \vdots \\ \text{S}_n \\ \text{S in E}\} \end{array}
$$

$$
\text{S} ::= \text{I} = \text{E} \mid \text{I}_1,\text{I}_2 = \text{E} \mid \text{I}[\text{E}_1] = \text{E}_2 \mid \text{I}![\text{E}_1] = \text{E}_2 \mid \text{I}!![\text{E}_1] = \text{E}_2 \mid \text{S}_1 ; \ldots ; \text{S}_n
$$

---

[1]The reader may enjoy extending our definitions to cover some of the features we have left out. Some of these, such as recursively defined types, will require some facility with the theory; some, such as the use of parentheses to limit the scope of barriers, will require facility in the manipulation of semantic definitions; others are merely a matter of small print.

C is a constant from the syntactic category **Con**, not further defined, and I is an identifier from the syntactic category **Ide**. Ω is a dyadic operator, and "$E_1[E_2]$" represents I-structure array selection. "$E_1![E_2]$" and "$E_1!![E_2]$" deal with M-structures: the first represents a "**take**" from an M-structure array element, and the second represents a "read" which does not remove the value (it may be thought of as **take**-ing it and immediately **put**-ting it back). "(E_1, E_2)" is a "tuple"; and the following two productions are for function definition[2] and application. "S **in** E" is a block: the expression E is to be evaluated in the environment produced by the bindings in the statement S. The next two productions contain barriers: *all* the computation required to evaluate the bindings above the line must be completely terminated before anything below the line is allowed to start. (Note that all the bindings in $S_1 ; \ldots ; S_n$ and possibly S are evaluated as one mutually recursive set: the barriers affect evaluation order, not scope. It is therefore quite easy to use them in a way which causes deadlock.)

The statement productions provide respectively for simple binding of variables, binding of names to elements of tuples, assignments to I-structure and M-structure components, an M-structure assignment that overwrites the previous value (again to be thought of as a **take** immediately followed by a **put**), and grouping several statements into a mutually recursive set (not a sequence, for in the absence of barriers the order is immaterial).

22.1.4   Semantic definitions of Id

There is as yet no complete formal definition of the Id language. Zena Ariola's thesis [2] contains an operational semantic definition of the first two layers, based on Graph Rewriting Systems [3]. This definition involves constant use of a whole-sale renaming and substitution mechanism, so that (as with many other operational definitions) it becomes difficult to keep track of the contribution to the total behaviour made by a particular part of the program. It has, however, been a useful basis for the development of compilers for Id. Paul Barth introduces in his thesis [5] a partial time-ordering on events, in order to discuss the constraints required for the correct use of M-structures, but the integration into a full semantic definition has yet to be done.

---

[2]We are ignoring the business of curried function definitions, such as **def** f a b = $a + b$; such a definition may be regarded as syntactic shorthand for the higher-order function definition f = **fun** $a \cdot$ (**fun** $b \cdot a + b$). That is not how a compiler would treat it, of course; but we think of that as a question of compiler optimisation, not semantics.

```
DEF member?_and_insert_list ys x =
  IF (MNil? ys) THEN
    (False, MCons x MNil)
  ELSE IF (x == ys.MCons_1) THEN
    (True, ys)                                          % 5
  ELSE
    { (b,ys´)      = member?_and_insert_list ys!MCons_2 x ;
      ys!MCons_2  = ys´ ;
    IN
      (b,ys)  };                                        % 10
```

Figure 22.1 Mutable lists.

22.2   The CSP Semantics of Id

22.2.1   Example

Consider the example (in the complete Id language, not our chosen subset) shown in Figure 22.1. This example is discussed by Barth [5] (though not with respect to the point discussed here), and concerns mutable lists used in the implementation of a parallel hash table. It is intended that several invocations of this function be allowed to scan the same list in parallel. It is obviously important to establish that the M-structure protocol is being properly observed, and for this we must show that the M-structure **take** on line 7 happens before the **put** on line 8. One easy way of ensuring this would be to put a barrier between the two lines; but this would prevent any parallel scans, as no other invocation would be able to **take** from ys!MCons_2 until the recursive call on line 7 had completed. As the program stands, however, the argument has to be much more complicated. The **put** will not occur until the expression on the right-hand side of line 8 has produced a result; but this will not happen until the variable ys´ has been initialised, which in turn will not happen until the recursive call on line 7 has produced at least part of its result. But this function happens to be strict in its first argument (because of the test on line 2), so there will be no result until the **take** has taken place.

This concentration on the ordering of events, and the synchronisation of events happening in different places, suggests that Hoare's Communicating Sequential Processes might be an appropriate vehicle for describing Id semantics. Accordingly, we now turn to the task of defining the semantics of Id in CSP.

22.2.2   Communicating Sequential Processes

We shall use CSP as set out in Hoare's book [18], deviating only in a couple of respects. For reasons of notational simplicity, we prefer not to include the alphabet of a process as one of the process's intrinsic parts; the notation for parallel composition must therefore be amended to include a specification of which events are to be synchronised (that is, to require the simultaneous participation of both processes involved) and which are to be interleaved (and in which, therefore, only one of the processes participates). We use the notation

$$P \parallel_A Q$$

for this purpose, where P and Q are processes and A is a set of events: only the events in A are to be synchronised (if both processes are sequential – that is, they have the terminating event "$\checkmark$" in their alphabets – then "$\checkmark$" must be an element of A). More formally, in the traces model, we define

$$(P \parallel_A Q) = \{s \mid \exists\, t \in P \cdot \exists\, u \in Q \cdot s \; synchint(t, u, A)\}$$

where *synchint* is very similar to Hoare's *interleaves* [18, Section 1.9.3] and is defined recursively as follows:

$$
\begin{aligned}
\langle\rangle \; synchint(t, u, A) \;\; &\Leftrightarrow \;\; t = \langle\rangle \wedge u = \langle\rangle \\
\langle x \rangle^\frown s \; synchint(t, u, A) \;\; &\Leftrightarrow \;\; (x \in A \wedge t = \langle x \rangle^\frown t_1 \wedge u = \langle x \rangle^\frown u_1 \\
&\qquad\qquad \wedge \; s \; synchint(t_1, u_1, A)) \\
&\quad \vee \; (x \notin A \wedge t = \langle x \rangle^\frown t_1 \wedge s \; synchint(t_1, u, A)) \\
&\quad \vee \; (x \notin A \wedge u = \langle x \rangle^\frown u_1 \wedge s \; synchint(t, u_1, A))
\end{aligned}
$$

At one point in the definition of congruence relations below, we shall find ourselves defining processes with traces where "$\checkmark$" occurs other than at the end. Readers whom this offends may without ill effect introduce for themselves a function which removes all such malformed traces from processes which have them.

22.2.3   The model for CSP

For the purposes of this paper, the traces model for CSP will be adequate for our needs: so, since we are omitting the alphabet from our representation of a process, a process is simply a prefix-closed set of traces. The definition of Id is, however, independent of which model is chosen; so if the more sophisticated failures-divergences model proves necessary for some future investigation of nondeterministic programs, it can then be adopted.

We are non-standard, however, in having higher-type values in our traces. This means that where CSP theory talks about processes as sets of traces, we should instead think of elements of the appropriate powerdomain. As we are using the traces model, the Hoare powerdomain [15] is, appropriately enough, the right one to use; that would no longer be true if we were to change to the failures-divergences model. In fact, however, we shall continue to use set notation for processes, relying on the structure of traces to make all the operations in our definitions safely computable.

Id expressions and statements on the one hand, and "memory cells" on the other, will all be represented as processes, and the events in their traces will mainly be for communication between these two classes. Processes which are the denotations of expressions may also indulge in the event "**result**.v", where v is an element of the expression's type; no trace of a simple expression may contain more than one of these events. (For multiple-valued expressions we have events "**result**.$\langle i \rangle.v$" and even "**result**.$\langle i, j \rangle.v$", and traces may contain one such event for each applicable sequence of indices; "**result**.v" is formally a synonym of "**result**.$\langle \rangle.v$".)

We may attach type subscripts to processes: to call a process P_τ means

$$\forall\, t \in P \bullet \langle \mathbf{result}.v \rangle \;\mathbf{in}\; t \Rightarrow v \in \mathbf{V}_\tau$$

where $\mathbf{V}_\tau$ is defined below. $\mathbf{P}_\tau$ means the domain of such processes.
The values of expressions are merely "sets" of traces; so

$$\mathbf{E}_\tau = \mathbf{P}_\tau$$

$\mathbf{V}_\tau$, the values of result events in those expressions which have them, is defined as follows:

$$
\begin{aligned}
\mathbf{V_B} &= \mathbf{B} \\
\mathbf{V}_{\tau_1 \to \tau_2} &= [V_{\tau_1} \to \mathbf{E}_{\tau_2}] \\
\mathbf{V}_{(\tau_1 \times \ldots \times \tau_n) \to \tau_k} &= [V^n \to \mathbf{E}_{\tau_k}]
\end{aligned}
$$

where V_{τ_1}, the set of variables of type τ_1, is defined below, and V^n is the set of n-tuples of appropriately typed variables. $\mathbf{B}$ is the basic domain of values of constants, not further defined here.

22.2.4 The "memory"

The process denoted by a program will run concurrently with the "memory", which is itself a collection of processes, a countable number each of variable cells, I-structure cells and M-structure cells. As usual with semantic definitions, provisions to deal with "catastrophic failure" complicate things: an error-handler and reporter run concurrently with the whole shebang.

In what follows, we shall assume that each cell has an associated type, which we shall refer to as τ or τ_n, and that the cell allocator always provides a cell with type appropriate for the context.

Variables

We shall regard variables as cells forming a set $\{V_n \mid n \in \mathbb{N}\}$. Each element of this set has its own associated type τ_n.

$$\alpha(V_n) = \bigcup\{\{\mathbf{v}_n.\mathbf{put}.x, \mathbf{v}_n.\mathbf{read}.x\} \mid x \in \mathbf{V}_{\tau_n}\} \cup \{\mathbf{prog\text{-}ok}\}$$
$$V_n = (\mathbf{v}_n.\mathbf{put}.x : (x \in \mathbf{V}_{\tau_n}) \longrightarrow (\mu\, X \bullet \mathbf{v}_n.\mathbf{read}.x \longrightarrow X$$
$$\mid \mathbf{prog\text{-}ok} \longrightarrow STOP)$$
$$\mid \mathbf{prog\text{-}ok} \longrightarrow STOP)$$

We may also refer to the process

$$(\mu\, X \bullet \mathbf{v}_n.\mathbf{read}.x \longrightarrow X \mid \mathbf{prog\text{-}ok} \longrightarrow STOP)$$

as $V_n(x)$. V is the set of event tags $\{\mathbf{v}_n \mid n \in \mathbb{N}\}$.

I-structures

The I-structure cells form a similar set $\{I_n \mid n \in \mathbb{N}\}$, each element of which has its own associated type τ_n. They differ from simple variables in that they have to cope with the possibility of double initialisation, which has to cause catastrophic failure: it signals "**drastic-error**" and then continues to return error values if asked. Their definition is omitted: it is similar to, but simpler than, that for M-structures, which immediately follows.

M-structures

The M-structure cells are defined similarly:

$$\alpha(M_n) = \bigcup\{\{\mathbf{m}_n.\mathbf{put}.x, \mathbf{m}_n.\mathbf{take}.x\} \mid x \in \mathbf{V}_{\tau_n}\}$$
$$\cup\{\mathbf{prog\text{-}ok}, \mathbf{drastic\text{-}error}\}$$
$$M_n = (\mathbf{m}_n.\mathbf{put}.x : (x \in \mathbf{V}_{\tau_n}) \longrightarrow MM_n(x)$$
$$\mid \mathbf{prog\text{-}ok} \longrightarrow STOP)$$
$$MM_n(x) = (\mathbf{m}_n.\mathbf{take}.x \longrightarrow M_n$$
$$\mid \mathbf{m}_n.\mathbf{put}.y : (y \in \mathbf{V}_{\tau_n}) \longrightarrow T_M$$
$$\mid \mathbf{prog\text{-}ok} \longrightarrow STOP)$$
$$T_M = \mathbf{drastic\text{-}error} \longrightarrow (\mu\, X \bullet (\mathbf{m}_n.\mathbf{take}.\top_{\tau_n} \longrightarrow X)$$
$$\mid \mathbf{m}_n.\mathbf{put}.y : (y \in \mathbf{V}_{\tau_n}) \longrightarrow X)$$

The complete system

The memory cells run almost independently: the "**prog-ok**" event is the only one in which they must all synchronise.

$$MEMORY = \underset{\{\mathbf{prog\text{-}ok}\}_{n \in \mathbb{N}}}{\|} (V_n \underset{\{\mathbf{prog\text{-}ok}\}}{\|} I_n \underset{\{\mathbf{prog\text{-}ok}\}}{\|} M_n)$$

The alphabet of this is, of course, the union of all the individual alphabets.

$$\alpha(MEMORY) = \bigcup_{n \in \mathbb{N}} (\alpha(V_n) \cup \alpha(I_n) \cup \alpha(M_n))$$

Two events in this alphabet are distinct from the others, and concern error-handling. So we let

$$A_E = \{\textbf{prog-ok, drastic-error}\}$$
$$A_M = \alpha(MEMORY) - A_E$$

Then we define the processes

$$ERROR\text{-}HANDLER = \textbf{drastic-error} \longrightarrow (\mu\,X \bullet \textbf{drastic-error} \longrightarrow X$$
$$|\ \textbf{prog-top} \longrightarrow STOP)$$
$$REPORTER = (\textbf{prog-ok} \longrightarrow SKIP\ |\ \textbf{prog-top} \longrightarrow STOP)$$

and the complete system to run the program process $PROG$ may finally be defined as follows:

$$SYSTEM(PROG) = (PROG\,;\,REPORTER) \underset{A_M \cup \{\textbf{prog-ok, prog-top}, \checkmark\}}{\|}$$
$$(MEMORY \underset{\{\textbf{drastic-error}\}}{\|} ERROR\text{-}HANDLER)$$

After $PROG$ terminates, $REPORTER$ either collects the "**prog-ok**" confirmation from the entire memory and successfully terminates, or, together with *ERROR-HANDLER*, produces "**prog-top**" as the final event, indicating that something in the program, and therefore the whole program, has failed catastrophically.

22.2.5 Semantic equations

Environments
In the CSP semantics, an environment is a finite mapping

$$\rho\ :\ \textbf{Ide} \rightarrow_{\textbf{m}} V$$

which respects type, in that if the identifier x is of type τ then so is the variable $\rho(x)$. The domain of ρ, $\mathrm{dom}(\rho) \subset \textbf{Ide}$, is always well-defined.

The equations
The semantic equations are given in Section 22.6.1 below. We use the subscript T in $\mathcal{E}_T$ to indicate that we are referring to the "trace" semantics. $\mathcal{V} : \textbf{Com} \rightarrow \textbf{B}$ and $\mathcal{W} : \textbf{Op} \rightarrow ((\textbf{B} \times \textbf{B}) \rightarrow \textbf{B})$ are not further defined.

The equations, and the discussion in the remainder of this paper, extensively mention "new variables", "variables new to an expression" and so on. It would be possible to formalise all this, for example by having the memory part of the system contain an allocation process which returned unused indices of variables on request; phrases like "where **v** is a new variable" occurring in the semantic equations would then be replaced by an interaction with this process and subsequent use of the index so allocated. But this would considerably and unnecessarily complicate the exposition, and we avoid it here.

The treatment of tuples in this definition is limited to pairs. They are included really only by way of example: a full treatment of multiple values would involve us in the mechanism of pattern matching, which we have determined to avoid.

An Id program is an expression. The effect of running an expression E as a program is to evaluate the process

$$SYSTEM(E_T[\![E]\!]\rho)$$

where ρ is some suitable environment. The trace of this evaluation may or may not contain a "**result**" event; if it does so, there may or may not subsequently be either a "$\checkmark$" event, denoting successful termination, or the "**prog-top**" event, signifying that the program has resulted in catastrophic failure. It is necessary to wait for one of these final indications before deciding whether to place any reliance in a result. As a matter of fact, all existing implementations of Id wait for termination before displaying the result (though they might display intermediate output, generated by explicit output statements, which are beyond the purview of this paper).

22.3   The Semantics of the Functional Layer

In the remainder of this paper we shall be considering only the functional layer of Id (but including barriers, since they affect the functional semantics). The syntax that remains is therefore:

$$E ::= C \mid I \mid \text{if } E_1 \text{ then } E_2 \text{ else } E_3 \mid E_1\Omega E_2 \mid (E_1, E_2)$$

$$\mid \text{fun } (I_1, \ldots, I_n) \bullet E \mid E_f(E_1, \ldots, E_n) \mid S \text{ in } E \mid \begin{matrix} \{S_1 \\ \vdots \\ S_n \\ \text{in } E\} \end{matrix} \mid \begin{matrix} \{S_1 \\ \vdots \\ S_n \\ S \text{ in } E\} \end{matrix}$$

$$S ::= I = E \mid I_1, I_2 = E \mid S_1 ; \ldots ; S_n$$

22.3.1   Examples

We begin this part by illustrating some of the subtleties which may be encountered in the functional-layer semantics of Id. We are interested in the question whether an Id expression produces a result and then terminates. This is partly because, as we have said, all existing implementations wait for termination before displaying a result; but even if a less strict implementation were available, the question of termination would still be of interest, for the expression

```
{ x = E
  ---
  IN x }
```

produces a result if and only if the expression E does so and terminates.

Suppose we are in the scope of the definition

```
DEF f a b c = IF a THEN b ELSE c;
```

so that f is functionally equivalent to a conditional operator, except that all its parameters are eagerly evaluated. Then the expression {x = f True 1 x IN x} will have the expected value *1* and will terminate[3], though it would do neither if f were strict. On the other hand, the expression

```
{ DEF g x = f (x==0) 1 (g (x-1))
  IN g 0 }
```

will produce the result *1* (which it would not were f strict), but will not terminate (as it would if evaluation were lazy). Similarly, {ones = 1:ones IN ones} will terminate successfully, having produced an infinite list (implemented as a cycle), and so will {DEF id x = x; ones = 1:(id ones) IN ones}. But

```
{ DEF copy []      = []
  | copy (x:xs) = x:(copy xs);
  ones = 1:(copy ones)
  IN ones }
```

will not terminate (though the beginnings of an ever-growing result will be produced).

In a standard denotational semantics, the evaluation rule is not explicitly specified: the distinction between strict and non-strict functions is the only tool we have. Clearly we need sometimes one and sometimes the other. Our final example shows that sometimes we need both. Consider the two programs

```
{ DEF h x = f True x z;          { DEF h x = f True x z;
  ---                              ---
  b = h 3;                         b = h 3;
                                   ---
  z = b;                           z = b;
  ---                              ---
  IN b}                            IN b}
```

in which the function f has the same definition as before. The left-hand one terminates (with the result *3*), but the right-hand one produces neither a result nor termination. Clearly, whether h is strict or not makes no difference, since its argument is always proper; but the *body* of h (that is, the call of f) has to be evaluated non-strictly on the left, but strictly on the right.

These considerations lead us to propose *two* sets of semantic equations for the functional layer. The intention is that one set should specify the non-strict semantics and the other the strict version, though the presence of barriers will cause each

---

[3]The stated behaviour of these examples may, of course, be checked from the CSP semantics.

to involve the other. Then the non-strict version may be used to tell whether an expression produces a result, while the strict version tells whether it also terminates. To deal properly with problems like our final example, however, we shall make Id functions denote a *pair* of functional values: the non-strict semantics will use one and the strict semantics the other.

22.3.2 Domains and environments

Because the two sets of equations refer to each other, we shall use the same domains in each. We accordingly define the set $[\![\tau]\!]$ of values of expressions of type τ to be $(\mathbf{E}_\tau)_\perp$, where

$$\mathbf{E_B} = \mathbf{B}$$
$$\mathbf{E}_{\tau_1\times\tau_2} = (\mathbf{E}_{\tau_1})_\perp \times (\mathbf{E}_{\tau_2})_\perp$$
$$\mathbf{E}_{\tau_1\to\tau_2} = [(\mathbf{E}_{\tau_1})_\perp \to (\mathbf{E}_{\tau_2})_\perp] \times [\mathbf{E}_{\tau_1} \to (\mathbf{E}_{\tau_2})_\perp].$$

Notice the pairs of functions, one strict and one not, in the third line. We shall frequently use ε (possibly with various kinds of decoration) to range over $(\mathbf{E}_\tau)_\perp$, and υ to range over $\mathbf{E}_\tau$.

Environments are now finite mappings

$$\rho \;:\; (\mathbf{Ide} \to_\mathbf{m} \bigcup_\tau [\![\tau]\!])_\perp$$

which also respect type, in that if x is of type τ then $\rho(x) \in ([\![\tau]\!])_\perp$. Except when $\rho = \perp$, $\mathrm{dom}(\rho) \subset \mathbf{Ide}$ is well-defined. (Note that the undefined environment, $\perp$, is quite different from the empty environment ρ in which $\mathrm{dom}(\rho) = \{\}$.)

22.3.3 The semantic equations

The semantic equations are given in Sections 22.6.2 and 22.6.3 below.

Many of these equations will be as expected. In the non-strict semantics for "S in E", ρ' is defined recursively: either of the following definitions is equivalent to the one given there.

$$\rho' = \mathit{fix}(\lambda\rho' \bullet \mathcal{S}_N[\![\mathbf{S}]\!](\rho+\rho'))$$
$$\rho' = \bigsqcup_{n\in\mathbb{N}}(\lambda\rho' \bullet \mathcal{S}_N[\![\mathbf{S}]\!](\rho+\rho'))^n(\perp_D)$$

where D is the domain of maps m such that $\mathrm{dom}(m) = \mathit{variables}[\![\mathbf{S}]\!]$.

In the strict semantics for the same clause, notice that ρ' is again defined recursively, exactly as in the previous version; but then the recursion is unfolded one final time, using the strict semantics. Thus non-strict semantics are used to give the variables their values; then strict semantics are used to insist on termination. The equations for the clauses with barriers are iterated versions using the same technique.

22.4   The Congruence of the Two Definitions

In order to increase our confidence in these definitions, we now embark on a proof that they define the same language. To avoid confusion when comparing values arising from the two definitions, we shall make use of the so-called "diacritical convention", introduced by Robert Milne [24] to help explicate much more complicated proofs of congruence. Values arising in the CSP semantics will be decorated with grave accents, and values arising in the functional semantics with acutes. Functions (such as $\mathcal{E}_T$ and $\mathcal{E}_N$) defined in the semantic equations will also gain accents, to emphasise their provenance, but they still denote exactly the same functions as they did before. Sometimes we shall also use circumflex accents, writing for example $\hat{\varepsilon}$ as an abbreviation for $\langle \grave{\varepsilon}, \acute{\varepsilon} \rangle$. (We also, when there is no danger of confusion, sometimes use abbreviations such as ε^n for $\langle \varepsilon_1, \varepsilon_2, \ldots, \varepsilon_n \rangle$.)

For comparing corresponding values from the two definitions, the appropriate tool is the *logical relation*. These are families of typed relations, defined by structural induction on types. (We are ignoring recursively defined types in this paper, so we do not need to discuss the extra complications of defining logical relations when such structural induction is inadequate.) Good introductions to logical relations are to be found in [27] and [31]; these relations amount to a more systematic version of the "inclusive predicates" used in congruence proofs by Milne [24, 25], and in considerably simpler examples by the present author [29, 30].

For brevity's sake, we shall make no further mention of multiple values. In particular, functions will be assumed to have but one argument, and the relevant semantic equations will be assumed to have been recast accordingly.

22.4.1   Some preliminary properties

Theorem 1 For all E, $\mathcal{E}_S[\![\mathbf{E}]\!]$ is strict (that is to say, in the expected next parameter ρ).

Proof: Structural induction.

Definition 2 If E is an expression, $FV(\mathbf{E})$ means the set of free variables of E.

Definition 3 A value in $[\![\tau]\!]$ is said to be *OK* if it equals $\bot$ or if it satisfies the following predicate at the appropriate type:

$$
\begin{aligned}
OK_{\mathbf{B}}(v_{\mathbf{B}}) \;\Leftrightarrow\;& true \\
OK_{\tau_1 \to \tau_2}(v_{\tau_1 \to \tau_2}) \;\Leftrightarrow\;& (\forall\, v' \in \mathbf{E}_{\tau_1} \bullet OK_{\tau_1}(v') \;\Rightarrow \\
& \quad (OK_{\tau_2}(v_1 v') \,\wedge\, (v_2 v' \neq\, \bot \;\Rightarrow\; v_1 v' = v_2 v')) \\
& \text{where } v_1 = \mathbf{fst}\ v \text{ and } v_2 = \mathbf{snd}\ v).
\end{aligned}
$$

Since Id functions denote a pair of functions in the functional semantics, this predicate is to express the fact that the components of such a pair are both the "same" function, at least whenever the strict version gives a proper result. Note that it is our first example of a logical relation – though unlike most of our others it is unary rather than binary.

Theorem 4 For all E and ρ, if $OK(\rho(\mathbf{I}))$ for all $\mathbf{I} \in FV(\mathbf{E})$, and if $\mathcal{E}_S[\![\mathbf{E}]\!]\rho \neq \bot$, then $\mathcal{E}_S[\![\mathbf{E}]\!]\rho = \mathcal{E}_N[\![\mathbf{E}]\!]\rho$.

Proof: Structural induction.

Note that this result implies that if E has no free variables, then its value under the two sets of functional semantic equations will be the same, at least whenever the strict semantics give a proper value. As is to be expected, sometimes the non-strict semantics give a proper value when the strict semantics do not.

Next we define a property of processes analogous to an expression's having no free variables.

Definition 5 A process P is said to be "*closed*" if the traces of $SYSTEM(P)$ contain no events in A_M other than those involving its own new variables.
We say that a process $\grave{\varepsilon}$ is "closed by B", where B is a process, if $(\grave{\varepsilon} \underset{\{\checkmark\}}{\|} B)$ is closed.

A closed process communicates with no variable processes which it does not itself initialise; so for any such process P, the values in the "**result**" events of the traces of $SYSTEM(P)$ are independent of the traces of variable processes already in use. It is easy to see that if E is a term with free variables $x_1, \ldots, x_n$ and $P_1, \ldots, P_n$ are processes closed by B, then

$$\grave{\mathcal{E}}_T[\![E]\!](\grave{\rho} + [x^n \mapsto \mathbf{v}^n]) \underset{\{\checkmark\}}{\|} B \underset{\{\checkmark\}}{\|} (\underset{\{\checkmark\}_{1 \leqslant i \leqslant n}}{\|} bind(\mathbf{v}_i, P_i))$$

is also closed, where $\mathbf{v}^n$ are n new variables.

Finally we define two criteria of good behaviour on the part of processes representing expressions. An expression should not assign values to any variables except for its own internal local definitions; and an expression should not terminate without producing a result.

Definition 6 A process is said "*to respect the memory*" if its possible traces contain no "**put**" events to any variables which are not new to it.

Lemma 7 For any E and ρ, $\mathcal{E}_T[\![E]\!]\rho$ respects the memory.

Proof: Structural induction.

Definition 8 We say that a process P has "well-formed traces" if

$$\forall t \in P \bullet \langle \checkmark \rangle \text{ in } t \Rightarrow \langle \mathbf{result}.\grave{v} \rangle \text{ in } t$$

for some $\grave{v}$.

A function value $\grave{v}$, possibly closed by a process B, has "well-formed traces" if $SYSTEM(\grave{v}\mathbf{v} \underset{\{\checkmark\}}{\parallel} bind(\mathbf{v},\grave{\varepsilon}))$ or $SYSTEM(\grave{v}\mathbf{v} \underset{\{\checkmark\}}{\parallel} bind(\mathbf{v},\grave{\varepsilon}) \underset{\{\checkmark\}}{\parallel} B)$ has well-formed traces whenever $SYSTEM(\grave{\varepsilon})$ or $SYSTEM(\grave{\varepsilon} \underset{\{\checkmark\}}{\parallel} B)$ has well-formed traces.

A process is "well-formed" if it has well-formed traces and, if it has functional type, the function values in its "**result**" events have well-formed traces.

Theorem 9 Let $\mathbf{E}_\tau$ be any expression and let $\{x_1,\dots,x_n\}$ be $FV(\mathbf{E})$. Then for any $\grave{\rho}$, and well-formed closed processes $\grave{\varepsilon}_1,\dots,\grave{\varepsilon}_n$, the process

$$SYSTEM(\grave{\mathcal{E}}_T[\![\mathbf{E}]\!](\grave{\rho} + [x^n \mapsto \mathbf{v}^n]) \underset{\{\checkmark\}}{\parallel} (\underset{\{\checkmark\}}{\parallel} \{bind(\mathbf{v}_i,\grave{\varepsilon}_i) \mid 1 \leqslant i \leqslant n\}))$$

is also well-formed, where the $\mathbf{v}^n$ are n new variables.

Proof: Structural induction, using a lemma (also proved by structural induction) to the effect that for all expressions of functional type, their functional values have well-formed traces.

22.4.2   The congruence relations

We now define a number of relations to express agreement between the CSP semantics and the functional semantics. e will be used to express the proposition that the CSP semantics produces a result just when the non-strict semantics give a proper value, and that the two results agree. t will be used for the proposition that the CSP semantics produces a result and terminates just when the strict semantics give a proper value, and that the two results again agree. In the proof of these propositions we shall also need a weaker form of t: wt (pronounced "weak tea") is to express the idea that the evaluation (in the CSP semantics) of some expression itself terminates, without insisting too, as t does, that the evaluation of all the expression's free variables also terminate. v is the logical relation expressing what it means for the results to agree.

Note that e, t and wt are each defined as the conjunction of implications in each direction: the congruence proof will not infrequently have to deal with these two directions separately.

Definition 10

$$\vec{e}_\tau (B)\,\grave{\varepsilon}_\tau \iff (\forall \acute{v} \bullet \varepsilon = \lfloor \acute{v} \rfloor \Rightarrow$$
$$(\exists\, t \in SYSTEM(\grave{\varepsilon} \underset{\{\checkmark\}}{\parallel} B) \bullet (\langle\mathbf{result}.\acute{v}\rangle \text{ in } t) \wedge v_\tau(B)\,\hat{v}_\tau))$$

$$\overleftarrow{e}_\tau (B)\, \hat{\varepsilon}_\tau \quad \Leftrightarrow \quad (\forall\, t \in SYSTEM(\grave{\varepsilon} \underset{\{\checkmark\}}{\parallel} B) \bullet (\langle \mathbf{result}.\grave{\upsilon}\rangle \text{ in } t) \Rightarrow$$
$$(\exists\, \acute{\upsilon} \bullet \acute{\varepsilon} = \lfloor \acute{\upsilon} \rfloor \wedge v_\tau (B)\, \hat{\upsilon}_\tau))$$
$$e_\tau(B)\, \hat{\varepsilon}_\tau \quad \Leftrightarrow \quad \overrightarrow{e}_\tau (B)\, \hat{\varepsilon}_\tau \;\wedge\; \overleftarrow{e}_\tau (B)\, \hat{\varepsilon}_\tau$$

Definition 11

v_τ is defined inductively as follows.

$$v_{\mathbf{B}}(B)\, \hat{\upsilon}_{\mathbf{B}} \quad \Leftrightarrow \quad \acute{\upsilon} = \grave{\upsilon}$$
$$v_{\tau_1 \to \tau_2}(B)\, \hat{\upsilon}_{\tau_1 \to \tau_2} \Leftrightarrow$$
$$\forall\, \hat{\varepsilon}'_{\tau_1} \bullet e_{\tau_1}(B)\, \hat{\varepsilon}'_{\tau_1} \Rightarrow e_{\tau_2}(B)\langle (\mathbf{fst}\ \acute{\upsilon})\acute{\varepsilon}', (\grave{\upsilon}\mathbf{v} \underset{\{\checkmark\}}{\parallel} bind(\mathbf{v}, \grave{\varepsilon}'_{\tau_1}))\rangle$$
$$\wedge\ wt_{\tau_1}(B)\, \hat{\varepsilon}'_{\tau_1} \Rightarrow wt_{\tau_2}(B)\langle (\mathbf{snd}\ \acute{\upsilon})\acute{\varepsilon}', (\grave{\upsilon}\mathbf{v} \underset{\{\checkmark\}}{\parallel} bind(\mathbf{v}, \grave{\varepsilon}'_{\tau_1}))\rangle$$
$$\wedge\ t_{\tau_1}(B)\, \hat{\varepsilon}'_{\tau_1} \Rightarrow t_{\tau_2}(B)\langle (\mathbf{snd}\ \acute{\upsilon})\acute{\varepsilon}', (\grave{\upsilon}\mathbf{v} \underset{\{\checkmark\}}{\parallel} bind(\mathbf{v}, \grave{\varepsilon}'_{\tau_1}))\rangle$$

where $\mathbf{v}$ is a new variable.

Definition 12

$$\overrightarrow{t}_\tau (B)\, \hat{\varepsilon}_\tau \quad \Leftrightarrow \quad (\forall\, \acute{\upsilon} \bullet \acute{\varepsilon} = \lfloor \acute{\upsilon} \rfloor \Rightarrow$$
$$(\exists\, t \in SYSTEM(\grave{\varepsilon} \underset{\{\checkmark\}}{\parallel} B) \bullet \langle \checkmark \rangle \text{ in } t \wedge e_\tau(B)\, \hat{\varepsilon}_\tau))$$
$$\overleftarrow{t}_\tau (B)\, \hat{\varepsilon}_\tau \quad \Leftrightarrow \quad (\forall\, t \in SYSTEM(\grave{\varepsilon} \underset{\{\checkmark\}}{\parallel} B) \bullet (\langle \checkmark \rangle \text{ in } t) \Rightarrow$$
$$(\exists\, \acute{\upsilon} \bullet \acute{\varepsilon} = \lfloor \acute{\upsilon} \rfloor \wedge e_\tau(B)\, \hat{\varepsilon}_\tau))$$
$$t_\tau(B)\, \hat{\varepsilon}_\tau \quad \Leftrightarrow \quad \overrightarrow{t}_\tau (B)\, \hat{\varepsilon}_\tau \;\wedge\; \overleftarrow{t}_\tau (B)\, \hat{\varepsilon}_\tau$$

Definition 13

$$\overrightarrow{wt}_\tau (B)\, \hat{\varepsilon}_\tau \quad \Leftrightarrow \quad (\forall\, \acute{\upsilon} \bullet \acute{\varepsilon} = \lfloor \acute{\upsilon} \rfloor \Rightarrow$$
$$(\exists\, t \in SYSTEM(\grave{\varepsilon} \,|||\, (B/\{\checkmark\})) \bullet \langle \checkmark \rangle \text{ in } t \wedge e_\tau(B)\, \hat{\varepsilon}_\tau))$$
$$\overleftarrow{wt}_\tau (B)\, \hat{\varepsilon}_\tau \quad \Leftrightarrow \quad (\forall\, t \in SYSTEM(\grave{\varepsilon} \,|||\, (B/\{\checkmark\})) \bullet (\langle \checkmark \rangle \text{ in } t) \Rightarrow$$
$$(\exists\, \acute{\upsilon} \bullet \acute{\varepsilon} = \lfloor \acute{\upsilon} \rfloor \wedge e_\tau(B)\, \hat{\varepsilon}_\tau)$$
$$wt_\tau(B)\, \hat{\varepsilon}_\tau \quad \Leftrightarrow \quad \overrightarrow{wt}_\tau (B)\, \hat{\varepsilon}_\tau \;\wedge\; \overleftarrow{wt}_\tau (B)\, \hat{\varepsilon}_\tau$$

Notice that the definition of wt gives rise to processes with traces containing "$\checkmark$" other than as their final event.

Note, too, that $\overrightarrow{e}\,(B)\,\langle \bot, \grave{\varepsilon}\rangle$, where $\grave{\varepsilon}$ and B are arbitrary; and $\overleftarrow{e}\,(B)\,\langle \acute{\varepsilon}, STOP\rangle$, where $\acute{\varepsilon}$ and B are arbitrary. So, in particular, $e(B)\,\langle \bot, STOP\rangle$. Similar facts hold for t and wt.

Lemma 14 The relation $e(B)\hat{\varepsilon}$ is inclusive in $\hat{\varepsilon}$: that is to say, if $\acute{\varepsilon}_1 \sqsubseteq \acute{\varepsilon}_2 \sqsubseteq \ldots \sqsubseteq \acute{\varepsilon}_n \sqsubseteq \ldots$ is a chain in $(\mathbf{\acute{E}})_\bot$, and $\grave{\varepsilon}_1 \subseteq \grave{\varepsilon}_2 \subseteq \ldots \subseteq \grave{\varepsilon}_n \subseteq \ldots$ a chain in $\mathbf{\grave{E}}$ such that $e(B)\hat{\varepsilon}_n$ for all $n \in \mathbb{N}$, then $e(B)\langle \bigsqcup_{n\in\mathbb{N}} \acute{\varepsilon}_n, \bigcup_{n\in\mathbb{N}} \grave{\varepsilon}_n\rangle$.

Proof. The proof is by induction on the structure of types. It is easy to see that it holds for $e_\mathbf{B}$. For $e_{\tau_1 \to \tau_2}$, suppose that we have chains in $(\mathbf{\acute{E}})_\perp$ and $\mathbf{\grave{E}}$ as set out in the statement of the lemma. Then either $\acute{\varepsilon}_n = \perp$ for all n, in which case no $\grave{\varepsilon}_n$ contains any trace with a **"result"** event. Then nor does $\bigcup_n \grave{\varepsilon}_n$; and since $\bigsqcup_n \acute{\varepsilon}_n = \perp$ too, the result holds. Or there is some m such that for all $n \geqslant m$ there is a t in $SYSTEM(\grave{\varepsilon}_n \parallel_{\{\checkmark\}} B)$ such that $\langle \mathbf{result}.\grave{\upsilon}_n \rangle$ **in** t, and $\acute{\varepsilon}_n = \lfloor \acute{\upsilon}_n \rfloor$ where $v_{\tau_1 \to \tau_2}(B)\hat{\upsilon}_n$.

Thence, if $e_{\tau_1}(B)\hat{\varepsilon}'$, we have, for all $n \geqslant m$, $e_{\tau_2}(B')\langle \acute{\upsilon}_n \acute{\varepsilon}', \grave{\upsilon}_n \mathbf{v} \rangle$, where $\mathbf{v}$ is a new variable and $B' = (B \parallel_{\{\checkmark\}} bind(\mathbf{v}, \grave{\varepsilon}'))$. By induction, $e_{\tau_2}(B')\langle \bigsqcup_n(\acute{\upsilon}_n \acute{\varepsilon}'), \bigcup_n(\grave{\upsilon}_n \mathbf{v}) \rangle$, and hence by continuity, $e(B')\langle(\bigsqcup_n \acute{\upsilon}_n)\acute{\varepsilon}', (\bigcup_n \grave{\upsilon})\mathbf{v}\rangle$, provided $e_{\tau_1}(B)\hat{\varepsilon}'$. That is, $v_{\tau_1 \to \tau_2}(B)\langle \bigsqcup_n \acute{\upsilon}_n, \bigcup_n \grave{\upsilon} \rangle$, and hence $e_{\tau_1 \to \tau_2}(B)\langle \bigsqcup_n \acute{\varepsilon}_n, \bigcup_n \grave{\varepsilon} \rangle$, as required.

Definition 15 A process B *terminates* if $\exists t \in SYSTEM(B) \bullet \langle \checkmark \rangle$ **in** t.

Lemma 16 If B terminates and $wt(B)\hat{\varepsilon}$, then $t(B)\hat{\varepsilon}$.

Proof: If B terminates, then $(\grave{\varepsilon} \mathbin{|||} (B/\{\checkmark\}))$ terminates just when $(\grave{\varepsilon} \parallel_{\{\checkmark\}} B)$ does. The definitions of t and wt therefore become equivalent.

22.4.3   The congruence theorem

We are now ready to state the main theorem. We wish to prove that the CSP semantics predict that a closed expression will give a result just when the non-strict semantic equations give a proper value; that the CSP semantics predict termination just when the strict semantics give a proper value; and that in both cases the results agree. This result will actually be a corollary of the theorem, which must be somewhat more complicated in order for the proof by induction to be successful.

Theorem 17 Let $\mathbf{E}_\tau$ be any expression and let $\{x_1, \ldots, x_m\}$ be $FV(\mathbf{E})$. Then for any $\hat{\rho}$ for which $\acute{\rho}$ is proper, and for any $\grave{\varepsilon}'_1, \ldots, \grave{\varepsilon}'_m$ which are OK, and for any well-formed processes $\grave{\varepsilon}'_1, \ldots, \grave{\varepsilon}'_m$ closed by B,

$$(e(B)\hat{\varepsilon}'_1 \wedge \ldots \wedge e(B)\hat{\varepsilon}'_m) \Rightarrow e_\tau(B')\langle \acute{\mathcal{E}}_N[\![\mathbf{E}]\!](\acute{\rho} + [x^n \mapsto \acute{\varepsilon}'^n]), \grave{\mathcal{E}}_T[\![\mathbf{E}]\!](\grave{\rho} + [x^n \mapsto \mathbf{v}^n])\rangle$$
$$(e(B)\hat{\varepsilon}'_1 \wedge \ldots \wedge e(B)\hat{\varepsilon}'_m) \Rightarrow wt_\tau(B')\langle \acute{\mathcal{E}}_S[\![\mathbf{E}]\!](\acute{\rho} + [x^n \mapsto \acute{\varepsilon}'^n]), \grave{\mathcal{E}}_T[\![\mathbf{E}]\!](\grave{\rho} + [x^n \mapsto \mathbf{v}^n])\rangle$$
$$(t(B)\hat{\varepsilon}'_1 \wedge \ldots \wedge t(B)\hat{\varepsilon}'_m) \Rightarrow t_\tau(B')\langle \acute{\mathcal{E}}_S[\![\mathbf{E}]\!](\acute{\rho} +_s [x^n \mapsto \acute{\varepsilon}'^n]), \grave{\mathcal{E}}_T[\![\mathbf{E}]\!](\grave{\rho} + [x^n \mapsto \mathbf{v}^n])\rangle$$

where in each case the $\mathbf{v}^n$ are n new variables, and

$$B' = (B \parallel_{\{\checkmark\}} (\parallel_{\{\checkmark\}1 \leqslant i \leqslant n} bind(\mathbf{v}_i, \grave{\varepsilon}'_i))).$$

Proof. The proof is by structural induction on the syntax of expressions. The case "S **in** E" needs a subsidiary fixed-point induction to handle the recursion; and the cases involving barriers involve a numerical induction for the sequence of barriers[4].

Corollary 18 If E_τ is any closed expression (that is, having no free variables), then for any $\hat{\rho}$ for which $\acute{\rho}$ is proper,

$$e_\tau(SKIP)\langle \acute{\mathcal{E}}_N[\![E]\!]\acute{\rho}, \grave{\mathcal{E}}_T[\![E]\!]\grave{\rho}\rangle \;\wedge\; t_\tau(SKIP)\langle \acute{\mathcal{E}}_S[\![E]\!]\acute{\rho}, \grave{\mathcal{E}}_T[\![E]\!]\grave{\rho}\rangle.$$

22.5   Conclusion

Corollary 18 gives us the result we sought. For purely functional Id programs, in the absence of barriers, it implies that we can safely use all the conventional techniques for constructing programs in a non-strict functional programming language, since all the mutually recursive equations and definitions are solved in the non-strict semantics. We merely have to make one final check, having assigned all our variables their prescribed values, to be sure that all the expressions involved then terminate according to the strict version of the semantics.

Matters are more complicated with barriers, of course: we have to go through this process for each set of definitions between barriers, keeping track at each stage which variables have been assigned proper values and which have not. Note that it should not be assumed, once a variable acquires a proper value during this procedure, that the value remains unchanged. A function value, for example, albeit always proper, may become defined on more and more arguments as its free variables subsequently acquire proper values.

It is to be hoped that the semantic definitions given here will be the basis of equally useful tools for constructing and reasoning about programs using the non-functional features of Id.

Acknowledgements

Much of this work was done while the author was on sabbatical leave at MIT, supported in part by the Advanced Research Projects Agency of the Department of Defense under the Office of Naval Research contract N00014-92-J-1310. He is most grateful to the Department of Electrical Engineering and Computer Science and to the Laboratory for Computer Science for their kind hospitality.

---

[4]The proof is given in the expanded version of this paper, available from the Oxford University Computing Laboratory as a PRG Technical Report.

22.6   Equations

22.6.1   The CSP semantics

Auxiliary functions

For all $n \in \mathbb{N}$, $rand_n(c) = \begin{cases} \mathbf{rand}_n.x & \text{if } c = \mathbf{result}.x \text{ for some } x \\ c & \text{otherwise} \end{cases}$

$rand_n$ may also be applied to processes, as described in [18, Section 2.6].
The alphabet $A_R = \{\mathbf{rand}_n.x \mid n \in \mathbb{N}\}$, where x ranges over all appropriate types.

$bind(\mathbf{v}, E) = (rand_1(E) \underset{A_R \cup \{\checkmark\}}{\|} BIND(\mathbf{v})) \setminus A_R$
where $BIND(\mathbf{v}) = (\mathbf{rand}_1.x : (x \in \tau) \longrightarrow \mathbf{v}.\mathbf{put}.x \longrightarrow SKIP)$.

$bind_2(\mathbf{v}_1, \mathbf{v}_2, E) = (E \underset{A \cup \{\checkmark\}}{\|} (\mathbf{result}.\langle 1 \rangle.x : (x \in \tau) \longrightarrow \mathbf{v}_1.\mathbf{put}.x \longrightarrow SKIP$
$\underset{\{\checkmark\}}{\|} \mathbf{result}.\langle 2 \rangle.x : (x \in \tau) \longrightarrow \mathbf{v}_2.\mathbf{put}.x \longrightarrow SKIP)) \setminus A.$
where $A = \{\mathbf{result}.\langle n \rangle.x \mid n \in \mathbb{N}\}$.

We introduce an operator for combining environments[5]:

$$\rho + \rho' = \begin{cases} \text{if } \rho = \bot, & \bot \\ \text{otherwise,} & \lambda I \bullet \begin{cases} \rho'(I), & \text{if } I \in \mathrm{dom}(\rho') \\ \text{otherwise} & \rho(I), & \text{if } I \in \mathrm{dom}(\rho) \\ \text{otherwise} & \bot \end{cases} \end{cases}$$

Expressions

$\mathcal{E}_T[\![\mathrm{C}]\!]\rho = (\mathbf{result}.c \longrightarrow SKIP)$
where $c = \mathcal{V}[\![\mathrm{C}]\!]$.

$\mathcal{E}_T[\![\mathrm{I}]\!]\rho = (\mathbf{v}.\mathbf{read}.x : (x \in \tau) \longrightarrow \mathbf{result}.x \longrightarrow SKIP)$
where $\mathbf{v} = \rho(\mathrm{I})$.

$\mathcal{E}_T[\![\mathbf{if}\ \mathrm{E}_1\ \mathbf{then}\ \mathrm{E}_2\ \mathbf{else}\ \mathrm{E}_3]\!]\rho =$
$\quad (rand_1(\mathcal{E}_T[\![\mathrm{E}_1]\!]\rho)$
$\quad \underset{A_R \cup \{\checkmark\}}{\|} \mathbf{rand}_1.x : (x \in bool) \longrightarrow (\mathbf{if}\ x\ \mathbf{then}\ \mathcal{E}_T[\![\mathrm{E}_2]\!]\rho\ \mathbf{else}\ \mathcal{E}_T[\![\mathrm{E}_3]\!]\rho))) \setminus A_R$

$\mathcal{E}_T[\![\mathrm{E}_1 \Omega \mathrm{E}_2]\!]\rho = ((rand_1(\mathcal{E}_T[\![\mathrm{E}_1]\!]\rho) \underset{\{\checkmark\}}{\|} rand_2(\mathcal{E}_T[\![\mathrm{E}_2]\!]\rho)) \underset{A_R \cup \{\checkmark\}}{\|} \mathcal{O}_T[\![\Omega]\!]) \setminus A_R$

$\mathcal{E}_T[\![\mathrm{E}_1[\mathrm{E}_2]]\!]\rho = ((rand_1(\mathcal{E}_T[\![\mathrm{E}_1]\!]\rho) \underset{\{\checkmark\}}{\|} rand_2(\mathcal{E}_T[\![\mathrm{E}_2]\!]\rho)) \underset{A_R \cup \{\checkmark\}}{\|} READI) \setminus A_R$
where $READI = (\ \mathbf{rand}_1.x : (x \in \tau_1) \longrightarrow \mathbf{rand}_2.y : (y \in \tau_2) \longrightarrow RI(x, y)$
$\quad \mid \mathbf{rand}_2.y : (y \in \tau_2) \longrightarrow \mathbf{rand}_1.x : (x \in \tau_1) \longrightarrow RI(x, y))$
in which $RI(x, y) = \begin{cases} \mathbf{i}_j.\mathbf{read}.r : (r \in \tau_3) \longrightarrow \mathbf{result}.r \longrightarrow SKIP, \\ \qquad\qquad \text{if } \mathbf{i}_j \text{ exists such that } \mathbf{i}_j = x(y) \\ STOP, \qquad\qquad\qquad\qquad\qquad\qquad \text{otherwise.} \end{cases}$

---

[5]This is more complicated than is needed here, as in this semantics it is never the case that $\rho = \bot$, but it will save introducing a different version of $\rho + \rho'$ for the functional layer semantics which follow.

where $\tau_1 = \mathbb{N}^n \to I$, $\tau_2 = \mathbb{N}^n$.

$$\mathcal{E}_T[\![E_1![E_2]]\!]\rho = ((rand_1(\mathcal{E}_T[\![E_1]\!]\rho) \underset{\{\checkmark\}}{\|} rand_2(\mathcal{E}_T[\![E_2]\!]\rho)) \underset{A_R \cup \{\checkmark\}}{\|} TAKE) \setminus A_R$$

where $TAKE = (\quad \mathbf{rand}_1.x : (x \in \tau_1) \longrightarrow \mathbf{rand}_2.y : (y \in \tau_2) \longrightarrow T(x,y)$

$\qquad\qquad | \quad \mathbf{rand}_2.y : (y \in \tau_2) \longrightarrow \mathbf{rand}_1.x : (x \in \tau_1) \longrightarrow T(x,y))$

in which $T(x,y) = \begin{cases} \mathbf{m}_j.\mathbf{take}.r : (r \in \tau_3) \longrightarrow result.r \longrightarrow SKIP, \\ \qquad\qquad\qquad\qquad \text{if } \mathbf{m}_j \text{ exists such that } \mathbf{m}_j = x(y) \\ STOP, \qquad\qquad\qquad\qquad\qquad\qquad\qquad \text{otherwise.} \end{cases}$

where $\tau_1 = \mathbb{N}^n \to M$, $\tau_2 = \mathbb{N}^n$.

$$\mathcal{E}_T[\![E_1!![E_2]]\!]\rho = ((rand_1(\mathcal{E}_T[\![E_1]\!]\rho) \underset{\{\checkmark\}}{\|} rand_2(\mathcal{E}_T[\![E_2]\!]\rho)) \underset{A_R \cup \{\checkmark\}}{\|} READM) \setminus A_R$$

where $READM = (\quad \mathbf{rand}_1.x : (x \in \tau_1) \longrightarrow \mathbf{rand}_2.y : (y \in \tau_2) \longrightarrow R(x,y)$

$\qquad\qquad\quad | \quad \mathbf{rand}_2.y : (y \in \tau_2) \longrightarrow \mathbf{rand}_1.x : (x \in \tau_1) \longrightarrow R(x,y))$

in which $R(x,y) = \begin{cases} \mathbf{m}_j.\mathbf{take}.r : (r \in \tau_3) \longrightarrow \mathbf{m}_j.\mathbf{put}.r \longrightarrow result.r \longrightarrow SKIP, \\ \qquad\qquad\qquad\qquad\qquad\qquad \text{if } \mathbf{m}_j \text{ exists such that } \mathbf{m}_j = x(y) \\ STOP, \qquad\qquad\qquad\qquad\qquad\qquad\qquad\qquad \text{otherwise.} \end{cases}$

where $\tau_1 = \mathbb{N}^n \to M$, $\tau_2 = \mathbb{N}^n$.

$$\mathcal{E}_T[\![(E_1, E_2)]\!]\rho = (res_1(\mathcal{E}_T[\![E_1]\!]\rho) \underset{\{\checkmark\}}{\|} res_2(\mathcal{E}_T[\![E_2]\!]\rho))$$

where res_n are the symbol-changing functions on processes induced by

$res_n(c) = \begin{cases} \mathbf{result}.t^\frown \langle n \rangle.x & \text{if } c = \mathbf{result}.t.x \text{ for some } x \\ c & \text{otherwise.} \end{cases}$

$$\mathcal{E}_T[\![\mathbf{fun} \ (I_1, \ldots, I_n) \bullet E]\!]\rho = (\mathbf{result}.f \longrightarrow SKIP)$$

where $f = \lambda(\mathbf{v}_1, \ldots, \mathbf{v}_n) \bullet \mathcal{E}_T[\![E]\!](\rho + [I_1, \ldots, I_n \mapsto \mathbf{v}_1, \ldots, \mathbf{v}_n])$

$$\mathcal{E}_T[\![E_f(E_1, \ldots, E_n)]\!]\rho = A \underset{\{\checkmark\}}{\|} (rand_1(\mathcal{E}_T[\![E_f]\!]\rho) \underset{A_R \cup \{\checkmark\}}{\|} \mathbf{rand}_1.f : (f \in \tau) \longrightarrow f(\mathbf{v}_1, \ldots, \mathbf{v}_n)) \setminus A_R$$

where $\mathbf{v}_1, \ldots, \mathbf{v}_n$ are n new variable cells, and $A = \underset{\{\checkmark\}_{1 \leqslant i \leqslant n}}{\|} bind(\mathbf{v}_i, \mathcal{E}_T[\![E_i]\!]\rho)$

$$\mathcal{E}_T[\![S \ \mathbf{in} \ E]\!]\rho = \mathcal{S}_T[\![S]\!]\rho' \underset{\{\checkmark\}}{\|} \mathcal{E}_T[\![E]\!]\rho'$$

where $\rho' = \rho + [variables[\![S]\!] \mapsto \mathbf{v}_1, \ldots, \mathbf{v}_j]$,
in which $variables[\![S]\!]$ are the new variable names (j of them) declared in S, and $\mathbf{v}_1, \ldots, \mathbf{v}_j$ are new variables.

$$\mathcal{E}_T[\![\ \begin{matrix} \{S_1 \\ \vdots \\ S_n \\ \mathbf{in} \ E\} \end{matrix} \ ]\!]\rho = (\mathcal{S}_T[\![S_1]\!]\rho' ; \ldots ; \mathcal{S}_T[\![S_n]\!]\rho') ; (\mathcal{E}_T[\![E]\!]\rho')$$

where $\rho' = \rho + [variables[\![S_1 ; \ldots ; S_n]\!] \mapsto \mathbf{v}_1, \ldots, \mathbf{v}_j]$,
in which $variables[\![S_1 ; \ldots ; S_n]\!]$ are the new variable names (j of them) declared in $(S_1 ; \ldots ; S_n)$, and $\mathbf{v}_1, \ldots, \mathbf{v}_j$ are new variables.

$$\mathcal{E}_T[\![\ \begin{matrix} \{S_1 \\ \vdots \\ S_n \\ S \ \mathbf{in} \ E\} \end{matrix} \ ]\!]\rho = (\mathcal{S}_T[\![S_1]\!]\rho' ; \ldots ; \mathcal{S}_T[\![S_n]\!]\rho') ; (\mathcal{S}_T[\![S]\!]\rho' \underset{\{\checkmark\}}{\|} \mathcal{E}_T[\![E]\!]\rho')$$

where $\rho' = \rho + [variables[\![S_1 ; \ldots ; S_n ; S]\!] \mapsto \mathbf{v}_1, \ldots, \mathbf{v}_j]$,
in which $variables[\![S_1 ; \ldots ; S_n ; S]\!]$ are the new variable names (j of them) declared in $(S_1 ; \ldots ; S_n ; S)$, and $\mathbf{v}_1, \ldots, \mathbf{v}_j$ are new variables.

Operators

$\mathcal{O}_T[\![\Omega]\!] =$
$$(\mathbf{rand}_1.x : (x \in \tau) \longrightarrow \mathbf{rand}_2.y : (y \in \tau) \longrightarrow \mathbf{result}.(\omega(x, y)) \longrightarrow SKIP)$$
$$\mid \ \mathbf{rand}_2.y : (y \in \tau) \longrightarrow \mathbf{rand}_1.x : (x \in \tau) \longrightarrow \mathbf{result}.(\omega(x, y)) \longrightarrow SKIP)$$
where $\omega = \mathcal{W}[\![\Omega]\!]$.

Statements

$$\mathcal{S}_T[\![\mathtt{I} = \mathtt{E}]\!]\rho = bind(\rho(\mathtt{I}), \mathcal{E}_T[\![E]\!]\rho)$$

$$\mathcal{S}_T[\![\mathtt{I}_1, \mathtt{I}_2 = \mathtt{E}]\!]\rho = bind_2(\rho(\mathtt{I}_1), \rho(\mathtt{I}_2), \mathcal{E}_T[\![E]\!]\rho)$$

$$\mathcal{S}_T[\![\mathtt{I}[\mathtt{E}_1] = \mathtt{E}_2]\!]\rho = ((rand_1(\mathcal{E}_T[\![\mathtt{E}_1]\!]\rho) \underset{\{\checkmark\}}{\parallel} rand_2(\mathcal{E}_T[\![\mathtt{E}_2]\!]\rho)) \underset{A_R \cup \{\checkmark\}}{\parallel} PUTI(\rho(\mathtt{I}))) \setminus A_R$$
where $PUTI(\mathbf{v}) = (\mathbf{v}.\mathbf{read}.x : (x \in \tau_1) \longrightarrow SKIP \underset{\{\checkmark\}}{\parallel} \mathbf{rand}_1.y : (y \in \tau_2) \longrightarrow SKIP$
$$\underset{\{\checkmark\}}{\parallel} \mathbf{rand}_2.z : (z \in \tau_3) \longrightarrow SKIP) \, ; PI(x, y, z)$$
in which $PI(x, y, z) = \begin{cases} \mathbf{i}_j.\mathbf{put}.z \longrightarrow SKIP, & \text{if } \mathbf{i}_j \text{ exists such that } \mathbf{i}_j = x(y) \\ STOP, & \text{otherwise.} \end{cases}$
where $\tau_1 = \mathbb{N}^n \to I$, $\tau_2 = \mathbb{N}^n$.

$$\mathcal{S}_T[\![\mathtt{I}![\mathtt{E}_1] = \mathtt{E}_2]\!]\rho = ((rand_1(\mathcal{E}_T[\![\mathtt{E}_1]\!]\rho) \underset{\{\checkmark\}}{\parallel} rand_2(\mathcal{E}_T[\![\mathtt{E}_2]\!]\rho)) \underset{A_R \cup \{\checkmark\}}{\parallel} PUT(\rho(\mathtt{I}))) \setminus A_R$$
where $PUT(\mathbf{v}) = (\mathbf{v}.\mathbf{read}.x : (x \in \tau_1) \longrightarrow SKIP \underset{\{\checkmark\}}{\parallel} \mathbf{rand}_1.y : (y \in \tau_2) \longrightarrow SKIP$
$$\underset{\{\checkmark\}}{\parallel} \mathbf{rand}_2.z : (z \in \tau_3) \longrightarrow SKIP) \, ; P(x, y, z)$$
in which $P(x, y, z) = \begin{cases} \mathbf{m}_j.\mathbf{put}.z \longrightarrow SKIP, & \text{if } \mathbf{m}_j \text{ exists such that } \mathbf{m}_j = x(y) \\ STOP, & \text{otherwise.} \end{cases}$
where $\tau_1 = \mathbb{N}^n \to M$, $\tau_2 = \mathbb{N}^n$.

$$\mathcal{S}_T[\![\mathtt{I}!![\mathtt{E}_1] = \mathtt{E}_2]\!]\rho = ((rand_1(\mathcal{E}_T[\![\mathtt{E}_1]\!]\rho) \underset{\{\checkmark\}}{\parallel} rand_2(\mathcal{E}_T[\![\mathtt{E}_2]\!]\rho))$$
$$\underset{A_R \cup \{\checkmark\}}{\parallel} UPDATE(\rho(\mathtt{I}))) \setminus A_R$$
where $UPDATE(\mathbf{v}) = (\mathbf{v}.\mathbf{read}.x : (x \in \tau_1) \longrightarrow SKIP$
$$\underset{\{\checkmark\}}{\parallel} \mathbf{rand}_1.y : (y \in \tau_2) \longrightarrow SKIP$$
$$\underset{\{\checkmark\}}{\parallel} \mathbf{rand}_2.z : (z \in \tau_3) \longrightarrow SKIP) \, ; U(x, y, z)$$
in which $U(x, y, z) = \begin{cases} \mathbf{m}_j.\mathbf{take}.w : (w \in \tau_3) \longrightarrow \mathbf{m}_j.\mathbf{put}.z \longrightarrow SKIP, \\ \qquad\qquad \text{if } \mathbf{m}_j \text{ exists such that } \mathbf{m}_j = x(y) \\ STOP, \qquad\qquad\qquad\qquad\qquad\qquad\qquad \text{otherwise.} \end{cases}$
where $\tau_1 = \mathbb{N}^n \to M$, $\tau_2 = \mathbb{N}^n$.

$$\mathcal{S}_T[\![\mathtt{S}_1, \ldots, \mathtt{S}_n]\!]\rho = \underset{\{\checkmark\}_{1 \leqslant i \leqslant n}}{\parallel} \mathcal{S}_T[\![\mathtt{S}_i]\!]\rho$$

22.6.2   The non-strict semantics

Auxiliary functions

$$Cond(\varepsilon_1, \varepsilon_2, \varepsilon_3) = \begin{cases} \varepsilon_2 & \text{if} & \varepsilon_1 = \lfloor true \rfloor, \\ \varepsilon_3 & \text{if} & \varepsilon_1 = \lfloor false \rfloor, \\ \bot & \text{otherwise.} \end{cases}$$

$$strict(f)(x) = \begin{cases} \bot & \text{if } x = \bot, \\ f(x) & \text{otherwise.} \end{cases}$$

$$vstrict(f)(x_1, \ldots, x_n) = \begin{cases} \bot & \text{if any of } x_1, \ldots, x_n \text{ is } \bot, \\ f(x_1, \ldots, x_n) & \text{otherwise.} \end{cases}$$

$$\rho +_s \rho' = \begin{cases} \bot, & \text{if } \rho = \bot \text{ or if } \rho'(I) = \bot \text{ for any } I \in \text{dom}(\rho') \\ \rho + \rho', & \text{otherwise.} \end{cases}$$

Expressions

$\mathcal{E}_N[\![\mathrm{C}]\!]\rho = \lfloor \mathcal{V}[\![\mathrm{C}]\!] \rfloor$

$\mathcal{E}_N[\![\mathrm{I}]\!]\rho = \rho(\mathrm{I})$

$\mathcal{E}_N[\![\textbf{if } \mathrm{E}_1 \textbf{ then } \mathrm{E}_2 \textbf{ else } \mathrm{E}_3]\!]\rho = Cond(\mathcal{E}_N[\![\mathrm{E}_1]\!]\rho, \mathcal{E}_N[\![\mathrm{E}_2]\!]\rho, \mathcal{E}_N[\![\mathrm{E}_3]\!]\rho)$

$\mathcal{E}_N[\![\mathrm{E}_1\Omega\mathrm{E}_2]\!]\rho = \omega(\mathcal{E}_N[\![\mathrm{E}_1]\!]\rho, \ \mathcal{E}_N[\![\mathrm{E}_2]\!]\rho) \text{ where } \omega = \mathcal{V}[\![\Omega]\!].$

$\mathcal{E}_N[\![(\mathrm{E}_1, \mathrm{E}_2)]\!]\rho = \lfloor\langle\mathcal{E}_N[\![\mathrm{E}_1]\!], \ \mathcal{E}_N[\![\mathrm{E}_2]\!]\rangle\rfloor$

$\mathcal{E}_N[\![\textbf{fun } (\mathrm{I}_1, \ldots, \mathrm{I}_n) \bullet \mathrm{E}]\!]\rho = \ \langle\lfloor\lambda(v_1, \ldots, v_n) \bullet \mathcal{E}_N[\![\mathrm{E}]\!](\rho + [\mathrm{I}_1, \ldots, \mathrm{I}_n \mapsto v_1, \ldots, v_n])\rfloor,$
$\qquad\qquad\qquad\qquad\qquad \lfloor\lambda(v_1, \ldots, v_n) \bullet \mathcal{E}_S[\![\mathrm{E}]\!](\rho +_s [\mathrm{I}_1, \ldots, \mathrm{I}_n \mapsto v_1, \ldots, v_n])\rfloor\rangle$

$\mathcal{E}_N[\![\mathrm{E}_f(\mathrm{E}_1, \ldots, \mathrm{E}_n)]\!]\rho = strict \, (\lambda f \bullet (\textbf{fst } f)(\mathcal{E}_N[\![\mathrm{E}_1]\!]\rho, \ldots, \mathcal{E}_N[\![\mathrm{E}_n]\!]\rho)) \, (\mathcal{E}_N[\![\mathrm{E}_f]\!]\rho)$

$\mathcal{E}_N[\![\mathrm{S} \textbf{ in } \mathrm{E}]\!]\rho = \mathcal{E}_N[\![\mathrm{E}]\!](\rho + \rho')$
where $\rho' = \mathcal{S}_N[\![\mathrm{S}]\!](\rho + \rho').$

$$\mathcal{E}_N[\!\![\begin{array}{c} \{\mathrm{S}_1 \\ \vdots \\ \underline{\mathrm{S}_n} \\ \textbf{in } \mathrm{E}\} \end{array}]\!\!]\rho = \mathcal{E}_N[\![\mathrm{E}]\!]\rho_n$$

where, for $1 \leqslant i \leqslant n$, $\quad\rho_i = \rho_0 +_s \rho_i''$
$\qquad\qquad\qquad\qquad \rho_i'' = \bigcup_{1 \leqslant j \leqslant i} \mathcal{S}_S[\![\mathrm{S}_j]\!](\rho_{i-1} + \rho_i')$
$\qquad\qquad\qquad\qquad \rho_i' = \mathcal{S}_N[\![\mathrm{S}_i]\!](\rho_{i-1} + \rho_i')$
and $\rho_0 = \rho + [\mathrm{I} \mapsto \bot \mid \mathrm{I} \in variables[\![\mathrm{S}_1 ; \ldots ; \mathrm{S}_n]\!]].$

$$\mathcal{E}_N[\!\![\begin{array}{c} \{\mathrm{S}_1 \\ \vdots \\ \underline{\mathrm{S}_n} \\ \mathrm{S} \textbf{ in } \mathrm{E}\} \end{array}]\!\!]\rho = \mathcal{E}_N[\![\mathrm{E}]\!](\rho_0 + \rho'')$$

where $\quad\rho_i'' = \mathcal{S}_N[\![\mathrm{S}]\!](\rho_n + \rho') \cup (\bigcup_{1 \leqslant j \leqslant n} \mathcal{S}_S[\![\mathrm{S}_j]\!](\rho_n + \rho'))$
$\qquad\quad\; \rho' = \mathcal{S}_N[\![\mathrm{S}]\!](\rho_n + \rho')$
and, for $1 \leqslant i \leqslant n$, $\quad\rho_i = \rho_0 +_s \rho_i''$
$\qquad\qquad\qquad\qquad\qquad \rho_i'' = \bigcup_{1 \leqslant j \leqslant i} \mathcal{S}_S[\![\mathrm{S}_j]\!](\rho_{i-1} + \rho_i')$
$\qquad\qquad\qquad\qquad\qquad \rho_i' = \mathcal{S}_N[\![\mathrm{S}_i]\!](\rho_{i-1} + \rho_i')$

where $\rho_0 = \rho + [\mathrm{I} \mapsto \bot \mid \mathrm{I} \in \textit{variables}[\![\mathrm{S}_1 ; \ldots ; \mathrm{S}_n ; \mathrm{S}]\!]]$.

Statements

$\mathcal{S}_N[\![\mathrm{I} = \mathrm{E}]\!]\rho = [\mathrm{I} \mapsto \mathcal{E}_N[\![E]\!]\rho]$

$\mathcal{S}_N[\![\mathrm{I}_1, \mathrm{I}_2 = \mathrm{E}]\!]\rho = [\mathrm{I}_1 \mapsto v_1, \mathrm{I}_2 \mapsto v_2]$ where $\langle v_2, \ v_2 \rangle = \mathcal{E}_N[\![E]\!]\rho$.

$\mathcal{S}_N[\![\mathrm{S}_1 ; \ldots ; \mathrm{S}_n]\!]\rho = (\mathcal{S}_N[\![\mathrm{S}_1]\!]\rho \cup \ldots \cup \mathcal{S}_N[\![\mathrm{S}_n]\!]\rho)$

22.6.3 The strict semantics

Expressions

$\mathcal{E}_S[\![\mathrm{C}]\!] = \textit{strict}(\lambda \rho \bullet \lfloor \mathcal{V}[\![\mathrm{C}]\!] \rfloor)$

$\mathcal{E}_S[\![\mathrm{I}]\!]\rho = \rho(\mathrm{I})$

$\mathcal{E}_S[\![\mathbf{if}\ \mathrm{E}_1\ \mathbf{then}\ \mathrm{E}_2\ \mathbf{else}\ \mathrm{E}_3]\!]\rho = \textit{Cond}(\mathcal{E}_S[\![\mathrm{E}_1]\!]\rho, \mathcal{E}_S[\![\mathrm{E}_2]\!]\rho, \mathcal{E}_S[\![\mathrm{E}_3]\!]\rho)$

$\mathcal{E}_S[\![\mathrm{E}_1 \Omega \mathrm{E}_2]\!]\rho = \omega(\mathcal{E}_S[\![\mathrm{E}_1]\!]\rho, \ \mathcal{E}_S[\![\mathrm{E}_2]\!]\rho)$ where $\omega = \textit{vstrict}(\mathcal{V}[\![\Omega]\!])$.

$\mathcal{E}_S[\![(\mathrm{E}_1, \mathrm{E}_2)]\!]\rho = \textit{vstrict}(\lambda \langle v_1, v_2 \rangle \bullet \lfloor \langle v_1, v_2 \rangle \rfloor)(\mathcal{E}_S[\![\mathrm{E}_1]\!], \ \mathcal{E}_S[\![\mathrm{E}_2]\!])$

$\mathcal{E}_S[\![\mathbf{fun}\ (\mathrm{I}_1, \ldots, \mathrm{I}_n) \bullet \mathrm{E}]\!] = \ \textit{strict}(\lambda \rho \bullet$
$\langle \lfloor \lambda(v_1, \ldots, v_n) \bullet \mathcal{E}_N[\![\mathrm{E}]\!](\rho + [\mathrm{I}_1, \ldots, \mathrm{I}_n \mapsto v_1, \ldots, v_n]) \rfloor,$
$\lfloor \lambda(v_1, \ldots, v_n) \bullet \mathcal{E}_S[\![\mathrm{E}]\!](\rho +_s [\mathrm{I}_1, \ldots, \mathrm{I}_n \mapsto v_1, \ldots, v_n]) \rfloor \rangle)$

$\mathcal{E}_S[\![\mathrm{E}_f(\mathrm{E}_1, \ldots, \mathrm{E}_n)]\!]\rho = \textit{strict}\,(\lambda f \bullet (\textit{vstrict}\,(\mathbf{snd}\ f))(\mathcal{E}_S[\![\mathrm{E}_1]\!]\rho, \ldots, \mathcal{E}_S[\![\mathrm{E}_n]\!]\rho))\,(\mathcal{E}_S[\![\mathrm{E}_f]\!]\rho)$

$\mathcal{E}_S[\![\mathrm{S}\ \mathbf{in}\ \mathrm{E}]\!]\rho = \mathcal{E}_S[\![\mathrm{E}]\!](\rho +_s \rho'')$
where $\rho'' = \mathcal{S}_S[\![\mathrm{S}]\!](\rho +_s \rho')$ and $\rho' = \mathcal{S}_N[\![\mathrm{S}]\!](\rho + \rho')$.

$$\mathcal{E}_S[\![\begin{array}{c}\{\mathrm{S}_1 \\ \vdots \\ \mathrm{S}_n \\ \mathbf{in}\ \mathrm{E}\}\end{array}]\!]\rho = \mathcal{E}_S[\![\mathrm{E}]\!]\rho_n$$

where, for $1 \leqslant i \leqslant n$,
$$\begin{aligned}\rho_i &= \rho_0 +_s \rho_i'' \\ \rho_i'' &= \bigcup_{1 \leqslant j \leqslant i} \mathcal{S}_S[\![\mathrm{S}_j]\!](\rho_{i-1} + \rho_i') \\ \rho_i' &= \mathcal{S}_N[\![\mathrm{S}_i]\!](\rho_{i-1} + \rho_i')\end{aligned}$$
and $\rho_0 = \rho + [\mathrm{I} \mapsto \bot \mid \mathrm{I} \in \textit{variables}[\![\mathrm{S}_1 ; \ldots ; \mathrm{S}_n]\!]]$.

$$\mathcal{E}_S[\![\begin{array}{c}\{\mathrm{S}_1 \\ \vdots \\ \mathrm{S}_n \\ \mathrm{S}\ \mathbf{in}\ \mathrm{E}\}\end{array}]\!]\rho = \mathcal{E}_S[\![\mathrm{E}]\!](\rho_0 +_s \rho'')$$

where
$$\begin{aligned}\rho_i'' &= \mathcal{S}_S[\![\mathrm{S}]\!](\rho_n + \rho') \cup (\bigcup_{1 \leqslant j \leqslant n} \mathcal{S}_S[\![\mathrm{S}_j]\!](\rho_n + \rho')) \\ \rho' &= \mathcal{S}_N[\![\mathrm{S}]\!](\rho_n + \rho')\end{aligned}$$

and, for $1 \leqslant i \leqslant n$, $\quad \rho_i \;\; = \;\; \rho_0 +_s \rho_i''$
$$\rho_i'' \;\; = \;\; \bigcup\nolimits_{1 \leqslant j \leqslant i} \mathcal{S}_S[\![\mathtt{S}_j]\!](\rho_{i-1} + \rho_i')$$
$$\rho_i' \;\; = \;\; \mathcal{S}_N[\![\mathtt{S}_i]\!](\rho_{i-1} + \rho_i')$$
where $\rho_0 = \rho + [\mathtt{I} \mapsto \bot \mid \mathtt{I} \in \mathit{variables}[\![\mathtt{S}_1 \,;\dots; \mathtt{S}_n \,; \mathtt{S}]\!]]$.

Statements
$$\mathcal{S}_S[\![\mathtt{I} = \mathtt{E}]\!]\rho = [\mathtt{I} \mapsto \mathcal{E}_S[\![E]\!]\rho]$$

$$\mathcal{S}_S[\![\mathtt{I}_1, \mathtt{I}_2 = \mathtt{E}]\!]\rho = [\mathtt{I}_1 \mapsto v_1, \mathtt{I}_2 \mapsto v_2]$$
where $\langle v_2,\; v_2 \rangle = \mathcal{E}_S[\![E]\!]\rho$.

$$\mathcal{S}_S[\![\mathtt{S}_1 \,;\dots; \mathtt{S}_n]\!]\rho = (\mathcal{S}_S[\![\mathtt{S}_1]\!]\rho \;\cup\; \dots \;\cup\; \mathcal{S}_S[\![\mathtt{S}_n]\!]\rho)$$

References

[1] W.B. Ackerman and J.B. Dennis. VAL—a value-oriented algorithmic language: Preliminary reference manual. Technical Report TR-218, Computation Structures Group, MIT Lab. for Computer Science, Cambridge, MA, June 1979.

[2] Z.M. Ariola. An algebraic approach to the compilation and operational semantics of functional languages with I-structures. Technical Report TR-544, MIT Laboratory for Computer Science, Cambridge, MA, 1992.

[3] Z.M. Ariola and Arvind. Graph rewriting systems. In M.R. Sleep, M.J. Plasmeijer, and M.C.J.D. van Eekelen, editors, *Term Graph Rewriting: Theory and Practice*, chapter 6, pages 77–90. John Wiley, Chichester, 1993.

[4] Arvind, K.P. Gostelow, and W. Plouffe. The (preliminary) Id report. Technical Report 114, Department of Information and Computer Science, University of California, Irvine, CA, 1978.

[5] P.S. Barth. Atomic data structures for parallel computing. Technical Report 532, MIT Laboratory for Computer Science, Cambridge, MA, 1992.

[6] R. Bird and P. Wadler. *Introduction to Functional Programming*. Prentice Hall International Series in Computer Science. Prentice Hall, New York, 1988.

[7] A.P.W. Bohm, D.C. Cann, J.T. Feo, and R.R. Oldehoeft. Sisal 2.0 reference manual. Technical Report CS-91-118, Colorado State University, November 12 1991.

[8] C. Böhm and W. Gross. Introduction to the Cuch. In E. Caianiello, editor, *Theory of Automata*, pages 35–65. Academic Press, London, 1965.

[9] A. Church. *The Calculi of Lambda Conversion*. Princeton University Press, Princeton, 1941.

[10] A. Church and J.B. Rosser. Some properties of conversion. *Transactions of the American Mathematical Society*, 39:472–482, 1936.

[11] J.B. Dennis. Programming generality, parallelism and computer architecture. In *Information Processing 68*, pages 484–492. North-Holland, Amsterdam, 1969.

[12] J.B. Dennis. First version of a dataflow procedure language. In B. Robinet, editor, *Programming Symposium; proceedings. Colloque sur la Programmation*, pages 362–376. Springer-Verlag, Berlin, 1974.

[13] A.D. Gordon. An operational semantics for I/O in a lazy functional language. In *Functional Programming Languages and Computer Architecture*, pages 136–145, New York, 1993. Association for Computing Machinery.

[14] M.J.C. Gordon, R. Milner, L. Morris, M. Newey, and C. Wadsworth. A metalanguage for interactive proof in LCF. In *Proc 5th ACM Symp. on Principles of Programming Languages*, pages 119–130. Association for Computing Machinery, 1978.

[15] C.A. Gunter and Dana S. Scott. Semantic domains. In Jan van Leeuwen, editor, *Handbook of Theoretical Computer Science*, volume B, chapter 12, pages 633–674. Elsevier Science Publishers and the MIT Press, Amsterdam and Cambridge, MA, 1990.

[16] R. Hindley. The principal type-scheme of an object in combinatory logic. *Transactions of the American Mathematical Society*, 146:29–60, 1969.

[17] C.A.R. Hoare. Communicating sequential processes. *Communications of the ACM*, 21(8):666–677, August 1978.

[18] C.A.R. Hoare. *Communicating Sequential Processes*. Prentice Hall International Series in Computer Science. Prentice Hall, New York, 1985.

[19] P. Hudak (editor), S. Peyton Jones (editor), P. Wadler (editor), Arvind, B. Boutel, J. Fairbairn, J. Fasel, M.M. Guzman, K. Hammond, J. Hughes, T. Johnsson, R. Kieburtz, R. Nikhil, W. Partain, and J. Peterson. Report on the functional programming language Haskell, version 1.2. *ACM SIGPLAN Notices*, 27, May 1992.

[20] P.J. Landin. The next 700 programming languages. *Communications of the ACM*, 9(3):157–164, March 1966.

[21] J. McCarthy. History of LISP. In R.L. Wexelblat, editor, *History of Programming Language*, pages 173–191, New York, 1981. Association for Computing Machinery, Academic Press.

[22] J. McCarthy et al. *LISP 1.5 Programmer's Manual*. MIT Press, Cambridge, MA, 1962.

[23] J. McGraw, S. Skedzielewski, S. Allan, D. Grit, R. Oldehoeft, J. Glauert, P. Hohensee, and I. Dobes. Sisal reference manual. Technical report, Lawrence Livermore National Laboratory, 1984.

[24] R.E. Milne. *The Formal Semantics of Computer Languages and their Implementations*. PhD thesis, University of Cambridge, 1974.

[25] R.E. Milne and C. Strachey. *A Theory of Programming Language Semantics*. Chapman and Hall and John Wiley, London and New York, 1976.

[26] R. Milner. A theory of type polymorphism in programming. *Journal of Computer and System Sciences*, 17:348–375, 1978.

[27] J.C. Mitchell. Type systems for programming languages. In J. van Leeuwen, editor, *Handbook of Theoretical Computer Science*, volume B, chapter 8, pages 365–458. Elsevier Science Publishers and the MIT Press, Amsterdam and Cambridge, MA, 1990.

[28] R.S. Nikhil. Id (version 90.1) reference manual. CSG Memo 284-2, MIT Laboratory for Computer Science, Cambridge, MA, 1991.

[29] J.E. Stoy. *Denotational Semantics: The Scott-Strachey Approach to Programming Language Theory*. MIT Press, Cambridge, MA, 1977.

[30] J.E. Stoy. The congruence of two programming language definitions. *Theoretical Computer Science*, 13:151–174, 1981.

[31] G. Winskel. *The Formal Semantics of Programming Languages: an Introduction*. MIT Press, Cambridge, MA, 1993.

Chapter 23

Correctness of Data Representations in Algol-like Languages

R. D. Tennent

23.1 Introduction

One of C. A. R. Hoare's most influential contributions to programming methodology and language design is a method for verifying data refinements [8]. The context is as follows: a programmer is supposed to have composed a program using a set A of "abstract" entities and a number of primitive operations f_i on them, but, in order to achieve a suitable implementation, wants to substitute a set C of "concrete" entities and corresponding operations p_i. The programmer's problem is to verify that the program obtained from this substitution is semantically equivalent to the original.

Essentially the following method is suggested for achieving this.

1. Define a suitable "representation" relation $R: A \leftrightarrow C$ between the abstract and concrete sets; i.e., $a[R]c$ exactly when $c \in C$ is considered to be a correct representation of $a \in A$. Actually, Hoare required R to be a (possibly partial) *function* from C to A; but R. Milner had already pointed out in [13] that the generalization to *arbitrary* relations is possible, and the usefulness of this generalization has become increasingly evident [33, 35, 4, 11, 6, 22, 36, 16].

2. Prove that corresponding pairs of primitive operations on the two sets preserve R; i.e.,

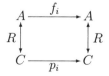

This is not a conventional commuting diagram; note the double-headed arrows. It should be interpreted as asserting that f_i and p_i map related arguments to related results; i.e., $f_i(a)[R]p_i(c)$ whenever $a[R]c$.

405

3. Prove that any initializations of the abstract and concrete variables from other program variables X yield related values; i.e.,

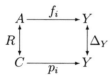

where Δ_X is the diagonal binary relation on X: $x[\Delta_X]x' \iff x = x'$.

4. Prove that any finalization operations from the abstract and concrete variables yield the same values when applied to related values:

$$
\begin{array}{ccc}
A & \xrightarrow{\;f_i\;} & Y \\
R \big\uparrow & & \big\downarrow \Delta_Y \\
C & \xrightarrow[\;p_i\;]{} & Y
\end{array}
$$

It is claimed in [8] that these are sufficient to ensure equivalence of the programs, and that this is "a fairly obvious theorem". A rigorous proof of this, however, is not so obvious, at least not for full Algol-like languages [34], which have both local-variable declarations and (possibly higher-order) procedures.

Consider the following equivalence of Algol 60 blocks; P is an arbitrary non-local procedure with a procedural parameter, and a_0 and c_0 are arbitrary **integer** constants.

$$
\begin{array}{lll}
\textbf{begin} & & \textbf{begin} \\
\quad \textbf{integer } a; & & \quad \textbf{integer } c; \\
\quad \textbf{procedure } \mathit{inc}; & & \quad \textbf{procedure } \mathit{dec}; \\
\quad\quad \textbf{begin } a := a + 1 \textbf{ end}; & \equiv & \quad\quad \textbf{begin } c := c - 1 \textbf{ end}; \\
\quad a := a_0; & & \quad c := c_0; \\
\quad P(\mathit{inc}) & & \quad P(\mathit{dec}) \\
\textbf{end} & & \textbf{end}
\end{array}
\qquad (23.1)
$$

The blocks are observationally equivalent, regardless of how the variables are initialized or what P does, because P cannot access the values of the local variables. Furthermore, this equivalence can be formally "verified" using (the relational form of) Hoare's method. Consider the relation $R\colon A \leftrightarrow C$ on the sets A and C of states for the two blocks such that

$$
s_A[R]s_C \iff (s_A \setminus a) = (s_C \setminus c);
$$

i.e., all variables except for a and c have equal values, but the values of variables a and c are unconstrained. This relation is clearly achieved from any state by the two initializations, and preserved by executions of procedures inc and dec; hence the states after execution of the calls to P also satisfy the relation (or both calls diverge). The local variables are then discarded, leaving equal states, and so the blocks have equivalent behaviours.

The problem is that this equivalence *fails* semantically for the conventional denotational semantics of local-variable declarations and procedures, and also for a number of more sophisticated interpretations [18, 25]. This means that Hoare's method *cannot* be validated using any of these semantic interpretations.

This paper addresses this issue. Section 23.2 shows how the theory of *logical* (families of) relations provides a simple and convenient framework for treating representation independence, and leads to a natural adaptation of (the relational form of) Hoare's method to *functional* languages; this material is based on [35]. Section 23.3 briefly reviews several unsatisfactory approaches to the semantics of local variables in Algol-like languages; this material is based on [25]. Finally, Section 23.4 describes some recent work by the author and P. W. O'Hearn [26] which, essentially, incorporates the relational form of Hoare's method into a new semantics of Algol, allowing the method to be validated for full Algol-like languages.

23.2 Logical Relations

If S and T are sets,

- $S \times T$ is the set of all ordered pairs (s, t) with $s \in S$ and $t \in T$;
- $S \to T$ is the set of all functions from S to T.

If A, A', C, and C' are sets, and $R\colon A \leftrightarrow C$ and $R'\colon A' \leftrightarrow C'$ are relations,

- $R \times R'\colon A \times A' \longleftrightarrow C \times C'$ is defined by

$$(a, a')[R \times R'](c, c') \iff a[R]c \text{ and } a'[R']c';$$

- $R \to R'\colon A \to A' \longleftrightarrow C \to C'$ is defined by

$$f[R \to R']p \iff \text{ for all } a \in A, c \in C, \text{ if } a[R]c \text{ then } f(a)[R']p(c);$$

i.e.,

$$
\begin{array}{ccc}
A & \xrightarrow{\ f\ } & A' \\
R \uparrow\downarrow & & \uparrow\downarrow R' \\
C & \xrightarrow{\ p\ } & C'
\end{array}
$$

Notice that, even when R and R' are *functional* relations, $R \to R'$ is *not* in general functional; this is one of the reasons that the *relational* generalization of Hoare's method is important.

Consider now the following simple language of type expressions over a type variable T, regarded as being an "abstract" type:

$$\theta ::= \omega \mid T \mid \theta \times \theta' \mid \theta \to \theta'$$

where ω ranges over some collection of primitive type names. Suppose that the primitive types are interpreted by a collection of fixed sets S_ω; then, for any set S regarded as the representation of type T, the interpretation can be extended to all type expressions θ by the following inductive definition:

- $\llbracket \omega \rrbracket S \;=\; S_\omega$
- $\llbracket T \rrbracket S \;=\; S$
- $\llbracket \theta \times \theta' \rrbracket S \;=\; \llbracket \theta \rrbracket S \times \llbracket \theta' \rrbracket S$
- $\llbracket \theta \to \theta' \rrbracket S \;=\; \llbracket \theta \rrbracket S \to \llbracket \theta' \rrbracket S$

Similarly, if A and C are sets, any binary relation $R\colon A \leftrightarrow C$ induces binary relations $\llbracket \theta \rrbracket R\colon \llbracket \theta \rrbracket A \longleftrightarrow \llbracket \theta \rrbracket C$ for all type expressions θ as follows:

- $\llbracket \omega \rrbracket R \;=\; \Delta_{S_\omega}$ (the diagonal relation on S_ω)
- $\llbracket T \rrbracket R \;=\; R$
- $\llbracket \theta \times \theta' \rrbracket R \;=\; \llbracket \theta \rrbracket R \times \llbracket \theta' \rrbracket R$
- $\llbracket \theta \to \theta' \rrbracket R \;=\; \llbracket \theta \rrbracket R \to \llbracket \theta' \rrbracket R.$

This is known as a *logical* family of (binary) relations [14, 29, 32, 30, 38, 15].

Let P be any closed term of the pure simply-typed lambda calculus having type θ. For any set S, let $\llbracket P \rrbracket S \in \llbracket \theta \rrbracket S$ be the usual set-theoretic meaning of P when S is the interpretation of the type variable T. As shown in [14, 29, 30, 35], the $\llbracket P \rrbracket S$ have the following uniformity property: for any sets A and C, and any relation $R\colon A \leftrightarrow C$,

$$\llbracket P \rrbracket A \big[\llbracket \theta \rrbracket R \big] \llbracket P \rrbracket C$$

In particular, if P has type $\theta \to \theta'$, we have that

In [35], this is termed the *Abstraction Theorem*, and interpreted as asserting that the meanings of lambda calculus terms are *representation independent*, where this notion is characterized (for the standard set-theoretic model) by preservation of arbitrary binary relations between alternative implementations of a type variable T; see also [16]. Following [40, 35], the uniformity criterion is now termed *relational parametricity*; cf. [27].

It should now be clear how the relational form of Hoare's method can be adapted to (possibly higher-order) functional languages: for any primitive operation of type $\theta \to \theta'$, the programmer must prove that where A, C, R, f_i and p_i are as before. This encompasses the three diagrams of Section 23.1 as special cases, and also allows for higher-order primitives. The Abstraction Theorem ensures that the programs obtained by replacing an abstract type and primitive operations on it by "abstract" and "concrete" representations, respectively, will map related inputs to related outputs; in particular, if the input and output types are independent of the abstract type, the programs will be extensionally equivalent.

We note in passing that the theory of logical relations generalizes straightforwardly to n-ary relations for any n. On the other hand, logical relations do *not* in general preserve relational composition; i.e.,

$$[\![\theta]\!](R_0 \mathbin{;} R_1) \;=\; [\![\theta]\!]R_0 \mathbin{;} [\![\theta]\!]R_1$$

may fail, where ; here denotes the usual composition of (binary) relations. This does not seem to be a disadvantage; in particular, it in no way precludes *stepwise* data refinement. There are frameworks for data refinement in which compositions of "simulations" *are* preserved [9, 10, 31, 20]; however, languages with both local-variable declarations and higher-order procedures have not been treated in these frameworks.

23.3 Semantics of Local Variables

Our aim is to ensure that Hoare's method, appropriately generalized, remains valid when applied in full Algol-like languages. According to [34], an Algol 60-like language *is* a higher-order functional language, but with "imperative" primitive types and operations. But, surprisingly, the local-variable declaration, one of the first features most programmers learn to use, is problematical in the context of higher-order procedures; see [18, 25] for further discussion.

The traditional denotational-semantic approach to local-variable declarations [37, 17, 39] is to assume a denumerable set L of "locations" (abstract storage addresses) and construct a set of states (also known as "stores") along the following lines:

$$S \;=\; L \to (V + \{unused\}) \,,$$

where V is the set of *storable values*. (For simplicity, we assume there is a *single* type of storable value, say, integers.) The idea is that each state $s \in S$ records, for every location $\ell \in L$, *either* the $v \in V$ currently stored at that location, *or* the fact that location ℓ is not currently "in use". Then the effect of a variable declaration is to bind the declared variable identifier to any currently unused location for the execution of the block body.

This kind of interpretation of local variables is adequate to show the correctness of the usual style of implementation of block structure [17]; however, many authors [3, 34, 23, 7, 24, 1, 18] have criticized it as being insufficiently abstract. For example, consider the simple equivalence

$$
\begin{array}{ll}
\textbf{begin} & \\
\quad \textbf{integer } z; & \\
\quad C & \equiv \quad C \\
\textbf{end} &
\end{array}
\qquad (23.2)
$$

when identifier z is not free in command C. The equivalence is a consequence of the inaccessibility of the "new" location to non-local entities in Algol-like languages. Unfortunately, the equivalence fails in the traditional semantics. To see the problem, assume that the initial state marks a location ℓ as being unused and ℓ is chosen as the meaning of z in the block; but in general the meaning of C need not respect the convention that ℓ is not accessible to non-local entities and might, for example, branch on whether it is "unused".

Some researchers [17, 7] have addressed this kind of difficulty by attempting to define the set of "accessible" locations or *storage support* of semantic entities, in order to ensure that the "new" location allocated for a variable declaration is not already accessible in the block body. However, this has proved to be technically complex and delicate. Phrases of basic type, such as expressions and commands, can be treated fairly straightforwardly; but the storage support of a procedure is much more difficult to define, particularly if an extensional treatment of procedures is desired.

An alternative is to adopt a semantical approach in which the set S of states is a *parameter* of the semantic interpretation, rather than a fixed global "constant"; this was first proposed in [34]. In logic, semantic parameters that determine certain "local" aspects of meanings have traditionally been termed *possible worlds* [12]. The meaning of a declaration block at one world can then be defined in terms of the meaning of the body of the block at an "expanded" world where states have an additional component to hold the value of the locally-declared variable. Hence if $S(W)$ is the set of states appropriate to any world W and W' is a world that allows for an additional integer-valued variable, we would have $S(W') = S(W) \times Z$, for Z the set of integers. Furthermore, each such change of world must induce suitable changes of meaning, so that non-local entities can be mapped into meanings appropriate to local contexts.

Reynolds and F. J. Oles [23, 24] formalized these intuitions using some of the most basic concepts of category theory [2, 28].

- Possible worlds and changes of world form a *category*.
- Types and type assignments are interpreted as *functors* from the category of possible worlds to a category of domains and continuous functions.
- Phrases are interpreted as *natural transformations* of these functors.

Procedures can be treated using the fact that, if $\mathbf{D}$ is the category of complete posets and continuous functions, and $\mathbf{W}$ is *any* small category, the functor category $\mathbf{D^W}$ is cartesian closed [21, 23]; this provides interpretations of procedural abstraction and application that validate the usual laws of the typed lambda calculus and formal extensionality [19].

This functor-category approach to the semantics of local variables is a great improvement on the traditional treatment; for example, equivalence (23.2) is easily validated. However, some fairly simple equivalences involving higher-type entities continue to fail. For example, equivalence (23.1) fails when P denotes the procedural meaning that diverges when executing its argument increases the value of the local variable, and terminates normally otherwise. Of course, such procedural meanings are not actually *defineable* in an Algol program, but they do exist in the functor-category model; the naturality requirement on the valuations does not exclude them. Because the equivalence can be formally verified by (the relational form of) Hoare's method, no semantic interpretation in which it fails can validate the method, and until very recently, this was the case with every published extensional semantics.

23.4   Parametric Semantics of Local Variables

In [26], the possible-world approach to local variables is refined by adopting relational parametricity as an *additional* uniformity criterion on valuations in order to "internalize" the representation-independence properties of intuitive local-variable semantics. This yields a much more satisfactory semantics for Algol, which we sketch here.

We assume a small collection of worlds that includes all desired data types, such as $\{false, true\}$ and $Z = \{\ldots, -2, -1, 0, 1, 2, \ldots\}$, and is closed with respect to finite products; then, for any world W, the set $S(W)$ of states appropriate to W is just W.

For each phrase type θ, the interpretation specifies

- a domain $[\![\theta]\!]W$ for every world W;
- a continuous function $[\![\theta]\!]f\colon [\![\theta]\!]W \to [\![\theta]\!](W \times X)$ for every "expansion" morphism $f\colon W \to W \times X$; and
- a relation $[\![\theta]\!]R\colon [\![\theta]\!]W_0 \longleftrightarrow [\![\theta]\!]W_1$ for every relation $R\colon W_0 \leftrightarrow W_1$,

For example, the basic type **comm** (of possibly non-terminating, deterministic commands) is interpreted as follows:

- for any world W, $[\![\textbf{comm}]\!]W = W \to W_\bot$, where $W_\bot$ is the domain obtained from W by adjoining a new least element;
- for any expansion $f\colon W \to W \times X$ and $c \in [\![\textbf{comm}]\!]W$, $[\![\textbf{comm}]\!]f\,c$ is the command that acts like c on non-local variables (W) and preserves local variables (X) invariant; and
- for any $R\colon W_0 \leftrightarrow W_1$, $[\![\textbf{comm}]\!]R = R \to R_\bot$, where $R_\bot$ is the relation defined by $s[R_\bot]s' \iff s = s' = \bot$ or $s[R]s'$.

For product types,

- for any world W, $[\![\theta \times \theta']\!]W \ = \ [\![\theta]\!]W \times [\![\theta']\!]W$;
- for any change of world morphism f, $[\![\theta \times \theta']\!](f)\langle a, a'\rangle \ = \ \langle [\![\theta]\!]f\,a, [\![\theta']\!]f\,a'\rangle$; and
- for any relation R, $[\![\theta \times \theta']\!]R \ = \ [\![\theta]\!]R \times [\![\theta']\!]R$,

as might be expected. However, *procedural* types are more complicated.

The difficulty is that new variables might be declared between the definition of a procedure and its uses. An interpretation that allows a procedure defined in world W to be used in all "expanded" worlds $W \times X$, but also precludes representation-dependent access to the new local variables, is as follows: For any world W, any $p \in [\![\theta \to \theta']\!]W$ is a *family* of functions

$$p(f\colon W \to W \times X)\colon [\![\theta]\!](W \times X) \to [\![\theta']\!](W \times X)$$

indexed by expansions $f\colon W \to W \times X$, satisfying not only the usual "naturality" condition, as in [23], but also the following additional parametricity constraint:

- for all expansions $f_0\colon W \to W \times X_0$ and $f_1\colon W \to W \times X_1$ and relations $R\colon X_0 \leftrightarrow X_1$,

$$
\begin{array}{ccccc}
X_0 & & [\![\theta]\!](W \times X_0) & \xrightarrow{\ p(f_0)\ } & [\![\theta']\!](W \times X_0)\\[2pt]
R\big\downarrow & [\![\theta]\!](\Delta_W \times R)\big\uparrow & & & \big\downarrow[\![\theta']\!](\Delta_W \times R)\\[2pt]
X_1 & & [\![\theta]\!](W \times X_1) & \xrightarrow[\ p(f_1)\ ]{} & [\![\theta']\!](W \times X_1)
\end{array}
$$

Function $p\ (f : W \to W \times X)$ models the behaviour of the procedure in the "expanded" world $W \times X$; the parametricity constraint ensures that the procedural meaning is independent of the representation of local variables. Despite the apparently *ad hoc* nature of this definition, it is an instance of a general categorical construction with appropriate properties; see [26], which also discusses $[\![\theta \to \theta']\!]f$ and $[\![\theta \to \theta']\!]R$.

The interpretation of types can then be extended to *type assignments* in the obvious way. Let $\pi = \{\iota_1 \mapsto \theta_1, \ldots, \iota_n \mapsto \theta_n\}$ be an assignment of types to a finite set $\mathrm{dom}\,\pi = \{\iota_1, \ldots, \iota_n\}$ of (distinct) identifiers; if $\pi(\iota)$ stands for the type assigned to $\iota \in \mathrm{dom}\,\pi$ by π, then,

- for any world W,

$$[\![\pi]\!]W \ = \ \prod_{\iota \in \mathrm{dom}\,\pi} [\![\pi(\iota)]\!]W$$

is the domain of π-compatible environments in world W;

- for any change of world $f\colon W \to X$, $[\![\pi]\!]f\colon[\![\pi]\!]W \to [\![\pi]\!]X$ defined by

$$[\![\pi]\!]f\,u\,\iota \;=\; [\![\pi(\iota)]\!]f\big(u(\iota)\big) \text{ for every } \iota \in \operatorname{dom}\pi$$

  is the function mapping π-compatible environments from world W to world X induced by f; and,
- for any $R\colon W_0 \leftrightarrow W_1$, $[\![\pi]\!]R\colon[\![\pi]\!]W_0 \longleftrightarrow [\![\pi]\!]W_1$ defined by

$$u_0\big[[\![\pi]\!]R\big]u_1 \iff u_0(\iota)\big[[\![\pi(\iota)]\!]R\big]u_1(\iota) \text{ for every } \iota \in \operatorname{dom}\pi$$

  is the relation between π-compatible environments in worlds W_0 and W_1 induced by R.

Finally, for any phrase P of type θ in the context of type assignment π, the interpretation specifies, for every world W, functions

$$[\![P]\!]_{\pi\theta}W\colon[\![\pi]\!]W \to [\![\theta]\!]W$$

satisfying naturality and the following additional parametricity condition: for all $R\colon W_0 \leftrightarrow W_1$,

$$
\begin{array}{ccc}
W_0 & [\![\pi]\!]W_0 \xrightarrow{\;[\![P]\!]_{\pi\theta}W_0\;} [\![\theta]\!]W_0 \\[2pt]
\uparrow R & \;\uparrow[\![\pi]\!]R \qquad\qquad\quad \uparrow[\![\theta]\!]R \\[2pt]
W_1 & [\![\pi]\!]W_1 \xrightarrow[\;[\![P]\!]_{\pi\theta}W_1\;]{} [\![\theta]\!]W_1
\end{array}
$$

In particular,

$$[\![\mathbf{begin}\ \tau\ \iota\,;\ C\ \mathbf{end}]\!]_{\pi\,\mathbf{comm}}W$$

(i.e., the meaning of the local-variable declaration block in world W) can be *parametrically* defined in terms of

$$[\![C]\!]_{\pi'\,\mathbf{comm}}(W \times [\![\tau]\!])$$

for $\pi' = (\pi \mid \iota \mapsto \mathbf{var}[\tau])$, where $\mathbf{var}[\tau]$ is the type of τ-valued variables and $[\![\tau]\!]$ is the set of τ-values for every data type τ.

In this semantics, equivalences such as (23.1) and (23.2) are easily validated. For example, to show (23.1), let W be any set of states, $X_0 = X_1 = Z$ (the set of integers), and R be the universally true binary relation on Z; then, taking inc and dec to stand for the meanings of $a := a + 1$ and $c := c - 1$, respectively, it is clear that

$$inc\big[[\![\mathbf{comm}]\!](\Delta_W \times R)\big]dec,$$

and then parametricity of any meaning p for $P\colon\mathbf{comm} \to \mathbf{comm}$ in world W ensures that

$$p(X_0)(inc)\big[[\![\mathbf{comm}]\!](\Delta_W \times R)\big]p(X_1)(dec)$$

This states that the procedure calls in the two blocks preserve relation $\Delta_W \times R$ (or both calls diverge). The desired equivalence follows because the initial states satisfy the relation and the final values of the local variables are discarded immediately after the procedure calls. Every test equivalence for local variables proposed to date has been similarly validated.

23.5   Discussion

That Hoare's method is indeed correct has never really been in doubt; but it has not been so obvious how this could be rigorously proved for realistic programming languages. The parametric semantics sketched in the preceding section and described in detail in [26] provides an interpretation that, for the first time, can be used to validate Hoare's method in a language with local-variable declarations and higher-order procedures. But perhaps this should be turned around: it was not possible to provide a satisfactory semantic interpretation of local-variable declarations in Algol-like languages without taking account of Hoare's insights into data representation published some twenty years earlier!

Acknowledgements

I have had innumerable discussions on these topics with Peter O'Hearn, and I am also grateful to him for comments on my presentation. David Naumann discussed with me the significance of simulation composition. Cliff Jones and Tobias Nipkow helped with references and historical information.

References

[1] S. D. Brookes. A fully abstract semantics and a proof system for an ALGOL-like language with sharing. In A. Melton, editor, *Mathematical Foundations of Programming Semantics*, volume 239 of *Lecture Notes in Computer Science*, pages 59–100, Manhattan, Kansas, 1985. Springer-Verlag, Berlin.

[2] M. Barr and C. Wells. *Category Theory for Computing Science*. Prentice-Hall International, London, 1990.

[3] J. Donahue. Locations considered unnecessary. *Acta Informatica*, 8:221–242, 1977.

[4] D. Gries and J. Prins. A new notion of encapsulation. In *Proceedings of the Symposium on Language Issues in Programming Environments*, Seattle, Washington, June 1985. *ACM SIGPLAN Notices*, 20:131–139, 1985.

[5] D. Gries, editor. *Programming Methodology, A Collection of Articles by IFIP WG 2.3*. Springer-Verlag, New York, 1978.

[6] J. He, C. A. R. Hoare, and J. W. Sanders. Data refinement refined (resumé). In B. Robinet and R. Wilhelm, editors, *1st European Symposium on Programming*, volume 213 of *Lecture Notes in Computer Science*, pages 187–196, Saarbrüken, March 1986. Springer-Verlag, Berlin. Also revised as Prespecification and Data Refinement, by He Jifeng and C. A. R. Hoare, in [10].

[7] J. Y. Halpern, A. R. Meyer, and B. A. Trakhtenbrot. The semantics of local storage, or what makes the free-list free? In *Conf. Record 11th ACM Symp. on Principles of Programming Languages*, pages 245–257, Austin, Texas, 1984. ACM, New York.

[8] C. A. R. Hoare. Proof of correctness of data representations. *Acta Informatica*, 1:271–281, 1972. Reprinted in [5], pages 269-281.

[9] C. A. R. Hoare. Data refinement in a categorical setting. Unpublished manuscript, June 1987.

[10] H. Jifeng and C. A. R. Hoare. Data refinement in a categorical setting. Technical monograph PRG-90, Programming Research Group, Oxford University Computing Laboratory, November 1990.

[11] C. B. Jones. *Systematic Software Development Using VDM*. Prentice-Hall International, London, 1986.

[12] S. A. Kripke. Semantical analysis of intuitionistic logic I. In J. N. Crossley and M. A. E. Dummett, editors, *Formal Systems and Recursive Functions*, pages 92–130. North-Holland, Amsterdam, 1965.

[13] R. Milner. An algebraic definition of simulation between programs. In *Proceedings of the Second International Joint Conference on Artificial Intelligence*, pages 481–489. The British Computer Society, London, 1971. Also Technical Report CS-205, Computer Science Department, Stanford University, February 1971.

[14] R. E. Milne. *The Formal Semantics of Computer Languages and their Implementations*. Ph.D. thesis, University of Cambridge, 1973.

[15] J. C. Mitchell. Type systems for programming languages. In J. van Leeuwen, editor, *Handbook of Theoretical Computer Science*, volume B, pages 365–458. Elsevier, Amsterdam, and The MIT Press, Cambridge, Mass., 1990.

[16] J. C. Mitchell. On the equivalence of data representations. In V. Lifschitz, editor, *Artificial Intelligence and Mathematical Theory of Computation: Papers in Honor of John McCarthy*, pages 305–330. Academic Press, 1991.

[17] R. E. Milne and C. Strachey. *A Theory of Programming Language Semantics*. Chapman and Hall, London, and Wiley, New York, 1976.

[18] A. R. Meyer and K. Sieber. Towards fully abstract semantics for local variables: preliminary report. In *Conf. Record 15th ACM Symp. on Principles of Programming Languages*, pages 191–203, San Diego, California, 1988. ACM, New York.

[19] J. C. Mitchell and P. J. Scott. Typed lambda models and cartesian closed categories (preliminary version). In J. W. Gray and A. Scedrov, editors, *Categories in Computer Science and Logic*, volume 92 of *Contemporary Mathematics*, pages 301–316. American Mathematical Society, 1989.

[20] D. A. Naumann. *Two-categories and Program Structure: Data Types, Refinement Calculi, and Predicate Transformers*. Ph.D. thesis, University of Texas at Austin, May 1992.

[21] E. Nelson. On exponentiating exponentiation. *J. of Pure and Applied Algebra*, 20:79–91, 1981.

[22] T. Nipkow. Are homomorphisms sufficient for behavioural implementations of deterministic and nondeterministic data types? In F. J. Brandenburg et al., editors, *STACS 87, 4th Annual Symposium on Theoretical Aspects of Computer Science*, volume 247 of *Lecture Notes in Computer Science*, pages 260–271, Passau, Germany, February 1987. Springer-Verlag, Berlin.

[23] F. J. Oles. *A Category-Theoretic Approach to the Semantics of Programming Languages*. Ph.D. thesis, Syracuse University, Syracuse, N.Y., 1982.

[24] F. J. Oles. Type algebras, functor categories and block structure. In M. Nivat and J. C. Reynolds, editors, *Algebraic Methods in Semantics*, pages 543–573. Cambridge University Press, Cambridge, England, 1985.

[25] P. W. O'Hearn and R. D. Tennent. Semantics of local variables. In M. P. Fourman, P. T. Johnstone, and A. M. Pitts, editors, *Applications of Categories in Computer Science*, volume 177 of *London Mathematical Society Lecture Note Series*, pages 217–238. Cambridge University Press, Cambridge, England, 1992.

[26] P. W. O'Hearn and R. D. Tennent. Relational parametricity and local variables. In *Conf. Record 20th ACM Symp. on Principles of Programming Languages*, pages 171–184, Charleston, South Carolina, 1993. ACM, New York.

[27] G. Plotkin and M. Abadi. A logic for parametric polymorphism. In *Proceedings of the International Conference on Typed Lambda Calculi and Applications*, Lecture Notes in Computer Science, Utrecht, The Netherlands, March 1993. Springer-Verlag, Berlin.

[28] B. C. Pierce. *Basic Category Theory for Computer Scientists*. The MIT Press, Cambridge, Mass., 1991.

[29] G. D. Plotkin. Lambda-definability and logical relations. Memorandum SAI-RM-4, School of Artificial Intelligence, University of Edinburgh, October 1973.

[30] G. D. Plotkin. Lambda-definability in the full type hierarchy. In J. P. Seldin and J. R. Hindley, editors, *To H. B. Curry: Essays in Combinatory Logic, Lambda Calculus and Formalism*, pages 363–373. Academic Press, 1980.

[31] A. J. Power. An algebraic formulation for data refinement. In M. Main et al., editors, *Mathematical Foundations of Programming Semantics, Proceedings of the 5th International Conference*, volume 442 of *Lecture Notes in Computer Science*, pages 390–401, Tulane University, New Orleans, 1989. Springer-Verlag, Berlin.

[32] J. C. Reynolds. On the relation between direct and continuation semantics. In J. Loeckx, editor, *Proc. 2nd Int. Colloq. on Automata, Languages and Programming*, volume 14 of *Lecture Notes in Computer Science*, pages 141–156. Springer-Verlag, Berlin, 1974.

[33] J. C. Reynolds. *The Craft of Programming.* Prentice-Hall International, London, 1981.

[34] J. C. Reynolds. The essence of Algol. In J. W. de Bakker and J. C. van Vliet, editors, *Algorithmic Languages*, pages 345–372. North-Holland, Amsterdam, 1981.

[35] J. C. Reynolds. Types, abstraction and parametric polymorphism. In R. E. A. Mason, editor, *Information Processing 83*, pages 513–523. North Holland, Amsterdam, 1983.

[36] O. Schoett. Behavioural correctness of data representations. *Science of Computer Programming*, 14:43–57, 1990.

[37] D. S. Scott. Mathematical concepts in programming language semantics. In *Proc. 1972 Spring Joint Computer Conference*, pages 225–34. AFIPS Press, Montvale, N.J., 1972.

[38] R. Statman. Logical relations and the typed λ-calculus. *Information and Computation*, 65:85–97, 1985.

[39] J. E. Stoy. *Denotational Semantics: The Scott-Strachey Approach to Programming Language Theory.* The MIT Press, Cambridge, Massachusetts, and London, England, 1977.

[40] C. Strachey. *Fundamental Concepts in Programming Languages.* Unpublished lecture notes, International Summer School in Computer Programming, Copenhagen, August 1967.

Chapter 24

Software is History!

Jim Welsh

24.1 Introduction

Seminal works by Dahl, Dijkstra and Hoare [1] and by Wirth [2] in the early
seventies fundamentally altered the computing world's view of programming. The
essential ingredients of the approach demonstrated in both cases were

- a systematic stepwise approach to program design, in which subproblems
  were isolated and solved one by one;
- an improved programming notation in which constructs reinforced the data
  and control structures chosen as the solution;
- a narrative presentation of the design decisions taken at each step, which
  analysed the issues involved, identified the options available, and justified
  the choices made.

In the decade that followed, the first two of these ingredients became the foundation stones of structured programming as practised throughout the eighties. The
stepwise approach to program design was embodied in a variety of so-called structured methodologies, all of which can be seen as variations on the same basic theme.
The programming notations were embodied in Wirth's own widely used programming languages, Pascal and Modula 2, and were acknowledged as the starting point
for almost every other procedural programming language developed in that period.
By these two observations alone, the influence of Hoare and his colleagues on the
development of programming is clearly established.

Here, however, we choose to focus on the third ingredient identified above, which
we called the narrative presentation of design decisions. Such a narrative can be
interpreted in two ways.

One simple interpretation is as a purely informal account of the thought process
which led the author to the design choices concerned. Such a narrative we call an
ideal design history. It is a history in the sense that it records the sequence of
decisions taken by the author in designing the program. It is ideal in that it need

not necessarily record all of the mistakes and blind alleys pursued by the author in arriving at the final design.[1] Most histories are ideal in this sense. The minutes recorded by a committee secretary capture all significant decisions taken and issues considered by the committee, but not necessarily the possibly acrimonious debate involved. Likewise a parliamentary historian records the issues debated and acts passed in the lifetime of a parliament, but not necessarily the day to day cut and thrust of political life.

In the programming context, the essential requirement is that a design history captures all significant issues considered and decisions taken in arriving at the program concerned. As such, the design history encapsulates all productive intellectual effort invested in the program's development, in effect the intellectual property that the program represents. We note, however, that intellectual property inherent in such a design history is much more complete, and more amenable to reuse, than that inherent in the program code itself. It is this design history, therefore, which should be considered as the product of the development process rather than the program itself.

An alternative interpretation of the narrative presentation is as an explicit justification, to a chosen degree of formality, that the program developed does in fact meet its specification. It was implicit in the writings of Hoare and his colleagues of the period that a program's correctness with respect to its specification can be demonstrated by formal reasoning with respect to known properties of the programming languages concerned – the principle had been established in earlier papers by Hoare [4] and Floyd [5]. In the context of software development by fully formal methods, however, the concept of a design history must include the initial formal specification of the program concerned, all formal or informal design steps which advance its development from initial specification to final code, all proof obligations inherent in the design steps chosen, and the discharge of all these obligations in a theory appropriate to the program and programming language concerned. As such the design history may attain a size and complexity several orders of magnitude greater than the program it produces.

In subsequent sections of this paper, we consider further the capture and use of design histories, both informal and formal, and the implications that these have for the tool support needed by effective software development.

24.2   Capturing History

While the development of structured programming methodologies and programming languages can be linked closely to the ideas published by Hoare and his colleagues in the early seventies, the way in which design histories have evolved is more related to technological constraints than conceptual innovations.

---

[1]Parnas and Clements advocated essentially the same kind of record in 1986 – they called it "faking a rational design process" [3].

24.2.1   The early approach

In the early seventies, interactive computing was in its infancy. Computers could be accessed from interactive teletypes or CRT terminals of equivalent functionality and speed, but the system functionality accessible to the software developer via such terminals was very limited. Simple line editors could be used to edit text files, compilations could be invoked, and low-level facilities for interaction with running programs were available.

In this limited technological context, program specification and design evolved as paper-based processes, to be carried out prior to any interaction with the computer itself. Documentation of each activity was seen to be important, but the forms taken by the documents corresponding to each phase were distinct. Graphical notations were preferred to textual or symbolic notations in many cases. Data flow diagrams or their equivalent were used to analyse the required system functionality. Structure charts or their equivalent were used to capture the overall organisation of program modules, and either data and control diagrams or some form of pseudocode were used to express the code requirements within each module. Between them, these documents could be seen as a form of design history, though in practice they often concentrated on the functionality involved rather than the reasons for a particular design choice. In addition, because of the disparate representations used in each, the necessary correspondence between them was primarily the developer's responsibility.

Without computer-based assistance, the preparation of the graphical representations adopted by these structured methodologies was expensive, and their modification equally so. Because of this, and the separation of the representations arising at each phase of development, the seeds of a considerable maintenance problem were also sown. It was always tempting to change only the final code versions of the programs developed, leaving the analysis and design documents unchanged, to the long-term detriment of the software's understandability and maintainability.

24.2.2   Literate programs

By the early eighties, interactive computing was well established. Access was still primarily via character-based terminals, but at much higher speeds, and relatively sophisticated computer-based facilities for (textual) document preparation were available. In this context the first significant example of computer-based support for narrative design histories emerged. This was Knuth's WEB system in support of "literate programming" [6]. WEB's development was in fact motivated by its author's need to document his major opus of that period, the TEX document processing system, and WEB's characteristics mirror the strengths and weaknesses of such systems.

WEB enabled the capture of a Pascal program's design history as a narrative sequence of development steps, with explicit relations determining how the development fragments came together to form a compilable program. Using the associated WEB utilities *weave* or *tangle*, the developer could either generate a high quality typeset copy of this narrative with automatic generation of additional cross referencing and indexing material, or extract a consolidated copy of the Pascal program for compilation. The quality of the typeset narrative produced by WEB compared favourably with those hand-crafted by Hoare and his colleagues in the early seventies, as can be seen from the published version of the TEX and Metafont implementations [7, 8].

In contrast, the input representation required by WEB reflected the relatively limited input capabilities of computers at that time. To use WEB, the developer prepared a text file in which the narrative commentary and code were interleaved in the required narrative sequence, with embedded commands to indicate the required structural relationships between code fragments. To prepare or review this input file the developer used a normal text editor, with no specific support for tracing or checking the consistency of the structural links represented by the embedded commands. When a WEB program was compiled and tested, the compilers and debuggers produced feedback in terms of the "tangled" compilable program, leaving the developer to interpret this in terms of the WEB narrative text file.

In overall terms, therefore, the WEB system effectively exploited the relatively sophisticated capacity of computers at that time to produce typeset publication-quality documents, but the developer's interaction with a WEB program during its development was constrained by the relatively primitive interaction capabilities available.

24.2.3   Current capabilities

Ironically, the WEB system's development and release coincided with a radical change in computer interaction technology. Character-based terminals were rapidly superseded by workstations with pointing devices, bitmapped displays and powerful graphical capabilities. Such facilities had the capacity to overcome the interaction limitations of systems like WEB, but in practice their most immediate impact from the software developer's viewpoint was to breathe new life into the structured methodologies' use of graphical representations.

Following the advent of these new interaction capabilities, CASE tools quickly emerged to provide computer-based facilities for the preparation and maintenance of dataflow diagrams, structure charts and other graphical representations used in each phase of the existing structured methodologies. These tools reduce the cost of preparing and, more dramatically, of maintaining the charts and diagrams involved. By doing so, they also reduce the temptation to maintain software at code level only, and thereby contribute to its long-term maintainability.

The separation of, and relatively informal relationship between, the representations used at each phase of development remains a problem, however. For this reason, the development of fully integrated CASE tool sets covering the entire development cycle has proved much more difficult than the provision of preparation and maintenance tools for each phase. This remains an essentially unsolved problem for the CASE tool industry, but may be seen as a flaw in the methodologies which the industry seeks to support, rather than a deficiency in the technology on which the tools are based.

With current interaction technology, there is no reason why fully integrated, fully effective support for software development cannot be provided in a way which more closely reflects the ideal design history concept. Such support would be based on an abstract representation of the overall design history in which the linkage between development steps would be explicitly recorded. For offline perusal, segments or views of this history would be sequentialised and typeset in a form similar to that originally illustrated by Hoare and his colleagues, and subsequently automated by the WEB system. For preparation and online perusal, however, the history would be presented by a blend of graphical and hypertext techniques, with navigation and interrogation mechanisms based on the relationships captured by the abstract representation.[2]

24.3   Rewriting History

Software is by definition amenable to change, and in practice most software systems are subject to continuing change throughout their lifetime. If software is seen to be embodied in its ideal design history then any change to software must imply some change of, or extension to, its history. Since the design history preserved is "ideal", however, it does not necessarily reflect the state of the software prior to the most recent change.[3] In this sense software change involves *rewriting* its ideal history, but without the adverse connotations normally associated with rewriting history!

24.3.1   Why design histories are rewritten

Rewriting of a design history may occur during development of a new software product, during maintenance of an existing product, or during reuse of an existing product or component in the development of a new product.

During development of a software product, software review may be used as a

---

[2]For the purposes of project organisation and management, the overall representation may be partitioned into "documents" which are subject to versioning, concurrent access and process controls, but the underlying abstract representation would be fully integrated in the sense that all relationships relevant to the software's development would be explicitly represented in the overall structure maintained. Versioning, access and process controls are not considered further here.

[3]In practice, an associated version control system may ensure that the old version of the design history is still available, but this is not seen as part of the ideal design history of the new version.

quality assurance procedure. The natural subject of such review is the product's design history to that point, or the segment of that history representing some component of the overall product. The outcome of the review may be a change request which is fed back to the developer, and the developer's response is to modify the design history to reflect the changes involved. Obviously, similar revision of a design history arises during a product's maintenance throughout its lifetime. Only the origin of the change request varies, according to whether the change arises from corrective, perfective or adaptive maintenance.

The overall aim of software reuse is to minimise cost and maximise quality by reuse of intellectual property invested in existing software components. In practice, such reuse may be achieved by reusing the end-product of a prior development, i.e., by avoiding redeveloping the same product, or by reusing intellectual property inherent in the design history itself to develop a similar but different product. Reuse of the end-product implies that the prior development has been structured so that (components of) it can be reused without change. The feasibility of such reuse depends on the way in which the prior development has separated the overall function of its product into separately reusable parts, and the extent to which each of these components has been parameterised to enable its reuse without change in a different context. The development of programming methods which maximise potential reuse has been a significant research focus in recent years – the apparent capability of object-oriented programming in this respect has been a major factor in its recent development.

In practice, however, effective code reuse is difficult to achieve. The functionality of any given development can be decomposed in many non-orthogonal ways, and anticipating which is most likely to enable reuse in future, as yet unforeseen, developments is not easy. In general, the smaller a component the more likely it is to be reused, but the greater the cost of composing such components into a worthwhile application. In general we can observe that the benefit of successfully reusing a component is proportional to its size, but the probability that it will be reusable is inversely proportional to its size!

For these reasons it is foolish to suppose that maximum software reuse can be achieved simply by facilitating code reuse. Effective provision for design reuse, i.e. reuse by rewriting of design histories, is essential if the overall benefits of software reuse are to be achieved.

24.3.2   How design histories are rewritten

Whether it arises during initial software development, subsequent software maintenance or software reuse, rewriting of design histories is a vital part of software engineering. To provide effective support for such rewriting, we must analyse what is actually involved.

Consider some change which is required in a software product initially developed by stepwise refinement. The corresponding design history is, conceptually at least, a tree structure of refinement steps, each of which decompose a particular component problem into one or more subproblems until leaf problems are reached, i.e. those directly expressible in program code. The standard strategy for changing a program developed in this way is to identify the highest node in the tree at which the need for change is implied, and then to redevelop the entire refinement subtree rooted at this node. By virtue of the stepwise refinement strategy, areas of the original refinement tree lying outside this subtree are unaffected by the change. Conversely any node or subtree lying within the subtree identified is liable to be affected by the change. In carrying out such a change, the first requirement of a developer is therefore a means of traversing the refinement tree with a view to identifying and delimiting the subtree of steps affected.

In many cases, however, much of the affected subtree does not actually need to change. In carrying out the change, therefore, the developer does not wish to redevelop the entire subtree from scratch, but rather to traverse the existing subtree in a systematic fashion and to *edit* the content of individual nodes or component subtrees as required. In some cases the change required may be as simple as replacing all occurrences of a particular identifier in a particular region by another. In others it may involve a non-trivial rebuilding of overall subtree structure.

The strategy which identifies, traverses and edits the affected subtree of a stepwise refinement tree is a particular case of the more general dependency-based strategy for revising design histories. With stepwise refinement the potential dependency of one component on a change in another is reflected by their relative position in the refinement tree. In general, such dependencies between software components arise in a number of ways, and these dependencies must be accessible to the developer via the rewriting tools if systematic rewriting of design histories is to be achieved.

In carrying out each set of related changes, the developer wishes to make maximum use of the prior intellectual property inherent in the software being changed. No existing component which can be reused without change should have to be reconstructed, and adaptation of any component which needs to change should be achievable with minimum rewriting of its existing history as perceived by the developer.

In achieving this latter goal, a particular issue is the consistency strategy enforced by the rewriting tools. In general, the components of a design history are subject to a variety of consistency constraints, syntactic, semantic and methodological, and the overall goal of development tools is to ensure that all such constraints are observed. To achieve this goal, a particular rewriting tool may adopt

- an error-preventing strategy, in which changes which violate the relevant constraints are simply precluded,
- an automatic error-signalling strategy, in which inconsistencies are allowed but immediately signalled to the developer, or

- an on-demand error-signalling strategy, in which inconsistencies are only signalled when the developer asks for them.

Error-preventing strategies have the obvious appeal that the consistency of the software is assured at all times. If they are enforced, however, changes to existing software often require more than minimum effort from the developer's viewpoint. Automatic signalling of inconsistencies can also be a source of significant irritation to the developer in some cases.

In summary, therefore, efficient, reliable rewriting of a design history requires

- a mechanism for identifying and tracing the dependency relations between components of the design history that determine which components are potentially affected by a change in a given component,
- an editing mechanism which allows changes to be made at relevant points in the design history without unnecessary reconstruction of any existing part of the history concerned,
- an overall consistency strategy which combines error-prevention with automatic and on-demand error-signalling to achieve minimum overall effort and irritation from the developer's viewpoint.

24.4   Reliving History

In the preceding sections, we have assumed that the developer is wholly responsible for all decisions which extend or amend the design history in any way. Within this assumption, tools like pretty-printers or syntax-directed editors may relieve the developer of responsibility for determining low-level detail of the history's physical presentation, but its underlying abstract structure is wholly determined by the developer.

In more advanced forms of software engineering, however, this is not necessarily the case. In these cases, computer-based development tools may play a significant role in determining parts of this abstract structure. Software development by formal methods is a typical case to consider.

To progress from an initial formal specification to a corresponding verified implementation, a systematic transformation process is often advocated in which the correctness of each transformation or refinement step is guaranteed, or verified before development continues. Morgan's refinement calculus [9] is a typical example of this approach. For development of software of any significant size or complexity, such a method is only feasible with the assistance of a refinement tool, which at each step identifies the possible applicable refinements, accepts the developer's choice from these, computes the refined components that arise, and generates the proof obligations necessary to ensure correctness of the refinement.

In fulfilling the proof obligations that arise, an interactive proof tool plays a similar role, accepting feasible proof steps from the developer as determined by the proof development to date, and generating the updated proof state, including further possible proof obligations.

Since the refinement and proof steps involved in such a process must be regarded as an integral part of the software's design history, the refinement and proof tools therefore play a significant role in determining the structure and significant content of that history. In this sense they are constructive rather than purely analytic tools. The consequent question arising is how the contribution of such constructive tools should be represented in the design history.

One option is to record only the developer inputs – since the constructive tools are presumably deterministic, the full design history can clearly be regenerated from this minimal information. As a reviewable record of the development, however, the sequence of developer inputs by themselves are incomprehensible. Review can only be achieved in this case by involving the constructive tools in an animated replay of the original development, i.e., by actually *reliving* the history concerned. Rewriting of such a history would be achieved in a similar way, i.e., by reliving it up to some point, making some alternative developer contribution, and then reliving or replacing further parts of the original history as appropriate.

In practice, however, the responses from constructive tools, such as refinement and proof tools, are often computationally intensive and hence slow. The developer also has a natural need to look ahead in the existing history before committing to a particular change, which could necessitate multiple replays of parts of the developer input record, as rewriting progresses. For these reasons, this approach could lead to a fairly tedious process for rewriting design histories.

The alternative option, of course, is to regard all contributions made by the constructive tools as an integral part of the design history. In this case the history is a static record which is fully comprehensible for review purposes. For rewriting, the developer's paradigm is one of simply editing (relevant parts of) this record, and looking ahead or back is a natural part of the same paradigm. To achieve the same level of verification as during initial development, the constructive tools again have to reprocess the developer's changes incrementally, i.e, they must be tightly coupled to the editing process itself.

In practice, refinement and proof tools sometimes produce a large volume of detail in response to single developer inputs, e.g., when a high-level proof tactic is invoked. Such detail is not always necessary to understanding the overall development involved. In such cases, judicious control on the level of detail captured, or presented, as the design history may be appropriate. The basic developer paradigm, of the design history as a complete, reviewable and editable record, is not affected by such detail control.

In summary, maintaining the design history view of software whose development involves the use of constructive tools, requires a careful integration of these tools with the basic review and rewrite mechanisms for design histories.

24.5   Conclusion

The concept of capturing a software product as its ideal design history has been apparent since the early seventies. The way in which the capture of design histories has evolved, however, has not maintained the integrated view apparent in the writing of Hoare and his colleagues at that time. Technological limitations have played some part in determining that evolution, but those limitations clearly no longer apply. Achieving the capture of a software product as an appropriately integrated design history, with presentation and manipulation mechanisms consistent with both offline and interactive use, is both relevant to current software engineering environment research and consistent with the foundational work of Hoare and his colleagues some twenty years ago.

24.6   Acknowledgements

The views presented here have their origins in the author's work under Tony Hoare at the Queen's University of Belfast in the early seventies. Their subsequent development has been influenced by collaboration with colleagues in Belfast, Manchester, Brisbane, and elsewhere; these include Brad Broom, Dave Bustard, David Carrington, Anthony Cheng, Maurice Clint, John Elder, Wolfgang Emmerich, Jun Han, Atholl Hay, Ian Hayes, Dan Johnston, Cliff Jones, Derek Kiong, Melfyn Lloyd, Mike McKeag, Gordon Rose, Wilhelm Schäfer, Mark Toleman, Mark Woodman and Yun Yang. Attempts to implement many of the ideas have been assisted by Warwick Allison, Paul Bakker, Alistair Edwards, Ian Fogg, Paul O'Keeffe, Cameron Strom, Luke Wildman and Andrew Wood, but the overall goal has yet to be achieved.

References

[1] O.-J. Dahl, E. W. Dijkstra and C. A. R. Hoare. *Structured Programming*, Academic Press, London, 1972.

[2] N. Wirth. *Program Development by Stepwise Refinement*, Communications of the ACM **14**, pp. 221–227, 1971.

[3] D. L. Parnas and P. C. Clements. *A Rational Design Process: How and why to fake it*, IEEE Transactions on Software Engineering **12**, pp. 251-257, 1986.

[4] C. A. R. Hoare. *An Axiomatic Basis for Computer Programming*, Communications of the ACM **12**, pp. 576–583, 1969.

[5] R. Floyd. *Assigning Meaning to Programs.* Proceedings of the Symposium in Applied Mathematics, pp 19–32, 1967.

[6] D. E. Knuth. *Literate Programming*, The Computer Journal **27** pp. 77–111, 1984.

[7] D. E. Knuth. *T_EX: The Program*, Addison-Wesley, 1986.

[8] D. E. Knuth. *METAFONT: The Program*, Addison-Wesley, 1986.

[9] C. Morgan. *Programming from Specifications*, Prentice-Hall International, 1990.

Chapter 25

A Mean Value Calculus of Durations

Zhou Chaochen and Li Xiaoshan

With this paper published in the Festschrift, the authors would like to express their gratitude to Professor C. A. R. Hoare. It may be hard to formulate how his academic work has inspired us to start and pursue our careers in Computing Science and even to write this paper – but it is there and in great measure.

25.1   Introduction

The Duration Calculus, proposed by C. Zhou, C.A.R. Hoare and A.P. Ravn [11], is a formal logic for describing and reasoning about requirements of real-time systems. It is a state-based logic, where states are piecewise continuous Boolean functions: $\mathbf{R} \to \{0, 1\}$. ($\mathbf{R}$ stands for the reals which models continuous time.) A *piecewise continuous* function has only a finite number of discontinuities in any interval. A requirement is expressed by a formula that constrains durations of system states. The applications of Duration Calculus show that the state-based logic works elegantly at top levels of system designs, where instant actions such as events are ignored. The original Duration Calculus (in the sequel called the Integral Calculus) uses integrals of Boolean functions as primitive interval temporal variables. However, all integrals over point intervals degenerate into zero, no matter what the point values of the integrated functions are. So it is impossible in the Integral Calculus to *directly* specify instant actions. When specification of communication events becomes essential for refinement of system designs, events are specified indirectly through an additional non-Boolean function, called *Trace* [9]. It records the communication histories. Another approach is simply to reject instantaneous actions, and to let all communications last for non-zero durations [10].

Event and state are dual concepts of automata theory. We can hardly have a preference for one rather than the other. The purpose of the paper is to develop a calculus to accommodate both states and events, while maintaining the properties of the Integral Calculus. In mathematical analysis, the mean value of function F

431

over an interval $[a, b]$, where the interval is not a point interval, is equal to the integral of F over the interval divided by the length $(b - a)$, otherwise it is equal to the value of F at the point. Thus we can define the integral by multiplying the mean value and the interval length, and the Mean Value Calculus in this paper becomes an extension of the Integral Calculus.[1] The Mean Value Calculus can also specify events by using mean values of Boolean δ-functions. They take value 1 at isolated points where events occur. Since mean values and integrals follow similar mathematical laws, like finite additivity, etc., the Mean Value Calculus is very close to the Integral Calculus, but with additional axioms to define the relationship between mean value and point values. Similar to the Integral Calculus [4], the Mean Value Calculus is (relatively) complete also.

The most primitive events with respect to a given state P are taken to be the rising edge and falling edge of P, denoted by $\uparrow P$ and $\downarrow P$. They determine the absence/presence of P in a neighbourhood of the events: changing from $\neg P$ to P or the other way round. In topology, the neighbourhood properties of functions are characterised by so-called function germs [2]. A function germ at a point is an equivalence class of functions which have the same value in an arbitrarily small neighbourhood of the point. States are piecewise continuous Boolean functions, so there are only eight possible state germs at any point. For point t, they are depicted in Figs. 1–8.

Since P is a *state* (not an event), the value of P at a single point is of no interest. We identify Figs. 1 and 2, and use $\mathcal{G}_1$ to denote the union of these two germs. $\mathcal{G}_1$ is the set of states which change from 0 to 1 around the concerned point. Similarly we use $\mathcal{G}_2$ for the union of the germs of Figs. 3 and 4. It is the set of states changing from 1 to 0 around the point. We use $\mathcal{G}_3$ for the germs of Figs. 5 and 6, and $\mathcal{G}_4$ for the germs of Figs. 7 and 8. The latter two are the states which do not change the value around the point. Their mathematical definitions for a point t are

$\mathcal{G}_1(t)$: $\{P | \exists \delta \forall x : (0, \delta).P(t - x) = 0 \wedge P(t + x) = 1\}$,
$\mathcal{G}_2(t)$: $\{P | \exists \delta \forall x : (0, \delta).P(t - x) = 1 \wedge P(t + x) = 0\}$,
$\mathcal{G}_3(t)$: $\{P | \exists \delta \forall x : (0, \delta).P(t - x) = 0 \wedge P(t + x) = 0\}$, and
$\mathcal{G}_4(t)$: $\{P | \exists \delta \forall x : (0, \delta).P(t - x) = 1 \wedge P(t + x) = 1\}$.

$\uparrow P$ becomes a state 'germship', which discriminates the membership of P for germ $\mathcal{G}_1$: $\uparrow P(t) = 1$ iff $P \in \mathcal{G}_1(t)$. Similarly $\downarrow P(t) = 1$ means $P \in \mathcal{G}_2(t)$. The other two germships corresponding to $\mathcal{G}_3$ and $\mathcal{G}_4$ are introduced in Section 3. A transition of a system from state S_1 to state S_2 can be considered a composite germship: $(\downarrow S_1 \wedge \uparrow S_2)$. That is, leaving S_1 and at the same time entering S_2. The behaviour of an automaton is determined by the correspondence between its events and state transitions. It can be specified in the Mean Value Calculus with formulas over events and state germships. The specification turns out to be very simple and

---

[1] We distinguish between *Integral Calculus*: the integral calculus of durations presented in [11], *Mean Value Calculus*: the mean value calculus of durations presented in this paper and *Duration Calculus*: calculus of durations in general.

intuitive. In the paper, combinational circuits and timed automata are taken as examples to explain state germs and their applications.

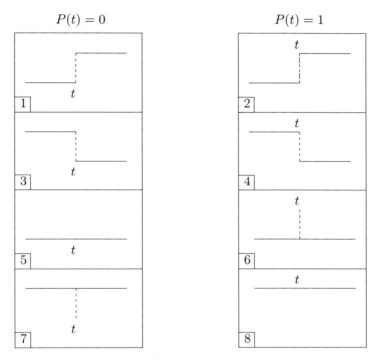

Figs. 1–8: Eight possible state germs.

25.2   A Mean Value Calculus

The Mean Value Calculus, like the Integral Calculus, is an extension of Interval Temporal Logic (ITL) [7] but adding a different structure to interval temporal variables.

25.2.1   Interval temporal logic

We briefly recall that ITL reasons about interval temporal variables. They are functions from intervals to reals: $\mathbf{I} \to \mathbf{R}$, where $\mathbf{I}$ is the set of all *closed* intervals, including point intervals. The variable l denotes the length of an interval. For an arbitrary interval $[a, b]$

$$l[a, b] \mathrel{\widehat{=}} (b - a) \qquad a \leq b$$

With the arithmetic operators and relations such as $+, -, *$ and $=, \leq, \geq$, etc., ITL constructs its *terms* and *atomic formulas* from the interval temporal variables. For example,

$$l = 0$$

is an atomic formula which is true of any point interval, and is abbreviated as

$$\lceil\,\rceil$$

in this paper. ITL also employs the connectives of the propositional logic and predicate logic to build its formulas. But the main feature of ITL is that ITL uses the modality: *chop*, here denoted ';'. For an arbitrary interval $[a, b]$ and formulas A and B, the meaning of *chop* is defined by

$$(A; B)[a, b] \,\widehat{=}\, \exists m : [a, b].A[a, m] \wedge B[m, b]$$

Thus $(A; B)$ is true of any interval $[a, b]$ which can be divided into two subintervals such that A is true of the first interval and B is true of the second interval. The conventional modalities $\Diamond$ and $\Box$ can be defined by *chop*.

$$\Diamond A \,\widehat{=}\, true; A; true$$

which reads: holds for an interval in which some subinterval satisfies A. The dual is

$$\Box A \,\widehat{=}\, \neg\Diamond\neg A$$

which reads: holds for an interval in which every subinterval satisfies A.
The *chop* operator is associative and monotonic, and has the point interval $\lceil\,\rceil$ as unit, *false* as zero, and distributes through disjunction.

- *Asscociativity:* $(A; B); C \Leftrightarrow A; (B; C)$
- *Monotonicity:* if $A1 \Rightarrow A2$ and $B1 \Rightarrow B2$, then $(A1; B1) \Rightarrow (A2; B2)$
- *Unit:* $(A; \lceil\,\rceil) \Leftrightarrow (\lceil\,\rceil; A) \Leftrightarrow A$
- *Zero:* $(A; false) \Leftrightarrow (false; A) \Leftrightarrow false$
- *Distributivity:* $(A; (B \vee C)) \Leftrightarrow ((A; B) \vee (A; C))$ and
  $\qquad\qquad\quad ((A \vee B); C) \Leftrightarrow ((A; C) \vee (B; C))$

Lengths of intervals are non-negative, and form a continuum.

- *Non-negative:* $l \geq 0$
- *Continuum:* $(l = r + s) \Leftrightarrow (l = r); (l = s) \qquad r, s \geq 0$

Induction rules of ITL are very useful. They allow reasoning about intervals adjacently covered by a finite number of formulas. Let $A_1, ..., A_k$ be formulas of ITL which are *positive* and *subinterval-closed*. That is

1. *Positive:* $\bigwedge_{i=1}^{k}(A_i \Rightarrow (l > 0))$ holds, and
2. *Subinterval-closed:* $\bigwedge_{i=1}^{k}(A_i \Rightarrow \Box(\lceil \: \rceil \vee \bigvee_{j=1}^{k} A_j))$ holds.

Intervals that are covered by a finite number of A_i's can be formulated by

$$\Box(\lceil \: \rceil \vee (\bigvee_{i=1}^{k}(A_i; true) \wedge \bigvee_{i=1}^{k}(true; A_i)))$$

here denoted A. To infer the intervals of A, we can start from point intervals ($\lceil \: \rceil$), and then extend the inference over adjacent subintervals of A_i's. Let X be a formula letter in the formula $R(X)$.

- *Induction:* If $R(\lceil \: \rceil)$ holds, and $\bigwedge_{i=1}^{k} R(X \vee X; A_i)$ is provable from $R(X)$, then $R(A)$ holds.

The base of the induction rule proves R to be true of point intervals, and the induction step proves that if the intervals of X satisfy R then attaching the intervals of A_i's to their ends will keep R satisfied. The rule concludes that, in this case, R will hold for the intervals which can be covered by a finite sequence of intervals of A_i's. The *Induction* rule has a symmetric form which uses $A_i; X$ for $X; A_i$.

- *Induction:* If $R(\lceil \: \rceil)$ holds, and $\bigwedge_{i=1}^{k} R(X \vee A_i; X)$ is provable from $R(X)$, then $R(A)$ holds.

We can derive rules to make induction on the length of intervals, by taking $k = 1$ and A_1 as $(0 < l \leq \varepsilon)$ for $\varepsilon > 0$. Since

$$(\lceil \: \rceil \vee (true; (0 < l \leq \varepsilon) \wedge (0 < l \leq \varepsilon); true))$$

can be proved by the axioms *Non-negative* and *Continuum*, the derived rules are

- If $R(\lceil \: \rceil)$ holds, and $R(X \vee X; (l \leq \varepsilon))$ is provable from $R(X)$, then $R(true)$ holds.
- If $R(\lceil \: \rceil)$ holds, and $R(X \vee (l \leq \varepsilon); X)$ is provable from $R(X)$, then $R(true)$ holds.

25.2.2 Mean value calculus

In the Mean Value Calculus, the interval temporal variables are mean values of Boolean functions, denoted F, G, etc. The Boolean functions are defined for every instant of time $\mathbf{R}$, and are *piecewise continuous* (called *finite variability* in [1]) in any intervals. 0 and 1 are constant functions. With the usual Boolean operators, we can construct composite functions. They are also Boolean functions, and preserve piecewise continuity. When the function is a step function (i.e. a Boolean function without *isolated* values), it can represent a *state*, denoted P, Q, S, etc.[2] When it is a δ-function (i.e. a Boolean function with value 1 at isolated points), it can represent an *event*, here denoted e, e', etc.

For an arbitrary function F and an arbitrary interval $[a, b]$, the mean value of F, denoted $\overline{F}$, is defined

$$\overline{F}[a, b] = \left\{ \begin{array}{ll} \int_a^b F(t)dt/(b-a) & \text{if } b > a \\ F(b) & \text{if } b = a \end{array} \right.$$

According to the definition, we lift point functions F ($\mathbf{R} \to \{0, 1\}$) to interval functions $\overline{F}$ ($\mathbf{I} \to [0, 1]$). In the Mean Value Calculus, interval temporal variables are restricted to mean values of functions and the interval-length l. The integral of function F can be defined by $\overline{F}$ and l.

$$\int F \triangleq \overline{F} * l$$

By replacing $\int F$ with $\overline{F} * l$ in the axioms of the Integral Calculus, we can obtain the axioms for the Mean Value Calculus. After simplification, they are[3]

Axiom 1 $\overline{0} = 0$
Axiom 2 $\overline{F} \geq 0$
Axiom 3 $\overline{F \vee G} = \overline{F} + \overline{G} - \overline{F \wedge G}$
Axiom 4 $(\overline{F} * l = r + s) \Leftrightarrow (\overline{F} * l = r); (\overline{F} * l = s)$ $r, s \geq 0$

The Mean Value Calculus is not a plain extension of the Integral Calculus. It needs additional axioms to define point values. Before listing these additional axioms, we introduce three more abbreviations:

$$\begin{array}{lll} \lceil F \rceil^0 & \triangleq & \lceil \; \rceil \wedge (\overline{F} = 1) \\ \lceil F \rceil & \triangleq & (l > 0) \wedge \neg((l > 0); (\lceil \; \rceil \wedge \overline{F} = 0); (l > 0)) \\ \lceil F \rceil^* & \triangleq & \lceil F \rceil \vee \lceil F \rceil^0 \end{array}$$

$\lceil F \rceil^0$ means: F has value 1 at a point. $\lceil F \rceil$ means that the function F has value 1 everywhere *inside* a non-point interval.[4]

The axioms relating point values assert that at any point the value of F is either 0 or 1, and, if F takes value 1 everywhere in a non-point interval, the mean value of F in this interval is 1.

Axiom 5 $\lceil \; \rceil \Rightarrow (\lceil F \rceil^0 \vee \lceil \neg F \rceil^0)$

---

[2]We can prove that composite functions built from a *complete* set of *exclusive* step functions are also step functions. In this sense, the Boolean operators preserve step functionality.
[3]Since the main idea behind the Mean Value Calculus is similar to the one behind the Integral Calculus, we do not explain in detail the meaning of the following axioms and do not show the proofs of the theorems. One can refer to [11], if one has difficulty in understanding this section.
[4]In the Integral Calculus, we used the same notation to mean that F takes value 1 *almost* everywhere in a non-point interval. Obviously the present one implies the former.

Axiom 6 $\lceil F \rceil^* \Rightarrow (\overline{F} = 1)$

Accepting these axioms we can prove

Theorem For point intervals,

1. $\lceil 1 \rceil^0$
2. $\lceil \neg F \rceil^0 \Leftrightarrow \neg \lceil F \rceil^0$, and
3. $\lceil F \vee G \rceil^0 \Leftrightarrow (\lceil F \rceil^0 \vee \lceil G \rceil^0)$

The theorem demonstrates that the truth of $\lceil F \rceil^0$ in a point interval is equivalent with the truth of the function F at the point. Therefore, to simplify notations of the Mean Value Calculus, we will use F as abbreviation of $\lceil F \rceil^0$ in the rest of the paper.

The following theorem can help us to understand the meaning of $\overline{F}$ and $\lceil F \rceil^*$.

Theorem

1. $\lceil 1 \rceil^*$
2. $\overline{1} = 1$
3. $\overline{F} + \overline{\neg F} = 1$
4. $\lceil F \Rightarrow G \rceil^* \Rightarrow (\overline{F} \leq \overline{G})$
5. $\lceil F \Rightarrow G \rceil^* \Rightarrow (\lceil F \rceil^* \Rightarrow \lceil G \rceil^*)$
6. $\lceil F \wedge G \rceil^* \Leftrightarrow (\lceil F \rceil^* \wedge \lceil G \rceil^*)$
7. $\lceil F \rceil \Leftrightarrow (\lceil F \rceil; F; \lceil F \rceil)$

Since the functions are discrete, the piecewise continuity means piecewise constancy. So the piecewise continuity of functions is formalised:

Axiom 7 $(\lceil \ \rceil \vee true; \lceil F \rceil \vee true; \lceil \neg F \rceil)$
Axiom 8 $(\lceil \ \rceil \vee \lceil F \rceil; true \vee \lceil \neg F \rceil; true)$

Combining the piecewise continuity axioms with the induction rules of ITL, we can derive induction rules for the Mean Value Calculus. For example, let $k = 2$, A_1 be $\lceil F \rceil$ and A_2 be $\lceil \neg F \rceil$:

Rule 1 If $R(\lceil \ \rceil)$ holds, and
$(R(X \vee X; \lceil F \rceil) \wedge R(X \vee X; \lceil \neg F \rceil))$ is provable from $R(X)$
then $R(true)$ holds.
Rule 2 If $R(\lceil \ \rceil)$ holds, and
$(R(X \vee \lceil F \rceil; X) \wedge R(X \vee \lceil \neg F \rceil; X))$ is provable from $R(X)$
then $R(true)$ holds.

The previous eight axioms constitute a (relatively) *complete* calculus. That is, any valid formulas of the Mean Value Calculus can be derived from the eight axioms, provided ITL is complete. We do not present here the proof of the relative completeness, since it is similar to the proof of completeness for the Integral Calculus in [4].

It is trivial to see that the Mean Value Calculus is a *conservative* extension of the Integral Calculus. We do not repeat all the application examples for the Integral Calculus in this paper. In the rest of the paper, we are exploring new applications of the Mean Value Calculus. They are beyond the expressiveness of the Integral Calculus, and involve events.

25.2.3   States and events

States have no isolated points, and events are δ-functions. A δ-function with piecewise continuity is *finitely convergent*. That is, in any interval, there is only a finite number of points where the function value is 1. To define the attributes of states and events, we stipulate two additional axioms:

Axiom 9 If P is a state, then

$$\lceil P \rceil; \lceil P \rceil \Rightarrow \lceil P \rceil$$

Axiom 10 If e is an event, then

$$\neg \Diamond \lceil e \rceil$$

Theorem If P is a state, then

$$\lceil P \rceil \Leftrightarrow (l > 0 \wedge \overline{P} = 1)$$

The theorem shows that $\lceil P \rceil$ in the Mean Value Calculus has the same meaning as in the Integral Calculus when P is a state (step function). The theorem can be proved using the induction rules.

25.3   State Germs

The behaviour of a system can be considered a sequence of system states as well as a sequence of system events. Both of them record the history of the system but from different angles. State sequences record state transitions of a system, and event sequences record interactions among system components and the environment. States and events are complementary, and in some systems, such as automata, both are employed to give a full picture of system behaviour.

25.3.1   Germs and germships

The most primitive events relating to an arbitrarily given state P are its *rising* and *falling* edges. In the introduction, they are denoted $\uparrow P$ and $\downarrow P$, and called *germships*: $\uparrow P(t) = 1$ iff $P \in \mathcal{G}_1(t)$, and $\downarrow P(t) = 1$ iff $P \in \mathcal{G}_2(t)$, where $\mathcal{G}_1$ and $\mathcal{G}_2$ are state germs. Corresponding to germs $\mathcal{G}_3$ and $\mathcal{G}_4$ we can introduce two more state germships $\bot P$ and $\top P$ such that $\bot P(t) = 1$ iff $P \in \mathcal{G}_3(t)$ and $\top P(t) = 1$ iff $P \in \mathcal{G}_4(t)$. So, for an arbitrarily given state P, we define four new Boolean functions:

$$
\begin{aligned}
\uparrow P(t) &\cong 1 &&\text{iff}& P &\in \mathcal{G}_1(t) \\
\downarrow P(t) &\cong 1 &&\text{iff}& P &\in \mathcal{G}_2(t) \\
\bot P(t) &\cong 1 &&\text{iff}& P &\in \mathcal{G}_3(t) \\
\top P(t) &\cong 1 &&\text{iff}& P &\in \mathcal{G}_4(t)
\end{aligned}
$$

The definitions of the germships can easily be formalised in the Mean Value Calculus. For $r > 0$[5]

Axiom $\uparrow$ $(l = r); \uparrow P; (l > 0) \Leftrightarrow ((l = r) \wedge true; \lceil \neg P \rceil); \lceil P \rceil; true$
Axiom $\downarrow$ $(l = r); \downarrow P; (l > 0) \Leftrightarrow ((l = r) \wedge true; \lceil P \rceil); \lceil \neg P \rceil; true$
Axiom $\bot$ $(l = r); \bot P; (l > 0) \Leftrightarrow ((l = r) \wedge true; \lceil \neg P \rceil); \lceil \neg P \rceil; true$
Axiom $\top$ $(l = r); \top P; (l > 0) \Leftrightarrow ((l = r) \wedge true; \lceil P \rceil); \lceil P \rceil; true$

Introducing new "citizens" into the Mean Value Calculus, one is obliged to prove the *piecewise continuity* and the *attributes* of the four new functions.

Theorem

1. $(\lceil \ \rceil \vee (\lceil \neg \uparrow P \rceil; true \wedge true; \lceil \neg \uparrow P \rceil))$
2. $(\lceil \ \rceil \vee (\lceil \neg \downarrow P \rceil; true \wedge true; \lceil \neg \downarrow P \rceil))$
3. $(\lceil \ \rceil \vee \lceil \top P \rceil; true \vee \lceil \neg \top P \rceil; true)$
   $(\lceil \ \rceil \vee true; \lceil \top P \rceil \vee true; \lceil \neg \top P \rceil)$
   $(\lceil \top P \rceil; \lceil \top P \rceil \Rightarrow \lceil \top P \rceil)$
4. $(\lceil \ \rceil \vee \lceil \bot P \rceil; true \vee \lceil \neg \bot P \rceil; true)$
   $(\lceil \ \rceil \vee true; \lceil \bot P \rceil \vee true; \lceil \neg \bot P \rceil)$
   $(\lceil \bot P \rceil; \lceil \bot P \rceil \Rightarrow \lceil \bot P \rceil)$

The first two formulas in the theorem state more than piecewise continuity. In fact, they imply the attribute of δ-functions. So $\uparrow P$ and $\downarrow P$ are events. The theorem also shows that $\top P$ and $\bot P$ comply with *Axiom 9*, and therefore are states. To prove the theorem, we apply to the piecewise continuity of P (*Axioms* 7 and 8) the following lemma which can be directly derived from the axioms of the germships.

---

[5]Notice that, in the following axioms and the rest of the paper, we will employ very often the abbreviations indicated in Section 2.2, by using $\uparrow P, \downarrow P, \bot P$, and $\top P$ to stand for the heavy notations $\lceil \uparrow P \rceil^0, \lceil \downarrow P \rceil^0, \lceil \bot P \rceil^0$ and $\lceil \top P \rceil^0$.

Lemma

1. $\lceil P \rceil \Rightarrow (\lceil \neg \uparrow P \rceil \wedge \lceil \neg \downarrow P \rceil \wedge \lceil \top P \rceil \wedge \lceil \neg \bot P \rceil)$,
2. $\lceil \neg P \rceil \Rightarrow (\lceil \neg \uparrow P \rceil \wedge \lceil \neg \downarrow P \rceil \wedge \lceil \neg \top P \rceil \wedge \lceil \bot P \rceil)$.

A *composite* germship is a germship of composite states or a combination of germships such as $\uparrow(P \wedge Q)$ and $(\uparrow P \wedge \downarrow Q)$. Composite germships follow a set of rules which can be derived from the germship axioms with a fact known from ITL. The fact states that an assertion is true by itself if the assertion is true in an arbitrary neighbourhood of the assertion. We formulate the fact as a new rule in ITL.

Neighbourhood rule

If $(l = r; A; l = s) \Rightarrow (l = r; B; l = s)$, then $A \Rightarrow B$. $(r, s \geq 0)$

Using the germship axioms and the *Neighbourhood* rule, we can prove the following theorem (called *Germship Calculus*) for composite germships.

Theorem (germship calculus) For any point intervals,

1. Completeness and Exclusiveness
   $\bigvee_\alpha \alpha P$ $\alpha \in \{\uparrow, \downarrow, \top, \bot\}$
   $\bigwedge_{\alpha \neq \alpha'} (\alpha P \Rightarrow \neg \alpha' P)$ $\alpha, \alpha' \in \{\uparrow, \downarrow, \top, \bot\}$
2. Constant Zero
   $\neg \uparrow 0$
   $\neg \downarrow 0$
   $\neg \top 0$
   $\bot 0$
3. Negation
   $\uparrow \neg P \Leftrightarrow \downarrow P$
   $\downarrow \neg P \Leftrightarrow \uparrow P$
   $\top \neg P \Leftrightarrow \bot P$
   $\bot \neg P \Leftrightarrow \top P$
4. Conjunction
   $\uparrow(P \wedge Q) \Leftrightarrow (\uparrow P \wedge \top Q) \vee (\uparrow Q \wedge \top P) \vee (\uparrow P \wedge \uparrow Q)$
   $\downarrow(P \wedge Q) \Leftrightarrow (\downarrow P \wedge \top Q) \vee (\downarrow Q \wedge \top P) \vee (\downarrow P \wedge \downarrow Q)$
   $\top(P \wedge Q) \Leftrightarrow (\top P \wedge \top Q)$
   $\bot(P \wedge Q) \Leftrightarrow \bot P \vee \bot Q \vee (\uparrow P \wedge \downarrow Q) \vee (\downarrow P \wedge \uparrow Q)$

The theorem has a series of corollaries for various composite germships. We list three which are used later in the paper.

Corollaries

1. $\uparrow(P \vee Q) \Leftrightarrow (\uparrow P \wedge \uparrow Q) \vee (\uparrow P \wedge \bot Q) \vee (\bot P \wedge \uparrow Q)$

2. $\downarrow(P \vee Q) \Leftrightarrow (\downarrow P \wedge \downarrow Q) \vee (\downarrow P \wedge \top Q) \vee (\top P \wedge \downarrow Q)$
3. If $P \Rightarrow \neg Q$, then $\neg(\uparrow P \wedge \uparrow Q)$ and $\neg(\downarrow P \wedge \downarrow Q)$

Proof: We only present part of the proof of (3):

$$
\begin{aligned}
\uparrow P \wedge \uparrow Q \quad &\Rightarrow \uparrow(P \wedge Q) && \text{(germ cal. 4)}\\
&\Leftrightarrow \uparrow(\neg(P \Rightarrow \neg Q)) && \text{(prop. logic)}\\
&\Leftrightarrow \uparrow 0 && \text{(prop. logic)}\\
&\Rightarrow false && \text{(germ cal. 2)}
\end{aligned}
$$

25.3.2 Combinational circuit

We illustrate one of the applications of the *Germship Calculus* using combinational circuits. A combinational circuit is a circuit made from logic gates, and its output voltage/signals are determined by its *current* inputs (i.e. no storages in the circuit).

In terms of circuits, let state P stand for a wire named P. $P(t) = 1$ means that wire P connects to power at time t, and $P(t) = 0$ means wire P connecting to ground at t. Germships $\uparrow P$ and $\downarrow P$ represent changes of voltage of wire P, and the other two germships $\top P$ and $\bot P$ represent stable voltage of the wire. Thus they describe the dynamic behaviour of a wire.

Example
Fig. 9 shows a NOR circuit made from an OR gate and an inverter NEG.

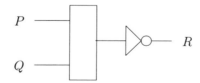

Fig. 9: NOR circuit $R = \neg(P \vee Q)$.

Using the *Germship Calculus* we can calculate the behaviour of the output wire R in terms of the behaviour of the inputs P and Q. For instance:

$$
\begin{aligned}
\uparrow R \quad &\Leftrightarrow \quad \uparrow \neg(P \vee Q)\\
&\Leftrightarrow \quad \uparrow(\neg P \wedge \neg Q)\\
&\Leftrightarrow \quad (\uparrow \neg P \wedge \uparrow \neg Q) \vee (\uparrow \neg P \wedge \top \neg Q) \vee (\uparrow \neg Q \wedge \top \neg P) && \text{(germ cal. 4)}\\
&\Leftrightarrow \quad (\downarrow P \wedge \downarrow Q) \vee (\downarrow P \wedge \bot Q) \vee (\downarrow Q \wedge \bot P) && \text{(germ cal. 3)}
\end{aligned}
$$

The calculation shows that the output rises just when both inputs fall or one falls and the other stays low. Similarly we can calculate the other three germships of the output with the calculus. The calculus formalizes the conventional theory of combinational circuits.

The Integral Calculus can be applied to sequential circuits [5]; so can the Mean Value Calculus. We are not discussing timing issues of circuits in the paper, yet we mention here that the transmission delay d of the rising signal of R in the example can be formulated as

$$\uparrow\neg(P \vee Q); (l = d) \Rightarrow (l = d); \uparrow R$$

and the inertial delay d as

$$\uparrow\neg(P \vee Q); (\lceil\neg(P \vee Q)\rceil \wedge (l = d)) \Rightarrow (l = d); \uparrow R$$

25.4   Timed Automata

An automaton is a system of events and states, where events cause state transitions. The behaviour of an automaton is determined by relations between its events and state transitions. Suppose S_1 and S_2 are two states of an automaton, then the composite germship $(\downarrow S_1 \wedge \uparrow S_2)$ is true at time t when the automaton is leaving S_1 at t and simultaneously entering S_2. So state transitions of automata are the germships of automata states, and the behaviour of automata can be defined by formulas of germships and events in the Mean Value Calculus.

We use a Gas Burner as an example to demonstrate how to specify and reason about timed automata in the calculus.

25.4.1   Gas burner

Let us recall the gas burner example [11]. The critical real-time requirement of the gas burner is that the proportion of time spent in the leak state is not more than one twentieth of the elapsed time, whenever the burner is observed for at least one minute. In the Integral Calculus, the requirement is encoded as

$$l \geq 60 \Rightarrow 20 * \int Leak \leq l$$

where *Leak* is a Boolean function which stands for the leak state of the burner. Since $\int Leak \mathrel{\hat{=}} \overline{Leak} * l$ in the Mean Value Calculus, the formulation of the requirement can be translated to

$$l \geq 60 \Rightarrow 20 * \overline{Leak} \leq 1$$

In [11], two design decisions are also presented in order to meet the requirement.

Des-1 $\Box(\lceil Leak \rceil \Rightarrow l \leq 1)$

Des-2 $\Box(\lceil Leak \rceil; \lceil \neg Leak \rceil; \lceil Leak \rceil \Rightarrow l \geq 30)$

The first decision guarantees that any leak is detectable and stoppable within one second, and the second one guarantees that, after a leak, the burner waits for at least thirty seconds before risking another leak. The Integral Calculus proves that the conjunction of these two decisions implies the requirement. We can use the same formulas to encode the decisions in the Mean Value Calculus and follow the same reasoning to prove the correctness of the design decisions. However the second decision can be expressed more intuitively in the Mean Value Calculus by using events.

Des-2′ $\Box(\downarrow Leak; \lceil \neg Leak \rceil; \uparrow Leak \Rightarrow l \geq 30)$

The proof of **Des-2′** $\Rightarrow$ **Des-2** can be derived from the following *Lemma* 2.1.

In [9], the design decisions are refined to an automaton with time-out signals as part of its events (Fig. 10).

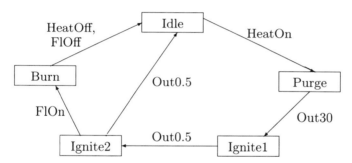

Fig. 10: The gas burner automaton.

The automaton has five states. The gas burner is in one and only one of these states at any time and changes from one to another driven by either of the six events. The behaviour of the automaton can be explained informally as follows.

Idle: Awaits heat request; no gas and ignition. Enters the Purge state on heat request *HeatOn*.

Purge: Pauses for 30 seconds, and then enters Ignite1. The event which starts the transition is a time-out signal: *Out30*, and the 30 seconds' pause ensures a sufficient distance among the periods of gas leaks.

Ignite1: Supplies gas and ignites the burner. After half a second, enters the Ignite2 state. Here time-out signal *Out0.5* starts the transition.

Ignite2: Monitors the flame and enters the Burn state if flame is sensed within 0.5 second. Otherwise turns off gas and returns to the Idle state. The two events which start the two transitions are *FlOn* and time-out signal *Out0.5* respectively.

Burn: Ignition is switched off, but gas is still supplied. The Burn state is stable until heat request goes off, *HeatOff*, or a flame failure occurs. The gas is then turned off and the Idle state is entered. Here the flame failure is immediately reported by event *FlOff*.

From the previous explanation we can assume that the only critical states are *Ignite1* and *Ignite2*, where the gas is on, but the flame may be off.

The formal specification consists of several groups of non-logical axioms. Let the five automaton states be step functions, and the six automaton events be δ-functions. Hence

$$Leak \triangleq Ignite1 \vee Ignite2$$

Let S and S' be variables over the state set $\{Idle, Purge, Ignite1, Ignite2, Burn\}$, and e and e' be variables over the event set $\{HeatOn, Out30, Out0.5, FlOn, FlOff, HeatOff\}$.

1. **State Completeness and Exclusiveness**

   - At any time the automaton is in one of its states

     $$\bigvee_{S} S$$

   - At any time the automaton is in at most one of its states

     $$\bigwedge_{S \neq S'} (S \Rightarrow \neg S')$$

2. **State Transitions**

   - State transitions are started by events

     $$(\downarrow S \wedge \uparrow S') \Rightarrow \bigvee_{e} e$$

   - The transition from Idle to Purge is started by *HeatOn*, and similarly for the other five legal state transitions

     $$
     \begin{aligned}
     \downarrow Idle \wedge \uparrow Purge &\Rightarrow HeatOn \\
     \downarrow Purge \wedge \uparrow Ignite1 &\Rightarrow Out30 \\
     \downarrow Ignite1 \wedge \uparrow Ignite2 &\Rightarrow Out0.5 \\
     \downarrow Ignite2 \wedge \uparrow Idle &\Rightarrow Out0.5 \\
     \downarrow Ignite2 \wedge \uparrow Burn &\Rightarrow FlOn \\
     \downarrow Burn \wedge \uparrow Idle &\Rightarrow HeatOff \vee FlOff
     \end{aligned}
     $$

     where the last one states that transition from Burn to Idle is started either by event *HeatOff* or event *FlOff*.

3. Event Drivings

Event *HeatOn* drives the automaton from Idle to Purge, and similarly for the other five events

$$
\begin{aligned}
HeatOn &\Rightarrow \downarrow Idle \wedge \uparrow Purge \\
Out30 &\Rightarrow \downarrow Purge \wedge \uparrow Ignite1 \\
Out0.5 &\Rightarrow (\downarrow Ignite1 \wedge \uparrow Ignite2) \vee (\downarrow Ignite2 \wedge \uparrow Idle) \\
FlOn &\Rightarrow \downarrow Ignite2 \wedge \uparrow Burn \\
HeatOff &\Rightarrow \downarrow Burn \wedge \uparrow Idle \\
FlOff &\Rightarrow \downarrow Burn \wedge \uparrow Idle
\end{aligned}
$$

Out0.5 drives the automaton either from Ignite1 to Ignite2 or from Ignite2 to Idle.

4. Real-time Transition Constraints

- Once the automaton reaches Purge, a timer is set, and time-out signal *Out30* occurs after exactly 30 seconds. Similarly for the other two transitions caused by time-out signal *Out0.5*.

$$
\begin{aligned}
\uparrow Purge; \lceil Purge \rceil; Out30 &\Rightarrow l = 30 \\
\uparrow Ignite1; \lceil Ignite1 \rceil; Out0.5 &\Rightarrow l = 0.5 \\
\uparrow Ignite2; \lceil Ignite2 \rceil; Out0.5 &\Rightarrow l = 0.5
\end{aligned}
$$

- Event *FlOn* has effect, only if it appears before *Out0.5*

$$
\uparrow Ignite2; \lceil Ignite2 \rceil; FlOn \Rightarrow l < 0.5
$$

5. Inevitability of Time-out Signals

Time-out signals are different from *synchronized* events. They are *autonomous* events, so that once they are set, their presence is inevitable. In case of *Out30*, the inevitability of the presence of the signal prevents the automaton from remaining in Purge for longer than 30 seconds.

$$
\lceil Purge \rceil \Rightarrow l \le 30
$$

Similarly for *Out0.5*

$$
(\lceil Ignite1 \rceil \vee \lceil Ignite2 \rceil) \Rightarrow l \le 0.5
$$

The above five groups of non-logical axioms constitute a complete specification of the automaton.

Now we can verify, in the Mean Value Calculus, that the automaton satisfies the two design decisions, **Des-1** and **Des-2′**, by proving that they are theorems under the non-logical axioms. First, we prove the lemmas.

Lemma 1

1. $\uparrow Ignite1 \Leftrightarrow \downarrow Purge$
2. $\uparrow Ignite2 \Leftrightarrow \downarrow Ignite1$

   3. $\downarrow Ignite2 \Leftrightarrow (\uparrow Burn \lor \uparrow Idle)$

Lemma 1 is about state transitions. The first asserts that the automaton enters Ignite1 iff it leaves Purge. Similarly we can explain the other two. Here we do not list more assertions about the state transitions of the automaton, since we do not use them in the verification. The proof consists of the following steps:

$$
\begin{aligned}
\uparrow S \quad & \Leftrightarrow \uparrow \neg \bigvee_{S' \neq S} S' && \text{(state comp. and excl.)} \\
& \Rightarrow \downarrow \bigvee_{S' \neq S} S' && \text{(germship calculus 3)} \\
& \Rightarrow \bigvee_{S' \neq S} \downarrow S' && \text{(corollary 2)} \\
& \Rightarrow \bigvee_{S' \neq S} (\uparrow S \land \downarrow S') && \text{(prop. logic)} \\
& \Rightarrow \bigvee_e e && \text{(the first axiom of state trans.)}
\end{aligned}
$$

and similarly

$$
\downarrow S \Rightarrow \bigvee_e e
$$

Combining these two results with **Event Drivings** and the Germship Calculus, we can prove the lemma. For example,

$$
\begin{aligned}
\uparrow Ignite1 \quad & \Rightarrow \bigvee_e e \\
& \Rightarrow \uparrow Ignite1 \land \bigvee_e e \\
\uparrow Ignite1 \land HeatOn \quad & \Rightarrow \uparrow Ignite1 \land \downarrow Idle \land \uparrow Purge && \text{(event drivings)} \\
& \Rightarrow \uparrow Ignite1 \land \uparrow Purge \\
& \Rightarrow false && \text{(corollary 3)} \\
\uparrow Ignite1 \land Out30 \quad & \Rightarrow \uparrow Ignite1 \land \downarrow Purge && \text{(event drivings)} \\
& \Rightarrow \downarrow Purge \\
\uparrow Ignite1 \land Out0.5 \quad & \Rightarrow false && \text{(similar to the above)} \\
\uparrow Ignite1 \land FlOn \quad & \Rightarrow false \\
\uparrow Ignite1 \land HeatOff \quad & \Rightarrow false \\
\uparrow Ignite1 \land FlOff \quad & \Rightarrow false \\
\uparrow Ignite1 \quad & \Rightarrow \downarrow Purge && \text{(from the all above)}
\end{aligned}
$$

Lemma 2

   1. $\lceil \neg S \rceil; true; \lceil S \rceil \Rightarrow true; \uparrow S; \lceil S \rceil$
   2. $\lceil Ignite1 \lor Ignite2 \rceil \Rightarrow (\lceil Ignite1 \rceil \lor \lceil Ignite2 \rceil \lor (\lceil Ignite1 \rceil; \lceil Ignite2 \rceil))$

The first proposition of the lemma states a fact: when the automaton changes from $\neg S$ to S, it must go through a rising edge of S. It can be proved by induction on state S. Let $R(X)$ be

$$
\lceil \neg S \rceil; X; \lceil S \rceil \Rightarrow true; \uparrow S; \lceil S \rceil
$$

The second proposition can be proved by induction on Ignite1. Let $R(X)$ be X implying the proposition. In the proof we have to use the results in *Lemma 1* to reject the illegal state transition $\lceil Ignite2 \rceil; \lceil Ignite1 \rceil$. *Axiom* 9 is needed in both of the proofs.

Now we are ready to prove the theorem.

Theorem

1. $\lceil Ignite1 \vee Ignite2 \rceil \Rightarrow l \leq 1$
2. $(\downarrow(Ignite1 \vee Ignite2); true; \uparrow(Ignite1 \vee Ignite2)) \Rightarrow l \geq 30$

The first proposition is a translation of *Des-1* by replacing *Leak* with its definition $Ignite1 \vee Ignite2$. The second one is stronger than the translation of *Des-2*. The proof of the first proposition is simple by using *Lemma* 2.2, *Axiom* 4 and the axioms of **Inevitability of Timeout Signals**. The proof of the second proposition can be given as follows:

$$
\begin{aligned}
\downarrow(Ignite1 \vee Ignite2) \Rightarrow\ & (\downarrow Ignite1 \wedge \downarrow Ignite2) \vee && \text{(corollary 2)}\\
& (\downarrow Ignite1 \wedge \sqcup Ignite2) \vee \\
& (\sqcup Ignite1 \wedge \downarrow Ignite2) \\
\Rightarrow\ & \downarrow Ignite2 && \text{(lemma 1.2, germ. cal. 1)}\\
\Rightarrow\ & \uparrow Burn \vee \uparrow Idle && \text{(lemma 1.3)}
\end{aligned}
$$

$$
\begin{aligned}
\uparrow(Ignite1 \vee Ignite2) \Rightarrow\ & (\uparrow Ignite1 \wedge \uparrow Ignite2) \vee && \text{(corollary 1)}\\
& (\uparrow Ignite1 \wedge \sqcup Ignite2) \vee \\
& (\sqcup Ignite1 \wedge \uparrow Ignite2) \\
\Rightarrow\ & \uparrow Ignite1 && \text{(lemma 1.2, germ. cal. 1)}\\
\Rightarrow\ & \downarrow Purge \wedge \uparrow Ignite1 && \text{(lemma 1.1)}
\end{aligned}
$$

$$
\begin{aligned}
& \downarrow(Ignite1 \vee Ignite2); true; \uparrow(Ignite1 \vee Ignite2) \\
\Rightarrow\ & (\uparrow Burn \vee \uparrow Idle); true; (\downarrow Purge \wedge \uparrow Ignite1) && \text{(the above)}\\
\Rightarrow\ & (\uparrow Burn \vee \uparrow Idle); true; (Out30 \wedge \downarrow Purge) && \text{(state trans.)}\\
\Rightarrow\ & (\lceil Burn \rceil \vee \lceil Idle \rceil); true; \lceil Purge \rceil; Out30 && \text{(axiom } \uparrow, \downarrow)\\
\Rightarrow\ & \lceil \neg Purge \rceil; true; \lceil Purge \rceil; Out30 && \text{(state exclusiveness)}\\
\Rightarrow\ & true; \uparrow Purge; \lceil Purge \rceil; Out30 && \text{(lemma 2.1)}\\
\Rightarrow\ & l \geq 30 && \text{(real-time constraints)}
\end{aligned}
$$

25.4.2 Notes

In order to generalize the approach used in the Gas Burner example, we have to specify *idle* transitions of states. By definition, an idle transition of an automaton from state S is a transition of the automaton from S to S itself. It corresponds to germship $\sqcap S$. However $\sqcap S$ is also true when the automaton stays at S and no events happen. So the specification of idle transition of state S started by event e' consists of

State Transitions

$$TS \Rightarrow e' \vee \varepsilon$$

where $\varepsilon \triangleq \neg \bigvee_e e$. $\varepsilon(t) = 1$ iff no events happen at t.

Event Drivings

$$e' \Rightarrow TS \vee Tran$$

where $Tran$ stands for all other transitions of the automaton started by e'.

25.5   Event Traces

In *event-based* specification, traces are used to capture system behaviour. To introduce traces into the calculus, one can follow [9]. It uses a new non-Boolean function Tr to record the event traces. Thus events become *trace* germships. For example, event e can be defined by the axiom: for $r > 0$

$$(l = r); e; (l > 0) \Leftrightarrow \exists x.((l = r) \wedge (true; \lceil Tr = \langle x \rangle \rceil)); \lceil Tr = \langle x, e \rangle \rceil; true$$

But in this paper we confine ourselves to Boolean functions, and consider traces to be abbreviations of formulas which define the traces. Let F and F_i be functions and tr and tr_i be non-empty sequences of functions

$$F_1, F_2, \ldots, F_n \qquad\qquad (n \geq 1)$$

Then we define

$$\langle F \rangle \triangleq F$$

$$\langle tr_1, tr_2 \rangle \triangleq \langle tr_1 \rangle; \lceil \varepsilon \rceil; \langle tr_2 \rangle$$

When $tr = e_1, e_2, \ldots, e_n$, $\langle tr \rangle$ defines intervals where the n events take place one by one in the specific order, and between any two consecutives there is a non-zero 'silent' period. When $tr = \ldots, e \wedge e', \ldots$, $\langle tr \rangle$ defines intervals where events e and e' take place simultaneously. It is easy to prove the following theorems about traces.

Theorems

1. $\langle tr_1, \varepsilon, tr_2 \rangle \Leftrightarrow \langle tr_1, tr_2 \rangle$
2. $\langle tr, e_1 \vee e_2 \rangle \Leftrightarrow \langle tr, e_1 \rangle \vee \langle tr, e_2 \rangle$
3. $\langle tr, e_1 \wedge e_2 \rangle \Leftrightarrow \langle tr, e_1 \rangle \wedge \langle tr, e_2 \rangle$
4. $\langle tr_1, e \rangle; \langle e, tr_2 \rangle \Leftrightarrow \langle tr_1, e, tr_2 \rangle$

The specification of the phase transition automaton of the gas burner, given in Section 4.1 in an event/state mixed manner, can be refined into event-based one.

1. Event Exclusiveness

   If $(e \neq e') \wedge (e \neq HeatOff \vee e' \neq FlOff)$, then $(e \Rightarrow \neg e')$

   which replaces the non-logical axioms of **State Completeness and Exclusiveness** in the event/state mixed specification.[6]

2. Event Ordering

   $$\langle HeatOn, e \rangle \Rightarrow \langle HeatOn, Out30 \rangle$$

   which defines that only *Out30* can directly follow *HeatOn*. Similarly

   $$\langle Out30, Out0.5, e \rangle \quad \Rightarrow \quad \langle Out30, Out0.5, FlOn \vee Out0.5 \rangle$$
   $$\langle Out0.5, Out0.5, e \rangle \quad \Rightarrow \quad \langle Out0.5, Out0.5, HeatOn \rangle$$
   $$\langle FlOn, e \rangle \quad \Rightarrow \quad \langle FlOn, HeatOff \vee FlOff \rangle$$
   $$\langle HeatOff \vee FlOff, e \rangle \quad \Rightarrow \quad \langle HeatOff \vee FlOff, HeatOn \rangle$$

   The first two formulas above needs explanation. The successors of event *Out0.5* are not unique. They are determined by the states that *Out0.5* leads to. When it leads to state Ignite2 that corresponds to the trace $\langle Out30, Out0.5 \rangle$, its successor is either *FlOn* or another *Out0.5*. That is stipulated by the first formula. The second one stipulates the successor of *Out0.5*, when it leads to state Idle. The group of **Event Ordering** replaces the groups of **State Transitions** and **Event Drivings**.

3. Real-Time Event Constraints

   Time-out event *Out30* occurs in exact 30 seconds after *HeatOn*.

   $$\langle HeatOn, \varepsilon \rangle \quad \Rightarrow \quad l < 30$$
   $$\langle HeatOn, Out30 \rangle \quad \Rightarrow \quad l = 30$$

   Similarly for time-out event *Out0.5*

   $$\langle Out30, \varepsilon \rangle \quad \Rightarrow \quad l < 0.5$$
   $$\langle Out30, Out0.5 \rangle \quad \Rightarrow \quad l = 0.5$$
   $$\langle Out30, Out0.5, \varepsilon \rangle \quad \Rightarrow \quad l < 1$$
   $$\langle Out0.5, Out0.5 \rangle \quad \Rightarrow \quad l = 0.5$$

   Please read the explanation for event *Out0.5* in **Event Ordering**, if you cannot understand the third formula. We need one more formula to express the time constraint for event *FlOn*.

   $$\langle Out0.5, FlOn \rangle \Rightarrow l < 0.5$$

   This group of non-logical axioms replaces the groups of **Real-Time Transition Constraints** and **Inevitability of Time-out Signals**.

To verify the event specification of the automaton with respect to the event/state specification, we can adopt the approach presented in [9] to define states by traces.

---

[6] *Event Completeness* becomes a logical tautology: $\varepsilon \vee \bigvee_e e$.

25.6   Conclusion

By using mean values of durations, this paper establishes a calculus which can describe real-time properties of both states and events. By introducing germs and germships, this paper tries to explore relations between states and events. In [7], ↑P and ↓P were specified by their neighbourhood properties. Unfortunately it used discrete time, and expressed events as one-unit (not point) actions. In [6], events were defined as state transitions that were expressed by pre-states and post-states. In [8], a similar narrative was formulated in terms of *limit* temporal operators. We here clarify all these ideas by tracing them back to the concept of function germs in topology, and establish a calculus for reasoning about events and state transitions.

As an application, the paper develops an interface between real-time automata and the Mean Value Calculus by specifying automata with the Mean Value Calculus in a simple and intuitive way. Another approach to the combination of automata with duration calculus is via model checking algorithms for verifying satisfaction of automata with respect to duration formulas [3]. It is practically useful, if one discovers efficient, mechanical algorithms. However it may not help designers to synthesize automata from duration formulas. As a complement to that approach, we expect that the Mean Value Calculus can be used not only to verify but also to refine real-time requirements.

Acknowledgements
The authors are grateful to Hans Rischel, who drew the first author's attention to the topological concept of function germs, and to Michael Hansen, who made a preliminary attempt with the first author to develop a mean value calculus. We thank Dines Bjørner, Amir Pnueli, Anders Ravn *et al.* for their valuable comments and suggestions.

References

[1] H. Barringer, R. Kuiper, and A. Pnueli: A Really Abstract Concurrent Model and its Temporal Logic, *Proceedings 13th ACM Symposium on the Principles of Programming Languages*, 173-183, 1986.

[2] N. Bourbaki: Elements of Mathematics: General Topology, Part 1, pp 65-58, Addison-Wesley Publishing Company, 1966.

[3] M.R. Hansen: Duration Calculus and Trace Specifications: a Model Checking Point of View, *ProCoS II, ESPRIT BRA 7071*, Fachbereich Informatik, Universität Oldenburg, Oct. 1992

[4] M.R. Hansen and Zhou Chaochen: Semantics and Completeness of Duration Calculus, *J.W. de Bakker, C. Huizing, W.-P. de Roever, G. Rozenberg, (Eds) Real-Time: Theory in Practice, REX Workshop, LNCS 600*, pp 209-225, 1992

[5] M.R. Hansen, Zhou Chaochen, J. Staunstrup: A Real-Time Duration Semantics for Circuits, *Proc. of the Workshop on Timing Issues in the Specification and Synthesis of Digital Systems, Princeton,* March 1992

[6] L. Lamport: Hybrid Systems in TLA$^+$. *to appear in Proceedings of the Workshop on Theory of Hybrid Systems, 19-21 Oct. 92, Lyngby, Denmark.*

[7] B. Moszkowski: A Temporal Logic for Multi-level Reasoning about Hardware. In *IEEE Computer, Vol. 18(2),* pp 10-19, 1985.

[8] A. Pnueli: System Specification and Refinement in Temporal Logic, *R.K. Shyamasunder (ed), Foundations of Software Technology and Theoretical Computer Science, LNCS 652,* pp 1-38, 1992

[9] A.P. Ravn, H. Rischel, K.M. Hansen: Specifying and Verifying Requirements of Real-Time Systems, *ACM Software Engineering Notes, Vol 15, No 5,* pp 44-54, 1991 (accepted also for *IEEE Trans. Software Eng.,* 1993)

[10] Zhou Chaochen, M.R. Hansen, A.P. Ravn, H. Rischel: Duration Specifications for Shared Processors, *Proc. of the Symposium on Formal Techniques in Real-Time and Fault-Tolerant Systems, Nijmegen,* January 1992, *LNCS 571,* pp 21-32, 1992

[11] Zhou Chaochen, C.A.R.Hoare, and A.P.Ravn: A Calculus of Durations. In *Information Processing Letters* 40(5), 1991, pp 269-276.